Consultants / Reviewers

Academic Consultants

Robert B. Blair, Ph.D.
Director, Center for Economic
    Education
Middle Tennessee State
    University
Murfreesboro, Tennessee

Martin E. Bookbinder, Ph.D.
Professor of Economics and
    Political Science
Passaic County College
Paterson, New Jersey

Sanford D. Gordon, Ph. D.
Director Emeritus of New York
    State Council of Economic
    Education
Albany, New York

Don R. Leet, Ph. D.
Professor of Economics
California State University,
    Fresno
Fresno, California

**Barbara A. Moore, M.Ed.,
    M.A.A.E.**
Instructor, Department of
    Economics
University of Central Florida
Orlando, Florida

Eleanor T. von Ende, Ph.D.
Associate Professor of
    Economics
Texas Tech University
Lubbock, Texas

Teacher Reviewers

deLyn R. Alumbaugh, II
Carver Vocational-Technical
    High School
Baltimore City, Maryland

Rick Bensman
Linworth Alternative Program,
    Worthington City Schools
Worthington, Ohio

Darcy K. Brodison
Coronado High School
Scottsdale, Arizona

Elizabeth B. Chadwick
Upper St. Clair High School
Upper St. Clair, Pennsylvania

Susie Fogarty
Martin County High School
Stuart, Florida

Kathryn L. Gustafson
Farmington High School
Farmington, Michigan

Marjorie J. Hunter
West Memphis High School
West Memphis, Arkansas

Ed Lucero
Del Norte High School
Albuquerque, New Mexico

Deborah Maynard
Eden Area ROP/San Leandro
    High School
San Leandro, California

Dana J. Mehl
Goshen High School
Goshen, Indiana

Gary N. Petmecky
Parkview High School
Lilburn, Georgia

Lee Ferrell Polk
LaVergne High School
LaVergne, Tennessee

Amanda C. Sausman
Louisville Male High School
Louisville, Kentucky

Gail Sloan
Whitehouse High School
Whitehouse, Texas

Don Stancavish
Montgomery High School
Montgomery Township, New
    Jersey

Vincent Stigler
Dundee-Crown High School
Carpentersville, Illinois

Glenn R. Stirrat
John H. Reagan High School
Austin, Texas

Robert M. Wedge
Collegiate School
Richmond, Virginia

James L. Willmann
Baker High School
Mobile, Alabama

Contents

Contents

Contents

Features

Case Study — ECONOMICS AND CULTURE

Debating Economic Issues

Global Economy

Graphs, Charts, and Maps

Graphs In MOtion

Graphs and charts labeled with the In Motion icon have been specially enhanced on the StudentWorks™ Plus CD-ROM and on glencoe.com. These In Motion graphics allow you to interact with layers of displayed data and to listen to audio components.

Entries in blue indicate In Motion graphics.

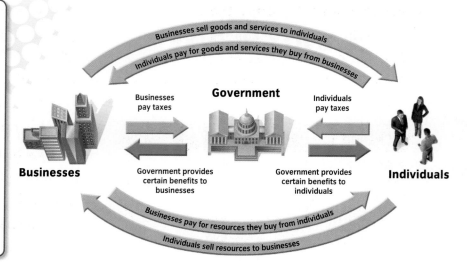

GRAPHS

CHARTS and TABLES

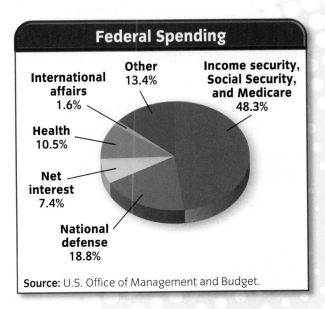

Federal Spending

International affairs 1.6%

Other 13.4%

Income security, Social Security, and Medicare 48.3%

Health 10.5%

Net interest 7.4%

National defense 18.8%

Source: U.S. Office of Management and Budget.

Graphs, Charts, and Maps

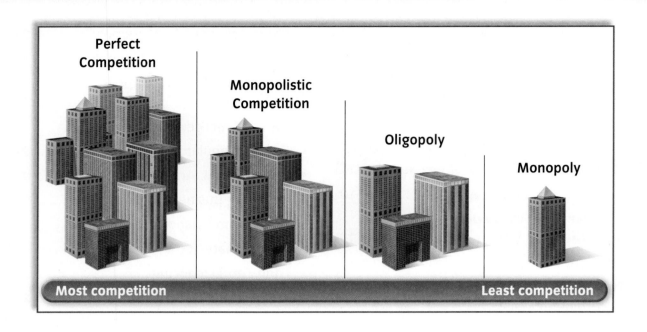

Perfect Competition — Monopolistic Competition — Oligopoly — Monopoly

Most competition — Least competition

Scavenger Hunt

GET TO KNOW YOUR BOOK!

Economics Today and Tomorrow contains a wealth of information—the trick is to know where to find it. If you go through this scavenger hunt, either alone, with a fellow student, or with your teacher or parents, you will quickly learn how the textbook is organized and how to get the most out of your reading and study time. Let's get started!

1. How many units and chapters are in the book?

2. What is the difference between the glossary and the index?

3. Unit 2 of the book contains a great deal of information on how to handle the economic aspects of your personal life. Where in the book can you find further information on how economics impacts you on a day-to-day basis?

4. Which feature provides information on current controversial topics in economics?

5. How can you find out how each Main Idea in the book relates to your life?

6. If you want to quickly find all the charts and graphs about supply and demand, where in the front of the book do you look?

7. What is the quickest way to find information on detailed, specific topics like gross domestic product and the national debt?

8. Where can you find the topic of Marketing and Distribution summarized in a visual way?

9. The Web site for the book is referred to at least four times in each chapter. Choose one chapter and find all of the references. How can the Web site help you?.

10. Which of the special features provides information about economics in other countries?

Big Ideas in ECONOMICS
Today and Tomorrow

As you read *Economics Today and Tomorrow*, you will be given help in sorting out all the information you encounter. This textbook organizes economic concepts around Big Ideas. These Big Ideas are the keys that will help you unlock all of the concepts you will study. By recognizing the Big Ideas and how they relate to the different concepts, you will better understand how economics affects you, your family, and your community today and in the future.

▶ **Scarcity is the basic economic problem that requires people to make choices about how to use limited resources.**

As much as we would like to do and buy anything we want at any time, this is not always possible because there are not enough resources to produce all the things people would like to have. Scarcity forces us to make choices about what, how, and for whom we produce.

▶ **Every society has an economic system to allocate goods and services.**

All societies develop economic systems to provide for the wants and needs of their citizens. In the market economy of the United States, buyers and sellers make economic decisions in their best interest.

▶ **The profit motive acts as an incentive for people to produce and sell goods and services.**

In a market economy, people open businesses because they hope to be successful and make a profit. They are free to produce any good or service they wish.

▶ **Buyers and sellers voluntarily interact in markets, and market prices are set by the interaction of demand and supply.**

Sellers can freely choose what to sell, and buyers are free to choose what to buy in a market economy. The price for a product is set by the forces of demand and supply.

▶ **Governments strive for a balance between the costs and benefits of their economic policies to promote economic stability and growth.**

The federal government uses a number of economic policies to further economic growth. The government tries to limit the negative effects of its policies while expanding the benefits.

▶ **Governments and institutions help participants in a market economy accomplish their financial goals.**

There are a number of organizations that help people accomplish their financial goals. Governments develop regulations, and institutions such as banks and nonprofits offer ways to save and grow money.

▶**Economists look at a variety of factors to assess the growth and performance of a nation's economy.**
Over time, economists have devised different ways to measure economic performance. These measures range from factors that affect individuals to those that assess the economies of countries, regions, and the world.

▶**The labor market, like other markets, is determined by supply and demand.**
The forces of supply and demand influence labor as much as any other market. Factors such as skills required and competition for various jobs determine wages.

▶**All levels of government use tax revenue to provide essential goods and services.**
We have to pay taxes at the local, state, and federal levels. The governments, in turn, use these revenues to provide goods and services that the market economy does not offer. Generally, local governments provide goods and services at the local level, states work statewide, and the federal government focuses on national needs.

▶**Trade and specialization lead to economic growth for individuals, regions, and nations.**
The more we practice a particular skill, the better we tend to get at it. The same is true in economics. When companies, regions, or nations specialize in the production of goods and services, they become better at it and both the seller and the buyer profit.

▶**The study of economics helps us deal with global economic issues and global demand on resources.**
Scarcity is an issue not just on a local or national level—it provides challenges on a global scale. Understanding how economics works helps us learn how we can address global problems such as population growth, pollution, and limited resources.

Using the Big Ideas ••••

You will find Big Ideas at the beginning of each chapter of your text. You are asked questions that help you put it all together to better understand how economic concepts are connected—and to see why economics is important to you.

Voluntary National Content Standards in Economics

Economics Today and Tomorrow incorporates the 20 **Voluntary National Content Standards** developed by the National Council on Economic Education.

Standard 1 Scarcity

Productive resources are limited. Therefore, people cannot have all the goods and services they want; as a result, they must choose some things and give up others.

Related concepts: Capital Resources, Choice, Consumer Economics, Consumers, Goods, Human Resources, Natural Resources, Opportunity Cost, Producers, Production, Productive Resources, Scarcity, Services, Wants, Entrepreneurship, Inventors, Entrepreneur, Factors of Production

Standard 2 Marginal Cost/Benefit

Effective decision making requires comparing the additional costs of alternatives with the additional benefits. Most choices involve doing a little more or a little less of something: few choices are "all or nothing" decisions.

Related concepts: Decision Making, Profit Motive, Benefit, Costs, Marginal Analysis, Profit, Profit Maximization, Cost/Benefit Analysis

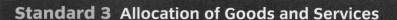

Standard 3 Allocation of Goods and Services

Different methods can be used to allocate goods and services. People acting individually or collectively through government must choose which methods to use to allocate different kinds of goods and services.

Related concepts: Economic Systems, Market Structure, Supply, Command Economy, Market Economy, Traditional Economy

Standard 4 Role of Incentives

People respond predictably to positive and negative incentives.

Related concepts: Choice, Incentive

Standard 5 Gain from Trade

Voluntary exchange occurs only when all participating parties expect to gain. This is true for trade among individuals or organizations within a nation, and usually among individuals or organizations in different nations.

Related concepts: Barriers to Trade, Barter, Exports, Imports, Voluntary Exchange, Exchange, Exchange Rate

Standard 6 Specialization and Trade

When individuals, regions, and nations specialize in what they can produce at the lowest cost and then trade with others, both production and consumption increase.

Related concepts: Division of Labor, Production, Productive Resources, Specialization, Factor Endowments, Gains from Trade, Relative Price, Transaction Costs, Factors of Production, Full Employment

Standard 7 Markets–Price and Quantity Determination

Markets exist when buyers and sellers interact. This interaction determines market prices and thereby allocates scarce goods and services.

Related concepts: Market Structure, Markets, Price Floor, Price Stability, Quantity Demanded, Quantity Supplied, Relative Price, Exchange Rate

Standard 8 Role of Price in Market System

Prices send signals and provide incentives to buyers and sellers. When supply or demand changes, market prices adjust, affecting incentives.

Related concepts: Non-price Determinants, Price Floor, Price Stability, Supply, Determinants of Demand, Determinants of Supply, Law of Demand, Law of Supply, Price Ceiling, Substitute Good, Price

Standard 9 Role of Competition

Competition among sellers lowers costs and prices, and encourages producers to produce more of what consumers are willing and able to buy. Competition among buyers increases prices and allocates goods and services to those people who are willing and able to pay the most for them.

Related concepts: Market Structure, Non-price Competition, Levels of Competition

Standard 10 Role of Economic Institutions

Institutions evolve in market economies to help individuals and groups accomplish their goals. Banks, labor unions, corporations, legal systems, and not-for-profit organizations are examples of important institutions. A different kind of institution, clearly defined and enforced property rights, is essential to a market economy.

Related concepts: Legal and Social Framework, Mortgage, Borrower, Interest, Labor Union, Legal Forms of Business, Legal Foundations of a Market Economy, Nonprofit Organization, Property Rights, Banking, Economic Institutions

Voluntary National Content Standards in Economics

Standard 11 Role of Money

Money makes it easier to trade, borrow, save, invest, and compare the value of goods and services.

Related concepts: Exchange, Money Management, Money Supply, Currency, Definition of Money, Money, Characteristics of Money, Functions of Money

Standard 12 Role of Interest Rates

Interest rates, adjusted for inflation, rise and fall to balance the amount saved with the amount borrowed, which affects the allocation of scarce resources between present and future uses.

Related concepts: Interest Rate, Monetary Policy, Real vs. Nominal, Risk, Investing, Savers, Savings

Standard 13 Role of Resources in Determining Income

Income for most people is determined by the market value of the productive resources they sell. What workers earn depends, primarily, on the market value of what they produce and how productive they are.

Related concepts: Human Resources, Derived Demand, Functional Distribution of Income, Labor, Labor Market, Marginal Resource Product, Personal Distribution of Income, Wage, Aggregate Demand (AD), Aggregate Supply (AS), Demand, Prices of Inputs, Functional Distribution

Standard 14 Profit and the Entrepreneur

Entrepreneurs are people who take the risks of organizing productive resources to make goods and services. Profit is an important incentive that leads entrepreneurs to accept the risks of business failure.

Related concepts: Taxation, Costs, Costs of Production, Entrepreneur, Risk, Taxes, Cost/Benefit Analysis, Innovation, Entrepreneurship, Inventors

Standard 15 Growth

Investment in factories, machinery, new technology, and in the health, education, and training of people can raise future standards of living.

Related concepts: Incentive, Interest Rate, Opportunity Cost, Production, Technological Changes, Trade-off, Trade-offs among goals, Human Capital, Intensive Growth, Investment, Physical Capital, Productivity, Risk, Standard of Living, Economic Efficiency, Economic Equity, Economic Freedom, Economic Growth, Economic Security, Investing, Business, Businesses and Households, Factors of Production, Health and Nutrition, Savers, Savings, Stock Market

Standard 16 Role of Government

There is an economic role for government in a market economy whenever the benefits of a government policy outweigh its costs. Governments often provide for national defense, address environmental concerns, define and protect property rights, and attempt to make markets more competitive. Most government policies also redistribute income.

Related concepts: Externalities, Income, Natural Monopoly, Role of Government, Taxation, Bonds, Income Tax, Maintaining Competition, Monopolies, Property Rights, Public Goods, Maintaining Regulation, Taxes, Regulation, Government Expenditures, Government Revenues

Standard 17 Using Cost/Benefit Analysis to Evaluate Government Programs

Costs of government policies sometimes exceed benefits. This may occur because of incentives facing voters, government officials, and government employees, because of actions by special interest groups that can impose costs on the general public, or because social goals other than economic efficiency are being pursued.

Related concepts: Cost/Benefit Analysis, Benefit, Costs, Special Interest Group, Barriers to Trade

Standard 18 Macroeconomy-Income/Employment, Prices

A nation's overall levels of income, employment, and prices are determined by the interaction of spending and production decisions made by all households, firms, government agencies, and others in the economy.

Related concepts: Gross Domestic Product (GDP), Macroeconomic Indicators, Nominal Gross Domestic Product (GDP), Per Capita Gross Domestic Product (GDP), Potential Gross Domestic Product (GDP), Real Gross Domestic Product (GDP), Circular Flow

Standard 19 Unemployment and Inflation

Unemployment imposes costs on individuals and nations. Unexpected inflation imposes costs on many people and benefits some others because it arbitrarily redistributes purchasing power. Inflation can reduce the rate of growth of national living standards because individuals and organizations use resources to protect themselves against the uncertainty of future prices.

Related concepts: Types of Unemployment, Causes of inflation, Consumer Price Index (CPI), Deflation, Labor Force, Unemployment, Unemployment Rate, Inflation

Standard 20 Monetary and Fiscal Policy

Federal government budgetary policy and the Federal Reserve System's monetary policy influence the overall levels of employment, output, and prices.

Related concepts: Inflation, National Debt, Tools of the Federal Reserve, Discount Rate, Federal Budget, Fiscal Policy, Monetary Policy, Open Market Operations, Reserve Requirements, Budget, Budget Deficit, Central Banking System, Budget Surplus, Causes of inflation

unit 1

An Introduction to Economics

In this unit, read to find out...

- what role economics plays in your life.

- what role you play in the economic system of the United States.

- what kinds of different economic systems operate around the world.

## chapter 1

What Is Economics?

The **BIG Idea**

Scarcity is the basic economic problem that requires people to make choices about how to use limited resources.

Why It Matters

Have you ever wanted to buy something or to participate in an activity, but you couldn't because you didn't have enough income or time? How do scarce resources like time and income affect you and everyone around you? In this chapter, read to learn about what economics is and how it is part of your daily life.

Economics ONLINE

Chapter Overview Visit the *Economics Today and Tomorrow* Web site at glencoe.com and click on *Chapter 1—Chapter Overviews* to preview chapter information.

The Basic Problem in Economics

GUIDE TO READING

Section Preview
In this section, you will learn that the driving forces behind economics are scarcity and choices.

Content Vocabulary
- economics *(p. 6)*
- microeconomics *(p. 6)*
- macroeconomics *(p. 6)*
- scarcity *(p. 7)*
- factors of production *(p. 8)*
- land *(p. 8)*
- labor *(p. 8)*
- goods *(p. 8)*
- services *(p. 8)*
- capital *(p. 9)*
- productivity *(p. 9)*
- entrepreneurship *(p. 9)*
- technology *(p. 10)*

Academic Vocabulary
- utilize *(p. 6)*
- focus *(p. 6)*

Reading Strategy
Organizing As you read the section, complete a table like the one below by providing two examples for each of the terms listed in the chart.

Term	Example 1	Example 2
Needs		
Wants		
Goods		
Services		

ISSUES IN THE NEWS
—from *The Guardian*

ECONOMICS IS EVERYWHERE Harry Potter may seem like he lives in a world where wizards have a wand and receive instant gratification, but that's a view that needs to be demolished by the Womping Willow.

Scarcity exists in the magic world just as much as in the Muggle world. There are a limited number of tickets to the Quidditch World Cup, magical creatures only shed so many feathers or hairs to go into wands, and not everyone has an invisibility cloak.

J.K. Rowling's fictional world . . . has its own central government (the Ministry of Magic), owl postal system, jail, hospital, news media, and public transport, not to mention Gringotts Bank and a special wizard currency. There are enough institutions to make Adam Smith salivate.

With scarcity and a monetary system, the Harry Potter series should be a case study for any economics course.

Starting at a very young age, many Americans use the words *want* and *need* interchangeably. How often do you think about what you "want"? How many times have you said that you "need" something? When you say, "I need some new clothes," do you *really* need them, or do you just want them? As you read this section, you'll find that economics deals with questions such as these.

Wants, Needs, and Choices

Main Idea The basic problem in economics is how to satisfy unlimited wants with limited resources.

Economics & You Think of the last time you said that you needed something. Was the object really necessary for your survival? Read on to learn that people must make choices about how to spend their limited resources.

economics: the study of how people make choices about ways to use limited resources to fulfill their wants

microeconomics: the branch of economic theory that deals with behavior and decision making by small units such as individuals and firms

macroeconomics: the branch of economic theory dealing with the economy as a whole and decision making by large units such as governments

Careers Handbook

See pages R76–R80 to learn about becoming an economist.

What, exactly, is economics? **Economics** is the study of how individuals, families, businesses, and societies use limited resources to fulfill their unlimited wants. Economics is divided into two parts. **Microeconomics** deals with behavior and decision making by small units such as individuals and firms. **Macroeconomics** deals with the economy as a whole and decision making by large units such as governments.

People often confuse *wants* with *needs.* When they use the word *need,* they really mean that they want something they do not have. Obviously, everyone needs certain things, such as food, clothing, and shelter, to survive. To economists, however, anything other than what people need for basic survival is a *want.* People *want* such items as new cars and electronics, but they often convince themselves they *need* these things. In a world of limited resources, individuals satisfy their unlimited wants by making choices.

Like individuals, businesses must also make choices. Businesspeople make decisions daily about what to produce now, what to produce later, and what to stop producing. Societies, too, face choices about how to **utilize** their resources. How these choices are made is the **focus** of economics.

Reading Check **Explaining** What do people have to do when faced with unlimited wants and limited resources?

▼Consumers often feel that *wants,* such as concert tickets, are actually *needs.*

ZITS

Zits partnership. Reprinted with permission of King Feature Syndicate.

| Figure 1.1 | Scarcity and Choices |

■ When many people think of making economic choices, they consider how they will spend their *income*. However, economic choices also involve how we choose to spend our limited *time*.

B. Time ▶
Choosing whether to play basketball or study for a test is another economic choice.

A. Money ▶
Choosing whether to save your income or spend it on a new computer game is one economic choice.

Economic Analysis

Explaining *Other than individuals, what groups of people make economic choices?*

The Problem of Scarcity

Main Idea Scarcity exists because people's incomes and time are limited.

Economics & You If you were very wealthy, would your resources be unlimited? Read on to learn why scarcity exists for everyone.

The need to make choices arises because everything that exists is limited, although some items (such as trees in a large forest) may appear to be in abundant supply. At any single moment, a fixed amount of resources is available. At the same time, people have competing uses for these resources. This situation results in scarcity—the basic problem of economics.

Scarcity means that people do not and cannot have enough income and time to satisfy their every want. What you buy as a student is limited by the amount of income you have. Even if everyone in the world were rich, however, scarcity would continue to exist, because even the richest person in the world does not have unlimited time. (See **Figure 1.1** above.)

Do not confuse scarcity with *shortages*. Scarcity always exists because of competing alternative uses for resources, whereas shortages are temporary. Shortages often occur, for example, after hurricanes or floods destroy goods and property.

scarcity: basic economic problem that results from a combination of limited resources and unlimited wants

✔**Reading Check** **Identifying** What two specific resources create scarcity?

The Factors of Production

Main Idea Scarce resources require choices about uses of the factors of production: land, labor, capital, and entrepreneurship.

Economics & You If you have a job, how does the work you do fit in with the bigger economic picture? Read on to learn that labor is one of the factors of production.

factors of production: resources of land, labor, capital, and entrepreneurship used to produce goods and services

land: natural resources and surface land and water

labor: human effort directed toward producing goods and services

goods: tangible objects that can satisfy people's wants or needs

services: actions that can satisfy people's wants or needs

When economists talk about scarce resources, they are referring to the **factors of production,** or resources needed to produce goods and services. Traditionally, economists have classified these productive resources as land, labor, capital, and entrepreneurship. (See **Figure 1.2** below.)

Land As an economic term, **land** refers to natural resources that exist without human intervention. "Land" includes actual surface land and water, as well as fish, animals, trees, mineral deposits, and other "gifts of nature."

Labor The work people do is **labor**—which is often called a human resource. Labor includes any work people do to produce goods and services. **Goods** are tangible items that people can buy, such as medicine, clothing, or computers. **Services** are activities done for others for a fee. Doctors, hair stylists, and Web-page designers all sell their services.

Figure 1.2 | Factors of Production

■ The four general categories of resources needed in the production of all goods and services include land, labor, capital, and entrepreneurship.

▶ **B. Labor** Labor includes any work done by people, whether they are doing manual labor or performing services.

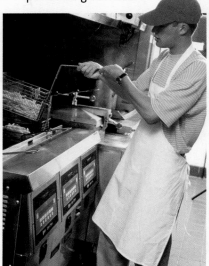

▲ **A. Land** Land includes all "gifts of nature," or any natural resource not created by people.

Capital Another factor of production is **capital**—the manufactured goods used to make other goods and produce other services. The machines, buildings, and tools used in making automobiles, for example, are *capital goods*. The newly assembled goods are not considered capital unless they, in turn, produce other goods and services, such as when an automobile is used as a taxicab.

When capital is combined with land and labor, the value of all three factors of production increases. Think about the following situation. If you combine an uncut diamond (land), a diamond cutter (labor), and a diamond-cutting machine (capital), you end up with a highly valued gem.

Capital also increases **productivity**—that is, greater quantities of goods and services are produced in better and faster ways. Consider how much faster an optical check-reading scanner—a capital good—can sort checks as compared to an individual worker reading each one.

Entrepreneurship The fourth factor of production is **entrepreneurship.** This refers to the ability of individuals to start new businesses, introduce new products and processes, and improve management techniques. Entrepreneurship involves initiative and willingness to take risks in order to reap profits. Entrepreneurs must also incur the costs of failed efforts. About 30 percent of new business enterprises fail. Of the 70 percent that do survive, only a few become wildly successful.

capital: previously manufactured goods used to make other goods and services

productivity: the amount of output (goods and services) that results from a given level of inputs (land, labor, capital, and entrepreneurship)

entrepreneurship: when individuals take risks to develop new products and start new businesses in order to make profits

▲ **C. Capital** Capital includes all manufactured goods, such as buildings, tools, and computers, used to make other goods or perform other services.

▲ **D. Entrepreneurship** Entrepreneurs are people who take risks by creating new products or starting new businesses.

Economic Analysis

Contrasting *In what way is land different from the other factors of production?*

technology: the use of science to develop new products and new methods for producing and distributing goods and services

Technology Some economists add technology to the list of factors of production. **Technology** includes any use of land, labor, and capital that produces goods and services more efficiently. For example, computerized word processing was a technological advance over the typewriter. Today, the word *technology* is commonly used to describe new products and new methods of producing goods and services.

U.S. Household Income Distribution

$100,000 and over 15.7%

Under $10,000 8.7%

$10,000–$24,999 19.6%

$50,000–$99,999 29.3%

$25,000–$49,999 26.7%

Source: U.S. Census Bureau, 2005.

Effect on Income and Wealth How much of each of the factors of production an individual has determines his or her wealth. The more land and capital you have, the richer you will probably be. The greater your entrepreneurial skills, the more income you might earn. In other words, the distribution of factors of production affects a nation's income distribution—what percentage of Americans are rich and what percentage are poor. The same holds true across nations as well. Nations with many natural resources at their disposal, for example, tend to be wealthier than nations with few natural resources.

✔ **Reading Check** **Identifying** What are the four factors of production?

section 1 Review

Vocabulary

1. **Explain** the significance of: economics, microeconomics, macroeconomics, scarcity, factors of production, land, labor, goods, services, capital, productivity, entrepreneurship, technology.

Main Ideas

2. **Making Distinctions** Wants and needs are not always easy to separate. Identify each of the following as a want or a need, and tell why you made that choice.

Choices	Want or Need	Reason
Food		
Car		
Yearly physical exam		
Cell phone		

Critical Thinking

3. **The BIG Idea** Explain why scarcity and choice are basic problems in economics.

4. **Identifying** Scarcity leads to economic choices. Give an example of an economic decision you made and what you gave up when you made your choice. Then think of a choice our country has made and what we may have given up in making that choice.

Applying Economics

5. **Microeconomics** For every purchase you make, you affect the economy. List three items you bought recently. For each item, list three businesses that benefited from your purchase.

Adam Smith

● **Founder of Classical Economics**

■ Professor of Moral Philosophy, University of Glasgow
■ Author of *The Theory of Moral Sentiments* (1759)
■ Author of *An Inquiry Into the Nature and Causes of the Wealth of Nations* (1776)

Adam Smith was born in Kirkcaldy, Scotland, in 1723. In school he proved himself a good scholar as he studied the usual subjects of the period—English, Latin, Greek, history, and arithmetic. At 14, along with other boys the same age, he entered Glasgow University, and in 1740 went on to Oxford.

Throughout his student years he encountered many ideas and individuals that would prepare him for the eventual writing of his important work, *An Inquiry into the Nature and Causes of the Wealth of Nations*. In it he brought together the economic concepts and theories that established the basis of modern economics.

Smith's main argument was that the general welfare of society is best promoted by allowing individuals to pursue their own self-interest within the law, because this alone is "capable of carrying on the society to wealth and prosperity." People should be able to do so through voluntary and mutually beneficial exchanges in free markets, with limited regulation by government officials:

> **[E]very individual . . . intends only his own gain, and he is in this, as in many other cases, led by an invisible hand to promote an end which was no part of his intention.**

Smith also believed that any attempt by government to force the economy beyond this "system of natural liberty" is counterproductive:

"It retards, instead of accelerating, the progress of the society towards real wealth and greatness; and diminishes, instead of increasing, the real value of the annual produce of its land and labor."

Because of the original ideas Smith put forth in his works, he is considered the founder of classical economics.

Checking for Understanding

1. **Explaining** What did Smith mean when he referred to an "invisible hand" that guides people's economic choices?

2. **Extending** List three examples in which a person's pursuit of his or her own self-interest might benefit society as a whole.

Global Economy

Pencils—An International Product

As you've learned, the "land" factor of production includes natural resources. The natural resources that make up a pencil come from all over the world. So a pencil—yes, the simple writing tool you hold in your hand—is an international product.

Manufacturers
The Eberhard Faber Division makes its pencils in Lewisburg, Tennessee. The company produces almost a billion pencils every year. The J.R. Moon Pencil Company is also located in Lewisburg.

The Casing
The casing (material around the lead) of most wooden pencils is made from incense cedar. Most of this cedar comes from the High Sierras in California, but some of it comes from Oregon and Washington.

Wax
Wax from Brazil coats the lead and soaks into the wood. The wax on the lead helps the pencil write more smoothly. Wax in the wood makes the wood easier to run through the machines at the factory and also makes the finished pencil easier for you to sharpen.

The Eraser
Rubber and pumice are the traditional ingredients of erasers. Pumice is the part that actually erases—the rubber just holds it together. The pumice comes from Italy, and the rubber comes from Malaysia. Modern erasers mix pumice with either vinyl or synthetic rubber.

Yellow Pencils
Pencils were first painted yellow to honor China, where the best graphite came from. In China, yellow is a color of royalty and respect.

The Lead
The lead in a pencil is not really lead at all. It's a mixture of graphite and clay. The best graphite comes from Sri Lanka, Madagascar, and Mexico. Many pencil makers prefer the graphite from Mexico because it makes the blackest marks. Clay comes from Germany and Georgia.

Thinking Globally

1. **Identifying** Producing pencils requires several different raw materials. Which ones come from within the United States? Which ones are obtained from other countries?
2. **Analyzing** What do you think might happen to the price of pencils if Brazil decided to double the price of wax?
3. **Critical Thinking** When we buy raw materials from a foreign country to make pencils, how does the exchange benefit the foreign country? What might be a drawback of this exchange?

13

GUIDE TO READING

Section Preview

In this section, you will learn about the relationship between trade-offs and opportunity costs, and how a production possibilities curve can help people make informed economic choices.

Content Vocabulary

- trade-off *(p. 15)*
- opportunity cost *(p. 16)*
- production possibilities curve *(p. 17)*

Academic Vocabulary

- alternative *(p. 16)*
- reveal *(p. 17)*

Reading Strategy

Organizing Imagine that you have just received your first paycheck from a new job. Using the information from this section, complete a table like the one below by listing the trade-off and opportunity cost of each economic decision you might make.

Decision	Trade-Off	Opportunity Cost
Buying something you want		
Saving your money		

ISSues In ThE NeWS

HEALTH AND SAFETY TRADE-OFFS Public health measures always involve trade-offs. . . . Health economists are typically concerned with finding policies that maximize the total number of life years, or . . . the average life expectancy of the population, leaving aside quality-of-life issues. A focus on life years recognizes that there are inevitable trade-offs involved in health and safety policies.

. . . If government policy always erred on the side of life, the speed limit would be reduced to 5 miles per hour to eliminate all fatal accidents. Of course, voters would not stand for a 5 mph speed limit, so . . . policy makers recognize that there is a trade-off between risk and the time required to transport goods and people on the highways.
—from the *New York Times*

As you learned in Section 1, scarcity forces people to make choices about how they will use their resources. In this section, you'll learn that the effects of these choices may be far-reaching and long-lasting. For example, one day you may choose to either go to work for a company or open your own business. Such a decision would affect many aspects of your life, including how much you earn and how you manage your time.

Trade-Offs

Main Idea Economic decisions always involve trade-offs that have costs.

Economics & You Think about the last time you spent an hour watching television. Were there other ways you could have spent your time? Read on to learn about how using resources one way means giving up other alternatives.

The economic choices people make involve exchanging one good or service for another. If you choose to buy an iPod, you are exchanging your income for the right to own the iPod. Exchanging one thing for another is called a **trade-off.**

Individuals, families, businesses, and societies are forced to make trade-offs every time they use their resources in one way and not another.

trade-off: sacrificing one good or service to purchase or produce another

The Cost of Trade-Offs The cost of a trade-off is what you give up in order to get or do something else. Time, for example, is a scarce resource—there are only so many hours in a day—so you must choose how to use it. When you decide to study economics for an hour, you are giving up any other activities you could have chosen to do during that time.

Trade-Offs

If you decide to go to college rather than work full-time right after high school, you are giving up the opportunity to start making money right away. You also may have to take on the burden of student loans. These are the trade-offs you make to gain a college education and increase your potential earning power later.

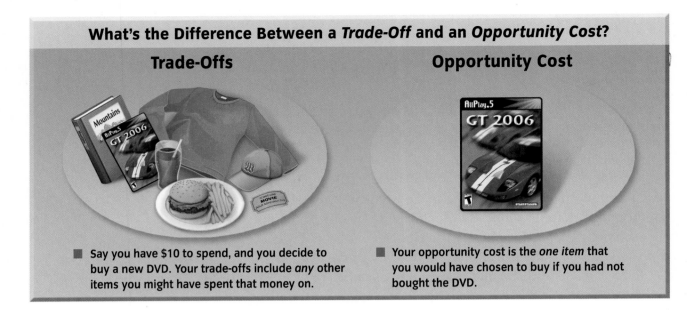

What's the Difference Between a *Trade-Off* and an *Opportunity Cost*?

Trade-Offs

■ Say you have $10 to spend, and you decide to buy a new DVD. Your trade-offs include *any* other items you might have spent that money on.

Opportunity Cost

■ Your opportunity cost is the *one item* that you would have chosen to buy if you had not bought the DVD.

opportunity cost: value of the next best alternative given up for the alternative that was chosen

Personal Finance Handbook
See pages **R4–R5** to learn about **budgeting**.

In other words, there is a cost involved in time spent studying this book. Economists call this an **opportunity cost**—the value of the next best **alternative** that had to be given up to do the action that was chosen. You may have many trade-offs when you study—exchanging instant messages with your friends, going to the mall, watching television, or practicing the guitar, for example. But whatever you consider the *single next best alternative* is the opportunity cost of your studying economics for one hour.

A good way to think about opportunity cost is to realize that when you make a trade-off (and you *always* make trade-offs), you lose something. What do you lose? You lose the ability to engage in your next highest valued alternative. In economics, therefore, opportunity cost is always an opportunity that is given up.

Considering Opportunity Costs Being aware of trade-offs and their resulting opportunity costs is vital in making economic decisions at all levels. Whether they are aware of it or not, individuals and families make trade-offs every day. Businesses must consider trade-offs and opportunity costs when they choose to invest funds or hire workers to produce one good rather than another.

Consider an example at the national level. Suppose Congress approves $220 billion to finance new highways. Congress could have voted instead for increased spending on medical research. The opportunity cost of building new highways, then, is less medical research.

Reading Check **Describing** What is an opportunity cost?

Production Possibilities Curve

Main Idea A production possibilities curve shows the maximum combinations of goods and services that can be produced with a given amount of resources.

Economics & You Imagine that you are taking two classes—economics and math. You can spend 10 hours per week studying. How will you decide how many hours to study for each subject? Read on to learn how a production possibilities curve helps people make such decisions.

Skills Handbook

See page **R49** to learn about *Using Line Graphs.*

Obviously, many businesses produce more than one type of product. An automobile company, for example, may manufacture several makes of cars per plant in a given year. What this means is that the company produces combinations of goods, which results in an opportunity cost.

Economists use a model called the **production possibilities curve** to show the maximum combinations of goods and services that can be produced from a fixed amount of resources in a given period of time. This curve can help determine how much of each item to produce, thus **revealing** the trade-offs and opportunity costs involved in each decision.

Imagine that you run a jewelry-making business. Working 20 hours a week, you have enough resources to make either 10 bracelets or 5 pairs of earrings. If you want to make some of both, **Figure 1.3** below shows your production possibilities.

production possibilities curve: graph showing the maximum combinations of goods and services that can be produced from a fixed amount of resources in a given period of time

Figure 1.3 | A Production Possibilities Curve

■ The curve here represents the production possibilities between bracelets and pairs of earrings during a 20-hour workweek. Note that if you make 10 bracelets (point A on the curve), you have no resources or time to make earrings. If you make only 6 bracelets (point B on the curve), you have enough resources and time to also make 2 pairs of earrings. Therefore, the opportunity cost of making 2 pairs of earrings is the 4 bracelets not made. Although you are making both bracelets and earrings, you—and businesses and nations—cannot produce more of one thing without giving up producing something else.

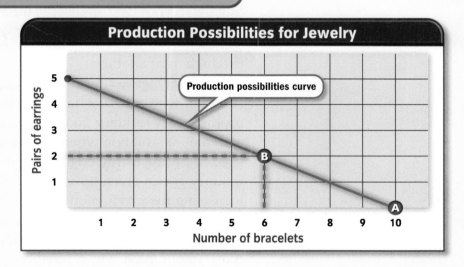

Production Possibilities for Jewelry

Production possibilities curve

Pairs of earrings

Number of bracelets

Economic Analysis

Using Graphs *What is the opportunity cost of making 3 pairs of earrings in a 20-hour workweek?*

Figure 1.4 | **Production Possibilities—Guns vs. Butter**

■ Nations produce combinations, or mixes, of goods. We often refer to the production of military goods as "guns" and the production of civilian goods as "butter." If a nation starts with all gun production and no butter production (point A), it can only get to some butter production (point B) by giving up some gun production. In other words, the cost of having some civilian goods (represented by the horizontal distance from point y to point z) is giving up some military goods (represented by the vertical distance from point A to point x).

Economic Analysis

Using Graphs *If a nation wanted to produce $5 billion in civilian goods, what would be the approximate cost in military goods?*

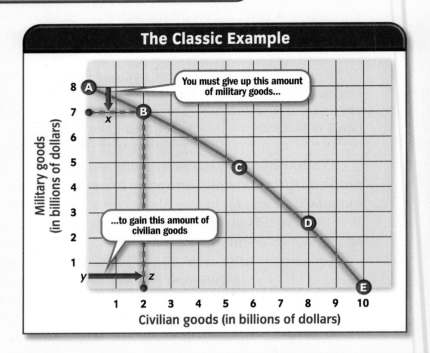

The classic example for explaining production possibilities in economics is the trade-off between spending on military defense and civilian goods, sometimes referred to as *guns* versus *butter.* The extreme situation for any nation would be to use all of its resources to produce only military goods or only civilian goods. Of course, in reality, nations always produce some of both. Governments, like businesses, face production possibilities curves all of the time, so they know they have to give up production of one type of good or service in order to get more production of another.

Look at **Figure 1.4** above. Point A on the graph represents a situation where all of a nation's resources are being used to produce only military goods (guns). Point E represents the other extreme—a situation where all the nation's resources are being used to produce only civilian goods (butter). The amount of military goods given up in a year is the opportunity cost for increasing the production of civilian goods, and vice versa.

In the United States, Congress and the president decide where on this curve the nation will be in terms of production of each type of good. The government collects revenue from citizens through taxes, and then it must decide how to use the revenue to best serve the nation. A production possibilities curve is useful in determining what the opportunity cost will be if a particular course of action is taken.

FOXTROT

▲ Mr. Fox just saw the production possibilities between saving $1,000 per year in expenses versus how much he had to pay the consultant for that information.

Of course, the real world doesn't work exactly as our graphs predict. In the real world, it takes time to move from point A to point B on the curve. Also, in terms of nations, leaders must take factors other than economics into consideration when allocating resources; they also look at the political and social concerns of citizens. The important point to remember is that a production possibilities curve can help nations, businesses, and individuals decide how best to use their resources.

✔ Reading Check **Examining** What is the classic example economists often use to explain production possibilities in economics?

section 2 Review

Vocabulary

1. **Explain** the significance of: trade-off, opportunity cost, production possibilities curve.

Main Ideas

2. **Explaining** What is the opportunity cost of any trade-off?

3. **Determining Cause and Effect** Individuals, families, and businesses make trade-offs. Create a chart like the one below, and for each example given, add a likely opportunity cost.

	Economic Decision	Likely Opportunity Cost
Individual	Gets second job	
Family	Purchases car	
Business	Paves parking lot	

Critical Thinking

4. **The BIG Idea** A politician promises to increase funding for both the space program and education. Knowing about opportunity costs, what question should you ask as a citizen?

Applying Economics

5. **Analyzing** Imagine that an independent supermarket owner decides to expand and builds another store in a neighboring town. However, it is now difficult to supervise employees in both stores. Explain how each of the following concepts might be applied to this situation:

   trade-off   *opportunity cost*
   production possibilities curve   *scarcity*

What Do Economists Do?

GUIDE TO READING

Section Preview
In this section, you'll learn about how economists use models to explain and predict economic behavior, and that economists may not always agree on which model or theory is the best one.

Content Vocabulary
- economy *(p. 21)*
- economic model *(p. 21)*
- hypothesis *(p. 22)*

Academic Vocabulary
- analyze *(p. 20)*
- complex *(p. 22)*
- theory *(p. 22)*

Reading Strategy
Contrasting As you read, complete a table like the one below by listing the benefits and drawbacks of using models to predict economic behavior.

Benefits	Drawbacks
1. _____	1. _____
2. _____	2. _____
3. _____	3. _____

ISSues In ThE NeWS
—from *TIME*

A NATION OF CONSUMERS If you made a graph of American life since the end of World War II, every line concerning money and the things money can buy would soar upward.

The size of the typical new house has more than doubled. A two-car garage was once a goal; now we're nearly a three-car nation. Designer everything, personal electronics and other items that didn't even exist a half-century ago are now affordable.

. . . That money never satisfies, [though,] is suggested by this telling fact: polls show that Americans believe that, whatever their income level, they need more to live well. Even those making large sums said  still larger sums were required. We seem conditioned to think we do not have enough, even if . . . our lives are comfortable.

As you've learned, economics is concerned with the ways individuals and nations choose to use their scarce resources. Economists might **analyze** how the super-rich spend their income, for example, and the effect this spending has on the economy. As you read this section, however, you'll find that something economists *don't* do is judge whether there *should* be a social class of super-rich people.

Economic Models

Economists construct models to investigate the way that economic systems work.

Economics & You Have you ever tried to predict the outcome of a sports match? On what information did you base your prediction? Read on to learn how economists use models to help them explain and predict economic behavior.

Remember that economics is concerned with the ways individuals, businesses, and nations choose to use their limited resources. To economists, the word **economy** means all the activity in a nation that together affects the production, distribution, and use of goods and services. When economists study specific parts of the economy—teenage employment rates or spending habits, for example—they often formulate theories and gather data from the real world. The theories that economists use in their work are called **economic models.** The study of these models can help explain and predict economic behavior.

You may be familiar with other types of models, such as model trains or airplanes, or models of buildings that architects have designed. Like these other types of models, economic models are simplified representations of the real world. Economists test these economic models, and the solutions that result from these tests often become the basis for actual decisions by private businesses or government agencies. Keep in mind, though, that no economic model records every detail and relationship that exists about a problem to be studied. A model will show only the basic factors needed to analyze the problem.

economy: the production and distribution of goods and services in a society

economic model: a theory or simplified representation that helps explain and predict economic behavior in the real world

Models

Model airplanes, like economic models, are simplified representations of objects or concepts in the real world.

What Models Show Physicists, chemists, biologists, and other scientists use models to understand in simple terms the **complex** workings of the world. One purpose of economic models is to show visual representations of consumer, business, or other economic behavior. Economic models all relate to the way individuals (as consumers) and businesspeople react to changes in the world around them. The most common economic model is a line graph explaining how consumers react to changes in the prices of goods and services. You'll learn about this model in Chapter 7.

Economic models assume that some factors remain constant. In studying the production possibilities curve for making jewelry in Section 2, for example, we assumed that the price of inputs (beads, wire, and so on) would not increase. We also assumed that inclement weather would not close schools for a day, which would have enabled you to work more than 20 hours a week on jewelry.

Why are these constant-factor assumptions important? Economists realize that, in the real world, several things may be changing at once. Using a model holds everything steady except the variables assumed to be related. In the same way that a map does not show every alley and building in a given location, economic models do not record every detail and relationship that exists about a problem to be studied. A model will show only the basic factors needed to analyze the problem at hand.

Creating a Model Models are useful if they help us analyze the way the real world works. An economist begins with some idea about the way things work, then collects facts and discards those that are not relevant. Let's assume that an economist wants to find out why teenage unemployment rises periodically. Perhaps this unemployment occurs when the federal minimum wage goes up, thereby forcing employers to pay their teenage workers more or to lay some workers off. The economist can test this **theory**, or model, in the same way that other scientists test a **hypothesis**—an educated guess or prediction.

Testing a Model Testing a model, or hypothesis, allows economists to see if the model does a good job of representing reality. Suppose an economist has developed the model shown in *Graph A* of **Figure 1.5** on the next page. The economist would collect data on the amount of teenage unemployment every year for the last 30 years. He or she would also gather 30 years of information on federal legislation that increased the legal minimum wage paid to teenagers.

Skills Handbook

See page **R39** to learn about **Formulating Questions**.

hypothesis: an assumption involving two or more variables that must be tested for validity

Help Wanted

Economic models can be used to study teenage unemployment.

Figure 1.5 Economic Models

■ The purpose of economic models is to show visual representations of consumer, business, or other economic behavior. Economic models, however, must be tested to see if they are useful.

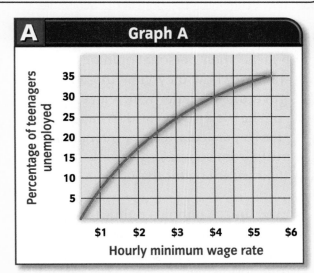

A Graph A

▲ **Graph A** This graph supports the theory that a direct relationship exists between increases in the minimum wage rate and increases in teenage unemployment.

▼ **Graph B** This graph does not support the theory that a direct relationship exists between the two factors studied.

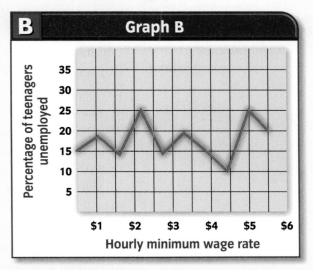

B Graph B

Economic Analysis

Predicting *If an economist's data supported the model in Graph A, what would happen if the federal minimum wage was raised?*

The economist can be fairly satisfied with the model if teenage unemployment rose every time the minimum wage rate increased. But suppose that the data instead resulted in *Graph B* of **Figure 1.5.** In that case, the economist would have to develop another model to explain changes in teenage unemployment.

Applying Models to Real Life Much of the work of economists involves attempts at predicting how people will react in a particular situation. Consider, for example, that some economists believe that to stimulate the economy, taxes should be cut and government spending increased. Cutting taxes, these economists believe, will put more income into consumers' pockets, which will increase both spending and production. People's fears concerning higher taxes in the future, though, might cause them to save the extra income rather than spend it. As this example illustrates, some models take into account several factors that may influence people's behavior.

✓ **Reading Check** **Describing** What is an economic model?

Schools of Economic Thought

Main Idea Competing economic theories are supported by economists from different schools of thought.

Economics & You Have you and a friend ever read the same book or seen the same movie and then disagreed about what it was trying to say? Read on to learn about how economists disagree about economic theories.

Economics ONLINE

Chapter Overview Visit the *Economics Today and Tomorrow* Web site at glencoe.com and click on **Chapter 1—Student Web Activities** to learn about famous economists and their contributions.

Economists deal with facts. Their personal opinions and beliefs may nonetheless influence how they view those facts and fit them to theories. The government under which an economist lives also shapes how he or she views the world. As a result, not all economists will agree that a particular theory offers the best prediction. Often, economists from competing schools of thought claim that their theories are better than others' theories in making predictions.

During a given period of time, a nation's political leaders may agree with one school of economic thought and develop policies based on it. Later, other leaders may agree with another group of economists. Throughout American history, for example, many economists have stressed the importance of the government maintaining a "hands off" (or *laissez-faire*) policy in business and consumer affairs to prevent increased unemployment and inflation. Other influential economists have proposed that the federal government should intervene in the economy to reduce unemployment and prevent inflation. (See **Figure 1.6** below.)

Figure 1.6 | Politicians and Schools of Economic Thought

■ Members of different political parties tend, in general, to follow different schools of economic thought. The two major parties in the United States, Democrats and Republicans, reflect this concept. A nation's economic policy can be heavily influenced by the economic thinking of the political party in control.

B. Republicans ▶
Republicans, like George W. Bush, tend to think that free markets will take care of themselves and that government intervention in the workings of the market should be minimal.

◀ A. Democrats
Democrats, like former president Bill Clinton, tend to believe that free markets are unstable and that the federal government sometimes needs to intervene in the economy to help the nation's citizens.

Economic Analysis

Evaluating *Which major political party tends to support laissez-faire economic policy?*

Learning about economics will help you predict what may happen if certain events occur or certain policies are followed. Economics will not tell you, however, whether the results will be good or bad. Judgments about results depend on a person's values. *Values* are the beliefs or characteristics that a person or group considers important, such as religious freedom, equal opportunity, individual initiative, freedom from government meddling, and so on. Even having the same values, however, does not mean that people will agree about strategies, interpretation of data, or solutions to problems.

For example, those in favor of decreasing teenage unemployment in order to bring about economic opportunity may disagree about the best way to solve this problem. If you were a legislator, you might show your commitment to this value by introducing a bill to decrease teenage unemployment. The economists who help you research the causes of teenage unemployment will tell you, based on their expertise, whether they think the proposed solution will actually reduce teenage unemployment.

Remember always that the science of economics is not used to judge whether a certain policy is good or bad. Economists only inform us as to likely outcomes of these policies.

Skills Handbook
See page **R47** to learn about **Making Predictions.**

✓**Reading Check** **Explaining** What factors may cause economists to disagree about economic theory?

section 3 Review

Vocabulary
1. **Explain** the significance of: economy, economic model, hypothesis.

Main Ideas
2. **Sequencing** Create a diagram like the one below to show how economists use models to study the real world.

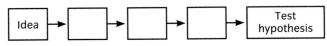

Idea → ☐ → ☐ → ☐ → Test hypothesis

Critical Thinking
3. The **BIG Idea** No one can change the fact that scarcity exists. Assume, however, that scarcity did not exist. How would your life be different?

4. **Explaining** Give an explanation about why models can never be completely realistic.

Applying Economics
5. **Examining** Which of the statements below would be a valid hypothesis to research, according to what you learned in this section? Explain why.

   a. Given an income of $150 per month, a teenager will spend more on food than he or she will save.

   b. Given an income of $150 per month, a teenager should save at least 50% of this money.

   c. Given an income of $150 per month, a teenager will spend too much on music.

BusinessWeek SPOTLIGHT on the Economy

THE GREASE PITS OF ACADEMIA

Taking the trade-off between work or a college education to the racetrack.

Check It Out! In this chapter you learned about trade-offs. A huge trade-off you will make after high school is whether to begin working or to attend college. This article discusses a new college degree that may interest you.

Students at Belmont Abbey College may have a head start in the race for post-graduation jobs—at least jobs that go vroom! Starting this fall, the 1,000-student school outside Charlotte, N.C., will offer the nation's first four-year bachelor's degree in Motorsports Management. . . . "The program will be NASCAR-focused but will have a broad application to all portions of the motor sports industry," says Philip Bayster, chair of the school's business department.

▲ A NASCAR race

The idea originated with H. A. "Humpy" Wheeler, president of racetrack owner Speedway Motorsports. He saw a need to boost management talent in the booming race-car business. . . .

Pay is anything but the pits: A 2005 study by two University of North Carolina-Charlotte professors found that annual salaries for the region's 14,000 motor sports jobs, not including drivers, averaged $72,000. Ladies and gentlemen, turn your tassels.

—Reprinted from *BusinessWeek*

Trade-Offs

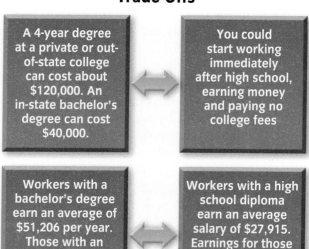

A 4-year degree at a private or out-of-state college can cost about $120,000. An in-state bachelor's degree can cost $40,000.

⟷

You could start working immediately after high school, earning money and paying no college fees

Workers with a bachelor's degree earn an average of $51,206 per year. Those with an advanced degree earn an average of $74,602 yearly.

⟷

Workers with a high school diploma earn an average salary of $27,915. Earnings for those without a high school diploma average $18,734.

Think About It

1. **Identifying** What is the opportunity cost of earning a Motorsports Management degree?
2. **Evaluating** How does the annual salary in a motorsports job compare to the average salary of a person with a bachelor's degree?

■ **Scarcity** exists because people's income and time are limited. Consumers seek a balance between satisfying their needs and wants and allocating their time and income.

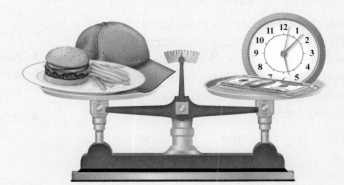

■ Economic decisions always involve **trade-offs** that have costs. Whenever you make an economic choice, you are sacrificing other goods or services that you may have purchased with your limited resources.

Trade-Offs

■ Economists use **economic models** to investigate the ways in which economic systems work.

Economic Model

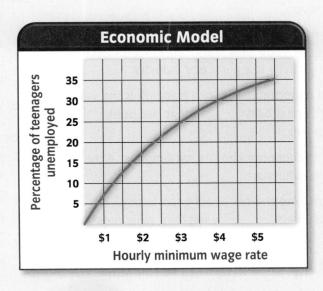

Review Content Vocabulary

1. *Think about any business in the United States, such as a company that produces computers or one that paints people's houses. Write a paragraph explaining how this business would use the factors of production. Use all of the following terms.*

factors of production	entrepreneurship
land	scarcity
labor	productivity
capital	technology

2. *Thinking of the same business, now write a short paragraph about how an economist might use economic models to help the business owner make decisions about trade-offs and opportunity costs. Use all of the following terms.*

economy	hypothesis
economic model	trade-off
production possibilities curve	opportunity cost

Review Academic Vocabulary

Choose the letter of the term that best completes each sentence.

a. utilize	e. analyze
b. focus	f. theory
c. alternative	g. complex
d. reveal	

3. An economist might use an economic model to _____ how new technology might affect productivity in a particular industry.

4. The opportunity cost of a trade-off is the value of the next best _____ that had to be given up.

5. Some economic choices are simple or easy, while others are _____.

6. By making choices about what to buy, consumers _____ what they value most.

7. Studying how people use limited resources to fulfill their unlimited wants is the _____ of economics.

8. An economist might use an economic model to formulate a _____, or hypothesis, about some aspect of the economy.

9. Different societies might _____ the same resource in different ways.

Review the Main Ideas

Section 1 (pp. 5–10)

10. What is the difference between microeconomics and macroeconomics?

11. How does scarcity differ from a shortage?

12. Your friend says, "I need some new clothes." Under what conditions would this be expressing a need? A want?

13. Complete the chart below by listing the four factors of production and an example of each.

Factors of Production	Examples

Section 2 (pp. 14–19)

14. What does making a trade-off require you to do?

15. If a person chooses to buy a pair of shoes instead of a new jacket, what does the jacket represent in economic terms?

16. What does a production possibilities curve show?

Section 3 (pp. 20–25)

17. For what purposes do economists use real-world data in building models?

18. What do economists and other scientists call the educated guesses that they make and test?

19. When does an economist consider an economic model useful?

Math Practice

The production possibilities curve below shows the production possibilities for a carpenter's typical workweek and supply of wood. Refer to this production possibilities curve to answer the following questions.

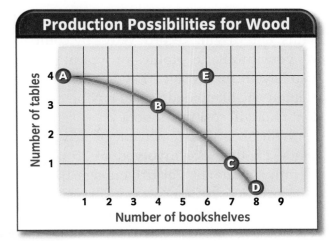

Production Possibilities for Wood

Number of tables (y-axis)
Number of bookshelves (x-axis)

20. What is the opportunity cost of making 7 bookshelves with the time and wood available?

21. What must happen in order to move from point B to point C?

Economics ONLINE

Self-Check Quiz Visit the *Economics Today and Tomorrow* Web site at glencoe.com and click on *Chapter 1—Self-Check Quizzes* to assess your knowledge of chapter content.

22. What would happen to the curve if the carpenter got sick for a couple of days or his wood supply was delivered a bit late? Why?

23. Point E represents an impossible situation—the carpenter would not be able to produce 6 bookshelves and 4 tables. Why?

Critical Thinking

24. **The BIG Idea** Imagine that the Guevara family buys a large piece of land suitable for growing grapes or oranges. They decide to ask an economist for advice about their options for turning the land into a money-making resource for the family. What are some examples of the kinds of hypotheses the economist might offer the family? Based on the economist's hypotheses, how will the Guevaras know whether the economic decisions they make are right or wrong?

Analyzing Visuals

25. Study the cartoon on the right, and then answer the following questions.

   a. Who are the two men in the cartoon, and what transaction are they discussing?

   b. Why would the car pictured be exceptionally fuel efficient?

   c. What is the trade-off to which the man on the left is referring?

"*Naturally, there's a trade-off for its exceptional fuel economy.*"

Why do males under 25 pay more for car insurance?

THE ISSUE

Although some insurance companies have started to base their rates on the number of years of driving experience rather than age, on average, it still costs young men more to insure their cars than young women or other age groups. A family that adds a teenage daughter to its insurance policy will pay about twice as much as before. If the same family adds a teenage son to the policy, the premiums may triple. Why do young men have to pay more for car insurance?

THE FACTS

To insurers, you're not a person—you're a set of risks. Before quoting a price for insuring your car, they consider the type of car, number of miles you drive per year, where you live, and who you are: age, gender, marital status, and driving record. Why? By comparing your profile to profiles of typical people who have been involved in crashes, they can estimate the likelihood of you having an accident that will cost them money.

While less than 7 percent of drivers are under 25, they are involved in 25 percent of traffic accidents. For drivers age 16 to 19, the crash risk is four times higher than for older drivers. Men of all ages are involved in twice as many crashes as women, and fatal crashes are twice as common among teenage males as teenage females. Check the chart below for more facts about young drivers.

Some companies also consider educational level and occupation. People with advanced degrees have fewer accidents than those with high-school diplomas. Who are the best drivers? They include editors, judges, firefighters, health technicians, homemakers, teachers, secretaries, and artists. The riskiest? Students, doctors, attorneys, architects, and real-estate agents.

Unsafe Driving Practices*

* Figures represent the percentage of poll respondents who admitted engaging in the listed unsafe driving practices.

Practice	16- to 25-year-olds	All drivers
Speeding	74%	69%
Aggressive driving	33%	16%
Cell phone use	65%	43%
Eating	73%	52%
Text messaging	25%	6%

Source: Mason-Dixon Polling & Research, 2005.

- 16- to 25-year-olds
- All drivers

THE ECONOMIC CONNECTION: PROFIT INCENTIVE

Like all businesses, insurance companies have a profit motive: they must make a profit to stay in business. When a clothing company sells you a pair of jeans, it's not taking a financial risk. But when an insurance company sells its service, it's taking a big risk. If you have an accident, the medical care, court costs, car repairs, and other expenses you might have will more than wipe out any profit the company might have made from the premiums you pay.

Successful companies do research to find out which types of customers generate the most—and the least—profit. Based on their research, auto insurers know it's less risky— and more profitable—to insure a 40-year-old woman teacher who owns a station wagon and has been driving and paying premiums for 20 years without having an accident. On the other hand, a 16-year-old male student with six months' experience driving a sports car carries a much larger risk. Traffic accidents involving teens cost society about $40 billion a year. Insurance companies must offset the losses

did you know? The most dangerous time to drive is midnight to 3:00 AM on Saturdays and Sundays. The second-largest number of accidents occur while driving to and from school.

they sustain on accident claims in order to make a profit. Since a few young men cause most of these accidents, all young men pay higher insurance premiums. But they are not the only ones. Companies usually also distribute some of the higher costs among all of their customers.

CONCLUSION

The profit incentive that drives all businesses in a market economy determines the prices consumers pay for goods and services. To ensure that profits (premiums) are greater than losses (accident claims), insurance companies charge all customers more, so all buyers of car, mortgage, or health insurance pay for the mistakes of others. When some young men drive recklessly, some homeowners cause fires by leaving lit candles unattended, or medical patients continue to live unhealthy lifestyles—everyone pays more for insurance.

Analyzing the Impact

1. **Synthesizing** Why would insurance rates be affected by where a driver lives?

2. **Critical Thinking** Which of the activities in the chart on the previous page do you think are the most dangerous? Why do you think more young people than older people engage in these activities while driving?

## chapter 2

Economic Systems and the American Economy

The **BIG Idea**

Every society has an economic system to allocate goods and services.

Why It Matters

As an American, you have many economic choices available to you. Not all nations offer their citizens the same economic choices that most Americans enjoy. In this chapter, read to learn how the American economy is different from the economies of some other countries.

Economics ONLINE

Chapter Overview Visit the *Economics Today and Tomorrow* Web site at glencoe.com and click on *Chapter 2—Chapter Overviews* to preview chapter information.

Economic Systems

GUIDE TO READING

Section Preview
In this section, you will learn about the four basic types of economic systems and how each one answers the three basic questions of what, how, and for whom to produce.

Content Vocabulary
- economic system *(p. 34)*
- traditional economy *(p. 36)*
- command economy *(p. 37)*
- market economy *(p. 38)*
- market *(p. 38)*
- circular flow of income and output *(p. 39)*
- mixed economy *(p. 40)*

Academic Vocabulary
- available *(p. 34)*
- distribute *(p. 35)*
- incentive *(p. 37)*

Reading Strategy
Describing As you read the section, use a web diagram like the one below to briefly describe each of the four basic types of economic systems.

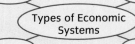

Types of Economic Systems

ISSues In ThE NeWS
—from *BusinessWeek*

MORE THAN A JOB Maybe it seems like you spend half your life on the phone with a call center in India. But in India itself, call centers actually are seeping into everyday life, appearing in a wave of popular sitcoms and books. *India Calling*, a hot Indian TV show … depicts a small-town girl who lands in Bombay in search of her missing sister. She finds a job in a call center instead. Viewers follow the highs and lows of the work, which attracts thousands of young Indians.

▲ **Call Center in India**

"Call center jobs are now part of India's social fabric, offering immense scope for romance, politics, … all creating high drama," says Shristi Behl Arya, who is the show's producer.

The economy of India is expanding, thanks in large part to growth in industries like call centers and software development. The economies of many other nations are changing as well, while others, like that of the United States, have remained relatively stable for many years. In this section, you'll learn that each nation's economy depends on how that nation chooses to use its resources to satisfy people's wants and needs.

Three Basic Questions

Main Idea All economic systems face the same basic questions: What should be produced? How should it be produced? For whom should it be produced?

Skills Handbook

See page R35 to learn about Identifying Main Ideas.

economic system: way in which a nation uses its resources to satisfy its people's needs and wants

Economics & You Do you think it's fair that some people have more than others, or should everyone share equally in what a society produces? Read on to learn about this and other questions that all economic systems must answer.

The way a nation determines how to use its resources to satisfy its people's needs and wants is called an **economic system.** Although nations have different economic systems, each one is faced with answering the same three basic questions: What goods and services should be produced? How should they be produced? Who should share in what is produced? (See **Figure 2.1** below.)

What Should Be Produced? As you've learned, we live in a world of scarcity and trade-offs. If more of one particular item is produced, then less of something else will be produced. If the government decides to use resources to build new roads, then fewer resources are **available** to maintain national parks. If a city decides to hire more police officers, fewer funds are available to add teachers to classrooms. Similarly, an automobile manufacturer must decide whether to produce pickup trucks, minivans, sport utility vehicles, or luxury cars—and how much of each.

Figure 2.1 | The Three Basic Economic Questions

■ In any economic system, the same three basic economic questions need to be addressed.

A. What to Produce? Because of scarcity, no nation can produce every good it needs or wants. Often, what a nation produces depends upon its natural resources. For example, because its soil and climate are good for growing coffee, Colombia produces a great deal of that product.

B. How to Produce? Trade-offs exist among the available factors of production. In factory settings, producers often need to decide whether piecemeal work or assembly line production would be more efficient.

How Should It Be Produced? After deciding what to produce, an economic system must then decide how those goods and services will be produced. How many laborers will be hired? Will skilled laborers or unskilled laborers do the work? Will capital goods be used to manufacture the products, thereby reducing the number of laborers needed? What kinds of technology will be used in the production process? For each good and service produced, there are always trade-offs possible among the available factors of production. Decisions must be made as to what the best combination of available inputs will be to get the job done for the lowest possible cost.

For Whom Should It Be Produced? After goods or services are produced, the type of economic system under which people live determines how the goods and services will be **distributed** among its members. Who receives the new cars? Who benefits from a new city school? Who lives in new apartment buildings? As you will read, the answers to these economic questions vary greatly depending on where you live. In the United States and in many other countries, most goods and services are distributed to individuals and businesses through a price system. Other economies may distribute products through majority rule, through a lottery, on a first-come-first-served basis, by sharing equally, by military force, and in a variety of other ways.

Reading Check **Identifying** What is an economic system, and what basic questions does it address?

C. For Whom to Produce? Economic systems determine how people will receive goods and services. In the United States, anyone who is willing and able to pay the price of a good or service is usually able to do so.

Economic Analysis

Explaining *Why can't businesses or nations produce as much as they want?*

Types of Economic Systems

Main Idea There are four basic types of economic systems: traditional, command, market, and mixed.

Economics & You How would you feel if the government told you where you could work and how much income you would make? Read on to learn about the four types of economic systems and the differences among them.

Economists have identified four types of economic systems. They differ from one another based on how they answer the three basic questions of what, how, and for whom to produce. The four general types of economic systems are traditional, command (or controlled), market (or capitalist), and mixed. Keep in mind that the four systems described here are theoretical representations of economies found throughout the world. No "pure" systems really exist—they are all mixed economies to some degree.

traditional economy: system in which economic decisions are based on customs and beliefs that have been handed down from generation to generation

Traditional System
A pure **traditional economy** answers the three basic questions according to tradition. In such a system, things are done "the way they have always been done." Economic decisions are based on customs and beliefs—often religious—handed down from generation to generation.

If you lived in a traditional economic system, your parents would teach you to perform the same tasks that they learned from their parents. As a male, if your father was a fisherman, you would become a fisherman. You would learn to make fishing nets the same way that he was taught, and you would distribute your catch in the manner that it had always been done.

Traditional Economy

The Mbuti of the Democratic Republic of the Congo in central Africa retain the elements of a traditional economy. They are hunter-gatherers, and the roles of the group members are set by custom and tradition.

An advantage of living in a traditional economy is that you know what is expected of you. In addition, family and community ties are usually very strong. Disadvantages include an economy in which change is discouraged and perhaps even punished, and in which the methods of production are often inefficient. Consequently, choices among consumer goods are rare. Also, people living and working in traditional economies rarely experience an increasing level of material well-being. Things tend to stay the same.

Traditional economies exist to some extent in very limited parts of the world today. The Inuit of North America, the Mbuti of the Democratic Republic of the Congo, and the Aborigines of Australia are organized into traditional economic systems.

Command Economy

In a command economy, government leaders decide how goods and services will be distributed. Here, women in North Korea stand in line to receive corn at a public distribution center.

Command System The pure **command economy** is somewhat similar to the traditional economy in that the individual has little, if any, influence over how the basic economic questions are answered. However, in a command or controlled system, government leaders—not tradition—control the factors of production and, therefore, make all decisions about their use.

Decisions in government may be made by one person, a small group of leaders, or a group of central planners in an agency. These people choose what is to be produced and how resources are to be used at each stage in production. They also decide how goods and services will be distributed. If you lived in a command economy, you would be paid according to what the central planners decide, and you might not be allowed to choose your own career. Through a series of regulations about education, the government guides people into certain jobs.

Disadvantages of such a controlled economy include a lack of **incentives** to work hard or to show inventiveness, as well as a lack of consumer choices. Because the government sets workers' salaries, there is no reason to work efficiently.

Only a few countries in the world today still have much of a command economy. North Korea and parts of the People's Republic of China are the two main examples because so much economic activity there is government-planned.

command economy: system in which the government controls the factors of production and makes all decisions about their use

Economics ONLINE

Student Web Activity
Visit the *Economics Today and Tomorrow* Web site at glencoe.com and click on *Chapter 2—Student Web Activities* to learn more about the command economy of the former Soviet Union.

market economy: system in which individuals own the factors of production and make economic decisions through free interaction while looking out for their own and their families' best interests

market: the process of freely exchanging goods and services between buyers and sellers

Market System The opposite of a pure command economy is a pure **market economy**—also called capitalism. In a market system, economic decisions are made not by government, but by individuals looking out for their own and their families' best interests. A limited government makes it possible for individuals to decide for themselves the answers to the three basic questions. Individuals own the factors of production, and therefore choose what to produce and how to produce it. Individuals also choose what to buy with the income received from selling their labor and other resources. All of these choices are guided not by tradition or a central planning agency, but by information in the form of market prices.

A **market** is not necessarily a place. Rather, it is the *voluntary exchange* of goods and services between buyers and sellers. This exchange may take place in a worldwide market for a good such as crude oil. It may also take place in a neighborhood market for services such as paper delivery, snow shoveling, and baby-sitting.

Prices in a market coordinate the interaction between buyers and sellers. As prices change, they act as signals to everyone within the system as to what should be bought and what should be produced. A high price for a good generally means that it is relatively scarce. A low price suggests that it is relatively abundant. The freedom of prices to rise and fall results in a neutral, self-organizing, incentive-driven system.

Market Economy

In a market economy, individuals make the economic decisions, and prices act as signals to buyers and sellers about what should be bought and what should be produced.

Figure 2.2 | Circular Flow of Income and Output

Charts In Motion
See StudentWorks™ Plus or
go to glencoe.com.

■ The circular flow of economic activity shows the relationship between different economic groups in a market system.

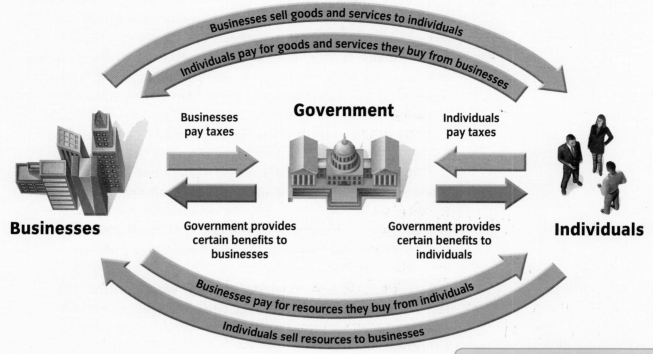

Businesses sell goods and services to individuals

Individuals pay for goods and services they buy from businesses

Government

Businesses pay taxes

Individuals pay taxes

Businesses

Government provides certain benefits to businesses

Government provides certain benefits to individuals

Individuals

Businesses pay for resources they buy from individuals

Individuals sell resources to businesses

Economic Analysis

Using Charts *What is one example of a resource a business might buy from an individual?*

The flow of resources, goods and services, and income in a market system is actually circular, as shown in **Figure 2.2** above. Economists use this model, called a **circular flow of income and output,** to illustrate how the market system works. Note how dollars flow from businesses to individuals and back to businesses again. The factors of production flow from individuals to businesses, which use them to produce goods and services that flow back to individuals.

The advantages of a pure market system are many. People have freedoms—to choose a career, to spend their income how they wish, to own property, and to take risks and earn profits. Also, the existence of competition provides consumers with a wide array of goods and services from which to choose, as well as an efficient system of determining costs. One disadvantage of a pure market system involves concern about those too young, too old, or too sick to work. Many fear that survival for these people would be difficult unless the government, churches, family members, or other organizations stepped in to provide goods and services for them.

circular flow of income and output: economic model that pictures income as flowing continuously between businesses and consumers

mixed economy: system combining characteristics of more than one type of economy

Mixed System

A **mixed economy** combines basic elements of a pure market economy and a command economy. Most countries of the world have a mixed economy in which private ownership of property and individual decision making are combined with government intervention and regulations. In the United States, most decisions are made by individuals reacting as participants within the market. Federal, state, and local governments, however, make laws protecting private property and regulating certain areas of business. Such regulations include certain environmental protections, safety guidelines for workers, and laws to protect consumers. In Section 2, you'll learn more about the United States's mixed economy, and the role of government in it.

To summarize, consider why a society has one type of economic system and not another. The goals that individuals set for their society help determine their economic system. The amount of government involvement in allocating scarce resources also determines a society's economic system.

✓ Reading Check **Summarizing** Who or what controls the factors of production in each of the four types of economic systems?

section 1 Review

Vocabulary

1. **Explain** the significance of: economic system, traditional economy, command economy, market economy, market, circular flow of income and output, mixed economy.

Main Ideas

2. **Explaining** An economic system answers what three basic questions?

3. **Summarizing** In a chart like the one below, fill in the answers to the questions about each major type of economic system.

Type of System	Who Answers 3 Basic ?'s	Advantages	Disadvantages
Traditional			
Command			
Market			
Mixed			

Critical Thinking

4. **The BIG Idea** Go back to the web diagram you made at the beginning of the section. For each economic system you listed, write down the name of a country that uses that system. Use examples from the text or your own knowledge.

5. **Contrasting** In the circular flow of income and output model in this section, consumers and businesses pass income back and forth freely. Which of the four economic systems would not be represented by this model, and why?

Applying Economics

6. **Political Systems** Some economic systems work better with democracies and some work better with authoritarian rule. Which political system best matches each economic system? Why?

ECONOMIST
(1806–1873)

John Stuart Mill

● **English Philosopher and Radical Reformer**

■ Author of *System of Logic (1843)*, *Principles of Political Economy* (1848), *On Liberty* (1859), *Utilitarianism* (1861), and *The Subjection of Women* (1869)

■ Member of Parliament

■ Godfather to the philosopher Bertrand Russell

John Stuart Mill was very much a product of home schooling. His father, James Mill, spent a great deal of time educating his nine children, but it was to John, the first born, that he devoted the most attention. By the time John was six, he had been reading Greek for three years and was an accomplished reader of Latin. As the eldest, John was forced to take a large part in the education of his younger siblings.

Mill went on to make important contributions to both political philosophy and economics. His essay *On Liberty* is considered a classic defense of personal freedom and individuality. In it he states, "[T]he only purpose for which power can be rightfully exercised over any member of a civilized community, against his will, is to prevent harm to others. His own good, either physical or moral, is not a sufficient warrant. . . . The only freedom which deserves the name, is that of pursuing our own good in our own way, so long as we do not attempt to deprive others of theirs. . . ."

Although Mill favored individual freedom in general, he was prepared to make numerous exceptions based on the philosophy of *utilitarianism*, the idea that society should adopt policies promoting "the greatest happiness of the greatest number." His *Principles of Political Economy*, for example, emphasized production and distribution as separate processes, with distribution to be regulated by the government in order to achieve the utilitarian goal:

> **The distribution of wealth . . . depends on the laws and customs of society. . . . Society can subject the distribution of wealth to whatever rules it thinks best.**

Checking for Understanding

1. **Clarifying** What is the goal of utilitarianism?

2. **Extending the Content** How did Mill think society should go about achieving "the greatest happiness of the greatest number"?

Characteristics of the American Economy

GUIDE TO READING

Section Preview
In this section, you will learn about the major characteristics of a market economic system.

Content Vocabulary
- capitalism *(p. 43)*
- laissez-faire *(p. 43)*
- free-enterprise system *(p. 44)*
- profit *(p. 45)*
- profit incentive *(p. 45)*
- competition *(p. 45)*
- private property *(p. 46)*

Academic Vocabulary
- regulate *(p. 43)*
- license *(p. 45)*

Reading Strategy
Organizing Complete a table similar to the one below by listing the six major characteristics of the U.S. economy.

U.S. Economy
1.
2.
3.
4.
5.
6.

PrODUCTS In ThE NeWS
*—from **Money***

GET THEM WHILE THEY'RE YOUNG Question: At what age do children start to develop "brand loyalty"?

Answer: Two years old. By the age of two—really, two—kids can recognize a favorite brand on store shelves and let you know they want it, with words or gestures, says James McNeal, a former marketing professor at Texas A&M. (In fact, his research shows that babies as young as six months are able to recognize some corporate logos and mascots.)

Once the brand light bulb goes on, children quickly learn the art of the nag: Kids ages four to twelve influence—that's putting it nicely—an estimated $300 billion of their parents' purchases annually. That's nearly as big as 2004's $319 billion federal budget deficit.

Careers Handbook
*See pages **R76–R80** to learn about becoming an advertising manager.*

In a market economy, producers often spend large amounts to make sure that consumers—even very young children—know the names and logos of their products. This is because free-market consumers have freedom of choice, and they will often choose brand names they recognize. In this section, you'll learn more about freedom of choice and the other major charactistics of a market economic system.

Limited Role of Government

Main Idea Under capitalism, government plays a relatively limited role in the allocation of resources.

Economics & You Do you think the government has a right to control a nation's resources, or should decisions about economic activity be left up to individuals? Read on to learn about the relatively limited role of government in a capitalist system.

In his book *An Inquiry into the Nature and Causes of the Wealth of Nations,* economist Adam Smith in 1776 described a system in which government has little to do with a nation's economic activity. He said that individuals left on their own would work for their own self-interest. In doing so, they would be guided as if by an "invisible hand" to use resources efficiently and thus achieve the maximum good for society.

Smith's version of the ideal economic system is called **capitalism,** another name for the market system. Pure capitalism has also been called a **laissez-faire** system. This French term means "let [people] do [as they choose]." A pure capitalist system is one in which the government lets people and businesses make their own economic decisions without government interference. Capitalism as practiced in the United States today would be best defined as an economic system in which private individuals own the factors of production but use them within certain legislated limits.

capitalism: economic system in which private individuals own the factors of production

laissez-faire: economic system in which the government minimizes its interference with the economy

Smith's ideas influenced the Founders of the United States, who limited the role of government mainly to national defense and keeping the peace. Since the 1880s, however, the role of government—federal, state, and local—has increased significantly. Among other things, federal agencies **regulate** the quality of various foods and drugs, watch over the nation's money and banking system, inspect workplaces for hazardous conditions, and guard against damage to the environment. The federal government also uses tax revenues to provide social programs such as Social Security and Medicare. State and local governments have expanded their roles in such areas as education, job training, recreation, and care for the elderly.

Reading Check **Describing** What is meant by a laissez-faire economic system?

"It's a new FCC regulation. You have to wear it if you are using your headset in public."

Other Characteristics

Main Idea In a free market, economic activity is coordinated by private businesses and individuals responding to market signals.

Economics & You Have you ever bought something you were unhappy with? Would you ever buy that product again? Read on to learn how buyers influence the market.

The government's relatively limited role in capitalist economies is only one characteristic of these economic systems. Now we will look at some of these systems' other features.

free-enterprise system: economic system in which individuals own the factors of production and decide how to use them within legal limits; same as capitalism

Freedom of Enterprise The American economy, besides being termed *capitalist*, is also known as a **free-enterprise system.** This term emphasizes that individuals are free to own and control the factors of production. If you go into business for yourself, you may become rich selling your product. You may instead end up losing money, however, because you—or any entrepreneur—have no guarantee of success.

The government places certain legal restrictions on freedom of enterprise. For instance, just because you know how to fix cars does not mean that you can set up an automobile-repair business in your backyard. Zoning regulations, child-labor laws, hazardous waste disposal rules, and other regulations limit free enterprise to protect you and your neighbors.

Freedom of Choice Freedom of choice is the other side of freedom of enterprise. It means that buyers, not sellers, make the decisions about what should be produced. The success or failure of a good or service in the marketplace depends on individuals freely choosing what they want to buy. If a computer game company releases a new game, but few people buy it, the company most likely will not use that particular game designer again. Buyers have signaled that they do not like that game designer's work.

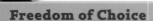

Freedom of Choice

If consumers buy a certain product at its current price, producers can maintain the current production level and price, or they can try raising the price to see if consumers will still buy the product. If the product still sells, the producers' profits will go up. If the product doesn't sell, producers will have to lower the price.

Although buyers are free to make choices in a free-market economy, the marketplace has become increasingly complex. At times, the government has intervened in various areas of the economy to protect buyers. Laws set safety standards for such things as toys, electrical appliances, and automobiles. In industries dominated by just a few companies—such as public utilities selling natural gas or electricity—the government sometimes regulates prices.

Profit Incentive When a person invests time, know-how, money, and other capital resources in a business, the goal is to make a profit. **Profit** is the amount left after all the costs of production have been paid, including wages, rents, interest, and taxes. The desire to make a profit is called the **profit incentive,** or profit motive. The profit incentive motivates entrepreneurs to produce new goods and services.

The risk of failing is also part of the free-enterprise system. What happens when profits are *not* realized—when businesses fail? Losses signal entrepreneurs that they should move resources elsewhere. Thus, the interaction of both profits and losses leads to an economy that is more efficient, adaptable to change, and continually growing.

Competition

Because of competition, similar products such as fast-food hamburgers will generally have similar prices.

Competition In a free-enterprise system, the lure of profits encourages **competition**—the rivalry among producers of similar products to win more business by offering lower prices or better quality. Effective competition often requires a large number of independent sellers, which means that no single company can noticeably affect the price of a particular product or service. If one company raises its prices, potential customers can simply go to other sellers.

Competition leads to an efficient use of resources. How so? Businesses have to keep prices low enough to attract buyers, yet high enough to make a profit. This forces businesses to keep their costs of production as low as possible.

For competition to exist, barriers to entry into, and exit from, industries must be weak. For the most part, the United States has weak barriers to entry and exit, but there are exceptions. For example, a person cannot become a physician until he or she has received a **license** from a state government.

profit: amount earned after a business subtracts its costs from its revenues

profit incentive: desire to make money that motivates people to produce and sell goods and services

competition: rivalry among producers or sellers of similar goods and services to win more business

private property: whatever is owned by individuals rather than by government

Private Property One of the most important characteristics of capitalism is the existence of **private property,** or property that is owned by individuals or groups rather than by the federal, state, or local governments. You as an individual are free to buy whatever you have the funds to do so, whether it is land, a business, an automobile, or baseball cards. You can also control how, when, and by whom your property is used. What are called the rights of property, however, are actually the rights of humans to risk investment, own productive assets, learn new ways of producing, and then to enjoy the benefits if these choices result in profits.

The Founders of the United States recognized that such rights must not be violated, because these rights are the invisible engine for creating wealth and prosperity for all. The Constitution guarantees an owner's right to private property and its use. Thus, in principle, no level of government in the United States can seize or use private property, at least not without paying the owners.

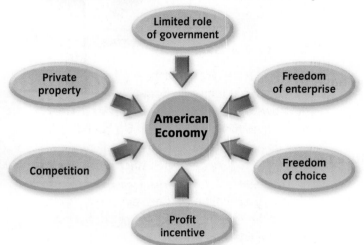

Characteristics of the American Economy

- Limited role of government
- Private property
- Freedom of enterprise
- Competition
- **American Economy**
- Freedom of choice
- Profit incentive

✓ **Reading Check** **Explaining** Who makes the decisions about what should be produced in a free-market system?

section 2 Review

Vocabulary
1. **Explain** the significance of: capitalism, laissez-faire, free-enterprise system, profit, profit incentive, competition, private property.

Main Ideas
2. **Identifying** Study the list of goods and services below. Then identify who you believe controls most decisions involved with each example, and explain your choice.

Goods and Services	Who Controls?	Why?
Electricity		
Lawn mowing service		
Ice cream store		

Critical Thinking
3. **The BIG Idea** Look back at the chart you made at the beginning of the section. Then think of a grocery store near your neighborhood, and give examples of how the store represents three of the characteristics of a pure market system.

4. **Summarizing** In a capitalist system, why might business owners resist government intervention in their business?

Applying Economics
5. **Extending the Content** Describe a situation in which a lack of competition caused you to pay more for a good or service than you would have otherwise.

section 3 The Goals of the Nation

GUIDE TO READING

Section Preview
In this section, you will learn about the goals of the American free-enterprise system and the rights and responsibilities that individual Americans face as members of this system.

Content Vocabulary
- economic efficiency *(p. 48)*
- economic equity *(p. 49)*
- standard of living *(p. 49)*
- economic growth *(p. 49)*

Academic Vocabulary
- element *(p. 48)*
- expand *(p. 49)*

Reading Strategy
Identifying Complete a table like the one below by listing the individual's rights and responsibilities in the American free-enterprise system.

Rights	Responsibilities
1.	1.
2.	2.
3.	3.

ISSues In ThE NeWS
—from *BusinessWeek*

THE INCOME GAP We can debate a lot of economic data but not income inequality. Every serious study shows that the U.S. income gap has become a chasm. Over the past 30 years, the share of income going to the highest-earning Americans has risen steadily to levels not seen since before the Great Depression. . . .

Growing inequality helps explain why so many Americans feel so vulnerable even as the overall economy begins to expand. Moods understandably darken when many have to take second jobs and go into debt to improve their living standards. . . .

If we don't pursue policies to fix inequality, social pressures may force unwise, even extremist moves, like protectionism. . . .

▲ **Low-income neighborhood in Detroit, Michigan**

Nations have values, and they set goals for themselves based on those values. The United States is no exception. Its goals are evident in the supreme law of the land—the Constitution—as well as in its government policies and in the actions of people like you. In this section, you'll learn how the nation strives both to reach its economic goals and treat its citizens fairly.

Goals of Free Enterprise

Main Idea The economic goals of free enterprise are freedom, efficiency, equity, security, stability, and growth.

Economics & You Take a moment to think about the values of the United States that are most important to you. Then read on to learn about the economic values of the American free-enterprise system.

The United States has a free-enterprise, or capitalist, system. Therefore, the major characteristics of a market economy should be evident in its goals. Among the national goals of Americans are freedom, efficiency, equity, security, stability, and growth. Although these goals have ethical, social, and religious **elements,** let's focus on their economic implications instead.

The goal of economic freedom is to allow each member of society to make choices. Americans have one of the highest degrees of freedom in the world to start their own businesses, to own private property, to make decisions in the marketplace, and to pursue other economic choices. Residents of the United States may choose to work nights or part-time, to have several jobs, and to move from place to place in search of work.

Along with this freedom come certain costs, as shown in **Figure 2.3.** In particular, individuals must normally accept the consequences of their decisions in our free-enterprise system. If an entrepreneur starts a business that fails, for example, the government usually won't help out.

Using our limited resources wisely is the goal of **economic efficiency.** Because of scarcity, if the factors of production are wasted, fewer goods and services overall will be produced. We must always be watchful to use the lowest-cost way to produce any given amount of output.

economic efficiency: wise use of available resources so as to obtain the greatest benefits possible

Economic Freedom

In the United States almost all people, including teenagers, have the right to open their own businesses and try to become successful entrepreneurs.

The issue of fairness underscores the goal of **economic equity**. Americans want their economic system to be fair and just. That's why we encourage our policy makers to pass laws such as those dealing with equal pay for equal work, fairness in hiring practices, and help for disabled workers. Another goal is *economic security*. Americans want protection against risks beyond our control—accidents on the job, natural disasters, business and bank failures, poverty in old age. Our economic system provides such security through a number of government social programs. The goal of *economic stability* seeks to reduce extreme ups and downs in the **standard of living**—the material well-being of an individual, group, or nation. The standard of living is measured by the average value of goods and services used by the average citizen during a given period of time. The United States has more individuals enjoying a high standard of living than almost anywhere else in the world. Finally, **economic growth** means producing increasing amounts of goods and services over the long term. As the population increases, the economy must also **expand** in order to provide for additional needs and wants. All nations have economic growth as a goal because it helps meet other goals.

economic equity: the attempt to balance an economic policy so that everyone benefits fairly

standard of living: the material well-being of an individual, group, or nation, measured by how well their necessities and luxuries are satisfied

economic growth: expansion of the economy to produce more goods, jobs, and wealth

Reading Check **Evaluating** Why is economic growth an important goal of the free-enterprise system?

| **Figure 2.3** | **Trade-Offs Among Goals** |

◼ In a world of scarcity, achieving national goals requires trade-offs. Understanding this will help you realize that not all political desires can be turned into economic reality.

▲ **A. Economic Freedom** The trade-off for the freedom to start a business and try to make a profit is the possibility that the business will fail.

▼ **B. Economic Security** The trade-off for programs that provide economic security, such as unemployment compensation, is the cost of resources that could have been used elsewhere.

Economic Analysis

Synthesizing *What might some trade-offs be for economic equity?*

Economic Systems and the American Economy **49**

Rights and Responsibilities

Main Idea Individuals have both rights and responsibilities within a free-enterprise system.

Economics & You Think about a time in your life when you received greater rights, such as the right to stay out later at night. Did you also experience greater responsibilities as a result? Read on to learn about the rights and responsibilities of Americans in the free-enterprise system.

The American free-enterprise system bestows numerous economic rights and protections on individuals like you. You have the right to enter into just about any profession or business you want. You have the right to work very little or to become a "workaholic." You have the right to buy those products and brands that you like and to reject all others.

A free-enterprise system will not work, however, if individuals do not take on certain responsibilities. The first is to be able to support yourself and your family. You have a responsibility to use your education in a way that helps you become a productive member of the free-enterprise system.

Also, because government has become such an important part of our economy, individuals in our system have the responsibility of electing responsible government officials. This requires both the knowledge of government policies and the ability to analyze the consequences of those policies.

✔ Reading Check **Summarizing** What are the economic responsibilities of Americans?

---

section 3 Review

Vocabulary

1. **Explain** the significance of economic efficiency, economic equity, standard of living, economic growth.

Main Ideas

2. **Identifying** Create a diagram like the one below and list the major goals of a market economy.

Goals of U.S. Economy

Critical Thinking

3. **The BIG Idea** How might economic freedom and a rising standard of living be related to each other?

4. **Contrasting** List three examples of ways that economic freedom and economic equity might conflict.

Applying Economics

5. **Synthesizing** Research three articles that reflect three different economic goals that you've read about. For each article, write a short paragraph explaining how the article fits the goal you selected.

Socialism and Capitalism

GUIDE TO READING

Section Preview
In this section, you will compare the characteristics of socialism and capitalism.

Content Vocabulary
- socialism *(p. 52)*
- proletariat *(p. 52)*
- communism *(p. 53)*
- democratic socialism *(p. 53)*
- authoritarian socialism *(p. 53)*

Academic Vocabulary
- continual *(p. 52)*
- initiative *(p. 54)*

Reading Strategy
Organizing As you read, complete a table like the one below by comparing the advantages and disadvantages of socialist and capitalist economic systems.

	Advantages	Disadvantages
Socialism		
Capitalism		

ISSues In ThE NeWS
—from *Novosti (Russian News and Information Agency)*

A NEW TAKE ON TOURISM The speaker of Ukraine's parliament suggested that the Chernobyl nuclear power plant, whose breakdown 20 years ago had far-reaching consequences for public health and the environment, should become a tourist destination. . . .

▲ **Chernobyl nuclear plant**

He said offering tours of the area surrounding the Chernobyl plant would make people more aware of the impact that man-made disasters could have on life on Earth.

Following the 1986 accident, the worst in the history of nuclear engineering, the facility was shut down and residents from within an 18-mile radius were evacuated. The aftermath included radioactive contamination that spread not only across Ukraine (then part of the Soviet Union), but also into neighboring Russia and Belarus and even some countries of northern and western Europe.

Some government intervention occurs in the American economy, but generally the marketplace answers the three basic economic questions of *what, how,* and *for whom* goods and services should be produced. In command (controlled) economies, however, the government (and not the market) answers these three basic questions. Read on to learn about the major alternative to market capitalism.

Pure Socialism

Main Idea Pure socialism is characterized by centralized economic planning and state ownership of the factors of production.

Economics & You Have you or a family member ever been treated unfairly in a job? Do you think that workers in general receive fair treatment under the American capitalist system? Read on to learn about socialism, the major alternative to free-enterprise systems.

socialism: a system in which the government owns the major factors of production and attempts to manage output and the distribution of goods

Pure command **socialism** is an economic system in which there is little private property and the state owns virtually all the factors of production, such as big factories. In a socialist economic system, the government attempts to manage production and especially the distribution of goods. Few examples of pure command socialism exist. Perhaps the most extensively controlled economies today are in North Korea and Cuba. See **Figure 2.4** below for a list of the characteristics of pure socialism.

The Marxian View of Socialism Socialism as a modern economic system grew out of protests against the problems caused by the Industrial Revolution of the 1800s. Karl Marx viewed history as a **continual** struggle between various groups, or classes, in society. In his own day, he saw this struggle as going on between capitalists—owners of the land, machines, and factories—and the **proletariat**, or workers.

proletariat: term Karl Marx used to refer to workers

Figure 2.4 | Pure Socialism

■ Socialism can be defined as an economic system that stresses government ownership of the major factors of production and control of the distribution of goods.

Characteristics of Pure Socialism

1. Most prices are set by the state, rather than by forces of supply and demand.

2. The movement of resources, particularly labor, is strictly controlled. The central planning authority makes all decisions.

3. Most of the major factors of production are owned by the state. Private property rights are strictly limited to small tools that an individual needs for an occupation.

4. Individual risk taking is not allowed. The state takes all of the risk when it decides which new companies shall be formed. All citizens pay for unsuccessful risk taking.

5. Economic decisions about what, how, and for whom to produce are all made by state officials through central planning agencies and other administrative units.

6. Taxation is often used to redistribute income.

Economic Analysis

Contrasting *How is life different for individual workers under pure socialism compared to under capitalism?*

Marx believed that capitalists exploited the proletariat, or used them unfairly. According to Marx, the value of goods depends only on how much labor is used in producing them. He believed that when capitalists sold a good and kept the profit, they were taking income that rightly belonged to the proletariat, the people who were actually doing the work.

Despite capitalism's dominance in the nineteenth century, Marx believed that it was ultimately doomed to fail. He outlined the eventual collapse of capitalism and predicted the evolution of socialism into **communism**—an idealized system with no need for a government. Today *communism* has come to mean any authoritarian socialist system that supports revolution as a means to overthrow capitalism and bring about socialist goals. Ironically, instead of "no government," communist systems have historically demonstrated that a central government ends up controlling the entire economy. The proletariat, whom Marx envisioned owning and controlling the means of production, actually end up with little to no power at all.

The Change From Capitalism to Socialism According to Marx

Step 1
Capitalism would suffer extreme recessions and depressions that would harm workers. A few rich capitalists would have all industrial power.

Step 2
The wide gap between the rich and the poor would cause workers to unite and overthrow capitalism.

▲ Karl Marx

Step 3
The victorious workers would establish a new socialist system. Workers, through the state, would own and control the means of production.

Step 4
The system would evolve into pure communism. Workers would contribute to society to their full abilities and, in return, take only what they needed.

communism: term used by Karl Marx for his idealized society in which no government is necessary

Socialism Since Marx In the twentieth century, socialism split into two major trends: democratic socialism and authoritarian socialism. **Democratic socialism** is a type of socialist system that works within the constitutional framework of a nation to elect socialists to office. In democratic socialist nations, government usually controls only some areas of the economy.

Authoritarian socialism, in contrast, more closely follows Marx's beliefs. Its supporters advocate revolution as the means to overthrow capitalism and bring about socialist goals. In authoritarian socialist nations, a central government controls the entire economy. *Communism,* the term Marx applied to his ideal society, came to mean any authoritarian socialist system. Few countries today have such a system.

democratic socialism: system that works within the constitutional framework of a nation to elect socialists to office; the government usually controls only some areas of the economy

authoritarian socialism: system that supports revolution as a means to overthrow capitalism and bring about socialist goals; the entire economy is controlled by a central government; also called *communism*

✔ Reading Check **Comparing and Contrasting** How does democratic socialism differ from authoritarian socialism? How are they similar?

The Benefits of Capitalism

Main Idea The main benefits of capitalism are economic efficiency and individual freedom.

Economics & You Which do you value more: personal freedom and individuality, or fairness and equality for all? Why? Read on to learn the values of a capitalist system.

Skills Handbook

*See page **R43** to learn about **Comparing and Contrasting.***

Many economists like to compare the advantages and disadvantages of capitalism and socialism. Often such comparisons are based on individual values.

Supporters of Capitalism Those who place a high value on personal freedom, **initiative,** and individuality prefer capitalism. They point out that socialism often brings extensive government intervention in all parts of the economy and, by necessity, in people's personal lives.

Supporters of capitalism point out that capitalism allows for more efficiency in the marketplace and for greater rates of economic growth. Indeed, considerable evidence shows that unregulated economic systems—those that are closer to pure capitalism—have *much higher* rates of economic growth.

Figure 2.5 | Planning in Market and Command Economies

■ Planning is unavoidable, no matter what the economic system. The United States has a highly planned economy. The difference between economic planning in the United States and in command economies is who does the planning.

Planning in Market and Command Economies

Market System: Decentralized	Command System: Centralized
In the U.S. market system, planning is undertaken by private firms, individuals, and elected government representatives. Economic activity is coordinated by private businesses and individuals responding to market signals.	In pure socialist systems, central planners undertake the planning on behalf of everyone. Planners also control the movement of resources, particularly labor.

Pyongyang, North Korea ▲

New York City, U.S.A. ▼

Economic Analysis

Explaining *Under which system is risk-taking by individuals encouraged?*

All Economies Are Planned It is often said that pure socialism requires centralized planning, and pure capitalism does not. In reality, all economies are planned in one way or another. (See **Figure 2.5**.) The United States has a highly planned economy. The difference between economic planning here versus that in socialist countries is who does the planning. Private firms, individuals, and elected government officials do the planning in the American economy. In pure socialist systems, central planners make decisions on behalf of everyone.

Real-world capitalism has some problems. Critics note that income is unequally distributed throughout the economy. They also say that although capitalist nations generally have enough government-provided goods such as highways, they do not have enough schools and museums for the general public. Such critics value some of the political goals of socialism.

No System Is Perfect

Some critics of capitalism claim that capitalist nations do not provide enough funds for schools and other institutions that benefit the public.

✔ Reading Check) **Identifying** What are some criticisms of socialism?

section 4 Review

Vocabulary
1. **Explain** the significance of: socialism, proletariat, communism, democratic socialism, authoritarian socialism.

Main Ideas
2. **Sequencing** Create a diagram like the one below to show the major steps in the development of socialism.

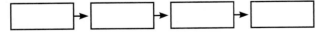

3. **Contrasting** Write a short paragraph contrasting authoritarian and democratic socialism.

Critical Thinking
4. **The BIG Idea** Look back at the chart you filled in listing the pros and cons of socialism and capitalism. Then list four reasons why authoritarian socialism seems to be ending while capitalism thrives.

Applying Economics
5. **Economics & You** Think of how you spend your time each day. Some goods and services you encounter are a result of our capitalist economy; someone made these items for a profit. Government provides other goods and services. Of the goods and services you used over the past 24 hours, which were made for a profit, and which were provided by the government?

RUSSIA: SHOPPERS GONE **WILD**

Russian consumers are on a buying spree.

Check It Out! In this chapter you learned about economic systems. This article discusses the changes in consumer buying habits after Russia's transition from a command to a market economy.

▲ A Mega mall in Russia

It's midday on Saturday, and the Mega-1 mall in southern Moscow is packed. Shoppers have come to stock up on groceries at the mall's French-owned Auchan hypermarket, buy furniture at Swedish retailer IKEA, and browse dozens of boutiques selling everything from Yves Rocher cosmetics to Calvin Klein underwear. Although crammed with expensive Western merchandise, Mega has been a hit since it opened its doors in December 2002. Last year it was the world's most frequented shopping center, with 52 million visitors. . . .

What makes the buying surge all the more remarkable is that the average income per person, while growing fast, is still just $300 a month. Yet a surprising number of Russians live as well or better than their Western counterparts. . . .

That's because some 70% of Russians' income is disposable, versus around 40% for a typical Western consumer. "We have 13% flat income tax, subsidized housing and utilities, and 10% savings. The rest of it is pretty much out there being spent," says Natalia Zagvozdina, a consumer-goods analyst at Moscow investment bank Renaissance Capital.

—Reprinted from *BusinessWeek*

Growing Consumerism in Russia		
Ownership by share of households		
	2001	**2006**
Mobile phone	6%	50%
Computer	5%	20%
Washing machine	16%	35%
Stereo	15%	31%
Video recorder	39%	50%
Car	25%	31%
Imported TV	58%	71%
Apartment or house	71%	82%

Source: GfK Rus Market Research, Moscow.

Think About It
1. **Identifying** What percentage of Russian households now own a computer? A car?
2. **Explaining** What has enabled Russians to buy more consumer products?

STUDY TO GO Study anywhere, anytime! Download quizzes and flash cards to your PDA from glencoe.com.

■ All economic systems answer **three basic questions:** what to produce, how to produce, and for whom to produce.

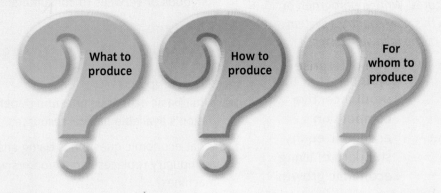

What to produce

How to produce

For whom to produce

■ There are four basic types of **economic systems:** traditional, command, market, and mixed.

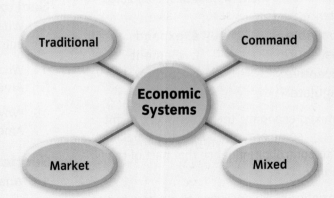

Traditional

Command

Economic Systems

Market

Mixed

■ The **American economy** is defined by six basic characteristics.

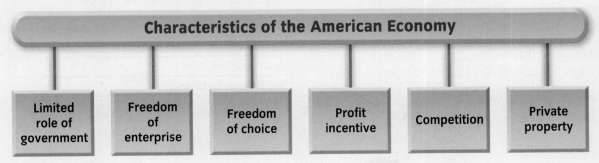

Characteristics of the American Economy

| Limited role of government | Freedom of enterprise | Freedom of choice | Profit incentive | Competition | Private property |

Review Content Vocabulary

1. *Imagine that a new country is being formed and wants to set up an economic system similar to that of the United States. Write a paragraph or two explaining how this new country's system might work. Use all of the following terms.*

economic system
mixed economy
market
circular flow of income and output
capitalism
laissez-faire

free-enterprise system
profit incentive
competition
economic equity
standard of living
economic growth

Review Academic Vocabulary

Choose the letter of the term that best completes each sentence.

a. available
b. distribute
c. incentive
d. regulate

e. expand
f. element
g. continual
h. initiative

2. In a mixed economy, the government might _____ some areas of business by making laws to control or influence that part of the economy.

3. All societies make decisions about how to use _____ resources.

4. A market economy experiences _____ changes as market forces influence the factors of production.

5. An entrepreneur is someone who sees a need and takes the _____ by starting a new business.

6. Competition is usually the _____, or motivation, for businesses to lower prices.

7. If a business is doing well, it might _____, or grow larger.

8. Competition is an important _____ of capitalism.

9. Every business must decide how best to _____ its goods or services to consumers.

Review the Main Ideas

Section 1 (pp. 33–40)
10. What basic economic question depends on a nation's available natural resources?

11. What economic question is being answered if an industry replaces some workers with machines?

12. How does a traditional economy answer the basic question, "How should it be produced?"

Section 2 (pp. 42–46)
13. What are six important characteristics of free enterprise?

14. What is government's role in the modern American version of capitalism?

15. Why is private property important in the American economic system?

Section 3 (pp. 47–50)
16. What are the six goals of free enterprise?

17. What are two examples of individuals' economic responsibilities in a free-enterprise system?

Section 4 (pp. 51–55)
18. Complete the graphic organizer by filling in characteristics of each economic system.

Economic System	Characteristics
Capitalism	
Democratic socialism	
Authoritarian socialism	

19. Who did Karl Marx believe should control the means of production in an economy?

Thinking Like an Economist

20. Imagine that a school club to which you belong wants to raise money to go on a group trip. Write two or three paragraphs explaining how your club would answer the three basic economic questions as they relate to the fund-raiser. Consider these questions: If your school represents an economic system, what type would it be (traditional, command, market, mixed)? Within that system, how would the club answer the three basic economic questions? How might concepts like competition and profit incentive influence the outcome of the fund-raiser?

Critical Thinking

21. **The BIG Idea** Karl Marx predicted that capitalism would collapse and evolve into socialism and then communism. The opposite has proved to be true—capitalism has thrived in the world and no society has yet evolved into pure communism. Why do you think this is so? Support your answer with facts and examples.

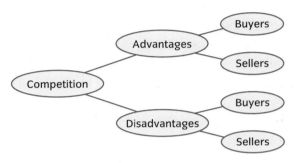

Economics ONLINE

Self-Check Quiz Visit the *Economics Today and Tomorrow* Web site at glencoe.com and click on **Chapter 2—Self-Check Quizzes** to assess your knowledge of chapter content.

22. **Comparing** Create a diagram like the one below to list the advantages and disadvantages of competition to buyers and sellers.

```
                              ┌─ Buyers
                   Advantages ─┤
                              └─ Sellers
Competition ─┤
                              ┌─ Buyers
                Disadvantages ─┤
                              └─ Sellers
```

23. **Interpreting** Explain what U.S. economic goal is being met by each of the following actions:
   (a) The government regulates the amount that an electric company can charge you for energy.
   (b) Juan moves to Seattle to work for a Web page designer.
   (c) Your savings account is insured up to $100,000.

Analyzing Visuals

24. Study the cartoon on the right, and then answer the following questions.

   a. What does the line on the graph represent?

   b. Why is making a profit more difficult now for ABX Corp.?

   c. Toward what economic system are other countries apparently moving?

"MAKING A PROFIT WAS A LOT EASIER BEFORE SO MANY COUNTRIES ABANDONED SOCIALISM AND STARTED COMPETING!"

Harley Schwadron/CartoonStock

Should the best event tickets go to the highest bidder?

Suppose your favorite team makes the playoffs, or the hottest band is coming to play in your town. Should the best seats be available to everyone on a lottery or first-come, first-served basis? Or should they go to whomever pays the most? The major ticket seller, Ticketmaster, recently adopted a policy of selling the best seats through online auctions. Some economists predict that, once a concert's true market value—its value to customers—is clear, the prices of all tickets go up. Others say early auctions allow promoters to assess demand, so remaining tickets may cost more or less. Should tickets go to the highest bidder?

NO! The true fans can't afford good seats

Who can afford a $1,000 ticket? Certainly not most loyal, long-time fans or teenagers looking to get as close as possible to their favorite pop idol. So instead of people who enjoy and respect the particular band or team getting a once-in-a-lifetime opportunity to see their favorite act up close, it'll be the highest bidder. Or fans will go to the poor house just to get a glimpse of their favorite artist.

It'll be just like [Georgia] Tech football games, where most of the prime chair-back seats are empty because those seats belong to the biggest contributors and not fans. The "true" fans will be stuck in nosebleed seats, itching for a closer look the whole time.

—Kimberly Rieck, Sports Editor, *Technique* newspaper, Georgia Institute of Technology

YES! It's more efficient and means more revenue for artists and promoters

Concert promoters like full venues. Big crowds buy more CDs and t-shirts, and maybe they also make the concert experience more enjoyable. So historically, tickets in general were priced too low . . . and the best seats were particularly underpriced. . . . But the economics of the music industry are changing. There is less money to be made in selling CDs [now], so bands are no longer willing to under-price live shows to support record sales. Rather, the concerts themselves have become the cash cow. Consequently, the artists want to squeeze as much money as possible out of them. Combine that with technological advances that make it possible to carry out online [ticket] auctions, and you now have a much more efficient market. More efficient in the sense that the people willing to pay the most end up in the expensive seats, and those extra revenues go to the artists (and the promoters and Ticketmaster), rather than scalpers.

—Steven D. Levitt, co-author, *Freakonomics*

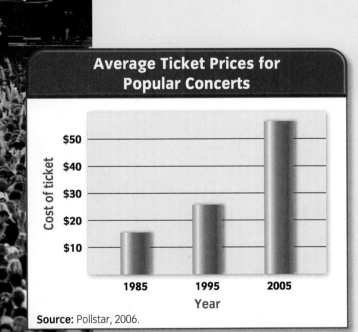

Average Ticket Prices for Popular Concerts

Source: Pollstar, 2006.

Debating the Issue

1. **Explaining** Why does the second writer believe that historically, concert tickets have actually been under-priced?

2. **Choosing Sides** The two writers disagree on whether the highest bidders should get the best event tickets. Which writer do you agree with? Why?

Find Out More!

3. **Analyzing** Using the Internet or other sources, check the difference between the prices of the best seats and the cheapest seats at an upcoming event you might like to attend. How do you think the promoters arrived at those prices? Is a better seat worth the difference in price?

Practical Economics: How Theory Works for You

In this unit, read to find out...

- how basic economic principles can help you in your daily life.

- what pitfalls to avoid when going into debt.

- what you should be aware of before buying a vehicle or house.

- why saving and investing are sound economic habits to learn.

The **BIG Idea**

Buyers and sellers voluntarily interact in markets, and market prices are set by the interaction of demand and supply.

Why It Matters

Think about how you spend your money on things such as transportation, entertainment, food, and clothing. How do you make these economic choices? In this chapter, read to learn about what it means to be a consumer and make rational consumer choices.

Economics **ONLINE**

Chapter Overview Visit the *Economics Today and Tomorrow* Web site at glencoe.com and click on *Chapter 3—Chapter Overviews* to preview chapter information.

Consumption, Income, and Decision Making

GUIDE TO READING

Section Preview
In this section, you will learn about factors that influence you as a consumer and how to make rational consumer decisions.

Content Vocabulary
- consumer (p. 66)
- disposable income (p. 66)
- discretionary income (p. 66)
- rational choice (p. 69)

Academic Vocabulary
- region (p. 66)
- perceive (p. 69)

Reading Strategy
Organizing As you read, complete a diagram like the one below by listing the factors that affect your ability to earn income and the factors you should consider when deciding how to spend your income.

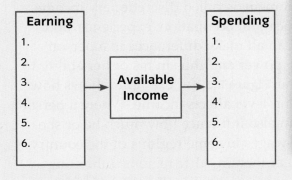

Earning		Spending
1.		1.
2.		2.
3.	**Available Income**	3.
4.		4.
5.		5.
6.		6.

ISSues In ThE NeWS
—from the *New York Times Magazine*

CREDIT LESSON IN A CARD Teaching your kids the basics of personal finance is important but also, let's face it, sort of a drag. Isn't there some entity you could outsource this chore to? Sure there is: Visa. In fact, Visa Buxx, a prepaid card aimed at 13- to 17-year-olds, is explicitly pitched as "a powerful financial education tool" that "helps your teen learn budgeting."

But how does putting $100 on such a card teach a teenager anything more about living within a budget than, say, doling out five $20 bills? . . . Thanks to an itemized online account, teenagers can see how they've spent their money and learn that the reason they can't afford that new pair of Nikes is that they're spending "$8 on a mochachino every other day."

Do you spend a lot of money on small, day-to-day items such as coffee, fast food, and candy, or do you prefer to save up your money for larger purchases? Either way, wise buying decisions will help you get the most out of the products you buy now and will enable you to meet your long-term financial goals. In this section, you'll learn how to spend—or not spend—your income wisely.

Personal Finance Handbook
See pages R4–R5 to learn about budgeting.

Disposable and Discretionary Income

Main Idea After people pay taxes, their remaining income may be saved or spent on essential or nonessential items.

Economics & You What do you plan to do after high school? How important is money to you when you consider your career plans? Read on to learn about the factors that affect how much income a person earns.

consumer: any person or group that buys or uses goods and services to satisfy personal needs and wants

disposable income: income remaining for a person to spend or save after all taxes have been paid

discretionary income: money income a person has left to spend on extras after necessities have been bought

You and everyone around you are consumers and, as such, play an important role in the economic system. A **consumer** is any person or group that buys or uses goods and services to satisfy personal needs and wants. Consumers spend on a wide variety of things—food, clothing, housing, automobiles, and movie tickets, for example.

A person's role as a consumer depends on his or her ability to consume. This ability to consume, in turn, depends on available income and how much of it a person chooses to spend now or save.

Income can be both disposable and discretionary. **Disposable income** is the money income a person has left after all taxes have been paid. People spend their disposable income on many kinds of goods and services. First, they buy the necessities: food, clothing, and housing. Any leftover income, which can be saved or spent on extras such as luxury items or entertainment, is called **discretionary income.**

Education, occupation, experience, and health can all make differences in a person's earning power and thus in his or her ability to consume. **Figure 3.1,** for example, shows how education level affects income. Where a person lives can also influence how much he or she earns—wages in some **regions** of the country are higher than in other regions. Inheriting money or property also affects earning power.

Reading Check **Identifying** On what two things does the ability to consume depend?

Spending Choices

Discretionary income can be spent on entertainment, such as movie tickets.

Decision Making as a Consumer

Main Idea Consumer decisions involve comparing available alternatives.

Economics & You Think about a recent purchase you made. What were your reasons for buying the item? Read on to learn the steps to making good consumer decisions.

Spending choices involve several decisions. The initial decision a consumer must make is whether to buy an item in the first place. This may sound so basic as to be unnecessary to mention, but how many times do you actually think about the reasons for the purchase you are about to make? When deciding how to spend your money, do you concentrate on items you *need* first, and then consider items you *want*? Do you consider the trade-offs involved? As we will see, consumer decisions involve three main considerations.

Scarce Resources After you have decided to make a purchase, at least two scarce resources are involved—income and time. Before you spend your money, you need to invest time in obtaining information about the product you wish to buy. Suppose, for example, that you wish to buy a mountain bike. How can you obtain information about the characteristics of the numerous brands and models and the prices of each? You should first visit retail stores and do some research on the Internet to compare prices. The time spent researching online or visiting stores to check models and prices is a cost to you. This time, and the money you eventually spend on the mountain bike, cannot be used for anything else.

Skills Handbook

See page **R51** to learn about *Using Tables and Charts.*

Figure 3.1 | Earning Power

■ Several factors can influence how much income a person has. One important factor is education. As you can see, the number of years of education you have has a direct effect on your income.

Economic Analysis

Using Charts *How much can you expect to make per year if you graduate from high school but do not attend college?*

How Education Affects Income

Amount of Education	Median Income	
	Males	Females
Not a high school graduate	$19,802	$10,613
High school graduate	$27,526	$15,972
Some college	$35,023	$20,602
Bachelor's degree	$55,188	$34,292
Professional degree	$88,216	$44,748

Source: *Statistical Abstract of the United States,* 2006.

Figure 3.2 | Consumer Spending

■ This circle graph shows how Americans, as a whole, spend their income. Note that both needs, like food, and wants, like entertainment, are included in consumer spending.

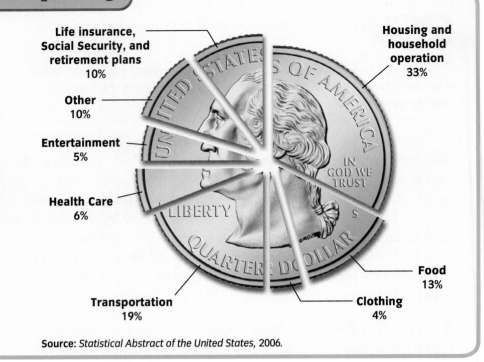

Life insurance, Social Security, and retirement plans 10%

Other 10%

Entertainment 5%

Health Care 6%

Transportation 19%

Clothing 4%

Food 13%

Housing and household operation 33%

Source: *Statistical Abstract of the United States, 2006.*

Economic Analysis

Identifying *What are the top three categories of consumer spending?*

Graphs In MOtion
See StudentWorks™ Plus or go to glencoe.com.

Opportunity Cost How U.S. consumers spend their income is shown in **Figure 3.2** above. Almost all of the steps in consumer decision making, like the choices represented in the graph, involve an opportunity cost. Remember from Chapter 1 that opportunity cost is the value of the highest alternative choice that you did not make. When considering this cost, you should think not only about whether you should buy an item in the first place, but also about the quality of the item if you do choose to buy it.

In general, a high-quality product costs more than a medium- or low-quality product. Suppose that you want to buy new cross-training shoes and are trying to decide between two different pairs. One model has a pump system that allows you to get a closer fit on your ankle, and the other does not. The pump system model costs $80 more than the other model. If you choose the higher-priced shoe, you will sacrifice $80. The opportunity cost of the pump model over the lesser-quality model shoe is whatever else you would have chosen to buy with that $80.

When considering opportunity costs, you should think carefully about whether the features of the higher-quality product are important to you, or whether you would rather spend the extra money elsewhere. In our training shoes example, for instance, think about whether a pump system is really something you need or want in a shoe. Is this feature really important to you? Or would you rather spend the $80 on something else?

68 Chapter 3

Rational Choice When you make consumer decisions based on opportunity cost, you are engaging in **rational choice.** Economists define rational choice as the alternative that has the greatest **perceived** value.

Rational choice involves choosing the best-quality item that is the least expensive from among comparable-quality products. As a consumer, you will make rational choices when you purchase the goods and services you believe can best satisfy your wants.

Do not get the impression that wise consumers will all make the same choices. Remember the definition: A rational choice is one that generates the greatest perceived value for any given expenditure. Each person's value system for his or her expenditures is different. Rational choices that are based on careful consumer decision making will still lead to billions of different consumer choices yearly.

Buying Decisions

If you choose the higher-priced product, you must believe that the opportunity cost for the higher quality is worth it—that nothing else at that instant will give you as much value.

rational choice: choosing the alternative that has the greatest value from among comparable-quality products

Reading Check **Explaining** What does it mean to make a rational consumer choice?

---

section 1 Review

Vocabulary

1. **Explain** the significance of: consumer, disposable income, discretionary income, rational choice.

Main Ideas

2. **Identifying** Copy the diagrams below, and in them list four items you would like to purchase now (Spending) and four items you would like to save for and buy later (Saving).

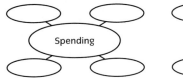

Critical Thinking

3. **The BIG Idea** From your spending web in question 2, list the items you are willing to give up in order to buy items in your savings web, and explain why.

4. **Explaining** What kinds of products are purchased with disposable income?

Applying Economics

5. **Rational Choice** Choose a product you like and create two advertisements. The first ad should emphasize why buying this product is a rational choice. The second ad should appeal to the fun or light side of the product and the desire to buy it, even if it's not a rational purchase.

Buying Principles and Strategies

GUIDE TO READING

Section Preview
In this section, you will learn the three basic buying principles that will help you to make effective consumer choices.

Content Vocabulary
- competitive advertising (p. 72)
- informative advertising (p. 72)
- bait and switch (p. 72)
- comparison shopping (p. 73)
- warranty (p. 74)
- brand name (p. 74)
- generic brand (p. 74)

Academic Vocabulary
- principle (p. 70)
- accurate (p. 71)
- similar (p. 74)

Reading Strategy
Outlining Complete an outline like the one below by listing the important points of the section.

Three Basic Buying Principles
1. Gathering information
A.
B.
2. Using advertising wisely
A.
B.
C.
3. Comparison shopping
A.
B.

ISSues In ThE NeWS

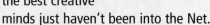

—from *BusinessWeek*

INTERNET ADS The 30-second television ad. To the creative directors at Madison Avenue's largest ad agencies, it is their focus, their world, their definition of happiness. Such spots are the means to glory, whether it's from a showy debut during the Super Bowl or a prestigious award at the annual Cannes Advertising Festival.

Online ads, on the other hand, have largely been ignored. Top agencies often outsource them to specialists or give them to separate in-house staffs. Some of the best creative minds just haven't been into the Net.

. . . [Advertisers] have to devote more creative talent to cyberspace. What they have found is that sparking people's interest online is as challenging as keeping them engaged when they're watching TV with a remote control.

The goal of advertisements is to win your consumer dollars, and advertisers are willing to spend millions of dollars to attract your attention to their products. Because of the problems of scarce income and time, however, *your* goal should be to obtain the most satisfaction from your limited income and time. In this section, you'll learn about three basic buying **principles** that can help you and all consumers achieve this goal.

Gathering Information

Main Idea Consumers should be well informed before making a purchase.

Economics & You Why do you think many people are reluctant to spend time researching a potential purchase? Read on to learn about why it is important to gather information before buying a product.

Suppose again that you want to buy a mountain bike. How should you go about selecting one? First, you have to obtain information about mountain bikes. You could ask for friends' opinions, or you could go to different stores and discuss the good and bad points of various brands and models with salespeople. You could also conduct online research. Actually, as a wise consumer, you would do all of these things before making your purchase.

Careers Handbook
See pages *R76–R80* to learn about becoming a *buyer.*

How Much Information Should You Obtain?

Information is costly because obtaining it involves your time. How much time should you spend? The buying principle to follow is: Obtain only as much information as is worthwhile. What, however, does *worthwhile* mean? The value of your time and effort spent gathering information should not be greater than the value you receive from making the best choice of product for yourself.

Developing a Consumer Knowledge Base

As you shop for different products, you will begin to develop a consumer knowledge base. Information you obtain looking for a mountain bike might help you someday to make decisions about choosing a car or a laptop. Simply getting salespeople to give you **accurate** information is a skill that you can acquire and sharpen over time.

One relatively easy way to obtain much information in a short amount of time is to use a standard search engine on the Internet. You might also want to read reviews other people have written about different brands and models of the product you wish to buy. Also, visit numerous sites that offer the product for sale and compare prices, warranties, and other information.

Help for Consumers

Many publications, in print and on the Internet, can help you learn about a product before you buy it. One good print publication is the magazine *Consumer Reports*, which tests and rates a wide variety of products.

Reading Check **Analyzing** Why is it important to develop a consumer knowledge base?

Using Advertising Wisely

Main Idea Consumers should carefully consider the claims of advertisers.

Economics & You Has an advertisement ever persuaded you to buy a product you weren't planning to buy? Why? Read on to learn about how to use advertising wisely.

Advertising is all around you—on television, the Internet, billboards, and so on. In general, advertising can be classified as competitive or informative. Advertising that attempts to persuade consumers that a product is different from and better than any other is **competitive advertising.** Companies use it to take customers away from competitors or to keep customers they already have. **Informative advertising** aids consumers by providing useful information about a product. See **Figure 3.3** below for more information on these types of advertising. Some companies use false advertising that misrepresents the quality, features, or true price of goods. A common example of this is **bait and switch.** The bait is an advertised item at an unrealistically low price. Then, when the consumer gets to the store, a salesperson points out all the bad features of the advertised item. The salesperson then shows the customer higher-priced models and points out all their good features—the switch. This practice is both deceptive and illegal.

competitive advertising: advertising that attempts to persuade consumers that a product is different from and superior to any other

informative advertising: advertising that benefits consumers by providing useful information about a product

bait and switch: ad that attracts consumers with a low-priced product, then tries to sell them a higher-priced product

Reading Check **Contrasting** Explain the difference between competitive and informative advertising.

Figure 3.3 | Advertising

■ When you are studying an advertisement for a product, it is important to carefully evaluate the information presented in the ad.

A. Competitive Advertising ►
Ads for well-established brand names and products, such as Dell computers and Nike shoes, are often of this type. Competitive ads, which may also be called persuasive ads, generally concentrate on appealing to people's emotions.

Comparison Shopping

Main Idea The best price for an item can be found through comparison shopping.

Economics & You What factors influence where you shop? Do you always "shop around" for the best price? Read on to learn about the importance of comparison shopping.

After you have gathered as much information as possible about the make and model of the product you want, you must decide *where* to buy it. It is generally worthwhile to get information on the types and prices of products available from different stores or companies. This process is known as **comparison shopping.**

To efficiently comparison shop, read newspaper advertisements, make telephone calls, browse the Web, visit different stores, and talk with friends who already have the product. Armed with prices that you have obtained from these sources, negotiate with local merchants to get them to match (or come close to) the lowest price.

Comparison shopping can be time-consuming. As with gathering information on a product, the value of your time and effort spent comparison shopping should not be greater than the value you receive from making the best choice of product for yourself. Comparison shopping can be especially useful under certain circumstances, such as when you are buying a very expensive or complex item, or when the quality or price of the product varies greatly.

Skills Handbook

See page R53 to learn about Comparing Data.

comparison shopping: getting information on the types and prices of products available from different stores and companies

B. Informative Advertising This type of advertising may contain information about the price, quality, and special features of a product. Be careful, though—informative advertising may also be competitive in nature.

What to Look For

Some stock seats are crotch-killers, but any good shop will swap saddles; some women prefer a wider seat. The main thing is to minimize friction and pressure while pedaling.

Nine sprockets back here add up to 27 speeds on top-end bikes. Why? Closer gear ratios mean smoother shifting.

Rear suspension: heavy, pricey, so smooth.

Smooth, easy-squeezing V-brakes (the cable enters the caliper from the side) are virtually standard nowadays. Disc brakes are an option for downhillers and muck-lovers.

You can't lose in this department. Both trigger- and throttle-style shifters get you in gear with equal deftness.

Unless your trails are a lot smoother than ours, go for front suspension. We like the rebound damping you get with air-oil setups.

Clipless pedals: You'll want them soon enough, so you might as well look for a bike that has them.

At the risk of begging the frame question, the right material boils down to personal preference. Aluminum and carbon fiber are stiff and responsive, but can rattle the bones of lighter riders. Steel's more forgiving. Titanium may be the best of all worlds, if you can afford it.

CANNONDALE F500 $900
Cannondale must chuckle at...
because this company...
A nearly fle...

Economic Analysis

Comparing *What do competitive and informative advertising have in common?*

warranty: promise made by a manufacturer or a seller to repair or replace a product within a certain time period if it is found to be faulty

brand name: word, picture, or logo on a product that helps consumers distinguish it from similar products

generic brand: general name for a product rather than a specific brand name given by the manufacturer

When you comparison shop, the most obvious influence on your decision will be price. Don't forget, however, to find out which store offers the best **warranty**, or the promise made by a manufacturer or seller to repair or replace a product if it is found to be faulty within a certain period of time.

Another consumer choice is between buying brand-name and generic products. A **brand name** is a word, picture, or logo on a product that helps consumers distinguish it from **similar** products. Brand-name products are usually sold nationwide and are backed by major companies. With **generic brands,** there is no brand name at all, and it is difficult to know who made the product.

"Well, it figures! We're seven-tenths of a mile past the warranty!"

▲ Be sure to check out a product's warranty, but remember that all warranties expire.

✔ **Reading Check** **Summarizing** What are some ways that a consumer can comparison shop efficiently?

---

section 2 # Review

Vocabulary

1. **Explain** the significance of: competitive advertising, informative advertising, bait and switch, comparison shopping, warranty, brand name, generic brand.

Main Ideas

2. **Summarizing** List at least three ways you might go about developing a consumer knowledge base.

3. **Organizing** Create a chart like the one below, and list some key characteristics of each type of ad.

Competitive	Informative	Bait and switch

Critical Thinking

4. **The BIG Idea** Go back and study the outline you made while reading this section. Then explain why some people might make "unreasonable" purchases even if they are aware of basic buying principles.

Applying Economics

5. **Negotiating** Think of an item you would like to purchase. Construct an argument to present to a merchant to get a better price for this item than the one advertised. Consider using the Internet, checking prices at other merchants, warranties, brand names, and other issues discussed in this section. Write or record what you would say to the merchant.

Oprah Winfrey

● **Chairperson of HARPO Entertainment Group**

■ Popular television host and magazine publisher

■ One of the 100 most influential people in the world (*TIME*, 2005)

■ First African American woman to become a billionaire

Oprah Winfrey emerged from an underprivileged childhood in rural Mississippi to become one of the wealthiest and most powerful women in the United States. Today, she heads the HARPO Entertainment Group—a movie, television, and video production company headquartered in Chicago. Winfrey also hosts the widely acclaimed *The Oprah Winfrey Show*, the number-one television talk show in the world for more than 20 years. It is seen by 9 million viewers a day in the United States and is broadcast in 117 countries.

Oprah believes that her success can be attributed, in part, to her philosophy of helping others:

"As a rule, we are a society that has based our lives and importance in our lives on how much we can accomplish through material goods. In the end what matters is how were you able to serve and who were you able to love."

Because she believes that education is the door to freedom, she has donated millions of dollars to provide for students who have merit but no means. In 2002 she expanded her global humanitarian efforts in South Africa, where 50,000 children received gifts of food, clothing, athletic shoes, school supplies, books, and toys.

On her Web site, www.oprah.com, viewers of *The Oprah Winfrey Show* can find, in addition to advice on many topics, a comprehensive list of resources related to the show.

> **This show's still the thing for me. It gives me the platform to try to figure out how do you get people to lead better lives? How do you get fathers to spend more time with their children?**

Checking for Understanding

1. **Explaining** What is meant by the phrase "students who have merit but no means"?

2. **Synthesizing** Why would Oprah care whether or not fathers spend more time with their children?

GUIDE TO READING

Section Preview
In this section, you will learn about your rights and responsibilities as a consumer.

Content Vocabulary
- consumerism *(p. 77)*
- ethical behavior *(p. 79)*

Academic Vocabulary
- assume *(p. 77)*
- guarantee *(p. 77)*

Reading Strategy
Organizing As you read the section, complete a chart like the one below by listing a consumer's rights and responsibilities.

Consumer Rights	Consumer Responsibilities
1.	1.
2.	2.
3.	3.
4.	4.
5.	5.
	6.
	7.
	8.

PrODUCTS In ThE NeWS
······················
—from *PR Newswire Association*

PROTECTING THE PUBLIC The Consumer Product Safety Commission (CPSC) recently announced a recall of nearly 12,000 plasma flat-panel televisions due to "arcing by capacitors" that "can pose a [fire] safety risk." The CPSC noted that in nine incidents, results "were contained within the TVs due to the use of flame retardant materials . . . [and] there have been no injuries reported."

"This is yet another example of how flame retardants work to contain the spread of fire and reduce the potential for catastrophic loss of life and property," said Laura Ruiz, chairperson of the American Fire Safety Council.

. . . Whether in television sets, airplanes, furniture, or mattresses, flame retardants work silently to safeguard the public, as well as fire fighters.

Most Americans are concerned with the reliability of the products and services they use. Many private groups and government agencies work to ensure the well-being of consumers. Consumers themselves, however, must be well informed about potential issues with products and services they purchase, and they must be proactive in their buying habits. In this section, you'll read more about consumer rights and responsibilities.

Consumer Rights

Main Idea Legislative protection of consumer rights has grown steadily since the 1960s.

Economics & You Have you ever been dissatisfied with a product you bought? Did you take steps to fix the problem? Read on to learn about your rights as a consumer.

Consumerism is a movement that started in the 1960s to educate buyers about the purchases they make and to demand better and safer products from manufacturers. Businesses can no longer **assume** it is the buyer's responsibility to know whether a product is safe, food is healthful, or advertising is accurate.

consumerism: movement to educate buyers about the purchases they make and to demand better and safer products from manufacturers

In 1962 President John F. Kennedy sent the first consumer protection message to Congress. In the message, he outlined four consumer rights:

- the right to safety—protection against goods that are dangerous to life or health.
- the right to be informed—information for use not only as protection against fraud but also as the basis for reasoned choices.
- the right to choose—the need for markets to be competitive and for government to protect consumers in markets where competition does not always exist, such as electric service.
- the right to be heard—the **guarantee** that consumer interests will be listened to when laws are being written.

President Richard Nixon later added a fifth right:

- the right to redress—the ability to obtain from the manufacturers adequate payment in money or goods for financial or physical damages caused by their products.

The Right to Safety

The United States Department of Agriculture (USDA) is a federal agency that aids consumers by inspecting and grading meat, fish, poultry, dairy products, and fruits and vegetables.

Reading Check **Examining** What effect did consumerism have on businesses?

Consumer Responsibilities

Main Idea Consumers can resolve problems most effectively by accepting certain responsibilities.

Economics ONLINE

Student Web Activity Visit the *Economics Today and Tomorrow* Web site at glencoe.com and click on *Chapter 3—Student Web Activities* to learn more about federal agencies that aid consumers.

Economics & You Take a moment to think about your responsibilities at home, work, and school. Then read on to learn about your responsibilities as a consumer.

Using President Kennedy's list, Congress passed consumer-protection legislation. Today, consumers dissatisfied with a specific product can complain to the store manager or to the manufacturer. They also may take the case to small-claims court. In addition, many private and government agencies are available to help consumers.

Among the private groups that aid consumers are local citizens' action groups and local chapters of the Better Business Bureau, found in many major cities and some smaller ones. These bureaus give consumers information on products and selling practices and help settle disagreements between buyers and sellers. Numerous state and federal agencies also have programs to aid consumers.

You have consumer responsibilities as well as rights. If a product or service is faulty, it is the consumer's responsibility to initiate the problem-solving process. See **Figure 3.4** below for a list of steps for consumers to take, as recommended by the Bureau of Consumer Protection.

Figure 3.4 | The Consumer's Role

■ Chances are, one day you will have a problem with a product or service and will need to seek a replacement product or a refund. This process will be much simpler if you keep careful records of your purchases and always retain your receipts. If you do have a problem with a product or service, the Bureau of Consumer Protection suggests you take the steps listed in the chart on the right.

Consumer Responsibilities

1. Report the problem immediately. Do not try to fix a product yourself, because doing so may cancel the warranty.

2. State the problem and suggest a fair and just solution—replacement, refund, etc.

3. Include important details and copies of receipts, guarantees, and contracts to support your case.

4. Describe any action you have taken to try to correct the problem.

5. Keep an accurate record of your efforts to get the problem solved. Include the names of people you have spoken to or written to and the dates on which you communicated.

6. Allow each person reasonable time to solve the problem before contacting another source.

7. If you need to contact the manufacturer in writing, type your letter or send an e-mail directly. Keep a copy.

8. Keep cool. The person who will help you solve your problem is probably not responsible for causing the problem.

Economic Analysis

Explaining *Why is it important to retain copies of receipts of all major purchases?*

The era of online shopping has presented some new challenges for consumers who use the Internet to make purchases. If you choose to shop online, you have the responsibility to make sure you are buying from a reputable, trustworthy source. Be sure to read any confidentiality and disclosure agreements. Also, remember that you should never enter your personal and financial information into a link that was sent to you by a business or company.

Another responsibility of consumers is to exhibit **ethical behavior** by respecting the rights of producers and sellers. For example, a responsible consumer will not try to return a used item just because it has been advertised elsewhere for a lower price. It's better to research various prices *before* you make a purchase.

Sellers' Rights

You have the responsibility to behave ethically if you need to return a product or get a refund on a service. You should not return a product just because you find the item at a lower price elsewhere. Also, you should never try to return a product that has been damaged through your own actions.

ethical behavior: acting in accordance with moral convictions about right and wrong

✔ **Reading Check** **Describing** What actions can dissatisfied consumers take?

Review

Vocabulary

1. **Explain** the significance of: consumerism, ethical behavior.

Main Ideas

2. **Synthesizing** Create a chart like the one below, and for each consumer right listed, think of an example that demonstrates it.

Consumer Right	Example
Right to safety	
Right to be informed	
Right to choose	
Right to be heard	
Right to compensation	

Critical Thinking

3. **The BIG Idea** Think of what it means for consumers and businesses to act ethically, and write three examples of each.

4. **Synthesizing** Some people assume that businesses will take advantage of them. Pretend that you own a business, and write a letter to a newspaper explaining why you would not take advantage of customers.

Applying Economics

5. **Consumer Activism** Suppose the people of an area are upset with water pollution caused by a local business. What are three ways that they might address this issue? Use the Internet or contact a consumer agency to help answer this question.

REVENGE OF THE IRATE **SHOPPER**

Retailers are hurt by word-of-mouth complaints.

Check It Out! In this chapter you learned about consumer rights and responsibilities. The following article highlights how stores are affected by disgruntled customers.

Caveat Vendor: That disgruntled shopper snarling at the manager isn't the problem. It's the customer who complains about the store to friends. A new study shows that people told about a friend's or relative's bad shopping experience are up to five times as likely to avoid the store in question as the original unhappy customer.

One reason is that the tales of annoyance tend to be embellished with each telling. By the fifth rendition or so, "the sales clerk who was just unresponsive has become abusive," says Paula Courtney, president of Verde Group, a Toronto retail consultant that conducted the study with the Jay H. Baker Retailing Initiative at the Wharton School.

The survey of roughly 1,200 U.S. shoppers . . . delivers some particularly bad news to the big-box stores. It seems that customers of mass merchandisers like Wal-Mart, Target, and Kmart share their negative experiences with an average of six people, double to triple the audience sought by customers who've had negative experiences at other retailers.

—Reprinted from *BusinessWeek*

Top Shopping Frustrations	
Shoppers say they are frustrated by:	**Total percent frustrated**
Merchandise stacked too high	77%
Delays in checkout	68%
Items out of stock	72%
Sales and coupons restricted to multiples or largest sizes	68%
Uninformed store employees	66%
Dirty restrooms	62%
Display blocking aisles	64%

Source: www.consumernetwork.org.

Think About It

1. **Making Connections** According to the story above, why does one person's bad shopping experience lead to a fivefold reduction in customers to the store?

2. **Extending** As a responsible consumer, what should you do if you have a negative experience at a store?

■ **Consumer decision making** deals with consumers' choices about how to spend their income.

Income $ — Taxes = Disposable income $ — Necessities = Discretionary income $

Can be spent or saved

■ Before making purchases, especially of big-ticket items, consumers should **gather information** and compare products from different sources.

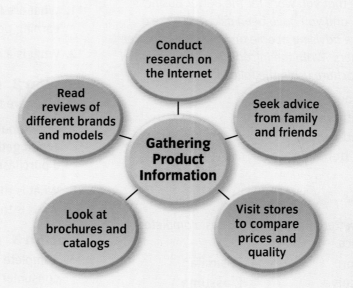

Conduct research on the Internet

Read reviews of different brands and models

Seek advice from family and friends

Gathering Product Information

Look at brochures and catalogs

Visit stores to compare prices and quality

■ In the United States, **consumer rights** are protected by congressional legislation. Along with these rights, though, come **consumer responsibilities.** Savvy consumers are aware of both and seek a balance between the two.

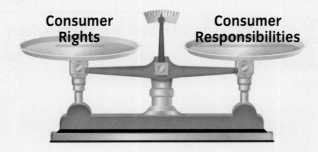

Consumer Rights

Consumer Responsibilities

Review Content Vocabulary

1. *Imagine that you earn $100 mowing lawns. You decide to spend it rather than save it. Write a paragraph explaining what factors will help you decide how to spend your money. Use all of the following terms.*

consumer

disposable income

discretionary income

rational choice

informative advertising

comparison shopping

warranty

brand name

generic brand

2. *Imagine that you work for the Better Business Bureau, and you have been asked to write a brochure advising people on how to be smarter consumers. Write the introductory paragraph of your brochure using the following terms.*

consumerism

competitive advertising

bait and switch

ethical behavior

Review Academic Vocabulary

Choose the letter of the term that best completes each sentence.

a. region
b. perceive
c. principles
d. accurate
e. similar
f. assume
g. guarantee

3. Wages might be higher in one _____ than they are in another part of the country.

4. Consumers can spend their money more wisely by following simple _____, or rules.

5. A generic product might be very _____ to a competing brand-name product.

6. Consumers need _____ information to make informed buying decisions.

7. Consumerism seeks to _____, or ensure, consumer rights in the marketplace.

8. Advertising seeks to change the way buyers _____ products and competitors.

9. Buyers should not _____ that advertising is accurate and fair.

Review the Main Ideas

Section 1 (pp. 65–69)

10. What is the difference between disposable and discretionary income?

11. What are four factors that affect a person's earning power?

12. What is a rational consumer choice?

Section 2 (pp. 70–74)

13. What are three important buying principles?

14. How should you decide how much time to spend gathering information before you make a purchase?

15. What is the goal of competitive advertising? What is the goal of informative advertising?

Section 3 (pp. 76–79)

16. Complete the graphic organizer by listing some consumer rights and responsibilities discussed in this chapter.

Consumer Rights	Consumer Responsibilities

17. Who protects consumers' rights?

18. What changes did the consumerism movement bring about?

Problem Solving

Jolene, a high school student, has $200 that she would like to spend on electronics. She could choose to buy an MP3 player for entertainment or a used computer of her own to help her do her homework. She wants to make a rational choice about her purchase based on opportunity costs.

19. What steps might Jolene take to help her decide which product to buy?

20. What would be the opportunity cost of choosing to buy an MP3 player?

21. Imagine you are in Jolene's situation, and conduct research on the steps you listed in question 19. Use a chart like the one below to record any information you find. Finally, write down what your decision would be, and then explain why.

Problem: MP3 player or used computer?	
Step 1:	Information:
Step 2:	Information:
Step 3:	Information:
Decision:	

Economics ONLINE

Self-Check Quiz Visit the *Economics Today and Tomorrow* Web site at glencoe.com and click on *Chapter 3—Self-Check Quizzes* to assess your knowledge of chapter content.

Critical Thinking

22. **The BIG IDEAS** Why do some people buy mostly brand-name products while other people buy mostly store-label products?

23. **Examining** Examine the advertisement below, then answer the questions that follow.

Buy Fantastic Fitness Water

Doctors say that staying hydrated is the most important part of exercising. The average adult needs at least 64 ounces of fluid per day to stay healthy! *Fantastic Fitness Water* is specially formulated to be absorbed quickly by the body, making your workout as effective as it can be.

a. What type of advertisement is this—competitive or informative? Why?

b. What audience does the advertisement target? How do you know?

Analyzing Visuals

24. Study the cartoon below, and then answer the following questions.
   a. What is a demographic?
   b. According to the cartoon, why do retailers value consumers in the demographic to which the boy apparently belongs?

Global Economy

A Day on the Town First, you go downtown to meet a friend for lunch. Later, a friend invites you to a movie. On the way to the theater, you stop and buy gasoline for your car. Check the map below to see what your day might cost in various cities around the world.*

London, England
Subway fare, one way	$2.00
Fast food hamburger	$4.50
Gasoline, one gallon	$6.36
Movie ticket	$11.00

Vancouver, Canada
Subway fare, one way	$1.13
Fast food hamburger	$2.79
Gasoline, one gallon	$4.35
Movie ticket	$13.43

New York City, United States
Subway fare, one way	$1.50
Fast food hamburger	$4.50
Gasoline, one gallon	$3.15
Movie ticket	$12.00

*All prices have been converted to U.S. $.

Buenos Aires, Argentina
Subway fare, one way	$0.15
Fast food hamburger	$1.58
Gasoline, one gallon	$2.21
Movie ticket	$3.21

Moscow, Russia

Subway fare, one way	$0.22
Lunch, per person	$22.70
Gasoline, one gallon	$1.59
Movie ticket	$7.63

Tokyo, Japan

Subway fare, one way	$1.32
Fast food hamburger	$2.99
Gasoline, one gallon	$4.93
Movie ticket	$21.65

Mumbai, India

Subway fare, one way	$0.15
Fast food hamburger	$2.23
Gasoline, one gallon	$4.87
Movie ticket	$2.30

Beijing, China

Fast food hamburger	$1.46
Gasoline, one gallon	$2.40
Movie ticket	$15.17

Johannesburg, South Africa

Subway fare, one way	$1.14
Fast food hamburger	$1.84
Gallon of gasoline	$2.62
Movie ticket	$9.62

Sydney, Australia

Subway fare, one way	$1.06
Fast food hamburger	$2.74
Gasoline, one gallon	$3.76
Movie ticket	$7.45

Thinking Globally

1. **Comparing** In which city would your day on the town cost the most? The least?

2. **Making Inferences** Look at the prices for Mumbai. How do you think most people get around the city—by car or by public transportation? Why?

3. **Critical Thinking** Which items seem to vary the most in price? Why do you think this is?

chapter **4**

Going Into Debt

The **BIG Idea**

Governments and institutions help participants in a market economy accomplish their financial goals.

Why It Matters

Have you ever taken out a loan or used a credit card? If so, why did you make the decision to borrow? Were you able to easily pay back the amount? In this chapter, read to learn how to apply for credit and how to use credit wisely.

Economics ONLINE

Chapter Overview Visit the *Economics Today and Tomorrow* Web site at glencoe.com and click on *Chapter 4—Chapter Overviews* to preview chapter information.

Americans and Credit

Section Preview
In this section, you will learn about the advantages and disadvantages of using credit to make purchases.

Content Vocabulary
- credit *(p. 88)*
- principal *(p. 88)*
- interest *(p. 88)*
- installment debt *(p. 88)*
- durable goods *(p. 88)*
- mortgage *(p. 89)*

Academic Vocabulary
- enormous *(p. 87)*
- period *(p. 88)*

Reading Strategy
Contrasting As you read the section, complete a table similar to the one below by listing the advantages and disadvantages of using credit to purchase a good or service.

Using Credit	
Advantages	**Disadvantages**

ISSUES IN THE NEWS
—from the **Associated Press**

'TIS THE SEASON TO CHARGE Shoppers are racing from store to store this holiday season, with credit cards clutched tightly in hand and visions of future bills dancing in their heads.

One-half of Americans say they worry about the money they owe, and many say they worry most of the time about their overall debts, an Associated Press poll found.

Those debts can come from home and car loans as well as credit cards. . . . Three-fourths [of people polled] said they have credit cards. Four in 10 of those with  credit cards said they will use plastic to help pay for their holiday spending this year.

. . . Most people with credit cards said they carefully manage the debts on those cards, which often have high finance charges on unpaid balances. A sizable minority of them admitted to having serious problems with credit cards.

Americans use credit to make many purchases. The total amount of funds borrowed and lent each year is **enormous**. In addition to individuals borrowing funds, the federal, state, and local governments all borrow funds, too. The nation's economy, in fact, depends on individuals and groups being able to buy and borrow on credit. In this section, you'll learn what credit is and why people use it.

Credit and Installment Debt

Main Idea The price of credit is the interest charged on the amount borrowed.

Economics & You Have you ever purchased something using credit? Why or why not? Read on to learn about the price of credit.

credit: receipt of funds either directly or indirectly to buy goods and services in the present with the promise to pay for them in the future

principal: amount originally borrowed in a loan

interest: amount the borrower must pay for the use of someone else's funds

installment debt: type of loan repaid with equal payments, or installments, over a specific period of time

durable goods: manufactured items that have a life span longer than three years

Credit is the receiving of funds either directly or indirectly to buy goods and services today with the promise to pay for them in the future. The amount owed—the debt—is equal to the principal plus interest. The **principal** is the amount originally borrowed. The **interest** is the amount the borrower must pay for the use of someone else's funds. That "someone else" may be a bank, credit union, credit card company, or store.

Any time you receive credit, you are borrowing funds and going into debt. Taking out a loan is the same as buying an item on credit. In both cases, you must pay interest for the use of someone else's purchasing power.

One of the most common types of debt is **installment debt**. Consumers repay this type of loan with equal payments, or installments, over a **period** of time; for example, 36 equal payments over 36 months. Many people buy **durable goods,** or manufactured items that last longer than three years, on an installment plan. Automobiles, refrigerators, washers, and other appliances are considered durable goods. People can also borrow cash and pay it back in installments. **Figure 4.1** below shows the growth in consumer installment debt.

| Figure 4.1 | Increase in Borrowing |

Graphs In MOtion
See StudentWorks™ Plus or go to glencoe.com.

■ More and more Americans are choosing to buy durable goods on credit.

Economic Analysis

Using Graphs *By about how much did consumer debt increase between 1997 and 2006?*

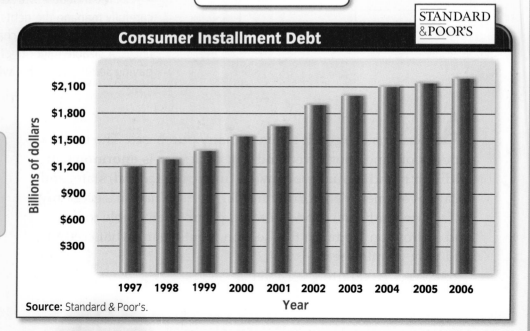

STANDARD &POOR'S

Consumer Installment Debt

Billions of dollars

$2,100
$1,800
$1,500
$1,200
$900
$600
$300

1997 1998 1999 2000 2001 2002 2003 2004 2005 2006

Year

Source: Standard & Poor's.

Figure 4.2 Pay Now or Pay Later?

■ Say you want to borrow $1,000 to buy a flat-screen television. Your monthly payment will be lower if you choose the 36-month loan over the 24-month loan. The amount of interest you pay, however, will be higher.

$1,000 Installment Loan at 9% Interest		
Term of loan	24 Months	36 Months
Monthly payments	$45.69	$31.80
Total interest	$96.56	$144.80
Total payments	$1,096.56	$1,144.80

Economic Analysis
Using Tables *How much more will you pay if you choose the 36-month loan?*

The length of the installment period is important in determining the size of the borrower's monthly payments and the total amount of interest he or she must pay. A longer repayment period results in a smaller monthly payment. For example, **Figure 4.2** above shows that if the repayment of a loan is spread over three years (36 months), the monthly payments will be smaller than if the loan were repaid in two years (24 months). There is a trade-off, however. The longer it takes to repay an installment loan, the greater the total interest the lender charges, and so the total payment will be greater.

The largest form of installment debt in this country is what people owe on mortgages. A **mortgage** is an installment debt owed on real property—houses, buildings, or land. Interestingly, most people who owe a mortgage on their home do not consider themselves deeply in debt. Because people must have housing, they think of a mortgage as being a necessary monthly payment not similar to other kinds of debt. A mortgage is a debt, however, because somebody has provided the owner with funds to purchase property. In return, the owner must repay the loan with interest in installments over a number of years. As with other forms of installment debt, the longer the repayment period is, the greater the final total payment will be.

Personal Finance Handbook
See pages R10–R15 to learn more about managing credit.

mortgage: installment debt owed on houses, buildings, or land

✔ **Reading Check** **Explaining** What is installment debt? Give one example of a common form of installment debt.

Why People Use Credit

Main Idea The use of credit allows the borrower to enjoy consumption now rather than later.

Economics & You Imagine that you want to buy a new car. Would you rather use credit to buy it now, or save your money and pay cash for it later? Why? Read on to learn about why people decide to use credit.

Many things that Americans buy on credit are "big-ticket" items—products such as automobiles, electronics equipment, and major home appliances. People often feel forced to buy such items on credit because they believe these products are essential and they want them immediately. They do not want to wait. Of course, consumers are not really "forced" to buy most goods and services on credit. They could decide instead to save the funds needed to make their purchases.

Some might say that you would be better off saving and waiting to buy a pickup truck, for example. During the years you are saving for the truck, however, you forgo the pleasure of driving it. Many people do not want to postpone purchasing an important durable good. They would rather buy on credit and enjoy the use of the item now rather than later.

Another reason for going into debt is to spread the payments over the service life of the item being purchased. For example, people do not buy a truck or car to have it sit in the garage. What they buy is the availability of the vehicle each day, week, month, and year that they own it.

Figure 4.3 | Buying on Credit

■ No hard-and-fast rules can tell you whether or not to buy on credit. This list of questions, however, can help you determine if you are making a wise decision.

Checklist for Buying on Credit

❶ Do I really require this item? Can I postpone purchasing the item until later?

❷ If I pay cash, what will I be giving up that I could buy with these funds?

❸ If I borrow or use credit, will the satisfaction I get from the item I buy be greater than the interest I must pay?

❹ Have I done comparison shopping for credit? (In other words, after you have determined that you are not going to pay cash for something, you should look for the best loan or credit deal, including the lowest interest rate and other conditions of repayment.)

❺ Can I afford to use credit now?

Economic Analysis

Synthesizing *Read number 2 in the list on the right. In economic terms, what would you call the other item that you must give up buying if you pay cash now for the first item?*

The decision to borrow or use credit involves whether the satisfaction the borrower gets from the purchases is greater than the cost of the interest payments. It is basically a question of comparing costs and benefits. The benefit of borrowing is being able to buy and enjoy the good or service now rather than later. The cost is whatever the borrower must pay in interest or lost opportunities to buy other items or earn interest on the amount put into a savings account or investment.

The benefit of borrowing is something only you can decide. You and every other borrower, however, should be aware of the costs involved. **Figure 4.3** can help you decide when to use credit. It can also help you avoid the improper use of credit by overspending.

Spreading Payments

Suppose you want to buy a pickup truck that costs $15,000. You have a choice. You could borrow $15,000 right now and buy the truck, but you would have to make interest payments on the borrowed funds for three to five years. You can also enjoy using it, though, at the same time you are paying for it. Alternatively, you could start saving now, earn interest on your savings, and pay cash for the truck in several years.

✔ **Reading Check** **Analyzing** On what question should the decision to use credit be based?

---

section **1** Review

Vocabulary

1. **Explain** the significance of: credit, principal, interest, installment debt, durable goods, mortgage.

Main Ideas

2. **Summarizing** Why do people go into debt?

3. **Organizing** Create a diagram like the one below to list the factors you should consider when deciding whether to use credit.

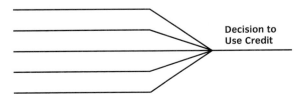

Decision to Use Credit

Critical Thinking

4. **The BIG Idea** Look back at the table you made at the beginning of the section listing the advantages and disadvantages of using credit. Study your lists, and then explain why some people are overwhelmed by debt.

5. **Explaining** Why are banks willing to lend funds to people?

Applying Economics

6. **Calculating Interest** Imagine that you buy a used car for $10,000 and the simple interest rate on the loan is 11%. What will your total payments be at the end of 24 months?

Sources of Loans and Credit

GUIDE TO READING

Section Preview
In this section, you will learn about the major types of credit and the cost of credit.

Content Vocabulary
- commercial bank *(p. 93)*
- savings and loan association *(p. 93)*
- savings bank *(p. 93)*
- credit union *(p. 94)*
- finance company *(p. 94)*
- charge account *(p. 95)*
- credit card *(p. 96)*
- finance charge *(p. 97)*
- annual percentage rate *(p. 98)*

Academic Vocabulary
- previous *(p. 95)*
- access *(p. 96)*

Reading Strategy
Organizing As you read, complete a web diagram like the one below by filling in the institutions discussed.

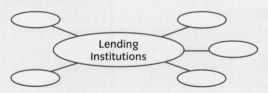

ISSues In ThE NeWS
—from *The Wall Street Journal*

WHEN THE BILL COMES DUE Thanks to low interest rates and easy ways to borrow, consumers have been on an all-out spending spree for several years. Now, there are signs that the bills may be piling up too high.

The portion of Americans' disposable income  devoted to paying off debt recently hit a record high, even as interest rates have stayed low. That could put a financial squeeze on many households if and when long-term interest rates finally start to go up.

. . . Nearly half of all consumer debt and 26% of all mortgage debt is now adjustable, estimates Joe Abate, senior economist at Lehman Brothers. . . . "When all these [adjustable-rate] mortgages reset soon, some of these people are going to see their monthly payments rise by a few hundred dollars a month," Mr. Abate says.

There are two major types of credit—using credit cards and borrowing directly from a financial institution. Although they differ in their services, they all charge interest on the funds they lend. In this section, you'll learn about financial institutions, charge accounts, and credit cards—and why you should be aware of the high interest rates they sometimes charge.

Types of Financial Institutions

Main Idea Financial institutions borrow funds at one interest rate and lend it at a higher rate.

Economics & You Chances are, you will have to take out a loan in the future, whether to pay for college, buy a car, or purchase a home. From whom should you borrow? Read on to learn about the different types of financial institutions available to consumers.

Once you have decided to take out a loan, you should first comparison shop. To gather information about borrower requirements, interest rates, and payment schedules, check various lending agencies in person, over the phone, or at their Web sites.

Commercial Banks The first place you might think to go for a loan is a **commercial bank**. Commercial banks today control the largest amount of funds and offer the widest range of services. These services include offering checking and savings accounts and loans to individuals. They also transfer funds among banks, individuals, and businesses.

commercial bank: bank whose main functions are to accept deposits, lend funds, and transfer funds among banks, individuals, and businesses

Savings and Loan Associations A **savings and loan association (S&L)**, like a commercial bank, accepts deposits and lends funds. S&Ls make many mortgage loans to families. They also finance commercial mortgages and auto loans. Their interest rates for loans are often slightly less than those for commercial banks.

savings and loan association (S&L): depository institution that accepts deposits and lends funds

savings bank: depository institution originally set up to serve small savers overlooked by commercial banks

Savings Banks **Savings banks** were first set up to serve the small savers who were overlooked by the large commercial banks. Most savings banks, like S&Ls, lend funds for home mortgages, along with personal and auto loans. Since 1980, savings banks, like commercial banks, have also been able to offer services similar to checking accounts.

Commercial Banking

At some point, you have probably been inside a commercial bank, one of the most popular of the common financial institutions for consumers.

Credit Unions

credit union: depository institution owned and operated by its members to provide savings accounts and low-interest loans only to its members

Credit Unions Union members and employees of many companies often have a credit union. A **credit union** is owned and operated by its members to provide savings accounts and low-interest loans only to its members. Credit unions primarily make personal, auto, and home improvement loans, although larger credit unions offer home mortgages as well. In general, credit unions offer higher interest rates on savings and charge lower interest rates on loans than other financial institutions.

finance company: company that takes over contracts for installment debts from stores and adds a fee for collecting the debt; a *consumer finance company* makes loans directly to consumers at high rates of interest

Finance Companies A **finance company** takes over contracts for installment debts from stores and adds a fee for collecting the debt. The consumer pays the fee in the form of slightly higher interest than he or she would pay to the retailer. Retailers use this method to avoid the risks involved in lending money to consumers.

A *consumer finance company* makes loans directly to consumers at relatively high rates of interest—often as much as 15 percent a year or more. The people who use consumer finance companies are usually unable to borrow from other sources with lower rates because they have not repaid loans in the past or have an uneven employment record.

Reading Check **Contrasting** What is the difference between a commercial bank and a credit union?

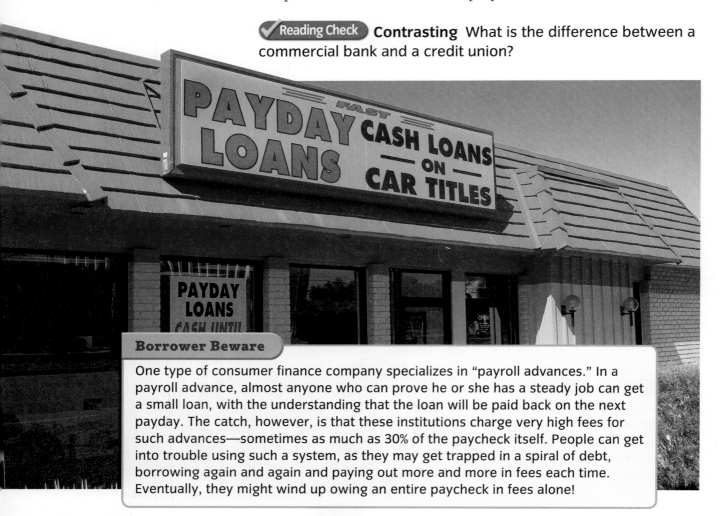

Borrower Beware

One type of consumer finance company specializes in "payroll advances." In a payroll advance, almost anyone who can prove he or she has a steady job can get a small loan, with the understanding that the loan will be paid back on the next payday. The catch, however, is that these institutions charge very high fees for such advances—sometimes as much as 30% of the paycheck itself. People can get into trouble using such a system, as they may get trapped in a spiral of debt, borrowing again and again and paying out more and more in fees each time. Eventually, they might wind up owing an entire paycheck in fees alone!

Charge Accounts and Credit Cards

Main Idea Charge accounts and credit cards extend credit directly to an individual or business.

Economics & You Do you own a credit card? Does having such a card affect your spending habits? Read on to learn more about this type of direct credit.

A second major type of credit is extended directly to an individual or business, without that person or business having first to borrow any funds. This credit may be in the form of a charge account or a credit card.

Charge Accounts A **charge account** allows a customer to buy goods or services from a particular company and pay for them later. Department stores generally offer three main types of charge accounts. A *regular charge account,* also known as a 30-day charge, has a credit limit, or a maximum amount of goods or services a person or business can buy on the promise to pay in the future. At the end of every 30-day period, the store sends a bill for the entire amount. No interest is charged if the entire bill is paid at that time. If it is not, interest is charged on the unpaid amount, often at a high interest rate.

A *revolving charge account* allows you to make additional purchases from the same store even if you have not paid the **previous** month's bill in full. Usually you must pay a certain portion of your balance each month. Interest is charged on the amount you do not pay. Of course, if you pay everything you owe each month, no interest is charged. This type of account also has a credit limit.

Major items such as sofas, televisions, and refrigerators are often purchased through an *installment charge account.* The items are purchased and paid for through equal payments spread over a period of time. Part of the amount paid each month is applied to the interest, and part is applied to the principal. This continues until the item is paid in full.

charge account: credit extended to a consumer allowing the consumer to buy goods or services from a particular company and to pay for them later

Other Charge Options

Sometimes you will hear stores offering special deals, such as "90 Days Same as Cash." This means that the store will give you longer than the usual 30-day period to pay off a bill—in this case, 90 days—without charging interest. Often, though, if a person fails to pay the balance within the extended time period, the store will charge a higher interest rate than usual.

credit card: credit device that allows a person to make purchases at many kinds of stores, restaurants, and other businesses without paying cash

Credit Cards A **credit card**, like a charge account, allows a person to make purchases without paying cash. The difference is that credit cards can be used at many kinds of stores, restaurants, hotels, and other businesses throughout the United States and even foreign countries. Visa, MasterCard, and others issue cards through banks. These cards can be used to purchase items in stores that accept them, or they may be used to borrow funds up to a certain limit. This gives consumers **access** to loans at all times without having to apply for them.

There is another method of payment known as a debit card. Although debit cards look like credit cards, they do not provide a loan or extend credit. See **Figure 4.4** below for more information on debit cards.

✓ Reading Check **Comparing and Contrasting** How are charge accounts and credit cards similar? How are they different?

Figure 4.4 | Debit Cards

■ Debit cards make cashless purchases easier by letting customers transfer funds electronically from their bank accounts directly to stores, restaurants, gas stations—almost anywhere transactions take place. Debit cards were first available in the 1970s, but they did not catch on with the public until the 1990s. By 2006, debit cards had become a more popular payment method than checks.

Remember when using a debit card that it is not the same as a credit card. The funds will be taken directly from your checking account, usually within 72 hours. Debit cards **do not** provide loans or credit.

A. Using a Debit Card
When you use a debit card in a store, the card reader will usually ask you to select "debit" or "credit."

B. Selecting "Debit"
If you select "debit," you will need to type in a PIN number. You will not have to provide a signature, and from many stores, you can get cash back from your account when you use this payment method.

C. Selecting "Credit"
Remember that if you select "credit," the money will still come directly out of your account. By selecting credit, you usually do not need to type in a personal identification number (PIN). Instead, you will sign a receipt.

Economic Analysis
Contrasting How are debit cards different from credit cards?

Finance Charges and Annual Percentage Rates

Main Idea The cost of credit can be expressed as a finance charge or as an annual percentage rate.

Economics & You Do you think that lenders should be allowed to charge fees to customers who use credit, in addition to what the customer originally paid for the item? Why or why not? Read on to learn about the cost of credit.

The terms *finance charge* and *annual percentage rate* tell the consumer the same thing—the cost of credit. Each, however, is expressed in a different way.

Finance Charges The **finance charge** is the cost of credit expressed in dollars and cents. It must take into account interest costs plus any other charges connected with credit. For example, yearly membership fees for the use of a credit card are included in the finance charge.

The way finance charges are computed is an important factor in determining the cost of credit. Store charge accounts and credit cards use one of four methods to determine how much people will pay for credit: previous balance, average daily balance, adjusted balance, or past due balance. Each method applies the interest rate to an account's balance at a different point during the month. The different methods can result in widely varying finance charges. In order to determine which method is used, you may have to call or write to the credit issuer.

finance charge: cost of credit expressed monthly in dollars and cents

Methods of Computing Finance Charges	
Type of Method	**How Finance Charge Is Computed**
Previous balance	Charge is computed on the month's opening balance, even if the bill has been paid in full by the time the finance charge is figured. There is no benefit in paying off a debt early with this method.
Adjusted balance	Payments made during the month are deducted from the opening balance. Charge is then computed on the balance due the last day of the month. With this method you can save the most if you pay your bill as soon as possible.
Average daily balance	Charge is applied to the sum of the actual amounts owed each day during the billing period, divided by the number of days in that period. Payments and credits–return of goods–are subtracted on the exact date of payment. With this method you can save the most if you pay your bill as soon as possible.
Past due balance	No finance charge is applied if full payment is received within a certain period, usually within 25 days after the date of the last billing statement. If full payment is not received, then a finance charge for the unpaid amount is added to the next month's bill.

annual percentage rate (APR): cost of credit expressed as a yearly percentage

Annual Percentage Rates

The **annual percentage rate (APR)** is the cost of credit expressed as a yearly percentage. Like the finance charge, the APR must take into account any noninterest costs of credit, such as a membership fee.

Knowing which creditor is charging the most for credit would be very difficult without some guide for comparison. The APR provides that guide by allowing consumers to compare costs regardless of the dollar amount of those costs or the length of the credit agreement. Suppose creditor A is charging an APR of 16 percent, while creditor B is charging 17 percent, and creditor C is charging 18½ percent. On a yearly basis, creditor C is charging the most for credit and creditor A the least.

Skills Handbook

See page R54 to learn about Understanding Percentages.

Credit Card Trade-Off

Using credit cards is convenient but costly. Stores must pay a percentage of credit purchases to the company that issued the card. This cost is then included in the prices stores charge customers.

Reading Check **Summarizing** What are four ways that lenders can determine finance charges?

---

section 2 Review

Vocabulary

1. **Explain** the significance of: commercial bank, savings and loan association, savings bank, credit union, finance company, charge account, credit card, finance charge, annual percentage rate (APR).

Main Ideas

2. **Summarizing** Create a diagram like the one below to list the types of financial institutions discussed in this section and describe their main functions.

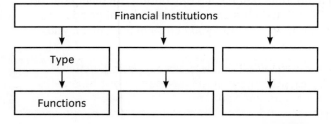

Financial Institutions		
Type		
Functions		

Critical Thinking

3. **The BIG Idea** Although credit abuse can cause serious financial problems, credit is an important part of our economy. What are advantages of allowing people and businesses to borrow money?

4. **Determining Cause and Effect** What is the disadvantage of not paying a total bill at the time it is due?

Applying Economics

5. **Synthesizing** Imagine you are the parent of a teenager about your age, and you are instructing him or her to use credit in a safe and wise way. Write or record one paragraph that would relate the pros and cons of what you have learned about credit.

Applying for Credit

GUIDE TO READING

Section Preview
In this section, you will learn about how to obtain credit and about your responsibilities after becoming a borrower.

Content Vocabulary
- credit bureau *(p. 100)*
- credit check *(p. 100)*
- credit rating *(p. 100)*
- collateral *(p. 100)*
- secured loan *(p. 101)*
- unsecured loan *(p. 101)*

Academic Vocabulary
- accumulate *(p. 100)*
- concentrate *(p. 102)*

Reading Strategy
Organizing As you read the section, complete a chart like this one by listing steps to obtaining credit and borrowers' responsibilities.

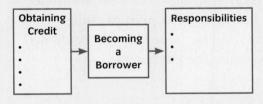

Obtaining Credit		Becoming a Borrower		Responsibilities
•				•
•				•
•				•
•				

ISSUes In ThE NeWS

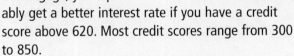
—from *CNNMoney.com*

TRACKING YOUR CREDIT If you're looking for a loan, it's a very scary time. Interest rates are on the rise and with them, mortgage delinquencies are increasing.

. . . Your credit report basically determines how loan-worthy you are, and the report is based on your credit history. That includes how many credit cards you have, how well you make your payments, your debt load, your available credit, and whether other lenders have inquired into your report.

So if you're looking to buy a car or take out a mortgage, you'll probably get a better interest rate if you have a credit score above 620. Most credit scores range from 300 to 850.

. . . Two years ago Congress passed a law that said lenders must notify consumers when their credit scores have negative information that triggers a less favorable rate quote. Guess what? Affected consumers still haven't gotten their letters.

How do you apply for credit? What factors determine whether or not you will be approved for credit? Perhaps more importantly, how can you dig yourself *out* of debt if your payments are more than you can handle? In this section, you'll learn what makes a person eligible for credit. You'll also learn ways to handle your debts before they get out of control.

Will You Be Able to Get Credit?

Main Idea Lenders determine creditworthiness by evaluating a borrower's credit history.

Economics & You If a friend wanted to borrow money, would you lend it to him or her? Read on to learn about how a borrower's creditworthiness is determined.

Careers Handbook

See pages R76–R80 to learn about becoming a consumer loan officer.

credit bureau: private business that investigates a person to determine the risk involved in lending to that person

credit check: investigation of a person's income, current debts, personal life, and past history of borrowing and repaying debts

credit rating: rating of the risk involved in lending to a specific person or business

collateral: something of value that a borrower lets the lender claim if a loan is not repaid

Several factors determine a person's creditworthiness. When you apply for credit, you usually will be asked to fill out a credit application. Then the lender will hire a **credit bureau,** a private business, to do a **credit check.** This investigation will reveal your income, any current debts, details about your personal life, and how well you have repaid debts in the past.

The information supplied by the credit bureau provides the creditor with a **credit rating** for you. This is a rating of the risk—good, average, or poor—involved in lending funds to a specific person or business. (See **Figure 4.5**.)

Though past history of credit use is important in deciding a person's creditworthiness, the creditor also looks at three other factors: your capacity to pay, your character, and any collateral you may have.

Capacity to pay considers how much debt you have in relation to your income. If you have changed jobs frequently or been unemployed for long periods, your capacity to pay will be considered questionable. *Character* refers to a person's reputation as a reliable and trustworthy person. Lenders also consider **collateral**, or the size of your capital or personal wealth. Collateral is important because it indicates your past ability to save and **accumulate**. It also indicates your present ability to pay off a loan, because even if you lose your job, you could sell off some collateral in order to make the payments.

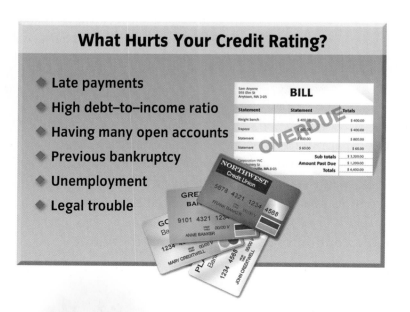

What Hurts Your Credit Rating?

- Late payments
- High debt–to–income ratio
- Having many open accounts
- Previous bankruptcy
- Unemployment
- Legal trouble

Figure 4.5   Your Credit Score

■ A credit score is a mathematical model that evaluates many types of information in a credit file. It is used by a lender to help determine whether a person qualifies for a particular credit card, loan, or service. Generally, the higher the score, the less risk the person represents. People with higher scores are also able to get better interest rates than people with low scores. How can you obtain your credit score?

Step 1 One easy way to find out your credit score is to log on to AnnualCreditReport.com and request a free copy of your credit report. Federal law states that you can receive one free credit report every 12 months from each of the three national consumer credit reporting companies: Equifax, TransUnion, and Experian.

Step 2 When you order your credit report from one of the three reporting companies, you may purchase your credit score at the same time. Credit scores generally range from 300 to 850. This table shows where your credit stands depending on your credit score. Any score above 620 is considered respectable.

General Credit Score Ratings

Credit Score	Rating
700+	Excellent
680–699	Good
620–679	Fair
580–619	Poor
Under 580	Very Poor

Economic Analysis

Determining Cause and Effect *What factors might negatively affect your credit score?*

Usually when a financial institution makes a loan, it will ask for collateral from the borrower. The collateral may be the item being purchased or something of value the borrower already owns. The borrower then signs a legal agreement allowing the lender to claim the collateral if the loan is not repaid. A loan that is backed up with collateral in this way is called a **secured loan**. Sometimes financial institutions will lend funds on a person's reputation and a promise to repay. Such a loan is called an **unsecured loan**. The interest rate charged on unsecured loans is usually much higher than the rate for secured loans.

A bank will also sometimes lend funds to a person if he or she has a cosigner. A *cosigner* is a person who signs a loan contract along with the borrower and promises to repay the loan if the borrower does not.

secured loan: loan that is backed up by collateral

unsecured loan: loan guaranteed only by a promise to repay it

Reading Check **Evaluating** Why is collateral important to lenders?

Responsibilities as a Borrower

Main Idea Maintaining a good credit rating is important for obtaining credit at favorable interest rates.

Economics & You Have you ever borrowed from a friend or parent and not paid them back? What were the consequences? Read on to learn about your responsibilities as a borrower.

Credit use carries responsibilities. If you do not pay your debts on time, the lender may have to hire a collection agency to help recover the funds. If you never pay, the lender has to write it off and take a loss. These costs are passed on to all consumers in the form of higher interest rates. Also, you will get a bad credit history. You will then have a difficult time when you really need credit in the future—to buy a house, for example.

Another responsibility as a borrower is to keep a complete record of all the charges you have made. You also must notify the credit-card issuer immediately if your card is lost or stolen.

What if you've lost control of your debt? Financial planners advise you to make a list of everything you owe, what the interest rate is, and what the payments are. **Concentrate** on paying the high-interest credit cards first, and pay more than the minimum payment, or it will take you years to reduce the debt.

Reading Check **Predicting Consequences** Why is it a bad idea not to pay off your debts?

section 3 Review

Vocabulary

1. **Explain** the significance of: credit bureau, credit check, credit rating, collateral, secured loan, unsecured loan.

Main Ideas

2. **Summarizing** Use a diagram like the one below to list the three factors, besides previous credit history, that a credit bureau will check to determine creditworthiness.

Obtaining Credit

Critical Thinking

3. **The BIG Idea** What are three possible consequences of not meeting your responsibilities as a borrower?

4. **Contrasting** What is the difference between a secured loan and an unsecured loan?

Applying Economics

5. **Synthesizing** Business owners, like consumers, have credit concerns. Allowing customers to buy on credit can be risky, but businesses lose customers if they do not accept credit. Write a policy that you would post in your store for credit customers. Use terms you learned in this chapter.

BAD CREDIT:
BREAKING THE CYCLE

Young adults can learn to control credit card spending.

Check It Out! In this chapter you learned about credit and going into debt. In this article, read to learn why charging everything from your cell phone to pizza is a bad idea.

▲ Paying off debt takes hard work.

Kristy Wilson and her husband had a nagging feeling that their spending might have spiraled out of control. When they finally sat down to look at their finances, they realized they'd racked up $30,000 in credit card debt. Wilson and her husband aren't the only young adults whose debt has daunted them in recent years. The average credit card debt among 25- to 34-year-olds was $5,200 in 2004, 98% higher than in 1992.

For many, credit card debt can seem insurmountable. But don't despair. These strategies may help ease the burden:

1. Assess the Situation. Before you can start cutting your debt, you need to itemize all your financial obligations.

2. Play Hardball. Your creditors want their money back, and they may be more flexible than you think. Explain what you can afford, and see if you can negotiate a modified payment plan.

3. Get Good Information. Your local state attorney general, Better Business Bureau, or consumer-protection agency might have information about resources near you.

4. Lose the Expensive Debt. Keep paying your minimums on all your cards, but focus your buying power on getting rid of one creditor at a time, starting with the card that's charging you the highest rates.

5. Knuckle Down. Kristy Wilson transferred higher-interest-rate credit debt to more affordable cards while she and her husband were grappling with their $30,000 burden. They did another little thing: the magic secret. "We just spent less," Wilson says.

—Adapted from *BusinessWeek*

How Much Debt?

Of 1,500 21- to 35-year-old college grads surveyed:

◆ **Nearly one-third had to move back in with parents because of education-related debt.**

◆ **Over one-third sold personal possessions to make ends meet.**

◆ **Over one-fourth delayed a medical or dental procedure due to lack of funds.**

Source: AllianceBernstein Investments, 2006.

Think About It
1. **Recalling** What is the average credit card debt among 25- to 34-year-olds?
2. **Summarizing** Describe five strategies to help ease debt burden.

Government Regulation of Credit

GUIDE TO READING

Section Preview
In this section, you will learn about laws that protect consumers from unfair credit practices, as well as those that regulate personal bankruptcy.

Content Vocabulary
- usury law *(p. 105)*
- bankruptcy *(p. 106)*

Academic Vocabulary
- series *(p. 105)*
- contrast *(p. 105)*

Reading Strategy
Identifying As you read, complete a diagram similar to the one below by listing some of the ways the government regulates credit.

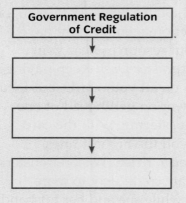

Government Regulation of Credit

ISSues In ThE NeWS
—from *MSNBC.com*

GET THE SITE RIGHT Beginning September 1, [2005], all U.S. adults will be able to request one free copy of their credit report from each of the nation's three credit bureaus. Consumers were granted the free reports as part of the Fair and Accurate Transaction Act, passed by Congress in December 2003.

. . . Probably the biggest glitch has been the site's name. While there's only one place for consumers to get their Congressionally-mandated free credit report—AnnualCreditReport.com—there are over 100 web sites with similar-sounding names. Most attempt to sell consumers subscription services that offer repeated peeks at their credit report.

The Web site is operated by the three credit bureaus—Equifax, Experian and TransUnion. . . .

"There have been some glitches, but we think all in all it's gone fairly well," said Peggy Tui, who monitors the site for the Federal Trade Commission.

EQUIFAX   **experian**   **TransUnion**

To protect consumers, the federal and state governments regulate the credit industry. Some states have set a maximum on the interest rates charged for certain types of credit. The federal government has also passed laws designed to increase the flow of credit information to consumers. In this section, you'll learn about these laws and how they protect consumers from unfair credit practices.

Laws Protecting Borrowers

Main Idea Laws have been enacted to protect borrowers against unfair lending practices and to help them make informed decisions.

Economics & You What do you think might happen if there were no laws protecting people who borrow? Read on to learn about these laws and how they protect your rights as a consumer.

Economics ONLINE

Student Web Activity Visit the *Economics Today and Tomorrow* Web site at glencoe.com and click on *Chapter 4—Student Web Activities* to learn more about government regulation of credit.

There are many laws designed to protect consumers who borrow. Here we look at some important federal laws and then explore state laws in general.

The Truth in Lending Act The Truth in Lending Act of 1968 was the first of a **series** of major federal laws that greatly expanded the government's role in protecting users of consumer credit. This act requires creditors to keep consumers fully informed about the costs and conditions of borrowing.

The Equal Credit Opportunity Act In 1974 Congress enacted the Equal Credit Opportunity Act (ECOA) as an addition to the Truth in Lending Act. Among other things, those who provide credit cannot deny you such credit solely on the basis of your race, religion, national origin, gender, marital status, or age. Also, no one can deny you credit simply because your income might come from public assistance benefits.

usury law: law restricting the amount of interest that can be charged for credit

State Usury Laws A law restricting the amount of interest that can be charged for credit is called a **usury law**. Some states set up different maximum rates for different types of consumer credit. Maximum rates on charge accounts and credit cards, for example, are often about 18 percent a year, or 1½ percent per month. Consumer finance agencies, in **contrast**, can often charge higher rates because their loans involve higher risks.

✓ Reading Check **Identifying** The Equal Credit Opportunity Act prohibits discrimination in giving credit on the basis of what six characteristics?

Women and Credit

Before the Equal Credit Opportunity Act of 1974, many creditors would not approve a married woman for credit unless her husband signed the application as well. Now, only joint applications require the signatures of both spouses.

Personal Bankruptcy

Main Idea Personal bankruptcy should be used only as a last resort to relieve the financial burden of debt.

Economics & You Have you ever found yourself in the position of owing someone more than you were able to quickly pay back? What steps did you take to fix the situation? Read on to learn about personal bankruptcy.

Every day in the United States, thousands of families get into financial trouble because they have ignored the total costs of all their borrowing. They have too many credit cards, too many charge accounts, and own a home that has too large a mortgage. Just because someone offers you credit or allows you to borrow does not mean that you should accept. Buying on credit is a serious consumer activity.

If debtors take out too many loans, use too many credit cards, and pile up debts that they cannot pay off, they may have to file personal **bankruptcy.** When a bankruptcy is approved through a bankruptcy court, debtors must give up most of what they own, which is then distributed to their creditors. The Constitution authorizes Congress to establish bankruptcy laws. Certain debts, such as taxes, must continue to be paid, however.

bankruptcy: the state of legally having been declared unable to pay off debts owed with available income

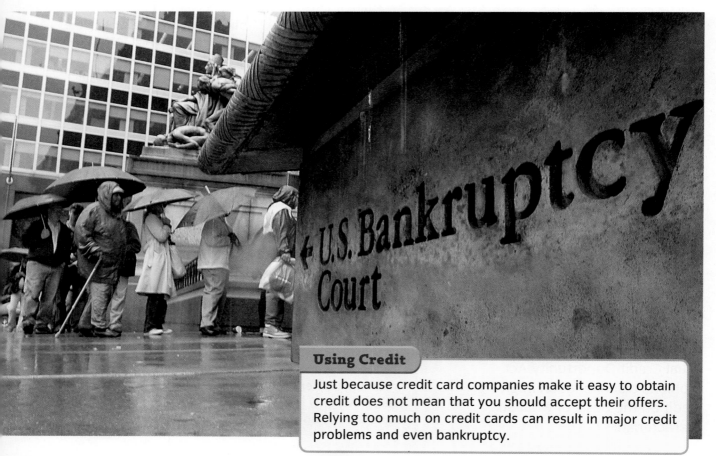

Using Credit

Just because credit card companies make it easy to obtain credit does not mean that you should accept their offers. Relying too much on credit cards can result in major credit problems and even bankruptcy.

FOXTROT

▲ Borrowers can run into trouble if they do not understand how credit works.

If you declare personal bankruptcy, be aware that the bankruptcy proceedings remain on your credit record for 10 years. During this period, it is very difficult to reestablish credit and borrow funds for items such as a new car or home. That is why choosing bankruptcy to get out of credit problems should be a last resort. Also, when you declare bankruptcy, you are making sure that your creditors will never be paid off (at least not in full) for what they loaned out.

In 2005, Congress passed extensive amendments to federal bankruptcy laws. It is now more difficult to avoid paying off student loans, for example.

✔ **Reading Check** **Explaining** Why is declaring bankruptcy considered a "last resort" for people in financial trouble?

section 4 Review

Vocabulary

1. **Explain** the significance of: usury law, bankruptcy.

Main Ideas

2. **Identifying** Tracking your credit rating is increasingly important. Using a chart like the one below, list the three credit bureaus that give free credit reports.

AnnualCreditReport.com

Critical Thinking

3. The **BIG Idea** Why does the U.S. government set rules for the regulation of credit?

4. **Summarizing** Why are consumer finance agencies often permitted to charge higher interest rates than other lending institutions?

Applying Economics

5. **Bankruptcy** Research the two types of bankruptcy known as Chapter 7 and Chapter 13. Which requires debtors to set up a repayment plan? Which deletes the debt completely? What are the long-term effects of each type on one's future?

Going Into Debt **107**

ENTREPRENEUR/ CREDIT COUNSELOR (1960–)

Dave Ramsey
● Financial Guru

■ Host of the nationally syndicated radio talk show *The Dave Ramsey Show*

■ Author of the best-selling books *Financial Peace* and *The Total Money Makeover*

■ Creator of Financial Peace University, a program to help people get out of debt

Dave Ramsey claims that he has an unusual way of looking at the world:

"My wife, Sharon, says I'm weird, and truthfully— I am weird. But there's a reason. Starting from nothing, by the time I was 26 I had a net worth of a little over a million dollars."

And then he lost it all, including a $4 million real estate portfolio. The reason? He had borrowed millions of dollars, and when the loans were called in, he couldn't pay them.

After considerable study and introspection, Ramsey came to the realization that before he could manage money, he had to manage himself. He also realized there were millions of other Americans in the same fix:

"We have become a nation of consumers instead of a nation of producers. We are spoiled. No one wants to wait and save money for purchases. . . . There's so much money to be made by the credit [card] companies that consumers are always

going to be encouraged to spend, spend, spend beyond their means through the use of credit."

In 1988 he established a consumer counseling service to help others who were suffering from financial stress. He reaches them through broadcasting, publishing, and seminars. His message is simple:

> **"Live on a written monthly plan—a budget. . . . It's not hard to add and subtract and to understand that if you spend more than you make you're going to be broke all your life and deeply in debt."**

Checking for Understanding

1. **Describing** What led to Dave Ramsey's financial problems?

2. **Theorizing** In what ways could a budget help someone stay out of debt?

STUDY TO GO → Study anywhere, anytime! Download quizzes and flash cards to your PDA from glencoe.com.

■ The **cost of credit** is the interest charged on the amount borrowed. The longer the loan period, the higher the amount of interest paid.

$1,000 Installment Loan at 9% Interest		
Term of loan	24 Months	36 Months
Monthly payments	$45.69	$31.80
Total interest	$96.56	$144.80
Total payments	$1,096.56	$1,144.80

Cost of credit

■ The two main **sources of credit** are credit cards/charge accounts and financial institutions.

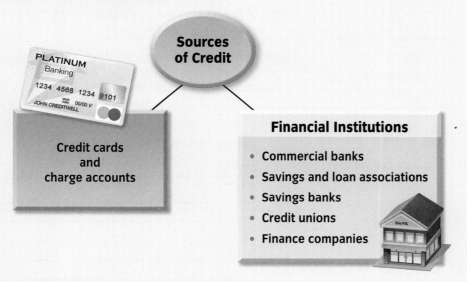

Sources of Credit

PLATINUM Banking
1234 4568 1234 9101
JOHN CREDITWELL

Credit cards and charge accounts

Financial Institutions
- Commercial banks
- Savings and loan associations
- Savings banks
- Credit unions
- Finance companies

■ Lenders look at your credit history to determine your **creditworthiness**. It is important to manage your credit wisely and avoid situations that will hurt your credit rating.

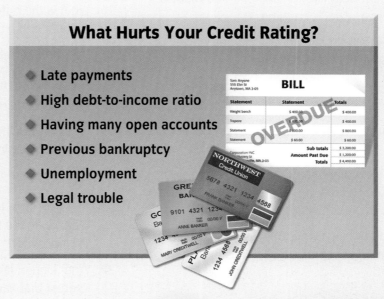

What Hurts Your Credit Rating?
- Late payments
- High debt-to-income ratio
- Having many open accounts
- Previous bankruptcy
- Unemployment
- Legal trouble

Review Content Vocabulary

1. *Write a paragraph or two explaining credit and debt to young people. Use all of the following terms.*

   credit
   principal
   interest
   charge account
   credit card
   finance charge
   annual percentage rate (APR)

2. *Now write a paragraph explaining to young people how they can get credit and what protects them from unfair credit practices or uncontrollable circumstances. Use all of the following terms.*

   credit check
   credit rating
   collateral
   secured loan
   unsecured loan
   usury law
   bankruptcy

Review Academic Vocabulary

Choose the letter of the term that best completes each sentence.

   a. enormous
   b. period
   c. previous
   d. access
   e. accumulate
   f. concentrate
   g. series
   h. contrast

3. Installment debt allows consumers to repay a loan over a _____ of time.

4. A person in debt should _____ on paying off high-interest credit cards first.

5. Loans give people _____ to goods that they might not be able to afford otherwise.

6. The Truth in Lending Act was the first of a _____ of laws dealing with consumer credit.

7. The credit rating of a person who has declared bankruptcy would _____ sharply with the rating of a person with good credit.

8. A consumer can always improve his or her credit rating, despite _____ mistakes.

9. The total amount of consumer debt in the United States is _____.

10. Debt can _____ quickly when a consumer has multiple credit cards, car loans, student loans, and a mortgage.

Review the Main Ideas

Section 1 (pp. 87–91)

11. What do you have to pay when you borrow?

12. How is taking out a loan similar to buying an item on credit?

13. What type of goods do people typically use installment debt to buy?

14. Why do people use credit?

Section 2 (pp. 92–98)

15. Fill in a chart like the one below to list and describe the types of lending institutions in the American economy.

Type of Institution	Description

16. What is the difference between a charge account and a credit card?

17. How does a debit card work?

Section 3 (pp. 99–102)

18. What does a credit check reveal?

19. What is the difference between a secured and an unsecured loan?

20. What are your responsibilities as a borrower?

Section 4 (pp. 104–107)

21. What does the Equal Credit Opportunity Act of 1974 prohibit?

22. What kind of law restricts the amount of interest that can be charged for credit?

Math Practice

Imagine that you charge $1,000 on a credit card and stop using it. The interest rate is fixed at 15%. You can pay $50 per month. Answer the following questions about credit card debt.

23. If there were no interest charges, how long would it take to pay off the balance?

24. With interest charges included, it would in fact take you 35 months to pay off the debt. Why?

25. When you finish paying off your debt, you will have paid a total of about $1,140. What is the extra $140 above your original $1,000 charge? Why do you pay this?

Critical Thinking

26. **The BIG Idea** In deciding whether to pay cash or use credit for a purchase, what are the benefits and drawbacks of each choice?

Economics ONLINE

Self-Check Quiz Visit the *Economics Today and Tomorrow* Web site at glencoe.com and click on **Chapter 4—Self-Check Quizzes** to assess your knowledge of chapter content.

27. **Determining Cause and Effect** If John declares personal bankruptcy, how does it affect him? How does it affect his creditors? Other consumers? Retailers? Fill in a graphic organizer like the one below to answer these questions.

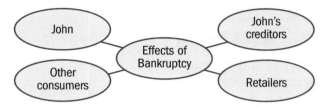

28. **Predicting** What might happen if a person took out a payroll advance for several weeks in a row?

Analyzing Visuals

29. Study the two "Terms and Conditions" statements for credit cards on the right, and then answer the following questions.

   a. Why would you want to avoid getting cash advances with either card?

   b. Why do you think Credit Card A has a 0% APR for six months?

   c. Based on the annual and monthly fees, which card costs more per year to have?

   d. Which offer is the better deal overall? Why do you think so?

TERMS AND CONDITIONS

Credit Card A

Annual Percentage Rate (APR) for Purchases	**0%** for six months, then **14.99%**
Other APRs	Cash advances: **19.99%** Balance transfers: **9.99%**
Annual Fee	**$50.00**
Other Fees	Cash advance fee: **3%** of amount Late payment fee: **$25.00** Over-limit fee: **$25.00**

Credit Card B

Annual Percentage Rate (APR) for Purchases	**9.99%**
Other APRs	Cash advances: **19.99%** Balance transfers: **9.99%**
Annual Fee	**none**
Other Fees	Monthly maintenance fees: **$10.95** Late payment fee: **$30.00** Over-limit fee: **$50.00**

chapter 5

Buying the Necessities

The **BIG Idea**

Scarcity is the basic economic problem that requires people to make choices about how to use limited resources.

Why It Matters

What are the costs of owning a car? How much should you budget for clothes and food? In this chapter, read to learn how to shop wisely for the necessities.

Economics ONLINE

Chapter Overview Visit the *Economics Today and Tomorrow* Web site at glencoe.com and click on *Chapter 5—Chapter Overviews* to preview chapter information.

Shopping for Food

GUIDE TO READING

Section Preview
In this section, you will learn about a variety of ways to save when shopping for food.

Content Vocabulary
- club warehouse store *(p. 115)*
- convenience store *(p. 115)*
- private-labeled products *(p. 116)*

Academic Vocabulary
- potential *(p. 115)*
- regional *(p. 116)*

Reading Strategy
Comparing and Contrasting As you read, complete a table like the one below by listing the benefits and costs of the money-saving habits discussed in the section.

Shopping for Food		
Habit	**Benefit(s)**	**Cost(s)**
Comparison shopping		
Using club warehouse stores		
Using convenience stores		
Buying store brands		
Using coupons		

PRODUCTS In ThE NeWS
—from *Time*

A NEW TAKE ON PIZZA Hold the ice cream!

How do you reinvent one of the world's favorite quick snacks? Competing teams of culinary inventors think they have a novel answer: pizza in a cone. Eating a slice on the run can be messy, so food scientists have cooked up a new conical concept that is catching on in Europe and will soon hit the U.S.

This summer, Konopizza expects to open shops in Indonesia, Kuwait, Spain, and Greece.

But Konopizza has an American competitor in Crispy Cones, [which] features not just pizza but also a range of conical chow, including chicken, chili, and fruit. Besting the Konopizza prep time of three minutes, Crispy Cones is counting on partially prebaked cones to cut retail oven-to-plate time to just 45 seconds.

"Food should be as portable as a phone," [says Nir Adar, founder of Crispy Cones.]

▲ **Crispy Cone Pizza**

Americans consume a great variety of foods. They can choose from thousands of different food products and buy them at thousands of stores. Hundreds of brands offer numerous choices. With pizza alone, Americans can choose fresh-baked or frozen, deep dish or thin crust, meat lovers' or vegetarian, or even pizza in a cone. In all, American consumers spend hundreds of billions of dollars a year on food. In this section, you'll learn how to get the most from your food dollars.

Comparison Shopping

(Main Idea) **Shopping for food involves many considerations, including brands, sizes, quantities, unit prices, freshness, the availability of coupons, and store locations.**

Economics & You How much do you spend per week on food? Is there any way you could spend less? Read on to learn about ways to save on food by comparison shopping and planning ahead.

Because American families spend so much on food, comparison shopping is important. It involves making comparisons among brands and sizes before you buy. You need to decide not only what to shop for but where to shop as well.

A consumer should do only as much comparison shopping as is worthwhile, however. It does not pay for a shopper to go far out of his or her way to shop at a store that has only a few needed items at low prices. The additional costs of time and transportation would outweigh any potential savings.

Remember, your time has an opportunity cost. The more time you spend comparison shopping for food, the less time you have to do anything else.

✔ **Reading Check** **Predicting Consequences** What is the opportunity cost of comparison shopping?

Figure 5.1 | Club Warehouse v. Convenience Stores

■ There are different trade-offs involved when you choose to shop at a club warehouse or convenience store rather than a regular grocery store.

(**A. Club Warehouse Stores**) Although these stores generally offer lower prices than grocery stores, you must buy most items there in bulk. Also, these stores often require people to become members in order to shop in them, and there is usually a membership fee involved. You need to make sure your potential savings on the items you will buy will be more than the other costs. Two popular club warehouse stores in the United States are Costco and Sam's Club.

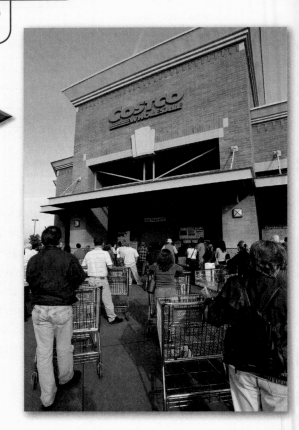

Trade-Offs in Stores

Main Idea Deciding what food to buy involves numerous trade-offs.

Economics & You Which resource is more important to you: time or money income? Read on to learn about trade-offs between saving time and saving money income when shopping for food.

Americans typically do their food shopping either in grocery stores or in **club warehouse stores**, which charge lower prices than grocery stores do. Club warehouse stores sell a limited number of brands and items. Although these stores offer the largest **potential** savings for your food dollars, there is a trade-off. Most food items are only available in large quantities, such as a "value-pack" of soup with 24 cans. Unless your family is large and eats canned soup regularly, you will have unused cans of soup in your cupboard for a long time. Therein lies an opportunity cost. You have tied up your funds in an inventory of food.

Occasionally, you may want to use a **convenience store**, such as 7-Eleven, for just that reason—because it's convenient. These stores are usually open 16 to 24 hours a day, but they carry only a limited selection of items, and they are considerably more expensive than grocery stores. See **Figure 5.1** for more information on club warehouse and convenience stores.

club warehouse store: store that carries a limited number of brands and items in large quantities and is less expensive than grocery stores

convenience store: store open 16 to 24 hours a day, carrying a limited selection of relatively higher-priced items

B. Convenience Stores Although these stores are easily accessible, the selection of items is very limited, and you will pay a much higher price for most items than you would in a regular grocery store. You should shop in these stores only when you really need to save time.

Economic Analysis

Explaining *What are the benefits and drawbacks of buying items in bulk?*

Brand-Name, Private-Labeled, and Bulk Foods

When you go grocery shopping, many of the food items have well-known brand names. Some food stores also carry **regional** brands that are found only in certain areas of the country.

As an alternative to relatively more expensive national brands, some grocery stores and club warehouse stores carry their own store-brand products. These are also called **private-labeled products.** According to some consumer surveys, it is possible to save as much as 40 percent by buying such products. You can often save even more by purchasing bulk items. See **Figure 5.2** below for more information on these kinds of items.

There is often a trade-off between quality and price in the products you buy. A lower-priced store-brand dishwasher soap might leave a slight film on your drinking glasses, for example, compared to a more expensive national-brand alternative.

Often you will find that the larger the quantity of any item you buy in a supermarket, the lower the per-unit price. Most states require stores to provide unit pricing for food and other products. This practice makes it easy to compare prices not only for different brands, but for different sizes of the same brand. For example, the price of milk might be expressed in terms of cents per ounce. You can then tell how much you save per ounce if you buy milk in larger containers.

private-labeled products: lower-priced store-brand products carried by some supermarket chains and club warehouse chains

Figure 5.2 | Store-Brand and Bulk Foods

■ Some food products are available in store-brand and bulk forms. Both store-brand and bulk foods usually have a lower price than brand-name products.

A. Bulk Products
Bulk products are sold in large quantities, usually at club warehouse stores. Also, as shown here, they can be sold loosely—that is, you can take as much or as little as you want, and you will generally pay a lower price per unit.

B. Store-Brand Products Store-brand products are the products retailers sell as their own brands. They may bear the name of the retailer selling them, such as Kroger or Safeway, or they may be sold under an entirely different name such as "Best Yet," which is sold only at KMart.

Economic Analysis
Contrasting *What is the difference between store-brand and bulk products?*

Cents-Off Coupons Many manufacturers give cents-off coupons. The use of cents-off coupons, however, requires time—the time to collect and match them to items when shopping. Because time is a scarce resource, you have to decide if the amount you save using coupons is worth the time you spend. In addition, coupons tempt you to buy brand-name products you might not otherwise buy—thus not saving you much at all.

Store Discount Cards Most grocery-store chains now issue store discount cards, which they might refer to as "advantage cards" or "loyalty cards." Using these cards is optional, but customers who choose to use the cards pay lower prices on some items. Store owners say the cards reward their loyal customers by offering discounts. The cards have drawn criticism from consumers' groups, though, who claim that rather than paying reduced prices, card holders are really paying the usual price, and non-card holders are paying an inflated price. Also, the cards are used to track customers' spending habits for marketing purposes. Some people feel that this practice is an invasion of customers' privacy.

Unit Pricing

Unit pricing allows you to compare like amounts: ounces to ounces, pounds to pounds, and so on. In this example, the item on the right has a lower price, but if you study the unit pricing, you will see that it actually costs more per ounce than the item on the left.

Skills Handbook

See page R53 to learn about Comparing Data.

Reading Check **Summarizing** What are the alternatives to paying full price for national-brand food products?

section 1 Review

Vocabulary
1. **Explain** the significance of: club warehouse store, convenience store, private-labeled products.

Main Ideas
2. **Compare and Contrast** Use a diagram like the one below to list an advantage and a disadvantage of each item listed.

	Advantage	Disadvantage
Club warehouse store		
Convenience store		
Buying in bulk		

Critical Thinking
3. **The BIG Idea** What trade-offs are involved in comparison food shopping?
4. **Determining Cause and Effect** Why should you not shop when you are hungry or thirsty?

Applying Economics
5. **Variable Pricing** Choose three food items and compare their prices at four different stores by looking at ads or by visiting the stores. Explain why you believe each store had similar or different prices for each item.

ENTREPRENEUR
(1957–   )

Russell Simmons

● **Founder, Def Jam Records and Phat Farm Clothing**

■ Chairman, President, and CEO, Rush Communications, Inc.

■ Chairman, Hip-Hop Summit Action Network

■ Winner of the 2003 Tony Award for *Def Poetry Jam on Broadway* and the 2002 Peabody Award for the HBO production, *Russell Simmons Presents Def Poetry*

While still in college, Russell Simmons became manager of his brother Joseph's rap group, Run-DMC. This was in the late 1970s, and the music industry considered hip-hop to be a temporary fad. As Simmons later noted, "If the music business understood hip-hop in the beginning, I wouldn't have built Def Jam." He was referring to the wildly successful recording company that he cofounded with Rick Rubin in the 1980s and which was eventually sold in 1999 to Universal Music Group. Simmons's share of the profits from the sale came to $100 million.

Def Jam was just the beginning of Simmons's hip-hop-based business ventures that included the Phat Farm clothing company (sold in 2004 for $140 million), television shows, a credit-card company, a movie production house, an advertising agency, and more. He explains his success by crediting others:

"I've been blessed to find people who are smarter than I am, and they help me to execute the vision I have."

Even though he has been referred to as an "extreme entrepreneur," there's more to Russell Simmons than making huge amounts of money. He's a dedicated practitioner of yoga and a vegan, for example. ("I don't eat anything that runs away from me.") He also devotes considerable amounts of time and money to helping correct what he sees as social ills:

> **❝I think we're all connected. In fact, you realize as you grow older that you're the least important as just a single individual, that you're a part of the whole, as opposed to the whole being you.❞**

Checking for Understanding

1. Why does Simmons believe he has been successful in achieving his vision?

2. **Extending the Content** What did Simmons mean when he said, "If the music business understood hip-hop in the beginning, I wouldn't have built Def Jam."?

Clothing Choices

GUIDE TO READING

Section Preview
In this section, you will learn methods to help you make wise consumer choices when shopping for clothes.

Content Vocabulary
- durability *(p. 121)*
- service flow *(p. 121)*

Academic Vocabulary
- factor *(p. 119)*
- equivalent *(p. 122)*

Reading Strategy
Organizing Complete a web diagram like the one below by listing the factors discussed in this section that determine clothing value.

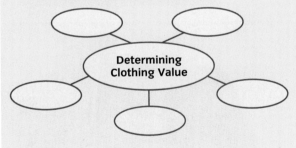

Determining Clothing Value

PRODUCTS In ThE NeWS
—from *CNN.com*

WHO CARES ABOUT PAIRS? It's one of life's greatest mysteries: What ever happened to the other sock?

Some cite rogue washing machines that feed on the helpless foot-warmers. Others blame mischievous sock fairies who spirit away the otherwise understated fashion fundamentals.

. . . People have been losing and clashing socks since they first appeared on people's feet. A little more than two years ago, a few friends met in San Francisco, California, intent on turning the phenomenon into a business.

. . . Conceived of in 2003, LittleMissMatched has exploded in the past year. . . . The fledgling company sells socks that do not match, in a variety of colors and patterns. . .

The patterned socks come in four color systems, characterized . . . as "fabulous," "marvelous," "kooky," and "zany." It adds up to 8,911 possible combinations—enough that a person could wear a different pair of LittleMissMatched socks every day for 24 years.

▲ **LittleMissMatched socks**

Americans spend over $400 billion annually on clothing and other personal products. Most people could reduce clothing expenditures by purchasing only a few very durable items. The clothes, however, would not serve another purpose—variety. In this section, you'll learn that variety, for Americans, is typically the motivating **factor** involved in clothing choice.

Comparing Clothing Value

Main Idea Clothing value depends on style, durability, and cost of care, as well as purchase price.

Economics & You Do you look for comfort, style, or certain brand names when shopping for clothes? How important are price and durability? Read on to learn how to make wise clothing choices.

Comparison shopping is an important part of buying wisely. Comparing value in clothing means more than simply purchasing an item from the store that offers the best price. Clothing value depends on at least three other factors: style, durability, and cost of care. (See **Figure 5.3** below.)

Style Clothing styles and trends change often, especially for young people. Today, many department stores offer very trendy clothes at reasonable prices. Some of these department stores also offer store-brand clothing labels that are similar to the store-brand grocery items discussed in the previous section. Store-brand clothing, like store-brand food, is generally less expensive than national brands. Nevertheless, it often represents the latest trends.

Careers Handbook

See pages R76–R80 to learn about becoming a fashion designer.

Figure 5.3 | Clothing Value

■ When making clothing purchases, many people want to have different looks for different occasions. Also, people who live in places where the climate changes need different wardrobes for summer and winter.

A. Style We often buy clothing that we believe reflects our self-image. Personal taste also has a big influence on the types of clothing people buy. For some people, wearing designer-label clothing, such as Abercrombie & Fitch, is important, and they will often spend more on clothing that bears this label than they would have spent on a similar, nondesigner product.

Durability The ability of an item to last is known as **durability**. The longer a piece of clothing—or any item—lasts, the more durable it is. When you purchase an item of clothing, you are purchasing it for the service flow that it yields. **Service flow** is the amount of time you will be able to use a product and the value you place on this use. If you buy a jacket that will last three years and costs $300, the cost per annual service flow is $100.

Before you shop, you may want to research what kinds of fabrics tend to last longer. Keep in mind, though, that if you are purchasing trendy, inexpensive clothing, durability might not be a very important factor. If you believe the item may be in fashion for only a year or two, you might not care whether it lasts much longer than that.

Cost of Care The cost of care is another factor in assessing value. Two shirts or blouses may cost the same, but one may require dry cleaning, which is more expensive than machine washing. Also, if an item requires hand washing, this will cost you in terms of the time that it will take to physically wash the item. When deciding on the best choice in a clothing purchase, you must consider these kinds of maintenance costs.

durability: ability of an item to last a long time

service flow: amount of use a person gets from an item over time and the value a person places on this use

✔ **Reading Check** **Explaining** What is service flow?

▼ **B. Durability** When comparison shopping for clothing, you should try to determine how long an item will last and how long you will need it. Then you should compare prices. If Shirt A is made of a more durable fabric than Shirt B, then Shirt A might be a better buy even if it costs a little more.

▲ **C. Cost of Care** Dry-cleaning costs can vary widely, from $4 per shirt to $12 or more for a skirt or sweater. Be sure to check clothing labels to determine if an item you are buying is dry-clean only.

Economic Analysis

Synthesizing *Why might a person who lives in Ohio spend more on clothes than a person who lives in Florida?*

More for Less

(Main Idea) **Consumers have many alternatives to buying clothing at full retail price.**

Economics & You Do you look for sales when you shop for clothing? Read on to learn about ways to spend less on clothing.

The cost of clothing has decreased significantly over the years. Seventy years ago, a good suit cost about $40, which took an average consumer almost 80 hours to earn. Today a comparable suit sells for just over $500, but costs the average worker the **equivalent** of about 40 hours of work.

Even though a smaller percentage of one's budget goes to clothing purchases now than in the past, it is still the wise consumer who looks for ways to save on clothing. Over the last couple of decades, *consignment stores,* or stores that sell used clothing at lower prices than new, have grown in popularity. Often, you can find very trendy clothing at low prices at consignment stores.

One Way to Save

At a consignment store, you can bring in used clothing of your own, and if the store accepts it, you will be given either cash or a credit on any future purchase you make at the store. These stores will generally grant you a higher amount in credit than in cash, to encourage you to shop at their store.

Another way to save on clothing is to buy it on sale. Most major department stores have frequent clothing sales, and holidays are often good times to look for clothing as stores will hold more sales when they think people will be off work and shopping.

Stores also frequently hold seasonal sales. For example, at the end of winter, a store might have a big sale on winter coats in order to get rid of their coat inventory and make room for spring and summer items. If you plan ahead on your wardrobe, you can save a lot through seasonal sales.

You can also sometimes save when you shop online, where there are thousands of clothing Web sites. Just enter "discount clothing" in any search engine, and you will find a great many sites that offer deals on clothes. Because clothing sales are so numerous throughout the year, however, it is easy to become a bargain fanatic—buying sale items that you don't need just because they are on sale. Before going shopping, make a list of the clothing you require. Having this list along may help you keep your spending within limits.

How Can You Save on Clothes?

◆ Comparison shopping
◆ Avoiding designer labels
◆ Buying items on sale
◆ Shopping at consignment stores
◆ Seasonal shopping

Personal Finance Handbook
See pages R4–R5 to learn about budgeting.

Reading Check **Determining Cause and Effect** Why do Americans spend a smaller percentage of their budget on clothing now than in the past?

section 2 Review

Vocabulary
1. **Explain** the significance of: durability, service flow.

Main Ideas
2. **Identifying** In a diagram like the one below, list one consideration you should keep in mind for each clothing value factor listed.

Style	Durability	Care

Critical Thinking
3. **The BIG Idea** What is your opportunity cost of comparison shopping for clothes?
4. **Explaining** When are the best times, usually, for taking advantage of clothing sales?

Applying Economics
5. **Evaluating Purchases** Think of the last article of clothing you bought and how much you paid for it. Then make a chart listing how the article rates in terms of style, durability, and cost of care. Do you think you made a good purchase? Why or why not?

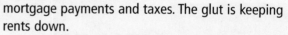

section 3 · To Rent or to Buy

GUIDE TO READING

Section Preview
In this section, you will discover the costs and responsibilities involved in both renting and buying a place to live.

Content Vocabulary
- lease *(p. 126)*
- security deposit *(p. 126)*
- closing costs *(p. 128)*
- points *(p. 129)*

Academic Vocabulary
- obtain *(p. 128)*
- involve *(p. 128)*

Reading Strategy
Organizing Complete a web diagram like the one below by listing the major costs involved in buying a home.

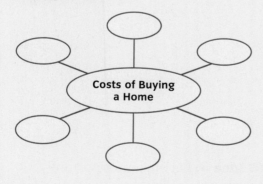

Costs of Buying a Home

ISSues In ThE NeWS
—from *Fortune*

A RENTER'S MARKET Why are rents keeping cool while prices keep getting hotter? Because a large [number] of today's buyers aren't purchasing homes to live in. The U.S. is creating 1.2 million new households a year, yet we're building about two million homes and condos. So 800,000 units are serving not as primary residences but as investments or as second and third homes.

These houses and condos often go back on the market as rentals, since owners need the income to cover the mortgage payments and taxes. The glut is keeping rents down.

In most big coastal cities, it now costs 40% to 70% as much to rent as to own. Home prices in those places have either doubled or almost doubled since 2000. But in most of them, rents have barely budged.

Deciding whether or not to buy a house is one of the most important financial decisions most people will make. Some people will save for years in order to buy a small house. Others take out huge mortgages to purchase large homes. Still others are content to rent a house, condo, or apartment most of their lives. In this section, you'll learn about the advantages and disadvantages of both renting and buying.

Should You Rent or Buy?

Main Idea There are advantages and disadvantages both to buying a home and renting a place to live.

Economics & You Have you ever thought about where you will live when you get out on your own? Read on to learn about the pros and cons of renting or buying a home.

The average American family spends about one-fourth to one-third of its income on housing. Therefore, deciding whether to rent or buy is one of the most important decisions a person can make.

When young adults first start out on their own, they will often rent an apartment or small house before they think about buying. There are many reasons why people often initially rent. First, buying a house generally requires a substantial down payment of many thousands of dollars. Renting an apartment, on the other hand, usually requires only a security deposit and one or two months' rent up front. Renters also do not have to pay maintenance costs or real estate taxes. Renting also allows people greater mobility; if renters want to find a different place to live, or if they want to move to another town or state, they don't have to worry about trying to sell property first.

Careers Handbook

See pages R76–R80 to learn about becoming a real estate agent.

Eventually, though, many people will choose to buy a home. Again, financial benefits are a driving consideration. Ownership of a home provides significant income tax benefits to the owner. Also, houses build up *equity,* which is the market value of the property minus the mortgage amount still owed. Home ownership is often a good investment, as houses often *appreciate,* or go up, in value, although this can depend on the neighborhood and the housing market at the time.

Buying

In addition to the long-term financial benefits of home ownership, people who choose to buy also experience the pride of ownership, and they have the freedom to remodel or improve the property as they wish. In turn, they give up the freedom of easy mobility.

✓ Reading Check

Explaining Name two advantages of renting.

Renter Rights and Responsibilities

(Main Idea) **Renters should read their leases carefully to understand their rights and responsibilities.**

Economics & You Do you know anyone who lives in an apartment, or have you ever experienced a conflict with a landlord? Read on to learn about the rights and responsibilities of renters and landlords.

lease: long-term agreement describing the terms under which property is rented

If you decide to rent, you will most likely be asked to sign a **lease,** or contract, that contains several clauses. As a prospective tenant, you should read the lease carefully. Most leases are for one to three years, although sometimes you may pay extra to get a six-month or nine-month lease. Often a lease will limit how an apartment can be used. The lease may forbid pets, for example, or forbid anyone other than the person named on the lease from living there. In signing a lease, the tenant is usually required to give the owner a **security deposit,** or funds for the owner to hold in case the rent is not paid or the apartment is damaged. The security deposit, usually equal to one month's rent, is returned after the tenant has moved out. The amount returned depends on the condition of the apartment, as determined by the landlord.

security deposit: funds a renter lets an owner hold in case the rent is not paid or the apartment is damaged

Among the rights of tenants is the use of the property for the purpose stated in the lease. Tenants also have the right to a certain amount of privacy. A landlord usually needs the renter's permission to enter an apartment. In turn, the tenant's responsibilities include paying the rent on time, taking reasonable care of the property, and notifying the landlord if repairs are needed.

The tenant is also required to give *notice,* or a formal warning, if he or she plans to move before the term of the lease is up. In this event, the landlord may ask for several months' rent to pay for any time the apartment is empty before a new tenant moves in.

Restrictions May Apply

If you have pets and are trying to rent, be sure to ask the landlord about this issue. Some landlords do not allow pets at all, while others allow some animals but not others. You may have to put down an extra security deposit if you have pets.

Figure 5.4 | Before You Sign

■ Follow these tips if you are planning on signing a lease on an apartment or other rental unit.

Clauses in Rental Leases

Avoid these types of clauses in leases:

1. **Confession-of-judgment clause:** The lawyer for the rental owner has the right to plead guilty for you in court if the owner thinks his or her rights have been violated. With a confession-of-judgment clause—illegal in some states—you are admitting guilt before committing any act.

2. **Inability-to-sue clause:** You give up your right to sue the owner if you suffer injury or damage through some fault of the owner, such as neglected repair work.

3. **Arbitrary clauses, or those based on one's wishes rather than a rule or law:** The owner has the right to cancel the lease because he or she is dissatisfied with your behavior.

If possible, add these clauses to your lease:

1. A list of the appliances that come with the apartment—dishwasher, garbage disposal, and air conditioner, for example.

2. The apartment community facilities you have been promised—recreation room, parking space, swimming pool—and whether you must pay extra for their use.

3. Any other promises made by the owner, such as painting the apartment (and what color).

4. The right to cancel your lease if you are transferred to a job in another city. Usually you must agree to pay a certain amount to do this, which should be stated in the lease.

5. The right to put in lighting fixtures, shelves, and so on, and have them remain your property when you move.

Charts In Motion
See StudentWorks™ Plus or go to glencoe.com.

Economic Analysis
Using Charts Why are confession-of-judgment clauses bad for renters?

Landlords have responsibilities too. In many states, landlords must make sure that their apartments have certain minimum services, such as heat, and that they are fit to live in. Landlords may also have to obey building safety laws. For example, fire escapes and smoke detectors may be required. Leases usually call for the landlord to make repairs within a reasonable amount of time. In many states, a tenant has the right to pay for the repairs and withhold that amount of rent if the landlord does not make the repairs. **Figure 5.4** above details more important information about leases.

Personal Finance Handbook
See pages R28–R29 to learn more about renting an apartment.

Reading Check **Identifying** Whose responsibility is it to make repairs to an apartment?

Economics ONLINE

Student Web Activity Visit the *Economics Today and Tomorrow* Web site at glencoe.com and click on *Chapter 5—Student Web Activities* to compare home prices in your area and around the country.

Personal Finance Handbook

See pages R24–R27 and R32–R33 to learn more about taxes and insurance.

closing costs: fees involved in arranging for a mortgage or in transferring ownership of property

Purchasing a House

Main Idea Potential home buyers need to consider many different costs before deciding to purchase a house.

Economics & You Do you plan to own a house someday? Why or why not? Read on to learn about the financial obligations of owning a home.

When you decide to buy a house, it is important that you do not take on financial obligations that are beyond your budget. As a general rule, no more than a third of your total income should go toward your mortgage payment and other costs. (See **Figure 5.5** below.)

One of the major challenges facing any home buyer is **obtaining** the mortgage. You will remember from Chapter 4 that a mortgage is the installment debt that you take on when you buy a house or other piece of property. If you buy a house for $200,000 and make a $40,000 down payment, you will need to obtain a mortgage for the remaining $160,000. The mortgage will then be repaid in monthly installments that include interest on the loan. Property taxes, homeowner's insurance, and mortgage insurance are often included in your mortgage payment as well.

At the time of purchase, in addition to the down payment, you will need funds for **closing costs.** These are costs **involved** in arranging for the mortgage or in transferring ownership of the property. Closing costs can include fees for such items as the title search, legal costs, loan application, credit report, house inspections, and taxes. Although the person buying the house usually pays these fees, the seller may agree to pay part or all of them if this will make it easier to sell the house.

Figure 5.5 The Cost of Ownership

■ There are many expenses involved in owning a home apart from the mortgage payments. Remember, though, that owning a home builds equity and is often a good investment.

Economic Analysis

Explaining *Why do lenders often charge points when someone takes out a mortgage?*

Costs to Consider When Buying a House

◆ Down payment

◆ Mortgage payments

◆ Closing costs

◆ Points

◆ Property taxes

◆ Homeowner's insurance

◆ Mortgage insurance

◆ Utilities and upkeep

Freedom of Use

Owning a home provides the owner with the freedom to remodel, paint, or perform any other home improvements he or she wishes. Home owners should be careful, though, not to overextend their debt load on home-improvement projects.

When you are arranging for a mortgage, it is important to know about points, which are included in closing costs. **Points** are the fees paid to the lender and computed as a percentage of the loan. Each point the lender charges equals 1 percent of the amount borrowed. Lenders charge points— usually one to four—when they believe that the current interest rate is not high enough to pay the expenses involved in handling the mortgage and still make a profit. When interest rates are up, on the other hand, lenders will sometimes waive points to attract home buyers. In any event, you should attempt to negotiate points with the lender. You also have the option of going to a different lender.

Reading Check **Analyzing** Aside from the down payment on the house itself, what other fees must you pay up front when buying a home?

points: fees paid to a lender and computed as a percentage of a loan

section 3 Review

Vocabulary
1. **Explain** the significance of: lease, security deposit, closing costs, points.

Main Ideas
2. **Comparing** In a chart like the one below, list the advantages of buying and renting.

Buying Advantages	Renting Advantages

Critical Thinking
3. The **BIG Idea** Based on the advantages and disadvantages of buying and renting that you've read about in this section, do you think you would like to rent or buy a house when you live independently? Explain your choice.

Applying Economics
4. **Analyzing a Lease** Go to an apartment complex office and ask for a copy of a lease. Bring the lease to class and read the contents. Then make one list of the renter's responsibilities and another list of the penalties for breaking the lease. Do you think the terms of the lease are fair? Why or why not?

Buying and Operating a Vehicle

GUIDE TO READING

Section Preview
In this section, you will learn how to go about buying and operating a vehicle, along with the costs involved.

Content Vocabulary
- registration fee *(p. 131)*
- liability insurance *(p. 133)*

Academic Vocabulary
- period *(p. 132)*
- status *(p. 133)*

Reading Strategy
Describing As you read, complete a diagram like the one below by listing the costs involved in buying and operating a car.

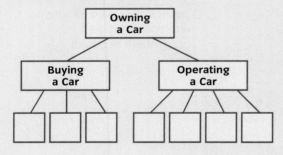

PRODUCTS In ThE NeWS
—from *CNNMoney.com*

SAFER ROADWAYS It used to be that if you wanted a car that was really safe, you paid for it. Safety was a luxury you found in expensive European cars like Volvo and BMW.

No longer. With crash test results and other safety data now widely available, no car company wants one of its models tagged as unsafe. And few are.

There are still some vehicles that are safer than others, but it's surprising how many really safe cars there are these days at non-luxury prices. Cost is no longer the issue. Newness is.

. . . Making cars safer does cost money. . . . Head-protecting side airbags generally cost $600 to $800 as an option, but more vehicles are offering them as standard equipment.

. . . Provided they are equipped with head-protecting side airbags, few vehicles today do poorly in . . . crash tests. [This translates into] comparatively low real-world fatalities.

▲ Toyota Camry

As with every decision in life, when you decide to buy a car, you are going to make a trade-off that involves an opportunity cost. You will have to decide what type of vehicle to buy, whether to buy new or used, and whether gas efficiency or engine size is more important to you, for example. In this section, you will learn about some of the important things to consider when shopping for a car.

Buying a Car

Main Idea Buying a car involves comparing many variables, such as the initial purchase prices, repair histories, warranties, and styles of different makes and models.

Economics & You Have you ever bought or considered buying a car? If so, what factors did you consider? Looks? Safety? Fuel efficiency? Price? Read on to learn about what to look for when buying a car.

Buying a car involves several considerations. One is the amount of money and time spent shopping for the car. Another is the amount of money and time spent in actually purchasing the car. Because of limited resources, most people have to borrow funds to buy a car. The costs of the loan are the down payment, the monthly payments on the principal, and the interest on the loan.

New or Used? The first decision you must make is whether to buy a new or used car. New cars are more expensive, of course, but they will generally cost less in repairs over the first several years. If you buy a used car, be sure to check out the vehicle's history first and make sure the car is in good condition. It's a good idea to have a used car checked over by an independent mechanic before purchasing it.

Registration Fee The owner of an automobile must pay a state licensing fee, or a **registration fee**, to use the car. Usually the fee must be paid annually. Some states now offer a two-year registration option. In many states, the amount of the fee varies depending on the car's age, weight, type, and value.

Extended Warranty One way to guard against having to pay for major repairs is to buy extended warranty coverage. New-car warranties generally protect owners for all major repairs except tune-ups and damage resulting from improper use of the automobile. New-car warranties usually last only a few years, or up to a certain limit of miles or kilometers. These warranties, however, can often be extended for another one, two, or three years by paying additional money when the car is purchased.

Reading Check **Evaluating** On what factors does a car registration fee generally depend?

Personal Finance Handbook
*See pages **R30–R31** to learn more about **buying a car**.*

registration fee: licensing fee, usually annual, paid to a state for the right to use a car

▼Fuel efficiency should be one factor you consider when buying a car.

Cornered

GUZZLER

"Backseat folds out to a bed in case you run out of gas on the way home."

Operating a Car

Main Idea Operating a car is expensive, involving the costs of gasoline, routine maintenance, major repairs, depreciation, and insurance.

Economics & You Do you own a car? Aside from the initial purchase, how much do you spend every month on the car's day-to-day use? Read on to learn the costs involved in operating a vehicle.

Normal Maintenance and Major Repairs

The amount of normal maintenance—oil and filter changes and minor tune-ups—depends on the amount the car is driven and how carefully the owner maintains the car. Major repairs are those that are normally unexpected and expensive. They include rebuilding the transmission and replacing the exhaust system. No one can guarantee that an automobile will not require major repairs while you own it, but you can follow certain steps to reduce the probability.

You should check the repair records of different cars before deciding on a particular make and model. If you are considering a used car, you should also take it to a diagnostic center, or have a mechanic check it. Sometimes dealers offer warranties on used cars for a limited time **period**, such as 30 days, or you can purchase a warranty covering a longer period of time.

Figure 5.6 | How Car Insurance Rates Are Set

■ When you buy automobile insurance, the rate you are charged is determined by your gender, driving experience, and a range of other factors.

Factors Affecting Automobile Insurance Rates

1. **The type of car you drive.** Insurance companies consider the safety record of a car and the costs to repair it if it is involved in an accident.

2. **Where you drive.** If the rate of thefts and accidents is high in an area, the risk to the insurance company is greater. A city, for example, would have more thefts and accidents than would a rural area. Therefore, the rate the insurance company charges in a city will be higher.

3. **What you use the car for.** If you drive your car for business on a daily basis, the rate will be higher than if you use it only for errands and occasional trips.

4. **Marital status.** In general, married men and women have lower accident rates than single men and women and, therefore, pay lower insurance rates.

5. **Safety record.** If you have a history of accidents and traffic tickets, then you will be charged a high rate. Whether a new driver has had driver education is often considered in determining a rate.

6. **Grades.** Many insurance companies offer better rates to teenage drivers who get good grades.

7. **Number of drivers.** The more drivers who use a particular car, the higher the insurance rate will be.

Economic Analysis

Analyzing Why do you think some insurance companies give lower rates to students with good grades?

Depreciation *Depreciation*—a decline in value over time—takes place as an item wears out or becomes outdated. Age is the major factor. A car loses value every year even if it is not driven because an automobile is a durable good. All durable goods deteriorate, or become worse over time. Another cause of depreciation is the technology and features of new makes and models. These changes make older models obsolete.

The amount of depreciation caused by physical wear and tear varies. It depends on how hard a car is driven, how far it is driven, and how well it is maintained. Generally, cars depreciate about 20 percent each year.

Insurance A major cost of owning an automobile, especially for new drivers, is insurance. Many states require that liability insurance be purchased before an automobile can be licensed. **Liability insurance** pays for bodily injury as well as property damage if you are in an accident.

Insurance companies classify drivers in various ways, usually according to age, gender, and marital **status**. Rates depend on the category into which a person fits. The categories, in turn, are based on statistics showing that different types of drivers have different accident rates. Young people, for example, almost always have to pay higher insurance rates.

Figure 5.6 shows factors in addition to age and gender that affect insurance rates. Rates cannot vary too widely, however, because states set limits on the rates that companies can charge.

liability insurance: insurance that pays for bodily injury and property damage

Personal Finance Handbook
See pages R32–R33 to learn more about insurance.

✔ **Reading Check** **Describing** What factors affect a car's rate of depreciation?

---

section 4 Review

Vocabulary
1. **Explain** the significance of: registration fee, liability insurance.

Main Ideas
2. **Identifying** Use a diagram like the one below to list six factors to consider when purchasing a vehicle.

Buying a Car

3. **Examining** What two costs of operating a vehicle are based on state requirements?

Critical Thinking
4. **The BIG Idea** What trade-offs are involved in buying a vehicle?

Applying Economics
5. **Insurance Rates** Choose a car you would like to purchase in the future, and then search the Internet for insurance rates in your area for that vehicle. Which company offers the best rate for your age group?

EAT YOUR HYBRID VEGGIES

From scarlet corn to tortilla-like lettuce, innovation is hitting the produce section.

Check It Out! In this chapter you learned about buying the necessities, including food. This article shows how shopping for healthy food has entered a whole new dimension.

▲ Colorful Harvest's orange, yellow, and red carrots

Even for shoppers used to the riot of colorful fruits and veggies in a suburban grocery store, a walk through the produce aisle at the Harris Teeter supermarket in Mount Pleasant, S.C., is a feast for the eyes. There are exotic fruits like the kiwanos, with orange skin and white flesh that tastes of banana, watermelon, and cucumber. The spiky fruits are so odd that when they roll through checkout, even the cashiers can't always I.D. them. But also piled high on the shelves are cobs of corn with scarlet kernels that look like old-fashioned wild maize…. The corn is custom-bred to have high levels of anthocyanin, an antioxidant usually found in blueberries. Down the way are some funny-looking artichokes—purple, thanks to a similar enrichment with anthocyanin.

Innovation is sweeping through the farm sector, bringing surprises that go beyond exotic fruits jet-shipped from the ends of the earth. In many cases it is consumers who are influencing produce breakthroughs, just as they forced agribusiness to take organic food seriously. Years ago seed companies courted farmers with new seed varieties that promised big harvests of veggies that could stay fresh for seemingly impossible lengths of time. Today's consumers are less interested in, say, rubbery tomatoes that last forever on a shelf, and more attracted to healthful produce that actually tastes good…. These new fruits and veggies aren't being cooked up using genetic engineering. Scientists employ older methods, such as crossbreeding different varieties of the same plant, but with a high-tech spin.

—Reprinted from *BusinessWeek*

Think About It

1. **Explaining** According to the article, who has influenced the rise of innovative fruits and vegetables?

2. **Theorizing** Which type of consumer would buy hybrid vegetables—one concerned with price, one concerned with taste, or one concerned with health? Explain your answer.

■ When buying any necessities, including food and clothing, there is often a trade-off between **quality and price**.

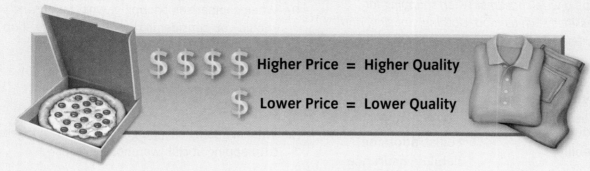

$$$$ Higher Price = Higher Quality

$ Lower Price = Lower Quality

■ When deciding whether to **rent or buy a home**, you should consider the advantages of each option.

Advantages of Renting

◆ Lower monthly costs
◆ Greater mobility
◆ No maintenance responsibilities

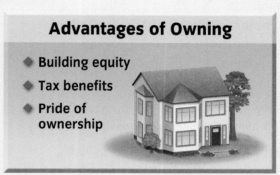

Advantages of Owning

◆ Building equity
◆ Tax benefits
◆ Pride of ownership

■ When buying a car, you will have many **trade-offs** to consider before deciding what type of vehicle is best for you.

◆ New
◆ Fuel efficient
◆ Under warranty
◆ Lower insurance

◆ Used
◆ Powerful engine
◆ No warranty
◆ Higher insurance

Review Content Vocabulary

1. *Write a paragraph or two explaining how one can be a wise consumer when shopping for necessities such as food, clothing, housing, and cars. Use all of the following terms.*

   club warehouse store
   convenience store
   private-labeled products
   durability
   service flow
   lease
   security deposit
   closing costs
   registration fee
   liability insurance

Review Academic Vocabulary

Choose the letter of the term that best completes each sentence.

   a. potential   e. equivalent
   b. significant   f. obtain
   c. regional   g. involved
   d. factor   h. status

2. Some brands are _____ because they are only available in certain areas of the country.

3. Trendiness is often a _____ in young people's clothing choices.

4. Insurance companies check drivers' marital _____ because married people tend to be safer drivers.

5. A security deposit is often _____ to one month's rent.

6. Leases protect both landlords and tenants from many _____ problems that might arise.

7. Customers can _____ necessities from a convenience store for a higher price.

8. There are many decisions _____ in buying a new car, including price, style, brand, and color.

9. The cost of a home is usually the most _____ expense in a family's budget.

Review the Main Ideas

Section 1 (pp. 113–117)

10. When comparison shopping, what factors should you consider in deciding where to shop and what to buy?

11. What is the trade-off involved when you buy a generic brand rather than a brand-name product?

12. What are some advantages and disadvantages to shopping at club warehouse stores?

Section 2 (pp. 119–123)

13. What four factors influence the kind of clothing choices people make?

14. In general, what is the relationship between how long an article of clothing will last and its price?

Section 3 (pp. 124–129)

15. Fill in a chart like the one below listing the advantages and disadvantages of owning a home versus renting.

	Owning	Renting
Advantages		
Disadvantages		

16. List three responsibilities of tenants and three responsibilities of landlords.

17. Name at least two things you should look for in a rental lease.

Section 4 (pp. 130–133)

18. If you get a loan to buy a car, what expenses must be included in the cost of buying the car?

19. What is included in the cost of operating an automobile?

Math Practice

20. Determine the per-unit price of each product listed in the chart below.

Product	Size or Quantity	Price	Price per Unit
Milk (national brand)	1/2 gallon (64 oz.)	$1.97	
Milk (store brand)	1 gallon (128 oz.)	$3.15	
Laundry Detergent X	70 oz. (40 loads)	$6.99	
Laundry Detergent X	210 oz. (120 loads)	$15.98	

21. Which milk is the better buy? Why?

22. Why might some people consider the other choice of milk to be better despite the price difference?

23. Which laundry detergent is the better buy? Why?

Economics ONLINE

Self-Check Quiz Visit the *Economics Today and Tomorrow* Web site at glencoe.com and click on **Chapter 5—Self-Check Quizzes** to assess your knowledge of chapter content.

Critical Thinking

24. **The BIG Idea** Most people's ability to spend is limited by the amount they earn. This means that income is a scarce resource, and people must make choices about how to use it. So, if a family's rent unexpectedly increases but their income does not, how might they adjust to this unavoidable change in their budget?

25. **Evaluating** Look over the expenses identified in this chapter as necessities (food, clothing, housing, vehicles). What other expenses in life would most people consider to be necessities? Why?

Analyzing Visuals

26. Study the cartoon on the right, and then answer the following questions.

   a. What necessary expenses are shown in this cartoon?

   b. Why does the man decide to stay home?

   c. How are oil prices affecting the man even if he does avoid driving?

Can you use your buying power to change society?

THE ISSUE

"Buying power" is the ability and willingness of a certain segment of the population to buy certain goods or services. America's 32 million teenagers spend about $159 billion a year. They also influence buying decisions for another $300 billion. That's a lot of buying power. Can teen buying power be used for more than acquiring things? That is, can individual shopping choices actually change American culture?

THE FACTS

Have you ever bought sneakers and later found out they were made by a child laborer in a developing country? Some people would refuse to buy that brand. Whenever you buy a product, you're endorsing the product and the company that made it.

Throughout history, consumer activists have used economic power to create social change, in everything from environmental issues to employee working conditions. One tactic used is the boycott, a practice in which consumers stop buying a company's products until the company changes the way it operates.

Another way to influence change is through investment choices. Some consumers invest only in companies they consider socially responsible. Still others protest what they consider over-commercialization of the culture by refusing to become "walking ads." They cover company names and logos on clothing, shoes, and other gear—or buy products without them.

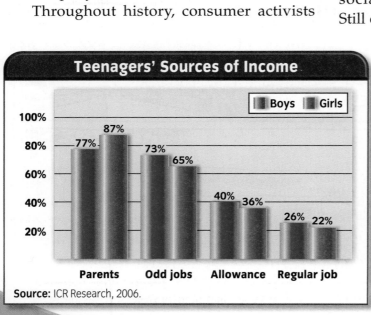

Teenagers' Sources of Income

	Boys	Girls
Parents	77%	87%
Odd jobs	73%	65%
Allowance	40%	36%
Regular job	26%	22%

Source: ICR Research, 2006.

▲ A boycott to protest wearing fur

THE ECONOMIC CONNECTION: YOUR ROLE AS A CONSUMER

As mergers create larger and larger corporations, the companies become so powerful that some people believe the average person cannot influence their activities. But consumers still have "the power of the pocketbook."

Just as product quality, availability, and opportunity cost affect purchasing and investment decisions, many people also take a company's ethics into consideration.

Whenever a group of consumers becomes a sizeable market—like teenagers—companies listen to what they want. That's why boycotts can succeed, if enough people support them. According to consumer advocate Ralph Nader, it doesn't take a huge drop in sales to convince companies to heed customers' wishes—2 to 5 percent will do it. In some cases, the mere threat of a boycott creates change.

One of the most famous boycotts occurred in 1955, when African Americans stopped using the Montgomery, Alabama, bus system after Rosa Parks was arrested for refusing to give her seat to a Caucasian man. What began as an economic boycott resulted in a U.S. Supreme Court ruling that ended bus segregation.

A nationwide boycott of table grapes from 1965 to 1970 achieved better living conditions and higher wages for migrant farmworkers. A 1986 boycott to protect Central American rain forests cut sales at a major fast-food chain by 12 percent, causing the company to stop importing beef from cattle raised on deforested land. Consumers working with nonprofit organizations have convinced several large clothing retailers not to sell fur. They also convinced a major pet-supply chain to stop selling parrots, and their activism has created a market for cosmetics that are not tested on animals. In 2006 students at 20 U.S. universities and in several other countries boycotted a soft-drink manufacturer for water pollution and union interference at bottling plants. Consumer campaigns also convinced cruise ship lines to stop dumping toxic waste into the oceans.

CONCLUSION

Companies spend a lot of money creating recognizable brands and making customers feel good about them so that they'll continue to buy their products. Just as citizens can use the power of the vote to change government, consumers can use the power of the dollar to change how companies do business. That's putting your money where your values are.

Analyzing the Impact

1. **Synthesizing** Have you ever chosen to buy or not to buy something because of the company's reputation, or would you do so in the future? Explain why or why not.

2. **Critical Thinking** Do you think consumer activism is necessary? Why or why not?

The **BIG Idea**

Governments and institutions help participants in a market economy accomplish their financial goals.

Why It Matters

In this chapter, read to learn about reasons for saving, as well as various investment possibilities and the risks associated with them.

Economics ONLINE

Chapter Overview Visit the *Economics Today and Tomorrow* Web site at glencoe.com and click on *Chapter 6—Chapter Overviews* to preview chapter information.

Why Save?

Section Preview
In this section, you will learn about the benefits of saving and the types of savings accounts available to you.

Content Vocabulary
- saving *(p. 142)*
- savings account *(p. 143)*
- money market deposit account *(p. 143)*
- time deposits *(p. 144)*
- maturity *(p. 144)*
- certificates of deposit *(p. 144)*

Academic Vocabulary
- require *(p. 142)*
- minimum *(p. 142)*

Reading Strategy
Identifying Complete a web diagram similar to the one below by identifying the different types of savings plans discussed in the section.

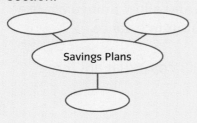

Savings Plans

ISSues In ThE NeWS
—from the *Dallas Morning News*

THE IMPORTANCE OF SAVING
Save your money.

Your parents and grandparents tried to teach you the concept when you were a kid. . . .

It's not a hard thing to understand. So why aren't more consumers doing it? No doubt, some consumers literally live hand to mouth financially. Every penny goes to pay for living expenses, and there's nothing left to stash away. But many others don't think enough about saving and aren't willing to slash unnecessary expenditures that could then translate into a fatter savings account. . . .

What most people don't realize is that they have more control than they think over their ability to save.

"I'm saying yes, you can [save], but I'm going against the grain, says Cynthia Nevels, executive director of the Jr. Finance Literacy Academy in Dallas, a financial-literacy program aimed at young people. "Too many people live in debt and worry about it later," she says.

If you have a part-time job, you may already be saving some of your income for a future use, such as buying the latest gaming system or continuing your education. Don't be discouraged if you can save only a small amount, as saving something is better than saving nothing. As you read this section, you'll learn why saving is important to you and the economy as a whole.

Deciding to Save

Economics & You Think of a time you wanted something that you couldn't afford. Did you save to buy it? Read on to learn about the benefits of saving.

saving: setting aside income for a period of time so that it can be used later

Economists define **saving** as the setting aside of income for a period of time so that it can be used later. Any saving that you do now may be only for purchases that **require** more funds than you have at one time. When you are self-supporting and have more responsibilities, you will probably save for other reasons.

When an individual saves, the economy as a whole benefits. Saving provides funds for others to invest or spend. Saving also allows businesses to expand, which provides increased income for consumers and raises the standard of living.

Generally, when people think of saving, they think of putting their funds in a savings bank or other financial institution where it will earn interest. Interest is the payment people receive when they lend funds, or allow someone else to use their funds. A person receives interest on a savings plan for as long as funds are in the account.

You have many options regarding places in which to put your savings. As you learned in Chapter 4, the most common places are commercial banks, savings and loan associations, savings banks, and credit unions. In shopping for the best savings plan, you need to consider the trade-offs. Some savings plans allow immediate access to your funds but pay a low rate of interest. Others pay higher interest and allow immediate use of your funds, but require a large **minimum** balance.

Personal Finance Handbook

See pages R6–R9 to learn more about saving.

Reading Check **Predicting Consequences** What are three benefits of saving?

▼ Savings accounts, like checking accounts, can be accessed electronically.

HI & LOIS

Figure 6.1 **Savings Basics**

■ Saving money can be difficult, but if you come up with a plan and stick with it, your overall financial situation will improve.

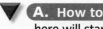 **A. How to Save** Following the steps listed here will start you on the road to saving.

Steps to Saving

◆ Determine reasons to save.

◆ Determine amount of funds to set aside.

◆ Decide what type of account you will use.

◆ Decide frequency of deposit.

◆ Decide when to invest a portion of what you have saved.

Where to Save?

Type of Account	Minimum Deposit?	Rate of Interest?	Availability of Funds?
Savings	No	Low	Immediate
Money market	$1,000 to $2,500	High	Immediate
Time deposit	$1,000	High	Depends on maturity; penalty for early withdrawal

▲ **B. Where to Save** You have several choices about the type of savings account to open first.

Economic Analysis

Analyzing *What type of account should you open if you have at least $1,000 to put away and you will not need the funds for a long time?*

Savings Accounts and Time Deposits

Main Idea Savings accounts and time deposits offer a variety of maturities and are insured by agencies of the federal government.

Economics & You Where do you keep what you save? At home, or in a bank? Read on to learn about the different types of saving plans available to you.

Figure 6.1 above outlines several options for saving. A basic **savings account** is an interest-earning account that has no set maturity. Funds from such accounts can be withdrawn at any time without penalty to the account owner.

A **money market deposit account** (MMDA) is another type of account that pays relatively high rates of interest and allows immediate access to one's funds through checks. The trade-off is that these accounts have a $1,000 to $2,500 minimum balance requirement. Customers can usually make withdrawals from a money market account in person at any time, but they are allowed to write only a few checks a month against the account.

savings account: account that pays interest, has no maturity date, and from which funds can be withdrawn at any time without penalty

money market deposit account: account that pays relatively high rates of interest, requires a minimum balance, and allows immediate access to funds

time deposits: savings plans that require savers to leave their funds on deposit for certain periods of time

maturity: period of time at the end of which time deposits will pay a stated rate of interest

certificates of deposit: time deposits that state the amount of the deposit, maturity, and rate of interest being paid

Skills Handbook

See page **R57** to learn about *Understanding Interest Rates.*

Time Deposits

The term **time deposits** refers to a wide variety of savings plans that require a saver to deposit his or her funds for a certain period of time. The period of time is called the **maturity**, and it may vary from seven days to eight years or more. Time deposits are often called **certificates of deposit** (CDs), or savings certificates. CDs state the amount of the deposit, the length of time until maturity is reached, and the rate of interest being paid.

Time deposits offer higher interest rates than regular savings accounts. (See **Figure 6.2** below.) The longer the maturity, the higher the interest rate that is paid. For example, a CD with a short-term maturity of 90 days pays less interest than a CD with a 2-year maturity. Savers who cash a time deposit before maturity pay a penalty.

Insuring Deposits

When the stock market collapsed in 1929, the resulting financial crisis wiped out many people's entire savings. Congress passed, and President Franklin Roosevelt signed, legislation to protect many types of deposits. This legislation created the Federal Deposit Insurance Corporation (FDIC). In addition to savings accounts, money market deposit accounts, and CDs, the FDIC also protects funds in regular checking accounts.

Figure 6.2 | Savings Choices

Charts In Motion
See StudentWorks™ Plus or go to glencoe.com.

■ While a regular savings account allows you ready access to your funds, a time deposit, such as a CD, earns more interest income. If you have funds that you will not need for a while, you should choose a time deposit, as it will pay you more in the long run.

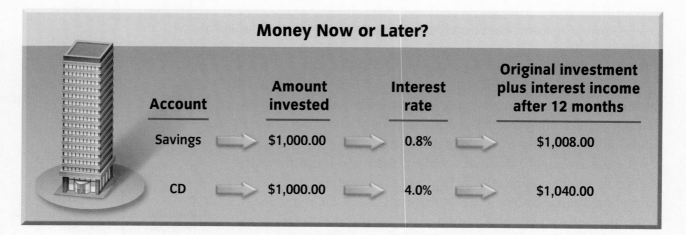

Money Now or Later?

Account	Amount invested	Interest rate	Original investment plus interest income after 12 months
Savings	$1,000.00	0.8%	$1,008.00
CD	$1,000.00	4.0%	$1,040.00

Economic Analysis

Using Charts *At the interest rates shown, at the end of a year, how much more will you have if you put your funds into a CD rather than a savings account?*

Today there are several federal agencies that insure most banks and savings institutions. The major one besides the FDIC is the National Credit Union Association (NCUA). Through these federal agencies, each depositor's funds in a particular savings institution are insured up to $100,000. If an insured institution fails, each depositor will be paid the full amount of his or her savings up to $100,000 for each legally separate account.

Federal deposit insurance has started to change with the times. Beginning on January 1, 2011, the $100,000 deposit insurance limit will be adjusted by the amount of inflation that occurred over the previous five years. Also, some special retirement accounts now have a limit of $250,000.

✓ Reading Check **Comparing** What are the benefits and drawbacks of savings accounts? Of time deposits?

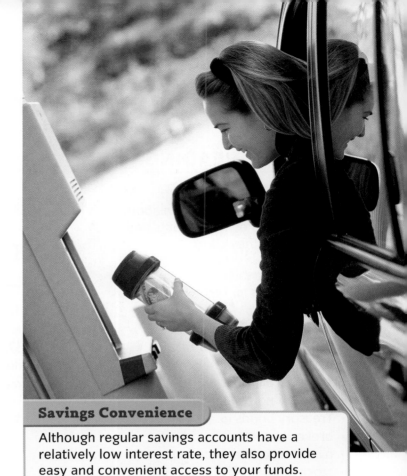

Savings Convenience

Although regular savings accounts have a relatively low interest rate, they also provide easy and convenient access to your funds.

---

section 1 Review

Vocabulary

1. **Explain** the significance of: saving, interest, savings account, money market deposit account, time deposits, maturity, certificates of deposit.

Main Ideas

2. **Summarizing** In a table like the one below, list one advantage and one disadvantage of each savings method listed.

	Savings Account	CD	Money Market
Advantage			
Disadvantage			

3. **Describing** How does interest make money for savers?

Critical Thinking

4. **The BIG Idea** Why is it best not to invest more than $100,000 in one account?

5. **Comparing and Contrasting** What is the difference between a basic savings account and a time deposit?

Applying Economics

6. **Calculating Interest** With $1000 in the bank at 0.5% simple interest monthly, how much will you make in one year? With $1,000 debt on your credit card at 2% simple interest each month, what will you pay that year?

Investing: Taking Risks With Your Savings

GUIDE TO READING

Section Preview
In this section, you will learn about different types of investments and the risks that they carry.

Content Vocabulary
- stockholders *(p. 147)*
- capital gain *(p. 147)*
- capital loss *(p. 147)*
- tax-exempt bonds *(p. 148)*
- savings bonds *(p. 149)*
- Treasury bills *(p. 149)*
- Treasury notes *(p. 149)*
- Treasury bonds *(p. 149)*
- broker *(p. 150)*
- over-the-counter market *(p. 151)*
- stock market indexes *(p. 151)*
- mutual fund *(p. 152)*
- money market fund *(p. 152)*

Academic Vocabulary
- design *(p. 153)*   • scheme *(p. 153)*

Reading Strategy
Comparing Use a chart like the one below to compare stocks and bonds.

Type of Investment	Definition	When Does It Pay?	Risks
Stocks			
Bonds			

ISSUES IN ThE NeWS
—from *Fortune*

THINKING AHEAD In 1891, Asa Candler, an Atlanta entrepreneur, paid pharmacist John Pemberton $2,300 for the formula to his weird brown health drink named Coca-Cola. Last year the company had revenue of $22 billion.

Back in 1961, $2.7 million seemed like a lot of money for a hamburger stand and some golden arches—in today's dollars, that would be $16.8 million—but Ray Kroc took the plunge. Forty-four years later,

▲ Tampa Bay Buccaneers

there are more than 30,000 McDonald's franchises throughout the world, and the company grossed $19.1 billion last year.

Malcolm Glazer was ridiculed when he paid $192 million for the hapless Tampa Bay Buccaneers in 1995. But after a 2003 Super Bowl win, the team is now valued at more than $700 million.

People keep their savings in banks and savings and loan associations because they want a safe rate of interest. If people are willing to take a chance on earning a higher rate of return, however, they can invest their savings in other ways. Stocks and bonds offer investors greater returns, but, at least for stocks, with more risk. As you read this section, you'll learn what stocks and bonds are, and why they carry a risk.

Stocks and Bonds

Main Idea Stockholders are owners of a corporation, and bondholders are creditors of a corporation.

Economics & You Would you rather save what you earn, or risk it in the hopes of earning more? Read on to learn about investing in different types of stocks and bonds.

Corporations are formed by selling shares of stock (also called securities). By issuing stock for sale, a company obtains funds for use in expanding its business. Shares of stock entitle the buyer to a certain part of the future profits and assets of the corporation selling the stock. The person buying stock, therefore, becomes a part owner of the corporation. As proof of ownership, the corporation issues stock certificates.

Stock Returns **Stockholders,** or owners of stock, benefit from stock in two ways. One is through *dividends,* the return a stockholder receives on the amount that he or she invested in the company. The corporation may declare a dividend at any time during a year. Dividends typically are paid only when the company makes a profit. The other way people benefit from stock is by selling it for more than they paid for it. Some people buy stock just to *speculate,* hoping that the price will increase greatly so they can sell it at a profit.

Capital Gains and Losses Suppose a person buys stock at $20 a share and sells it for $30. The profit of $10 per share is called a **capital gain**. Of course, the value of stock may also fall. If a person decides to sell stock at a lower price than he or she paid for it, that person suffers a **capital loss**. Money may be made or lost on bonds in much the same way.

Personal Finance Handbook
*See pages **R6–R9** to learn more about **investing.***

stockholders: people who have invested in a corporation and own some of its shares of stock

capital gain: increase in value of an asset from the time it was bought to the time it was sold

capital loss: decrease in value of an asset from the time it was bought to the time it was sold

Stockholders' Meeting

Corporations hold annual stockholders' meetings, where all stockholders are invited to come together to discuss issues of interest to the company, including plans for the future. Often, elections are held to determine the membership of the board of directors.

Bonds Instead of buying stock, people with funds to invest can buy bonds. A *bond* is a certificate issued by a company or the government in exchange for borrowed funds. It promises to pay a stated rate of interest over a stated period of time, and then to repay the borrowed amount in full at the end of that time. A bondholder lends for a period of time to a company or government and is paid interest on that amount. At the end of the period, the full amount of the borrowing is repaid. This period of time is called the bond's maturity.

Unlike buying stock, buying a bond does not make a bondholder part owner of the company or government that issued the bond. The bond becomes part of the debt of the corporation or government, and the bondholder becomes a creditor. **Figure 6.3** below lists these and some other differences between stocks and bonds.

Tax-Exempt Bonds Local and state governments also sell **tax-exempt bonds**. The interest on these types of bonds, unlike bonds issued by companies, is not taxed by the federal government. Interest that you earn on bonds your own city or state issues is also exempt from city and state income taxes. Tax-exempt bonds are good investments for wealthier people who would otherwise pay high tax rates on interest earned from investments.

tax-exempt bonds: bonds sold by local and state governments; interest paid on the bond is not taxed by the federal government

Figure 6.3 | Differences Between Stocks and Bonds

■ Stocks and bonds can both be good investments, but there are key differences between them that investors should be aware of before making any purchasing decisions. Be sure you have studied these differences before investing in either option.

Stocks

❶ All corporations issue or offer to sell stock. That act is what makes them corporations.

❷ Stocks represent ownership.

❸ Most stocks do not have a fixed dividend rate

❹ Dividends on stock are paid only if the corporation makes a profit.

❺ Stocks do not have a maturity date. The corporation issuing the stock does not repay the stockholder.

❻ Stockholders usually elect a board of directors who control the corporation.

❼ Stockholders have a claim against the property and income of a corporation only after the claims of all creditors (including bondholders and holders of preferred stock) have been met.

Savings Bonds The U.S. government issues **savings bonds** as one of its ways of borrowing money. They range in face value from $50 up to $10,000. The purchase of a U.S. savings bond is similar to buying a bank's certificate of deposit. Savings bonds are attractive because they are very safe, and because the interest earned is not taxed until the bond is turned in for cash.

A person buying a savings bond pays half the bond's face value. You could purchase a $50 bond, then, for only $25. The bond increases in value every 6 months until its full face value is reached. If you choose to redeem a U.S. savings bond before it matures, you are guaranteed a certain rate of interest, which changes depending on rates of interest in the economy.

T-Bills, T-Notes, and T-Bonds

The Treasury Department of the federal government also sells several types of larger investments. **Treasury bills** mature in a few days to 26 weeks. The minimum amount of investment for Treasury bills is $1,000. **Treasury notes** have maturity dates of 2 to 10 years, and **Treasury bonds** mature in 30 years. Notes and bonds are sold in minimums of $1,000. The interest on all three of these government securities is exempt from state and local income taxes, but not from federal income tax.

Reading Check **Explaining** What are two ways that investors can benefit from stocks?

savings bonds: bonds issued by the federal government as a way of borrowing money; they are purchased at half the face value and increase every 6 months until full face value is reached

Treasury bills: certificates issued by the U.S. Treasury in exchange for a minimum amount of $1,000 and maturing in a few days up to 26 weeks

Treasury notes: certificates issued by the U.S. Treasury in exchange for minimum amounts of $1,000 and maturing in 2 to 10 years

Treasury bonds: certificates issued by the U.S. Treasury in exchange for minimum amounts of $1,000 and maturing in 30 years

---

Bonds

1. Corporations are not required to issue bonds.
2. Bonds represent debt.
3. Bonds pay a fixed rate of interest.
4. Interest on bonds normally must always be paid, whether or not the corporation earns a profit.
5. Bonds have a maturity date. The bondholder is to be repaid the value of the bond, although if the corporation goes out of business, it does not normally repay the bondholders in full.
6. Bondholders usually have no voice in or control over how the corporation is run.
7. Bondholders have a claim against the property and income of a corporation that must be met before the claims of any stockholders, including those holding preferred stock.

Economic Analysis

Comparing *Of stocks and bonds, which investment option involves less risk?*

Stock and Bond Markets

(Main Idea) **Ownership of stocks and bonds can be transferred on centralized exchanges or in decentralized markets.**

Economics & You If you had $500 to invest in stocks or bonds, how would you decide what to do? Read on to learn about different investment markets.

Stocks are bought and sold through brokers or on the Internet. A **broker** is a person who acts as a go-between for buyers and sellers. If an investor is interested in buying or trading corporate shares, he or she can contact a brokerage firm, which will perform the service for a fee.

Thousands of full-service brokerage firms throughout the country buy and sell stocks daily for ordinary investors. The fees they charge to perform the trades—up to $500—depend on the dollar amounts invested or traded. Today, however, if an investor has an account with an Internet brokerage firm, the cost for the same trade may be as low as $7.

There are well over 100 online brokerage firms, with more springing up on the Web every day. It is estimated that 20 million American investors use the Internet to make trades every year.

Stock Exchanges Brokerage houses communicate with the busy floors of the stock exchanges. The largest stock exchange, or stock market, is the New York Stock Exchange (NYSE) in New York City. There are also supplemental stock exchanges and regional exchanges—such as the Chicago Exchange—and exchanges in other countries—such as the London and Tokyo stock exchanges. To be listed on these exchanges, a corporation offering stock must prove to the exchange that it is in good financial condition. Most of the companies traded on stock exchanges are among the largest, most profitable corporations in the country.

broker: person who acts as a go-between for buyers and sellers of stocks and bonds

Careers Handbook

See pages R76–R80 to learn about becoming a broker.

Buying Stocks or Bonds

If you decide to buy stocks or bonds, you will need to contact a broker. You pay the broker a fee to purchase the stock at one of the stock exchanges.

Over-the-Counter Markets

Stocks can also be sold on the **over-the-counter market**, an electronic marketplace for stocks not listed on the organized exchanges. The largest volume of over-the-counter stocks are quoted on the National Association of Securities Dealers Automated Quotations (NASDAQ) national market system, which merged with the American Stock Exchange in 1998.

Unlike organized stock exchanges, over-the-counter stocks are not traded in any specific place. Brokerage firms hold shares of stocks that they buy and sell for investors. For example, assume that XYZ Corporation is a company that sells computers. If an investor wanted to buy stock in it, he or she would check the NASDAQ listings in the local newspaper or on the Internet. This table of over-the-counter stocks would list XYZ Corporation, the number of shares of stock sold the day before, and the price at which shares were bought and sold that day. The investor would then call a broker or use the Internet to buy a certain number of shares. Usually stocks are sold in amounts of 100 shares, but some brokers will handle smaller amounts.

Trading on the Internet

Today, many people choose to use the Internet to buy and sell stocks and bonds rather than calling a broker on the phone. Many investors who trade this way assume they have a direct connection to the market in which they're trading, but this is not the case. The orders of Internet traders still go through a broker, just as call-in orders do.

over-the-counter market: electronic purchase and sale of stocks and bonds, often of smaller companies, which often takes place outside the organized stock exchanges

Stock Market Indexes   Almost every weekday, there is news about what happened to the **stock market indexes**, of which there are many. Such indexes are based on what happened to the stock prices of various listed companies. The most well known is the Dow Jones Industrial Average—often called "The Dow." This index involves 30 major industrial companies in the United States. There is also the Standard & Poor's 500 (S&P 500). The S&P 500 index tracks the stock prices of 500 companies.

stock market indexes: measures of what is happening to a given set of stock prices for a specified list of companies; the most well known is the Dow Jones Industrial Average

Bond Markets   The New York Exchange Bond Market and the American Exchange Bond Market are the two largest bond exchanges. Bonds, including U.S. government bonds, are sold over-the-counter and on the Internet.

There is an enormous variety of individual bonds to choose from. If you decide to invest in bonds, you will probably want to contact a financial adviser to help you find a bond that matches your needs and expectations.

Mutual Funds Many people invest in the stock market by placing some of their savings in a **mutual fund**, an investment company that pools the funds of many individuals to buy stocks, bonds, or other investments. Most mutual funds hold a variety of stocks or bonds. Losses in one area are likely to be made up by gains in another.

Most mutual funds use the S&P 500 as the yardstick against which they compare their returns on stocks. The long-run return from *index funds* is higher than can be expected from almost any other investment. By investing in a broad-based index fund, investors will almost surely do better over the long run than by investing in individual stocks or in a managed mutual fund. A *managed mutual fund* is one in which the managers adjust the mix of stocks and move often in and out of the market to try to generate the highest total return.

Money Market Funds One type of mutual fund, called a **money market fund**, normally uses investors' funds to buy the short-term debt of businesses and banks. Most of these funds allow investors to write checks against their account. Any check, however, must be above some minimum amount, usually $500. The investor then earns interest only on the amount left in the account.

Banks and savings and loan associations offer a similar service, called *money market deposit accounts* (MMDAs). A major advantage of MMDAs is that the federal government insures them against loss. Mutual funds and money market funds are not insured by the federal government.

Reading Check **Describing** What is a mutual fund? Name three types of mutual funds.

mutual fund: investment company that pools the funds of many individuals to buy stocks, bonds, or other investments

money market fund: type of mutual fund that uses investors' funds to make short-term loans to businesses and banks

Bull and Bear Markets

When listening to news about the stock market, you may have heard the terms "bull market" and "bear market." A bull market refers to a period of time when stock prices move up steadily. Investors expect this trend to continue, and they buy stock. In a bear market, stock prices have been dropping for a period of time, and investors sell stock in expectation of lower profits.

This famous bull statue stands near Wall Street in New York City.

Government Regulations

Main Idea Securities markets are heavily regulated to protect investors.

Economics & You Do you feel more comfortable investing, knowing that the federal government is able to regulate the stock market? Read on to learn about some of the laws controlling the stock market.

The stock market is heavily regulated today, at both the state and federal levels. The Securities and Exchange Commission (SEC), created by the Securities Exchange Act of 1934, is responsible for administering all federal securities laws. It also investigates any dealings among corporations, such as mergers, that affect the value of stocks.

Congress passed the Securities Exchange Act in an attempt to avoid another stock market crash like that of 1929. The act requires that, to inform investors, any institution issuing stocks or bonds must file a registration statement with the federal government. Also, a briefer description, called a *prospectus*, must be given to each potential buyer of stocks or bonds. It lists the amount offered, the price, and the company's projected use for the amount raised by the stocks or bonds.

States also have securities laws. These are **designed** to prevent **schemes** that would take advantage of small investors.

Reading Check **Identifying** What are the responsibilities of the SEC?

section 2 Review

Vocabulary

1. **Explain** the significance of: stockholders, capital gain, capital loss, tax-exempt bonds, savings bonds, Treasury bills, Treasury notes, Treasury bonds, broker, over-the-counter market, stock market indexes, mutual fund, money market fund.

Main Ideas

2. **Comparing** Use a Venn diagram like the one below to compare stocks and bonds.

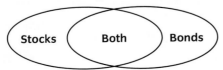

Critical Thinking

3. **The BIG Idea** Explain why stocks are riskier than bonds.

4. **Comparing** List five investments you could make if you had $10,000 in available funds. Rank them from highest to lowest in potential risk and return.

Applying Economics

5. **Stocks** In a newspaper or on the Internet, find the list of stock quotes in the NYSE and the NASDAQ. Analyze the quotes, and then choose a stock from each listing that you would buy if you had the available funds. Explain your choices.

Lilia Clemente

● Founder, Chairperson, and CEO of Clemente Capital, Inc.

■ At age 28, the first woman investment manager and youngest officer ever of the Ford Foundation

■ Author of *Achievement and Leadership for Women of Color in a Global World* (1986) and *Asian Capital Markets* (1996)

Lilia Clemente has been called the Woman Wizard of Wall Street, and for good reason. In 1976 she invested savings of $25,000 to launch her own financial consulting company. Today, through her offices in New York and half a dozen Asian capitals, she controls funds totaling more than $7.5 billion.

Clemente was born to a wealthy family in the Philippines and traveled widely throughout Asia as a child. Her father, a well-connected lawyer, was involved in the drafting of the new Philippine constitution, and her mother, in addition to being a psychology professor and provincial governor, was the first female holder of a seat on the Manila Stock Exchange.

"My mother was a real role model. I thought it was natural for women to go into business and politics."

Following her mother's example, she was active in politics at the University of the Philippines while earning a bachelor's degree in business administration. Later, at the University of Chicago, she was granted a master's degree in agricultural economics and international trade. In her academic department, she was one of only seven women among 400 students.

❝In a male world like finance, you have to think of yourself as a very special person. Each person has her own pluses and minuses. You have to turn your negatives into your own positives.❞

Her intimate knowledge of Asia was certainly a positive. She realized early on that countries such as China, Thailand, and the Philippines would develop into important economic markets.

Checking for Understanding

1. **Explaining** What kind of impact did Clemente's mother have on her life?

2. **Hypothesizing** Do you think Clemente would have achieved the same degree of financial success if she had been born poor? Explain your answer.

Special Savings Plans and Goals

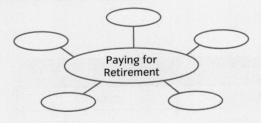

Paying for Retirement

ISSues In ThE NeWS
—from *Marketwatch*

PLANNING AHEAD If a teenager has a paying job outside the home—as do 40 percent of high-school students—it makes sense to put her earnings into a . . . retirement fund. This could pay off big later on.

There is no minimum age for contribution to an IRA. So as soon as [a teenager] has earnings from work—baby-sitting, helping [a parent] at the office, or mowing lawns— she can open an account.

"At a hypothetical annual return of 8 percent, four years of $4,000 contributions during high school ($16,000) could be worth over $750,000 when the child turns 65," says Kevin McKinley, author of *Make Your Kid a Millionaire—11 Easy Ways Anyone Can Secure a Child's Financial Future.*

. . . Of course, it's not always easy to get a teen to think about retirement, let alone persuade her to agree to save, rather than spend, her earnings.

One of the many reasons that people save is to send their children to college. Another is to make a down payment on a home. Yet another is for those years after people stop working. There are different methods of saving for retirement, each having different risks. As you read this section, you'll learn about special savings plans and the amount of risk involved in these investments.

Investing for Retirement

Skills Handbook

See page R41 to learn about Evaluating Information.

Main Idea Retirement is a major reason for saving and investing.

Economics & You Do you think much about retirement? Read on to learn ways to save for this time of life.

Although most people are eligible for Social Security when they retire, this plan does not provide enough income to live comfortably. It is important, therefore, for a person to save for and invest in his or her own retirement.

pension plans: company plans that provide retirement income for their workers

Many individuals have company-supported **pension plans** to save for retirement. One of the most common types is a 401(k) plan, in which a **portion** of your paycheck is withheld and the company matches the amount. A major benefit of such a plan is the tax savings. As long as your contribution does not exceed a certain amount, you do not have to pay federal income tax on the amount you put in—or on the amount the plan earns—until you withdraw funds from the plan at retirement.

Keogh plan: retirement plan that allows self-employed individuals to save a maximum of 15 percent of their income up to a specified amount each year, and to deduct that amount from their yearly taxable income

Individual Pension Plans

The Keogh Act of 1962 was passed to help self-employed people set up their own pension plans. The **Keogh plan** allows those people who are self-employed to set aside a maximum of 15 percent of their income up to a specified amount each year, and then deduct that amount from their yearly taxable income.

Figure 6.4 | Retirement Plan Options

■ Today people have several choices in retirement plans.

Types of Retirement Plans			
401(k)	**Keogh**	**IRA**	**Roth IRA**
◆ Company plan	◆ Self-employed plan	◆ Individual/married couple's plan	◆ Individual/married couple's plan
◆ Portion of pay withheld and matched by company	◆ Up to 15% of yearly income set aside	◆ Tax-deferred contributions	◆ Contributions taxed
◆ Tax deferred on income and interest	◆ Amount is tax deductible	◆ Tax-deferred interest income	◆ Interest income never taxed
◆ Maximum contribution limit	◆ Maximum contribution limit	◆ Maximum contribution limit	◆ Maximum contribution limit

Economic Analysis

Comparing *What do these retirement plans have in common?*

Another form of retirement plan is the **individual retirement account (IRA).** A person earning less than $30,000 can **contribute** up to $4,000 a year and deduct those contributions from taxable income. The benefit of an IRA is that the income you contribute to the IRA is not taxed in the year it is contributed. In addition, the interest you earn on that income is not taxed either. You pay the tax only when you take out funds from your IRA account, usually after age 59½.

A relatively new form of IRA is called the **Roth IRA.** Again, you are allowed to put up to $4,000 a year in a Roth IRA. You do not get to deduct your contributions from your taxable income, however. The benefit is that all of the interest you earn on your contributions to a Roth IRA is tax-free forever. Thus, when you take out funds from your Roth IRA account while you are retired, you pay no additional taxes. See **Figure 6.4** on the previous page for a summary of the major points of all of these retirement plans.

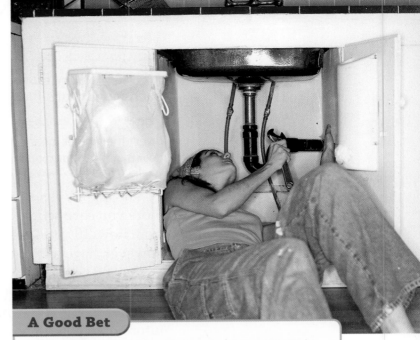

Real Estate as an Investment Buying real estate, such as land and buildings, is another form of investing. For the past 50 years or so, buying a home, condominium, or co-op has proven to be a wise investment in many parts of the country. Resale values have soared at times, especially during the late 1970s. Although the housing market fluctuates, buying a home is usually a good investment in the long run. Buying raw, or undeveloped, land is generally a much riskier investment. No one can guarantee that there will be a demand in the future for a particular piece of land.

Real estate, either as raw land or as developed land, is not very easy to turn into cash on short notice. Sometimes real property for sale stays on the market for long periods of time. This difficulty in getting cash for your investment is one of the trade-offs involved when investing in real estate. You cannot get your funds as quickly as you could if you had invested in stocks, bonds, a bank CD, or some other savings plan.

Reading Check **Contrasting** What is the difference between a 401(k) and an IRA?

individual retirement account (IRA): private retirement plan that allows individuals or married couples to save a certain amount of untaxed earnings per year with the interest being tax-deferred

Roth IRA: private retirement plan that taxes income before it is saved, but which does not tax interest on that income when funds are used upon retirement

Economics ONLINE

Student Web Activity Visit the *Economics Today and Tomorrow* Web site at glencoe.com and click on *Chapter 6—Student Web Activities* to learn more about Roth IRAs.

How Much to Save and Invest?

Main Idea How much to save and invest is determined by each individual's income, risk tolerance, and values.

Economics & You If you have money saved, would you be willing to invest it even if it meant risking losing it? Read on to learn how to decide how much of your money you should save and invest.

Saving involves a trade-off like every other activity. The more you save today, the more you can buy and consume a year from now, 10 years from now, or 30 years from now. You will, however, have less to spend today. Keep in mind that if you have debt, especially on a high-interest credit card, you may want to pay that off before diverting funds into savings. Also consider that if you expect to make a much higher income in the future than you do now, you have less reason to save a large percentage of today's income. (See **Figure 6.5** below.)

Amount of Risk So, how much of your savings should you risk in investment? When making this decision, remember that if you put a lesser amount in the more risky types of investments, you will have some security with your savings, and you will have some funds readily available should you need cash in a hurry. You may also have a chance of making high returns, but the higher the promised return, the greater the risk. Indeed, it's impossible to obtain higher returns without taking more risk.

Figure 6.5 | Savings Considerations

■ Periodically, you should reevaluate how much of your income you are saving. If you are at a point where you have accumulated debt on a credit card, for example, you may want to pay off your debt before putting funds into savings. At another time, if interest rates rise, you may want to save more and earn more interest.

How Much Should You Save?

Ask yourself the following questions when you are deciding how much of your income to save:

1. How much do I spend on fixed expenses?
2. What are my reasons for saving?
3. How much interest can I earn on my savings, and how fast will my savings grow?
4. How much income will I be earning in the future?
5. What degree of risk am I willing to take?
6. How important is it that my savings be readily available in case I need immediate cash?
7. Will my standard of living at retirement depend largely on my accumulated savings?

Economic Analysis

Explaining *From what sources other than savings might you get funds for retirement?*

Spreading Out Your Investments

Investing your savings in several different types of accounts lowers the **overall** risk. If one investment turns sour, the others may do better. Financial planners call spreading out your investments **diversification**. Mutual funds, for example, help you diversify.

When you have very little income and cannot afford any investment losses, you should probably put your savings in insured accounts in a local bank or savings and loan association, or you should buy U.S. government savings bonds. The greater your income and the more savings you have, the more you can diversify into stocks, corporate bonds, and so on.

Values Your values may also determine where you invest your savings. If you believe that your community needs more development, you might choose to put your savings in a local savings and loan that guarantees that a large percentage of its investments are made in community loans. You may also choose to invest in stocks issued by environmentally responsible companies or companies that have aggressive equal opportunity programs.

Risk and Return

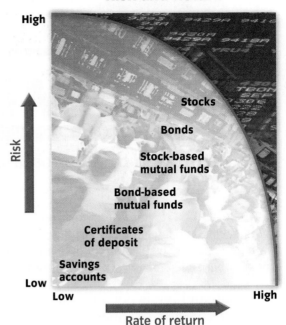

diversification: spreading of investments among several different types to lower overall risk

✔ Reading Check **Evaluating** What questions should you ask yourself when deciding how much to save and invest at any given time?

section 3 Review

Vocabulary

1. **Explain** the significance of: pension plans, Keogh Plan, individual retirement account (IRA), Roth IRA, diversification.

Main Ideas

2. **Summarizing** Copy the chart below, and for each investment option listed, give one advantage.

Investment Method	Advantage
Pension plan	
Keogh plan	
IRA	
Roth IRA	

Critical Thinking

3. **The BIG Idea** How does the federal government help people invest for retirement?

4. **Comparing and Contrasting** What is one advantage and one disadvantage of investing in real estate?

Applying Economics

5. **Evaluating Investment Options** Imagine you have $15,000 of funds to invest. Which type of funds or investments discussed in this section would you choose? Explain your answer.

FOLLOW MY MONEY

Sifting through the blogosphere for financial advice.

Check It Out! In this chapter you learned about saving and investing. In this article, read to learn about a new way young people are helping one another save and invest for the future.

Jonathan Ping is not a financial guru. He's not a certified financial planner. And he's not a millionaire (yet). He's simply a 27-year-old engineer living with his wife and dog in a rented house in Portland, Ore. Within the next 18 months he hopes to scrape up $100,000 for a down payment on a home, and he wants to build a net worth of $1 million by age 45. So far he's at $88,953.

How do I know this? It's in bold type in the top right-hand corner of his Web log, MyMoneyBlog.com, where Ping keeps a daily tally of his progress. He's one of more than 150 bloggers, mostly 22 to 35, who have adopted an open-source approach to personal finance. Most keep their names secret, but that's about all they hide. In stark contrast to their parents' generation, for whom comparing incomes can be awkward,

▲ Checking out MyMoneyBlog.com

if not downright taboo, bloggers list financial information down to the dollar in retirement, brokerage, and savings accounts. They recommend investments, decry credit-card debt, and wallow together over high taxes, commenting on one another's postings and leaving behind a road map for financial voyeurs. Ping writes: "If I mess up, you'll know. If I come across a neat way to make or save money, you'll read about it here. . . hopefully we'll learn from each other and meet up in the Caymans some day."

—Reprinted from *BusinessWeek*

Information Shared on Financial Blogs
What mistakes should I avoid when investing?
What credit cards offer the best incentives?
Should I first pay off debt or build up savings?
Which online savings accounts offer the best rates?
Where should I invest my 401(k)?

Think About It

1. **Summarizing** What financial information can bloggers provide?
2. **Contrasting** How are young financial bloggers different from their parents?

■ **Saving** some of your income allows you to earn interest and put away funds for future purchases.

Steps to Saving

◆ Determine reasons to save.

◆ Determine amount of funds to set aside.

◆ Decide what type of account you will use.

◆ Decide on frequency of deposits.

◆ Decide when to invest a portion of what you have saved.

■ After you have accumulated savings funds, you may want to **invest** some of it to try to earn greater returns.

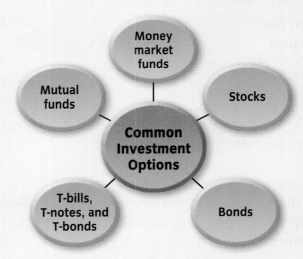

Money market funds

Mutual funds

Stocks

Common Investment Options

T-bills, T-notes, and T-bonds

Bonds

■ It is important to **diversify** your saving and investing, especially when looking toward retirement. In general, the greater the risk involved in any venture, the greater the potential return.

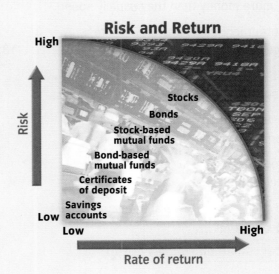

Risk and Return

High

Risk

Stocks
Bonds
Stock-based mutual funds
Bond-based mutual funds
Certificates of deposit
Savings accounts

Low

Low   High

Rate of return

Review Content Vocabulary

1. *Write a paragraph or two explaining some methods a person might choose to save or invest a $10,000 inheritance. Use all of the following terms.*

   savings account
   interest
   money market deposit account
   time deposit
   certificates of deposit
   stockholder
   broker
   savings bonds
   mutual fund
   Treasury bills

2. *Write a paragraph or two explaining some of the special methods a person might choose to save for retirement. Use all of the following terms.*

   pension plan
   Keogh plan
   individual retirement account (IRA)
   Roth IRA
   diversification

Review Academic Vocabulary

Choose the letter of the term that best completes each sentence.

   a. require
   b. minimum
   c. designed
   d. schemes
   e. portion
   f. contribute
   g. overall

3. Saving helps people prepare for expenses that _____ more money than they usually spend.

4. Special retirement plans are _____ to encourage people to save for the future.

5. One must keep a _____ balance in some types of savings accounts to avoid paying fees.

6. Having a variety of types of savings and investments lowers one's _____ risk.

7. It is a good idea to save a _____ of every paycheck for the future.

8. A person can _____ several thousand dollars to an IRA each year.

9. Securities laws help prevent _____ that try to take advantage of investors.

Review the Main Ideas

Section 1 (pp. 141–145)

10. What is interest on savings accounts? Why do banks pay interest?

11. Why is a bank certificate of deposit (CD) called a time deposit?

12. Why are deposits of up to $100,000 in banks and savings institutions often considered very safe?

Section 2 (pp. 146–153)

13. What is the basic difference between a stock and a bond?

14. What are two advantages of United States savings bonds?

15. What kind of investment company hires professionals to manage the investments of a pool of investors?

Section 3 (pp. 155–159)

16. What are three common types of retirement plans for individuals?

17. What are some of the factors one must consider when deciding how much to save in what kind of plan?

18. Fill in the graphic organizer below to show how a person might diversify (spread out) his or her retirement investments.

Type of Investment	Description

Problem Solving

Imagine that you are out of school and have started working and saving. You want to keep from using credit cards or unnecessary loans as much as possible, so you make savings plans for major purchases and expenses.

19. Write down a short-term savings goal, such as saving to buy a new portable MP3 player. Explain the typical ways in which you can save for such a purchase.

20. Now write down a long-term savings goal, such as saving for college, a house, or retirement. Explain some methods you might use to achieve this goal.

21. What is the major difference between the two ways of saving?

22. Why is saving up for major purchases and expenses better than using credit cards or taking out loans?

Economics ONLINE

Self-Check Quiz Visit the *Economics Today and Tomorrow* Web site at <u>glencoe.com</u> and click on *Chapter 6—Self-Check Quizzes* to assess your knowledge of chapter content.

Critical Thinking

23. **The BIG Idea** Suppose you have $300,000 that you want to save. The FDIC only insures up to $100,000. What can you do to make sure all your funds are insured by the FDIC?

24. **Determining Cause and Effect** How does buying a U.S. savings bond increase the U.S. government's debt?

25. **Synthesizing** Assume that you have $100,000 in savings. Create a chart like the one below to list the investments you might make and what percentage of the $100,000 you would invest in each. In the last column, explain how your choices will achieve investment diversification.

Investment Type	% of Funds	Diversification

Analyzing Visuals

26. Study the cartoon on the right, and then answer the following questions.

   a. According to the cartoon, what will the effect be of the drop in consumer confidence?

   b. What effect will consumer spending have on savings rates? Why?

   c. What is the relationship between consumer spending and saving?

Debating Economic Issues

Should colleges and universities ban credit-card companies from campuses?

Imagine being 30 years old and still paying off a slice of pizza you bought when you were in college. Sounds crazy, but for many people, credit-card debt built up in college stays with them for many years to come. Could the problem be solved by preventing credit-card companies from marketing to college students?

YES! Credit card providers use methods that take advantage of students.

When students arrive on college campuses across our nation, they are bombarded with credit card applications. . . Credit card companies have card table displays, offering free hats, T-shirts, or other token gifts for the student to sign the application. Some students have no interest in a credit card but can't refuse a free T-shirt or the peer pressure to do what "everyone is doing." When the credit card arrives in the student's campus mail, some are generally surprised and start using the card.

One student's story [shows] the problem. This student didn't believe he signed up for a credit card. He thought he'd entered a drawing when he filled out a small card in exchange for a T-shirt. . . . When the credit card arrived, he thought he'd won. He used it and was very surprised when a bill arrived.

He ignored the bill, and with interest, collection fees, and penalties, the student now has a considerable amount of debt. . . . When the student discussed the issue with the credit card issuer, they suggested he ask his parents for assistance—something they should have suggested when he signed up for the card. We should ban them!

— Linda Chuhran, faculty member, Schoolcraft College, Livonia, Michigan

NO! Credit cards are a reality our students must learn to live with.

Credit card vendors have been on my campus since at least 1989, when I was a freshman. There has to be some reason they were invited to campuses in the first place. . . . But now that there has been half a generation of former college students let loose on the world without the basic concepts of credit/debt management, everyone wants to yell "foul" instead of looking at any practical solutions or realities.

If there is true concern about stemming the tide of student debt, there needs to be credit/debt management initiatives established by schools. Solid credit habits can be built, with help, during college, and the benefits can be far reaching. Employers, as well as mortgage and loan companies, investigate credit histories. A poor credit rating can [hurt] a student's work prospects more than a poor grade point average.

Credit card companies can lend support to this effort by providing credit specialists from their organizations to provide training. If schools can rise to the occasion of training about alcohol consumption, sexual assault, and other areas of concern, then they should be able to help students learn better credit control.

—Eric Beck, coordinator, Center for East Asian and Pacific Studies, University of Illinois, Urbana-Champaign

Debating the Issue

1. **Explaining** How do many credit-card companies get college students to sign up for credit cards?

2. **Choosing Sides** The two writers disagree on whether or not college students are mature enough to handle credit cards. Which writer do you agree with? Why?

Find Out More!

3. **Synthesizing** Use the Internet or other resources to find out the average credit-card debt of a student graduating from college today. Does this information change your opinion on whether credit-card companies should be banned from campuses? Why or why not?

unit 3

Microeconomics: Markets, Prices, and Business Competition

In this unit, read to find out...

- how your consumer decisions affect prices.

- what risks and expectations you'll have when starting a business.

- why competition among businesses is vital to the price you pay for goods and services.

The **BIG Ideas**

1. Scarcity is the basic economic problem that requires people to make choices about how to use limited resources.

2. Buyers and sellers voluntarily interact in markets, and market prices are set by the the interaction of demand and supply.

Why It Matters

In this chapter, read to learn about how the relationship between supply and demand sets the prices you pay for goods and services.

Economics ONLINE

Chapter Overview Visit the *Economics Today and Tomorrow* Web site at glencoe.com and click on *Chapter 7—Chapter Overviews* to preview chapter information.

GUIDE TO READING

Section Preview
In this section, you will learn about the law of demand and how it affects choices you make.

Content Vocabulary
- demand *(p. 170)*
- supply *(p. 170)*
- market *(p. 170)*
- voluntary exchange *(p. 171)*
- law of demand *(p. 172)*
- quantity demanded *(p. 172)*
- real income effect *(p. 173)*
- substitution effect *(p. 173)*
- utility *(p. 174)*
- marginal utility *(p. 174)*
- law of diminishing marginal utility *(p. 174)*

Academic Vocabulary
- analysis *(p. 171)*
- alternate *(p. 173)*

Reading Strategy
Organizing As you read this section, use a diagram similar to the one below to list characteristics of demand.

PRODUCTS In ThE NeWS
—from *BusinessWeek*

THE DEMAND FACTOR Once the word hits the street, hundreds of teens start lining up at stores. So strong is demand that new releases happen only on weekends—so kids won't skip school. When the doors open, they sell out in hours. Tickets for the current Eminem tour? The new iPod music player? Nope. We're talking about a basic basketball sneaker, Nike Inc.'s Air Force 1.

How do you keep a basic sneaker hot for a quarter-century? . . . Nike creates consumer longing by keeping supplies tight and releasing collectible versions with minimal hype.

Every two months or so, Nike unleashes a newly tweaked shoe. . . . Each release involves roughly 350,000 to 500,000 pairs of shoes shipped nationwide, and each store gets only about 25 to 30.

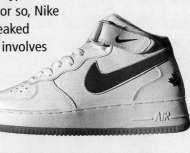

▲ Nike's Air Force 1 sneaker

The word *demand* has a special meaning in economics. Most American teenagers own a pair of sneakers. Because of high demand and high price, however, not everyone who wants a pair of Nike Air Force 1 sneakers is able to acquire this particular brand. As you read this section, you'll learn that the idea of demand centers on people being both willing *and* able to pay for a product or service.

Demand and Supply **169**

The Marketplace

Main Idea In a market economy, buyers and sellers set prices.

Economics & You Have you ever sold something on eBay? How did you decide what price to set? Read on to learn how people like eBay users follow basic ideas of demand and supply.

demand: the amount of a good or service that consumers are able and willing to buy at various possible prices during a specified time period

supply: the amount of a good or service that producers are able and willing to sell at various prices during a specified time period

market: the process of freely exchanging goods and services between buyers and sellers

When you buy something, do you ever wonder why it sells at the particular price you paid? People do not usually think that individual consumers have any influence over the price of an item. In a market economy, however, consumers collectively have a great deal of influence on the prices of all goods and services. To understand this, let's look first at how people in the marketplace decide what to buy and at what price. This is **demand**. Later, we'll examine how the people who want to sell goods and services decide how much to sell and at what price. This is **supply**.

What is the marketplace? A **market** represents the freely chosen actions between buyers and sellers of goods and services. A market for a particular item or service can be local, national, international, or a combination of these. (See **Figure 7.1** at the bottom of this page for more information on markets.)

Figure 7.1	Examples of Markets

■ When you hear the term "market," you probably think of a supermarket, clothing store, record shop, or other store you have visited. However, a "market" can be any place where buyers and sellers come together.

▲ **A. Stores** Any place where you can buy food, clothing, or other items is a market.

B. Services A service is any activity that one person performs for another for a fee. Examples of services include haircutting, tutoring, and dental checkups. Any time or place these services are performed is an example of a market.

In a market economy, individuals decide for themselves the answers to the WHAT?, HOW?, and FOR WHOM? economic questions that you studied back in Chapter 2.

The basis of activity in a market economy is the principle of **voluntary exchange**. A buyer and a seller exercise their economic freedom by working toward satisfactory terms of an exchange of goods or services. For example, the seller of an automobile sets a certain price based on his or her view of market conditions. The buyer, through the act of buying, agrees to the product and the price. In order to make the exchange, both the buyer and the seller must believe they will be better off—richer or happier—after the exchange than before.

In a market economy, buyers have many choices about how to spend their income, and sellers have many choices about how to sell their products. With voluntary exchange, the seller's problem of what to charge and the buyer's problem of how much to pay is solved voluntarily in the market. Supply and demand **analysis** is a model of how buyers and sellers operate in the marketplace. Such analysis is a way of explaining cause and effect in relation to price.

voluntary exchange: a transaction in which a buyer and a seller exercise their economic freedom by working out their own terms of exchange

✔ Reading Check **Explaining** How are prices set in a market economy?

▲ **C. Entertainment** Whenever we pay for entertainment, such as movies, concerts, and ball games, we are participating in a market.

▼ **D. Internet Shopping** Over the last several years, the Internet has created a huge virtual market, home to millions of buyers and sellers.

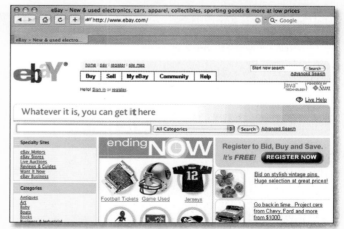

Economic Analysis

Making Comparisons *What characteristics do all these examples of markets have in common?*

The Law of Demand

Main Idea The law of demand states that as price goes up, quantity demanded goes down, and vice versa.

Economics & You Can you think of a common household item that was once very expensive but is now much cheaper? Read on to find out how demand affects the prices of items you buy and use every day.

Demand, in economic terms, represents all of the different quantities of a good or service that consumers will purchase at various prices. It includes both the willingness and the ability to pay. A person may say he or she wants a new DVD. Until that person is both willing *and able* to buy it, however, no demand for DVDs has been created by that individual.

The **law of demand** explains how people react to changing prices in terms of the quantities demanded of a good or service. (See **Figure 7.2**.) There is an *inverse*, or opposite, relationship between quantity demanded and price. For example, if the price of a DVD is $15 many people will buy it. If the price went up to $20 fewer people would buy it, but many people who wanted the DVD would still buy it. Only a few people would buy the DVD if the price went up to $75. This example shows how the law of demand works.

Several factors explain the inverse relation between price and **quantity demanded**, or how much people will buy of any item at a particular price. These factors include real income, possible substitutes, and diminishing marginal utility.

law of demand: economic rule stating that the quantity demanded and price move in opposite directions

quantity demanded: the amount of a good or service that a consumer is willing and able to purchase at a specific price

---

Figure 7.2 | The Law of Demand

■ Consumers react to price changes.

As price goes up . . .

Quantity demanded goes down.

As price goes down . . .

Quantity demanded goes up.

Economic Analysis

Determining Cause and Effect *What happens to the demand for an item if the price goes down?*

Real Income Effect No one—not even the wealthiest person in the world—will ever be able to buy everything he or she might possibly want. People's incomes limit the amount they are able to spend. Individuals cannot keep buying the same quantity of a good if its price rises while their income stays the same. This concept is known as the **real income effect** on demand. It forces consumers to make trade-offs.

Suppose that you normally fill your car's gas tank twice a month, spending $40 each time. If the price of gasoline rises, you may have to spend $50 each time. If the price continues to rise while your income does not, eventually you will not be able to fill the gas tank twice per month because your *real income*, or purchasing power, has dropped. To keep buying the same amount of gasoline, you would need to cut back on buying other things. The real income effect forces you to make a trade-off in your gasoline purchases. The same is true for every item you buy, particularly those you buy regularly.

The real income effect works in the opposite direction, too. If you are already buying $80 worth of gas each month, and the price of gas drops dramatically, your real income increases. You will have more purchasing power and will be able to spend the extra amount you save on gas on other things you want to buy.

Real Income Effect

If the price of gasoline rises but your income does not, you obviously cannot continue buying the same amount of gasoline and everything else you normally purchase.

Substitution Effect Suppose there are two items that are not exactly the same but which satisfy basically the same need. Their cost is about the same. If the price of one falls, people will most likely buy it instead of the other, now higher-priced, good. If the price of one rises in relation to the price of the other, people will buy the now lower-priced good. This principle is called the **substitution effect**.

Suppose, for example, that you listen to both CDs and downloaded music. If the price of CDs rises dramatically, you will probably buy more music downloads and fewer CDs. **Alternately,** if the price of music downloads increases, you will probably buy more CDs. If the prices of CDs and music downloads both increase, you will most likely buy fewer of each and look for other ways to listen to music—for example, you may start listening to the radio or borrowing CDs from the library.

real income effect: economic rule stating that individuals cannot keep buying the same quantity of a product if its price rises while their income stays the same

substitution effect: economic rule stating that if two items satisfy the same need and the price of one rises, people will buy more of the other

Diminishing Marginal Utility Almost everything that people like, desire, use, or think they would like to use, gives satisfaction. The term that economists use for satisfaction is *utility*. **Utility** is defined as the power that a good or service has to satisfy a want. Based on utility, people decide what to buy and how much they are willing and able to pay at any given time. In deciding to make a purchase, consumers think about the amount of satisfaction, or use, they think they will get from whatever item they are thinking about buying.

Consider the utility that can be derived from buying a cold soft drink at a baseball game on a hot day. At $4 per cup, how many will you buy? That decision depends on the additional utility, or satisfaction, you expect to receive from each additional soft drink. Your *total* satisfaction will rise with each one bought. The amount of *additional* satisfaction, or **marginal utility**, however, will lessen with each additional cup bought. This example illustrates the **law of diminishing marginal utility**.

At some point, you will stop buying soft drinks. Maybe you don't want to wait in line, or perhaps you are no longer thirsty.

utility: the ability of any good or service to satisfy consumer wants

marginal utility: an additional amount of satisfaction

law of diminishing marginal utility: rule stating that the additional satisfaction a consumer gets from purchasing one more unit of a product will lessen with each additional unit purchased

Diminishing Marginal Utility

Regardless of how satisfying the first taste of an item is, additional satisfaction declines with additional consumption. Assume, for example, that at a price of $3.00 per bag of peanuts, you have enough after buying two bags. Thus, the value you place on additional satisfaction from a third bag of peanuts would be less than $3.00. According to what will give you the most satisfaction, you will spend the $3.00 on something else. Eventually you would receive no additional satisfaction from more peanuts, even if the vendor gave them to you for free.

▲ As the cartoon shows, people often confuse *wants* with *needs*.

At that point, the satisfaction you get from the drink is less than the value you place on its cost. In general, people stop buying an item when the satisfaction from the next unit of the same item becomes less than the price they must pay for it.

What if, after the fifth inning, the price of soft drinks drops to $3? You might then buy at least one additional drink. Why? Remember, people will continue buying an item to the point at which the satisfaction from the last unit bought is equal to the price. At that point, people will stop buying. As the price of an item decreases, however, people will generally buy more.

> **Skills Handbook**
>
> *See page **R36** to learn about **Determining Cause and Effect**.*

Reading Check **Explaining** What happens to the quantity demanded for an item if the price of the item goes up?

section 1 Review

Vocabulary

1. **Explain** the significance of: demand, supply, market, voluntary exchange, law of demand, quantity demanded, real income effect, substitution effect, utility, marginal utility, law of diminishing marginal utility.

Main Ideas

2. **Determining Cause and Effect** Create a chart like the one below to show how each cause listed influences the quantity demanded for a given product or service.

Cause	Effect on Quantity Demanded
Increase in real income	
Decrease in real income	
Price of substitutes	
Utility	

Critical Thinking

3. **The BIG Ideas** Think about what you have learned about diminishing marginal utility. Then think of three examples from your own experience, and explain how they demonstrate this concept.

4. **Contrasting** Describe the difference between the real income effect and the substitution effect.

Applying Economics

5. **Real Income Effect** Imagine that you make $1,000 per month at a part-time job. Make a budget for yourself that lists how much you spend on food, clothing, gas, entertainment, etc. Now imagine that the price of gas rises by $1 per gallon. How will this affect your budget? Revise your budget to include this price change.

IT'S A **WHAT?**

The latest craze among dog fanciers: Poodles crossed with other breeds.

Check It Out! In this chapter you learned how demand can increase as tastes and preferences change. In the following article, read to learn how a new breed of dog has created explosive demand.

Roll over, rover: Make room for doodles, the latest designer dogs—a mix of a poodle with another breed. The most popular hybrids are goldendoodles (golden retriever mix), Labradoodles (Labrador retriever), schnoodles (schnauzer), and cockapoos (cocker spaniel).

Aside from their shaggy good looks and friendliness, doodles are in demand because they usually don't shed. "If you've ever lived with a golden or Lab, there's a lot of hair," says Rochelle Sundholm, owner of Spring Creek Labradoodles in Williamette Valley, Oregon. Another plus: They have poodle smarts without the stereotypical frou-frou

A goldendoodle is a mix of a ▲ poodle and a golden retriever.

yappiness. But doodles aren't standardized, so there's a lot of variability in appearance, personality, health—and price….

The American Kennel Club (AKC) doesn't recognize doodle crossbreeds—and may not for a long time. "The reason people pay thousands of dollars for a purebred dog is for the hundreds, if not thousands, of years of pedigree," says AKC spokeswoman Daisy Okas. Yet doodle pups fetch pedigree prices—anywhere from $400 to $3,000.

—Reprinted from *BusinessWeek*

Top Dog

If trends are any indication, the high demand for the Labradoodle is no surprise! Check out the most popular breeds of the last several decades.

Labrador Retriever ◀

Most Popular Dog Breeds	
1950s	Beagle
1960s and 1970s	Poodle
1980s	Cocker Spaniel
1990s to present	Labrador Retriever

Source: American Kennel Club, 2006.

Think About It

1. **Explaining** How are doodle dogs different from other breeds of dogs?

2. **Synthesizing** Why did demand for the newer breeds of doodle dogs grow so quickly? How did this affect the price of doodle dogs compared to the price of other non-AKC-accredited dogs?

The Demand Curve and Elasticity of Demand

GUIDE TO READING

Section Preview
In this section, you will learn more about the relationship between price and demand.

Content Vocabulary
- demand schedule *(p. 179)*
- demand curve *(p. 179)*
- complementary good *(p. 181)*
- elasticity *(p. 182)*
- price elasticity of demand *(p. 182)*
- elastic demand *(p. 183)*
- inelastic demand *(p. 183)*

Academic Vocabulary
- visual *(p. 178)*
- concept *(p. 178)*
- specific *(p. 180)*

Reading Strategy
Identifying As you read, complete a web diagram like the one below by listing the factors that contribute to the elasticity of demand for a good or service.

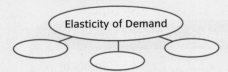

Elasticity of Demand

COMPANIES In ThE NeWS
—from *USA Today*

HARLEY'S RECORD PROFIT FAILS TO IMPRESS In recent years, Harley-Davidson has had a far greater demand for its products than supply. Dealers often have had long lists of buyers waiting for motorcycles. Now the company says the gap between supply and demand has been closing. It said its plans to cut production by 10,000 vehicles will help keep demand greater than supply.

. . . To reach its sales goals, Harley-Davidson needs to attract new customers, says UBS Investment Research analyst Robin Farley. That's why he was surprised at the company's promotions this winter aimed at current Harley owners.

. . . Harley-Davidson may not have a clear idea of what the true demand is for its motorcycles. Long waiting lists made it seem like the growth rate would be higher than it is turning out to be.

In Section 1, you learned that quantity demanded is based on price. Demand, however, can be affected by a variety of factors, including changes in general economic conditions, the existence and price of substitutes, and changes in people's tastes and preferences. Some of these other factors might explain the recent decrease in demand for Harley-Davidson motorcycles.

Graphing the Demand Curve

Main Idea A demand curve is a graph that shows the relationship between the price of an item and the quantity demanded.

Economics & You If the price of a movie ticket suddenly went up to $20, how often would you go to the movies? What if the ticket price dropped to 50 cents? Read on to learn how this relationship between price and demand can be illustrated visually.

Economics ONLINE

Student Web Activity
Visit the *Economics Today and Tomorrow* Web site at glencoe.com and click on **Chapter 7—Student Web Activities** to see how changes in population affect demand.

Skills Handbook

See page R51 to learn about Using Tables and Charts.

How can you learn to distinguish between a change in quantity demanded and a change in demand? And how do economists show these relationships in a **visual** way? It is said that a picture is worth a thousand words. In economics, the "picture" is often a graph that shows the relationship between two statistics or **concepts**.

The law of demand can be graphed. As you learned in Section 1, the relationship between the quantity demanded and price is inverse—that is, as the price of a good or service goes up, the quantity demanded goes down, and as the price goes down, the quantity demanded goes up.

Take a look at *Table A* and *Graph B* in **Figure 7.3**. These graphs show how the price of a particular good affects the quantity

Figure 7.3 Graphing the Demand Curve

■ Note how the table and the graph each use a different format to show the same thing. Each shows the law of demand—as price falls, quantity demanded increases. Also, note that in Graph B we refer to the quantity of DVDs demanded per year. We could also have used a time period of one day, one week, one month, two years, etc.

A **Demand Schedule**

Price per DVD	Quantity Demanded (in millions)	Points in Graph B
$20	100	A
$18	300	B
$16	500	C
$14	700	D
$12	900	E
$10	1,100	F

Table A. Demand Schedule ▶
The numbers in this demand schedule show that as the price per DVD decreases, the quantity demanded increases.

demanded at each price. *Table A* is a **demand schedule**—a table of prices and quantity demanded. The numbers show that as the price of DVDs decreases, the quantity demanded increases. For example, at a cost of $20 each, 100 million DVDs will be demanded. When the cost decreases to $12 each, 900 million DVDs will be demanded.

In *Graph B*, the numbers from the schedule in *Graph A* have been plotted onto a graph. The bottom (or horizontal) axis shows the quantity demanded. The side (or vertical) axis shows the price per DVD. Each pair of figures showing price and quantity demanded represents a point on the graph. These points are labeled A through K.

Finally, the line connecting points A through K is the **demand curve.** A demand curve shows the quantity demanded of a good or service at each possible price. Demand curves slope downward (that is, they fall from the left to the right). When you study *Graph B*, you can see clearly the inverse relationship between price and quantity demanded. As price falls, quantity demanded increases, and vice versa.

demand schedule: table showing quantities demanded at different possible prices

demand curve: downward-sloping line that shows in graph form the quantities demanded at each possible price

✓ Reading Check **Determining Cause and Effect** What causes a change in quantity demanded? How can this be shown visually using a demand curve?

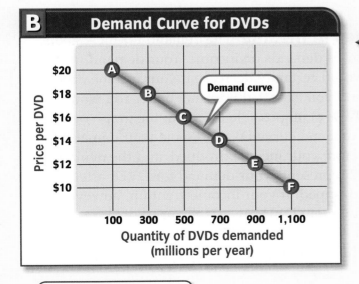

B **Demand Curve for DVDs**

Price per DVD / Quantity of DVDs demanded (millions per year)

◄ **Graph B.** Demand Curve
Here, the price and quantity demanded numbers from the demand schedule have been plotted on a graph and connected with a line. This line is the *demand curve*, which always falls from left to right.

Economic Analysis
Using Graphs *According to the demand curve, how many DVDs will be demanded at a price of $12 each?*

Graphs In MOtion
See StudentWorks™ Plus or go to glencoe.com.

Demand and Supply **179**

Determinants of Demand

Main Idea A change in the demand for a particular item shifts the entire demand curve to the left or right.

Economics & You Think of a product or service you used to buy a lot of but don't anymore. Did this happen because of changing trends, a change in your income, or something else? Read on to learn about various factors that affect demand.

Many factors can affect demand for a **specific** product or service. Among these factors are changes in population, changes in income, changes in people's tastes and preferences, the availability and price of substitutes, and the price of complementary goods.

If Population Increases

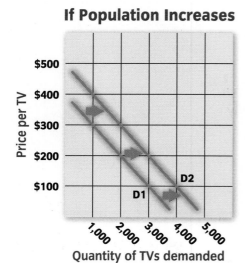

Changes in Population

When population increases, opportunities to buy and sell increase. Naturally, the demand for most products then increases. This means that the demand curve for, say, flat-screen televisions, shifts to the right. At each price, more flat-screen televisions will be demanded simply because the consumer population increases. This concept is shown in the graph on the left. The demand curve labeled D1 represents demand for televisions before the population increased. The demand curve labeled D2 represents demand after the population increased.

In contrast, if population decreases, overall demand for products also decreases. At each price, fewer flat-screen televisions will be demanded. When this happens, the demand curve shifts to the left.

If Income Decreases

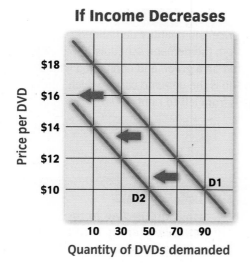

Changes in Income

The demand for most goods and services depends on income. Your demand for DVDs would certainly decrease if your income dropped in half and you expected it to stay there. You would buy fewer DVDs at all possible prices. In the graph on the left, the demand curve D1 represents your demand for DVDs before your income dropped, and the demand curve D2 represents your demand for DVDs after your income dropped. If your income went up, however, you might buy more DVDs even if the price of DVDs doubled. Buying more DVDs at all possible prices would shift the demand curve to the right.

Changes in Tastes and Preferences

One of the key factors that determine demand is people's tastes and preferences. Tastes and preferences refer to what people like and prefer to choose. When a product becomes a fad, more of the products are demanded and sold at every possible price. The demand curve then shifts to the right, as shown in the graph on the right. In the early 1990s, when Beanie Babies became a fad, the demand curve shifted from D1 to D2. As the popularity of this product died down, its demand curve then shifted back to the left.

Substitutes

As you learned in Section 1, substitutes are goods used in place of one another. The availability and price of substitutes also affect demand. For example, people often think of butter and margarine as substitutes. Suppose that the price of butter remains the same and the price of margarine falls. People will then buy more margarine and less butter at all prices of butter. This shift in the demand curve for butter is shown in the graph on the right. If, in contrast, the price of the substitute (margarine) increases, the demand for the original item (butter) also increases.

Complementary Goods

Complements are products that are generally bought and sold together. Digital cameras and flash memory, for example, are **complementary goods**. When two goods are complementary, the decrease in the price of one will increase the demand for it as well as its complementary good. If the price of digital cameras drops, for example, people will probably buy more of them. They will also probably buy more flash memory to use with the cameras. Therefore, a decrease in the price of digital cameras leads to an increase in the demand for flash memory. As a result, the demand curve for flash memory will shift to the right, as shown in the graph on the right. The opposite would happen if the price of digital cameras increased. In this case, the demand for the complement, flash memory, would decrease, and the demand curve would shift to the left.

Reading Check **Explaining** Why does a change in population affect the demand curve?

If Preferences Change

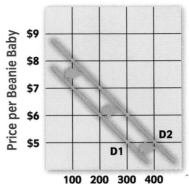

Quantity of Beanie Babies demanded (in millions)

If Price of Substitute Decreases

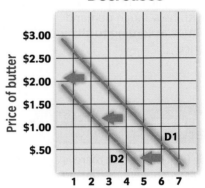

Quantity of butter demanded (in millions of pounds)

If Price of Complement Decreases

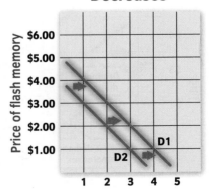

Quantity of flash memory demanded (in millions)

complementary good: a product often used with another product

The Price Elasticity of Demand

Main Idea Elasticity of demand measures how much the quantity demanded changes when price goes up or down.

Economics & You Do rising gas prices affect how much gas you are willing to buy? If not, then your demand for gas is inelastic. Read on to learn about price responsiveness, or elasticity.

elasticity: economic concept dealing with consumers' responsiveness to an increase or decrease in the price of a product

price elasticity of demand: economic concept that deals with how much demand varies according to changes in price

The law of demand is straightforward: The higher the price charged, the lower the quantity demanded—and vice versa. If you sold DVDs, how could you use this information? You know that if you lower prices, consumers will buy more DVDs. By how much should you lower the price, however? You cannot really answer this question unless you know how responsive consumers will be to a decrease in the price of DVDs. Economists call this price responsiveness **elasticity**. The measure of the **price elasticity of demand** is *how much* consumers respond to a given change in price.

Figure 7.4   Demand vs. Quantity Demanded

■ Remember that there is a difference between a change in *demand* and a change in *quantity demanded*.

▼ **Graph B.** Change in Quantity Demanded
This is caused by a change in the price of a good, and it is shown as a movement *along* the demand curve.

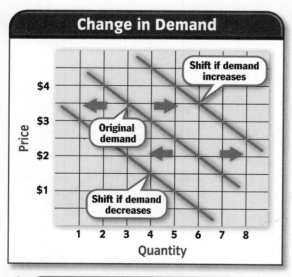

Graph A. Change in Demand   This is caused by something other than a change in the product's price, and it causes the entire demand curve to shift to the left or right.

Economic Analysis
Determining Cause and Effect *Which graph would be affected by the price of substitutes?*

Goods with . . .

. . . Elastic Demand

. . . Inelastic Demand

■ In general, goods with elastic demand are luxury items or have many substitutes.

■ In general, goods with inelastic demand are necessities or have few or no substitutes.

Elastic Demand For some goods, a rise or fall in price greatly affects the amount people are willing to buy. The demand for these goods is considered *elastic*—consumers can be flexible about buying or not buying these items. For example, specific brands of coffee probably have a very **elastic demand.** Consumers consider the many competing brands of coffee to be almost the same. A small rise in the price of one brand will probably cause many consumers to purchase the cheaper substitute brands instead.

Another example of goods that are generally considered to have elastic demand are luxury items. Luxury items are things people might want but do not really need to survive. Expensive cars, high-end electronic items, and exotic vacations are all examples of luxury items. Some foods, especially expensive foods such as steak and lobster, are also considered luxury items. Because people do not need these things to survive, the demand for them is usually elastic.

Inelastic Demand If a price change does not result in a substantial change in the quantity demanded, then demand for that particular good is considered *inelastic*. This means that consumers are usually not flexible with these items and will purchase some of the items no matter what they cost. In general, goods that are considered necessities, such as staple foods, spices like salt and pepper, and certain types of medicine, normally have **inelastic demand.**

Note that by using two demand curves together in one diagram—as shown in **Figure 7.5** on page 184—you can compare a relatively inelastic demand with a relatively elastic demand at a particular price.

elastic demand: situation in which a given rise or fall in a product's price greatly affects the amount that people are willing to buy

inelastic demand: situation in which a product's price change has little impact on the quantity demanded by consumers

Figure 7.5 Elasticity of Demand

■ **Curve A** at the price of $5.50 could represent the inelastic demand for pepper. Even if the price of pepper dropped dramatically, you would not purchase much more of it.

■ **Curve B** at $5.50 could represent the elastic demand for steaks. If the price drops just a little, many people will buy much more steak.

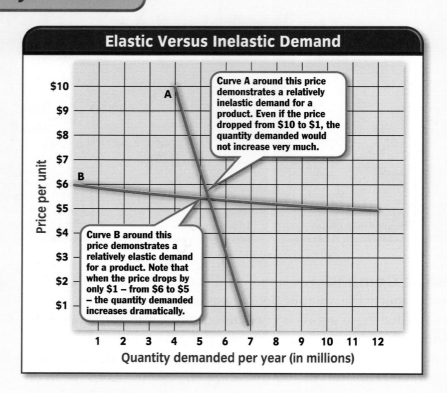

Elastic Versus Inelastic Demand

Curve A around this price demonstrates a relatively inelastic demand for a product. Even if the price dropped from $10 to $1, the quantity demanded would not increase very much.

Curve B around this price demonstrates a relatively elastic demand for a product. Note that when the price drops by only $1 – from $6 to $5 – the quantity demanded increases dramatically.

Price per unit

Quantity demanded per year (in millions)

Economic Analysis

Explaining *What determines whether goods have elastic or inelastic demand?*

Personal Finance Handbook
See pages R4–R5 to learn more about budgeting.

What Determines Price Elasticity of Demand?

Why do some goods have elastic demand and others have inelastic demand? At least three factors determine the price elasticity of demand for a particular item: the existence of substitutes; the percentage of a person's total budget devoted to the purchase of that good; and the time consumers are given to adjust to a change in price.

Clearly, the more substitutes that exist for a product, the more responsive consumers will be to a change in the price of that good. A diabetic needs insulin, which has virtually no substitutes. The price elasticity of demand for insulin, therefore, is very low—it is inelastic. The opposite is true for soft drinks. If the price of one goes up by very much, many consumers may switch to another.

The percentage of your total budget spent on an item will also determine whether its demand is elastic or inelastic. For example, the portion of a family's budget devoted to pepper is very small. Even if the price of pepper doubles, most people will keep buying about the same amount. The demand for pepper, then, is relatively inelastic. Housing demand, in contrast, is relatively elastic because it represents such a large proportion of a household's yearly budget.

Profits and the Law of Supply

Main Idea The law of supply states that as price goes up, quantity supplied goes up, and vice versa.

Economics & You Would you be willing to work more hours at your job for the same wages? Read on to learn that businesses are only willing to supply more of something if their profits also increase.

To understand how prices are determined, you have to look at both demand and supply—the willingness and ability of producers to provide goods and services at different prices in the marketplace. The **law of supply** states that as the price of a good rises, the quantity supplied generally rises; as the price falls, the quantity supplied also falls. (See **Figure 7.6** below.)

You may recall that with demand, price and quantity demanded move in opposite directions. With supply, a direct relationship exists between the price and **quantity supplied**. A direct relationship means that when prices rise, quantity supplied will rise, too. When prices fall, quantity supplied by sellers will also fall. Thus, a larger quantity will generally be supplied at higher prices than at lower prices. A smaller quantity will generally be supplied at lower prices than at higher prices.

The profit **incentive** is one of the factors that motivate people in a market economy. In the case of supply, the higher the price of a good, the greater the incentive is for a producer to produce more. The higher price not only returns higher revenues from sales but also covers the additional costs of producing more. This concept is the basis of the law of supply.

law of supply: economic rule stating that price and quantity supplied move in the same direction

quantity supplied: the amount of a good or service that a producer is willing and able to supply at a specific price

Reading Check **Explaining** What kind of relationship exists between price and quantity supplied?

Figure 7.6   The Law of Supply

■ Suppliers react to price changes.

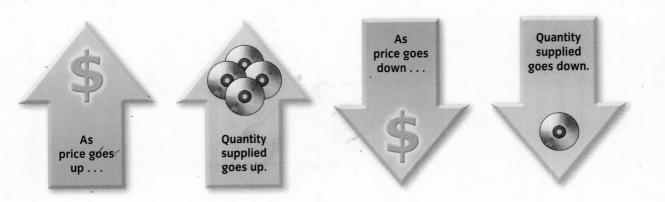

As price goes up . . .

Quantity supplied goes up.

As price goes down . . .

Quantity supplied goes down.

The Supply Curve

Main Idea A supply curve is a graph that shows the relationship between price and quantity supplied.

Economics & You How many extra hours would you be willing to work for $1? For $100? Read on to learn how the relationship between price and quantity supplied can be illustrated with a supply curve.

Remember that economists show the relationship between price and quantity demanded by using a demand schedule and a demand curve. Similarly, we can use special tables and graphs to illustrate the law of supply visually. (See **Figure 7.7** below.) Using the example of DVD producers, the graphs in this figure show a visual relationship between the price of each DVD and the quantity of DVDs that producers are willing to supply at each price.

Table A in Figure 7.7 is the **supply schedule**, which is a table showing that as the price per DVD increases, the quantity that producers are willing to supply also increases. For example, at a price of $10 per DVD, only 100 million DVDs will be supplied. When the price increases to $15 each, however, 600 million DVDs will be supplied.

supply schedule: table showing quantities supplied at different possible prices

Figure 7.7 | Graphing the Supply Curve

■ Note how each of the two graphs uses a different format to show the same thing. Each shows the law of supply—as price rises, quantity supplied increases.

Table A. Supply Schedule
The numbers in this supply schedule show that as the price per DVD increases, the quantity supplied increases. At $16 each, a quantity of 700 million DVDs will be supplied.

A | Supply Schedule

Price per DVD	Quantity Supplied (in millions)	Points in Graph B
$10	100	L
$12	300	M
$14	500	N
$16	700	O
$18	900	P
$20	1,100	Q

In *Graph B,* the numbers from the schedule in *Table A* have been plotted onto a graph. Note that the bottom (horizontal) axis shows the quantity supplied, and the side (vertical) axis shows the price per DVD. Each intersection of price and quantity supplied represents a point on the graph. We label these points L through V.

When we connect the points in *Graph B* with a line, we end up with the **supply curve** for DVDs at the particular prices shown. A supply curve shows the quantities that producers are willing to supply at each possible price. It slopes upward from left to right.

You can compare the supply curve to the demand curve in **Figure 7.3** on page 179. In doing so, you will see that the two curves are similar. The main difference between them is that in looking at the supply curve, you can see that the relationship between price and quantity supplied is direct—or moving in the same direction. In the case of the demand curve, the opposite is true—the relationship between price and quantity demanded is inverse. Because of this key point, the slopes of the two curves will always be different.

supply curve: upward-sloping line that shows in graph form the quantities supplied at each possible price

✔ Reading Check **Describing** What does a normal supply curve look like?

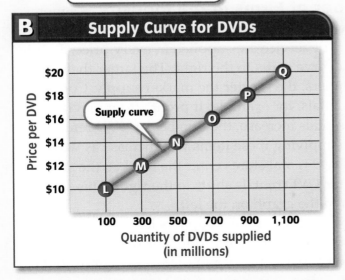

B **Supply Curve for DVDs**

◀ **Graph B. Supply Curve** Here the price and quantity supplied figures from the supply schedule have been plotted on a graph and connected with a line. This line is the *supply curve,* which rises from left to right.

Economic Analysis

Using Graphs *According to the supply curve, how many DVDs will be supplied at a price of $14 each?*

The Determinants of Supply

Main Idea A change in the supply of a particular item shifts the entire supply curve to the left or right.

Economics & You Why are iPods so much more common now than they were five years ago? Read on to learn about the factors that affect supply.

Many factors can affect the supply of a specific product. Four of the major determinants of supply (not *quantity supplied*) are the price of inputs, the number of firms in the industry, taxes, and technology.

If Inputs Become Cheaper

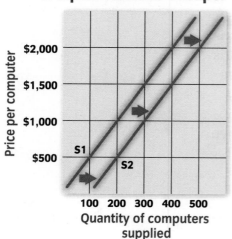

Price of Inputs If the price of the inputs needed to make a product—raw materials, wages, and so on—drops, a producer can supply more at a lower production cost. This causes the entire supply curve to shift to the right. This situation occurred, for example, when the price of memory chips used in making computers fell during the 1980s and 1990s. Look at the graph on the left. Line S1 shows the supply of computers *before* the price of memory chips fell. Line S2 shows the increased supply of computers *after* the price of memory chips fell. After the price drop, more computers were supplied at any given price than before.

In contrast, if the cost of inputs increases, then the cost of production also increases, and suppliers will offer fewer goods for sale at every possible price.

If Number of Firms Increases

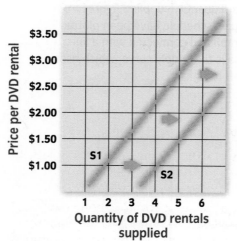

Number of Firms in the Industry As more firms enter an industry, greater quantities of their product or service are supplied at every price, and the supply curve shifts to the right. The larger the number of suppliers, the greater the market supply. Consider DVD rentals, for example. If profits from movie and game rentals increase, the number of DVD rental stores supplying these items will increase as well. As more DVD rental stores enter the market, the supply curve for DVD rentals shifts to the right. This shift is shown in the graph on the left.

Conversely, if some suppliers leave the market, fewer quantities of their product or service are supplied at every price, and the supply curve shifts to the left. Sellers in a free-market economy are entering and leaving the market all the time.

Taxes If the government **imposes** more taxes on the production of certain items, businesses will not be willing to supply as much as before because the cost of production will rise. The supply curve for products will shift to the left, indicating a decrease in supply. For example, if taxes on the production of silk scarves increased, businesses that sell silk scarves would supply fewer quantities at each and every price. Look at the graph on the right. Line S1 indicates the supply of silk scarves *before* the government raised taxes on this product. Line S2 equals the supply *after* the government raised taxes. Because of the increased cost of production caused by the taxes, the entire supply curve for silk scarves shifted to the left.

Technology The use of science to develop new products and new methods for producing and distributing goods and services is called **technology**. Any improvement in technology will increase supply, as shown in the graph on the right. This is because new technology usually allows suppliers to make more goods for a lower cost. The entire cost of production is cut, and the supply curve shifts to the right.

Reading Check **Analyzing** What happens to the supply curve when production costs increase?

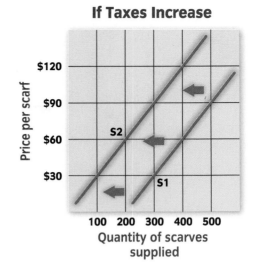

If Taxes Increase

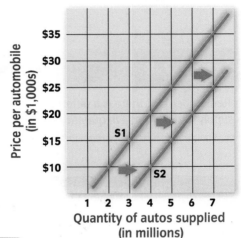

If Technology Improves Production

technology: the use of science to develop new products and new methods for producing and distributing goods and services

Advances in Technology

In the early 1900s, improved technology in the auto-making industry greatly reduced the amount of time and other resources needed to make many new automobiles. Therefore, a larger quantity supplied of autos was offered for sale at every price.

The Law of Diminishing Returns

Main Idea When a business wants to expand, it has to consider how much expansion will really help the business.

Economics & You Have you ever heard the expression, "Too many cooks spoil the soup"? Read on to learn why hiring more workers is not always the best option for businesses.

Imagine that you own a business, and you want to expand production. Assume you have 10 machines and employ 10 workers, and you hire an 11th worker. Now, production increases by 1,000 units per week. When you hire a 12th worker, however, production increases by only 900 per week. (See **Figure 7.9**.) If you continue to hire more workers, production will continue to increase, but the rate of increase will fall. Maybe there are not enough machines to go around, and perhaps the workers are getting in each other's way. If you continue to hire still more workers, your overall output will eventually decrease.

Figure 7.8 Supply vs. Quantity Supplied

■ Remember that there is a difference between a *change in supply* and a *change in quantity supplied*.

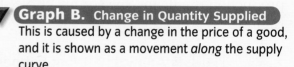
Graph B. Change in Quantity Supplied
This is caused by a change in the price of a good, and it is shown as a movement *along* the supply curve.

▲ **Graph A.** Change in Supply This is caused by something other than price, and it causes the entire supply curve to shift to the left or right.

Economic Analysis

Determining Cause and Effect *Which graph would be affected by a significant improvement in technology?*

Figure 7.9 | **Diminishing Returns**

■ Normally after some point, if you are expanding production, the additional workers that you hire do not add as much to total output as the previous workers that you hired. Eventually, adding more workers will not produce additional output.

Diminishing Marginal Returns

Number of Workers	Additional Output
11	1,000
12	900
13	800
14	700
15	600
16	500
17	400
18	300
19	200
20	100
21	0

Economic Analysis

Using Tables *If you start with 12 workers and hire 6 more, by how many units will your additional output decrease?*

This example illustrates the **law of diminshing returns**, which says that adding units of one factor of production increases total output. After a certain point, however, the extra output for each *additional* unit hired will begin to decrease.

law of diminishing returns: economic rule that says as more units of a factor of production are added to other factors of production, after some point total output continues to increase but at a diminishing rate

Reading Check **Explaining** Why is it important for business owners to understand the law of diminishing returns?

section 3 **Review**

Vocabulary

1. **Explain** the significance of: law of supply, quantity supplied, supply schedule, supply curve, technology, law of diminishing returns.

Main Ideas

2. **Summarizing** Create a diagram like this to list the four determinants of supply.

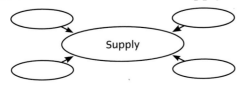

Critical Thinking

3. The **BIG Ideas** How does the incentive of greater profits affect supply?

4. **Analyzing Visuals** Study the charts on pages 190–191. Which one of the four charts is significantly different from the others? Why?

Applying Economics

5. **Synthesizing Information** Imagine that you produce baseball caps and distribute them to local stores. Create a graph showing the various prices and quantities supplied for your caps.

Putting Supply and Demand Together

Section Preview
In this section, you will learn about how supply and demand interact to affect prices and about restrictions the government sometimes places on this process.

Content Vocabulary
- equilibrium price *(p. 195)*
- shortage *(p. 197)*
- surplus *(p. 197)*
- price ceiling *(p. 198)*
- rationing *(p. 199)*
- black market *(p. 199)*
- price floor *(p. 199)*

Academic Vocabulary
- assume *(p. 196)*
- eliminate *(p. 197)*

Reading Strategy
Describing As you read this section, use a Venn diagram like the one below to define each of the economic terms listed.

Shortage — Equilibrium Price — Surplus

PRODUCTS In ThE NeWS
—from *BusinessWeek*

SEEKING A BALANCE Demand for Apple's iPod will be huge again this holiday season, no question. The only issue is supply—and how much revenue Apple will forgo because of shortages that look unavoidable.

Circuit City Stores says it expects shortages, and two smaller retailers say they're getting less than half of what they order each week. With demand expected to surge—analysts figure Apple could sell upwards of 10 million iPods in the final quarter—last-minute shoppers could be left with empty stockings.

Of most concern is the iPod Nano. Chief Operating Officer Tim Cook told analysts: "The demand for this product is staggering. At this point I can't project when supply will meet demand."

What do Beanie Babies, Cabbage Patch Kids, and iPods all have in common? At one point in time, they all were in short supply—and usually right before the December holiday season. Around that time of year, you can often see empty shelves in stores where the hot items have sold out. As you will read, shortages occur when the quantity demanded is larger than the quantity supplied at the current price.

Equilibrium Price

Main Idea In free markets, prices are determined by the interaction of supply and demand.

Economics & You When new video game systems first come out, they are often too expensive for most people to buy. What happens to the price of the systems over time? Read on to learn about equilibrium price, the point at which demand and supply meet.

In the real world, demand and supply operate together. As the price of a good goes down, the quantity demanded rises and the quantity supplied falls. As the price goes up, the quantity demanded falls and the quantity supplied rises.

Is there a price at which the quantity demanded and the quantity supplied meet? Yes. This level is called the **equilibrium price**. At this price, the quantity supplied by sellers is the same as the quantity demanded by buyers. One way to visualize equilibrium price is to put the supply and demand curves on one graph, as shown in **Figure 7.10.** Where the two curves intersect is the equilibrium price.

equilibrium price: the price at which the amount producers are willing to supply is equal to the amount consumers are willing to buy

Figure 7.10 | Equilibrium Price

■ How does the market reach an equilibrium price? Study the charts. If sellers think the price for DVDs will be $20, they will produce 1,100 million units, but buyers will purchase only 100 million. To get rid of the surplus, suppose sellers lower the price to $10 and are willing to supply 100 million DVDs. At this price, 100 million are supplied but 1,100 million are demanded, leaving a shortage. The price tends to change until it reaches equilibrium.

A | Market Demand and Supply Schedules

Quantity Demanded (millions)	Price	Quantity Supplied (millions)	Surplus/ Shortage (millions)
100	$20	1,100	1,000
200	$19	1,000	800
300	$18	900	600
400	$17	800	400
500	$16	700	200
600	$15	600	0
700	$14	500	−200
800	$13	400	−400
900	$12	300	−600
1,000	$11	200	−800
1,100	$10	100	−1,000

B Graphing the Equilibrium Price

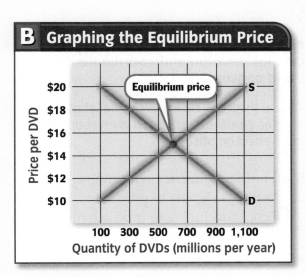

Equilibrium price

Price per DVD — $20, $18, $16, $14, $12, $10

Quantity of DVDs (millions per year) — 100 300 500 700 900 1,100

Economic Analysis

Using Graphs *According to the schedule and the graph, what is the equilibrium price and quantity demanded in this example?*

Figure 7.11 | Change in Equilibrium Price

■ When the supply or demand curves shift, the equilibrium price also changes. Note that the old equilibrium price was $15. But now the new demand curve intersects the supply curve at a higher price—$17.

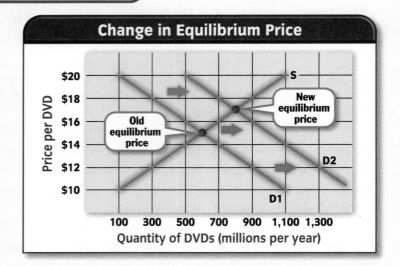

Change in Equilibrium Price

Economic Analysis

Cause and Effect *What might happen if scientists proved that watching movies decreases life span?*

What happens when there is an increase in the demand for DVDs? **Assume** that scientists prove that watching a lot of movies increases life span. This discovery will cause the entire demand curve to shift outward to the right, as shown in **Figure 7.11** above.

What about changes in supply? You can show these in a similar fashion. Assume that there is a major breakthrough in the technology of producing DVDs. The supply curve shifts outward to the right. The new equilibrium price will fall, and both the *quantity supplied* and the *quantity demanded* will increase.

Reading Check **Identifying** What is the equilibrium price of a good?

Prices as Signals

Main Idea Under a free-enterprise system, prices function as signals that communicate information and coordinate the activities of producers and consumers.

Economics & You Can you think of a recent event that affected the price of an everyday item such as gasoline? Read on to learn about shortages, surpluses, and their effect on prices.

In the United States and other countries with mainly free-enterprise systems, prices serve as signals to producers and consumers. Rising prices signal producers to produce more and consumers to purchase less. Falling prices signal producers to produce less and consumers to purchase more.

Shortages

A **shortage** occurs when, at the current price, the quantity demanded is greater than the quantity supplied. If the market is left alone—without government regulations or other restrictions—shortages put pressure on prices to rise. At a higher price, consumers reduce their purchases, whereas suppliers increase the quantity they supply.

shortage: situation in which the quantity demanded is greater than the quantity supplied at the current price

Surpluses

At prices above the equilibrium price, suppliers produce more than consumers want to purchase in the marketplace. Suppliers end up with **surpluses**—large, undesired inventories of goods—and this and other forces put pressure on the price to drop to the equilibrium price. If the price falls, suppliers have less incentive to supply as much as before, whereas consumers begin to purchase a greater quantity. The decrease in price toward the equilibrium price, therefore, **eliminates** the surplus.

surplus: situation in which quantity supplied is greater than quantity demanded at the current price

Market Forces

One of the benefits of the market economy is that when it operates without restriction, it eliminates shortages and surpluses. Whenever shortages occur, the market ends up taking care of itself—the price goes up to eliminate the shortage. Whenever surpluses occur, the market again ends up taking care of itself—the price falls to eliminate the surplus. (See **Figure 7.12** below for more information.) Now, let's take a look at what happens to the availability of goods and services when the government—not market forces—becomes involved in setting prices.

✔ **Reading Check** **Explaining** What causes shortages and surpluses to eventually disappear?

Figure 7.12 | **Shortages & Surpluses**

■ Shortages and surpluses can affect the price of a good or service.

B. Surplus ▶
If a business sets the price of a good too high or overestimates demand, it could wind up with a surplus of the good.

▲ **A. Shortage** Natural disasters, such as floods and hurricanes, can cause temporary shortages of water and other essential goods.

Economic Analysis

Predicting *What happens to prices during a shortage if the market is left alone?*

Demand and Supply **197**

Price Controls

Main Idea Under certain circumstances, the government sometimes sets a limit on how high or low a price of a good or service can go.

Economics & You Do you think there are times the government is justified in setting prices on certain goods and services? Read on to learn why this sometimes happens.

The government sometimes gets involved in setting prices if it believes such measures are needed to protect consumers or suppliers. Also, special interest groups sometimes exert pressure on elected officials to protect certain industries.

price ceiling: a legal maximum price that may be charged for a particular good or service

Price Ceilings

A **price ceiling** is a government-set maximum price that can be charged for goods and services. For example, city officials might set a price ceiling on what landlords can charge for rent. As *Graph A* of **Figure 7.13** below shows, when a price ceiling is set below the equilibrium price, a shortage occurs.

Figure 7.13   Price Ceilings and Price Floors

■ When the government gets involved in setting prices, price ceilings or price floors may result.

▼ **Graph B.** Price Floor
A fast-food restaurant wants to hire students at $4.15 an hour, but the government has set a minimum wage—a price floor—of $5.15 an hour.

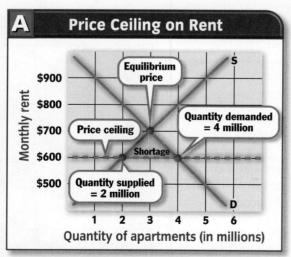

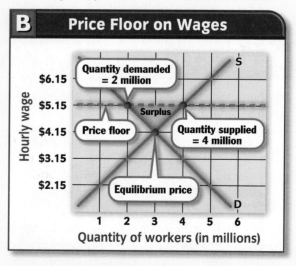

▲ **Graph A.** Price Ceiling
More people would like to rent at the government-controlled price, but apartment owners are unwilling to build more rental units if they cannot charge higher rent. This results in a shortage of apartments to rent.

Economic Analysis
Using Graphs *What is the surplus of workers when the hourly wage price floor is $5.15?*

Effective price ceilings—and resulting shortages—often lead to nonmarket ways of distributing goods and services. The government may resort to **rationing**, or limiting, items that are in short supply. Shortages also may lead to a **black market**, in which illegally high prices are charged for items that are in short supply.

Price Floors A **price floor**, in contrast, is a government-set minimum price that can be charged for goods and services. Price floors—more common than price ceilings—prevent prices from dropping too low. When are low prices a problem? Assume that about 30 of your classmates all want jobs after school. The local fast-food restaurant can hire 30 students at $4.15 an hour, but the government has set a minimum wage—a price floor—of $5.15 an hour. At that wage, not all of you will get hired, which will lead to a surplus of unemployed workers as shown in *Graph B* of Figure 7.13. If the market was left on its own, you and all of your classmates would be working at the equilibrium price of $4.15 per hour.

rationing: the distribution of goods and services based on something other than price

black market: "underground" or illegal market in which goods are traded at prices above their legal maximum prices or in which illegal goods are sold

price floor: a legal minimum price below which a good or service may not be sold

Skills Handbook

*See page **R47** to learn about Making Predictions.*

✔ **Reading Check** **Predicting Consequences** What two problems might be caused by price ceilings?

---

section 4 Review

Vocabulary
1. **Explain** the significance of: equilibrium price, shortage, surplus, price ceiling, rationing, black market, price floor.

Main Ideas
2. **Identifying Cause and Effect** Create a diagram like the one below to show how shortages and surpluses affect prices.

3. **Explaining** How does a shortage of tickets to a professional sports event determine the price of those tickets?

Critical Thinking
4. **The Big Ideas** How are equilibrium prices determined?
5. **Analyzing Visuals** Look at the charts in Figure 7.13 on page 198. What would happen to the equilibrium price on apartment rentals if the price ceiling was raised to $700?

Applying Economics
6. **Extending the Content** In a free-market economy, how much and how often do you believe the government should intervene by setting price floors and ceilings? Why?

Demand and Supply **199**

ECONOMIST
(1967–)

Steven Levitt

● **Rogue Economist**

■ Professor of Economics, University of Chicago

■ Editor, *Journal of Political Economy,* and Associate Editor, *Quarterly Journal of Economics*

■ Author of dozens of articles in scholarly journals

Economics is sometimes called "the dismal science," but it becomes anything but dismal when filtered through the mind of University of Chicago professor Steven Levitt. The topics that this Harvard-educated economist writes about include teachers who fix test results, sumo wrestlers who throw matches, and drug dealers who live with their mothers. In the process he has become a lightening rod for controversy.

In Levitt's view, economics is a science with excellent tools for gaining answers but a serious shortage of interesting questions. His particular gift is the ability to ask such questions. When asked why he investigates such problems as cheating sumo wrestlers, he replied, "Because it's fun. The kind of problems I like are problems which look hard but are easy. Finding cheaters often has that characteristic."

A popular approach to his research was published in 2005 in a book entitled *Freakonomics: A Rogue Economist Explores the Hidden Side of Everything,* which Levitt cowrote with Stephen J. Dubner. The book refers to Levitt as a "rogue" economist, meaning he tackles economic issues in an unconventional way. As he explains,

> **When the book calls me a rogue, we mean it in the 'mischievously playful' sense. . . . The rogue I have in mind is someone who strays from the subjects deemed appropriate for an economist, fails to treat economics with the necessary sense of seriousness. . . .**

Checking for Understanding

1. **Explaining** According to Levitt, what is the main problem with studying economics?

2. **Analyzing** What is meant by the term "rogue economist," and why does Levitt consider himself one?

■ The **law of demand** states that as price goes up, quantity demanded goes down. As price goes down, quantity demanded goes up.

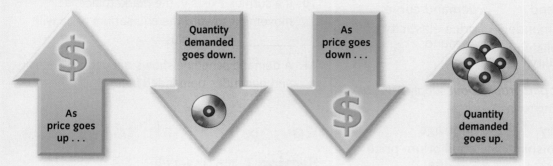

As price goes up . . .

Quantity demanded goes down.

As price goes down . . .

Quantity demanded goes up.

■ The **law of supply** states that as price goes up, quantity supplied also goes up. As price goes down, quantity supplied goes down.

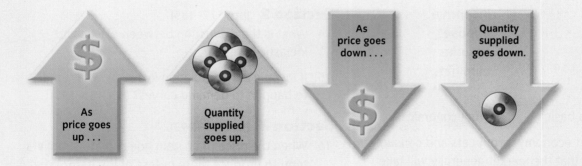

As price goes up . . .

Quantity supplied goes up.

As price goes down . . .

Quantity supplied goes down.

■ The point at which the quantity demanded and the quantity supplied meet is called the **equilibrium price**.

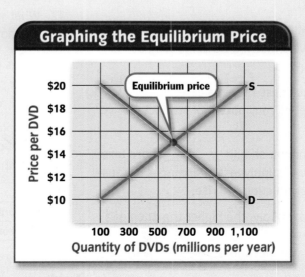

Graphing the Equilibrium Price

Equilibrium price

Price per DVD

$20 $18 $16 $14 $12 $10

S

D

Quantity of DVDs (millions per year)
100 300 500 700 900 1,100

Review Content Vocabulary

1. *Write a short paragraph about demand using all of the following terms.*

   law of demand   demand curve
   quantity demanded   price elasticity of
   law of diminishing   demand
   marginal utility

2. *Write a short paragraph about supply using all of the following terms.*

   law of supply   shortage
   law of diminishing   equilibrium price
   returns   surplus
   supply curve

Review Academic Vocabulary

Choose the term that best completes each sentence below.

   analysis   incentive
   alternate   impose
   visual   assume
   concept   eliminate
   specific

3. Choice is a basic _____ in economics.

4. In a market economy, producers and consumers _____ that the market generally will take care of itself.

5. A demand schedule shows the quantities of a good or service that will be demanded at _____ prices.

6. Opening a business requires careful _____ of the market of your potential product or service.

7. If the government should _____ more taxes, businesses will supply less at all prices because the cost of production will rise.

8. In the case of supply, the higher the price of a good, the greater the _____ is for a producer to produce more.

9. If the price of your favorite soft drink goes up, you may choose to purchase an _____ brand.

10. If a surplus exists in the marketplace, a movement toward the equilibrium price will _____ the surplus.

11. A demand schedule shows data about prices and quantities demanded in a _____ way.

Review the Main Ideas

Section 1 (pp. 169–175)

12. What is the basis of most activity in a market economy?

13. What generally happens to quantity demanded when the price of a good goes up (and other prices stay the same)?

Section 2 (pp. 177–185)

14. What is the distinction between elastic and inelastic demand?

15. If income and population increase, what tends to happen to demand curves? (pp. 186–193)

Section 3 (pp. 186–193)

16. When the price of an item goes up, do suppliers tend to produce more or less of the item? Why?

17. What would an increase in taxes do to the position of the supply curve?

Section 4 (pp. 194–199)

18. If the price of a product is above its equilibrium price, what is the result?

19. Complete the graphic organizer by listing how producers and consumers act during surpluses and shortages.

	Producers	Consumers
Surpluses		
Shortages		

Math Practice

20. **Using Graphs** Nancy, the owner of a small café, is trying to set a price for the new sandwich she is offering. In order to do so, she wants to find the equilibrium price. She collects information on how many sandwiches she can expect to sell at different prices. Using the information below, create a graph of the supply and demand curves. Use the graph in **Figure 7.10** on page 195 as an example. After you have created the graph, determine the equilibrium price of the new sandwich.

Nancy's Sandwiches

Quantity Demanded	Price	Quantity Supplied
1	$8.00	8
2	$7.50	7
3	$7.00	6
4	$6.50	5
5	$6.00	4
6	$5.50	3
7	$5.00	2
8	$4.50	1

Economics ONLINE

Self-Check Quiz Visit the *Economics Today and Tomorrow* Web site at glencoe.com and click on *Chapter 7—Self-Check Quizzes* to assess your knowledge of chapter content.

Critical Thinking

21. **The BIG IDEAS** Some prices in the American economy almost never change, whereas others change all the time, even daily. Make a list of products whose prices change slowly, if at all. Make another list of products whose prices change quickly. Finally, write a short paragraph summarizing why prices change slowly or quickly for various products.

22. **Making Predictions** How do you think the market demand curve for pizza would be affected by (1) an increase in everyone's pay, (2) a successful pizza advertising campaign, (3) a decrease in the price of hamburgers, and (4) new people moving into the community? Explain your answers.

23. **Making Comparisons** How do you think the price elasticity of demand for DVDs compares to that of insulin needed by diabetics? Why?

Analyzing Visuals

24. Study the cartoon on the right, and then answer the following questions.

   a. According to the cartoon, why has demand for movies dropped?

   b. What other reasons could there be for fewer people going to see the movies?

   c. If demand for movies continues to drop, how will movie producers most likely respond?

Rogers © 2005 Pittsburgh Post-Gazette/Dist. by United Features Syndicate

Why are the salaries of professional sports stars so high?

THE ISSUE

In the 2004–2005 basketball season, the Miami Heat's Shaquille O'Neal brought in a salary of almost 28 million dollars. Allan Houston of the New York Knicks and Chris Webber of the Philadelphia 76ers each earned over $17.5 million. Even on the pro basketball team with the lowest median salary, the New Jersey Nets, the players' average earnings were close to a million dollars. These are very large salaries. Why do professional sports stars make so much money?

THE FACTS

Have you ever heard people complain about how many important, worthy professions, such as teaching and nursing, are underpaid, while professional baseball, football, and basketball players often make huge amounts of money? Study the charts below to compare the salaries of the 10 highest-paid NBA players in 2005 with those of 10 common U.S. professions. As you can see, the difference between what a top NBA player makes and what "ordinary Americans" make is huge. Yet, some people would argue that nurses benefit society greatly by saving lives, and teachers have a tremendous impact on the nation's young people, while basketball players merely provide entertainment. So, from an economic standpoint, how can these salary differences be justified?

The NBA's Highest-Paid Players, 2004-2005		
Player	**Team**	**Salary**
1. Shaquille O'Neal	Miami Heat	$27,696,430
2. Allan Houston	New York Knicks	$17,531,250
3. Chris Webber	Philadelphia 76ers	$17,531,250
4. Kevin Garnett	Minnesota Timberwolves	$16,000,000
5. Jason Kidd	New Jersey Nets	$14,796,000
6. Jermaine O'Neal	Indiana Pacers	$14,796,000
7. Shareef Abdur-Rahim	Portland Trail Blazers	$14,625,000
8. Ray Allen	Seattle SuperSonics	$14,625,000
9. Anfernee Hardaway	New York Knicks	$14,625,000
10. Zydrunas Ilgauskas	Cleveland Cavaliers	$14,625,000
Median salary of all NBA players: around $2,500,000		

Source: usatoday.com.

Median Salaries of 10 Common Professions 2005	
Profession	**Salary**
1. Attorney	$94,930
2. Nurse	$52,330
3. High School Teacher	$43,660
4. Computer Support Technician	$40,430
5. Restaurant Manager	$39,610
6. Real Estate Agent	$35,670
7. Administrative Assistant	$34,970
8. Social Worker	$34,820
9. Machinist	$29,720
10. Child Care Worker	$14,669

THE ECONOMIC CONNECTION: SUPPLY AND DEMAND

To a certain extent, all salaries are determined by supply and demand. A high demand for a certain profession, combined with a low supply of people able to perform the job, will generally result in a high salary for the job, and vice versa.

In the case of professional ball players, the law of supply and demand is especially important in setting salaries. The public likes to watch professional sports, and so there is a high demand for professional sports players. However, the number of people who are able to meet the physical and mental challenges of playing professional sports—that is, the supply of players—is relatively small. In this case, the demand exceeds the supply, which drives salaries up.

Also, professional basketball players are usually allowed "free agency"—that is, they are allowed to sell their services to any team willing and able to pay them what they want. When teams really want talented and popular players to play for them, they will bid against each other for the player, thus driving the players' potential salaries higher and higher.

Compare that situation with the case of high-school teachers. Although teaching is a very difficult and demanding profession, many more people are able to meet the requirements to become a teacher than are able to play basketball at a professional level. Therefore, even though the nation needs many more teachers than pro ball players, the supply of certified teachers often meets or even exceeds demand—keeping teachers' salaries relatively low and stable.

CONCLUSION

Just as the laws of supply and demand interact in the market to determine prices, they also work to determine the salaries of various professions. The first round of the 2005 NBA playoffs was viewed by over 100 million people, demonstrating a high demand for professional basketball players. However, very few people are able to play at the NBA level, so the supply of players is small. Whenever you have a very high demand combined with a very small supply, you will wind up with a very high price—or, as in this case, a Shaq-sized salary.

Shaquille O'Neal

Analyzing the Impact

1. **Synthesizing** How do you think players' salaries would be affected if free agency was not allowed? Why?

2. **Critical Thinking** How do you think the high salaries of ball players affect the ticket prices you pay? What might happen in the market if players' salaries continue to rise?

## chapter 8

Business Organizations

The **BIG Idea**

The profit motive acts as an incentive for people to produce and sell goods and services.

Why It Matters

Imagine that you want to start a business. You will need to decide what your business will do, how you would like it to be structured, and whether you would like to work alone or with a partner. In this chapter, read to learn about the different ways that businesses are organized and what it takes to start a business.

Economics ONLINE

Chapter Overview Visit the *Economics Today and Tomorrow* Web site at glencoe.com and click on *Chapter 8—Chapter Overviews* to preview chapter information.

Starting a Business

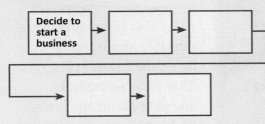
PrODUCTS In ThE NeWS
—from *Time*

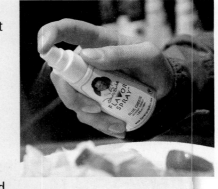

A NEW TAKE ON FLAVOR Looking for a way to add taste while cutting calories? Chef David Burke, known for his Willy Wonka-like creations at New York City restaurant davidburke & donatella, has created a line of flavor sprays that mimic the taste of high-cal foods but have no fat, calories, or carbs. Available in 18 varieties—such as Memphis BBQ, pesto and chocolate fudge—the sprays are concoctions of natural and artificial flavors. A shot of bacon can make scrambled eggs seem like a full breakfast feast, while root-beer-float or marshmallow spray may make you crave rice cakes.

How many times have you seen a product for sale and said, "That was *my* idea"? Or you see an item, nod your head, and think, "That's a good idea. I wonder how they thought of that"? Many new products and services arise from personal inspiration—as in the case of David Burke's flavor sprays. In this section, you'll learn how to take your idea and start a business.

Getting Started

Main Idea Businesses are started by entrepreneurs who are willing to take risks.

Economics & You What are your talents? Can you think of a way to turn these skills into a marketable business? Read on to learn about how to start your own business.

Careers Handbook

*See pages R76–R80 to learn about becoming an **electrician**.*

entrepreneur: person who organizes, manages, and assumes the risks of a business in order to gain profits

Imagine that you have been tinkering with electronic equipment since you were a child. By now you can take apart and reassemble CD and DVD players, most computers, and other electronic equipment without difficulty. You are so good at repairing this kind of equipment that you have been doing it for friends and relatives for some time. Then an idea occurs to you: Why not charge people for your services? Why not go into business for yourself?

A person who starts his or her own business is an **entrepreneur**—a person willing to take a risk. People usually decide to start a business to gain profits, to "do something on their own," or to be their own boss.

After making the decision to start a business, entrepreneurs must gather the **relevant** factors of production to produce their good or service and decide on the form of business organization that best suits their purposes. (You'll learn about the different types of business organizations in Sections 2 and 3.)

Anyone hoping to become an entrepreneur must also learn as much as possible about the business he or she plans to start. This process includes learning about the laws, regulations, and tax codes that will apply to the business. An entrepreneur should also investigate potential competition.

Entrepreneurship

Entrepreneurs are willing to take risks to gain a profit and be their own bosses.

Figure 8.1 — Sources of Help for Business Startups

■ If you want to start a small business, there are many sources of information available to you, and some may provide funding as well. You should investigate all of these sources in the beginning stages of your planning.

Small Business Administration

Local colleges and universities

Local departments of commerce

Small-business incubators

Business-related Internet sites

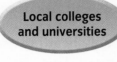

Economic Analysis

Explaining *What type of help might an entrepreneur get from a small-business incubator?*

Help From Government For a person who wants to start a small business, help is available. (See **Figure 8.1** above.) The federal government's Small Business Administration often helps finance **startups**, or new small businesses. State departments of commerce and community affairs also offer assistance. Many community college and university campuses have small-business development centers that are federally funded to help small businesses get started.

A **small-business incubator** might also aid businesses in your area. Just as incubators help hatch chicks, there are business incubators that help "hatch" small businesses. They are often operated with state and federal funds. A small-business incubator might provide a low-rent building, management advice, and computers. The incubator's goal is to **generate** job creation and economic growth, particularly in economically depressed areas.

Help From the Internet Although new entrepreneurs can get help from government agencies, the Internet also provides a huge amount of information on how to start a business. By using search engines, you can find Web sites that explain everything from putting together a business plan to learning the "secrets to success."

startup: a beginning business enterprise

small-business incubator: private- or government-funded agency that assists new businesses by providing advice or low-rent buildings and supplies

Economics ONLINE

Student Web Activity
Visit the *Economics Today and Tomorrow* Web site at glencoe.com and click on *Chapter 8—Student Web Activities* to learn more about the Small Business Administration.

✓ Reading Check **Analyzing** Why do entrepreneurs make the decision to start a business?

Elements of Business Operation

Main Idea There are four basic elements of business operation: expenses, advertising, record keeping, and risk.

Economics & You What stops you from starting your own business every time you have a good idea for a product or service? Read on to learn about the risks and expenses involved in business operation.

Every business must consider four basic elements: expenses, advertising, record keeping, and risk. (See **Figure 8.2** below.)

Expenses You've probably heard the saying, "You have to spend money to make money." This is true when considering business expenses: new equipment, wages, insurance, taxes, electricity, telephone service, and so on. And depending on the kind of job you do, you may need replacement parts. At first, you might buy parts only as you need them for a particular job. In time, you will find it easier to have an **inventory**, or supply of items that are used in your business.

inventory: extra supply of the items used in a business, such as raw materials or goods for sale

---

Figure 8.2 | Elements of Business Operation

■ Every small business presents its owner with unique issues and challenges, but they all have some elements in common as well. These common elements include expenses, advertising, record keeping, and risk.

▼ **B. Advertising** The cost of advertising can cut into profits, especially in the startup phase of a business.

▲ **A. Expenses** Expenses include the supplies you need to do your job. If you start a painting business, for example, your expenses will include brushes, paint, and ladders. As your business grows, you might buy more expensive equipment, like paint sprayers and sanders.

rainbow painting company

We Paint:
Houses,
Fences,
Decks,
and Trim.

Outdoor Work
Reasonable Rates

Pam Bowe and associates

Wages are an expense. Because you could be working for someone else and earning an income, you should pay yourself a wage equal to what you could earn elsewhere. It's important not to forget this *opportunity cost* when you figure out the true profits and losses that your new business is making.

Will your business make a profit? Add your wages to your other expenses, including taxes. Then subtract your total expenses from your **receipts,** or the money income you've received from customers, and you will have your profit. Keep records of how much you owe and to whom, and of how much your business is taking in. You will need this information to do your taxes.

receipts: income received from the sale of goods and/or services; also, slips of paper documenting a purchase

Advertising

When you start a business, you must make potential customers aware that your goods or services are available for a price. You could have flyers printed and distributed to advertise your business. You could also buy advertising space in newspapers, in community newsletters, or on various Web sites.

D. Risk Many startups fail. If you work for a boss, your overall risks are usually small. As your own boss, your risks are greater, but so are your potential rewards.

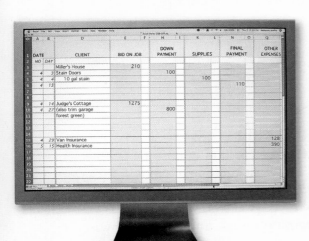

C. Record Keeping
Maintaining accurate records of your expenses and receipts is vital, especially when you're doing your taxes.

Economic Analysis

Examining *What expenses other than supplies might a small-business owner have?*

Record Keeping No matter how small your business, having a system to track your expenses and income is key to your success. Probably one of the first things you'll need is a computer. You should also purchase or download from the Internet the programs that will allow you to track your expenses and receipts. These programs write checks, calculate your monthly profits and losses, tell you the difference between what you own and what you owe (called *net worth*), and so on.

The slips of paper that **document** your purchases of supplies—also known as *receipts*—must be filed in a safe place. All legitimate business expenses can be deducted from business receipts before taxes owed are calculated. Taxes are assessed only on *net business income.* Here is where you see how important record keeping is.

Risk Every business involves risks. You must balance the risks against the advantages of being in business for yourself. For example, if you spend part of your savings to pay for advertising and equipment, you are taking a risk. You may not get enough business to cover these costs.

Farcus

by David Waisglass
Gordon Coulthart

Farcus® is reprinted with permission from Laughing Stock Licensing Inc., Ottawa, Canada. All Rights Reserved.

WAISGLASS/COULTHART

"Sure, I'd like to start my own business ... but, frankly, I think it's too risky."

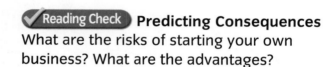 **Reading Check** **Predicting Consequences**
What are the risks of starting your own business? What are the advantages?

---

section 1 Review

Vocabulary
1. **Explain** the significance of: entrepreneur, startup, small-business incubator, inventory, receipts.

Main Ideas
2. **Identifying** Copy the diagram below, and list four ways the government provides funds for businesses.

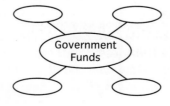

Government Funds

Critical Thinking
3. **The BIG Idea** Explain why some people would rather risk taking a loss in a business of their own rather than work for a wage.
4. **Determining Cause and Effect** Why is the government willing to provide start-up funds to entrepreneurs?

Applying Economics
5. **Entrepreneurship** Find a business in your area owned by an entrepreneur. Invite the person to speak to your class, or interview the person and read the interview aloud to the class.

Sole Proprietorships and Partnerships

GUIDE TO READING

Section Preview
In this section, you will learn about common ways to organize a business.

Content Vocabulary
- sole proprietorship *(p. 214)*
- proprietor *(p. 214)*
- unlimited liability *(p. 214)*
- assets *(p. 214)*
- partnership *(p. 215)*
- limited partnership *(p. 216)*
- limited liability company *(p. 216)*
- joint venture *(p. 216)*

Academic Vocabulary
- potential *(p. 215)*
- temporary *(p. 216)*

Reading Strategy
Comparing As you read, complete a table like the one below by listing the advantages and disadvantages of three common types of business organizations.

Business Type	Advantage(s)	Disadvantage(s)
Sole Proprietorship		
Partnership		
Limited Partnership		

PEOPLE In ThE NeWS
—from the *Fresno Bee*

YOUNG ENTREPRENEURS Travis Pierce hasn't graduated from high school yet, and he's already thinking about how many businesses he would like to own. The Clovis High School student wants to open an entertainment club for young people, become an accountant, and dabble in real estate investment.

▲ Young entrepreneurs' meeting

Although the 17-year-old student's ideas may seem lofty, Travis joins a growing number of American teenagers interested in becoming their own bosses.

. . . Hoping to fuel young people's interest in business, Junior Achievement and the U.S. Small Business Administration have created a Web site—www.mindyourownbiz.org—aimed at providing the tools and resources they need for becoming an entrepreneur. The SBA also has its own Web site, www.sba.gov/teens.

Businesses can be organized in a number of ways. As the story above shows, many young people dream of starting their own business and being their own boss. Single-owner businesses, however, are only one option available to people who want to work for themselves. In this section, you'll learn that the two most common ways of organizing businesses in the United States are sole proprietorships and partnerships.

Sole Proprietorships

Main Idea A sole proprietorship is a business owned and operated by one person.

Economics & You If you were to start a business, would you rather work alone or with a partner? Read on to learn about businesses owned and operated by one person.

sole proprietorship: business owned and operated by one person

proprietor: owner of a business

The most common form of business organization is the **sole proprietorship,** a business owned by one person. A **proprietor** is the owner of a business. The United States has about 18 million sole proprietorships. You probably have contact with many sole proprietorships without realizing it.

There are advantages and disadvantages to being a sole proprietor. A proprietor may get satisfaction from being the boss and creatively making the business into whatever he or she wants it to be. Running a business alone is demanding and time-consuming, however.

The financial risk also has advantages and disadvantages. If the business does well, the proprietor receives all the profits. Also, taxes on a sole proprietorship are usually low because a business owner pays income taxes only on profits. At the same time, the owner also has **unlimited liability**—complete legal responsibility for all debts and damages arising from doing business. Personal **assets,** or items of value such as houses, cars, jewelry, and so on, may be seized to pay off business debts.

unlimited liability: requirement that an owner is personally and fully responsible for all losses and debts of a business

assets: all items to which a business or household holds legal claim

Reading Check **Explaining** What is meant by unlimited liability? What effect does this have on a sole proprietor?

Figure 8.3 | Two Types of Businesses

■ Sole proprietorships and partnerships are two common ways that businesses are organized.

A. Sole Proprietorships
People who run their own businesses enjoy having creative control and being their own boss. Operating a sole proprietorship, though, is also a huge responsibility. The proprietor must handle all the decision making, even when the problem is unfamiliar.

Partnerships

Main Idea A partnership is a business owned and operated by two or more individuals.

Economics & You Have you ever worked with a partner on a school project? What were some of the advantages and disadvantages of this arrangement? Read on to learn about partnerships in business.

Earlier in this chapter, we imagined that you had started an electronics repair business. Suppose your business is doing so well that your workload becomes overwhelming, leaving you little time to do anything else. You could expand your business by hiring an employee. You also need financial capital to buy new equipment, but you would rather not take out a loan. So, you decide to take on a partner.

In a **partnership,** two or more individuals own and operate a business. Partners sign an agreement that is legally binding. It describes the duties of each partner, the division of profits, and the distribution of assets should the partners end the agreement.

Partnerships are usually more efficient than proprietorships because each partner can work in his or her area of expertise. As with sole proprietorships, taxes tend to be low because partners pay income tax only on their share of the profits. Because the partners have to work together, however, decision making is often slower, and disagreements can lead to problems.

A partnership's borrowing **potential** is generally very good. Because the combined value of the partners' personal and business assets is usually greater than that of a sole proprietor, creditors are willing to lend more because these same assets can be taken over if the partnership fails to repay the loan.

partnership: business that two or more individuals own and operate

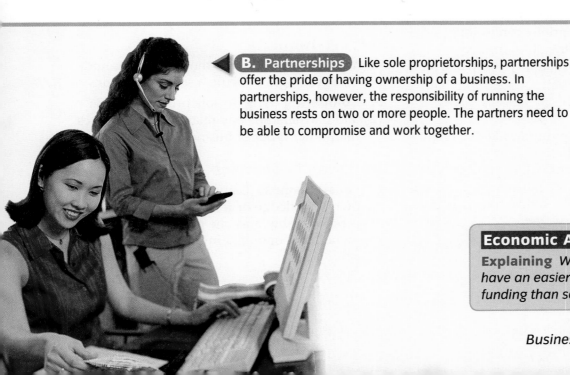

B. Partnerships Like sole proprietorships, partnerships offer the pride of having ownership of a business. In partnerships, however, the responsibility of running the business rests on two or more people. The partners need to be able to compromise and work together.

Economic Analysis

Explaining *Why do partners often have an easier time obtaining funding than sole proprietors do?*

limited partnership: special form of partnership in which one or more partners have limited liability but no voice in management

limited liability company: type of business enterprise that protects members against losing all of their personal wealth; members are taxed as if they were in a partnership

joint venture: partnership set up for a specific purpose for a short period of time

Some partnerships are specialized. In a **limited partnership,** not all of the partners are equal. One partner is called the *general partner.* This person (or persons) assumes all of the management duties and has full responsibility for the debts of the partnership. The other partners are *limited* because they only contribute funds or property to the business. They have no say in the management of the business, but they also have no liability for business losses other than their initial investment.

Another type of business structure that creates benefits for businesspersons is called a **limited liability company.** In this type of business enterprise, so-called members often do not have to worry about losing their personal wealth if the business fails with a lot of debts. Limited liability companies are similar to corporations (which you will read about in the next section), but they are taxed as if they were partnerships.

Finally, a **joint venture** is a **temporary** partnership created to accomplish a specific task for a short period of time. Once the task is completed, the joint venture is ended. A common example is when investors purchase real estate and then resell the property for a profit.

Reading Check **Determining Cause and Effect** Why would an entrepreneur want to take on a partner when starting a business?

section 2 Review

Vocabulary
1. **Explain** the significance of: sole proprietorship, proprietor, unlimited liability, assets, partnership, limited partnership, limited liability company, joint venture.

Main Ideas
2. **Synthesizing** In a pyramid like the one below, rank the following four types of businesses in order of risk to you, with the highest risk at the top: partnership, limited partnership, limited liability company, sole proprietorship.

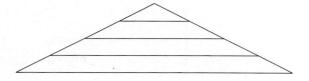

3. **Comparing** What is one advantage of a joint venture?

Critical Thinking
4. **The BIG Idea** Explain the advantages and disadvantages of being a sole proprietor.
5. **Comparing** Why do sole proprietorships and partnerships pay relatively lower taxes than other types of business organizations?

Applying Economics
6. **Local Business** Using the Internet or your own knowledge or research, list one sole proprietorship and one partnership that is owned and operated in your community or city.

People and Perspectives

Indra K. Nooyi

- President and Chief Financial Officer of PepsiCo, Inc.

- ■ Board member of Motorola, the International Rescue Committee, the Lincoln Center for the Performing Arts, and the Asia Society
- ■ Serves on the Advisory Boards of the Yale School of Management and the Greenwich Breast Cancer Alliance

At one time the lead guitarist in an all-female rock band in India, Indra Nooyi is now president and chief financial officer of Pepsico, Inc. How does a young woman from Chennai, India, become a top executive at the giant corporation that owns Pepsi-Cola, Frito-Lay, Gatorade, Tropicana, Quaker Oats, and hundreds of other brands around the globe?

"To the extent that I have succeeded in finding happiness as a sister, a wife, a mom, an Indian daughter and daughter-in-law (both have their own challenges!), and as a business leader, I found that five simple principles have guided me over the years.

The 1st Principle that helped guide my life, is: *Whatever you choose to do, aim high . . . and put your heart into it.*

The 2nd Principle . . . is: *Never stop learning.* Some people think learning ends when you leave school. They are terribly misguided.

The 3rd Principle . . . is: *Keep an open mind.* Treat others with the same respect and dignity that you want others to treat you.

The 4th Principle . . . is: It's important to remember that we're all individuals. . . . [N]ever hide what makes you, you. *Always be yourself.*

> **The 5th Principle that helped guide my life is the most important of all:** *Remember the three things that are most important in life . . . family . . . friends . . . and faith.*

Nooyi remains true to her Indian identity. She often wears a sari, and in her home in Connecticut there is a *puja,* or Hindu prayer room. And she still plays her electric guitar.

Checking for Understanding

1. **Discussing** Of the many roles Nooyi plays, which seem to be the most important to her? How can you tell?
2. **Defending** Which of Nooyi's five principles is the most important to you? Why?

The Corporate World and Franchises

GUIDE TO READING

Section Preview
In this section, you will learn about the characteristics and structure of corporations and franchises.

Content Vocabulary
- corporation *(p. 219)*
- stock *(p. 219)*
- limited liability *(p. 220)*
- articles of incorporation *(p. 220)*
- corporate charter *(p. 220)*
- common stock *(p. 221)*
- dividend *(p. 221)*
- preferred stock *(p. 221)*
- bylaws *(p. 221)*
- franchise *(p. 222)*

Academic Vocabulary
- visible *(p. 219)*
- distinct *(p. 219)*
- annual *(p. 221)*

Reading Strategy
Sequencing As you read, complete a flowchart like the one below by filling in the steps necessary to form a corporation.

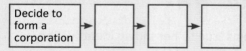

Decide to form a corporation → ☐ → ☐ → ☐

PeOPLE In ThE NeWS
—from *Entrepreneur.com*

YOUNG FRANCHISORS While practically everyone has heard of Subway, not many people know that its founder, Fred DeLuca, started the sandwich juggernaut as a 17-year-old college student in 1965. Nearly 40 years later, he's inspiring other young people to choose their own destinies. Working at the local Subway has become almost a rite of passage for teenagers, as it was for Devin Smith back in 1994. He, like DeLuca, was 17 when he began his relationship with Subway—Smith worked there part time during high school and college before graduating to the next level at Subway: ownership.

▲ Fred DeLuca, Subway founder, with employees

Smith isn't the only early achiever looking beyond the corporate path. Brandon Gough, president of Juice It Up! Franchise Corporation, notes a recent increase in younger applicants interested in the smoothie franchise.

Profits are a good thing. As a sole proprietor, you keep all the profits. In a partnership, you share the profits with one or several partners. In a corporation, however, the profits are dispersed among thousands of shareholders. So why do entrepreneurs incorporate, or form corporations? In this section, read to learn why and how corporations are formed.

Corporations and Their Structure

Main Idea Stock represents ownership rights to a certain portion of a corporation's profits and assets.

Economics & You What do you think of when you picture a corporation? Profit? A complicated structure? Read on to learn about the characteristics of corporations.

Suppose your electronics repair business that we discussed at the beginning of this chapter has grown. You now have several partners and have turned your garage into a shop. You would like to expand and rent a store so that your business is more **visible.** You would also like to buy the latest equipment, charge a little less than your competitors, and capture a larger share of the market. You need financial capital, however.

You have decided that you do not want any more partners. You no longer want to consult with them about every detail of the business. What you want are financial backers who will let you use their funds while letting you run the business. You are proposing a corporation.

What Is a Corporation?
A **corporation** is an organization owned by many people but treated by law as though it were a person. A corporation can own property, pay taxes, make contracts, sue and be sued, and so on. It has a separate and **distinct** existence from the stockholders who own the corporation's stock. **Stock** represents ownership rights to a certain portion of the future profits and assets of the company that issues the stock.

Skills Handbook

See page **R48** to learn about **Problems and Solutions.**

corporation: type of business organization owned by many people but treated by law as though it were a person; it can own property, pay taxes, make contracts, and so on

stock: share of ownership in a corporation that entitles the buyer to a certain part of the future profits and assets of the corporation

The Biggest of Them All

In the early 2000s, Wal-Mart became the biggest corporation in the United States. In 2005, $8.90 out of every $100 spent in U.S. retail stores was spent at Wal-Mart. Although Wal-Mart offers low prices to consumers and employs a large number of people, some critics maintain that small businesses suffer from the intense competition.

In terms of the amount of business done (measured in dollars), the corporation is the most significant type of business organization in the United States today. See **Figure 8.4** below to compare corporations with other forms of businesses.

One of the major advantages of a corporation is **limited liability.** If a corporation goes bankrupt or is sued, the stockholders' losses are limited to their investment in the firm. A major disadvantage of corporations is that they are taxed more heavily than other forms of business organizations. In order to form a corporation, its founders must do three things. First, they must register their company with the government of the state in which it will be headquartered. Second, they must sell stock. Third, along with the other shareholders, they must elect a board of directors.

Registering the Corporation Every state has laws governing the formation of corporations, but most state laws are similar. Suppose that you and your partners decide to form a corporation. You will have to file the **articles of incorporation** with the state in which you will run your corporation. In general, these articles include four items:

(1) Name, address, and purpose of the corporation;
(2) Names and addresses of the initial board of directors;
(3) Number of shares of stock to be issued;
(4) Amount of money capital to be raised through issuing stock.

If the articles are in agreement with state law, the state will grant you a **corporate charter**—a license to operate from that state.

limited liability: requirement in which an owner's responsibility for a company's debts is limited to the size of the owner's investment in the firm

articles of incorporation: document listing basic information about a corporation that is filed with the state where the corporation will be headquartered

corporate charter: license to operate granted to a corporation by the state where it is established

---

Figure 8.4 | **Comparing Corporations, Partnerships, and Proprietorships**

■ As you can see, although corporations make up only about 20 percent of all businesses in the United States, they earn about 85 percent of all business revenues.

Graphs In Motion
See StudentWorks™ Plus or go to glencoe.com.

Economic Analysis
Using Graphs *What percent of business revenues do nonincorporated businesses generate?*

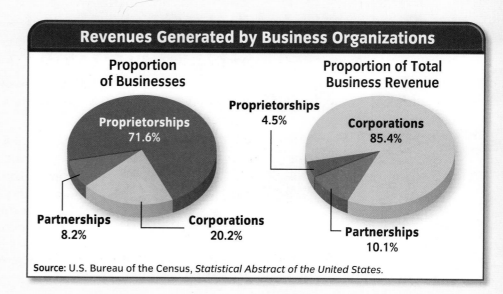

Revenues Generated by Business Organizations

Proportion of Businesses
- Proprietorships 71.6%
- Partnerships 8.2%
- Corporations 20.2%

Proportion of Total Business Revenue
- Proprietorships 4.5%
- Corporations 85.4%
- Partnerships 10.1%

Source: U.S. Bureau of the Census, *Statistical Abstract of the United States.*

Board of Directors' Meeting

Members of a corporation's board of directors are elected by the stockholders. The board will often meet to discuss corporate strategy, but it does not get involved in the day-to-day operations of a business.

Selling Stock To raise funds for the expansion of your electronics repair business, you could sell shares of stock in your new corporation. **Common stock** gives the investor part ownership in the corporation, a right to a percentage of the company's future profits, and voting rights at the **annual** stockholders' meeting. It does not, however, guarantee a **dividend**—a money return on the money invested in a company's stock. Holders of **preferred stock** do not have voting rights in the corporation, but they are guaranteed a certain amount of dividend each year. Plus, if the corporation goes out of business, holders of preferred stock have first claim on whatever value is left after creditors have been paid.

common stock: shares of ownership in a corporation that give stockholders voting rights and a portion of future profits (after holders of preferred stock are paid)

dividend: portion of a corporation's profits paid to its stockholders

Naming a Board of Directors To become incorporated, a company must have a board of directors. You and your partners, as founders of your corporation, would select the first board. After that, stockholders would elect the board. The bylaws of the corporation govern this election. **Bylaws** are a set of rules describing how stock will be sold and dividends paid, with a list of the duties of the company's officers. They are written after the corporate charter has been granted.

preferred stock: shares of ownership in a corporation that give stockholders a portion of future profits (before any profits go to holders of common stock), but no voting rights

The board is responsible for supervising and controlling the corporation. It does not run business operations on a day-to-day basis. Instead, it hires officers for the company—president, vice president(s), secretary, and treasurer—to run the business and hire other employees.

bylaws: a set of rules describing how stock will be sold and dividends paid

Reading Check **Examining** What are a major advantage and a major disadvantage of incorporating?

Franchises

Main Idea A franchise is an arrangement in which a person or group obtains the right to use the name and sell the products of another business.

Economics & You Can you find your favorite fast-food restaurant when you travel? If so, then the restaurant is probably a franchise. Read on to learn about franchising a business.

franchise: contract in which one business (the franchisor) sells to another business (the franchisee) the right to use the franchisor's name and sell its products

Many hotel, motel, gas station, and fast-food chains are franchises. A **franchise** is a contract in which a firm—usually a corporation—sells to a person or group of people the right to use its name and sell its products. In return, the person or group makes certain payments and meets certain requirements. The corporation, or parent company, is called the *franchisor*, and the person or group buying these rights is called the *franchisee*.

The franchisee pays a fee to the franchisor that may include a percentage of all revenues taken in. If a person buys a motel franchise, for example, that person agrees to pay the motel chain a certain initial fee plus a portion of the profits for as long as his or her motel stays in business. In return, the chain will help the franchisee set up the motel. Often, the chain will have a training program to teach the franchisee about the business and set the standards of business operations.

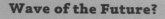

Wave of the Future?

Franchises exploded onto the retail scene in the 1950s with the development of fast-food chains. Their numbers have continued to increase over the years. Today, Subway sandwich shops are one of the most common and popular franchises in the United States.

Franchise Rules

Franchise agreements usually require the franchisee to meet certain quality standards decided on by the franchisor. For example, all Subway franchises are required to use freshly baked bread and fresh ingredients, and employees must assemble sandwiches in front of the customers.

Advantages of Franchising The main reasons people choose to open franchises rather than start their own businesses are name recognition and a proven way of doing business. If the parent company is already successful, it has figured out a way to market its products or services effectively. The franchisee can follow this method rather than coming up with an original plan that may or may not work. In addition, parent companies generally spend a great deal on advertising. Think of how often you see ads for popular franchises like McDonald's, Burger King, Wendy's, and Pizza Hut. The franchisee benefits from this advertising without having to pay for it. Because of these advantages, the success rate of franchises is much higher than that of independently owned businesses.

Disadvantages of Franchising For franchisees, the main disadvantage is a loss of control. While they gain the use of a business plan, training, and marketing, they give up the freedom to run their business as they'd like. Also, franchise arrangements sometimes run into legal trouble if one of the parties fails to hold up its side of the agreement.

✓ **Reading Check** **Analyzing** Why might someone purchase a franchise rather than start his or her own business?

section 3 Review

Vocabulary

1. **Explain** the significance of: corporation, stock, limited liability, articles of incorporation, corporate charter, common stock, dividend, preferred stock, bylaws, franchise.

Main Ideas

2. **Comparing and Contrasting** Copy the diagram below, and list the advantages and disadvantages of incorporating a business.

Incorporating	
Advantages	Disadvantages

3. **The BIG Idea** The goal of business is to make a profit. Who gets the profits in a proprietorship? A partnership? A corporation?

Critical Thinking

4. **Evaluating** Imagine you have $1,000 to invest. Would you buy preferred stock or common stock? Why?

Applying Economics

5. **Franchising** Successful entrepreneurship can be profitable but carries risk. Write a paragraph explaining why franchising is less risky than being a sole proprietor. Use at least four examples from the text.

PANERA **BREAD**

Giving Fast Food a Run for Its Money

Check It Out! In this chapter you learned about franchises and corporations. In the following article, read to learn how one franchise is "rolling in the dough."

▲ A Panera franchise in Orlando, Florida

Back in the 1980s, fast-food chains had turned into "self-serve gasoline stations for the body," says Ronald M. Shaich, CEO of Panera Bread Co. In 1993, he acquired Panera and began preaching its virtues as he opened branches across the country. "It's food you crave, food you trust." Actually, people are gobbling it up.

Panera attracts its crowds by focusing on freshness. Breads and pastries are baked at each site from dough that contains no unhealthy trans fats. Shaich revitalizes Panera's menu every two months with a new sandwich or salad. To cover the increased cost, it had to hike sandwich prices by 7%, to $4.99-plus. But the customers who frequent the chain didn't balk. Fans don't mind

paying a premium for its healthy alternatives. The average Panera patron spends $8.51 on lunch, vs. an industry average of $4.55. Panera has trounced many fast-food competitors in average sales per store.

Panera's expansion—and Shaich's eye for spotting trends early—has helped the chain withstand lean times. In 2003, Americans went on a low-carbohydrate kick. With "bread" in its name, Panera suddenly landed on the do-not-eat list of many Atkins Diet followers. So Shaich acted fast to boost the salad lineup and low-carb, whole-grain breads. High marks from customers are projected to push Panera's revenues to $1 billion in 2007.

—Reprinted from *BusinessWeek*

Annual Per-Store Sales of Some Major U.S. Chain Restaurants

Panera Bread
McDonald's
Denny's
Boston Market
Dunkin' Donuts

$1 $1.5 $2

Sales (in millions)

Source: Nation's Restaurant News.

Think About It

1. **Contrasting** How does Panera Bread differ from other fast-food franchises?
2. **Explaining** Owning a business means constantly tracking trends. How did Shaich avert disaster when low-carb diets emerged?

■ There are four main **elements of business operation:** expenses, advertising, record keeping, and risk.

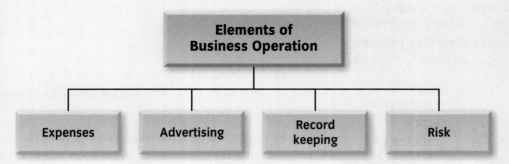

Elements of Business Operation

Expenses | Advertising | Record keeping | Risk

■ **Sole proprietorships** and **partnerships** are two common ways that businesses are organized.

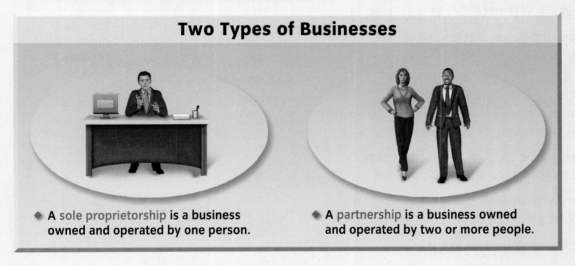

Two Types of Businesses

◆ A sole proprietorship is a business owned and operated by one person.

◆ A partnership is a business owned and operated by two or more people.

■ The majority of business revenues in the United States are brought in by **corporations,** which are owned by many people but treated by law as if they were individuals.

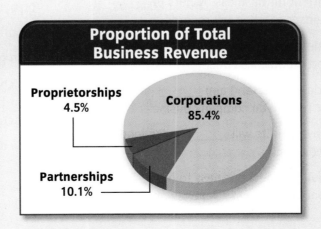

Proportion of Total Business Revenue

Proprietorships 4.5%

Corporations 85.4%

Partnerships 10.1%

Review Content Vocabulary

1. *Imagine that you are starting a business, such as a pet grooming business or a clothing store. Write a paragraph or two explaining the choices you will have to make about how your new business will be structured and run. Use all of the following terms.*

entrepreneur
startup
sole proprietorship
unlimited liability
partnership
limited partnership
joint venture

corporation
stock
articles of incorporation
limited liability
franchise

Review Academic Vocabulary

Choose the letter of the term that best completes each sentence.

a. relevant
b. generate
c. document
d. potential

e. temporary
f. visible
g. distinct
h. annual

2. Some partnerships are _____ because they are meant to end after a specific goal is met.

3. Retailers try to make their stores as _____ as possible so that more customers will see them.

4. Business owners strive to increase _____ revenue.

5. It is important for business owners to _____ their expenses for their tax records.

6. Stockholders must be informed about _____ and important business decisions.

7. Stockholders can attend a(n) _____ meeting each year to vote on company business.

8. A company's profits will _____ dividends for its stockholders.

9. It is helpful for a new business to be _____, or different in some way, from its competitors.

Review the Main Ideas

Section 1 (pp. 207–212)

10. Every business involves expenses, receipts, and record keeping. What are two other elements? Why are they important?

11. When you calculate your profits, it is especially important for you to include the value of your time. What is this called?

12. If you start a small business, you have to consider many things. Where can you look for help?

Section 2 (pp. 213–216)

13. What is the most common form of business organization?

14. Describe the characteristics of sole proprietorships, partnerships, limited partnerships, and joint ventures by filling in a diagram like the one below.

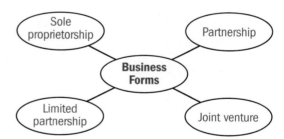

Section 3 (pp. 218–223)

15. What makes a corporation different from other forms of businesses such as sole proprietorships and partnerships?

16. Who grants corporate charters?

17. Which group within a corporation chooses the board of directors? What does the board of directors do?

18. How does a franchise operate?

Thinking Like an Economist

19. Use a chart like the one below to help you analyze and classify five or more businesses in your community. Write down a variety of businesses—retailers, service providers, "mom-and-pop" operations, businesses that serve other businesses, franchises, manufacturers, and so on. Conduct research or make educated guesses about each company's business form (sole proprietorship, partnership, corporation, franchise, etc.) and explain why you think the owner or owners chose each form.

Community Businesses		
Business name	Business form	Why owner(s) probably chose this form

Critical Thinking

20. **The BIG Idea** What is the main reason entrepreneurs are willing to take huge financial risks to start new businesses?

21. **Analyzing** Why might a person decide in favor of a partnership rather than a sole proprietorship?

22. **Determining Cause and Effect** Create a diagram like the one below, and identify three problems in a corporation that might be caused by its complex organizational structure.

Complex Corporate Structure

Problem | Problem | Problem

Analyzing Visuals

23. Study the cartoon below, and then answer the following questions.
    a. What type of business organization does Globo Tort represent?
    b. What kind of business is the Mom and Pop tortilla shop?
    c. What is the double meaning of the word *dough* in this cartoon?

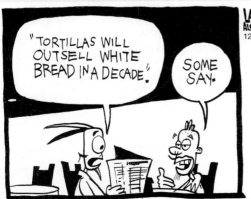

Global Economy

Demand for Oil Americans demand oil for many purposes, but mostly as a fuel for their automobiles. According to the Department of Energy, the average American drives a vehicle more than 12,000 miles and uses around 500 gallons of gasoline every year. The United States provides about 35 percent of its own oil. The remaining amount comes from various international sources, as shown in the map below.

Canada supplies 16 percent

Mexico supplies 16 percent

Caribbean Nations supply 2 percent
(Leading Sources: Virgin Islands, Trinidad and Tobago, Netherlands Antilles)

South America supplies 17 percent
(Leading Sources: Venezuela, Colombia, Ecuador)

On average, a barrel holding 42 gallons of crude oil produces 21 gallons of gasoline.

Europe supplies
4 percent
*(Leading Sources: Great
Britain, Norway, Belgium)*

Persian Gulf Region
supplies 24 percent
*(Leading Sources: Saudi
Arabia, Iraq, Kuwait)*

Other World Sources
supply 5 percent

Africa supplies
16 percent
*(Leading Sources: Nigeria,
Angola, Algeria)*

Thinking Globally

1. **Identifying** Which two regions of the world supply the most oil to the United States?

2. **Analyzing** How do you think the amount of oil supplied by a region affects the political situation between that region and the U.S.?

3. **Applying** Choose one country listed in the chart, and then use the Internet to research how much oil that country supplies to the United States. Then research the political relationship between that country and the U.S. How are the two related?

229

chapter 9

Competition and Monopolies

The **BIG Idea**

The profit motive acts as an incentive for people to produce and sell goods and services.

Why It Matters

Think about the products that you buy most frequently. Are they produced by just one company, or do you have choices about where to buy the items? In this chapter, read to learn how competition—or the lack of it—determines the prices you pay.

Economics ONLINE

Chapter Overview Visit the *Economics Today and Tomorrow* Web site at glencoe.com and click on *Chapter 9—Chapter Overviews* to preview chapter information.

GUIDE TO READING

Section Preview
In this section, you will learn about perfect competition and how this market structure benefits consumers.

Content Vocabulary
- market structure *(p. 232)*
- perfect competition *(p. 232)*

Academic Vocabulary
- initial *(p. 233)*
- interact *(p. 233)*
- unique *(p. 234)*

Reading Strategy
Organizing As you read, use a Venn diagram like the one below to explain how the concepts listed affect price under perfect competition.

Prices Under Perfect Competition

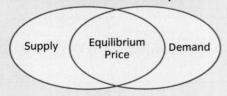

Supply — Equilibrium Price — Demand

PrODUCTS In ThE NeWS
—from *Fortune*

COCA-COLA FACES THE COMPETITION [Coca-Cola] CEO Neville Isdell has known for a long time that Coke must change if it is to prosper again. . . . The new Coca-Cola, he promised, will innovate, launching new products with strange-sounding names like Tab Energy (diet energy drink), Coca-Cola Blak (coffee Coke), and Full Throttle Fury (a citrus-flavored energy concoction).

. . . For too long Coke had stayed stubbornly, defiantly rooted in its past, holding on to the belief that its business model was as good as gold: Make cola concentrate for pennies, then sell it for dollars through a global bottling system to a mass market that still pretty much drank what it saw on TV.

. . . [However], it takes a lot more than Coke With Lime to impress the video iPod generation. They want Izzes and Starbucks and Red Bulls. They want choice, not a company telling them "Father knows best."

Competition happens when two or more companies strive against each other to convince consumers to buy their products or services. Competition is advantageous to consumers for several reasons. First, it provides us with choices. Competition is advantageous for another reason as well. Having many competing suppliers of a product, like coffee drinks, leads to lower prices. As you can imagine, for this reason each supplier would like to have as little competition as possible.

Market Structure and Perfect Competition

Main Idea Market structure refers to the extent of competition within particular markets.

Economics & You What if you could go to only one university, one doctor, or one grocery store? This situation is known as a monopoly. Read on to learn about this and other types of market structures.

market structure: the extent to which competition prevails in particular markets

perfect competition: market situation in which there are numerous buyers and sellers, and no single buyer or seller can affect price

In Chapter 8 you learned that businesses are often set up based on the number of owners—sole proprietorship, partnership, corporation. In this chapter, you'll learn that businesses are also categorized by **market structure**—or the amount of competition they face. **Figure 9.1** below shows the four basic market structures in the American economy: perfect competition, monopolistic competition, oligopoly, and monopoly. In this section you'll learn about the ideal market structure of perfect competition.

All businesses must engage in some form of competition as long as other businesses produce similar goods or services. When a market includes so many sellers of a particular good or service that each seller accounts for a small part of the total market, a special situation exists. Economists term it **perfect competition.** For perfect competition, also known as pure competition, to take place, five conditions must be met:

Figure 9.1 | Comparing Market Structures

■ Markets that are either perfectly competitive or pure monopolies are rare. Most industries in the United States fit one of the other two forms.

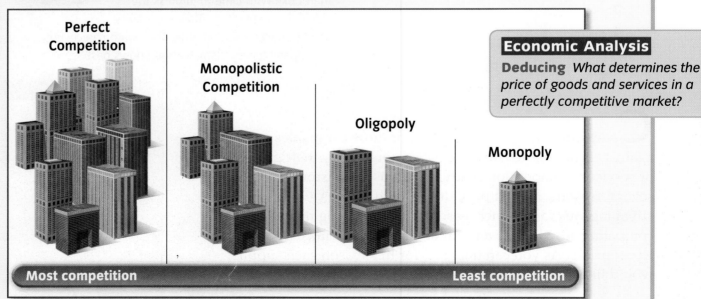

Perfect Competition

Monopolistic Competition

Oligopoly

Monopoly

Most competition · Least competition

Economic Analysis

Deducing *What determines the price of goods and services in a perfectly competitive market?*

(1) **A Large Market** Numerous buyers and sellers must exist for the product.

(2) **A Nearly Identical Product** The goods or services being sold must be nearly the same.

(3) **Easy Entry and Exit** Sellers already in the market cannot prevent competition, or entrance into the market. In addition, the **initial** costs of investment are small, and the good or service is easy to learn to produce.

(4) **Easily Obtainable Information** Information about prices, quality, and sources of supply is easy for both buyers and sellers to obtain.

(5) **Independence** The possibility of sellers or buyers working together to control the price is almost nonexistent.

No Control Over Price When the above five conditions are met, the workings of supply and demand, rather than a single seller or buyer, control the price. On the supply side, perfect competition requires a large number of suppliers of a nearly identical product. On the demand side, perfect competition requires a large number of buyers who know exactly what the market price is for the good or service.

In a perfectly competitive market, the market price is the equilibrium price. Total supply and total demand are allowed to **interact** to reach the equilibrium price—the only price at which quantity demanded equals quantity supplied. In a world of perfect competition, each individual seller would accept that price. Because so many buyers and sellers exist, one person attempting to charge a higher or lower price would not affect the market price.

Perfect Competition

At a farmers' market, you may see several different stands selling fruit, such as apples. Having a nearly identical product and easy entry into the market—such as fruit stands at farmers' markets do—are two conditions of perfect competition.

Information Is Key True perfect competition is rarely seen in the real world. Nonetheless, fierce competition does exist in many sectors of the economy. The ability of consumers to obtain information is key to sustaining competition. Today, virtually anyone with access to the Internet can find out the lowest prices of just about anything.

✓ Reading Check **Analyzing** How is the Internet important to maintaining a competitive market structure?

Agriculture as an Example

Main Idea Agricultural markets come close to a perfectly competitive market structure.

Economics & You How much does a loaf of bread cost? Does the price ever change much? Read on to learn about how the prices of many agricultural products are determined by the market.

Few perfectly competitive industries exist in the United States. One that comes close is the agricultural market. It is often used as an example of perfect competition because farmers have almost no control over the market price of their goods. (See **Figure 9.2**.)

No Control Over Wheat Prices No single wheat farmer has any great influence on wheat prices. The market price for wheat is determined by the interaction of supply and demand, and individual wheat farmers have to accept the market price. If the price is $3 per bushel, that is the price every farmer receives. Farmers who attempt to raise their price above $3 will find that no one will buy their wheat. Farmers will not be willing to sell their wheat for less than $3 per bushel.

Unique Situation The total demand for wheat and other agricultural products is somewhat different from the demand for many other products. People's demand for wheat is relatively inelastic—even if the price of wheat were to increase or drop, quantity demanded would not change significantly. The supply side of most agricultural markets is also **unique**. It is highly dependent on conditions over which farmers have little or no control, such as weather and crop disease.

Figure 9.2 — A Classic Example

■ Because the wheat market meets all of the conditions needed for perfect competition, as shown in this table, it is often used as an example of a perfectly competitive industry. True perfect competition, though, is rarely seen in the real world.

Economic Analysis

Analyzing *Do you agree that the wheat market meets all five of the conditions listed here? Why or why not?*

The Wheat Market as a Perfect Competitor

1. **A Large Market** Thousands of wheat farmers grow wheat, and thousands of wholesalers buy wheat.

2. **A Nearly Identical Product** All wheat is fairly similar.

3. **Easy Entry and Exit** The costs of renting farmland are relatively low, and farming methods can be learned.

4. **Easily Obtainable Information** Information about wheat prices is fairly easy to obtain. Indeed, it can be obtained on the Internet in a few seconds.

5. **Independence** The possibility of thousands of wheat farmers banding together to control prices is very small.

Benefits to Society The intense competition in a perfectly competitive industry forces the price down to one that just covers the costs of production plus a small profit. This price is beneficial to consumers because it means that they are paying only for what has been put in to make those products—the opportunity cost of the use of land, labor, capital, and entrepreneurship. The price that consumers pay for products under perfect competition is a correct signal about the value of those products in society.

Perfectly competitive industries yield economic efficiency. All inputs are used in the most advantageous way possible, and society therefore enjoys an efficient allocation of productive resources.

Effects on Supply

Variations in weather, including natural disasters like floods, can wipe out entire harvests. So can crop diseases and crop-destroying insects. This means that farmers may have a good harvest one year and a poor harvest the next. As a result, there are widely fluctuating supplies of goods in the agricultural market.

Reading Check **Explaining** What makes the demand for agricultural products unique?

section 1 Review

Vocabulary
1. **Explain** the significance of: market structure, perfect competition.

Main Ideas
2. **Summarizing** In a table like the one below, list the conditions that must be met for perfect competition to exist.

Perfect Competition
1.
2.
3.
4.
5.

Critical Thinking
3. **The BIG Idea** Explain how perfect competition tends to drive down profits.
4. **Analyzing** Is there any way for a seller in a perfectly competitive market to raise prices?
5. **Deducing** Why is perfect competition such a rare market structure?

Applying Economics
6. **Perfect Competition** Explain how a local fast-food restaurant manager faces almost perfect competition in the demand for high-school employee labor.

section 2 — Monopoly, Oligopoly, Monopolistic Competition

GUIDE TO READING

Section Preview
In this section, you will learn about three types of imperfect market structures: monopoly, oligopoly, and monopolistic competition.

Content Vocabulary
- monopoly *(p. 237)*
- barriers to entry *(p. 237)*
- economies of scale *(p. 238)*
- patent *(p. 238)*
- copyright *(p. 238)*
- oligopoly *(p. 240)*
- product differentiation *(p. 241)*
- cartel *(p. 241)*
- monopolistic competition *(p. 242)*

Academic Vocabulary
- revolution *(p. 239)*
- dominate *(p. 240)*

Reading Strategy
Comparing and Contrasting Use a table like the one below to describe how much competition the seller faces and how much control over price he or she has in each type of market structure listed.

	Competition	Control Over Price
Monopoly		
Oligopoly		
Monopolistic Competition		

Skills Handbook

See page R43 to learn about Comparing and Contrasting.

ISSues In ThE NeWS
——from *BusinessWeek*

TAMING THE GIANT For 14 years, one regulator or another has chased after Microsoft—mostly unsuccessfully. In 1990, the Federal Trade Commission launched an investigation into a long list of allegedly predatory practices. The probe was dropped. In 1998, the Justice Dept. tried to prevent Microsoft from using its Windows monopoly to corner the emerging web browser market. Microsoft fought back and got only a slap on the wrist. Now European regulators are taking their shot at restraining the software giant.

In its March 24 ruling, the European Union labeled Microsoft an abusive monopolist and issued a sweeping set of penalties. . . . The EU ruled that Microsoft must share their technical information with rivals that will help their server software work better with Windows.

▲ Microsoft founder Bill Gates

As mentioned in Section 1, perfect competition is an idealized type of market structure. Most industries in the United States, in contrast, represent some form of *imperfect* competition. Economists classify these three types of imperfect market structures as monopoly, oligopoly, or monopolistic competition. In this section, you'll learn how they differ from one another.

Monopoly

Main Idea A monopoly exists when a single seller controls the supply of a good or service and largely determines its price.

Economics & You Have you ever played the board game *Monopoly*? What is the object of the game? Read on to learn the characteristics and objectives of monopolies.

The most extreme form of imperfect competition is a pure **monopoly**, in which a single seller controls the supply of the good or service and thus determines its price. A few such markets do exist in the real world. For example, some local electric utility companies are the sole providers for a community. See **Figure 9.3** below for a description of the four characteristics of a monopoly.

In a pure monopoly, the supplier can raise prices without fear of losing business, because buyers have nowhere else to go to buy the good or service. A monopolist, however, cannot charge outrageous prices, as the law of demand is still operating. As the price of a good or service rises, consumers buy less.

If a monopoly is collecting all the profits in a particular industry, why don't other businesses rush in to get a share of those profits? A monopoly is protected by **barriers to entry**—obstacles that prevent others from entering the market. State laws that prevent competing utility companies from entering the market are one example of a barrier to entry.

Another barrier to entry is the cost of getting started. Called "excessive money capital costs," this barrier is found in industries such as automobiles and steel.

monopoly: market situation in which a single supplier makes up an entire industry for a good or service with no close substitutes

barriers to entry: obstacles to competition that prevent others from entering a market

Figure 9.3 A Monopoly Market Structure

■ A monopoly exists when a single seller controls the supply of a good or service and largely determines its price. Four major characteristics define a monopoly.

Characteristics of a Monopoly

1. **A Single Seller** Only one seller exists for a good or service.

2. **No Substitutes** There are no close substitutes for the good or service that the monopolist sells.

3. **Barriers to Entry** The monopolist is protected by obstacles to competition that prevent others from entering the market.

4. **Almost Complete Control of Market Price** By controlling the available supply, the monopolist can control the market price.

Economic Analysis

Listing *What are some examples of barriers to entry?*

Types of Monopolies Pure monopolies can be separated into four categories depending on why the monopoly exists. The four types of monopolies are natural, geographic, technological, and government, as shown in **Figure 9.4** below.

First, we have *natural monopolies,* where the government grants exclusive rights to companies that provide things like utilities, bus service, and cable TV. The justification for natural monopolies is that a larger firm can often use its factors of production more efficiently. The large size, or scale, of most natural monopolies gives them **economies of scale**—by which they can produce large amounts of their good or service at a relatively low cost.

A *geographic monopoly* is another kind of monopoly. A country store in a rural setting is an example of this. Because the setting of the business is isolated and the potential for profits is so small, other businesses choose not to enter the market.

If you invent something, you are capable of having a *technological monopoly* over your invention. A government **patent** gives you the exclusive right to manufacture, rent, or sell your invention for a specified number of years—usually 20. Similarly, a United States **copyright** protects art, literature, song lyrics, and other creative works for the life of the author plus 70 years.

economies of scale: low production costs resulting from the large size of output

patent: exclusive right to make, use, or sell an invention for a specified number of years

copyright: exclusive right to sell, publish, or reproduce creative works for a specified number of years

---

Figure 9.4   **Types of Monopolies**

■ Pure monopolies can be separated into four categories depending on why the monopoly exists.

▲ **A. Natural Monopoly** In many major U.S. cities, bus service is a natural monopoly, granted exclusive rights by local governments to provide this service.

B. Geographic Monopoly ▶
A country store in a lightly populated area is an example of a geographic monopoly. Other businesses choose not to enter the market because there is a small customer base and little potential for profits.

Finally, we have *government monopolies*. A government monopoly is similar to a natural monopoly, except the monopoly is held by the government itself. The construction and maintenance of roads and bridges, for example, are the responsibility of local, state, and national governments, who contract this work out to companies. In the United States, the postal service is a common example of a government monopoly.

Monopolies today are far less important than they once were. Geographic monopolies, for example, have much less effect now than they did in the past because of potential competition from mail-order businesses and electronic commerce on the Internet. More and more natural monopolies are being broken up by the introduction of new technologies and government deregulation.

Technological monopolies rarely last longer than the life of the patent—if even *that* long. Why? Competitors can make and patent slight variations in new products quickly. The microcomputer **revolution** in the early 1980s followed such a pattern. One company copied another's product, making changes and adding features to obtain a patent of its own.

✓ Reading Check **Summarizing** What are the four types of monopolies, and what are their major characteristics?

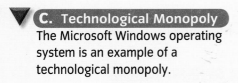

C. Technological Monopoly
The Microsoft Windows operating system is an example of a technological monopoly.

D. Government Monopoly In a government monopoly, local, state, and national governments themselves hold exclusive rights to contract out work like highway and bridge construction.

WINDOWS VISTA
BRINGS CLARITY TO
YOUR WORLD

EXPERIENCE
WINDOWS VISTA
CHECK YOUR EMAIL
BROWSE THE WEB

Economic Analysis
Determining Cause and Effect *What factors have led to the decline of the power of monopolies in recent years?*

Oligopoly

Main Idea An oligopoly exists when an industry is dominated by a few suppliers that exercise some control over price.

Economics & You How many domestic car companies can you name? How many soft drink companies? Read on to learn more about this type of industry, in which a few sellers dominate the market.

oligopoly: industry dominated by a few suppliers who exercise some control over price

Unlike a monopoly with just one supplier, an **oligopoly** is an industry **dominated** by *several* suppliers who exercise some control over price. See **Figure 9.5** below for a description of the five characteristics of an oligopoly.

Oligopolies are not considered as harmful to consumers as monopolies. Consumers may pay more than if they were buying in a perfectly competitive market, but oligopolistic markets tend to have generally stable prices. They also offer consumers a wider variety of products than would a perfectly competitive industry. (See **Figure 9.6.**)

Skills Handbook

See page R44 to learn about Detecting Bias.

Product Differentiation Oligopolists engage in nonprice competition. What does this mean? Let's use automobiles as an example. Several large auto manufacturers have an oligopoly on the domestic car market. They all make cars, trucks, and sport utility vehicles. They spend millions, if not billions, of advertising dollars per year to differentiate their products in your mind—and to win your consumer dollars.

Figure 9.5 | An Oligopoly Market Structure

■ An oligopoly exists when an industry is dominated by a few suppliers that exercise considerable control over price. Five major characteristics define an oligopoly.

Characteristics of an Oligopoly

1. **Domination by a Few Sellers** Several large firms are responsible for 70 to 80 percent of the market.

2. **Barriers to Entry** Capital costs are high, and it is difficult for new companies to enter major markets.

3. **Identical or Slightly Different Products** The goods and services provided by oligopolists—such as airline travel, domestic automobiles, and kitchen appliances—are very similar.

4. **Nonprice Competition** Advertising emphasizes minor differences and attempts to build customer loyalty.

5. **Interdependence** Any change on the part of one firm will cause a reaction on the part of other firms in the oligopoly.

Economic Analysis

Explaining *Why is advertising important in oligopolistic markets?*

Figure 9.6 **Oligopolies**

Charts In Motion
See StudentWorks™ Plus or go to glencoe.com.

■ Oligopolies exist in a few industries throughout the United States. Here several industries and their control of markets are highlighted. Economists would classify the top three as oligopolies.

Selected Oligopolies

Industry

Tobacco products	99%
Breakfast cereals	83%
Domestic motor vehicles	82%
Soft drinks	59%
Primary aluminum	47%

30 40 50 60 70 80 90 100

Percentage of Value of Total Domestic Shipments Accounted for by Top Four Firms in Each Industry

Source: U.S. Bureau of the Census

Economic Analysis

Contrasting *How are oligopolies different from monopolies?*

The price you pay for brand names is not just based on supply and demand. Rather, it is based on **product differentiation**—the real or perceived differences in the good or service that make it more valuable in consumers' eyes.

Interdependent Behavior With so few firms in an oligopoly, whatever one does, the others are sure to follow. When one domestic airline cuts its airfares to gain market share, for example, the other major domestic airlines lower theirs even more. Although this type of price war is initially good for consumers in the form of lower prices, it may force an airline out of business if prices drop too much. Fewer airlines leads to less competition, which may raise prices in the long run.

In contrast, if competing firms in an oligopoly secretly agree to raise prices or to divide the market, they are performing an illegal act called *collusion*. Heavy penalties, such as fines and even prison terms, are levied against companies found guilty of collusion in the United States. One significant form of collusion is the cartel. A **cartel** is an arrangement among groups of industrial businesses, often in different countries, to reduce international competition by controlling price, production, and the distribution of goods. Such firms seek monopolistic power.

product differentiation: manufacturers' use of minor differences in quality and features to try to differentiate between similar goods and services

cartel: arrangement among groups of industrial businesses to reduce international competition by controlling the price, production, and distribution of goods

✔ Reading Check **Predicting Consequences** What is a price war? What are its effects on the consumer?

Monopolistic Competition

Main Idea Monopolistic competition exists when a large number of sellers offer similar but slightly different products, and each firm has some control over price.

Economics & You What makes you buy one brand of toothpaste over another brand that costs the same? Read on to learn about the role that advertising plays in monopolistic competition.

monopolistic competition: market situation in which a large number of sellers offer similar but slightly different products and in which each has some control over price

The most common form of market structure in the United States is **monopolistic competition,** in which a relatively large number of sellers offer similar but slightly different products or services. Obvious examples are brand-name items such as toothpaste, cosmetics, and designer clothes. See **Figure 9.7** below for a description of the five characteristics of monopolistic competition.

Many of the characteristics of monopolistic competition are the same as those of an oligopoly. The major difference is in the number of sellers of a product. As you recall, in an oligopoly a few companies dominate an industry, and control over price is interdependent. In contrast, monopolistic competition has many firms, no real interdependence, and some slight difference among products. In this market structure, if a company succeeds in building brand loyalty for a product, the company gains a certain amount of influence over the market. It can raise the price of the product slightly without losing a great many customers.

Figure 9.7 | Market Structure of Monopolistic Competition

■ Monopolistic competition exists when a large number of sellers offer similar but slightly different products, and each firm has some control over price. Five major characteristics define monopolistic competition.

Characteristics of Monopolistic Competition

1. **Numerous Sellers** No single seller or small group dominates the market.

2. **Relatively Easy Entry** Entry into the market is easier than in a monopoly or oligopoly. One drawback is the high cost of advertising.

3. **Differentiated Products** Each supplier sells a slightly different product to attract customers.

4. **Nonprice Competition** Businesses compete by using product differentiation and by advertising.

5. **Some Control Over Price** By building a loyal customer base through product differentiation, each firm has some control over the price it charges.

Economic Analysis

Identifying *What is the main way companies achieve product differentiation?*

Because of the need to build brand loyalty, competitive advertising is even more important in monopolistic competition than it is in oligopolies. Advertising attempts to persuade consumers that the product being advertised is different from, and superior to, any other. When successful, advertising enables companies to charge more for their products. That's why companies like Nike, The Gap, and Procter & Gamble pour millions of dollars into their advertising budgets every year.

The heavy advertising required by monopolistic competition has both critics and defenders. Critics claim that it induces consumers to spend more on products than they normally would just because of the name associated with them. Defenders argue that brand names can represent a guarantee of quality, and that advertising helps reduce the cost to consumers of weighing the trade-offs of numerous competing brands.

Competitive Advertising

Advertising leads to product differentiation and competition for consumer dollars. It is more important in monopolistic competition than in any other market structure.

Reading Check **Contrasting** How is monopolistic competition different from an oligopoly?

Careers Handbook

See pages R76–R80 to learn about becoming an advertising manager.

section 2 Review

Vocabulary

1. **Explain** the significance of: monopoly, barriers to entry, economies of scale, patent, copyright, oligopoly, product differentiation, cartel, monopolistic competition.

Main Ideas

2. **Describing** Copy the diagram below, and under each box, write a characteristic that fits the type of monopoly listed.

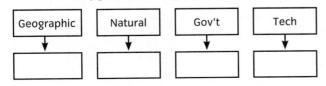

Geographic	Natural	Gov't	Tech
↓	↓	↓	↓

Critical Thinking

3. **The BIG Idea** Profits are determined by price. Explain how product differentiation is used to try to increase profits.

4. **Identifying** Name two barriers to entry that keep potential competitors out of a market.

Applying Economics

5. **Product Differentiation** Give three examples of products you bought recently because advertising convinced you to buy them. What was it about these products that convinced you to buy them rather than other, similar products?

ENTREPRENEUR
(1955–   )

Bill Gates

● **Cofounder and chairman of Microsoft Corporation**

■ Named the richest man in America by *Forbes* magazine

■ Along with his wife, started the Bill & Melinda Gates Foundation, the largest charitable foundation in the world, to promote global health and learning

■ Author of *Business @ the Speed of Thought* (1999), a best-seller translated into 25 languages

Bill Gates dropped out of Harvard in his junior year. He did so in order to devote all his time to the company he'd recently founded with his old school pal, Paul Allen. That company was Microsoft Corporation.

Gates and Allen became friends at Lakeside School in Seattle, Washington. Bill wasn't sure he wanted to attend that particular school:

"In those days, Lakeside was an all-boys school where you wore a jacket and tie, called your teachers 'master,' and went to chapel every morning. For a while, I even thought about failing the entrance exam [on purpose]."

But he decided to do his best and was admitted into the seventh grade. This was in the late 1960s, and there was no such thing as a personal computer. Nevertheless, Gates and Allen became early computer enthusiasts. Not only did the two learn more than anyone about the fundamentals of computing programming, but they invented it as they went along.

Even back then they were certain there was a future in personal computers, and together they wrote the first ever microcomputer BASIC program. They had guessed right, and 30 years after its founding, their once-tiny company had annual revenues of nearly $40 billion. Does Gates see an end in sight? Not at all.

> **"[S]oftware has moved to the center . . . for communications, for creativity, and for visualization, and it's amazing to see how far software has come and yet how much more we need to do."**

Checking for Understanding

1. **Explaining** What does Gates mean when he talks about "visualization" in the software industry?

2. **Speculating** Do you believe there is still a place for innovators in the software industry?

section 3

Government Policies Toward Competition

GUIDE TO READING

Section Preview
In this section, you will learn about steps the government has taken to regulate business practices.

Content Vocabulary
- interlocking directorate *(p. 246)*
- antitrust legislation *(p. 246)*
- merger *(p. 247)*
- conglomerate *(p. 247)*
- deregulation *(p. 248)*

Academic Vocabulary
- prohibit *(p. 246)*
- promote *(p. 248)*

Reading Strategy
Organizing As you read the section, complete a diagram like the one below by listing examples of federal regulatory agencies.

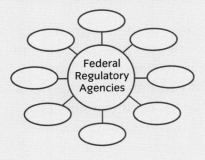

Federal Regulatory Agencies

ISSUES IN THE NEWS
—from *www.forbes.com*

AIRLINE BAILOUTS There isn't much precedent for U.S. government bailouts of private industry. The few that have occurred have generally been successful, but there are ways federal regulators could still muck up the $15 billion bailout [after September 11, 2001] of the airline industry.

For starters, regulators could guarantee loans for troubled airlines that will probably go belly-up, wasting potentially billions of tax dollars. "You'd hate to try to save an airline  that was going to go under anyway," says Daryll Jenkins, director of the aviation institute at George Washington University. . . .

. . . Economists say it's questionable whether the bailout will even improve liquidity for such high-cost carriers as US Air. The government therefore should demand that airlines that accept loan guarantees be far more disciplined on cost control and improving return on capital. Anything less will not help restore the industry. . . .

Historically, one of the goals of government in the United States has been to encourage competition in the economy. Does the federal government's bailout of various airlines work toward that goal? Should the government intervene in such cases? In this section, you'll learn about the federal laws and regulatory agencies that attempt to force monopolies to act more competitively.

Antitrust Legislation and Mergers

Economics ONLINE

Student Web Activity
Visit the *Economics Today and Tomorrow* Web site at glencoe.com and click on *Chapter 9—Student Web Activities* to learn more about antitrust legislation.

Main Idea The goal of antitrust legislation is to encourage competition in the economy and to prevent unfair trade practices.

Economics & You How do you think people in your community would react to an oil monopoly today? Why? Read on to learn about how public pressure caused the government to take the first steps to regulating business over a hundred years ago.

The industrial expansion after the Civil War fueled the rise of big businesses. John D. Rockefeller's Standard Oil Company at the end of the nineteenth century was the most notorious for driving competitors out of business and pressuring customers not to deal with rival oil companies. He also placed members of Standard Oil's board of directors onto the board of a competing corporation. Because the same group of people, in effect, controlled both companies, it was less tempting for them to compete with one another. This practice of creating **interlocking directorates** was perfected by Rockefeller.

interlocking directorate: a board of directors, the majority of whose members also serve as the board of directors of a competing corporation

antitrust legislation: federal and state laws passed to prevent new monopolies from forming and to break up those that already exist

Public pressure against Rockefeller's monopoly, or trust, over the oil business led Congress to pass the *Sherman Antitrust Act* in 1890. The law sought to protect trade and commerce against unlawful restraint and monopoly. This act was important **antitrust legislation,** or laws to prevent new monopolies or trusts from forming and to break up those that already exist.

Because the language of the Sherman Act was so vague, a new law was passed in 1914 to sharpen its antitrust provisions. The *Clayton Act* **prohibited** or limited a number of very specific business practices that lessened competition substantially. The Clayton Act, however, does not state what the term *substantially* means. As a result, it is up to the federal courts and agencies to make a subjective decision as to whether the merging of two corporations would substantially lessen competition.

A Former Monopoly

American Telephone & Telegraph (AT&T) was once the nation's largest corporation and held a natural monopoly on telephone service. In 1984, "Ma Bell," as the company was called, was broken up after the settlement of a lawsuit filed by the federal government. Today, the telephone service industry is highly competitive, especially since cell and digital phones have entered the market.

Figure 9.8 | Mergers

■ **Horizontal mergers** involve businesses that make the same product or provide the same service. **Vertical mergers** take place when firms taking part in different steps of manufacturing come together. A **conglomerate** is a firm that has many businesses, each providing unrelated products or services.

Horizontal Merger

Juan's Garden Shop

Shannon's Home and Garden

Lee's Nursery

Conglomerate Merger

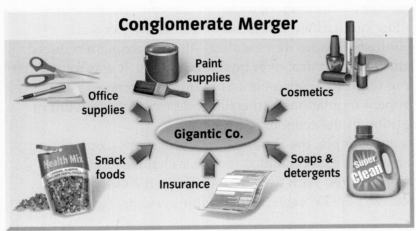

Office supplies

Paint supplies

Cosmetics

Gigantic Co.

Snack foods

Insurance

Soaps & detergents

Vertical Merger

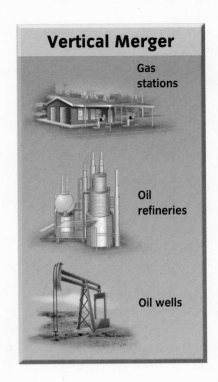

Gas stations

Oil refineries

Oil wells

Economic Analysis

Extending *In what ways might mergers benefit corporations?*

Most antitrust legislation deals with restricting the harmful effects of mergers. A **merger** occurs when two or more companies combine into one corporation. As shown in **Figure 9.8** above, three kinds of mergers exist: horizontal, vertical, and conglomerate.

When the corporations that merge are in the same business, a *horizontal merger* has occurred. An example of a horizontal merger occurs when DVD Store A buys DVD Store B. When corporations involved in a "chain" of supply merge, this is called a *vertical merger*. An example would be a paper company buying the lumber mill that supplies it with pulp or buying the office supply business that sells its paper. Another type of merger is the conglomerate merger. A **conglomerate** is a huge corporation involved in at least four or more unrelated businesses. Procter & Gamble, for example, is a multinational conglomerate, with operations in more than 160 countries.

merger: the legal combination of two or more companies that become one corporation

conglomerate: large corporation made up of smaller corporations dealing in unrelated businesses

✔ **Reading Check** **Contrasting** Explain the difference between horizontal and vertical mergers.

Government Regulation

Main Idea The aim of government regulatory agencies is to promote efficiency, competition, fairness, and safety.

Economics & You When you apply for a job, can an employer turn you down because of your race, gender, or ethnicity? Why or why not? Read on to learn about the government's regulatory agencies.

Besides using antitrust laws to foster a competitive atmosphere, the government uses direct regulation of business pricing and product quality. The chart below lists several regulatory agencies that oversee various industries and services. These agencies exist at the federal, state, and even local levels.

Although the aim of government regulations is to **promote** efficiency and competition, recent evidence indicates that something quite different has occurred. In the 1980s and 1990s, many industries were **deregulated**—the government reduced regulations and control over business activity. It was found that in trying to protect consumers from unfair practices, government regulations had actually *decreased* the amount of competition in the economy.

As an example, the Federal Communications Commission (FCC) had for years regulated the basic channels in the television market. With deregulation came the entry of competitive pay-TV, cable, and satellite systems.

deregulation: reduction of government regulation and control over business activity

Federal Regulatory Agencies	
Agency	**Function**
Federal Trade Commission (FTC) (1914)	Regulates product warranties, unfair methods of competition in interstate commerce, and fraud in advertising.
Food and Drug Administration (FDA) (1927)	Regulates purity and safety of foods, drugs, and cosmetics.
Federal Communications Commission (FCC) (1934)	Regulates television, radio, telegraph, and telephone; grants licenses, creates and enforces rules of behavior for broadcasting; most recently, partly regulates satellite transmissions and cable TV.
Securities and Exchange Commission (SEC) (1934)	Regulates the sale of stocks, bonds, and other investments.
Equal Employment Opportunity Commission (EEOC) (1964)	Responsible for working to reduce workplace discrimination based on religion, gender, race, national origin, or age.
Occupational Safety and Health Administration (OSHA) (1970)	Regulates workplace environment; makes sure that businesses provide workers with safe and healthful working conditions.
Environmental Protection Agency (EPA) (1970)	Develops and enforces environmental standards for air, water, and toxic waste.
Nuclear Regulatory Commission (NRC) (1974)	Regulates the nuclear power industry; licenses and oversees the design, construction, and operation of nuclear power plants.

Many economists speculate about what would happen if the government removed its watchdog responsibility toward mergers in general. Economists assume prices would rise. If, however, the price increases caused profits to be excessive, other sellers would find ways to enter the market. Consumers would benefit eventually from a competitive supply of goods and services. Also, with increased global competition, domestic firms cannot raise prices without attracting foreign rivals. Indeed, global competition has become the biggest competitive threat to many American companies. The few domestic car producers have been battered by foreign competitors. Toyota, Honda, and others have created financial problems for General Motors and Ford.

■ Government deregulation of the airline industry was designed to lower the price of air travel, but the cartoonist believes this deregulation also had negative consequences.

Reading Check **Determining Cause and Effect** What is one potentially negative result of government regulations?

section 3 Review

Vocabulary

1. **Explain** the significance of: interlocking directorate, antitrust legislation, merger, conglomerate, deregulation.

Main Ideas

2. **Comparing and Contrasting** Complete the chart below by listing some advantages and disadvantages of government control of business.

	Regulation	Deregulation
Advantages		
Disadvantages		

Critical Thinking

3. The **BIG Idea** Explain how the Sherman Antitrust Act and the Clayton Act limited profits for some businesses.

4. **Determining Cause and Effect** How might a merger help a business be more efficient and increase profits?

Applying Economics

5. **Conglomerates** Type "conglomerate" into an Internet search engine. Research one of the conglomerates that you find, and list all of the businesses or products owned by that conglomerate.

A WINDOW INTO MICROSOFT'S **BATTLE**

Antitrust rulings aim to open Microsoft's Windows to competitors' products.

Check It Out! In this chapter you learned about monopolies. This article discusses the technological monopoly that Microsoft holds and the antitrust cases trying to change that.

The long-running antitrust battle between Microsoft and the European Commission (EC) revolves around two separate issues: Microsoft's bundling of its Media Player into Windows, and whether the company must disclose secret software protocols to rivals. . . .

Microsoft's argument is analogous to shoes and shoelaces. While consumers can and do buy shoelaces separately, they also expect at least one pair to be included when they buy new shoes. The company will argue that modern consumers similarly now demand a media player built into the operating system. . . .

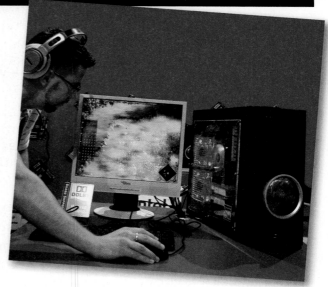

▲ High-end Windows operating system

The arguments over server interoperability are more complex. . . . Microsoft claims it shouldn't be forced to disclose its server interface information because the software makers who want to use it aim to enhance their existing products to compete against Microsoft.

Microsoft's rivals, naturally, take a different view. While courts largely lean towards protecting the intellectual property rights of inventors, things change when the holder of the copyright or patent is a monopolist with the ability to shape markets.

—Reprinted from *BusinessWeek*

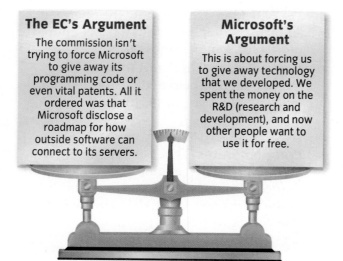

The EC's Argument

The commission isn't trying to force Microsoft to give away its programming code or even vital patents. All it ordered was that Microsoft disclose a roadmap for how outside software can connect to its servers.

Microsoft's Argument

This is about forcing us to give away technology that we developed. We spent the money on the R&D (research and development), and now other people want to use it for free.

Think About It

1. **Discussing** What arguments does Microsoft use to justify its technological monopoly?

2. **Assessing** According to the article, why might the intellectual property of Microsoft not be protected?

■ Of the **four basic market structures**, perfect competition and monopolies are rare, while monopolistic competition and oligopolies are much more common.

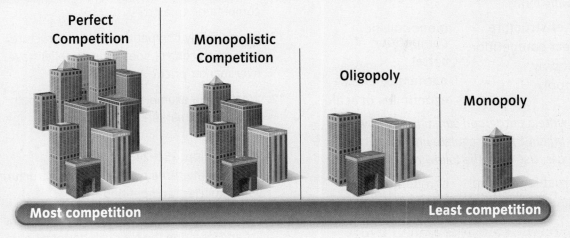

Perfect Competition

Monopolistic Competition

Oligopoly

Monopoly

Most competition   **Least competition**

■ The **level of competitiveness** in a particular market is determined by several factors.

Factors of Competitiveness in Markets

1. Size of the market
2. Number of sellers in the market
3. Whether or not there are barriers to entry
4. How differentiated the products are
5. How much control over price the sellers have
6. Whether or not substitutes exist for the product

■ **Government regulatory agencies** seek to promote efficiency, competition, fairness, and safety.

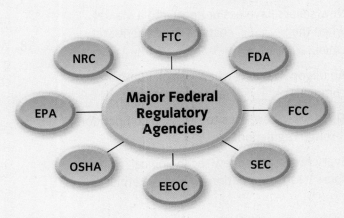

FTC

NRC

FDA

EPA

Major Federal Regulatory Agencies

FCC

OSHA

SEC

EEOC

Review Content Vocabulary

1. *Write a paragraph or two explaining market structures and their characteristics. Use all of the following terms.*

market structure
perfect competition
monopoly
oligopoly

monopolistic competition
cartel
barriers to entry
economies of scale

2. *Now write a paragraph summarizing how the government tries to regulate unfair business practices. Use all of the following terms.*

antitrust legislation
merger

conglomerate
deregulation

Review Academic Vocabulary

Choose the letter of the term that best completes each sentence.

a. initial
b. interact
c. unique
d. revolution

e. dominate
f. prohibit
g. promote

3. A completely _____ business would have no competition because there would be nothing else like it in the marketplace.

4. In perfect competition, there is nothing to _____ the entry of new sellers in a market.

5. Supply and demand _____ to reach an equilibrium price.

6. New sellers have easier entry into a market when the _____ costs of investment are small.

7. An oligopoly exists when a small number of companies _____ an industry.

8. The government tries to _____ competition through regulation.

9. Every few years, a new technological _____ spurs fresh competition in the marketplace.

Review the Main Ideas

Section 1 (pp. 231–235)

10. What five conditions are necessary for perfect competition to exist?

11. In a perfectly competitive market structure, how much control does a single seller have over market price?

12. What is one example of an almost perfectly competitive market?

Section 2 (pp. 236–243)

13. What are the three types of market structures with imperfect competition?

14. Fill in a graphic organizer like the one below to list and describe the four categories of pure monopolies.

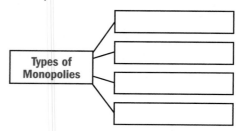

15. How much control does an oligopoly have over price? Why?

16. What are the differences between an oligopoly and monopolistic competition?

Section 3 (pp. 245–249)

17. What is the difference between a horizontal merger and a vertical merger?

18. What two methods does the federal government use to keep businesses competitive?

Thinking Like an Economist

List some industries that are regulated by government (common examples include electricity providers, broadcast television, airlines). Choose one, and then fill in a chart like the one below to help you analyze the advantages and disadvantages of government regulation of this industry. Then answer the questions that follow.

Regulation	
Advantages	**Disadvantages**

19. In your opinion, should this industry be regulated by the government? Why or why not?

20. What would happen if this industry were to be completely deregulated? Justify your opinion with logical arguments and examples.

Economics ONLINE

Self-Check Quiz Visit the *Economics Today and Tomorrow* Web site at glencoe.com and click on **Chapter 9—Self-Check Quizzes** to assess your knowledge of chapter content.

Critical Thinking

21. **The BIG Idea** Why is more competition generally good for consumers? What effect does competition have on suppliers?

22. **Explaining** Why are oligopolies typically interdependent?

23. **Contrasting** What are the basic differences between the goals of antitrust legislation and the goals of federal government regulatory agencies?

24. **Predicting** In a situation of perfect competition, what would happen if barriers to entry in the market suddenly sprang up?

Analyzing Visuals

25. Study the cartoon on the right, and then answer the following questions.

   a. Who do the two men pictured in this cartoon represent?

   b. What has happened to the speaker's competition?

   c. With what crime does the cartoon imply the man has been charged?

TOLES ©2000 The Washington Post. Reprinted with permission of UNIVERSAL PRESS SYNDICATE. All rights reserved.

Should price gougers be punished?

"**P**rice gouging" is what happens when businesses sharply raise the prices of essential goods such as food, clothing, shelter, medicine, gasoline, and equipment needed to preserve lives and property during emergencies. After Hurricane Katrina in 2005, oil companies hiked the average price of gasoline by one-third or more, blaming damage to refineries in the Gulf of Mexico and increases in the price they paid for crude oil. Consumers complained that the price increases amounted to unjustifiable profits for the oil companies. In some states, price gouging is a felony, but few companies are actually penalized. Should laws against price gouging be toughened and enforced?

NO! All prices should be determined by supply and demand

Prices are not just arbitrary numbers plucked out of the air. Nor are the price levels that you happen to be used to any more special or "fair" than other prices that are higher or lower. . . . The new prices make as much economic sense under the new conditions as the old prices made under the old conditions.

What do prices do? They not only allow sellers to recover their costs, they force buyers to restrict how much they demand. . . . What if [hotel] prices were frozen where they were before [Katrina] happened?. . . . At higher prices, a family that might have rented one room for the parents and another for the children will now double up in just one room because of the "exorbitant" prices. That leaves another room for someone else. It is essentially the same story when stores are selling ice, plywood, gasoline, or other things for prices that reflect today's supply and demand, rather than yesterday's supply and demand. Price controls will not cause new supplies to be rushed in nearly as fast as higher prices will.

—Thomas Sowell, economist

YES! The health of the nation's economy depends on regulating gas prices

At best, 10 percent of production was shut down [after Hurricane Katrina hit]. . . . That's 10 percent of one-fourth of U.S. demand—a tiny amount . . . while gas prices rose 25–35 percent and even more in some areas. Not often mentioned . . . was the fact that the world price of oil actually *fell* by almost 10 percent over the same period.

. . . When the per barrel price of crude falls, the price at the pump hangs at its high level, sometimes for weeks, but if crude goes up, so does the pump price. Consumers can't shop for bargains, because all gas stations behave the same way. For the most part, though, it's not the stations that are doing this gouging . . . but rather the oil companies themselves.

. . . If Congress and the White House were serious about combating price rigging, coordinated production slowdowns, and artificial scarcities, they would be changing the anti-trust laws so that the objective existence of anti-competitive pricing and production alone would be illegal, not just [the current requirement of] deliberate conspiring to fix prices.

—Dave Lindorff, author, *This Can't Be Happening: Resisting the Disintegration of American Democracy*

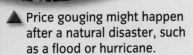

▲ Price gouging might happen after a natural disaster, such as a flood or hurricane.

Debating the Issue

1. **Explaining** How do high gasoline prices affect American families?

2. **Choosing Sides** Do you believe oil companies should be allowed to charge whatever people will pay for gasoline? Why or why not?

Find Out More!

3. **Analyzing** Using the Internet or other resources, learn more about alternatives to paying high prices for gasoline. Which solution or solutions do you think would best solve the problem?

unit 4

Microeconomics: American Business In Action

In this unit, read to find out...

- how businesses obtain financing and produce goods.
- how those goods are marketed and distributed to you as a consumer.
- who makes up the American labor force.

## chapter 10

Financing and Producing Goods

The **BIG Idea**

The profit motive acts as an incentive for people to produce and sell goods and services.

Why It Matters

Imagine that you want to start your own business. What type of good or service would you produce? In this chapter, read to learn how companies obtain the financing needed to open for business, and how they try to work efficiently to make profits.

Economics ONLINE

Chapter Overview Visit the *Economics Today and Tomorrow* Web site at glencoe.com and click on *Chapter 10—Chapter Overviews* to preview chapter information.

Investing in the Free-Enterprise System

GUIDE TO READING

Section Preview
In this section, you will learn about the factors companies evaluate when deciding whether to obtain financing for expansion.

Content Vocabulary
- financing *(p. 260)*
- cost-benefit analysis *(p. 261)*
- revenues *(p. 261)*
- profits *(p. 261)*

Academic Vocabulary
- sufficient *(p. 259)*
- integral *(p. 260)*
- instance *(p. 263)*

Reading Strategy
Sequencing As you read the section, complete a flowchart similar to the one below by listing the steps that savings dollars go through when financing business expansion.

Financing Business Expansion

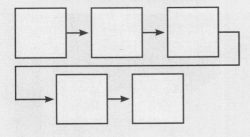

PeOPLE In ThE NeWS
—from *BusinessWeek*

INVESTING CLOSE TO HOME U.S. entrepreneurs are the engines that drive new companies—and financing is the fuel that propels them.

. . . Informal investors put up more money for startups and growing businesses than professional venture-capital firms. Indeed, informal investors are the lifeblood of U.S. entrepreneurship. If informal investors, sometimes called the 4Fs—founders, family, friends, and foolhardy strangers—dried up, entrepreneurship in the U.S. would wither.

[The Global Entrepreneurship Monitor found that:]

- Almost 5 in every 100 adults report they have invested in someone else's private business in the last three years.
- The more education people have, the more likely they are to be informal investors.

▲ **A family discusses investment options**

- Male informal investors are twice as prevalent as female investors, and they invest larger amounts of money.
- More than 50% of all informal investments are made in relatives' businesses.

If you were an entrepreneur, you would face many hurdles on your road to success. One hurdle would be finding **sufficient** financing to pay for your company's current needs, such as parts and tools, and its long-term needs, such as growth. As you read this section, you'll learn that both the short-term and long-term needs of businesses can be financed in a variety of ways.

Before You Pursue Financing

Main Idea Businesses should expand if the benefits of doing so exceed the costs.

Economics & You Have you ever taken a risk? Did you weigh the cost of the action against the potential benefits? Read on to learn about the factors businesses must consider before deciding to risk expansion.

financing: obtaining funds or money capital for business expansion

Financing refers to the obtaining of funds, or money capital. Financing business operations and growth is an **integral** part of our free-enterprise system. It all begins with people who save by depositing their funds in one of several types of financial institutions, which you learned about in Chapter 6. The financial institutions, in turn, make these deposits available to businesses to finance growth and expansion.

Let's assume that you own an electronics repair company that you have incorporated. You now have the opportunity to open additional repair shops in other locations, but you do not have enough extra funds to invest in the expansion. You can obtain this financing in many ways. These include digging into your own personal savings, asking your friends and family to loan funds to the company, borrowing from a financial institution, or selling more shares of stock. Even if you are able to finance the expansion, however, one important question remains. *Should* you expand?

Personal Finance Handbook

See pages R14–R15 for more information on taking out loans.

Staying in the Family

Many small businesses, such as neighborhood delis, receive financing from family and friends of the owner or owners.

Figure 10.1 | **Cost-Benefit Analysis**

Charts In Motion
See StudentWorks™ Plus or go to glencoe.com.

■ Remember that you should undertake an activity only up to the point at which the additional benefit equals the additional cost.

▼ **B. The Details** In going through each step, business owners should try to consider every possibility of costs and sources of revenue.

Five Steps of Cost-Benefit Analysis

Step ❶
Estimate the costs of expansion.

Step ❷
Calculate expected revenues.

Step ❸
Calculate expected profits.

Step ❹
Calculate cost of loan plus interest.

Step ❺
Expected profits should outweigh the costs of expansion.

▲ **A. The Overall Analysis** Businesses should follow these five steps first when deciding whether to expand.

Costs Could Include:

◆ Renting new stores	◆ Opportunity cost of more time spent working
◆ Training new workers	◆ New taxes
◆ Additional bookkeeping	◆ Additional inventory
◆ Additional insurance	◆ Meeting government regulations
◆ Utilities	

Economic Analysis

Explaining *What is the difference between revenues and profits?*

Businesses usually answer this question by making a standard **cost-benefit analysis.** (See **Figure 10.1** above.) You estimate the cost of any action and compare it with the benefits of that action. Developing a cost-benefit analysis involves five steps:
(1) Estimate the costs of expansion.
(2) Calculate expected **revenues,** or total income from sales.
(3) Calculate expected **profits,** or revenues minus costs.
(4) Calculate how much it will cost you to borrow funds to finance your proposed business expansion.
(5) If expected profits more than cover the cost of financing the expansion, then the expansion may be warranted.

Here is a simple numerical example: Suppose that you can borrow $1 million to finance your business expansion. Your bank will charge 10 percent per year for the loan. That equals $100,000 per year. If your expansion generates profits of $200,000 per year, then borrowing $1 million would be worthwhile.

cost-benefit analysis: a financial process in which a business estimates the cost of any action and compares it with the estimated benefits of that action

revenues: total income from sales of output

profits: the amount earned after a business subtracts its costs from its revenues

✔ **Reading Check** **Identifying** What are four methods businesses can use to obtain financing for expansion?

Why People Are Willing to Finance Investment

Main Idea Savings should be invested where they will get the highest expected rates of return in the form of interest or profits.

Economics & You Would you be willing to risk your savings gambling? Why or why not? Read on to learn about why people decide to risk financing business investments.

Economics ONLINE

Student Web Activity
Visit the *Economics Today and Tomorrow* Web site at glencoe.com and click on *Chapter 10—Student Web Activities* to learn how businesses can obtain financing through the Internet.

Businesses are interested in obtaining financing so that they can expand and make higher profits in the future. The people who finance such business investments—whether intentionally or unintentionally—are also seeking rewards. Such rewards can take several different forms.

Savers unintentionally finance business growth when they deposit funds in a savings account or certificate of deposit (CD). Their reward is the interest earned on the savings account or CD, as **Figure 10.2** below illustrates. For those who intentionally finance investment, the reward is the interest on a corporate bond that they purchase, or dividends from the stock that they buy in an expanding company.

Pursuing Investment Financing When one business succeeds at obtaining financing, it uses funds that might have helped another business. In a market economy, each business competes for scarce financial resources.

Figure 10.2 Financing Business Expansion

■ Businesses are able to obtain financing because you (and other income earners) do not spend all that you earn during a year. Through saving, you and others who save make resources available to finance business expansion in the United States.

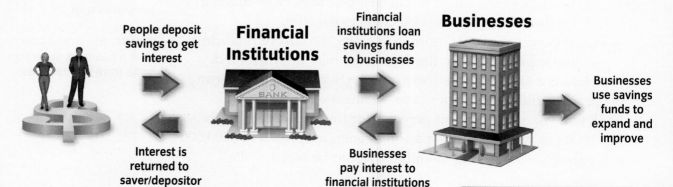

People deposit savings to get interest

Financial Institutions

Financial institutions loan savings funds to businesses

Businesses

Businesses use savings funds to expand and improve

Interest is returned to saver/depositor

Businesses pay interest to financial institutions

Economic Analysis

Synthesizing *On what specific things or activities might businesses spend financing funds?*

If the cost to finance business expansion is relatively high, only those businesses that believe they have the most profitable expansion projects will be willing to pay the high cost of financing. If the cost of financing is relatively low, on the other hand, more companies will decide that they, too, can profitably engage in additional business investment. In either **instance,** the lending institution makes the final decision regarding lending the business the funds to expand.

Methods of Financing There are several methods of financing business expansion. As you learned in Chapter 6, corporations offer stock and may sell bonds to finance investment. Businesses, just like individuals, can also borrow from banks, finance companies, or other institutions. Today businesses can even use the Internet to obtain financing. In Section 2, you'll learn more about the types of financing for business operations.

▲ Remember, not all investments guarantee a return.

✔ Reading Check **Predicting Consequences** When savers unintentionally finance business growth, what reward do they receive? What is the reward for those who intentionally finance investment?

section 1 Review

Vocabulary

1. **Explain** the significance of: financing, cost-benefit analysis, revenues, profits.

Main Ideas

2. **Identifying** Use a web diagram like the one below to list the steps involved in cost-benefit analysis.

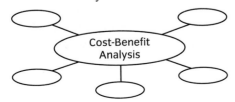

3. **Contrasting** What is the difference between profit and revenue?

Critical Thinking

4. **The BIG Idea** What is the profit rule used in cost-benefit analysis to decide whether or not to build or expand a business?

5. **Determining Cause and Effect** What are two ways people who finance a business can obtain profits?

Applying Economics

6. **Financial Institutions** Use your own specific saving habits to create a chart similar to the one in **Figure 10.2** on page 262. Include arrows showing in what type of financial institution your savings go or would go, and what your reward for saving is or would be.

Types of Financing for Business Operations

GUIDE TO READING

Section Preview
In this section, you will learn about the three types of financing available to businesses: short-term, intermediate-term, and long-term.

Content Vocabulary
- debt financing *(p. 265)*
- short-term financing *(p. 265)*
- intermediate-term financing *(p. 266)*
- long-term financing *(p. 267)*

Academic Vocabulary
- undergo *(p. 264)*
- adequate *(p. 266)*

Reading Strategy
Organizing As you read, complete a table similar to the one below by filling in definitions and examples for the types of financing listed.

Debt Financing		
Type of Financing	Definition	Examples
Short-term		
Intermediate-term		
Long-term		

ISSUES IN THE NEWS
—from Entrepreneur.com

MAXED OUT We asked our 2005 young millionaires how they financed their business, and what advice they could offer on getting financing. [Here's what] Joel Boblit, 29, the founder of BigBadToyStore Inc., an online toy retailer specializing in collectible action figures, [had to say]:

"It was financed through credit cards and mortgaging everything we owned for the first two years. We financially went all in. I was actually in debt when I started the business, and my family had no extra assets, so we did it all completely on credit and high-interest loans. . . . We were probably up to $300,000 at the highest point in short-term loan and credit card debt, but we were also growing exponentially the first few years, so I didn't feel too bad about it. But there is a definite risk involved."

▲ Power Rangers action figure from BigBadToyStore Inc.

Businesses, like individuals, must **undergo** a certain process when borrowing funds. A business that wants to borrow must show creditworthiness by undergoing a credit check. Also, a business, like an individual, must pay interest on loans and repay them within a stated period of time. As you read this section, you'll learn about the financing options from which businesses may choose.

Three Kinds of Financing

Main Idea When a business needs to borrow, it can use a variety of short-term, intermediate-term, or long-term financing.

Economics & You You many need to borrow to pay for college or other events. Is it better to borrow for the short term or long term? Read on to learn about the types of financing available to businesses.

Raising funds for a business through borrowing, or **debt financing,** can be divided into three categories: short-term, intermediate-term, and long-term financing.

Short-Term Financing When a business borrows funds for any period of time less than a year, it has obtained **short-term financing.** The chart below describes several types of short-term financing. A business may seek short-term financing for many reasons. A company may have excellent business during the month but not be paid until the beginning of the following month. In the meantime, the company needs funds to pay salaries and its bills. During a growing season, a farmer may have to borrow to buy seed, repair equipment, and pay workers.

debt financing: raising funds for a business through borrowing

short-term financing: funds borrowed by a business for any period of time less than a year

Short-Term Financing

Trade Credit

Trade credit is extended by one firm to another business buying the firm's goods. It allows the buyer to take possession of goods immediately and pay for them at some future date, usually 30 to 90 days later.

Businesses often receive a discount—2 percent, for example—if they pay their bill within 10 days. If a business does not pay the bill in that amount of time, it is, in effect, paying 2 percent interest for the use of trade credit.

Unsecured Loans

Most short-term bank credit for businesses is in the form of unsecured bank loans. These are loans not guaranteed by anything other than the promise to repay them. The borrower must sign a **promissory note** to repay the loan in full by a specified time and with a specified rate of interest. The usual repayment period is one year.

Secured Loans

Secured loans are backed by **collateral**—something of value that the borrowers will lose if they do not repay a loan. Businesses offer as collateral property such as machinery, inventories, or **accounts receivable**—amounts owed to a business by its customers.

Line of Credit

A **line of credit** is a maximum amount a company can borrow from a bank during a period of time, usually one year. Rather than apply each time for a loan, a company may automatically borrow up to the amount of the line of credit—$100,000, for example.

Short-Term Borrowing

Farmers sometimes seek short-term financing to repair equipment and buy supplies. Short-term loans generally must be paid off in less than a yea

intermediate-term financing: funds borrowed by a business for 1 to 10 years

Careers Handbook

*See pages **R76–R80** to learn about becoming a **loan officer**.*

Intermediate-Term Financing Borrowing for 1 to 10 years is considered **intermediate-term financing.** When a company wants to expand its business by buying more land, buildings, or equipment, short-term financing generally is not **adequate.** For example, imagine you want to expand your electronics repair business, and you decide the best way to do this would be to open another shop. In this case, you would not apply for a 90-day loan. In 90 days, you would not be able to do enough repair jobs to earn the additional revenue to repay the loan. Instead, you would look for intermediate-term financing. Forms of this type of financing are described in the chart below.

Intermediate-Term Financing

Loans

Intermediate-term loans have repayment periods from 1 to 10 years and generally require collateral such as stocks, bonds, equipment, or machinery. The loan is considered a mortgage if it is secured by property such as the building in which the business is located. Sometimes large, financially sound companies may be able to get unsecured intermediate-term loans.

Leasing

Leasing means renting rather than buying—whether it is a building, machinery, or the like. One advantage of leasing is that the leasing company will often service the machinery at low cost. Another advantage is that the business may deduct a part of the funds spent on a lease before figuring income taxes. A disadvantage is that a lease often costs more than borrowing to buy the same equipment.

Long-Term Financing Borrowing for longer than 10 years or issuing stock is called **long-term financing.** Long-term financing is used for major expansion, such as building a new plant or buying expensive, long-lasting machines to replace outdated ones. For financing investments like these lasting 10 to 15 years or more, corporations either issue stock or sell bonds. (See the chart below.) Usually only large corporations finance long-term debt by selling bonds. Unlike smaller companies, large corporations with huge assets appear to be better risks to investors who are interested in buying bonds.

long-term financing: funds borrowed by a business for a period of more than 10 years or funds raised by issuing stock

Reading Check **Determining Cause and Effect** In what cases might a business seek short-term financing?

Long-Term Financing	
Bonds	
Bonds promise to pay a stated rate of interest over a stated period of time and to repay the full amount borrowed at the end of that time.	
Stocks	
Selling stock is called **equity financing** because part of the ownership, or equity, of the company is being sold. Corporations may sell either preferred or common stock. The differences between these types of stock are explained below.	
Common Stock	**Preferred Stock**
❶ Common stock is issued by all public corporations; it is the stock most often bought and sold.	❶ Many corporations do not issue preferred stock.
❷ Holders of common stock have voting rights in a corporation. As a group they elect the board of directors.	❷ Holders of preferred stock generally have no voting rights.
❸ Common stock may pay dividends based on a corporation's performance. If the company does well, dividends may be high; if it does poorly, the dividends may be low or zero.	❸ Preferred stock pays a fixed dividend. This amount must be paid before holders of common stock receive any dividends. If a company cannot pay a fixed dividend on time, it must usually make up the missed payment later.
❹ The value of common stock rises and falls in relation to the corporation's performance and what investors expect it to do in the future.	❹ The value of preferred stock changes in relation to how well the company is doing.
❺ If a corporation fails, holders of common stock are the last to be paid with whatever funds are left after paying all creditors.	❺ If a corporation fails, holders of preferred stock must be paid before any holders of common stock are paid, but bondholders are paid before any stockholders.

Choosing the Right Financing

Main Idea Decisions regarding financing depend on the level of interest rates, the financial condition of the company, the overall economic climate, and the opinions of the stockholders.

Economics & You When it comes time for you to borrow funds, how will you decide how much to borrow, or how long you will need to pay the loan back? Read on to learn how businesses make similar decisions.

Financial managers try to obtain capital at a minimum cost to the company. To do so, they try to choose the best mix of financing. The length of a loan that a company takes out or a corporation's decision regarding whether to sell bonds or issue stock depends on four factors. These factors are the costs of interest, the financial condition of the company, the overall economic climate, and the opinions of the company's owners.

Skills Handbook

See page **R57** to learn about **Understanding Interest Rates**.

Interest Rates When interest rates in general are high, a business may be reluctant to take out a loan. A company may delay its expansion until it can borrow at better interest rates, or it may take out a series of short-term loans at high rates, hoping that interest rates will drop. When that happens, the company will then take out a long-term loan.

Interest rates also affect the decision to issue bonds. When rates are high, corporations must offer high rates of interest on their bonds to attract investors. When interest rates drop overall, corporations can offer lower rates of return on their bonds.

Financial Condition of the Company A company or corporation whose sales and profits are stable or are expected to increase can safely take on more debt—if its current debt is not too large. Financial managers use cost-benefit analysis to determine if the potential profits will more than cover the cost of financing expansion.

"Whoops! There go those darned interest rates again!"

Interest Rate Effects

The cost of interest is one factor that determines what type of financing a business will choose. In general, when interest rates are high, businesses will put off borrowing or seek short-term loans. When interest rates drop, businesses are more likely to take out long-term loans.

Market Climate Financial managers need to be aware of the market climate when determining whether to sell bonds or to issue stock to raise financing. If economic growth in the overall market appears to be slow, investors may prefer the fixed rate of return of bonds or preferred stock to the unknown return on common stock.

Control of the Company

Bonds do not have voting rights attached to them. Most preferred stocks also do not give voting rights to shareholders. The owners of common stocks, however, do have the right to vote in company elections. When debating issues of financing, financial managers may have to gain approval from the owners of common stock before taking action. Bondholders are not asked for their approval.

Factors Affecting Financing Decisions

Control of the company

Interest rates

Financing Decisions

Market climate

Company's financial condition

✔ Reading Check **Analyzing** How does the overall economic climate affect a business's decisions regarding financing?

---

section 2 **Review**

Vocabulary

1. **Explain** the significance of: debt financing, short-term financing, intermediate-term financing, long-term financing.

Main Ideas

2. **Comparing and Contrasting** Use a Venn diagram like the one below to compare and contrast the three types of financing discussed in this section.

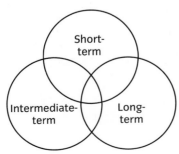

Short-term

Intermediate-term

Long-term

Critical Thinking

3. **The BIG Idea** Explain three ways interest rates affect the profits of a company.

4. **Contrasting** What are the major differences between common and preferred stock?

Applying Economics

5. **Financing Your Business** Imagine you are opening a pizza shop in a popular and busy location. You need to borrow $100,000. Check today's interest rates in a newspaper or on the Internet. Then list the four financing factors you should consider and describe how each would affect your business.

ECONOMIST
(1930–)

Thomas Sowell

● **Syndicated columnist and commentator**

■ Senior Fellow, Hoover Institution, Stanford University
■ Recent published books include *Affirmative Action Around the World* (2004) and *Basic Economics* (2004)
■ Recipient of the National Humanities Medal, 2002

Thomas Sowell spent his early years in Charlotte, North Carolina, where he grew up under very modest circumstances:

"Like most of the houses in the area ours had no such frills as electricity, central heating, or hot running water. . . . For heat in the winter we had the stove, a fireplace in the living room, and a kerosene heater. For light at night we used kerosene lamps. It never occurred to me that we were living in poverty, and in fact those were the happiest times of my life."

Sowell was an exceptionally intelligent child, and he already knew how to read when he entered school. In time, his family moved to Harlem, and he was eventually drafted into the Marine Corps. With the G.I. Bill to help pay his way, he entered prestigious Howard University and later transferred to Harvard, where he graduated *magna cum laude.* There followed a long career as a scholar and writer, during which time he churned out over thirty books, dozens of essays, and hundreds of newspaper columns.

As a young man, Sowell was a self-described Marxist, but he eventually converted to free market capitalism. Today, if he must be labeled, he prefers the term *libertarian*. In describing his political change of heart, Sowell has the following to say: "Back in the days when I was a Marxist, my primary concern was that ordinary people deserved better and that elites were walking all over them." In time, however, Sowell's view of the "elites" and their impact on others, both economically and politically, changed:

> **The passing decades have taught me that political elites and cultural elites are doing far more damage than the market elites could ever get away with doing.**

Checking for Understanding

1. **Synthesizing** Does Sowell believe that having lots of consumer goods is necessary for a child to be happy? How do you know?

2. **Interpreting** What do you think Sowell means by "political elites," "cultural elites," and "market elites"?

The Production Process

Section Preview
In this section, you will learn about the process that companies go through to produce goods and services that satisfy consumer needs and wants.

Content Vocabulary
- production *(p. 272)*
- consumer goods *(p. 272)*
- mechanization *(p. 274)*
- assembly line *(p. 274)*
- division of labor *(p. 275)*
- automation *(p. 275)*
- robotics *(p. 275)*

Academic Vocabulary
- process *(p. 271)*
- location *(p. 272)*

Reading Strategy
Organizing As you read, use a web diagram like the one below to list the production operations discussed in this section.

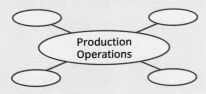

Production Operations

PEOPLE In ThE NeWS
—from *Fortune Magazine*

A PRODUCTION VISIONARY At a dinner party in Tokyo in the summer of 1950, 21 of Japan's most influential corporate leaders . . . [listened to] W. Edwards Deming, an obscure statistician who claimed he knew how to solve postwar Japan's economic problems.

The pursuit of quality, Deming said, was the key to higher productivity, bigger profits, more jobs, and therefore a richer society. Quality, he lectured, did not begin by finding defects at the end of the production line. It had to be pursued along every link of the supply chain, with the active cooperation of everyone from suppliers to the humblest worker on the factory floor.

. . . It wasn't until the '80s that U.S. manufacturers adopted his principles—largely to meet the competition from Japan. Deming's 14 points are now standard operating procedure around the world.

▲ W. Edwards Deming

After businesses obtain the necessary financing, they can get down to the work of producing goods or providing services. This may involve several steps of careful planning, including getting raw materials from suppliers on time. As you read this section, you'll learn about all the steps in the **process** businesses go through to satisfy consumer needs and wants.

Steps in Production Operations

Main Idea The production process involves the coordination of many steps, such as planning, purchasing of inputs, quality control, and inventory control.

Economics & You Has a store ever run out of a product that you wanted to buy? If so, then that store did not maintain its inventory. Read on to learn about this and other production operations of businesses.

production: process of changing resources into goods that satisfy the needs and wants of individuals and businesses

consumer goods: goods produced for individuals and sold directly to the public to be used as they are

Careers Handbook

See pages R76–R80 to learn about becoming a dispatcher.

Production refers to the process of changing resources into goods. One category is **consumer goods,** or goods sold directly to individuals to be used as they are. As you learned in Chapter 1, businesses may also produce *capital goods,* which are products used to make other goods. Besides the actual manufacturing of a good, the production process also involves planning, purchasing, and quality and inventory control. (See **Figure 10.3** below.) A fifth operation, product design, will be discussed in Chapter 11.

Planning includes choosing a location and scheduling production. Among the **location** factors to consider are nearness to markets, raw materials, labor supply, and transportation facilities. A business also needs to have access to a way to deliver its products—highways, railroads, airlines, and pipelines. Scheduling production operations involves setting start and end times for each step in the process. It includes monitoring labor, machinery, and materials so that production moves smoothly.

Figure 10.3 | Production Decisions

■ In setting up a production process, business must consider several other factors besides the actual manufacturing of the good or goods.

B. Purchasing A business's purchasing agent decides what to buy, from whom, and at what price.

A. Planning *Where* a business is located and *how* the business will get its products to consumers are directly related to how successful the business will be. Businesses that cater to teenagers, like music stores, often locate on college campuses.

The people who purchase goods for a business have to decide what to buy, from whom, and at what price. They are usually called purchasing agents. To get the best deal for the company, purchasing agents must consider the price and quality of raw materials, office supplies, machinery, and so on. They must also consider issues such as insurance and shipping rates and times.

Quality control involves overseeing the grade or freshness of goods, their strength or workability, their construction or design, safety, adherence to various standards, and other factors. Quality control systems can be as simple as testing one item per thousand produced or testing each product as it is finished.

Almost all manufacturers and many service businesses, such as dry cleaners, need inventories of the materials they use in making their products or offering their services. A production line can come to a complete halt if inventory runs out. Manufacturers and businesses, such as supermarkets, also keep stockpiles of finished goods on hand for sale.

Inventories are costly, however. The more inventory a business has, the less capital it has for other activities. For example, it costs money to warehouse and insure goods against fire and theft. Some goods, such as film and medicines, spoil if kept beyond a certain period of time. Other goods may become obsolete, or out of date.

✔ Reading Check **Identifying** What must purchasing agents consider before buying goods for a business?

C. Quality Control Conducting quality control is an essential part of the production process, but there is a trade-off. The more time spent on quality control, the higher the production costs.

D. Inventory Control Businesses must manage their inventories carefully. Maintaining too large an inventory can be costly and possibly wasteful.

Economic Analysis

Identifying *Besides choosing a location, what other major consideration goes into the planning stage of the production process?*

Technology and Production

Main Idea Productivity can be increased by utilizing technology and dividing labor.

Economics & You Have you ever purchased anything online? Read on to learn about how technology such as the Internet has impacted business and production.

Technology is the use of science to develop new products and new methods for producing and distributing goods and services.

mechanization: combined labor of people and machines

Mechanization In the 1700s, the Industrial Revolution—the beginning of the factory system—came about through **mechanization,** which combines the labor of people and large power-driven machines. With the introduction of spinning and weaving machines in factories, entrepreneurs replaced skilled handiwork with machines run by unskilled workers. The rate of output per labor hour greatly increased as a result.

assembly line: production system in which the good being produced moves on a conveyor belt past workers who perform individual tasks in assembling it

The Assembly Line An outgrowth of mechanization was the **assembly line.** An assembly line is a production system in which the good being produced moves on a conveyor belt past workers who perform individual tasks in assembling it.

Figure 10.4 | Continuing Advances

■ The development of the assembly line was a major leap forward in the efficiency of the production process. Constantly advancing technology continues to improve the process today. Within the assembly line itself, for example, advances in robotics and automation make today's assembly lines many times more efficient than those of Henry Ford's time.

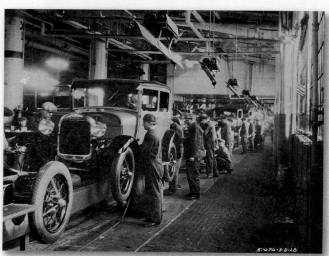

▲ Ford assembly line in Dearborn, Michigan, 1928

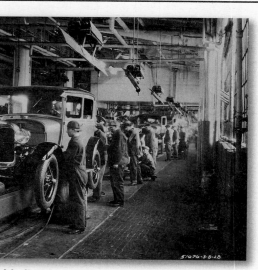

Modern Ford ▶ assembly line in Flat Rock, Michigan

Economic Analysis

Comparing and Contrasting *What similarities can you see between the two assembly lines? What differences do you notice?*

The Ford Motor Company developed the modern assembly-line process early in the twentieth century. Because the assembly line results in more efficient use of machines and labor, the costs of production drop. (See **Figure 10.4**.)

Division of Labor Assembly-line production is possible only with interchangeable parts made in standard sizes, and with the **division of labor,** or the breaking down of a job into small tasks. A different worker performs each task.

Automation Mechanization combines the labor of people and machines. In **automation,** machines do the work and people oversee them. Automation is so common in American society that most of us don't even think about the efficiency of automated traffic signals, doors, or teller machines anymore.

Robotics **Robotics** refers to sophisticated, computer-controlled machinery that operates the assembly line. In some industries, robotics regulate every step of the manufacturing process—from the selection of raw materials to processing, packaging, and inventory control.

division of labor: the breaking down of a job into small tasks performed by different workers

automation: production process in which machines do the work and people oversee them

robotics: sophisticated, computer-controlled machinery that operates an assembly line

✔**Reading Check** **Explaining** What is automation? What are some examples of automation in today's world?

---

section 3 Review

Vocabulary

1. **Explain** the significance of: production, consumer goods, mechanization, assembly line, division of labor, automation, robotics.

Main Ideas

2. **Determining Cause and Effect** What are the factors to consider when locating a business?

3. **Analyzing** Use a chart like the one below to explain how each adaptation helped increase business efficiency.

Business Adaptation	How Efficiency Increased
Mechanization	
Assembly line	
Division of labor	
Automation	
Robotics	

Critical Thinking

4. **The BIG Idea** How can poor inventory control affect profits?

5. **Contrasting** What is the difference between consumer goods and capital goods?

Applying Economics

6. **Purchasing** Imagine you are the purchasing agent for a pizza shop. List the items you would have to buy before opening, and research the cost of each item. Then make a list of additional items you would have to purchase on an ongoing basis. Finally, prepare a report you would submit to the owner of the business listing these costs.

WHAT **GREAT WALL?**

FedEx is taking off like a 'rocket ship.'

Check It Out! In this chapter you learned that businesses must make wise decisions when selecting a supplier to ship raw materials as well as finished goods. In this article, read to learn how FedEx is cutting costs for many small companies.

▲ FedEx bus billboard in China

As soon as Motion Computing Inc. in Austin, Texas, receives an order for one of its $2,200 tablet PCs, workers at a supplier's factory in Kunshan, China, begin assembling the product. When they've finished, they individually box each order and hand them to a driver from FedEx Corp., who trucks it 50 miles to Shanghai, where it's loaded on a jet bound for Anchorage before a series of flights and truck rides finally puts the product into the customer's hands. Elapsed time: as little as five days. Motion's inventory costs? Nada. Zip. Zilch. "We have no inventory tied up in the process anywhere," marvels Scott Eckert, Motion's chief executive. "Frankly, our business is enabled by FedEx."

There are thousands of other Motion Computings that, without FedEx, would be crippled by warehouse and inventory costs. That value proposition has made the Memphis shipping giant an indispensable partner for companies whose products are made in China. In the past two years, the volume of goods that FedEx has shipped over its vast international network has soared 40%, with much of the growth from Asia.

As far back as the 1980s, FedEx founder and CEO Frederick W. Smith predicted that Asia would become an economic powerhouse. These days, FedEx operates 120 flights weekly to and from Asia, including 26 out of China alone. . . .

—Reprinted from *BusinessWeek*

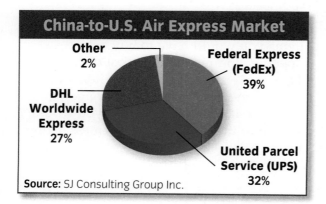

China-to-U.S. Air Express Market

- Other 2%
- Federal Express (FedEx) 39%
- DHL Worldwide Express 27%
- United Parcel Service (UPS) 32%

Source: SJ Consulting Group Inc.

Think About It

1. **Determining Cause and Effect** How does FedEx affect costs for Motion Computing, Inc.?

2. **Synthesizing** How has FedEx's planning decisions affected its success over the past several years?

■ Before undertaking expansion, a business should conduct a **cost-benefit analysis** and expand only if the benefits of doing so outweigh the costs.

Five Steps of Cost-Benefit Analysis				
Step ❶ Estimate the costs of expansion.	**Step ❷** Calculate expected revenues.	**Step ❸** Calculate expected profits.	**Step ❹** Calculate cost of loan plus interest.	**Step ❺** Expected profits should outweigh the costs of expansion.

■ When a business needs to borrow funds to expand, it can choose between **short-, intermediate-,** and **long-term financing** depending upon the kind of expansion it wants to do.

Type of Financing	Typical Repayment Term	Generally Used for:
Short-term	30–90 days	• Paying bills • Buying supplies • Emergencies
Intermediate-term	1–10 years	• Buying land, buildings, or equipment
Long-term	10–15 years or more	• Major expansion projects, such as building a new plant or buying expensive, long-lasting equipment

■ Once a business obtains funds to expand, it must consider the steps in **setting up the production process.**

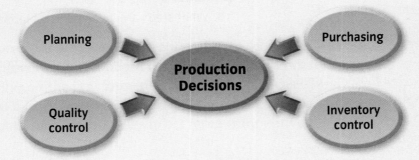

Planning → Production Decisions ← Purchasing

Quality control → Production Decisions ← Inventory control

Review Content Vocabulary

1. *A manufacturing business needs advice on how to pay for an expansion. Write a paragraph or two explaining some of the company's options for accomplishing this. Use all of the following terms.*

financing
cost-benefit analysis
revenues
profits
debt-financing

short-term financing
intermediate-term financing
long-term financing

2. *Now write a paragraph summarizing how companies go about producing goods and services. Use all of the following terms.*

production
consumer goods
mechanization
assembly line

division of labor
automation
robotics

Review Academic Vocabulary

Choose the letter of the term that best completes each sentence.

a. sufficient
b. integral
c. instance
d. undergo

e. adequate
f. location
g. process

3. An entrepreneur must find _____ financing, enough to pay for start-up costs.

4. If a company's process is no longer _____ for its production needs, the company might consider mechanization to speed things up.

5. In one _____, an entrepreneur decides to use credit cards to finance his business.

6. The production _____ usually has many steps.

7. A business must _____ a thorough credit check to borrow money.

8. Getting funding is a(n) _____ part of starting or expanding a business.

9. Business owners should consider _____ factors, such as nearness to markets, raw materials, and transportation facilities.

Review the Main Ideas

Section 1 (pp. 259–263)

10. How do individuals unintentionally invest in businesses? What is their reward for their investment?

11. What are the steps in a cost-benefit analysis? Why do businesses use it when they think about expanding?

Section 2 (pp. 264–269)

12. Fill in a graphic organizer like the one below to describe a situation in which a business might use each type of financing.

Examples of Business Financing	
Short-term	
Intermediate-term	
Long-term	

13. Issuing stocks is a form of what type of financing?

14. What might cause a business to be reluctant to take out a loan?

Section 3 (pp. 271–275)

15. What steps are involved in the production process?

16. What does assembly-line production require?

Problem Solving

17. Imagine that you own a business. Think of at least five business expansions you would like to make to your company that would require financing. List after each type of business expansion, such as buying 10 desktop computers, what the appropriate type of financing would be. Finally, explain your choices. Use a table like the one below to organize your thoughts.

Business Choices		
Expansion	Type of Financing	Explanation

Economics ONLINE

Self-Check Quiz Visit the *Economics Today and Tomorrow* Web site at glencoe.com and click on **Chapter 10—Self-Check Quizzes** to assess your knowledge of chapter content.

Critical Thinking

18. **The BIG Idea** What is the strongest motivation behind most entrepreneurs' efforts to start or expand their businesses? Explain.

19. **Explaining** What factors should a business owner consider when deciding where his or her business should be located?

20. **Analyzing** Assume that you have to buy new inventory that you plan to sell off completely by the end of each month. What is the most appropriate type of financing to use to buy this inventory? Why?

21. **Synthesizing** Imagine that you represent a bank that gives loans to businesses for expansions. What qualities would you look for in a business before approving a loan? Why are these particular qualities important?

Analyzing Visuals

22. Study the cartoon below, and then answer the following questions.
    a. What does the woman want to buy?
    b. What reasons does the coffee shop's owner give for not selling coffee by the pound?
    c. What does the shop owner's reaction imply about his experience as an entrepreneur?

Global Economy

Worldwide Advertising

Each year the United States spends approximately $500 billion on advertising. The map below shows advertising expenditures for five countries whose economies are at different levels of development.

Russia

Category	Spending (millions)
Television	$ 718.4
Radio	123.0
Print*	1,130.5
Outdoor**	58.7
Point of Purchase	374.6
Promotions***	2,773.0
Direct Mail	314.5
Other	4,117.0
Total	**$96.1 billion**
% of World Total	**10.1%**

Egypt

Category	Spending (millions)
Television	$119.7
Radio	4.8
Print*	188.4
Outdoor**	9.8
Point of Purchase	46.8
Promotions***	727.9
Direct Mail	30.3
Other	128.4
Total	**$12.6 billion**
% of World Total	**1.3%**

Kenya

Category	Spending (millions)
Television	$15.2
Radio	0.2
Print*	24.0
Outdoor**	1.2
Point of Purchase	2.0
Promotions***	88.7
Direct Mail	5.5
Other	11.5
Total	**$1.5 billion**
% of World Total	**0.16%**

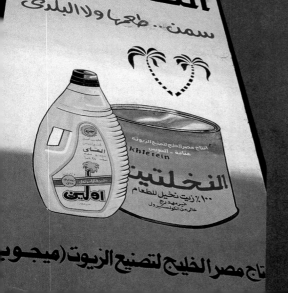

Vietnam

Category	Spending (millions)
Television	$15.5
Radio	0.8
Print*	24.4
Outdoor**	1.3
Point of Purchase	0.8
Promotions***	79.7
Direct Mail	7.2
Other	10.2
Total	**$1.4 billion**
% of World Total	**0.15%**

Singapore

Category	Spending (millions)
Television	$129.7
Radio	67.0
Print*	204.2
Outdoor**	10.6
Point of Purchase	261.6
Promotions***	535.7
Direct Mail	66.3
Other	244.6
Total	**$15.2 billion**
% of World Total	**1.6%**

*newspapers and magazines
**billboards, etc.
***coupons, give-aways, etc.

Thinking Globally

1. **Identifying** What is the largest category of advertising for each country?

2. **Defending** Which of the expenditures for specific countries surprised you the most? Explain your answer.

3. **Critical Thinking** Why do you think advertising expenditures for Kenya and Vietnam are so low compared to the other countries listed?

chapter 11

Marketing and Distribution

The BIG Idea

The profit motive acts as an incentive for people to produce and sell goods and services.

Why It Matters

Do you think advertisements influence your buying habits? In this chapter, read to learn how businesses market and distribute their goods and services.

Economics ONLINE

Chapter Overview Visit the *Economics Today and Tomorrow* Web site at glencoe.com and click on *Chapter 11—Chapter Overviews* to preview chapter information.

The Changing Role of Marketing

GUIDE TO READING

Section Preview
In this section, you will learn about the steps that companies take to figure out how to best meet consumer needs.

Content Vocabulary
- marketing *(p. 284)*
- consumer sovereignty *(p. 284)*
- utility *(p. 284)*
- market research *(p. 285)*
- market survey *(p. 287)*
- test-marketing *(p. 287)*

Academic Vocabulary
- estimate *(p. 284)*
- crucial *(p. 285)*
- individual *(p. 287)*

Reading Strategy
Organizing As you read the section, complete a web diagram similar to the one below by listing the four major types of utility (the ability of a good or service to satisfy consumer wants).

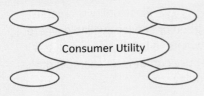

ISSueS In ThE NeWS

TARGETING TEENS Marketers spend a lot of time figuring out what teenagers want. Teenagers are their most desirable and fickle demographic, the arbiters of cool who set trends, influence brand health, and part with their discretionary income most freely.

So as part of Advertising Week 2005, interactive advertising agencies tried to answer the question . . . of what teenagers want.

. . . So what

▲ Advertising Week, 2005

do teenagers want? As one might expect, they want to have some fun. They want to customize products, they want to play games, and they want to socialize.

. . . Interactive advertising usually appeals to teenagers, the agency said, because it engages their desire to control what they buy. For marketers, it allows advertising to masquerade as a game and engage the customer.
—from the *New York Times*

In addition to financing and producing products, which you learned about in Chapter 10, businesses must promote and eventually sell their products and services. In doing so, they must conduct activities that provide information about their products or services to consumers. As you read this section, you'll learn that these activities include market research, advertising and promotion, and distribution.

The Development of Marketing

Main Idea The focus of marketing is to maximize sales by satisfying consumer wants and needs.

Economics & You Have you ever tried to buy something late at night and found the stores to be closed? A 24-hour store would have met your demand. Read on to learn how companies work to satisfy consumer needs.

marketing: all the activities needed to generate consumer demand and to move goods and services from the producer to the consumer

consumer sovereignty: the role of the consumer as ruler of the market when determining the types of goods and services produced

utility: the amount of satisfaction one gets from a good or service

Marketing involves all of the activities needed to generate consumer demand and to move goods and services from the producer to the consumer. Some economists **estimate** that about 50 percent of the price people pay for an item today is for the cost of marketing. The idea and importance of marketing in the United States have changed considerably since 1900. The development of marketing can be traced by analyzing what it has focused on: production, sales, advertising, and **consumer sovereignty**—or consumer as ruler.

Today, marketing's main purpose is to convince consumers that a certain product will add to their utility. **Utility** is the ability of any good or service to satisfy consumer wants. Utility can be divided into four major types: form utility, place utility, time utility, and ownership utility. (See **Figure 11.1** below.)

Reading Check **Explaining** What is the purpose of marketing?

Figure 11.1 | Types of Utility

■ Consumer utility can be divided into four major types.

A. Form Utility Form utility, created by production, is the conversion of raw materials to finished goods. Examples include transforming cotton cloth into clothing or refining crude oil into gasoline, as shown here.

B. Place Utility Place utility is created by having a good or service available where a consumer wants to buy it. Locating a gas station on a busy corner is an example of this type of utility.

Market Research

Main Idea Through market research, businesses can determine what products consumers are likely to buy and at what prices.

Economics & You Have you ever been asked to fill out a survey about a product or service? Read on to learn about this and other methods companies use to figure out what consumers want.

Finding out what consumers want can be difficult. It is **crucial** that businesses do so, however, because many markets today are national or even global. An increase in sales of a few percentage points can result in millions of dollars in increased profits. Therefore, before a product is produced or a service is offered, businesses research their market. Market in this sense means the people who are potential buyers of the good or service.

Through **market research** a company gathers, records, and analyzes data about the types of goods and services that people want. From automakers to producers of frozen foods, most companies producing consumer goods invest heavily in market research. They use this research to figure out how best to promote their product. Issues they consider include what their target audience should be and what advertising method will be most effective.

Careers Handbook

See pages R76–R80 to learn about becoming a market research analyst.

market research: gathering, recording, and analyzing data about the types of goods and services that people want

C. Time Utility Time utility is created by having a good or service available when a consumer wants to buy it. An all-night diner is an example of time utility.

D. Ownership Utility Ownership utility is the satisfaction one receives from simply owning the good or service. One might purchase a fine art painting or a piece of expensive jewelry just to have the satisfaction of owning the object. Luxury cars like the one shown here also provide ownership utility.

Economic Analysis

Contrasting *What is the difference between time utility and place utility?*

Marketing and Distribution **285**

When Should Market Research Be Done?

Market research may be done at several stages of product development. It can be done at the very beginning when the first ideas about a new product are being developed. It can be conducted again to test sample products and alternative packaging designs.

Early market research has several purposes. It helps producers determine whether there is a market for their good or service and what that market is. It can also indicate any changes in quality, features, or design that should be made before a product is offered for sale.

To investigate initial consumer response, market research is often done immediately after a product is released for sale. Some companies even test their advertising to make sure it is attracting the market segment for which the product was designed. Market researchers can also gather information about a product that has been on the market for a while. They then attempt to discover what should be done to maintain or increase sales.

Skills Handbook

See page **R40** to learn about *Analyzing Information.*

Figure 11.2 | **Types of Market Surveys**

A. Questionnaire Marketers often ask consumers to fill out questionnaires about a product. In such a questionnaire, the consumer provides information about how he or she learned about the product, when and where it was purchased, and how satisfied he or she is with the product.

B. Focus Groups Members of a focus group may test and discuss what they like and dislike about similar, and often competing, products. Generally, the people chosen to be part of the focus group do not know which company has hired them to test the products. The focus group is often observed through a one-way mirror by the marketers of one of the products.

Economic Analysis

Comparing and Contrasting *What do you think the benefits and drawbacks of each of these types of market surveys might be?*

Market Surveys The first step in market research is performing a **market survey,** in which researchers gather information about who might be possible users of the product. Such characteristics as age, gender, income, education, and location—urban, suburban, rural—are important to a producer in deciding which market a product should target.

A market survey typically involves a series of carefully worded questions. The questions may be administered in the form of a written questionnaire, which is mailed to consumers. Manufacturers of small appliances such as hair dryers and microwave ovens often put a questionnaire on the back of the warranty card that purchasers are to return. Another way to survey the market is by conducting **individual** interviews or querying focus groups. (See **Figure 11.2.**) Some market surveys are also done online.

market survey: information gathered by researchers about possible users of a product based on such characteristics as age, gender, income, education, and geographic location

Testing New Products As a final step before offering a product for national distribution, market researchers will often test-market a product such as a detergent or a toothpaste. **Test-marketing** means offering a product for sale in a small area, perhaps several cities, for two months to two years to see how well it sells before offering it nationally. (See **Figure 11.3.**) For example, before attempting to market a new energy drink, a company might sell it in several selected areas where the product is most likely to attract the target market segment.

test-marketing: offering a product for sale in a small area for a limited period of time to see how well it sells before offering it nationally

| Figure 11.3 | Testing New Products |

■ A new product might go through the cycle shown here several times before reaching national distribution. Many new products never make it that far.

Economic Analysis
Clarifying *Why are companies willing to take the risk of introducing new products to the market?*

SHOE

▲ The cost of marketing can significantly increase the price of a good or service.

Researchers keep track of the units sold and test different prices and ad campaigns within the test markets. If the product is successful, the company will offer it nationally. If sales are disappointing, the company has two choices. It can make changes or, rather than spend more funds redesigning the product, the company can abandon the idea.

Of all the new products introduced every year in the United States, most are not profitable and do not survive in the marketplace. It is the constant lure of owning a high-profit item that motivates companies to continue developing new products.

✔ **Reading Check** **Identifying** What are two steps involved in market research?

section 1 Review

Vocabulary

1. **Explain** the significance of: marketing, consumer sovereignty, utility, market research, market survey, test-marketing.

Main Ideas

2. **Outlining** Fill in the steps a new product goes through before reaching the market.

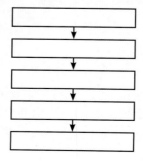

Critical Thinking

3. **The BIG Idea** Explain how test-marketing can increase profits.

4. **Interpreting** Why is marketing for consumer sovereignty successful?

5. **Explaining** What is meant by consumer utility?

Applying Economics

6. **Market Surveys** Imagine that you have the task of testing the market to see what people want in a new energy bar. What questions would you ask? Create a questionnaire for this product to distribute to consumers.

GUIDE TO READING

Section Preview
In this section, you will learn how companies develop a plan to sell their products effectively.

Content Vocabulary
- penetration pricing *(p. 291)*
- price leadership *(p. 291)*
- promotion *(p. 293)*
- direct-mail advertising *(p. 293)*
- product life cycle *(p. 294)*

Academic Vocabulary
- strategy *(p. 289)*
- accompany *(p. 290)*
- obvious *(p. 292)*

Reading Strategy
Clarifying As you read, complete a chart like the one below by explaining each of the four elements involved in developing an effective marketing strategy.

	The "Four Ps" of Marketing
Product	
Price	
Place	
Promotion	

ISSUES IN THE NEWS
—from *The Chief Executive*

UNWELCOME CHANGE An outcry . . . erupted in Britain recently over Nestlé's decision to alter the packaging of its popular Smarties candies.

After 67 years of being packaged in cardboard tubes, the M&M-like coated chocolates are to be sold in a hexagon-shaped box. It is part of a revamp that, if successful, could extend across the globe. A similar outcry came in 1999 when Nestlé reinvented the KitKat chocolate bar by giving it a chunkier shape.

Hullabaloo over candy packaging? It's true. Consumer attachment to the way a product looks on shelves underlines the significance of brand identity and marketing to Nestlé.

In today's highly competitive world, simply producing a product and offering it for sale is not enough. Through their marketing departments, companies plan a marketing **strategy,** which details how the company will sell the product effectively. As you read this section, you'll learn that a marketing strategy, or plan, combines the "four Ps" of marketing: product, price, place, and promotion.

The "Four Ps" of Marketing

Main Idea The "four Ps" of marketing are product, price, place, and promotion.

Economics & You Have you ever noticed magazines and other "impulse" items displayed near the checkout lines in grocery stores? Read on to learn about methods companies use to promote their products.

Product Market research helps determine *what* good or service to produce. It also helps a company determine what services to offer with the product, how to package it, and what kind of product identification to use.

Additional services that **accompany** a product often help make a sale. Warranties are customary with many manufactured products, but some manufacturers offer special services free or for a small charge. For example, if you buy a digital camera, you may be able to purchase from the manufacturer a 2-year extended warranty in addition to the 1-year warranty given by the store in which you bought the camera.

Packaging is also an important factor in selling a product. The "right" packaging combines size, design, and color to attract potential consumers. DVDs, books, and food are especially dependent on packaging. Such words as *New and Improved* or *Economy Size* are used to attract customers. Sometimes manufacturers add coupons and rebate offers to their packages. Coupons are used to persuade consumers to make a repeat purchase and develop the habit of buying the product.

Once a product is offered for sale, *product identification* becomes important. Product identification is meant to attract consumers to look at, buy, and remember a particular product. It can involve the use of a logo or certain colors on a package. It can also involve a song or jingle, a certain type of packaging, or anything that can be associated with and identify the product.

Skills Handbook

See page R44 to learn about Detecting Bias.

Product Identification

From the Pillsbury Doughboy to the familiar Cheerios logo, all of these items are good examples of packaging that achieves product identification.

Price Supply and demand ultimately determine the price of a good or service. Because of the laws of supply and demand, the price at which a product sells may help determine whether it is successful in attracting buyers while still being profitable to its maker. In setting a price, a company has to consider the costs of producing, advertising, selling, and distributing the product, as well as the amount of profit it hopes to make. (See **Figure 11.4** below.)

When companies first introduce a new product into the market, that product will often be priced low, initially, to lure customers away from better-known similar products. This strategy is called **penetration pricing.** Such pricing is an alternative to spending more on advertising.

penetration pricing: selling a new product at a low price to attract customers away from an established product

Another strategy companies employ is to offer coupons attached right to the new products themselves in the store. The coupons act as incentives to attract consumers to the new products. If a consumer likes a new product, he or she will probably buy it again even without a coupon.

Often companies sell similar goods at similar prices. This practice is known as **price leadership.** For example, one major airline may lower its prices, which causes all of the other major airlines to follow by lowering their fares. Conversely, if a certain product becomes very popular with consumers, all the manufacturers of the product may raise their prices.

price leadership: a practice in some industries in which the largest firm publishes its price list ahead of its competitors, who then match those announced prices

---

Figure 11.4 | **Factors of Price**

■ Companies must consider several factors when deciding on a price to set for new products. They must weigh these factors against the forces of supply and demand to arrive at a price at which the product will sell and also make a profit for the producer.

Expected profit

Cost of distributing

Cost of producing

Price Considerations

Cost of selling

Cost of advertising

Economic Analysis

Extending *What costs might be included in distributing a product?*

Place *Where* the product should be sold is another decision of the marketing department. Should it be sold through the mail, by telephone, in department stores, in specialty shops, in supermarkets, in discount stores, door-to-door, or on the Internet? Or should it be sold in a combination of many of these places? Often, the answer is **obvious** because of past experience with similar products. A cereal company, for example, would most likely market a new cereal in supermarkets.

The location of the product within the store itself is another consideration of both the manufacturer and the store owner. Cereals aimed at children, for example, are usually placed on lower shelves where children can see them. Also, more expensive items are placed on middle shelves at the eye level of adults of average height. This placement ensures that consumers will be more likely to notice the pricier products.

Sometimes a company will decide that its goods would appeal only to a limited market. Therefore, it may choose to sell the product or products only in specialty shops, through mail-order catalogs, or on the Internet.

Geographic location may also be a consideration when companies decide where to market products. Some products may be targeted specifically at large cities, while others may be more suitable for rural markets.

Impulse Buying
Product placement within a store is another factor marketers must consider. Often, companies will pay a high price to a store to have their products placed near the check-out counters, where people look at the products while they are waiting in line. Common products placed here include candy, gum, and magazines. People will often buy these products on impulse.

Sometimes companies will pay celebrities or famous athletes huge amounts to promote their products. For example, in 2003, Cleveland Cavalier LeBron James signed a 7-year, $90 million contract with Nike to promote basketball shoes.

Promotion Promotion is the use of advertising and other methods to inform consumers that a new or improved product or service is available. Promotion also seeks to convince consumers to purchase the new items. Businesses spend billions of dollars each year on promotional campaigns. Advertising methods may include ads in newspapers and magazines, radio spots, and television commercials. Increasingly, businesses are also advertising and promoting their products on the Internet.

The particular type of promotion that a producer uses depends on three factors: (1) the product, (2) the type of consumer that the company wants to attract, and (3) the amount the company plans to spend. If a product is going to be marketed to teenagers, for example, companies will often advertise in teen magazines and on teen Web sites.

Magazines and catalogs, credit card companies, and insurance companies also often use **direct-mail advertising.** The mailer usually includes a letter describing the product or service and an order blank.

Other promotional efforts include free samples, cents-off coupons, gifts, and rebates. Where and how products are displayed is important to promotion as well.

promotion: use of advertising to inform consumers that a new or improved product or service is available and to persuade them to purchase it

direct-mail advertising: type of promotion using a mailer that usually includes a letter describing the product or service and an order blank or application form

✔ Reading Check **Summarizing** What determines the type of promotion that a producer uses?

FOXTROT

▼ Most people are more influenced by product names and slogans than they realize.

Product Life Cycle

Introduction

Growth

Maturity

Decline

product life cycle: series of stages that a product goes through from first introduction to complete withdrawal from the market

Product Life Cycle

(Main Idea) **Most products go through a four-stage life cycle consisting of introduction, growth, maturity, and decline.**

Economics & You Can you think of a product that has been around since your childhood? What about a fad that passed quickly? Read on to learn about the life cycles of different products.

Most products go through what is known as a **product life cycle.** This cycle is a series of stages from first introduction to complete withdrawal from the market. The four stages of a typical product life cycle include introduction, growth, maturity, and decline.

People involved in marketing products need to understand the stages of each product's life cycle because marketing programs are different for each stage. A product in its introductory stage has to be explained and promoted much differently than one in its maturity stage. Also, pricing can vary depending on the stage. Prices of products tend to be relatively high during the growth stage.

Many marketers attempt to extend the life of old products. They may redesign the packaging or find new uses for the product. Advertisements attempt to persuade consumers that they need the product for its new uses.

✓ Reading Check **Explaining** How do marketers extend the life of old products?

section 2 Review

Vocabulary

1. **Explain** the significance of: penetration pricing, price leadership, promotion, direct-mail advertising, product life cycle.

Main Ideas

2. **Examining** Copy the chart below and explain how each concept listed affects price.

Concept	How It Affects Price
Supply and demand	
Penetration pricing	
Price leadership	

Critical Thinking

3. The **BIG Idea** Besides profit desired, list the factors a company must consider before setting a price.

4. **Evaluating** Think of a product you like and use regularly. Which advertising method discussed in this section would you use to promote the product? Why?

Applying Economics

5. **Product Life Cycle** Research the product life cycle of videocassette tapes, and make a chart showing the *introduction, growth, maturity,* and *decline* of that product's marketing.

SHAPING SHOPPERS' EMOTIONS

Shop 'Til You Feel It's a Full-Blown Experience.

Check It Out! In this chapter you learned about marketing's main purpose: to convince consumers that a certain product will add to their utility. The following article highlights how stores have taken this idea one step further.

Companies used to focus on making new, better, or cheaper products and services—and then selling them in the marketplace. Now, the game is to create wonderful and emotional experiences for consumers around whatever is being sold. It's the experience that counts, not the product. While that business model has long been the preserve of cult-like brands such as Starbucks and Apple, it's fast becoming the norm in all industries. . . .

▲ Starbucks understands emotional branding

Think of the emphasis on a consumer's individual experience as a final blow to the notion of mass marketing. It's the next step beyond customization of what you make—to shaping people's emotions with what you make. And there's good reason to take the leap. Profit margins are much higher on "experiences" than actual products or services. After all, customers aren't just paying for a cup of coffee at Starbucks. . . . They're paying admission to a club—one that delivers something to satisfy the soul.

—Reprinted from *BusinessWeek*

The 10 Commandments of *Emotional* Branding

1. Consumers buy, *people* live.
2. Products fulfill needs, *experiences* fulfill desires.
3. Honesty is expected. *Trust* is engaging and needs to be earned.
4. Quality for the right price is a given. *Preference* creates the sale.
5. Notoriety gets you known. To be desired, you must meet the customer's *aspirations*.
6. Identity is recognition. *Personality* is about character and charisma!
7. The functionality of a product is about practical qualities only. *Design* is about experiences.
8. Widespread presence is seen. *Emotional presence* is felt.
9. Communication is telling. *Dialog* is sharing.
10. Service is selling. *Relationship* is acknowledgment

Think About It

1. **Recalling** According to the story above, how has the goal of marketing changed?
2. **Synthesizing** What is the marketing advantage for companies that focus on experiences rather than just products?

Source: www.allworth.com

Distribution Channels

GUIDE TO READING

Section Preview
In this section, you will learn about the different ways in which goods are moved from producers to consumers.

Content Vocabulary
- channels of distribution (p. 297)
- wholesalers (p. 297)
- retailers (p. 298)
- e-commerce (p. 298)

Academic Vocabulary
- method (p. 298)
- valid (p. 299)

Reading Strategy
Sequencing As you read, complete a flowchart like the one below by listing and explaining the four steps involved in the distribution process.

Product Distribution

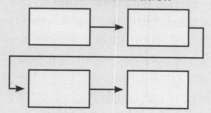

PrODUCTS In ThE NeWS
—from the *Arizona Daily Star*

COOKIE CRAZE If you don't think Girl Scout cookies have become a big business, the sight of 17,500 cases of cookies moving from a . . . warehouse last weekend would change your mind.

Troop leaders loaded the Thin Mints, Samoas, Do-Si-Dos, and other variations into a fleet of minivans, trucks, and U-Haul trailers for sale and delivery this week.

[A] growing percentage of those cookies are now sold from booths set up at shopping centers rather than through [door-to-door] cookie orders. . . .

"Some parents don't want their children going door-to-door, and it's also become a matter of convenience, . . . [said Dominick San Angelo, development manager for the Sahuaro Girl Scout Council]. "I've heard people say that they'd rather just buy the cookies on their way to the grocery store instead of ordering them and having them delivered later."

Decisions about distribution, or moving goods from where they are produced to the people who will buy them, is another function of marketing. As you read this section, you'll learn about various options for distribution and how decisions are made regarding how goods will be moved and distributed. You'll also learn about the increasing role of the Internet in this branch of marketing.

Wholesalers, Retailers, Storage, and Transportation

Main Idea Goods are usually moved from producers to consumers through middlemen such as wholesalers and retailers.

Economics & You Do you buy goods such as clothing and food in the same place where they are produced? Read on to learn how consumer goods get from producers to you.

The routes by which goods are moved are known as **channels of distribution.** (See **Figure 11.5** below.) Some consumer goods, such as clothing and farm products, are usually sold by a producer to a wholesaler and then to a retailer, who sells them to consumers. Other consumer goods, such as automobiles, are normally sold by the producer directly to a retailer and then to consumers. With each transaction, or business deal, the price increases. Few goods go directly from producer to consumer. An example of some that do would be vegetables sold at a farmer's roadside stand.

channels of distribution: routes by which goods are moved from producers to consumers

Wholesalers Businesses that purchase large quantities of goods from producers for resale to other businesses (not to consumers) are called **wholesalers.** Various types of wholesalers exist. Some may buy goods from manufacturers and sell them to retail stores that then deal directly with consumers. Others may also buy and sell raw materials or capital goods to manufacturers.

wholesalers: businesses that purchase large quantities of goods from producers for resale to other businesses

Figure 11.5 Distribution of Consumer Goods

Charts In Motion See StudentWorks™ Plus or go to glencoe.com.

■ In rare cases, consumer goods go directly from the manufacturer to the consumer. More often, goods first travel through other channels of distribution, such as wholesalers and retail stores.

① Manufacturer → Consumer

② Manufacturer → Retailer → Consumer

③ Manufacturer → Wholesaler → Retailer → Consumer

Economic Analysis

Synthesizing *If the same product moved through each of the three distribution channels shown, in which channel would consumers wind up paying the highest price? Why?*

Transporting Goods

Producers need to decide how best to transport their goods to where consumers can buy them. In the United States, trucking is a popular and widely utilized way to accomplish this task.

retailers: businesses that sell consumer goods directly to the public

e-commerce: business transactions conducted over the Internet

Retailers Businesses that sell consumer goods directly to the public are **retailers.** You are probably familiar with many of them: department stores, discount stores, supermarkets, club warehouses, mail-order houses, specialty stores such as bookshops, and so on.

Traditional retailers have also "set up shop" on the Internet. More and more, there are **e-commerce** retailers that have no physical store anywhere. They are "virtual companies."

Storage and Transportation Part of the distribution process includes storing goods for future sales. The producer, wholesaler, or retailer may perform this function. Most retailers keep some inventory on hand for immediate sales. Many have a two- to three-month supply, depending on the type of merchandise.

Transportation involves the physical movement of goods from producers and/or sellers to buyers. In deciding the **method** of transportation, businesspeople must consider the type of good, such as perishable food. The size and weight of the good are also important. Airfreighting tons of wheat is impractical, but airfreighting small machine parts is not. Speed may be necessary to fulfill a sale or to get fresh fruit to a food plant. The cost of the different types of transportation helps determine how to ship items.

Reading Check **Predicting Consequences** How has the Internet affected the retail sector?

Other Distribution Channels

Main Idea Direct marketing is done mainly through catalogs and over the Internet.

Economics & You Have you ever been to a club warehouse store? What are the benefits and challenges of this type of shopping? Read on to learn about this and other expanding distribution channels.

In the last 15 to 20 years, distribution channels have expanded rapidly because of the growth of club warehouse stores and direct marketing. A typical club warehouse store requires a membership fee—about $55 a year for individuals and more for businesses. The club warehouse formula is to buy a limited number of brands and models of each product in such huge quantities that the warehouse gets very favorable prices from the manufacturers. Direct marketing is done mainly through catalogs and over the Internet. Catalog shopping became a popular distribution channel to avoid state sales taxes. The purchaser normally does not pay sales tax if the catalog company is located in another state. The same holds true for goods purchased through the Internet, although this may change in the future.

Shopping on the Internet has become increasingly popular because of the ease with which it can be done. Anybody with access to the Internet and a **valid** credit card can order just about anything on the Web.

Reading Check **Evaluating** What are three reasons to shop on the Internet?

section 3 Review

Vocabulary

1. **Explain** the significance of: channels of distribution, wholesalers, retailers, e-commerce.

Main Ideas

2. **Identifying** In a web diagram like the one below, list three common distribution channels for products.

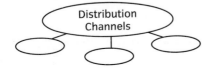

Critical Thinking

3. **The BIG Idea** Determine and list two ways an e-commerce company can boost profits, as compared to other distributors.

4. **Contrasting** What is the difference between a retailer and a wholesaler?

Applying Economics

5. **Catalog Marketing** Find four catalog displays, and then draw or describe specific changes you would implement to make the ad more appealing and convincing to yourself and other teenagers.

Margaret Whitman

● **President and Chief Executive Officer of eBay, Inc.**

■ Turned Internet auction house eBay into a truly global corporation with services in Europe, Asia, Australia, and Latin America

■ Serves on the board of directors of Procter & Gamble, Gap, and DreamWorks Animation

■ Ranked first in *Fortune* magazine's list of the 50 most powerful women in business, 2004 and 2005

Margaret Whitman—or "Meg," as everyone calls her—is considered one of the most powerful women on the planet. As a new MBA graduate in 1979, she took her first plunge into the corporate world with Procter & Gamble in Cincinnati. Following that she held important positions with several major corporations before making the most important career move of her life. Rather than continue holding top jobs with established companies, Whitman decided to hitch her wagon to a rising star.

While she was working at Hasbro in 1997, she was approached by a corporate recruiter and offered the CEO's position at eBay. At first she wasn't interested. In that year, eBay had only $5.7 million in revenues, a fairly small company by current standards. After conducting further research, however, Whitman became convinced that taking over leadership of eBay was the right move. Eventually, stockholders agreed. Under Whitman's direction, eBay's revenues grew from $5.7 million to over $4.5 billion in just eight years. During that same period, registered users on eBay rose from 2 million to 180 million.

In the process, Whitman has done quite well for herself. In 2005, she made the *Forbes* list of the 500 richest people in the world, coming in at slot 437 with an estimated net worth of $1.5 billion. What does Meg Whitman think about her job?

"I have one of the best jobs in corporate America. It's this unique blend of commerce and community. . . .[eBay] is one of the fastest-growing companies of any scale. Every week, there is a different set of issues, a different challenge, something new to think about."

Perhaps the best part of Whitman's job is the constant learning experience it provides:

> **"Probably at least a couple of times a week, I go, 'Huh! I didn't know that.'"**

Checking for Understanding

1. **Speculating** Do you think an advanced degree is needed in order to be a corporate executive? Why or why not?

2. **Defending** If you were an executive, would you take a position with a small, not-yet-established company? Why or why not?

■ The **main purpose of marketing** is to convince consumers that a certain product or service will add to their utility. Product testing helps marketers predict whether or not a new good will sell well.

New Product

Offered for sale in selected areas for specific time period

If sales are low

If product does well

Product is changed

Product is abandoned

National distribution

■ When introducing a new product, businesses need to keep the **"Four Ps" of marketing** in mind.

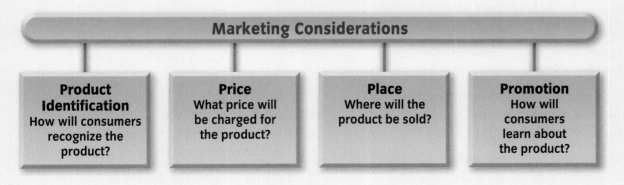

Marketing Considerations

Product Identification	**Price**	**Place**	**Promotion**
How will consumers recognize the product?	What price will be charged for the product?	Where will the product be sold?	How will consumers learn about the product?

■ Goods are usually moved from manufacturers to consumers through various **distribution channels** like wholesalers and retailers.

Manufacturer → Wholesaler → Retailer → Consumer

Review Content Vocabulary

1. *Write a paragraph or two explaining the process of marketing, promoting, and distributing a product. Use all of the following terms.*

marketing
utility
market research
penetration pricing
promotion
product life cycle

channels of distribution
wholesalers
retailers
e-commerce

Review Academic Vocabulary

Choose the letter of the term that best completes each sentence.

   a. estimate
   b. crucial
   c. individual
   d. strategy

   e. accompany
   f. obvious
   g. method
   h. valid

2. When a product becomes profitable, it proves that the company used a _____ marketing strategy.

3. One _____ of finding out what consumers want is sending out questionnaires.

4. Coupons that _____ advertisements are often very effective at bringing in new buyers.

5. After a product has been on the market for some time, stores can better _____ how many units of the product to order.

6. Knowing what customers want is _____ knowledge for marketers and producers.

7. Sometimes improvements that would help a product sell better are _____ and easy to do.

8. Marketers might try a new _____ for selling an older product.

9. Each _____ response to a market survey is important to help improve a product.

Review the Main Ideas

Section 1 (pp. 283–288)

10. What is the relationship between marketing and utility?

11. What are the four types of utility?

12. When is market research done, and how is it conducted?

Section 2 (pp. 289–294)

13. List and describe the "four Ps" of planning a marketing strategy.

14. What are two examples of how goods and services can be promoted?

15. Fill in a graphic organizer like the one below to show the four stages of a product's life cycle.

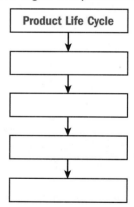

Section 3 (pp. 296–299)

16. What are distribution channels? Give two examples of common channels of distribution.

17. Who may perform the storage function of distribution?

18. What factors must a business consider in choosing a method of transporting the goods they sell?

Thinking Like an Economist

19. Suppose that you are in charge of marketing a new product.

   a. First, come up with a product to market, such as a new sports drink or a cell phone targeted at young users.

   b. Create a short questionnaire to use as a market-research tool to find out what people who might buy the product would want.

   c. Have as many people as possible answer the questionnaire.

   d. Analyze the results and create a simple visual presentation to show what the product should be like and how best to market it.

20. Now describe the cycle your new product will go through while it is being tested in the market.

Economics ONLINE

Self-Check Quiz Visit the *Economics Today and Tomorrow* Web site at glencoe.com and click on **Chapter 11—Self-Check Quizzes** to assess your knowledge of chapter content.

Critical Thinking

21. **The BIG Idea** How does the process of marketing (research, promotion, distribution, etc.) help producers? How does it help consumers?

22. **Evaluating** Think of a product that has been around for a very long time, such as a particular brand of candy or soft drink. Fill in a graphic organizer like the one below to evaluate various methods marketers might use (or have used) to try to extend the life of this older product.

Marketing method	How effective would it be? Why?
Redesign packaging	
New uses for product	
New advertising	
(Fill in another idea)	

Analyzing Visuals

23. Study the cartoon on the right, and then answer the following questions.

   a. Who are the two men pictured in this cartoon?

   b. What process is the speaker describing?

   c. What flaw in this process does the man point out?

AFTER A FAVORABLE RATING FROM THE FOCUS GROUP, IT UNDERWENT EXTENSIVE TEST MARKETING. NOW, AFTER MONTHS OF CLEARING LEGAL HURDLES, IT'S READY FOR MASS PRODUCTION. OF COURSE, THE DOWNSIDE IS THAT IT'S NOW OBSOLETE...

GIZMO INC.

Should advertising to kids be banned?

Advertisers spend billions of dollars each year targeting children as young as two years old. Between television, games, movies, the Internet, magazines, and other sources, kids get an average of 8.5 hours of media exposure a day. That's 40,000 ads per year. Childhood obesity has doubled in the past 20 years—as has the amount spent advertising junk food to kids. People who support banning ads directed at children say they create the desire for unhealthy foods and make socially inappropriate behavior seem cool. Opponents of a ban say parents should exert more control. Should advertising to children be against the law?

YES! Parents can't fight $15 billion worth of advertising

We can no longer stand by as our children's health is sacrificed for corporate profits. Children are especially vulnerable to the impact of advertising. . . . Children under eight aren't able to understand that ads are created to convince people to buy products. . . . Teens are particularly vulnerable because they are being marketed to in a way that preys on their desire to be older and to act older. It's harder and harder to find "unbranded" time for children, time that is not in their face selling them something.

. . . One family, alone, can't combat a $15 billion industry. . . . If Congress cared about the health and well-being of children, it would enact legislation that would support not the rights of . . . marketers, but the rights of children to grow up—and the rights of parents to raise them—without being undermined by greed.

—Susan Linn, author of *Consuming Kids: The Hostile Takeover of Childhood,* and Diane E. Levin, co-founders, Campaign for a Commercial-Free Childhood

NO! Parents and advertisers should be mutually responsible

Advertisers need to gain the trust of children and their parents through effective and honest advertising. In turn, parents must take responsibility for their children: monitor what they watch and read, determine how they spend their free time, and educate them to become responsible and informed consumers. Advertising to children will become less controversial only when advertisers and parents assume mutual responsibility for its content and exposure.

With respect to broadcast advertising, the industry believes that current guidelines—the careful review and approval process of commercials by the advertiser, its agency, and the station or network that will air the advertising—provide sufficient controls for children's advertising. According to the American Association of Advertising Agencies, whose member agencies place more than 80 percent of all national advertising in the U.S., product commercials aired during children's programming are designed to "show the product's features and explain its benefits in terms understandable to children and sensitive to their special attitudes and perceptions."

—Statement by the Advertising Educational Foundation, an organization of advertisers, advertising agencies, and media companies

Annual Advertising Spending by Food Manufacturers (in Millions)	
Prepared convenience foods	$1,563
Candy and snacks	$1,095
Soft drinks	$702
Cooking products, seasonings	$675
Coffee, tea, juices	$625
Dairy products	$505
Bakery goods	$408
Meat, poultry, fish	$210
Fruits, vegetables, grains, beans	$159
General promotions	$50

Source: Center for Science in the Public Interest

Debating the Issue

1. **Specifying** In what ways might advertising be linked to childhood obesity?

2. **Choosing Sides** Do you think advertising should be allowed in places like schools and on school buses, where they will be seen mainly by children? Why or why not?

Find Out More!

3. **Analyzing** Bring to class two examples of ads—one targeting children under 8 and one targeting teenagers. How does the advertiser in each ad appeal to the target audience?

The **BIG Idea**

The labor market, like other markets, is determined by supply and demand.

Why It Matters

In this chapter, read to learn about the major categories of the labor force, the role of unions in today's work force, and the factors that affect wages.

Economics ONLINE

Chapter Overview Visit the *Economics Today and Tomorrow* Web site at glencoe.com and click on *Chapter 12—Chapter Overviews* to preview chapter information.

section 1   Americans at Work

GUIDE TO READING

Section Preview
In this section, you will learn how workers are categorized and how their wages are determined.

Content Vocabulary
- civilian labor force *(p. 308)*
- blue-collar workers *(p. 309)*
- white-collar workers *(p. 309)*
- service workers *(p. 309)*
- unskilled workers *(p. 310)*
- semiskilled workers *(p. 310)*
- skilled workers *(p. 310)*
- professionals *(p. 310)*
- minimum wage law *(p. 313)*

Academic Vocabulary
- resource *(p. 307)*
- displace *(p. 309)*

Reading Strategy
Categorizing As you read, complete a diagram like this one to describe the types of workers discussed.

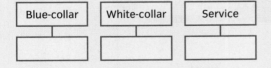

Blue-collar	White-collar	Service

ISSues In ThE NeWS
—from *CareerJournal.com*

CAREER OUTLOOK Your perfect job may . . . come with a trade-off or two. But the likelihood of having to accept trade-offs will be small if your abilities mesh well with any of the nation's best careers. Fortunately, there are many great jobs out there, which means the odds that you can find your perfect profession may be greater than you think.

According to the . . . *Jobs Rated Almanac* by Les Krantz, the nation's single best job in terms of low stress, high compensation, lots of autonomy, tremendous hiring demand and several other

▲ **Lumberjack**

key criteria, is biologist. . . . Other top-rated jobs [include financial planners, actuaries, computer-systems analysts, and accountants].

Lumberjacks were ranked at the bottom of the list. . . . Their careers couldn't be much rougher in terms of work, instability, poor pay, and pure danger.

Everyone—from a lumberjack to a biologist to the president of a corporation—belongs to the productive **resource** known as labor. As you read this section, you'll learn how workers are categorized, how wages are determined, and why employers need to pay more to get (and keep) good workers.

Personal Finance Handbook
See pages R20–R23 to learn about getting a job.

The Civilian Labor Force

Main Idea Workers can be categorized by the type of work they perform and by skill level.

Economics & You Do you have a job? What kinds of skills does it require? Read on to learn about how American workers are categorized according to their skill level or the type of work that they do.

civilian labor force: total number of people 16 years old or older who are either employed or actively seeking work

When discussing labor, economists use the term *labor force* in a specific way. The **civilian labor force** is the total number of people 16 years old or older who are either employed or actively seeking work. Individuals not able to work, such as disabled people or those in prisons or mental institutions, are not included in the civilian labor force. People in the armed forces or those not looking for a paying job, such as full-time students and homemakers, are excluded as well. **Figure 12.1** below shows the civilian labor force in comparison to the total working-age population.

Workers in the United States are categorized in several ways. One way is to group them according to the type of work they perform. Another way is by the level of training or education their jobs require.

Skills Handbook

*See page **R50** to learn about **Using Bar and Circle Graphs.***

Figure 12.1   Employment Status of U.S. Population

■ As shown here, most people age 16 and older in the United States are part of the civilian labor force.

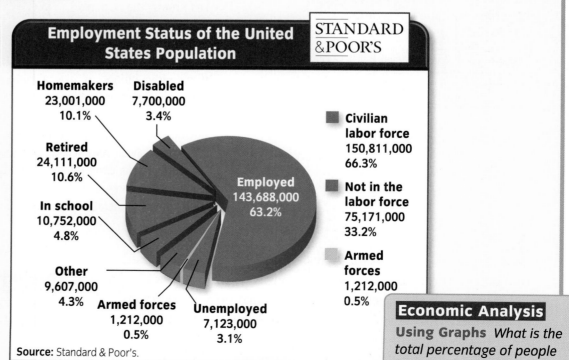

Employment Status of the United States Population

STANDARD &POOR'S

Homemakers 23,001,000 10.1%

Disabled 7,700,000 3.4%

Retired 24,111,000 10.6%

In school 10,752,000 4.8%

Other 9,607,000 4.3%

Armed forces 1,212,000 0.5%

Employed 143,688,000 63.2%

Unemployed 7,123,000 3.1%

■ **Civilian labor force** 150,811,000 66.3%

■ **Not in the labor force** 75,171,000 33.2%

■ **Armed forces** 1,212,000 0.5%

Source: Standard & Poor's.

Economic Analysis

Using Graphs *What is the total percentage of people who are not employed and not looking for work?*

Blue-Collar, White-Collar, and Service Workers

During the late 1800s and early 1900s, higher wages paid to workers in urban areas lured farmworkers there. **Displaced** farmers, and others who entered the workforce because of higher wages, often became **blue-collar workers**—craft and manufacturing workers and nonfarm laborers.

The largest sector of the labor force is **white-collar workers.** Office workers, salespeople, and highly trained individuals such as physicians and engineers are classified as white-collar workers. This sector experienced steady growth throughout the twentieth century.

In recent years, a shift away from farm work and blue-collar jobs to the service sector of the economy has occurred. **Service workers** are those who provide services directly to individuals. Cooks, piano tuners, health-care aides, computer repair specialists, and barbers are all service workers. See **Figure 12.2** below.

blue-collar workers: category of workers employed in crafts, manufacturing, and nonfarm labor

white-collar workers: category of workers employed in offices, sales, or professional positions

service workers: people who provide services directly to individuals

---

Figure 12.2 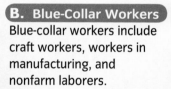 **Worker Categories by Type of Job**

■ Economists sometimes classify workers by their type of occupation, regardless of the skills necessary to perform the job.

B. Blue-Collar Workers Blue-collar workers include craft workers, workers in manufacturing, and nonfarm laborers.

A. White-Collar Workers White-collar workers include office workers, salespeople, and highly trained individuals such as engineers.

C. Service Workers Service workers provide services—haircuts, food service, child care, and so on—directly to individuals.

Economic Analysis

Extending *How do you think "white-collar" and "blue-collar" workers got their names?*

Jobs Categorized by Skill Level
Another way to categorize workers is by the skills required to perform their occupation. **Unskilled workers** are those whose jobs require no specialized training. Jobs such as waiting on tables, assembly-line work, and custodial work are generally considered unskilled, although obviously these types of work require skills such as patience and the ability to pace oneself or to work according to a schedule. Such jobs may also demand the ability to work well with people.

Semiskilled workers are those whose jobs require some training, often using modern technology. The job of nurse's aide, for example, is considered a semiskilled occupation.

Someone who has learned a trade or craft, either through a vocational school or as an apprentice to an experienced worker, is considered a **skilled worker.** Police officers and electricians engage in skilled occupations.

Professionals are those with college degrees and usually additional education or training. Also classified as white-collar workers, people who hold professional jobs include teachers, architects, and accountants.

Although such terms as *semiskilled, skilled,* etc., are helpful in picturing different areas of the labor force, individual workers do not always fall into a single category. The definition of *technician,* for example, has become increasingly vague, as some technicians today require professional-level training. Also, workers may move from one skill level to another as they gain training and experience.

unskilled workers: people whose jobs require no specialized training

semiskilled workers: people whose jobs require some training, often using modern technology

skilled workers: people who have learned a trade or craft either through a vocational school or as an apprentice to an experienced worker

professionals: highly educated individuals with college degrees and usually additional education or training

✔ Reading Check) **Identifying** Who is not included in the civilian labor force?

In Training
Often, people work in semiskilled occupations while they are training for a skilled profession. Nurses' aides, for example, may move on to become nurses.

Supply and Demand in the Labor Market

Main Idea In labor markets, wages are influenced by factors affecting supply and demand, such as variations in skill levels, job conditions, and work locations.

Economics & You In your opinion, do you get paid enough for the work that you do? Read on to learn how supply and demand determine wages in the labor market.

The labor market, like other markets, is affected by supply and demand. Suppliers are the workers who offer their services to employers, while the demand comes from the employers who require workers.

Supply and Demand Factors That Affect Wages

Three major factors affect how supply and demand determine prices, or in this case wages, in the labor market. These factors include skill, type of job, and location. **Figure 12.3** below discusses two of these factors.

Figure 12.3 | **Some Factors That Affect Wages**

■ The skill level a person brings to a job and the risk involved in performing a job are two major factors in determing how much a job will pay.

▼ **A. Skill** Alex Rodriguez, third baseman and power hitter for the New York Yankees, signed a $252 million 10-year contract. His wages are high because his types of skills are in high demand but short supply.

▲ **B. Type of Job** People with dangerous jobs, such as firefighters, receive higher wages than others who do not have life-threatening occupations.

Economic Analysis

Identifying *What kind of labor market exists when there is high demand and short supply for a certain occupation?*

Figure 12.4   Location

■ As you can see from the table, where a person lives can have a significant impact on wages. For example, workers in the Northeast tend to earn more than workers in the South.

Economic Analysis

Synthesizing *Who do you think generally earns more—workers in large cities or rural areas? Why?*

Income Comparison by State	
Five states with the highest median incomes:	
Connecticut	$56,409
New Jersey	$56,356
Maryland	$54,302
Massachusetts	$52,713
New Hampshire	$52,409
Five states with the lowest median incomes:	
Montana	$34,449
Lousiana	$33,792
Arkansas	$33,445
West Virginia	$32,967
Mississippi	$32,397

Source: U.S. Census Bureau, 2005.

Economics ONLINE

Student Web Activity
Visit the *Economics Today and Tomorrow* Web site at glencoe.com and click on *Chapter 12—Student Web Activities* to see how the Internet can help you find a job.

The first factor, *skill*, may come from talent, initiative, education and/or training, or experience. Because the demand for talented individuals is usually high, whereas the supply of such employees is often scarce, a type of "tight" labor market occurs. The evidence of such a "tight" labor market is that it usually results in high prices—or high wages. Highly educated brain surgeons, for example, are paid large sums because their skills are in high demand relative to supply.

The *type of job* also affects the amount an employer is willing to pay and a potential employee is willing to accept. Jobs that are unpleasant or dangerous, such as coal mining, often pay higher wages compared to other jobs requiring equal levels of skill. Again, the demand for workers might be high, but the supply of laborers willing to do the work may be low.

In contrast, some jobs are enjoyable or prestigious or desirable enough that people are willing to take them even at low wages. Many people take lower-paying jobs in industries such as filmmaking and publishing for these reasons. In these cases, the demand for workers might be low, whereas the supply of individuals waiting for prestigious positions is high.

The *location* of both jobs and workers is the third factor in determining wages. (See **Figure 12.4** above.) If workers are relatively scarce in an area, companies may have to pay high wages to attract workers to move there. In contrast, a company in a heavily populated area often can hire people at relatively low wages. Even professionals in such a location may not receive high wages.

Restrictions on Wages If the labor market were perfectly competitive, the changing supply and demand for labor would result in constantly shifting wage rates.

Two factors restrict supply and demand in terms of their influence on wages. One is the federal **minimum wage law,** which sets the lowest legal hourly wage rate that may be paid to certain types of workers. Some states and cities have their own minimum wage laws, too.

Although the purpose of the minimum wage is to help workers, some studies have shown that the opposite often occurs. An increase in the minimum wage causes some firms to hire fewer low-skilled workers. This can delay the acquisition of job skills by low-paid workers who may not have had much formal education. When this happens, these low-skilled workers are even less sought after in the labor market.

Another factor that restricts the influence of supply and demand on wages is the process of wage negotiations between organized labor (unions) and management. Supply and demand have less influence on wage negotiations than do such things as the company's ability to pay higher wages, the length of the negotiated contract, and seniority—length of time on the job. You'll learn more about organized labor in Sections 2 and 3.

minimum wage law: federal law that sets the lowest legal hourly wage rate that may be paid to certain types of workers

✔ **Reading Check** **Summarizing** List at least three factors, other than supply and demand, that influence wages.

section 1 Review

Vocabulary

1. **Explain** the significance of: civilian labor force, blue-collar workers, white-collar workers, service workers, unskilled workers, semiskilled workers, skilled workers, professionals, minimum wage law.

Main Ideas

2. **Synthesizing** In boxes like the ones below, list three examples of jobs that would fit into each category.

Service	Blue-collar	White-collar

Critical Thinking

3. **The BIG Idea** What kind of supply-and-demand situation creates a "tight" labor market?

4. **Determining Cause and Effect** Describe how type of job, skill level, and location affect wages.

Applying Economics

5. **Minimum Wage** Find the minimum wage in your state by using an Internet search engine. Then write a letter to the editor of the local paper explaining why you think the wage should be raised, lowered, or stay the same.

IPOD'ING AT **WORK?**

The boss is watching—so watch your iPod!

Check It Out! In this chapter you learned about job categories and their skill levels. In the following article, read to learn how some companies are using tech-toys to enhance the skills of their employees.

Trying to turn out productive workers as efficiently as possible, a few fast-food chains are using iPod video players to train new employees. Pal's Sudden Service, a regional chain with Tennessee and Virginia outlets, started iPod video training in its 20 restaurants in February. "We're looking to expedite the learning process through technology," says Pal's CEO Thom Crosby. Chuck E. Cheese, the pizza-and-games chain, is a few months into testing the video iPods in one of its Dallas outlets.

Both programs, developed by podTraining, a Flower Mound (Texas) startup, use short video clips to show new hires how to do their jobs. Unlike video or DVD-based training systems, the iPods can be updated quickly and cheaply by downloading new content. And the portability of the iPod allows training to be done on the job. New Pal's employees practice making the chain's trademark Big Pal burger while watching a video of the

▲ iPod training

process. Other videos address customer service, ethics, and cashier operations.

TJ Schier, president and founder of podTraining, says he is developing more fast-food training videos for the iPod, including troubleshooting segments produced with Coca-Cola to teach workers what to do when a soda machine breaks. . . . At Pal's, the iPod program has shaved a week and a half from new-employee training times, Crosby says, and has created a cool factor that has given a boost to recruitment.

—Reprinted from *BusinessWeek*

Corporate office produces training video for:
- New products
- New recipes
- New procedures
- Steps in repair

→ **Corporate office puts information on Internet** →

Individual stores immediately download new information onto iPods, saving time and paper

Think About It

1. **Explaining** What is the advantage of using iPods versus other training systems?

2. **Extending** What other benefits to using iPods besides the ones listed in the article can you think of?

section 2 | Organized Labor

GUIDE TO READING

Section Preview
In this section, you will learn about the history of labor unions and how they are organized.

Content Vocabulary
- labor union (p. 316)
- strike (p. 317)
- craft union (p. 317)
- industrial union (p. 317)
- local union (p. 318)
- closed shop (p. 318)
- union shop (p. 318)
- agency shop (p. 318)
- right-to-work laws (p. 318)

Academic Vocabulary
- regulate (p. 317)
- significant (p. 317)

Reading Strategy
Sequencing As you read the section, complete a time line like the one below by filling in at least five major events in the organized labor movement from the late 1800s to the mid-1900s.

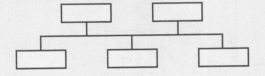

ISSues In ThE NeWS
—from *washingtonpost.com*

UNIONS IN ACTION Six months before the [2006] November elections, alarms sounded throughout the labor movement. A flurry of memos from the field warned that high-level rancor from the 2005 breakup of the AFL-CIO was gumming up political mobilization on the ground, threatening to blow the Democrats' opportunity to retake Congress.

"Let us continue to fight, together," pleaded a May 4 letter from 150 AFL-CIO state and local officials to the leaders of the breakaway unions known as Change to Win. "Let us live. Don't walk away."

The warnings now read like ancient history. The labor movement, despite being more divided and depleted than it has been in decades, produced record participation in the 2006 campaign, contacting 13.4 million voters in 32 battleground states and supplying 187,000 volunteers to help Democrats match the GOP's get-out-the-vote machine, which was far better financed.

In the late 1800s, some American workers began taking steps to try to improve their wages and working conditions. They believed that if they united in groups, they would have more influence on management than they would as individual workers acting alone. As you read this section, you'll learn about the steps that workers took to gain a voice in their working environments.

Development of Labor Unions

Main Idea Labor unions developed to attempt to improve working conditions and wages for their members.

Economics & You If you work, do you feel that working conditions in your job are fair? Read on to learn about how workers who wanted to change working conditions formed the first labor unions.

Working conditions in the 1800s were very different from those of today. Buildings were often poorly lighted and ventilated, and the machinery was sometimes dangerous to operate. The workweek was long, and wages were low. Health-care benefits, unemployment insurance, sick leave, and paid vacations and holidays did not exist. In an attempt to gain some control over their wages and working conditions, many American workers started forming labor unions. A **labor union** is an association of workers organized to improve wages and working conditions for its members. Unionism, however, met with strong resistance. In the 1800s, state legislatures passed laws against unions, and courts upheld them.

labor union: association of workers organized to improve wages and working conditions for its members

Figure 12.5 Labor's Early Struggle for Recognition

Maps in Motion See StudentWorks™ Plus or go to glencoe.com.

■ The major weapon for workers to use against management was the strike. More often than not, however, striking unions were viewed as dangerous by the public, who turned against them.

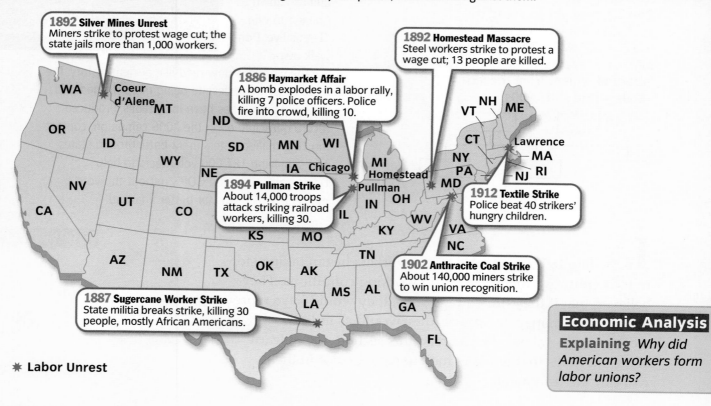

1892 Silver Mines Unrest Miners strike to protest wage cut; the state jails more than 1,000 workers.

1892 Homestead Massacre Steel workers strike to protest a wage cut; 13 people are killed.

1886 Haymarket Affair A bomb explodes in a labor rally, killing 7 police officers. Police fire into crowd, killing 10.

1894 Pullman Strike About 14,000 troops attack striking railroad workers, killing 30.

1912 Textile Strike Police beat 40 strikers' hungry children.

1902 Anthracite Coal Strike About 140,000 miners strike to win union recognition.

1887 Sugercane Worker Strike State militia breaks strike, killing 30 people, mostly African Americans.

✳ Labor Unrest

Economic Analysis

Explaining *Why did American workers form labor unions?*

Many businesses refused to hire union members or deal with unions. Workers who tried to unionize were fired and blacklisted—kept from being employed. **Strikes,** or deliberate work stoppages by workers to force an employer to give in to their demands, often resulted in violence between strikers and police, as described in **Figure 12.5**. Not until the mid-1930s did Congress begin to pass laws to **regulate** labor-management relations.

Labor-Management Legislation	
Legislation	**Description**
Norris-LaGuardia Act, 1932	Limits the power of the courts to stop picketing and boycotts, and makes yellow-dog contracts illegal. This type of contract is the practice in which employers require that employees pledge not to join a union.
Wagner Act, 1935	Guarantees labor's right to organize and bargain collectively. Sets up National Labor Relations Board (NLRB) to oversee the establishment and operation of unions.
Taft-Hartley Act, 1947	Outlaws certain strike tactics, permits states to pass laws making union shops illegal, and allows the president to delay a strike if it will threaten the nation's health and safety.
Landrum-Griffin Act, 1959	Increases government control over unions and guarantees union members certain rights, such as freedom of speech in union activities and control over union dues.

The American Labor Movement

For much of its history, organized labor in the United States has been split into two groups: craft unions and industrial unions. A **craft union** is made up of skilled workers in a specific trade or industry, such as carpentry or printing. The first permanent federation, or organization of national labor unions, was the American Federation of Labor (AFL), composed of craft unions and led by Samuel Gompers.

An **industrial union** is made up of all the workers in an industry regardless of job or skill level. Attempts to organize industrial unions date to the late 1800s and the leadership of Eugene V. Debs, founder of the American Railway Union. The first **significant** effort to unionize unskilled and semiskilled workers did not begin, however, until the formation of the Congress of Industrial Organizations (CIO) in 1938.

strike: deliberate work stoppage by workers to force an employer to give in to their demands

craft union: union made up of skilled workers in a specific trade or industry

industrial union: union made up of all the workers in an industry regardless of job or skill level

The AFL-CIO

During the late 1930s and early 1940s, both the AFL and the CIO launched organizing campaigns that made the lines between industrial and craft unions less clear. AFL unions began recruiting semiskilled and unskilled workers, while the CIO began organizing workers in the skilled trades. The resulting rivalry cost both union federations time and effort.

By the mid-1950s, union leaders realized that the labor movement would make greater gains if craft and industrial unions worked together. As a result, the two federations merged in 1955 to form the present AFL-CIO.

Reading Check **Determining Cause and Effect** What were some complaints of workers in the 1800s?

How Unions Are Organized

Main Idea Labor unions can exist as local unions, as national or international unions, or as federations.

Economics & You Do you think that today's workers should be required to join a local union? Why or why not? Read on to learn about both sides of this debate.

local union: members of a union in a particular factory, company, or geographic area

closed shop: company in which only union members could be hired

union shop: company that requires new employees to join a union after a specific period of time

agency shop: company in which employees are not required to join the union, but must pay union dues

right-to-work laws: state laws forbidding unions from forcing workers to join and pay union dues

Organized labor operates at three levels: the local union, the national or international union, and the federation.

Local Unions A **local union** consists of the members of a union in a particular factory, company, or geographic area. The local deals with a company by negotiating a contract and making sure the terms of the contract are kept. The influence that a local has often depends on the type of membership policy it has negotiated with management.

Not all local unions are alike. Membership requirements and the ways in which management relates to union members vary from one kind of shop to another. In a **closed shop,** companies could hire only union members. The Taft-Hartley Act of 1947 outlawed closed shops, however. In a **union shop,** a new employee must join the union after a specific period of time, usually three months. In an **agency shop,** employees are not required to join the union, but they must pay union dues.

Supporters of union and agency shops argue that employees in companies that are unionized should be required to pay union dues because they benefit from contracts the union negotiates. Opponents believe that a person should not be required to join a union. Since 1947 a number of states have passed **right-to-work laws** that forbid union shops. These laws allow workers to continue working in a particular job without joining a union. The benefits negotiated by the union must be made available to workers who do not join the union. Unions have less power in states with right-to-work laws than in other states.

The Big Three

Three of the largest unions in the United States are the Teamsters, the United Automobile Workers, and the United Steelworkers of America.

National Unions Above the locals are the national unions. These are the individual craft or industrial unions that represent locals nationwide. Those unions that also have members in Canada or Mexico are often called international unions.

National unions send in organizers to help employees set up locals. To help in negotiating a contract between a local and a particular company, the nationals provide lawyers and other staff members. In certain industries such as steel and mining, the national union negotiates the contract for the entire industry. After the majority of union members accept the contract, all the locals within the industry must work under the contract. Some of the largest unions are the International Brotherhood of Teamsters, the United Automobile Workers (UAW), and the United Steelworkers of America (USW).

Federation Level At the federation level is the AFL-CIO, which is made up of more than 50 national and international unions with about 9 million members.

Since 2005, the AFL-CIO has had to face competition from a new union organization. That organization is called the Change to Win Federation. It is composed of members of seven unions, including the Service Employees International and the International Brotherhood of Teamsters. Change to Win seeks to promote and increase U.S. union membership.

✔ **Reading Check** **Evaluating** How do right-to-work laws affect unions?

---

section 2 Review

Vocabulary
1. **Explain** the significance of: labor union, strike, craft union, industrial union, local union, closed shop, union shop, agency shop, right-to-work laws.

Main Ideas
2. **Summarizing** In a diagram like the one below, list the types of unionized shops described in this section, along with one characteristic of each shop.

Unionized Shops

Critical Thinking
3. **The BIG Idea** How do the laws of supply and demand relate to unionization?
4. **Contrasting** What is the difference between a craft union and an industrial union?

Applying Economics
5. **Professional Unions** Interview a teacher about the teacher's union in your school. Is it an agency shop? How much are the dues? What services does the union offer? Is the teacher satisfied with this union? If there is no union, how do teachers negotiate a contract?

Collective Bargaining

GUIDE TO READING

Section Preview
In this section, you will learn how unions and employers determine the conditions of employment, and about the role of unions today.

Content Vocabulary
- collective bargaining *(p. 321)*
- cost-of-living adjustment (COLA) *(p. 321)*
- mediation *(p. 321)*
- arbitration *(p. 321)*
- picketing *(p. 322)*
- boycott *(p. 322)*
- lockout *(p. 323)*
- injunction *(p. 323)*

Academic Vocabulary
- neutral *(p. 321)*
- resolve *(p. 321)*

Reading Strategy
Organizing As you read the section, complete a chart like the one below by listing the steps of the collective bargaining process that can occur if labor and management are unable to reach a compromise.

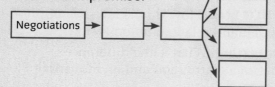

ISSues In ThE NeWS
—from *CNN.com*

HOCKEY SEASON CUT SHORT [In February 2005], the NHL canceled the remainder of the season . . . after a series of last-minute offers were rejected on the final day of negotiations.

The players had been locked out over a salary cap dispute since the season was scheduled to start in October. The NHL now becomes the first major professional sports league in North America to lose an entire season to a labor dispute. . . . The league and players' union traded

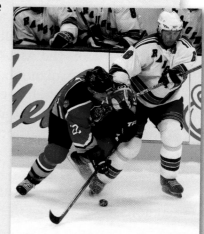

a flurry of proposals and letters . . . but could never agree on a cap. The players proposed $49 million per team; the owners said $42.5 million.

. . . Over the 10-year term of the last collective bargaining agreement, players' salaries went from just over $500,000 a season to $1.83 million. An economic study commissioned by the NHL determined that players got 75 percent of team revenues, the most of any of the four North American professional leagues.

At the core of negotiations between management and unions is compromise. Companies want to keep wages and benefits low to hold labor costs down and remain competitive in the market. Unions want to increase wages and benefits for their members as much as possible. As you read this section, you'll learn that both sides must be prepared to give and take a little.

Negotiations

Economics & You Have you ever had to compromise to get something you wanted? Read on to learn about how workers and management attempt to reach compromises on important labor issues.

Collective bargaining is the process by which unions and employers negotiate the conditions of employment.

In collective bargaining, labor and management meet to discuss a wide range of contract issues, including working hours, fringe benefits, and a **cost-of-living adjustment (COLA).** In most cases, negotiations are friendly and result in an agreement that satisfies all parties.

If negotiations become hostile or compromise breaks down, labor and management may try mediation. **Mediation** occurs when a **neutral** person steps in and tries to get both sides to reach an agreement. The mediator suggests possible solutions and works to keep the two sides talking with each other. The federal government, through the Federal Mediation and Conciliation Service (FMCS), provides a mediator free of charge upon request of either side. In a typical year, FMCS mediators are involved in thousands of negotiations. A number of state and private mediators also help **resolve** disputes.

If mediation fails, the negotiation process may go to **arbitration,** in which the two sides submit the issues they cannot agree on to a third party for a final decision. Both sides agree in advance to accept the arbitrator's decision, although one or both sides may not be completely happy with the outcome. The FMCS often helps in these cases by providing labor and management with a list of private arbitrators in their area.

Reading Check **Explaining** What is mediation? What role does the federal government play in this process?

collective bargaining: process by which unions and employers negotiate the conditions of employment

cost-of-living adjustment (COLA): provision calling for a wage increase each year if the general level of prices rises

mediation: a neutral person tries to get both sides to reach an agreement during negotiations

arbitration: union and management submit the issues they cannot agree on to a third party for a final decision

Seeking Compromise

In most cases, issues that arise between management and workers are settled to the satisfaction of all parties through collective bargaining.

Strikes and Management

Main Idea If labor negotiations break down, unions may resort to strikes or boycotts, and management may resort to lockouts or injunctions.

Economics & You Have you ever witnessed, or participated in, a strike? What did you experience? Read on to learn about what happens when negotiations between labor and management break down.

Most contracts are settled at the bargaining table. Sometimes, however, negotiations break down and a strike results. The number of strikes in the United States has declined sharply since the 1970s, as shown in **Figure 12.6**.

Strikers usually walk up and down in front of their workplace carrying picket signs that state their disagreement with the company. **Picketing** is meant to discourage workers from crossing the picket line to work for the employer. It is also aimed at embarrassing the company and building public support for the strike.

Striking unions may also use a boycott to exert more economic pressure. In a **boycott,** unions urge the public not to purchase goods or services produced by a company. In addition, unions may ask politicians to push management for a settlement or to support publicly the union's demands.

picketing: action of strikers who walk in front of a workplace carrying signs that state their disagreement with the company

boycott: economic pressure exerted by unions urging the public not to purchase the goods or services produced by a company

When Negotiations Fail

One of the biggest strikes in recent history involved the Transport Workers Union Local 100 (TWU) in New York City. In December 2005, negotiations between the union and the Metropolitan Transportation Authority broke down over retirement, pension, and wage issues. Most New York City transit authority personnel observed the strike, effectively ending all bus and subway service and affecting millions of commuters. The strike lasted for three days.

Figure 12.6 | Strikes

■ As you can see from the graph, strikes in the United States have declined sharply since the 1970s.

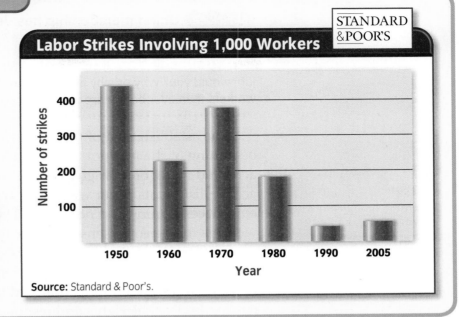

Labor Strikes Involving 1,000 Workers

STANDARD &POOR'S

Number of strikes (y-axis: 100, 200, 300, 400)

Year (x-axis: 1950, 1960, 1970, 1980, 1990, 2005)

Source: Standard & Poor's.

Economic Analysis

Explaining *What are workers trying to accomplish when they picket in a strike?*

Strikes can drag on for months and even years. After a long period of time, strikers sometimes become discouraged. Some may decide to go back to work without gaining what they wanted. In most cases, however, strikes are settled as management and labor return to the negotiating table and work out an agreement.

Lockouts When faced with a strike, management has methods of its own to use against strikers. One is the **lockout,** which occurs when management prevents workers from returning to work until they agree to a new contract. Another tactic is to bring in strikebreakers, called "scabs" by strikers. These are people willing to cross a picket line to work for the terms the company offers.

lockout: situation that occurs when management prevents workers from returning to work until they agree to a new contract

Injunctions Management sometimes requests a court injunction to limit picketing or to prevent a strike from continuing or even occurring. An **injunction** is a legal order of a court preventing some activity. Under the Taft-Hartley Act of 1947, the president of the United States can obtain an injunction to delay or halt a strike for up to 80 days if the strike will endanger the nation's safety or health. During this cooling-off period, the two sides must try to reach a settlement. Although settlements usually are reached in these cases, presidents have invoked the Taft-Hartley Act numerous times over the years.

injunction: court order preventing some activity

✔**Reading Check** **Describing** What is a scab?

Decline of Unions

Main Idea Union membership has declined steadily over the past several decades.

Economics & You If you had the option of joining a union for your job, would you? Why or why not? Read on to learn about why fewer workers than ever before are willing to become union members.

The establishment of the AFL in 1886 is considered the beginning of the modern union era. Since that time, unions have achieved many of their goals. Union supporters list among their accomplishments better wages and working conditions for all employees—union and nonunion. They point out that many workers now enjoy a sense of security that helps to maintain some control over their jobs and lives.

Union supporters also note that the collective bargaining process has brought more order and fairness to the workplace. It has made clear the rights and responsibilities of both management and labor.

Because working conditions have improved so dramatically over the years, many nonunion workers often see little to gain from joining a union. **Figure 12.7** below shows how much union membership has declined since the 1940s. In addition, the nature of the economy itself is changing. More jobs are opening in the white-collar and service sectors, whereas blue-collar jobs are decreasing due to automation.

Skills Handbook

See page R49 to learn about Using Line Graphs.

| Figure 12.7 | Declining Union Membership |

■ The labor movement today faces many problems. The percentage of the labor force who belong to a union reached a high in the mid-1940s and has been declining since 1955.

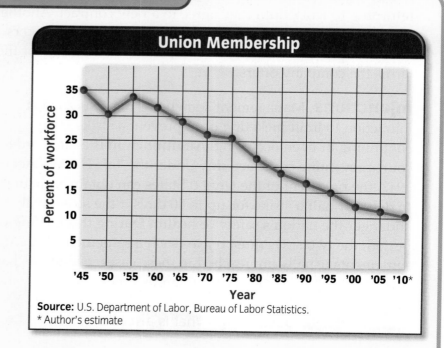

Union Membership

Percent of workforce

'45 '50 '55 '60 '65 '70 '75 '80 '85 '90 '95 '00 '05 '10*

Year

Source: U.S. Department of Labor, Bureau of Labor Statistics.
* Author's estimate

Economic Analysis

Comparing *Compare the trend in strikes with what is happening in union membership. How are the two related?*

LUCKY COW

▲ Unions' demands must be reasonable for the union to be effective.

The labor movement also has its critics. Some opponents charge that unions have grown so large and bureaucratic that they are out of touch with their members' needs. Others claim that increased wages are passed on to consumers in the form of higher prices.

Employers often argue that union rules decrease productivity. They point to rules that slow the introduction of new technology or require more employees than necessary to do a job. In addition, at times corruption among some labor leaders has damaged the reputation of organized labor.

✓ Reading Check **Analyzing** What are two reasons why workers are less willing to join unions today than in the 1940s?

section 3 Review

Vocabulary

1. **Explain** the significance of: collective bargaining, cost-of-living adjustment (COLA), mediation, arbitration, picketing, boycott, lockout, injunction.

Main Ideas

2. **Interpreting** From a worker's point of view, what are the advantages and disadvantages of each strategy listed in the table below?

	Advantages	Disadvantages
Picketing		
Boycott		
Lockout		
Injunction		

Critical Thinking

3. **The BIG Idea** How can collective bargaining overrule supply and demand for wages in a workplace?

4. **Contrasting** What is the difference between mediation and arbitration?

Applying Economics

5. **Collective Bargaining** Imagine that your student body is bargaining with your school administration about conditions for students. Using each term in this section's vocabulary list, write a newspaper article about what is happening in negotiations.

LABOR LEADER
(1927–1993)

César Chávez

● **Founder of the United Farm Workers of America**

■ Led successful international grape and lettuce boycotts in support of migrant farm workers

■ In 1975, helped push California's Agricultural Labor Relations Act through the state legislature, protecting the right of farm workers to unionize

■ Posthumous recipient of the Presidential Medal of Freedom

By the time César Chávez reached the eighth grade and dropped out of school to help support his family, he had attended more than 30 elementary and middle schools as the child of migrant farm workers. After a stint in the U.S. Navy, Chávez married, started a family, and returned to the life of an agricultural worker. He caught the eye of a community organizer and was recruited to work for a Latino civil-rights group. His goal, however, was to create a union for underpaid farm workers.

Chávez spent 10 years learning how to be an organizer, and in 1962, he began the difficult work of forming what would become the United Farm Workers of America.

"The organizer has to work more than anyone else. . . . and in the initial part of the movement, there's the fear that when the organizer leaves, the movement will collapse. So you have to be able to say, I'm not going to be here a year or six months, but an awful long time."

He did stay a long time, and in 1966 he negotiated the first genuine union contract between a grower and farm workers. For the next 27 years, he led boycotts, went on hunger strikes, and continued his organizing activities until his death in 1993. Though given great credit for his dedication, he acknowledged his reliance on the workers themselves:

> **❝I have always believed that, in order for any movement to be lasting, it must be built on the people. They must be the ones involved in forming it, and they must be the ones that ultimately control it.❞**

Checking for Understanding

1. **Assessing** Of what importance was César Chávez's work as a civil-rights organizer?

2. **Drawing Conclusions** Why does an organizer need to be dedicated to his or her cause?

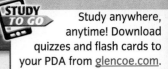

■ In labor markets, a variety of factors that affect **supply and demand for jobs** ultimately determine wages for those jobs.

| • Skill level required • Job conditions • Work location | → Affect → | Supply and demand | → Affect → | $ WAGES $ |

■ **Labor unions** formed in the United States to try to improve working conditions and wages for their members.

Unions May Work For:

◆ Higher wages
◆ Safer working conditions
◆ Shorter workweek
◆ Health-care benefits
◆ Child care
◆ Sick leave
◆ Paid vacations and holidays
◆ Unemployment insurance

■ Because working conditions in general have improved so much since the mid-1950s, many nonunion workers see little to gain by joining a union, and **union membership has declined.**

Union Membership

Percent of workforce (vertical axis): 5, 10, 15, 20, 25, 30, 35

Year (horizontal axis): '45 '50 '55 '60 '65 '70 '75 '80 '85 '90 '95 '00 '05 '10*

Source: U.S. Department of Labor, Bureau of Labor Statistics.
* Author's estimate

Review Content Vocabulary

1. *Write a paragraph or two describing the basic categories of workers. Use all of the following terms.*

   blue-collar workers   semiskilled workers
   white-collar workers   skilled workers
   service workers   professionals
   unskilled workers

2. *Write a paragraph or two explaining the role of organized labor in the United States, both past and present. Use all of the following terms.*

   minimum wage law   collective
   labor union   bargaining
   strike   mediation
   local union   picketing
   union shop   lockout
   right-to-work laws

Review Academic Vocabulary

Choose the letter of the term that best completes each sentence.

   a. resource   d. significant
   b. displaced   e. neutral
   c. regulate   f. resolve

3. Labor unions have had a _____ impact on improving working conditions and wages.

4. Human labor is a valuable productive _____.

5. Sometimes a _____ third party must mediate between workers and management.

6. When a person loses his job, he becomes _____.

7. Congress has passed laws to _____ labor-management relations.

8. Unions and management often _____ their disputes through negotiations.

Review the Main Ideas

Section 1 (pp. 307–313)

9. Which category of worker usually has a higher-education degree as well as additional training?

10. What is the difference between blue-collar and white-collar workers?

11. What factors determine how much a person is paid for his or her work?

12. What two main factors restrict the influence of supply and demand on wages?

Section 2 (pp. 315–319)

13. Why did workers start forming unions in the late 1800s?

14. What are the major kinds of labor unions, and what type(s) of workers belong to each?

15. What two union federations merged in 1955?

16. How do right-to-work laws affect workers who do not belong to unions?

Section 3 (pp. 320–325)

17. What kinds of issues are typically addressed in collective bargaining negotiations?

18. What is a strike, and what is it meant to accomplish?

19. How might management respond to strikes?

20. Create a diagram like the one below to explain the factors that have caused a decline in union membership in recent decades.

Declining Union Membership

Math Practice

Study this table about union membership in different occupations in the United States. Then answer the questions that follow.

Union Membership	
Occupation	**Percentage of workers who belong to unions**
Construction	13.3%
Financial (bankers, accountants, brokers, etc.)	2.3%
Local government (teachers, police, firefighters, etc.)	41.9%
Manufacturing	13.0%
Telecommunications	21.4%
Transportation and utilities	24.0%

21. Which group in the table is the most heavily unionized? Why do you think so many in this group belong to unions?

Economics ONLINE

Self-Check Quiz Visit the *Economics Today and Tomorrow* Web site at glencoe.com and click on *Chapter 12—Self-Check Quizzes* to assess your knowledge of chapter content.

22. Which occupation had the lowest percentage of union members? Why do you think this is so?

23. If 100,000 people are working in manufacturing jobs in one state, about how many of them belong to unions?

Critical Thinking

24. **The BIG Idea** How do supply and demand affect the labor market? Give an example.

25. **Determining Cause and Effect** Why do workers with more education and training generally get paid higher wages?

26. **Synthesizing** How might things be different for workers today if labor unions had never existed?

27. **Predicting Consequences** Do you think union membership will continue to decline in the future? Why or why not?

Analyzing Visuals

28. Study the cartoon below, and then answer the following questions.

   a. What is a CEO?

   b. What economic factors contribute to a CEO having a higher salary than the young women shown in the cartoon?

   c. Do you think it is fair that CEOs make more than fast-food workers? Why or why not?

How can young people run successful businesses?

THE ISSUE

In a recent survey, 90 percent of teachers and guidance counselors reported that students have expressed interest in starting their own businesses. Many say that they would prefer being their own boss to working for an employer, but there are other reasons to become an entrepreneur. First, there is the potential to earn more income than you would working for someone else. There's also the possibility of earning *passive money*—money you make even when you're not working, which could include royalties from books or income from sales made by employees you hire. Also, many people like the idea of being able to set their own hours and work in an environment of their own choosing. But how can young people without business experience operate successful businesses?

Profits Kept By Entrepreneurs	
Type of Company	**Percent of Profits Kept by Owner**
Real estate agents, brokers, managers, and appraisers	52.3%
Home health-care services	49.5%
Legal services	48.3%
Certified public accountants	45.7%
Child day-care services	45.6%
Personal laundry services	36.0%
Administrative and support services	35.0%
Advertising related services	30.7%
Clothing and accessories stores	13.6%
Freight trucking, local or long distance	18.0%

THE FACTS

Many successful companies were started by young people with a good idea. When Michael S. Dell was an 18-year-old freshman at the University of Texas, he thought buying computers and parts from retail stores was too expensive and that the service was generally poor.

Like all successful entrepreneurs, Michael saw a need in the market and met it: he began selling computer parts out of his dorm room. Without the expense of operating retail stores, he could offer lower prices. He borrowed $1,000 and founded Dell Computer Corporation (now Dell, Inc.) to sell computers directly to consumers. By 2006 Dell had become the world's top vendor of personal computers, with sales of almost $56 billion.

The Dell business model did not come from Michael Dell's experience in business but from his personal experience as a consumer. Other young entrepreneurs have taken similar paths. At age 16, for example, Richard Branson published a magazine in London called *Student*. It evolved into the Virgin Group, a conglomerate that now operates dozens

of companies in industries from entertainment and fitness to financial services and travel, including space tourism.

THE ECONOMIC CONNECTION: ENTREPRENEURSHIP

Almost three-fourths of American businesses—19.5 million—consist of one self-employed person. More than 6 million new businesses are started each year; after five years, almost 44 percent have survived. The rest usually fail because of poor management or inadequate financing.

Once you decide to start a business, the first step is to identify a good or service the public either wants or needs, or can be convinced it wants or needs—discovering or creating demand. Then, write a **business plan** detailing how you'll produce the product (production), who will buy it (market research), and how you'll reach them (marketing). Other key considerations include taxes, insurance, legal issues, and **cash flow**—the money coming into and going out of a business.

Learning to handle these functions as you go is called on-the-job training. That's how Michael Dell, Richard Branson, Mary Kay, Bill Gates, and many other entrepreneurs did it. Of course, the risk of learning as you go is that you may not learn the skills you need as quickly as you need them. But several organizations are available to help. Many universities offer entrepreneurship programs. Junior Achievement and the Young Entrepreneur Foundation provide advice, ideas, and annual awards. The Small Business Administration provides advice and tools to help young entrepreneurs get started.

CONCLUSION

Entrepreneurs are a large segment of the American labor force. They are people willing to take risks and rely on their own initiative—rather than an employer—for their livelihoods. While having the right skills and experience are valuable in any job, the essential qualities of successful entrepreneurs are determination, perseverance, the ability to hire good people, and the ability to learn from mistakes.

◄ Michael Dell of Dell, Inc.

Analyzing the Impact

1. **Synthesizing** In what ways might it be easier for young people to start businesses than older people who have already been in the workforce?

2. **Critical Thinking** Think of a product you could make or a service you could sell. If you decided to start a business, who would buy the product/service? What would you need to start?

unit 5

Macroeconomics: The Nation's Economy

In this unit, read to find out...

■ what statistics measure the economy's health.

■ how the American banking system works.

■ the role government plays in the nation's economy.

chapter 13

Measuring the Economy's Performance

The **BIG Idea**

Economists look at a variety of factors to assess the growth and performance of a nation's economy.

Why It Matters

Economists use an array of tools to evaluate the performance of the American economy. In this chapter, read to learn about GDP, the consumer price index, and other economic indicators.

Economics ONLINE

Chapter Overview Visit the *Economics Today and Tomorrow* Web site at glencoe.com and click on ***Chapter 13—Chapter Overviews*** to preview chapter information.

National Income Accounting

GUIDE TO READING

Section Preview
In this section, you will learn how economists calculate the overall success of the nation's economy.

Content Vocabulary
- national income accounting *(p. 336)*
- gross domestic product (GDP) *(p. 337)*
- net exports *(p. 338)*
- depreciation *(p. 338)*
- net domestic product (NDP) *(p. 338)*
- national income (NI) *(p. 339)*
- personal income (PI) *(p. 339)*
- transfer payments *(p. 340)*
- disposable personal income (DPI) *(p. 340)*

Academic Vocabulary
- statistic *(p. 336)*
- category *(p. 338)*

Reading Strategy
Organizing As you read, complete a web diagram like the one below by listing the five major statistics used to measure the national economy.

National Economy

ISSUES IN THE NEWS
—from *BusinessWeek*

UNTRACKED SPENDING Everyone knows the U.S. is well down the road to becoming a knowledge economy, one driven by ideas and innovation. What you may not realize is that the government's decades-old system of number collection and crunching captures investments in equipment, buildings, and software, but for the most part misses the growing portion of GDP that is generating the cool, game-changing ideas. . . .

▲ **Training new employees**

The statistical wizards at the Bureau of Economic Analysis in Washington can whip up a spreadsheet showing how much the railroads spend on furniture ($39 million in 2006, to be exact). But they have no way of tracking the billions of dollars companies spend each year on innovation and product design, brand-building, employee training, or any of the other intangible investments required to compete in today's global economy.

People can measure how economically successful they are by how much income they make and by their standard of living. These calculations include figuring out how much their disposable personal income will buy. In this section, you'll learn that the state of the nation's overall economy is measured in a similar way.

National Income Accounting, GDP, and NDP

Main Idea Gross domestic product is an estimate of the total dollar value of all final goods and services produced annually within a country.

Economics & You What tools and measurements does a physician use to decide whether you are healthy? Read on to learn about the factors economists use to determine the health of the American economy.

Skills Handbook

See page R53 to learn about Comparing Data.

national income accounting: measurement of the national economy's performance, dealing with the overall economy's output and income

The way we usually measure the national economy's performance is by using **national income accounting.** This area of economics deals with the overall economy's output, or production, and its income.

Five major **statistics** measure the national economy. These are gross domestic product, net domestic product, national income, personal income, and disposable personal income. Each will be examined separately, starting with the largest overall measurement—gross domestic product. **Figure 13.1** below shows gross domestic product and how it is related to the other four measurements.

Graphs In Motion
See StudentWorks™ Plus or go to glencoe.com.

Figure 13.1 Measuring the National Economy

■ Economists start with GDP and subtract various items until they reach the figure measuring disposable personal income—the amount people have left to spend after they pay taxes. This graph shows how five important measures of the national economy are calculated.

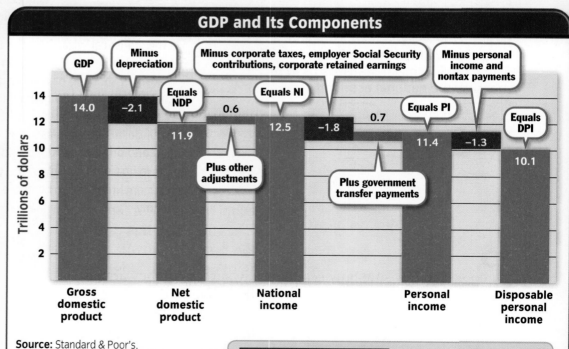

GDP and Its Components

GDP · Minus depreciation · Equals NDP · Minus corporate taxes, employer Social Security contributions, corporate retained earnings · Equals NI · Minus personal income and nontax payments · Equals PI · Equals DPI

14.0 · −2.1 · 11.9 · 0.6 · Plus other adjustments · 12.5 · −1.8 · 0.7 · Plus government transfer payments · 11.4 · −1.3 · 10.1

Trillions of dollars

Gross domestic product · Net domestic product · National income · Personal income · Disposable personal income

Source: Standard & Poor's.

Economic Analysis

Using Graphs *According to the graph, what is the difference in dollars between gross domestic product and disposable personal income?*

Measuring GDP The broadest measure of the economy's size is **gross domestic product (GDP).** This is the total dollar value of all *final* goods and services produced in the nation during a single year. This figure tells the amount of goods and services produced within the country's borders and made available for purchase in that year.

Avoiding Double Counting

When calculating GDP, economists count only the value of the final product. The intermediate products that go into making a flat-screen television, for example, are not counted in GDP. Only the price of the television itself is counted.

Measuring Value Note the word *value* in the definition of GDP. Simply adding up the quantities of different items produced would not mean much. Can we really measure the strength of the economy, for example, if we know that 3 billion safety pins and 2 space shuttles were produced?

What we need to know is the total value of the items, using some common measure. Economists use the dollar as this common measure of value. As a result, GDP is always expressed in dollar terms. For example, in 2006, GDP for the United States totaled more than $13 trillion.

gross domestic product (GDP): total dollar value of all final goods and services produced in a nation in a single year

Measuring Final Goods and Services The word *final* in the definition of GDP is also important. Measuring the economy's performance accurately requires that economists add up only the value of final goods and services to avoid *double counting*. For example, consider all the parts that go into computers. When calculating GDP, we do not take into account the price of memory chips and motherboards if those chips and motherboards are installed in computers for sale. The final price of the computer to the buyer already includes the price of these parts. When memory chips and motherboards are sold separately, however, they are included in GDP.

Also, only new goods are counted in GDP. The sale price of a used car or a secondhand refrigerator is not counted as part of GDP. Such a sale is not due to the production of the nation, but only transfers an existing product from one owner to another. If a new battery is put in an old car, however, that new battery is counted as part of GDP.

Economics ONLINE

Student Web Activity
Visit the *Economics Today and Tomorrow* Web site at glencoe.com and click on *Chapter 13—Student Web Activities* to learn about your gross state product.

Figure 13.2 **Computing GDP**

■ To compute GDP, economists add the total amount of expenditures from the consumer sector, the investment sector, the government sector, and net exports.

Four Categories of GDP

Consumer goods and services **71.0%**

Investment (business) goods and services **17.0%**

Government goods and services **18.8%**

Net exports **−6.8%**

C + I + G + X

Source: *Economic Indicators,* July 2006.

Economic Analysis

Contrasting *Why can net exports, unlike the other categories, sometimes be a negative figure?*

net exports: difference between what the nation sells to other countries and what it buys from other countries

Computing GDP To derive GDP, economists add the expenditures made in four economic **categories.** The first is the *consumer sector (C),* or those goods and services bought directly by consumers. The second category is the *investment sector (I),* or business purchases of items used to produce other goods. Goods and services bought by the *government sector (G)* make up the third category. The final category is **net exports** *(X),* or the difference between the nation's exports and imports. This figure may be a plus or minus depending on economic activity in a given year. (See **Figure 13.2.**) GDP measurements have weaknesses, though. Statistics about easily measurable things, such as government purchases, are reliable. Some workers, however, are given food, fuel, or housing as part of their wages, and GDP can include only an estimate of their value. Also, GDP omits certain areas of economic activity, such as unpaid work.

depreciation: loss of value because of wear and tear to durable goods and capital goods

net domestic product (NDP): value of the nation's total output (GDP) minus the total value lost through depreciation on equipment

Net Domestic Product (NDP) The loss of value because of wear and tear to durable or capital goods is called **depreciation.** GDP disregards depreciation. It does not take into account that some production merely keeps machines and equipment in working order and replaces them when they wear out. **Net domestic product (NDP)**—another way of measuring the economy—accounts for the fact that some production is lost to depreciation. NDP takes GDP and subtracts the total loss in value of capital goods caused by depreciation.

✓ Reading Check **Explaining** Why are only new and final goods counted in GDP?

Measurements of Income

Main Idea Disposable personal income is the total income that people have left after taxes are paid.

Economics & You If you have a job, how much do you earn there? Read on to learn about how personal income is a factor in determining the nation's economic health.

So far, you've learned about GDP and NDP—two major measurements of the value of the nation's output. Economists also look at three additional measurements dealing with income—national income, personal income, and disposable personal income.

National Income The total amount of income earned by everyone in the economy is called **national income (NI).** NI includes the income of those who use their own labor as well as those who earn income through the ownership of the other factors of production. NI is equal to the sum of all income resulting from five different sources. These sources include wages and salaries, income of self-employed individuals, rental income, corporate profits, and interest on savings and other investments.

national income (NI): total income earned by everyone in the economy

Personal Income The total income that individuals receive before personal taxes are paid is called **personal income (PI).** PI can be derived from NI through a two-step process. First, several items are subtracted: corporate income taxes, profits that businesses reinvest in business to expand, and Social Security contributions employers make. These items are subtracted because they represent income that is not available for individuals to spend.

personal income (PI): total income that individuals receive before personal taxes are paid

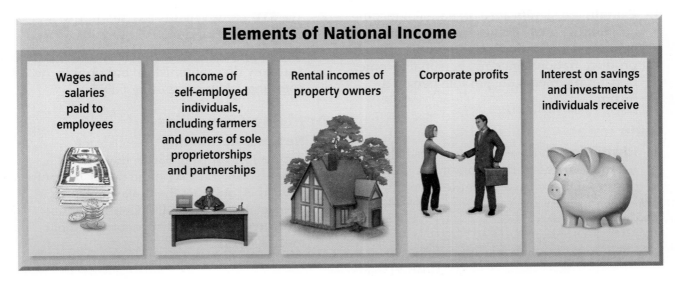

Elements of National Income

| Wages and salaries paid to employees | Income of self-employed individuals, including farmers and owners of sole proprietorships and partnerships | Rental incomes of property owners | Corporate profits | Interest on savings and investments individuals receive |

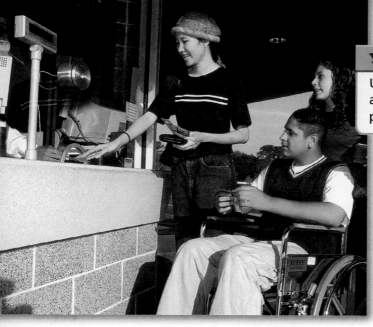

Your DPI

Usually, the dollars you spend on movies and popcorn are part of your disposable personal income.

Then government transfer payments are added to NI. **Transfer payments** are welfare payments and other assistance payments—unemployment compensation, Social Security, and food stamps—that a state or the federal government makes to individuals. These transfer payments add to an individual's income even though they are not exchanged for any current productive activity.

transfer payments: welfare and other supplementary payments that a state or the federal government makes to individuals

disposable personal income (DPI): income remaining for people to spend or save after all taxes have been paid

Disposable Personal Income The income that people have left after taxes, including Social Security contributions, is called **disposable personal income (DPI).** DPI equals PI minus personal taxes. DPI is an important indicator of the economy's health because it measures the actual amount of money income people have available to save and spend.

Reading Check **Identifying** What five sources of income make up the national income?

 section **1**

Review

Vocabulary

1. **Explain** the significance of: national income accounting, gross domestic product, net exports, depreciation, net domestic product, national income, personal income, transfer payments, disposable personal income.

Main Ideas

2. **Identifying** In boxes like the ones below, list the four categories economists use to derive GDP and two examples of each.

1.	1.	1.	1.
2.	2.	2.	2.

Critical Thinking

3. **The BIG Idea** What is the difference between GDP and NDP?

4. **Explaining** What is "double counting," and how do economists avoid double counting when computing GDP?

Applying Economics

5. **National Accounting** Reconstruct Figure 13.1 on page 336 in the form of a spreadsheet. Start with the dollar figure for GDP, then subtract the dollar figure of depreciation to get NDP. Continue until you have tabulated disposable personal income (DPI).

Correcting Statistics for Inflation

GUIDE TO READING

Section Preview
In this section, you will learn what price inflation is and how it is measured.

Content Vocabulary
- inflation *(p. 342)*
- purchasing power *(p. 342)*
- deflation *(p. 342)*
- consumer price index (CPI) *(p. 343)*
- market basket *(p. 343)*
- base year *(p. 343)*
- producer price index (PPI) *(p. 344)*
- GDP price deflator *(p. 344)*
- real GDP *(p. 344)*

Academic Vocabulary
- physical *(p. 342)*
- indicate *(p. 343)*

Reading Strategy
Explaining As you read, fill in a diagram like the one below by defining the three most commonly used measurements of inflation.

Measuring Inflation

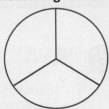

ISSues In ThE NeWS
—from *abcNEWS.com*

THE REAL PRICE OF GAS "Record high gas prices" has been the refrain of many in the media this past year while talking about the price at the pump. Jay Leno even said, "They don't even put the price on the sign any-more—it just says 'If you have to ask, you can't afford it.'"

Drivers . . . at a New York gas station agreed. "It's going up and up and up and it's the most expensive it's ever been," said [one] woman. But the reality is that the "record high gas prices" are a myth. The U.S. Department of Energy records show that when you adjust for inflation the price of gas is now lower than it's been for most of the twentieth century. Prices are lower now than they were 25 years ago. Yes, prices are up from the 1998 all-time low of $1.19, but they are a dollar lower than they were in the early 1980s. . . . The media keep telling us about the record high prices—they're just not adjusting for inflation!

In Section 1, you learned how GDP statistics measure the size of the national economy. You also learned that GDP figures can be misleading or incomplete because they do not measure unpaid work or depreciation. In this section, you'll learn about another factor that influences the current dollar value of GDP as well as your ability to purchase goods and services.

The Purchasing Power of Money

Main Idea The nominal value of GDP must be adjusted for changes in the purchasing power of money to determine changes in real output.

Economics & You Will one dollar buy you more or less food than it would have a year ago? Read on to learn about the changing purchasing power of money.

inflation: prolonged rise in the general price level of final goods and services

purchasing power: the real goods and services that money can buy; determines the value of money

deflation: prolonged decline in the general price level of goods and services

When thinking about GDP, economists need to take **inflation** into account. Inflation is a prolonged rise in the general price level of goods and services. When this situation occurs, the **purchasing power** of the dollar goes down. A dollar's purchasing power is the real goods and services that it can buy. In other words, if there is inflation, a dollar cannot buy the same amount as it did before the inflation occurred.

How does a drop in the dollar's purchasing power skew GDP? The higher GDP figures that result from inflation do not represent any increase in output. For example, last year an ice-cream cone may have cost $1.50. This year it may cost $2.00. The **physical** output has not changed; only its money value has. To get a true measure of the nation's output in a given year, inflation must be taken into account. **Deflation,** a prolonged *decline* in the general price level, also affects the dollar value of GDP, but deflation has rarely happened in modern times.

Reading Check **Examining** How is the value of a dollar determined?

Figure 13.3 — Selected Consumer Prices

■ Price indexes allow you to compare price levels from year to year. When the CPI rises, there is inflation.

▼ **A. Selected Categories** This table shows the CPI broken down into four major categories.

A	Consumer Price Index of Selected Categories		
	2003	**2004**	**2005**
Food	180.5	186.6	191.2
Clothing	120.9	120.4	119.5
Housing	184.8	189.5	195.7
Medical	297.1	310.1	323.2

Source: U.S. Department of Labor, Bureau of Labor Statistics.

B	The CPI	
1995	152.4
1996	156.9
1997	160.5
1998	163.0
1999	166.6
2000	172.2
2001	177.1
2002	179.9
2003	184.0
2004	188.9
2005	195.3

◀ **B. Overall CPI** This table shows the overall CPI for selected years.

Source: U.S. Department of Labor, Bureau of Labor Statistics.

Economic Analysis
Drawing Conclusions
What general trend do you notice in the overall CPI?

Measures of Inflation

Main Idea Inflation can be measured in several ways by calculating changes in different price indexes.

Economics & You Think of an item that costs more today than it did when your parents were your age. This is an example of inflation. Read on to learn how inflation is calculated.

The government measures inflation in several ways. The three most commonly used measurements are the consumer price index, the producer price index, and the implicit GDP price deflator.

Consumer Price Index (CPI)

Every month, the government measures the prices of a specific group of goods and services that the average household uses. This measurement is the **consumer price index (CPI).** The group of items that are priced, called a **market basket,** includes about 80,000 specific goods and services under general categories such as food, housing, transportation, clothing, education, recreation, medical care, and personal care. About every 10 years, the market basket is updated to include new products and services and to reflect more current spending patterns. (See **Figure 13.3.**)

Employees at the federal Bureau of Labor Statistics (BLS) compile the CPI monthly. They start with prices from a **base year** so that they have a point of comparison for current-day prices. For example, if you paid $2.00 for an ice-cream cone in 2006, and the price of the cone increased to $2.50 in 2007, the cost of an ice-cream cone has risen 50 cents since the base year 2006 ($2.50 – 2.00 = .50).

In compiling the CPI, the BLS's base year is really the average of prices that existed for the three years 1982 to 1984. This base is given a value of 100. CPI numbers for later years **indicate** the percentage that the market basket price has risen since the base year. For example, the 2004 CPI of 188.9 means that the average price of goods and services in the market basket has risen 88.9 percent since the period 1982–1984 (188.9 – 100 = 88.9). The price level, therefore, rose 88.9 percent since 1982–1984. The CPI can also be used to calculate inflation for any period.

consumer price index (CPI): a statistical measure of the average of prices of a specified set of goods and services purchased by typical consumers in city areas

market basket: representative group of goods and services used to compile the consumer price index

base year: year used as a point of comparison for other years in a series of statistics

Paying More Than Before

If you have to pay more for an ice cream cone now than you did a couple of years ago, then inflation may have affected the price of ice cream.

producer price index (PPI): measure of the change in price over time that U.S. producers charge for their goods and services

Producer Price Index

Another important measure of inflation is the **producer price index (PPI).** The PPI is actually a group of indexes that measures the average change in prices that United States producers charge their customers—whether these customers are other producers buying crude materials for further processing or wholesalers who will sell the products to retailers or directly to consumers. Most of the producer prices included in the PPIs are in mining, manufacturing, and agriculture.

The PPIs usually increase before the CPI. Apple producers, for example, may experience a weak harvest. Because of the reduced supply of apples, the price of apples rises. A bakery that buys apples will eventually increase the price of its apple pies to cover the higher price of apples. Eventually the CPI will increase because consumers will have to pay more for the final products—in this case, apple pies. Therefore, changes in the PPIs often are watched as a hint that inflation and the CPI are going to increase.

Skills Handbook

See page *R56* to learn about *Understanding Nominal and Real Values.*

GDP price deflator: price index that removes the effect of inflation from GDP so that the overall economy in one year can be compared to another year

real GDP: GDP that has been adjusted for inflation by applying the price deflator

GDP Price Deflator

Government economists account for inflation by issuing another measure of price changes in GDP, called the **GDP price deflator.** This index removes the effects of inflation from GDP so that the overall economy in one year can be compared to the overall economy in another year. When the price deflator is applied to GDP in any year, the new figure is called **real GDP.**

Graphs In MOtion See StudentWorks™ Plus or go to glencoe.com.

| Figure 13.4 | Nominal and Real GDP Over Time |

■ *Nominal GDP* is also called current GDP. *Real GDP* has been adjusted for inflation using 2000 as a base year.

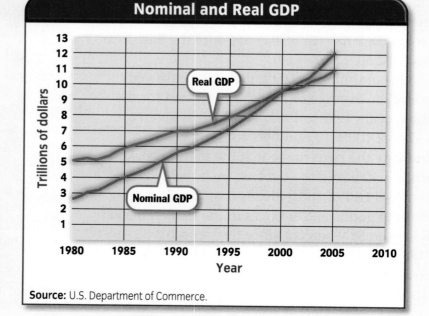

Nominal and Real GDP

Source: U.S. Department of Commerce.

Economic Analysis

Using Graphs By how much did nominal GDP rise between 1980 and 2005?

The federal government uses 2000 as its base year to measure real GDP. Each year the price deflator is used to change current, or nominal, GDP into real GDP. For example, GDP in current dollars for 2004 was $11,734.3 billion. To find real GDP for 2004, the government divides 2004 GDP by the 2004 price deflator (109.099) and multiplies the result by 100: ($11,734.3 billion ÷ 109.099) × 100 = $10,755.6 billion.

Real GDP for 2004 was $10,755.6 billion. This figure may now be compared to other years' real GDP figures. Such comparisons are more meaningful than those made by simply comparing nominal values. **Figure 13.4** on page 344 shows both nominal GDP and real GDP over time.

▲ Purchasing power is determined by more than just wages—inflation is also a factor.

✔ **Reading Check** **Determining Cause and Effect** How does the PPI affect the CPI?

---

section 2 Review

Vocabulary

1. **Explain** the significance of: inflation, purchasing power, deflation, consumer price index, market basket, base year, producer price index, GDP price deflator, real GDP.

Main Ideas

2. **Contrasting** In a chart like the one below, describe the difference between what the CPI and the PPI measure.

Index	What It Measures
CPI	
PPI	

Critical Thinking

3. **The BIG Idea** Why would real GDP be more accurate than nominal GDP when comparing one year's growth to another?

4. **Predicting Consequences** Producer prices are monitored to predict how the CPI might change. Explain how this works.

Applying Economics

5. **Market Basket** Choose six items you buy regularly, and list the price of each. Ask an adult what this item cost ten years ago. Write a paragraph to describe how inflation or deflation affects the price of each of your items today.

GDP: WHAT'S COUNTED, WHAT'S **NOT**

Figuring out the size of the U.S. economy is a tricky task.

Check It Out! In this chapter you learned about GDP. In this article, read to learn why economists debate this measurement's accuracy.

You might think that calculating the size of the U.S. economy is easy: Add up the value of all the goods and services that American workers produce, and you're done. Unfortunately, this simple procedure has a basic flaw: It leads to a lot of double-counting. For example, if [a person] sets up a factory making ceramic frogs and sells them to The Ceramic Frog Store, there's a real danger the frogs will be counted twice: when they leave the factory and again when they're sold to some frog-crazed consumer.

So here's what the government's statistical experts do. Everything that's bought is assigned to one of three bins. The "consumption bin" includes goods and services intended for use by households or the government today or in the near future. Food, haircuts, cell-phone service, and computer games all go into the consumption bin.

The "investment bin" includes all long-lived assets expected to contribute to production in the future. For example, shopping malls, airplanes, and business computers all go into the investment bin. Business software was put into the investment bin in 1999. Homes go there, too.

Finally, the "intermediate output" bin includes all purchases by a business that are used up today in the production of whatever it is the business produces. The classic case is the purchase of ingredients by a restaurant.

▲ Employee training is not counted in GDP.

Here's the problem: There are all sorts of anomalies where purchases are put into the wrong bin, either for historical reasons or because it's too hard to put them somewhere else. Education— human capital—is surely a long-lived asset, but government and personal spending on education is mostly put into the consumption bin. A big portion of the long-term output of American companies isn't being counted as part of GDP at all. And that, in a nutshell, is the problem.

—Adapted from *BusinessWeek*

Think About It

1. **Recalling** Into what three categories does the government organize purchases?

2. **Analyzing** According to the article, what part of the American economy is not being counted in GDP? What impact might this have on measuring the economy's output?

Aggregate Demand and Supply

GUIDE TO READING

Section Preview
In this section, you will learn how the laws of supply and demand apply to the economy as a whole.

Content Vocabulary
- aggregates *(p. 348)*
- aggregate demand *(p. 348)*
- aggregate demand curve *(p. 348)*
- aggregate supply *(p. 349)*
- aggregate supply curve *(p. 349)*

Academic Vocabulary
- output *(p. 348)*
- reverse *(p. 349)*

Reading Strategy
Determining Cause and Effect As you read the section, complete a table like the one below by listing the factors that cause changes in aggregate demand and aggregate supply.

	Increase	Decrease
Aggregate demand		
Aggregate supply		

ISSues In ThE NeWS
—from *abcNEWS.com*

WHEN THE PROFIT INCENTIVE ISN'T ENOUGH If you're in the market for Valentine's Day roses, don't bother going by Errol O'Brien's flower shop [in Manhattan]. It will be closed today.

. . . O'Brien's unorthodox decision appears to fly in the face of logic, especially because Valentine's Day is to florists what Thanksgiving weekend is to retailers. . . .

But O'Brien has his reasons. Foremost among them: His experience with disappointed consumers. . . .

Just like with any industry, the business revolves around supply and demand. . . . But to meet the unique spike in demand for Cupid's holiday, some wholesalers import large quantities of roses and stockpile them like Christmas trees for weeks.

That means by the time they get from the wholesalers' warehouse to a vase at home, those pricey bouquets might be up to a month old.

As we shall see, the laws of supply and demand can be applied to the economy as a whole, as well as to individual consumer decisions. Economists are interested in the demand by all consumers for all goods and services, and the supply by all producers of all goods and services. In this section, we'll learn about how economists study the economy as a whole in terms of supply and demand.

Aggregate Demand and Supply

Main Idea Aggregate demand and aggregate supply curves plot the price level versus total output.

Economics & You On any given day, you probably see people buying things. Read on to learn about aggregate demand and supply, which sums up all of the individual supply and demand in the economy.

In Chapter 7, you learned about demand and supply for individual goods and services. Here we look at demand and supply again, but in a different way. When we look at the economy as a whole, we are looking at **aggregates**—the summing up of all the individual parts in the economy. As you'll learn in this section, we call these sums aggregate demand and aggregate supply.

aggregates: summation of all the individual parts in the economy

aggregate demand: the total of all planned expenditures in the entire economy

aggregate demand curve: a graphed line showing the relationship between the aggregate quantity demanded and the average of all prices as measured by the implicit GDP price deflator

Aggregate Demand **Aggregate demand** can be defined as the total of all planned expenditures in the entire economy. To determine how much people, businesses, and governments plan to spend, we have to relate this planned spending to something. Because there are millions of different prices for all products, aggregate demand cannot be related to individual prices. Instead, aggregate demand is related to the *price level*—the average of all prices as measured by a price index. If we use the implicit GDP price deflator as our index, our measure of aggregate demand will be based on real (adjusted for inflation) domestic **output**. You can see this relationship in **Figure 13.5** below. It is called the **aggregate demand curve**.

Figure 13.5 | Aggregate Demand and Supply

■ Aggregate demand and supply deal with the summing up of all the individual parts in the economy.

A. The Aggregate Demand Curve Although the curve for aggregate demand resembles that for simple demand, it is for the entire economy, not just one good or service. Aggregate demand may increase (curve shifts to the right) if consumers collectively spend more and save less or if better economic conditions are forecast. Aggregate demand may decrease (curve shifts to the left) if higher taxes are imposed on the overall economy or if bleak economic conditions are forecast.

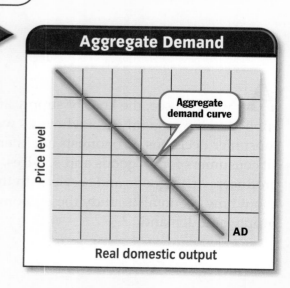

Aggregate Demand

Aggregate demand curve

Price level

AD

Real domestic output

Notice the similarity between the aggregate demand curve and the individual demand curve you studied in Chapter 7 (page 179). Both of them slope downward, showing an inverse relationship. As the price level in the economy goes down, a larger quantity of real domestic output is demanded per year. This change in quantity demanded is shown as a movement *along* the AD curve.

There are two main reasons for this inverse relationship. First, inflation causes the purchasing power of cash to go down, and deflation causes it to go up. Therefore, when the price level goes down, the purchasing power of all cash will go up. You and everyone else will feel slightly richer because you are able to buy more goods and services. Secondly, when the price level goes down in the United States, our goods become relatively better deals for foreigners who want to buy them. Foreigners then demand more of our goods as exports.

Aggregate Supply Aggregate demand is only one side of the story. Let us look at aggregate supply. As the price of a specific product goes up, and if all other prices stay the same, producers of that product find it profitable to produce more. The same is true for all producers in the economy over a short period of time. If the price level goes up and wages and other costs of production do not, overall profits will rise. Producers will want to supply more to the marketplace—they offer more real domestic output as the price level increases. The **reverse** is true as the price level falls. This is called **aggregate supply**. You can see this positive relationship in the graph in **Figure 13.5** below—the **aggregate supply curve.**

aggregate supply: real domestic output of producers based on the rise and fall of the price level

aggregate supply curve: a graphed line showing the relationship between the aggregate quantity supplied and the average of all prices as measured by the implicit GDP price deflator

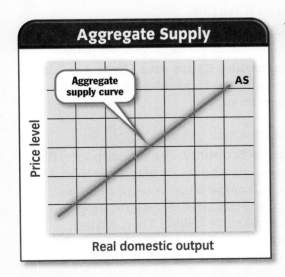

Aggregate Supply

Aggregate supply curve

AS

Price level

Real domestic output

◀ **B. The Aggregate Supply Curve** The aggregate supply curve shows the amount of real GDP that will be produced at various price levels. Aggregate supply increases (curve shifts to the right) when all firms experience lower costs of production due to lower taxes or interest rates or lower prices for foreign oil, for example. Aggregate supply decreases (curve shifts to the left) for the opposite reasons: higher taxes, higher interest rates, higher prices for foreign oil.

Economic Analysis

Extending *What other examples of lower production costs, besides the ones listed here, might occur and cause the aggregate supply curve to shift?*

Equilibrium Price Level

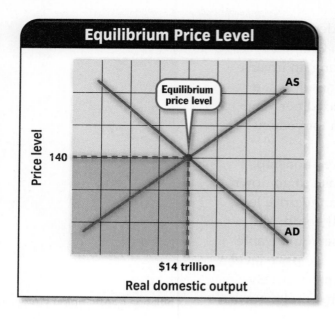

Putting Aggregate Demand and Aggregate Supply Together

Just as we are able to compare demand and supply for a given product to find an equilibrium price and quantity, we can compare aggregate demand and aggregate supply.

The equilibrium price level in our example is determined where the aggregate demand curve crosses the aggregate supply curve, or at a GDP price deflator of 140. The equilibrium quantity of real GDP demanded and supplied is $14 trillion. As long as nothing changes in this situation, the economy will produce $14 trillion of real domestic output, and the price level will remain at 140—there will be neither inflation nor deflation.

Now, if something pushes out the aggregate demand curve faster than the aggregate supply curve, the equilibrium price level will rise. If the aggregate supply curve shifts out faster than the aggregate demand curve, the equilibrium price level will drop.

Reading Check **Predicting Consequences** What will happen to the equilibrium price level if there is an increase in aggregate demand?

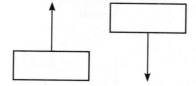 **Review**

Vocabulary

1. **Explain** the significance of: aggregates, aggregate demand, aggregate demand curve, aggregate supply, aggregate supply curve.

Main Ideas

2. **Synthesizing** Create a diagram like the one below to show why there is an inverse relationship between aggregate quantity demanded and the price level.

Critical Thinking

3. **The BIG Idea** Explain how a bad economic forecast can affect aggregate demand.

4. **Determining Cause and Effect** Explain how high taxes and interest rates hurt aggregate supply.

Applying Economics

5. **Today's Economy** Use a newspaper, the Internet, or a business magazine to make a list of all of the clues you see that show aggregate demand, aggregate supply, or prices rising or falling. Then write a paragraph explaining whether you think the current economy is inflationary, stable, or deflationary.

Business Fluctuations

GUIDE TO READING

Section Preview
In this section, you will learn about the forces that cause fluctuations, or "ups and downs," in the American economy.

Content Vocabulary
- business fluctuations *(p. 352)*
- business cycle *(p. 352)*
- peak *(p. 352)*
- boom *(p. 352)*
- contraction *(p. 352)*
- recession *(p. 352)*
- depression *(p. 352)*
- trough *(p. 352)*
- expansion *(p. 352)*
- recovery *(p. 352)*

Academic Vocabulary
- capacity *(p. 352)*
- precede *(p. 353)*

Reading Strategy
Sequencing As you read the section, complete a flowchart like the one below to list the steps of an idealized business cycle.

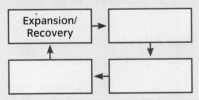

ISSUES IN THE NEWS
·············
—from *U.S. News & World Report*

A SURPLUS IN DESPERATE TIMES One of the ironies of the Great Depression was that an enormous surplus of food was being farmed around the country, while in the cities, people fought over rotting refuse in garbage cans. Government programs helped bail out farmers, buying up the unsold crops and burning them or using them as feed. But the International Apple Shippers Association approached the produce glut with city folk in mind, putting thousands of the unemployed to work by offering them crates of 100 apples for $2, usually on credit. By 1931, city streets around the nation were filled with apple vendors hawking their goods at a nickel apiece.

▲ **Depression-era apple vendor**

Some years inflation in the United States is high; other years it is not. The same holds true for unemployment and world trade. In any given year as well as over time, we have fluctuations in virtually all aspects of our economy. In this section, you'll learn about these ups and downs in the economy and how they relate to GDP.

Model of the Business Cycle

Main Idea Business cycles are characterized by periods of expansion and contraction in economic activity.

Economics & You Think about a time when you felt ill. Probably your symptoms worsened for a while, then leveled off and began to improve until you felt normal again. Read on to learn about similar fluctuations in the health of the economy.

business fluctuations: ups and downs in an economy

business cycle: irregular changes in the level of total output measured by real GDP

peak/boom: period of prosperity in a business cycle in which economic activity is at its highest point

contraction: part of the business cycle during which economic activity is slowing down

recession: part of the business cycle in which the nation's output (real GDP) declines for at least six months

depression: major slowdown of economic activity

trough: lowest part of the business cycle in which the downward spiral of the economy levels off

expansion/recovery: part of the business cycle in which economic activity slowly increases

The ups and downs in an economy are called **business fluctuations.** Some people associate them with what has been called the **business cycle**—irregular changes in the level of total output measured by real GDP. In a model of an idealized business cycle, growth leads to an economic **peak** or **boom**—a period of prosperity. Eventually, however, real GDP levels off and begins to decline. During this part of the cycle, a **contraction** of the economy occurs. If the contraction lasts long enough and is deep enough, the economy can continue downward until it slips into a recession.

A **recession** generally is defined as any period of at least six consecutive months in which real GDP declines. Business activity starts to fall rapidly. Factories scale back production, consumers cut back on purchases, and few new businesses open. If a recession becomes extremely bad, it deepens into a **depression.** Then millions of people are out of work, and the economy operates far below **capacity.**

At some point, the economy hits a **trough,** or the lowest point in the business cycle. This occurs when real GDP stops going down and slowly begins to increase. The increase in economic activity that follows the trough is called an **expansion** or **recovery.** Consumer spending picks up, signaling factories to increase production to meet demand. The recovery continues until the economy hits another peak, and a new cycle begins.

Reading Check **Determining Cause and Effect** What factors might cause a recession to deepen into a depression?

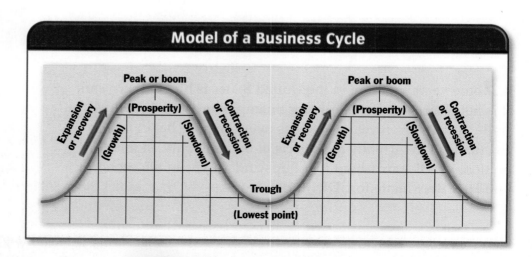

Model of a Business Cycle

Peak or boom
(Prosperity)
Expansion or recovery
(Growth)
(Slowdown)
Contraction or recession
Peak or boom
(Prosperity)
Expansion or recovery
(Growth)
(Slowdown)
Contraction or recession
Trough
(Lowest point)

Figure 13.6 **Business Activity**

Graphs In Motion
See StudentWorks™ Plus or go to glencoe.com.

■ As you can see, American business activity has undergone many cycles of change over the past several decades.

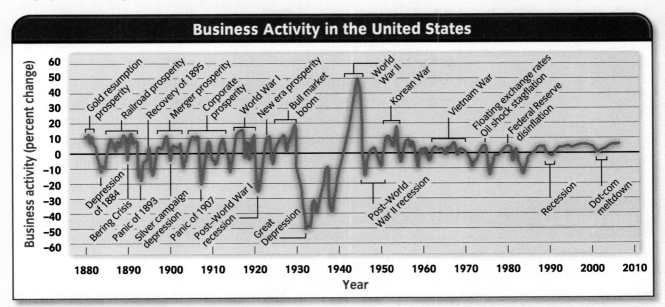

Business Activity in the United States

Economic Analysis

Using Graphs *At what point was U.S. business activity contracting most severely?*

Ups and Downs of Business

Main Idea Throughout its history, the United States has experienced business expansions and recessions of varying severity and frequency.

Economics & You What changes do you think occurred in the nation's economy after the September 11, 2001, terrorist attacks? Read on to learn about this and other business cycles in American history.

In the real world, as you can see from **Figure 13.6** above, business cycles occur irregularly. The periods of expansion and contraction are clear, however.

The largest drop that eventually resulted in a depression followed the stock market crash in October 1929. The **preceding** years had been a time of widespread prosperity. By September 1929, heavy speculation had driven stock prices to an all-time peak. Then stock prices started to fall in early October and continued to fall. Suddenly, on October 29, there was a stampede to unload stocks. In one day the total value of all stocks fell by $14 billion.

Skills Handbook

*See page **R59** to learn about **Reading Stock Market Reports**.*

Not long after the stock market crash, the nation fell into a recession. Factories shut down, laying off millions of workers. Businesses and banks failed by the thousands. Real GDP fell sharply over the next few years, pushing the nation into the depths of the Great Depression. (See **Figure 13.7** below.) A gradual upward rise climaxed in the boom period after World War II.

Quite naturally, the economic expansion during World War II has caused many to believe that war is "good" for the economy. It is true that the total national output of goods and services increased during the war. At the same time, though, much of this output went to the war effort—bombs, planes, and guns—rather than consumer goods. So, the average American's true standard of living didn't rise by much until the late 1940s.

Figure 13.7 | Prosperity, Depression, and Boom

■ From the 1920s through the 1940s, business activity in the United States underwent major swings.

▼ **A. Prosperity Before the Crash** The 1920s had been a decade in which Americans began buying increasing numbers of radios, stoves, and automobiles. During these years, prices remained stable, and the standard of living rose about 3 percent per year.

▲ **C. War Boom** The United States economy grew rapidly during World War II. There were 17 million new jobs created, and farmers shared in the prosperity as crop prices doubled between 1940 and 1945.

B. Depression Conditions ▶ The Great Depression of the 1930s forced millions of Americans out of work. Used to the prosperity of the 1920s, Americans during the bust era of the Depression often relied on handouts.

Economic Analysis
Summarizing *What happens in an economy during a recession?*

Until the 1980s, small ups and downs occurred. The 1980s started off with a small recession that developed into the most serious economic downturn by some measurements since World War II. This downturn ended in 1982 and was followed by relative prosperity, except for a severe stock market crash in October 1987. The economy boomed during the last half of the 1990s, but started to falter in March 2001, when the so-called dot-com meltdown occurred. Many Internet businesses failed then. The terrorist attacks in September caused further weakness in the economy. But the recession lasted a total of only eight months. Then, through the middle of the first decade of the 2000s, economic growth was the norm.

...SO THEN I GO, NO WAY! AND THEY'RE ALL, Y'KNOW, NEGATIVE AND STUFF, AND GO, YO...WAY, DUDE. SO THEN I GO, LIKE, BUMMER, MAN. I'M SURE YOU ALL UNDERSTAND...

FORMAL NOTICE of ANOTHER DOT-COM FAILURE

▲ Many dot-com entrepreneurs were young and inexperienced.

Reading Check **Identifying** What was the worst economic downturn in American history? What major event led to the nation's greatest economic boom?

section 4 Review

Vocabulary

1. **Explain** the significance of: business fluctuations, business cycle, peak, boom, contraction, recession, depression, trough, expansion, recovery.

Main Ideas

2. **Determining Cause and Effect** In a chart like the one below, explain how each event listed affected the nation's economy.

Event	Effect
Depression	
WWII	
Tech boom	
9/11	

Critical Thinking

3. **The BIG Idea** What happens during an economic expansion? During a contraction?

4. **Analyzing** Why does the economy expand during war times?

Applying Economics

5. **Government Assistance** Research and compile a list of the ways that government helped people during the Great Depression. Then write a paragraph telling why you believe tax dollars should or should not be used to assist people in this way.

Causes and Indicators of Business Fluctuations

GUIDE TO READING

Section Preview
In this section, you will learn how economists explain and predict changes or fluctuations in the economy.

Content Vocabulary
- innovation *(p. 357)*
- economic indicators *(p. 358)*
- leading indicators *(p. 358)*
- coincident indicators *(p. 359)*
- lagging indicators *(p. 359)*

Academic Vocabulary
- anticipate *(p. 357)*
- compile *(p. 358)*
- duration *(p. 359)*

Reading Strategy
Sequencing As you read the section, complete a time line similar to the one below by listing the three broad categories of economic indicators and when they occur relative to an economic change.

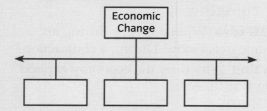

ISSues In ThE NeWS
—from Britannica Student Encyclopedia

TRYING TO EXPLAIN BUSINESS FLUCTUATIONS
Economists, politicians, and others have been puzzled by business cycles since at least the early 19th century. One of the more unusual explanations was proposed by English economist William Stanley Jevons in the 19th century. He believed the ups and downs of an economy were caused by sunspot cycles, which affected agriculture and caused cycles of bad and good harvests. This hypothesis is not taken seriously today. . . .

Shifts, changes, and temporary fluctuations do not constitute business cycles. They are adjustments that economies have always endured. The question that must be answered is, what causes a widespread buildup of prosperity followed by a sudden decline? Since money is the connecting link between all economic activities, the answer must be sought there.

▲ **William Stanley Jevons**

$\mathbf{F}$or as long as booms and recessions have existed, economists have tried to explain why business fluctuations occur. No single theory, however, seems to explain past cycles or to serve as an adequate measure to predict future ones. The difficulty arises because at any given time, several factors are working together to create business fluctuations.

Causes of Business Fluctuations

Main Idea Business cycles can be caused by changes in business investment, government policies, and the availability of key commodities, or by psychological factors.

Economics & You How has the Internet affected the economy in your lifetime? Read on to learn about how innovations such as the Internet, along with several other factors, contribute to business fluctuations.

For many years economists believed that business fluctuations occurred in regular cycles. Later, they thought changes in the rate of saving and investing caused the fluctuations. Today economists tend to link fluctuations to four main forces: business investment, government activity, external factors, and psychological factors.

Some economists believe that business decisions are the key to fluctuations. Suppose a firm believes that prospects for future sales are good and increases its capital investment. This expansion will create new jobs and more income for consumer spending. **Innovations**—usable inventions and new production techniques—can have a similar effect on the economy. When businesses **anticipate** an economic downturn, they cut back on capital investment, which could lead to a recession.

A number of economists believe that the changing policies of the federal government are a major reason for business cycles. The government affects business activity in two ways: through its policies on taxing and spending, and through its control over the supply of money available in the economy.

Factors outside a nation's economy also influence the business cycle. Wars in particular have an important impact, because of increased government spending during wartime. Another external factor—the availability of raw materials such as oil—may also have an effect.

Finally, it is possible that people's psychological reactions to events—such as the terrorist attacks of September 11, 2001—also cause business fluctuations.

innovation: transforming an invention into something useful to humans

External Factors

War, natural and environmental disasters, and crime waves are some external factors that affect business cycles.

✓ **Reading Check** **Analyzing** What are two major ways that the government influences business activity?

Economic Indicators

Main Idea Some economists use leading, coincident, and lagging indicators to assess the current state of the economy and to predict its future course.

Economics & You Have you ever made a prediction about something, such as the weather or the outcome of a sports match? How accurate were your predictions? Read on to learn about the tools economists use to predict changes in the economy.

economic indicators: statistics that measure variables in the economy

leading indicators: statistics that point to what will happen in the economy

Every day, business leaders are faced with trying to predict what will happen to the economy in the coming months and years. To aid decision makers, government and private economists study a number of economic indicators to learn about the state of the economy. **Economic indicators** are statistics that measure variables in the economy, such as stock prices or the dollar amount of loans to be repaid. Each month, the U.S. Department of Commerce, along with a private company called the Conference Board, **compiles** statistics for economic indicators covering all aspects of the U.S. economy.

Major Economic Indicators

Leading Indicators

1. Average weekly hours for production workers in manufacturing
2. Weekly initial claims for unemployment insurance
3. New orders for consumer goods
4. Speed with which companies make deliveries (the busier a company, the longer it will take to fill orders)
5. Number of contracts and orders for plants and equipment
6. Number of building permits issued for private housing units
7. Stock prices
8. Changes in money supply in circulation
9. Changes in interest rates
10. Changes in consumer expectations

Coincident Indicators

1. Number of nonagricultural workers who are employed
2. Personal income minus transfer payments
3. Rate of industrial production
4. Sales of manufacturers, wholesalers, and retailers

Lagging Indicators

1. Average length of unemployment
2. Size of manufacturing and trade inventories
3. Labor cost per unit of output in manufacturing
4. Average interest rate charged by banks to their best business customers
5. Number of commercial and industrial loans to be repaid
6. Ratio of consumer installment debt to personal income
7. Change in consumer price index for services

Leading Indicators

Statistics that point to what will happen in the economy are called **leading indicators.** They seem to lead to a change in overall business activity—whether it is an upward or a downward trend. The Conference Board keeps track of numerous leading indicators, but the ten listed in the chart are the ones that most concern American economists.

The number of hours per week logged by the average U.S. production worker is one of the major indicators that economists study to try to determine the direction the economy is heading.

Coincident Indicators

Other economic indicators, which usually change at the same time as changes in overall business activity, also help economists. When these **coincident indicators** begin a downswing, they indicate that a contraction in the business cycle has begun. If they begin an upswing, they indicate that the economy is picking up and a recovery is under way.

coincident indicators: economic indicators that usually change at the same time as changes in overall business activity

Lagging Indicators A third set of indicators seems to lag behind changes in overall business activity. For example, it may be six months after the start of a downturn before businesses reduce their borrowing. The amount of change in these **lagging indicators,** whether up or down, gives economists clues as to the **duration** of the phases of the business cycle.

lagging indicators: indicators that seem to lag behind changes in overall business activity

✔**Reading Check** **Contrasting** What is the difference between leading and lagging economic indicators?

---

section 5 **Review**

Vocabulary

1. **Explain** the significance of: innovation, economic indicators, leading indicators, coincident indicators, lagging indicators.

Main Ideas

2. **Summarizing** Copy the chart below, and in each box, explain how the term listed affects the business cycle.

Investment	Policy	Products	Psychology

Critical Thinking

3. **The BIG Idea** In what two ways does government affect business activity?

4. **Contrasting** Explain the difference between leading indicators, coincident indicators, and lagging indicators.

Applying Economics

5. **Innovations** Choose two innovations that you believe had the most influence on the American economy in your lifetime, and explain why.

ECONOMIST
(1946–   )

Janet Yellen

- President and Chief Executive Officer, Federal Reserve Bank of San Francisco

- Chair of President Clinton's Council of Economic Advisers, 1997–99
- Member, Board of Governors of the Federal Reserve System, 1994–97
- Author of many scholarly articles on economic issues

Recalling her appointment to the Board of Governors of the Federal Reserve System, Janet Yellen remarked, "I didn't even own a suit. I never felt I had to have a suit at Berkeley. . . . The minute after I got the call, I walked across the street and bought [one]."

But it wasn't just a new suit she took to Washington. Yellen is well known as someone who can understand and explain complicated economic issues. Until this point in her professional career, she had taught in universities, lectured at the London School of Economics, and held various positions advising the government. This was the first time when, as she put it, she had "the opportunity to apply ivory tower ideas to the real world[,] . . . a chance many scholars only dream of." But she didn't let her lofty position disrupt her normal life. "I made up my mind early on that my family would remain a priority."

Her goal, as head of one of the nation's 12 Federal Reserve Banks, is to help achieve and maintain "maximum employment and price stability."

Unlike some economists, Yellen does not believe that a free-market economy is best left to itself. In 1985 she and her Nobel Prize-winning husband, George Akerlof, coauthored a paper in which they demonstrated that the government could, in fact, smooth out business cycles, an idea that, at the time, was out of favor.

> **Capitalism is a terrific system for organizing economic activity. But the market system has some failures that necessitate or are helped by government intervention.**

Checking for Understanding

1. **Paraphrasing** What did Yellen mean when she said she had "the opportunity to apply ivory tower ideas to the real world"?
2. **Speculating** What does it mean to "smooth out business cycles"?

■ A nation's **gross domestic product (GDP)** is the total dollar value of all final goods and services produced annually.

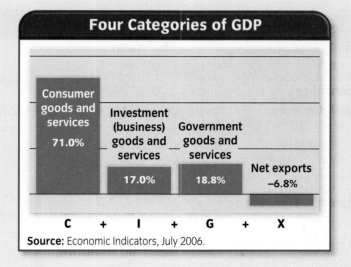

Four Categories of GDP

Consumer goods and services 71.0%

Investment (business) goods and services 17.0%

Government goods and services 18.8%

Net exports –6.8%

C + I + G + X

Source: Economic Indicators, July 2006.

■ GDP figures must be adjusted for **inflation**, which can be measured in several ways.

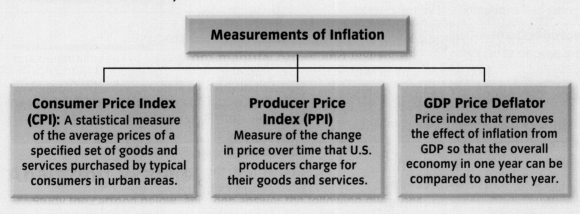

Measurements of Inflation

Consumer Price Index (CPI): A statistical measure of the average prices of a specified set of goods and services purchased by typical consumers in urban areas.

Producer Price Index (PPI) Measure of the change in price over time that U.S. producers charge for their goods and services.

GDP Price Deflator Price index that removes the effect of inflation from GDP so that the overall economy in one year can be compared to another year.

■ The **price level of the overall economy** is determined by the interaction of aggregate demand and aggregate supply.

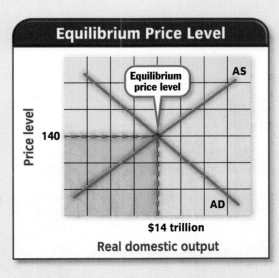

Equilibrium Price Level

Equilibrium price level

AS

Price level

140

AD

$14 trillion

Real domestic output

Measuring the Economy's Performance **361**

Review Content Vocabulary

1. *Write a paragraph or two explaining how economists measure the U.S. economy. Use all of the following terms.*

national income accounting

consumer price index

gross domestic product (GDP)

producer price index

net domestic product

GDP price deflator

inflation

aggregate demand

real GDP

aggregate supply

2. *Write a paragraph or two explaining business fluctuations and how they can be predicted. Use all of the following terms.*

business fluctuations

expansion

business cycle

recovery

boom

economic indicators

recession

leading indicators

depression

lagging indicators

Review Academic Vocabulary

Choose the letter of the term that best completes each sentence.

a. statistics
b. category
c. indicate
d. output
e. capacity
f. precede
g anticipate

3. What a factory produces is called its _____.

4. When a factory is producing all it can possibly produce, it has reached its _____.

5. Economists use _____ to measure the national economy.

6. The consumer sector is one _____ considered when computing GDP.

7. An increase in consumer spending might _____, or point to, an economic expansion.

8. A boom would _____ economic contraction.

9. Economists try to _____ coming changes in the economy by analyzing economic indicators.

Review the Main Ideas

Section 1 (pp. 335–340)

10. Net exports and government goods and services are two components of GDP. What are the other two components?

11. Fill in a chart like the one below to list the five categories that make up national income.

National Income	a. wages and salaries
	b.
	c.
	d.
	e.

Section 2 (pp. 341–345)

12. What is the difference between inflation and deflation?

13. How would you determine real GDP if you knew only GDP? Why would you do this?

Section 3 (pp. 347–350)

14. Why do the aggregate demand and supply curves slope the way they do?

15. What is the point where the aggregate demand and supply curves cross?

Section 4 (pp. 351–355)

16. What are the four main phases of a business cycle?

17. When the economy enters a recession, what normally happens?

Section 5 (pp. 356–359)

18. How might psychological factors affect the business cycle?

19. What two aspects of government activity affect business cycles?

Critical Thinking

20. **The BIG Idea** How might knowledge of nationwide economic statistics help you in your daily life?

21. **Summarizing** Create a diagram like the one below to summarize national income accounting. Start with the lowest statistic, disposable personal income, and work your way up to GDP—adding and subtracting the appropriate items.

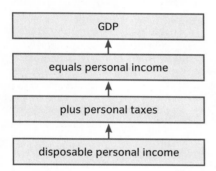

```
              ┌─────────────────────────────┐
              │            GDP              │
              └─────────────────────────────┘
                            ▲
              ┌─────────────────────────────┐
              │    equals personal income   │
              └─────────────────────────────┘
                            ▲
              ┌─────────────────────────────┐
              │     plus personal taxes     │
              └─────────────────────────────┘
                            ▲
              ┌─────────────────────────────┐
              │  disposable personal income │
              └─────────────────────────────┘
```

Economics ONLINE

Self-Check Quiz Visit the *Economics Today and Tomorrow* Web site at glencoe.com and click on **Chapter 13—Self-Check Quizzes** to assess your knowledge of chapter content.

Math Practice

22. To make comparisons between the prices of things in the past and those of today, you have to make the distinction between current prices (often called *nominal values*) and prices adjusted for inflation (*real values*). Use the following equation and statistics to find real 2000 GDP.

$$\frac{\text{Nominal GDP}}{\text{Implicit GDP Price Deflator}} \times 100 = \text{Real GDP}$$

- 2000 nominal GDP = $10.223 trillion
- 2000 price deflator = 107.7

Analyzing Visuals

23. Study the cartoon on the right, and then answer the following questions.

   a. What economic problem is shown in this cartoon?

   b. How does the employee think this problem could be solved?

   c. The boss implies that if wages were to increase more rapidly, inflation would worsen. Is the boss right? Why or why not?

Bruce Beattie/Copley News Service

Global Economy

A Brief History of Money Over the centuries such items as cattle, salt, large stones, seashells, metals, beads, tea, coffee, tobacco, fishhooks, and furs have served as money. Some of the more important developments in the history of money are described here.

Two Bits
Do you know why people sometimes call a quarter "two bits"? The origin of this term dates back to colonial times. The American colonists used Spanish silver dollar coins called "pieces of eight." Each coin was divided into eight pieces—or bits—so that it could be broken to make change. Four bits was equal to half a dollar, while two bits equaled a quarter.

Cowrie Shells
Cowrie shells have been used as money throughout Asia, Africa, and Oceania. The cowrie was still in use in some African countries as recently as the mid-1900s. The name for Ghana's monetary unit, the cedi, comes from the Ghanaian word meaning "cowrie shell."

The First Coins
The Lydians, who lived in what is now western Turkey, probably made the first coins during the 600s B.C. These coins were made of electrum, a mix of gold and silver, and were stamped with pictures of gods or emperors. The Greeks, Persians, and Romans adopted Lydian coining techniques and, in time, the use of coins spread throughout much of Western Europe.

The First Paper Banknotes
The Chinese may have begun to make coins around the same time as the Lydians. These coins were made of bronze and often had holes in them so that they could be carried on a string. The Chinese also began using paper banknotes—printed on paper made from mulberry bark—in the A.D. 800s.

Rings and Ingots
Perhaps as early as 2500 B.C., the people of ancient Egypt and Mesopotamia—the land between the Tigris and Euphrates Rivers—were using gold and silver as money. The money took the form of rings, small ornaments, and ingots, or bars.

Thinking Globally

1. **Identifying** Where did the use of coins develop?

2. **Analyzing** How is the history of money in Africa reflected in the currency of Ghana?

3. **Applying** How did coins in the United States develop from "two bits" to the quarters, dimes, and nickels we use today? Use the Internet to research the history of coins in the United States, and create a time line depicting when each of these coins was developed and put into use.

## chapter 14

Money and Banking

The **BIG Idea**

Governments strive for a balance between the costs and benefits of their economic policies to promote economic stability and growth.

Why It Matters

When you think of the word *money,* what comes to mind? Besides coins and cash, what other types of money can you name? In this chapter, read to learn about the functions of money and the role of the banking system.

Economics ONLINE

Chapter Overview Visit the *Economics Today and Tomorrow* Web site at glencoe.com and click on *Chapter 14—Chapter Overviews* to preview chapter information.

The Functions and Characteristics of Money

GUIDE TO READING

Section Preview
In this section, you will learn about the different uses, characteristics, and types of money.

Content Vocabulary
- money (p. 368)
- medium of exchange (p. 368)
- barter (p. 368)
- unit of accounting (p. 369)
- store of value (p. 369)
- commodity money (p. 371)
- representative money (p. 371)
- fiat money (p. 371)
- legal tender (p. 371)

Academic Vocabulary
- indicate (p. 369)
- convert (p. 371)
- transport (p. 370)

Reading Strategy
Taking Notes As you read the section, complete an outline like the one below identifying the functions, characteristics, and types of money.

Money	
I. Functions	D.
A. Medium of exchange	E.
B.	F.
C.	III. Types
II. Characteristics	A.
A.	B.
B.	C.
C.	D.

ISSues In ThE NeWS
—from *BusinessWeek*

EURO GROWS STRONG The surging euro is confounding critics who once doubted it could rival the U.S. dollar, British pound and Japanese yen—but Europe's shared currency still annoys some consumers [several] years after its introduction in cash form. . . .

"When it first started—and even before it hit markets properly—everyone was very skeptical and negative on the whole thing, and that's exactly the performance we saw," said David Jones, chief currency analyst for CMC Markets. . . .

"That initial negative view is history now," Jones said. "The euro is seen as a strong global currency now."

However, some consumers still grumble about using the euro. . . . Many still calculate large purchases in the old currencies.

And having a single currency hasn't closed the growth gap between Europe—where one or two percent annual growth constitutes an upswing—and more dynamic economies in the United States and Asia.

▲ Euro notes and coins

For thousands of years, money has made it possible for businesses to obtain easily what they need from suppliers and for consumers to obtain goods and services. What, however, is money, and how does it function in an economic system? As you read this section, you'll learn the answers to these questions.

The Functions of Money

Main Idea Money functions as a medium of exchange, a unit of accounting, and a store of value.

Economics & You What personal items do you value the most? Would you trade them in exchange for other goods? Read on to learn about how many items with a store of value can be used as money.

The basis of the market economy is voluntary exchange. Most Americans think of money as bills, coins, and checks. Historically, though, money has also been shells, gold, or sheep. Native Americans used wampum—beads made from shells. People in the Fiji Islands used whales' teeth.

Economists identify money by certain functions. Anything that is used as a medium of exchange, a unit of accounting, and a store of value is considered **money**. (See **Figure 14.1** below.)

money: anything customarily used as a medium of exchange, a unit of accounting, and a store of value

medium of exchange: use of money for exchange for goods or services

barter: exchange of goods and services for other goods and services

Medium of Exchange
To say that money is a **medium of exchange** simply means that a seller will accept it in exchange for a good or service. Without money, people would have to **barter**—exchange goods and services for other goods and services. Barter requires a double coincidence of wants. Each party to a transaction must want exactly what the other person has to offer. In the past, bartering was used extensively, both within and between societies. Today, however, bartering works only in small societies with fairly simple economic systems.

Figure 14.1 | Three Functions of Money

■ All money serves three functions.

▼ **A. Medium of Exchange** The money this person is holding serves as a medium of exchange; the vendor will accept it in exchange for a meal.

▲ **B. Unit of Accounting** Money is also a unit of accounting. The products in U.S. markets are all priced in dollars and cents, so people can easily compare values of different items.

Unit of Accounting Money is the yardstick that allows people to compare the values of goods and services in relation to one another. In this way, money functions as a **unit of accounting.** Each nation uses a basic unit to measure the value of goods, as it uses the foot or meter to measure distance. In the United States, this base unit of value is the dollar. In Japan, it is the yen, and in much of Europe, the euro. An item for sale is marked with a price that **indicates** its value in terms of that unit.

By using money prices as a factor in comparing goods, people can determine whether one item is a better bargain than another. A single unit of accounting also allows people to keep accurate financial records—records of debts owed, income saved, and so on.

unit of accounting: use of money as a yardstick for comparing the values of goods and services in relation to one another

Store of Value Money also serves as a **store of value.** You can sell something, such as your labor, and store the purchasing power that results from the sale in the form of money for later use. People usually receive their money income once a week, once every two weeks, or once a month. In contrast, they usually spend their income at different times during a pay period. To be able to buy things between paydays, a person can store some of his or her income in cash and some in a checking account. It is important to note that in periods of rapid and unpredictable inflation, money is less able to act as a store of value.

store of value: use of money to store purchasing power for later use

✓**Reading Check** **Explaining** What are the disadvantages of bartering?

C. Store of Value
Finally, money serves as a store of value—people can store their purchasing power in the form of dollars. Money income earned from a part-time job, like mowing lawns, for example, can be stored this way.

Economic Analysis
Synthesizing *Why is cash a more efficient medium of exchange than other items, like shells and beads, that people used in the past?*

Characteristics of Money

Main Idea Any item to be used as money must first meet certain criteria.

Economics & You What do you think of when you hear the term "money"? Read on to learn about the characteristics that define money.

Anything that people are willing to accept in exchange for goods can serve as money. At various times in history, cattle, salt, animal hides, gems, and tobacco have been used as mediums of exchange. Each of these items has certain characteristics that make it better or worse than others for use as money. Cattle, for example, are difficult to **transport,** but they are durable. Gems are easy to carry, but they are not easy to split into small pieces to use.

Figure 14.2 below lists the characteristics that to some degree all items used as money must have. Almost any item that meets most of these criteria can be and probably has been used as money. Precious metals like gold and silver work very well as mediums of exchange, and have often been used as such throughout history. It is only in more recent times that paper money has been widely used as a medium of exchange.

Skills Handbook
See page **R51** to learn about **Using Tables and Charts.**

Reading Check **Identifying** Name five items—other than paper bills, coins, or checks—that have been used as money.

Figure 14.2	Characteristics of Money

■ This table lists the traits that items must possess to be able to be used as money, whether those items are bills, coins, or some other item.

Characteristics of Money	
Characteristic	**Description**
Durable	Money must be able to withstand the wear and tear of being passed from person to person. Paper money lasts one year on average, but old bills can easily be replaced. Coins, in contrast, last for many years.
Portable	Money must be easy to carry. Though paper money is not very durable, people can easily carry large sums of paper money.
Divisible	Money must be easily divided into small parts so that purchases of any price can be made. Carrying coins and small bills makes it possible to make purchases of any amount.
Stable in value	Money must be stable in value. Its value cannot change rapidly, or its usefulness as a store of value will decrease.
Scarce	Whatever is used as money must be scarce. That is what gives it value.
Accepted	Whatever is used as money must be accepted as a medium of exchange in payment for debts. In the United States, acceptance is based on the knowledge that others will continue to accept paper money, coins, and checks in exchange for desired goods and services.

Economic Analysis

Analyzing In which of the categories listed does paper money have an advantage over cattle as a medium of exchange? Why?

Types of Money

Main Idea Today, all United States money is fiat money that is not backed by gold or any other commodity.

Economics & You What if your boss decided to pay you for a week's worth of work in cattle or IOUs? Would you accept either of these as a fair exchange? Read on to learn more about mediums of exchange.

Mediums of exchange such as cattle and gems are considered **commodity money.** They have a value as a commodity, or good, aside from their value as money. **Representative money** is money backed by—or exchangeable for—a valuable item such as gold or silver.

At one time, the United States government issued representative money in the form of silver and gold certificates. In addition, private banks accepted deposits of gold bars or silver ingots (called bullion) in exchange for paper money called banknotes. The notes were a promise to **convert** the paper money back into coin or bullion on demand. These banks were supposed to keep enough gold or silver in reserve—on hand—to redeem their banknotes. That did not always happen, however.

Today all United States money is **fiat money,** meaning that its face value occurs through government fiat, or order. It is in this way declared **legal tender.**

Reading Check **Contrasting** Explain the difference between commodity money and representative money.

commodity money: a medium of exchange such as cattle or gems that has value as a commodity or good aside from its value as money

representative money: money that is backed by an item of value, such as gold or silver

fiat money: money that has value because a government fiat, or order, has established it as acceptable for payment of debts

legal tender: money that by law must be accepted for payment of public and private debts

---

section 1 Review

Vocabulary

1. **Explain** the significance of: money, medium of exchange, barter, unit of accounting, store of value, commodity money, representative money, fiat money, legal tender.

Main Ideas

2. **Recalling** In a diagram like this one, list an example for each function of money.

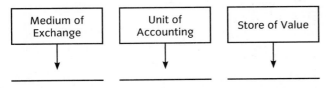

Critical Thinking

3. **The BIG Idea** Government policy has a significant effect on fiat money and legal tender. Explain why this is true.

4. **Determining Cause and Effect** Describe how inflation affects money as a store of value.

Applying Economics

5. **Bartering** Imagine that you live in a barter society. List five items you use and value. What would you be willing to trade each item for? Write a paragraph to explain why using money might be more convenient than barter.

People and Perspectives

Hector Barreto

- Former Administrator of the U.S. Small Business Administration (SBA)

■ Named one of America's 100 Most Influential Hispanics by *Hispanic Business* magazine

■ Founded his own company, Barreto Insurance and Financial Services, which specializes in providing financial services to California's Latino population

As a nine-year-old boy in Kansas City, Missouri, Hector Barreto's first job was waiting tables in his family's restaurant.

"I like to tell people that everything important that I learned about business I learned in a Mexican restaurant. And it's true. My father was an immigrant to this country in the late 1950s. . . . The greatest thing for [him] was the opportunity to be your own boss, and my father and mother saved their money and they were able to open up a little Mexican restaurant. . . . [T]his is a dream that really has defined our country for centuries, . . . that dream that tells us that it really doesn't matter where we start. It only matters where you end up. And if you work hard enough, and if you create an environment for yourself, you can accomplish anything that you want. . . . I learned that from my father."

After earning a bachelor's degree in business administration, Barreto went on to found, among other things, a small business institute providing technical assistance, education, and development opportunities to small businesses.

Eventually Barreto came to the attention of President George W. Bush, and in 2001 he was unanimously confirmed by the U.S. Senate as administrator of the U.S. Small Business Administration (SBA). This is a critical position, because small businesses are an important part of the economy and employ more than half of all workers in the United States. In interviews, Barreto has made it clear that he credits the spirit of American entrepreneurship for the success of small businesses:

> **Small business people are resilient. The same stubbornness that drives an entrepreneur to start a business of their own and be their own boss . . . also steels their resolve to survive in tough times.**

Checking for Understanding

1. **Defending** What is your opinion about a nine-year-old working in a family business? What do you think Barreto's opinion is?

2. **Drawing Conclusions** Do you believe it should be government's role to help people run small businesses? Why or why not?

History of American Money and Banking

PrODUCTS In ThE NeWS
—from *Fortune*

THE BIRTH OF ELECTRONIC BANKING John Reed was operating on faith. He knew he was right, though he didn't know why. Fortunately Reed's boss, Citibank chairman Walter Wriston, was also a believer in the possibilities that technology could bring to banking. So in 1975, Wriston agreed to sink an eye-popping $100 million into Reed's plan. Two years later the bank went public with it. Then, virtually overnight, Citi dotted the Big Apple with a network of more than 400 automatic teller machines.

▲ Early ATM

...The gamble paid off—with a little help from above. In early 1978, New York City was walloped with more than a foot of snow. Within three days a commercial ran showing New Yorkers trekking through the slush to Citibank ATMs. A catch phrase was born: "The Citi Never Sleeps." Use of the machines soared.

American banking has undergone many changes since our nation's founding. Its mediums of exchange have included everything from wampum to "virtual" money—banking in cyberspace on the Internet. In this section, you'll learn about the development of and changes in the United States banking industry.

History of American Banking

Main Idea Throughout history, instability in the banking system has contributed to business fluctuations.

Economics & You How has banking changed since your parents or guardians were in high school? Read on to learn about money and banking in the United States since the colonial period.

Because the history of money in the United States is so closely tied to the development of the nation's banking system, the time line in **Figure 14.3** below describes both. During the early colonial period of American history, England did not permit the new colonies to print money or mint coins. Therefore, bartering for goods was common. Colonists used various items in place of coins and paper money. In the Massachusetts Bay Colony, for a time, people used Native American wampum as a medium of exchange. In the Virginia Colony, tobacco became commodity money.

Though scarce, some European gold and silver coins also circulated in the colonies. The Spanish *dolár*, later called the "dollar" by colonists, was one of the more common coins.

Skills Handbook

See page R52 to learn about Sequencing Events.

Figure 14.3 Time Line of Money and Banking

■ When the United States was first established, it had no reliable medium of exchange or banking system. Over the years, the nation's monetary standard and banking regulations have undergone many changes.

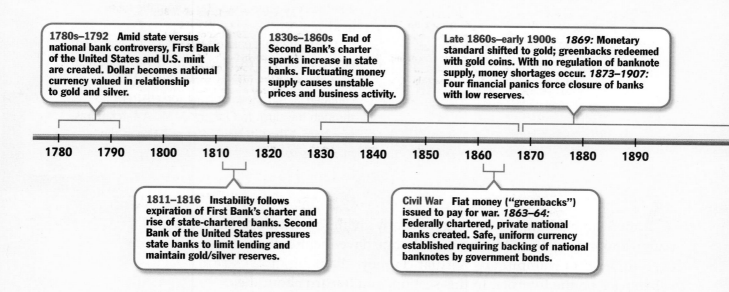

1780s–1792 Amid state versus national bank controversy, First Bank of the United States and U.S. mint are created. Dollar becomes national currency valued in relationship to gold and silver.

1830s–1860s End of Second Bank's charter sparks increase in state banks. Fluctuating money supply causes unstable prices and business activity.

Late 1860s–early 1900s *1869:* Monetary standard shifted to gold; greenbacks redeemed with gold coins. With no regulation of banknote supply, money shortages occur. *1873–1907:* Four financial panics force closure of banks with low reserves.

| 1780 | 1790 | 1800 | 1810 | 1820 | 1830 | 1840 | 1850 | 1860 | 1870 | 1880 | 1890 |

1811–1816 Instability follows expiration of First Bank's charter and rise of state-chartered banks. Second Bank of the United States pressures state banks to limit lending and maintain gold/silver reserves.

Civil War Fiat money ("greenbacks") issued to pay for war. *1863–64:* Federally chartered, private national banks created. Safe, uniform currency established requiring backing of national banknotes by government bonds.

The Revolutionary War brought even more confusion to the already haphazard colonial money system. To help pay for the war, the Continental Congress issued bills of credit, called Continentals, that could be used to pay debts. So many of these notes were **issued** that they became worthless, and people often refused to accept them. The phrase "not worth a Continental" became a way of describing something of little value.

After the war, establishing a reliable medium of exchange became a major concern of the new nation. The Constitution, ratified in 1788, gave Congress the power to mint coins, although private banks were still allowed to print banknotes representing gold and silver on deposit. Then in 1792, Congress passed the Coinage Act, which established the dollar as the basic unit of currency for the nation.

The nation's new leaders also had to decide on a banking system. Some supported a national banking system, while others argued for state-chartered banks. Today, we have both.

Economics ONLINE

Student Web Activity
Visit the *Economics Today and Tomorrow* Web site at glencoe.com and click on *Chapter 14—Student Web Activities* to see how online banking works.

✔ **Reading Check** **Determining Cause and Effect** What effects did the Revolutionary War have on the colonial money system? Why?

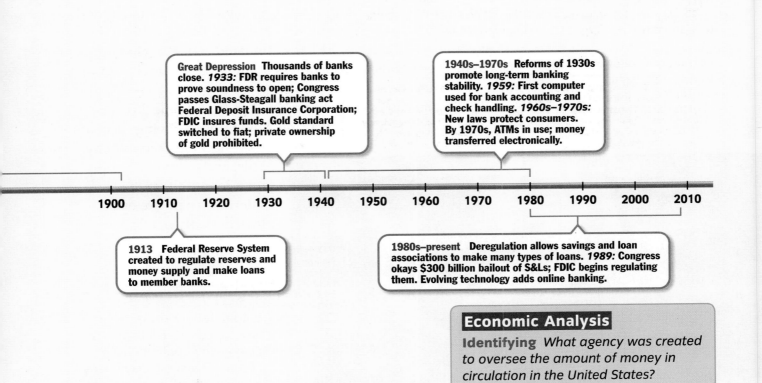

Great Depression Thousands of banks close. *1933:* FDR requires banks to prove soundness to open; Congress passes Glass-Steagall banking act Federal Deposit Insurance Corporation; FDIC insures funds. Gold standard switched to fiat; private ownership of gold prohibited.

1940s–1970s Reforms of 1930s promote long-term banking stability. *1959:* First computer used for bank accounting and check handling. *1960s–1970s:* New laws protect consumers. By 1970s, ATMs in use; money transferred electronically.

1900 1910 1920 1930 1940 1950 1960 1970 1980 1990 2000 2010

1913 Federal Reserve System created to regulate reserves and money supply and make loans to member banks.

1980s–present Deregulation allows savings and loan associations to make many types of loans. *1989:* Congress okays $300 billion bailout of S&Ls; FDIC begins regulating them. Evolving technology adds online banking.

Economic Analysis

Identifying *What agency was created to oversee the amount of money in circulation in the United States?*

Banking Services

Main Idea The efficiency of banking services has increased as computer technology has reduced the dependence on paper.

Economics & You Why do you choose to keep your money at one bank rather than another? What services or other benefits influence your decision? Read on to learn about many of the services offered by present-day banks.

Banks and savings institutions today offer a wide variety of services, including checking accounts, interest on certain types of checking accounts, automatic deposit and payment, storage of valuables, transfer of money from one person to another, and overdraft checking. **Overdraft checking** allows a customer to write a check for more money than exists in his or her account. The bank lends the needed amount and the customer pays the money back, usually at a relatively high rate of interest.

In general, the types of banking services are the same across the country. The exact terms and conditions of the services, however, **vary** from state to state according to each state's banking laws. When choosing a bank or savings institution, you should obtain information on the bank's service charges.

overdraft checking: checking account that allows a customer to write a check for more money than exists in his or her account

electronic funds transfer (EFT): system of transferring funds from one bank account directly to another without any paper money changing hands

automated teller machine (ATM): unit that allows consumers to do their banking without the help of a teller

Electronic Banking One of the most important changes in banking began in the late 1970s with the introduction of the computer. With it came **electronic funds transfer (EFT),** or a system of transferring funds from one bank account directly to another without any paper money changing hands. One of the most common features of EFT is **automated teller machines (ATMs).** These units let consumers do their banking without the help of a teller.

Today you can even do your banking from home. You can see your account balances, transfer funds from a savings account to a checking account, pay bills, and often even apply for a loan—all on the Internet. There are even Internet-only banks.

Banking Convenience

Since automated teller machines were developed in the late 1970s, their usage and popularity have grown tremendously. Today, many people do their banking exclusively through ATMs and the Internet.

EFT Concerns Although EFT can save time, trouble, and costs in making transactions, it does have some drawbacks. The possibility of tampering and lack of privacy are increased because all records are stored in a computer. A person on a computer terminal could call up and read or even alter the account files of a bank customer in any city, if he or she knew how to get around the safeguards built into the system. In response to these and other concerns, the Electronic Funds Transfer Act of 1978 describes the rights and responsibilities of participants in EFT systems. For example, EFT customers are responsible for only $50 in losses when someone steals or illegally uses their ATM cards, if they report the cards missing within two days. If they wait more than two days, they could be responsible for as much as $500. Users are also protected against computer mistakes.

▲ ATM and Internet banking is convenient but carries security concerns, such as identity theft.

✔ **Reading Check** **Evaluating** List at least one positive and one negative outcome of electronic banking.

section 2 Review

Vocabulary

1. **Explain** the significance of: overdraft checking, electronic funds transfer (EFT), automated teller machine (ATM).

Main Ideas

2. **Comparing and Contrasting** Electronic funds transfer is rapidly replacing paper or live transactions. In a chart like the one below, list two advantages and two disadvantages of EFT.

Electronic Funds Transfer	
Advantages	1.
	2.
Disadvantages	1.
	2.

Critical Thinking

3. **The BIG Idea** What do you believe are the two most significant laws affecting banking since the 1920s? Why?

4. **Analyzing** What is the significance of service charges, and how are they determined?

Applying Economics

5. **Service Charges** Go to three local banks and pick up information pamphlets on credit cards, checking accounts, and savings accounts at each bank. Bring these to class and make a list of charges that you would have to pay. Which bank offers the best terms for you?

Types of Money in the United States

GUIDE TO READING

Section Preview
In this section, you will learn about what counts as money and near money in the United States.

Content Vocabulary
- checking account (p. 380)
- checkable deposits (p. 380)
- thrift institutions (p. 380)
- debit card (p. 381)
- near moneys (p. 382)
- M1 (p. 383)
- M2 (p. 383)

Academic Vocabulary
- consist (p. 379)
- create (p. 381)

Reading Strategy
Listing As you read, complete a web diagram like the one below by listing five different forms that money can take in the United States.

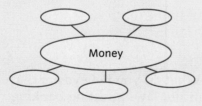

Money

ISSUES IN THE NEWS
··
—from the *Associated Press*

NEW MONEY Hooray for the red, yellow and orange! Those are the colors featured on the newly redesigned $10 bill, the third currency denomination to add splashes of color to the traditional green of U.S. currency.

Some 800 million of the new bills will be put into circulation starting [in 2006] in the government's latest effort to stay ahead of the tech-savvy counterfeiters.

. . . The makeover of the $10 bill follows similar colorization of the $20 bill in 2003 and the $50 bill [in 2004].

. . . Each bill denomination has different colors mixed in with the traditional green. For the $20, the additional colors are peach and blue, while the $50 bill has blue and red.

. . . [T]he government plans to redesign the currency every seven to ten years to keep ahead of counterfeiters armed with ever more sophisticated devices.

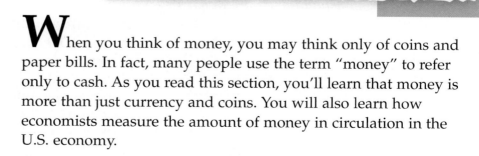

When you think of money, you may think only of coins and paper bills. In fact, many people use the term "money" to refer only to cash. As you read this section, you'll learn that money is more than just currency and coins. You will also learn how economists measure the amount of money in circulation in the U.S. economy.

Money and Near Moneys

Main Idea The money supply consists of not only bills and coins, but also checking and savings deposits and certain other liquid investments.

Economics & You Do you have a checking account or a savings account? Read on to learn about how these, in addition to the cash in your wallet, count as money.

Money in use today **consists** of more than just currency. It also includes deposits in checking and certain types of savings accounts, plus certain other investments.

Currency The Bureau of the Mint, which is part of the Treasury Department, makes all the coins in the United States. About 5 percent of the currency in circulation today is in the form of coins.

Most of the nation's currency consists of Federal Reserve notes issued by Federal Reserve banks. The Bureau of Engraving and Printing, also part of the Treasury Department, prints all Federal Reserve notes. They are issued in denominations of $1, $5, $10, $20, $50, and $100. (Larger notes used to be printed, but the practice was stopped to make it harder for criminals to hide large amounts of cash.)

Fighting Funny Money

Government printing officials employ several methods to try to make counterfeiting more difficult. Such methods include printing multicolored bills and using embedded devices such as strips, microprinting, and inks whose colors change depending on the angle of the light.

Checks A **checking account** consists of funds deposited in a bank that a person can withdraw at any time by writing a check. The bank must pay the amount of the check on demand, or when it is presented for payment. Such accounts used to be called *demand deposits.* Today we call these **checkable deposits,** and a variety of financial institutions offer them. Many banks provide checking accounts at no cost to the customer. The banks can still make a profit on such accounts, however, by charging very high fees when customers write checks for more than the balance of their accounts. These fees may be as high as $30 for a check that is only a few dollars more than the customer's checking account balance.

Commercial banks used to be the only financial institutions that could offer checkable deposits. Today all **thrift institutions**—mutual savings banks, savings and loan associations (S&Ls), and credit unions—offer checkable deposits. In addition, many brokerage houses offer the equivalent of checking accounts. Merrill Lynch and Fidelity Investments are two examples.

The largest part of the money supply in the United States consists of checkable accounts. **Figure 14.4** below provides information about how to manage checks and checking accounts, including how to write a check and balance a checkbook.

Figure 14.4 | Managing a Checking Account

■ When you write a check, the funds will not come out of your account until the receiving party deposits the check and it is processed through the Federal Reserve system. It is very important to manage your account carefully and to make sure the funds are there when the check finally clears.

A. Writing a Check Always fill out your checks completely and clearly in ink. Make sure the numeric amount in the box matches the written amount on the line below it.

B. Tracking Your Transactions Whenever you write a check to someone or make a deposit into your checking account, record the check number, date, and amount in your check register. Keep an accurate running total in the right-hand column.

Number	Date	Description	Payment of Debt	Fee	Deposit of Credit	Balance
						$ 827 91
132	4/25	Fashion shop	$ 73 16		$	$ 754. 75
133	5/1	Rent	462 50			292 25
134	5/7	Phone	83 00			209 25
135	5/14	Cash	50 00			159 25
136	5/15	J.W. Little	10 00			149 25
—	5/22	John's check			4 00	153 25
—	5/23	Paycheck			500 61	653 86
137	6/1	Rent	462 50			191 36

Credit Cards and Debit Cards Even though many people use their credit cards to purchase goods and services, the credit card itself is not money. It acts neither as a unit of accounting nor as a store of value. The use of your credit card is really a loan to you by the issuer of the card, whether it is a bank, retail store, gas company, or American Express. Basically, then, credit card "money" represents a future claim on funds that you will have later. Credit cards defer payments rather than complete transactions that ultimately involve the use of money.

A **debit card,** on the other hand, automatically withdraws funds from a checkable account. When you use your debit card to purchase something, you are in effect giving an instruction to your bank to transfer money directly from your bank account to the bank account of the grocery store, retail store, gas station, etc. (Debit cards can be used to make online purchases as well, and the process is the same.) The funds transfer usually happens within 72 hours of your purchase. The use of a debit card does not **create** a loan. Rather, debit card "money" is similar to checkable account money.

Debit cards have become increasingly popular in the United States. In some other countries, such as France, they are used almost exclusively in place of cash. An advantage to debit cards is that people who use them cannot spend more than they have in their checking accounts, and so they avoid overdraft fees.

Personal Finance Handbook

See pages **R10–R13** for more information on **Understanding Credit.**

debit card: device used to make cashless purchases; money is electronically withdrawn from the consumer's checkable account and transferred directly to the store's bank account

---

◄ FIRST NATIONAL BANK OF CHICAGO
P.O. Box 1234 Finance Place, Anytown U.S. 56789

Bernadette C. Dabney
12 Vico Lane
Haddonfield, NJ 08033

Statement Date:
1 June 2008

Account Number
123-456-7

Summary of Accounts

Account Number	Previous Balance	Total Credits	Total Debits	Total Charges	Current Balance
123-456-7	827.91	504.61	674.66	3.00	660.86

Previous Balance	827.91	Current Balance	660.86

Debits			Credits		Balance
May 4	132	73.16			754.75
8	133	462.50			292.25
15	134	83.00			209.25
	135	50.00			159.25
			May 22	4.00	163.25
			23	500.61	663.86
	SC	3.00			660.86

C. **Balancing Your Checkbook**

When you receive your monthly bank statement, follow these steps:

1. Check off your checks and deposit slips in your check register.

2. Deduct service charges and bank fees from your checkbook balance.

3. Add to the bank statement balance any deposits that have not cleared.

4. Total the amount of checks that have not cleared. Subtract this total from the amount on your bank statement.

Economic Analysis

Synthesizing *Why is the "Current Balance" shown on the bank statement different from the running balance shown on the check register?*

near moneys: assets, such as savings accounts, that can be turned into money relatively easily and without the risk of loss of value

Near Moneys Numerous other assets are almost, but not exactly, like money. These assets are called **near moneys.** Their values are stated in terms of money, and they have high liquidity in comparison to other investments, such as stocks. Near moneys can be turned into currency or into a means of payment, such as a checking deposit, relatively easily and without the risk of loss of value. For example, if you have a bank savings account, you cannot normally write a check on it. You can, however, go to the bank and withdraw some or all of your funds. You can then redeposit these funds in your checking account or spend it all as cash.

Time deposits and savings account balances are near moneys. Both pay interest, and neither can be withdrawn by check. Time deposits require that a depositor notify the financial institution within a certain period of time, often 10 days, before withdrawing money. Savings accounts do not usually require such notification.

✓ **Reading Check** **Explaining** What are near moneys? Name two examples of this type of asset.

Figure 14.5 | **M1 and M2**

Graphs In Motion
See StudentWorks™ Plus or go to glencoe.com.

■ With the deregulation of banking services in the early 1980s, the definition of the money supply was enlarged to include the new types of accounts.

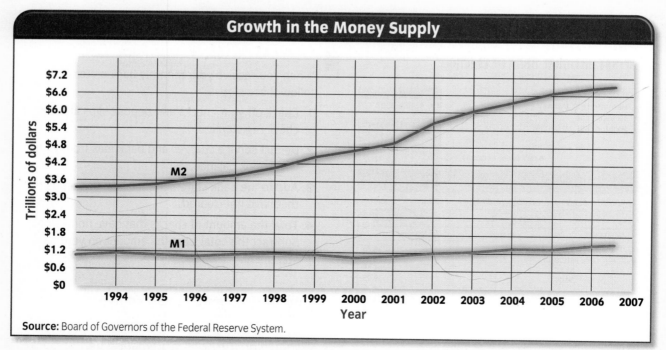

Growth in the Money Supply

Trillions of dollars

Year

Source: Board of Governors of the Federal Reserve System.

Economic Analysis

Using Graphs *In 2006, what was the difference between M2 and M1?*

The Money Supply

Main Idea Economists use both narrow and broad definitions of the money supply to measure the amount of money in circulation.

Economics & You In your opinion, what should count as money? Read on to learn about the two basic definitions of the U.S. money supply.

How much money is there in the United States today? That question is not so easy to answer. First, the definition of *money supply* must be agreed upon. Currently, two basic definitions are used, although others exist. The first is called M1, and the second M2.

M1 includes all currency (bills and coins), all checkable deposits, and traveler's checks. **M2** includes everything in M1 plus savings deposits, small-denomination time deposits, money market deposit accounts, retail money market mutual fund balances, and other more specialized account balances. **Figure 14.5** on the previous page shows the growth of M1 and M2 from 1994 to 2006.

Reading Check **Comparing** What does the M2 definition of the money supply include that the M1 does not?

M1: narrowest definition of the money supply; consists of moneys that can be spent immediately and against which checks can be written

M2: broader definition of the money supply; includes all of M1, plus such near moneys as savings deposits, small-denomination time deposits, money market deposit accounts, and retail money market mutual fund balances

---

section 3 Review

Vocabulary

1. **Explain** the significance of: checking account, checkable deposits, thrift institutions, debit card, near moneys, M1, M2.

Main Ideas

2. **Comparing and Contrasting** In a diagram like the one below, list the characteristics of each type of card in the outer circles and the traits they share in the inner circle.

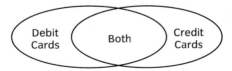

Critical Thinking

3. **The BIG Idea** What is the advantage of allowing thrift institutions to offer the same services as commercial banks?

4. **Explaining** Describe the difference between M1 and M2.

Applying Economics

5. **Counterfeiting** Contact the closest Secret Service office, and ask them for information about how money is coined and printed to prevent counterfeiting. Share the information you discover with your class.

BANKS: "PROTECTION" RACKET?

Overdraft and other fees become huge profit sources for banks.

Check It Out! In this chapter you learned about banking services. In this article, read to learn how consumers and critics are reacting to higher bank fees for those services.

Chris Keeley went on a shopping spree last Christmas Eve, buying $230 in gifts with his debit card. But his holiday mood soured a few days later when he received a notice from his bank that he had overdrawn the funds in his checking account. While the bank allowed each of his seven transactions to go through, it charged him $31 a pop—or a hefty $217 in fees for his $230 worth of purchases.

This fee frenzy may seem paradoxical with so many banks trying to lure new customers with offers of "free" checking. Sure, most don't carry monthly maintenance fees—instead, customers get hit with a myriad of other fees. Charges may include a $2 hit every time a customer with a low

▲ Banking charges can add up.

balance calls a service rep, $20 for closing an account within six months of opening it, and $30 per hour when a staffer helps a customer reconcile an account.

None of the new fees is more controversial than bounce protection. Critics contend that bounce-protection fees, as high as $37 per transaction, are little more than high-priced credit. For now consumers need to remember that at many banks there's no free lunch—or checking accounts.

—Adapted from *BusinessWeek*

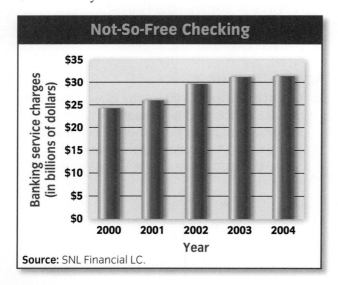

Not-So-Free Checking

Banking service charges (in billions of dollars)

| Year | 2000 | 2001 | 2002 | 2003 | 2004 |

Source: SNL Financial LC.

Think About It

1. **Explaining** What actions are banks taking to earn more profits?
2. **Problem Solving** How can you as a banking customer avoid paying fees?

■ Money functions as a **medium of exchange**, a **unit of accounting**, and a **store of value**.

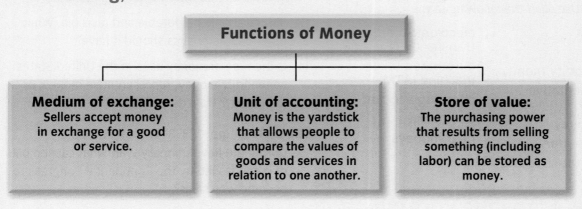

Functions of Money

Medium of exchange: Sellers accept money in exchange for a good or service.

Unit of accounting: Money is the yardstick that allows people to compare the values of goods and services in relation to one another.

Store of value: The purchasing power that results from selling something (including labor) can be stored as money.

■ All money, whether bills, coins, or some other item, must have specific **characteristics**.

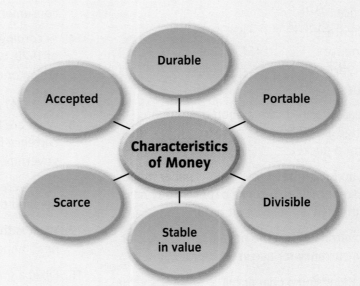

Durable

Accepted

Portable

Characteristics of Money

Scarce

Divisible

Stable in value

■ **Money and near moneys** include bills, coins, checkable deposits, savings accounts, debit and credit cards, and time deposits.

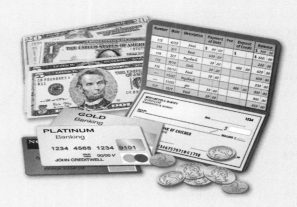

Money and Banking **385**

Review Content Vocabulary

1. *Write a paragraph or two explaining how money and the banking system work in the United States. Use all of the following terms.*

money
barter
commodity money
representative money
fiat money
legal tender
overdraft checking

electronic funds transfer (EFT)
automated teller machine (ATM)
checking account
debit card
near moneys

Review Academic Vocabulary

Choose the letter of the term that best completes each sentence.

a. indicate
b. transport
c. convert
d. issue

e. varies
f. consists
g. create

2. One reason coins make a good medium of exchange is that they are easy to _____ in a purse or a pocket.

3. Banks no longer need to _____ paper money into coin or bullion because paper money has value through a government order.

4. The government has the power to _____, or supply, currency for use in the United States.

5. The markings on a coin or bill _____ its value in the country in which it was made.

6. The size and shape of coins _____ from country to country.

7. A country cannot simply _____ money; it must be backed up by something of value or it is worthless.

8. Money _____ of currency, checking and savings deposits, and certain other investments.

Review the Main Ideas

Section 1 (pp. 367–371)

9. What is one alternative to using money?

10. Money should be durable and divisible. What other characteristics should it have?

11. Is the type of money used in the United States commodity money, representative money, or fiat money? How do you know?

Section 2 (pp. 373–377)

12. During the Revolutionary War, what caused bills of credit issued by the Continental Congress to become worthless?

13. Electronic banking is increasingly common today. What forms of this system do most consumers use?

14. According to the Electronic Funds Transfer Act of 1978, what happens if a person's ATM card is stolen or used illegally?

Section 3 (pp. 378–383)

15. What are the only denominations of paper currency being issued today by the federal government?

16. Why were checking accounts formerly called demand deposits?

17. What is the distinction between money and near moneys?

18. Fill in a graphic organizer like the one below to show what is included in M1 and M2 when defining the money supply.

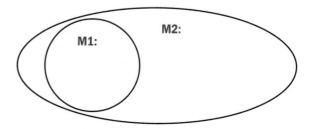

Thinking Like An Economist

19. The three functions of money are as a medium of exchange, a unit of accounting, and a store of value. Use a chart like the one below to keep track of any time you use money, see money used, or see dollar values written somewhere. Do this for three to five days. Try to determine in each instance what function the money is serving. For example, if you see a headline that says "Microsoft Corporation Sales Increased to $10 Billion," you know that money is being used as a unit of accounting.

Medium of Exchange	Unit of Accounting	Store of Value
	• Microsoft sales report	

Economics ONLINE

Self-Check Quiz Visit the *Economics Today and Tomorrow* Web site at glencoe.com and click on **Chapter 14—Self-Check Quizzes** to assess your knowledge of chapter content.

Critical Thinking

20. **The BIG Idea** Create a table like the one below to compare the costs and benefits of engaging in barter to the costs and benefits of using money.

	Costs	Benefits
Barter		
Money		

21. **Explaining** Why are debit cards similar to money, whereas credit cards are not?

22. **Defending** The U.S. government is considering discontinuing the production and use of pennies. Do you think pennies should be discontinued? Why or why not?

Analyzing Visuals

23. Study the cartoon below, and then answer the following questions.

   a. Where does Clare work? How do you know?

   b. What is the manager's concern about what Clare is doing online?

   c. Why does Clare seem unconcerned with the possibility of identity

How does identify theft impact consumers?

THE ISSUE

What if you went to the bank and were told you had no money in your account—even though you had deposited $300 last week? What if you tried to buy something with a credit card and the card was taken away by the store—even though you'd made all your payments on time? These are some of the problems encountered by victims of identity theft, the fastest-growing crime in the United States.

Just as your character, your appearance, and your personal traits make you unique as a person, your name, social security number, birth date, mother's maiden name, and other personal information give you a unique identity as a consumer. You need them to access your money and credit. How might the theft of your identity affect your life?

THE FACTS

Identity theft, or identity fraud, is the taking of a person's private information in order to use it for a variety of purposes. Identity thieves may steal funds from their victims' bank accounts, obtain credit and credit cards, apply for loans, establish accounts with utility companies, rent apartments, or even obtain jobs using their victims' names. The victims may not know what has happened for days, weeks, or even months—until they apply for credit, check their credit report, or begin receiving calls from collection agencies demanding payment for purchases they didn't make. Some thieves even use stolen identities to commit crimes ranging from traffic violations to felonies.

THE ECONOMIC CONNECTION: MONEY AND BANKING

Every 79 seconds, a thief steals someone's identity and goes on a buying spree. That's almost 9 million thefts a year. Victims each spend between 40 and 175 hours repairing the damage, trying to explain to banks and other financial institutions what has happened to them. The average theft amounts to $6,383. The victim usually loses about 7 percent of the fraudulent amount, plus additional expenses.

▲ The Internet has made identity theft easier.

For stolen credit cards, the consumer is liable for only the first $50 charged after reporting the theft to the company. But identity theft costs American businesses almost $53 billion annually.

How is identity theft accomplished? Thieves employ several methods to steal information. A "dumpster diver" may go through your trash, finding unshredded bank or credit card statements or offers. A dishonest sales clerk or server may write down your name, card number, and expiration date from the credit card you give them. Thieves might also divert your billing statements to another location by completing a change-of-address form, or simply steal your wallet, cards, or mail. About 35 percent of frauds reported to the Federal Trade Commission were initiated by e-mail or Web sites. Someone could hack into your computer, place links in a chat room, or clone a legitimate Web site to collect your information when you place an online order.

The fact is that anywhere your private information can be found is a potential theft site. All a criminal needs is your social security number, your birth date, and other identifying information such as your address and phone number. With this information and a false driver's license, they apply for credit, in person or through the mail, posing as you.

CONCLUSION

Anyone can become a victim of identity theft, but consumers are not helpless. Consumer pressure for privacy rights has caused more than 22 states to pass laws requiring companies to notify consumers when their data may have been exposed to theft. And 11 states have "credit freeze" laws, which make

Ways to Protect Your Identity

Do:

◆ Shred all documents containing private information before discarding them.

◆ Sign new credit cards as soon as they arrive.

◆ Keep a record of your account numbers, their expiration dates, and the phone number and address of each company in a secure place.

◆ Keep an eye on your card during purchases, and get it back as quickly as possible.

◆ Open bills promptly and reconcile accounts monthly, just as you would for your checking account.

◆ Report any questionable charges promptly and in writing to the card issuer.

◆ Check your credit report twice a year.

Don't:

◆ Lend credit card(s) to anyone, or leave cards, receipts, or account information lying around—even at home.

◆ Open suspicious e-mails or click on links on websites (type the address yourself).

◆ Sign a blank receipt. When you sign a receipt, draw a line through any blank spaces above the total.

◆ Write your account number on a postcard or the outside of an envelope.

◆ Provide private information to anyone over the Net unless you know it's a secure site.

identity theft nearly impossible when consumers actually exercise the right to freeze their credit files. Check the "Do" and "Don't" list above to learn about some of the ways you can reduce your susceptibility to identity theft.

Analyzing the Impact

1. **Synthesizing** How would having your identity stolen affect you?

2. **Critical Thinking** Is your private information as safe as it could be? If not, what changes might you make to protect your identity?

## chapter 15

The Federal Reserve System and Monetary Policy

The **BIG Idea**

Governments strive for a balance between the costs and benefits of their economic policies to promote economic stability and growth.

Why It Matters

In this chapter, read to learn about who is in charge of the U.S. money supply and how they decide how much currency to put into circulation.

Economics ONLINE

Chapter Overview Visit the *Economics Today and Tomorrow* Web site at glencoe.com and click on **Chapter 15—Chapter Overviews** to preview chapter information.

Organization and Functions of the Fed

GUIDE TO READING

Section Preview
In this section, you will learn about how the Federal Reserve System, or Fed, is organized, and its role in determining the nation's monetary policy.

Content Vocabulary
- Fed *(p. 392)*
- monetary policy *(p. 392)*
- Federal Open Market Committee (FOMC) *(p. 393)*
- check clearing *(p. 395)*

Academic Vocabulary
- assist *(p. 392)*
- network *(p. 392)*

Reading Strategy
Organizing As you read, complete a diagram similar to the one below to illustrate the organization of the Federal Reserve System.

Federal Reserve System

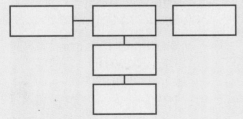

ISSues In ThE NeWS
—from The Federal Reserve: Purposes & Functions

WHY THE FED WAS CREATED During the nineteenth century and the beginning of the twentieth century, financial panics plagued the nation, leading to bank failures and business bankruptcies that severely disrupted the economy. The failure of the nation's banking system to effectively provide funding to

▲ **Early bank**

troubled depository institutions contributed significantly to the economy's vulnerability to financial panics. . . . A particularly severe crisis in 1907 prompted Congress to establish the National Monetary Commission, which put forth proposals to create an institution that would help prevent and contain financial disruptions of this kind. After considerable debate, Congress passed the Federal Reserve Act "to provide for the establishment of Federal reserve banks, to furnish an elastic currency, to afford means of rediscounting commercial paper, to establish a more effective supervision of banking in the United States, and for other purposes." President Woodrow Wilson signed the act into law on December 23, 1913.

Congress created the Federal Reserve System in 1913 as the central banking organization in the United States. Its major purpose was to end the periodic financial panics (recessions) that had occurred during the 1800s and into the early 1900s. In this section, you'll learn how the system is organized to carry out its many functions.

Organization of the Federal Reserve System

Main Idea The Federal Open Market Committee of the Federal Reserve is responsible for implementing monetary policy.

Economics & You Would you want power over the entire money supply to be concentrated in the hands of only a few people? Why or why not? Read on to learn about how the Fed is organized.

Fed: the Federal Reserve System created by Congress in 1913 as the nation's central banking organization

monetary policy: policy that involves changing the rate of growth of the supply of money in circulation in order to affect the cost and availability of credit

The Federal Reserve System, or **Fed,** as it is called, is made up of a Board of Governors **assisted** by the Federal Advisory Council, the Federal Open Market Committee, 12 Federal Reserve district banks, 25 branch banks, and many thousand banks and thrift institutions. (See **Figure 15.1** below.) As its name states, the Fed is a system, or **network,** of banks. Power is not concentrated in a single central bank but is shared by the governing board and the 12 district banks.

The Fed is responsible for monetary policy in the United States. **Monetary policy** involves changing the rate of growth of the supply of money in circulation in order to affect the amount of credit, thereby affecting business activity in the economy.

Figure 15.1 Organization of the Fed

■ Since the change in banking regulations in the early 1980s, nonmember banks are also subject to control by the Federal Reserve System.

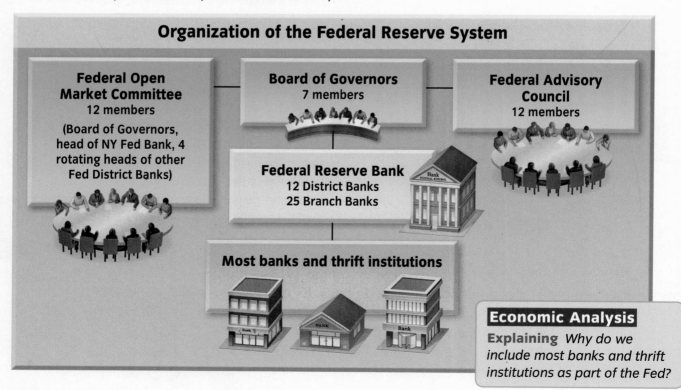

Organization of the Federal Reserve System

Federal Open Market Committee
12 members
(Board of Governors, head of NY Fed Bank, 4 rotating heads of other Fed District Banks)

Board of Governors
7 members

Federal Advisory Council
12 members

Federal Reserve Bank
12 District Banks
25 Branch Banks

Most banks and thrift institutions

Economic Analysis
Explaining *Why do we include most banks and thrift institutions as part of the Fed?*

Board of Governors The Board of Governors directs the operations of the Fed. It supervises the 12 Federal Reserve district banks and regulates certain activities of member banks and all other depository institutions.

The 7 full-time members of the Board of Governors are appointed by the president of the United States with the approval of the Senate. The president chooses one member as a chairperson. Each member of the board serves for 14 years. The terms are arranged so that an opening occurs every 2 years. Members cannot be reappointed, and their decisions are not subject to the approval of the president or Congress. Their length of term, manner of selection, and independence in working reduces their exposure to political pressures.

Federal Advisory Council The Board of Governors is assisted by the *Federal Advisory Council (FAC)*. It is made up of 12 members elected by the directors of each Federal Reserve district bank. The FAC meets at least 4 times each year and reports to the Board of Governors on general business conditions in the nation.

Federal Open Market Committee The 12 voting members on the **Federal Open Market Committee (FOMC)** meet 8 times a year to decide the course of action that the Fed should take to control the money supply. The FOMC determines such economic decisions as whether to raise or lower interest rates. It is this committee's actions that have a resounding effect throughout the financial world.

Federal Open Market Committee (FOMC): 12-member committee in the Federal Reserve System that meets 8 times a year to decide the course of action that the Fed should take to control the money supply

The Banks As shown in **Figure 15.2** below, the nation is divided into 12 Federal Reserve districts, with each district having a Fed district bank. Each of the 12 district banks is set up as a corporation owned by its member banks. The system also includes 25 Federal Reserve branch banks. These smaller banks act as branch offices and aid the district banks in carrying out their duties. All national banks are required to become members of the Federal Reserve System. State-chartered banks may join if they choose to do so.

In the past, only member banks were required to meet Fed regulations, such as keeping a certain percentage of their total deposits in reserve. Now all institutions that accept deposits from customers must keep reserves in their Fed district bank.

Today, the advantage of membership in the Fed is that member banks, as stockholders in their district bank, receive dividends on their stock in the district bank. Member banks also are able to vote for 6 of the district bank's 9 board members.

Reading Check **Identifying** What part of the Fed is responsible for raising or lowering interest rates?

Economics ONLINE

Student Web Activity
Visit the *Economics Today and Tomorrow* Web site at glencoe.com and click on *Chapter 15—Student Web Activities* to see how the Federal Reserve System functions.

Figure 15.2 | **The Federal Reserve System**

■ The 12 Federal Reserve district banks that serve the nation's banks are distributed throughout the country. Trillions of dollars a year pass through the Fed as it processes billions of checks. Note that the Fed is headquartered in Washington, D.C.

Each Federal Reserve district has an identifying letter and number. These are used on Federal Reserve Notes to identify the issuing bank for each note. This bill, labeled with an "E," was issued in Richmond.

- ★ Board of Governors
- ● Federal Reserve District Bank Cities
- — Federal Reserve District Boundaries

Source: *Federal Reserve Bulletin*, Board of Governors of the Federal Reserve System.

Economic Analysis
Explaining *How is each Fed district bank structured?*

Figure 15.3 | **How a Check Clears**

Maps In Motion
See StudentWorks™ Plus or go to glencoe.com.

■ All depository institutions may use the Federal Reserve's check-clearing system. The reserve accounts mentioned in the diagram refer to a bank's account in its Federal Reserve district bank.

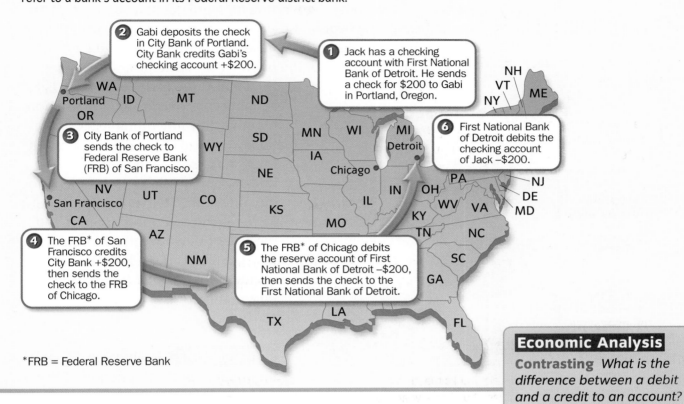

2 Gabi deposits the check in City Bank of Portland. City Bank credits Gabi's checking account +$200.

1 Jack has a checking account with First National Bank of Detroit. He sends a check for $200 to Gabi in Portland, Oregon.

3 City Bank of Portland sends the check to Federal Reserve Bank (FRB) of San Francisco.

6 First National Bank of Detroit debits the checking account of Jack −$200.

4 The FRB* of San Francisco credits City Bank +$200, then sends the check to the FRB of Chicago.

5 The FRB* of Chicago debits the reserve account of First National Bank of Detroit −$200, then sends the check to the First National Bank of Detroit.

*FRB = Federal Reserve Bank

Economic Analysis
Contrasting *What is the difference between a debit and a credit to an account?*

Functions of the Fed

Main Idea The primary function of the Federal Reserve is to control the money supply.

Economics & You What happens to a check after you write it? How is it turned into money? Read on to learn about this and other important functions of the Federal Reserve.

    Among the Fed's functions are check clearing, acting as the federal government's fiscal agent, supervising banks, holding reserves and setting reserve requirements, supplying paper currency, and regulating the money supply.

    The primary responsibility of the Fed is regulating the money supply. To do this, it determines the amount of money in circulation, which, in turn, affects the level of interest rates, the availability of credit, and business activity in general. You'll learn more about this process in Section 3. As you can see from **Figure 15.3** above, **check clearing**—the transferring of funds from one bank to another when you write or deposit a check—is also an important and complex function.

Personal Finance Handbook
*See pages **R2–R3** for more information on **checking accounts.***

check clearing: method by which a check that has been deposited in one institution is transferred to the issuer's depository institution

As the federal government's fiscal, or financial, agent, the Fed keeps track of federal deposits of tax revenues and holds a checking account for the United States Treasury. Checks for such payments as Social Security, tax refunds, and veterans' benefits are drawn on this account. The Fed also acts as a financial adviser to the federal government, regulates state banks that are members of the Federal Reserve System, holds reserves of checkable deposits and sets reserve requirements, and supplies and maintains much of the nation's paper money.

Finally, the Fed sets standards for certain types of consumer legislation, mainly truth-in-lending legislation. By law, sellers of goods and services must make some kinds of information available to people who buy on credit. This information includes the amount of interest and the size of the monthly payment to be paid. The Federal Reserve System decides what type of financial information must be supplied to consumers.

Functions of the Fed

Reading Check **Evaluating** What is the most important function of the Fed?

---

section 1 Review

Vocabulary
1. **Explain** the significance of: Fed, monetary policy, Federal Open Market Committee (FOMC), check clearing.

Main Ideas
2. **Interpreting** In a chart like the one below, explain how the Fed performs each function listed.

Federal Reserve Functions	
Clearing checks	
Supervising members	
Setting and managing reserves	
Supplying paper money	

Critical Thinking
3. **The BIG Idea** What is the major function of the Fed?
4. **Predicting Consequences** Which decision by the Federal Open Market Committee affects the entire financial world?

Applying Economics
5. **Learning About Money** Find the Web site of the Federal Reserve district bank for the region where you live. Then create a list of the kinds of information, such as facts about counterfeiting, that the Web site provides.

ECONOMIST
(1953–)

Ben S. Bernanke
● Chairman of the Federal Reserve

■ Former chair, Princeton University economics department, and professor of economics and public affairs at several universities for 23 years

■ Editor, *American Economic Review*

■ Author and coauthor of several books, including two textbooks and *Essays on the Great Depression*

It's not surprising that the nation's top banker showed an interest in numbers early in his life. At the age of three, Ben Bernanke played with pennies and could do basic math. A straight-A student, he taught himself calculus in high school, achieved a near-perfect score on the SAT, and then earned degrees in economics from both Harvard and the Massachusetts Institute of Technology.

Dr. Bernanke is an expert in monetary policy—managing the country's money supply by adjusting interest rates. His job is to help keep the economy growing while keeping inflation and unemployment low. He finds lessons for today by studying the U.S. stock market crashes of 1929 and 1987, as well as Japan's in 1990: "There's no denying that a collapse in stock prices today would pose serious macroeconomic challenges for the United States. . . . History proves, however, that a smart central bank can protect the economy and the financial sector from the nastier side effects of a stock market collapse."

Dr. Bernanke believes the hardships people suffered in the Great Depression could have been lessened if the central banks had taken control of deflation. He also believes the U.S. economy can withstand stock market crashes if the central banks can maintain a targeted inflation rate of about 2 percent:

> **A collapse in U.S. stock prices certainly would cause a lot of white knuckles on Wall Street. But what effect would it have on the broader U.S. economy? If Wall Street crashes, does Main Street follow? Not necessarily.**

Checking for Understanding

1. **Explaining** What does the Federal Reserve Bank do?

2. **Contrasting** What is the difference between inflation and deflation?

Money Supply and the Economy

Section Preview
In this section, you will learn how the Fed controls the money supply and interest rates.

Content Vocabulary
- loose money policy *(p. 399)*
- tight money policy *(p. 399)*
- fractional reserve banking *(p. 400)*
- reserve requirements *(p. 400)*

Academic Vocabulary
- function *(p. 398)*
- portion *(p. 401)*

Reading Strategy
Synthesizing As you read the section, complete a flowchart like the one below to contrast the effects that a loose or tight money policy can have on the economy.

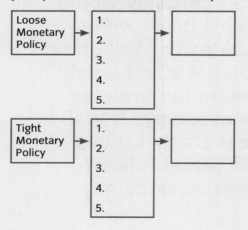

| Loose Monetary Policy | 1. 2. 3. 4. 5. | |

| Tight Monetary Policy | 1. 2. 3. 4. 5. | |

PeOPLE In ThE NeWS
—from the *Washington Post*

BERNANKE STANDS TOUGH Ben S. Bernanke rattled world financial markets . . . with his tough talk about combating inflation, but he also buffed up his image as a strong Federal Reserve chairman committed to the fight, analysts said. . . .

▲ Ben Bernanke

Gone, during Bernanke's remarks to a bankers' conference, was any mention of a Fed pause in its two-year series of interest rate increases. Gone was any fretting over the danger of pushing interest rates too far and triggering a slump. Instead, he declared the recent rise in inflation would not be tolerated. . . .

Bernanke's remarks followed extensive discussion within the central bank about its strategy for communicating with the public. Bernanke has long argued that Fed officials should be more open about their thinking to help the markets anticipate the likely course of interest rates.

As you learned in Section 1, the jobs of the Fed today range from processing checks to serving as the government's banker. As you read this section, however, you'll learn that the Fed's most important **function** involves control over the rate of growth of the money supply and, consequently, changes in interest rates.

Loose and Tight Money Policies

Main Idea The goal of monetary policy is to promote economic growth and employment without causing inflation.

Economics & You Have you ever wondered why the government doesn't eliminate poverty by printing money until everyone has enough? Read on to learn why this "loose" money policy would be problematic.

You may have read a news report in which a business executive complained that money is "too tight" or an economist warned that it is "too loose." In these cases, the terms *tight* and *loose* refer to the monetary policy of the Fed. Monetary policy, as you recall, involves changing the rate of growth of the money supply in order to affect the cost and availability of credit.

Credit, like any good or service, has a cost—the interest that must be paid to obtain it. As the cost of credit increases, the quantity demanded decreases. In contrast, if the cost of borrowing drops, the quantity of credit demanded rises.

Figure 15.4 below shows the results of monetary policy decisions. If the Fed implements a **loose money policy** (often called "expansionary"), credit is abundant and inexpensive to obtain. If the Fed follows a **tight money policy** (often called "contractionary"), credit is in short supply and is expensive to obtain. A loose money policy encourages economic growth, while a tight money policy controls inflation. If money becomes too plentiful too quickly, prices increase.

Reading Check **Analyzing** What happens to the availability of credit when the interest rate rises? When it falls?

Skills Handbook

See page R57 to learn more about Understanding Interest Rates.

loose money policy: monetary policy that makes credit inexpensive and abundant, possibly leading to inflation

tight money policy: monetary policy that makes credit expensive and in short supply in an effort to slow the economy

---

Figure 15.4 | **Balancing Monetary Policy**

■ This chart shows what happens in an economy under loose and tight money policies.

Loose Money Policy

Inflation

- Borrowing is easy
- Consumers buy more
- Businesses expand
- More people are employed
- People spend more

Tight Money Policy

- Borrowing is difficult
- Consumers buy less
- Businesses postpone expansion
- Unemployment increases
- Production is reduced

Recession

Economic Analysis

Contrasting *What is the difference between inflation and recession?*

Fractional Reserve Banking

Main Idea Banks are not required to keep 100 percent reserves to back their deposits.

Economics & You What happens to the money you deposit in your bank? Read on to learn how the Fed uses it to increase the money supply.

fractional reserve banking: system in which only a fraction of the deposits in a bank is kept on hand, or in reserve; the remainder is available to lend

reserve requirements: regulations set by the Fed requiring banks to keep a certain percentage of their checkable deposits as cash in their own vaults or as deposits in their Federal Reserve district bank

Before you can understand how the Fed regulates the nation's money supply, you need to understand the basis of the U.S. banking system and the way money is created. The banking system is based on what is called **fractional reserve banking.**

Since 1913 the Fed has set specific **reserve requirements** for many banks. This means that they must hold a certain percentage of their checkable deposits either as cash in their own vaults or as deposits in their Federal Reserve district bank. Banks must hold these reserves in case many of their banking customers decide to withdraw large amounts of cash from their checking accounts. Currently, many financial institutions must keep 10 percent of their checkable deposits as reserves with the Fed.

Figure 15.5 Expanding the Money Supply

■ The chart shows how $1,000 in new reserves expands to $5,000 by simple loans. In Round 1, the Fed deposits $1,000 of "new" money in Bank A. With a 20 percent reserve requirement, Bank A must hold $200 of the new deposit on reserve. This leaves the bank with $800 of excess reserves.

■ In Round 2, Mr. Jones applies to Bank A for an $800 loan to buy a computer. Bank A grants the loan, and Mr. Jones writes a check to Computer World, which deposits the funds at Bank B. Bank B's reserves increase by $800. Of this

amount, $160 (20 percent of $800) are required reserves, and the remaining $640 are excess reserves.

■ In Round 3, Bank B—to earn profits—loans its excess reserves to Ms. Wang, who wants to borrow $640. She, in turn, buys something from Mr. Diaz, who does his banking at Bank C. He deposits the funds from Ms. Wang. Bank C now has $640 in new deposits, of which $128 are required reserves. Bank C now loans $512 of excess reserves to Mrs. Fontana, who buys something from Mrs. Powers, and so on.

Round	Deposited by	Amount of Deposit	Required reserves (20%)	Excess reserves (80%)	Loaned to	Paid to
1	The Fed (Bank A)	$1,000.00	$200.00	$800.00	Mr. Jones	Computer World
2	Computer World (Bank B)	$800.00	$160.00	$640.00	Ms. Wang	Mr. Diaz
3	Mr. Diaz (Bank C)	$640.00	$128.00	$512.00	Mrs. Fontana	Mrs. Powers
4	Mrs. Powers (Bank D)	$512.00	$102.40	$409.60		
5	All Others					
Eventual totals		$5,000.00	$1,000.00			

Economic Analysis
Analyzing Why are banks required to hold a certain percentage of deposits in reserve, rather than loan them all out?

Currency is a small part of the money supply. A larger portion consists of funds that the Fed and customers deposit in banks. Because banks are not required to keep 100 percent of their deposits in reserve, they can use these reserves to create what is, in effect, new money. (See **Figure 15.5.**)

Suppose Bank A sells a government bond to the Fed and receives $1,000. This is $1,000 in "new" money because the Fed simply creates it by writing a check. With a 20 percent reserve requirement, the bank must hold $200 of that money in reserve. The bank is free to lend the remaining $800.

Suppose that Bank A now provides an $800 loan to an independent business. The business then deposits the $800 in Bank B, which must keep in reserve 20 percent of this new deposit, or $160. Bank B can then loan out the remaining $640. If the business or person receiving the $640 loan then deposits it in Bank C, that bank must keep 20 percent and can loan out the rest. The process continues—$1,000 of "new money" in the banking system becomes a $5,000 increase in the money supply.

So, as we see, each bank uses the nonrequired reserve **portion** of money deposits to make loans to businesses and individuals. This process is known as the *multiple expansion of the money supply.*

Careers Handbook

See pages R76–R80 to learn about becoming a loan officer.

✔ Reading Check **Explain** Explain the process of money expansion.

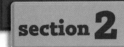

Review

Vocabulary

1. **Explain** the significance of: loose money policy, tight money policy, fractional reserve banking, reserve requirements.

Main Ideas

2. **Determining Cause and Effect** Copy the arrows below, and write at least three characteristics of loose and tight money inside the appropriate arrow.

Loose $ Tight $

Critical Thinking

3. **The BIG Idea** Why does the government require banks to keep reserves against certain deposits?

4. **Evaluating** What is the advantage to a bank of fractional reserves?

Applying Economics

5. **Inflation and the Money Supply** Check the newspaper or an online source for an article about either current interest rates (which are affected by the money supply) or inflation. Write a paragraph or create a chart to show how interest rates affect inflation.

Regulating the Money Supply

GUIDE TO READING

Section Preview
In this section, you will learn about several tools that the Fed uses to control the size of the U.S. money supply.

Content Vocabulary
- discount rate *(p. 404)*
- prime rate *(p. 404)*
- federal funds rate *(p. 405)*
- open-market operations *(p. 406)*

Academic Vocabulary
- precise *(p. 403)*
- contract *(p. 405)*

Reading Strategy
Listing As you read, complete a diagram similar to the one below by filling in the tools the Fed uses to regulate the money supply.

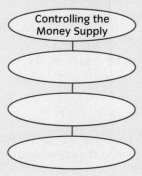

Controlling the Money Supply

ISSUES IN ThE NEWS
···
—from *BusinessWeek*

RATE DEBATE HEATS UP Federal Reserve meetings are about to get a lot more interesting than they have been in several years. Some policymakers are already raising questions about tightening too much, while others are concerned that labor market pressures and rising energy costs could fuel inflation out-

▲ **Globalization affects interest rates.**

side of energy. From here on, policy decisions will depend almost totally on what the economic data imply about growth and inflation, but different people can interpret data in different ways. . . .

One of the hottest topics around the Fed's table will be the role of globalization in policy decisions. U.S. prices of everything from copper to bonds to labor are now influenced by market forces overseas. Globalization ups the ante on finding the right level of interest rates that will keep U.S. inflation at bay.

The main goal of the Federal Reserve is to keep the money supply growing steadily and the economy running smoothly. The Fed attempts to control the money supply efficiently while avoiding both inflation and recession. As you'll learn in this section, the Fed uses several tools to achieve a smoothly running economy.

Changing Reserve Requirements

Main Idea The Fed can change the growth rate of the money supply by changing reserve requirements on bank deposits.

Economics & You If you have a job and save part of your paycheck, you cannot spend the part that you "reserve." Read on to learn about how the Fed uses a similar process to control the money supply.

The Federal Reserve can choose to control the money supply by changing the reserve requirements of financial institutions. One option the Fed has is to raise reserve requirements. When this happens, a bank can call in some loans, sell off investments, or borrow from another bank or from the Fed. Obviously, because all banks would have to increase their reserves, this action would decrease the amount of money in the economy. Raising reserve requirements, then, can be used to help slow down the economy if it is expanding too rapidly.

Even small changes in the reserve requirement can have major effects on the money supply. As a result, some believe that this tool is not **precise** enough to make frequent small adjustments to the money supply. In recent years, changing the reserve requirement has not been used to regulate the money supply.

Reading Check Determining Cause and Effect How does raising the reserve requirement slow down the economy?

Skills Handbook
See page **R36** to learn about **Determining Cause and Effect.**

Raising and Lowering Reserve Requirements

Bank Deposits	Reserve Requirement	$ Amount Bank May Loan	Fed Action
Part A **$1,000,000**	10% (10% × $1,000,000 = $100,000)	$900,000	Suppose a bank has $1 million in deposits, and the reserve requirement is 10%. The bank must keep at least $100,000 in reserves.
Part B **$1,000,000**	5% (5% × $1,000,000 = $50,000)	$950,000	If the Fed wanted to increase the money supply, it could lower the reserve requirement to 5%, for example. The bank would then need to keep only $50,000 in reserves. It could lend out the other $950,000. This additional $50,000 would expand the money supply many times over as it was lent and redeposited. This could help pull the economy out of a recession.
Part C **$1,000,000**	15% (15% × $1,000,000 = $150,000)	$850,000	Suppose instead that the Fed wanted to decrease the money supply, or at least slow down its rate of growth. It could do this by increasing the reserve requirement from 10% to 15%. The bank in this example would then need to keep $150,000 on reserve—$50,000 more than with a 10% reserve requirement.

Changing the Discount Rate

Main Idea The Fed can change the growth rate of the money supply by changing short-term interest rates.

Economics & You Have you ever borrowed money from a friend? Banks sometimes borrow from each other as well. Read on to learn about how this practice can also affect the money supply.

Sometimes a bank will find itself without enough reserves to meet its reserve requirement. This situation may occur if customers unexpectedly borrow a great deal or if depositors suddenly withdraw large amounts. The bank must then borrow funds to meet its reserve requirement. One of the ways it can do this is to ask its Federal Reserve district bank for a loan. The district bank, like any other bank, charges interest. The rate of interest the Fed charges banks is called the **discount rate.**

discount rate: interest rate that the Fed charges on loans to commercial banks and other depository institutions

If the bank does borrow from the Fed, this newly created money would then be available for lending to individuals or businesses, thus increasing the money supply. If the discount rate is high, the bank passes its increased costs on to customers in the form of higher interest rates on loans. For example, it might raise its **prime rate**—the interest rate it charges its best business customers. High discount rates, which discourage borrowing, might keep down the growth of the money supply.

prime rate: rate of interest that banks charge on loans to their best business customers

In contrast, if the discount rate is low, even a bank with sufficient reserves might borrow money to raise its reserves and increase its ability to make loans. Thus, a reduction in the discount rate may increase the total money supply.

Changing the discount rate, like changing the reserve requirement, is now rarely used by the Fed as a tool of monetary policy. Rather, either through its chair or its Federal Open Market Committee, the Fed periodically states that it is going to change "the" interest rate. Because there are many interest rates in the economy, which one does the Fed mean?

FOXTROT

▼ Smart consumers pay attention to interest-rate changes.

Figure 15.6 | **Federal Funds Rate**

■ When the media discuss a rate hike or reduction by the Fed, they are referring to the federal funds rate, or the interest rate that banks charge each other for overnight loans. This affects how much both banks and individuals will borrow.

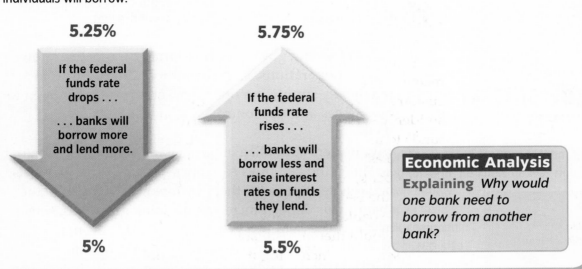

5.25%

If the federal funds rate drops . . .

. . . banks will borrow more and lend more.

5%

5.75%

If the federal funds rate rises . . .

. . . banks will borrow less and raise interest rates on funds they lend.

5.5%

Economic Analysis

Explaining *Why would one bank need to borrow from another bank?*

The interest rate the Fed is referring to is the **federal funds rate.** This is the interest rate that banks charge each other for short-term loans (usually overnight). Why would one bank need to borrow from another? Suppose a customer walks into Bank A late in the day and withdraws a large amount. In order to provide funds to the customer, the bank must dip into its required reserves. Before the banking day ends, Bank A must raise its reserves to the required amount or pay a penalty to the Federal Reserve.

Bank A could borrow from the Fed as discussed earlier, but the discount rate may be too high. Instead, Bank A approaches Bank B for a loan. Bank B happens to have excess reserves that day, so it loans Bank A the funds it needs, charging the federal funds rate. This federal funds market is active—billions of dollars of reserves are borrowed and loaned each business day.

If the Fed causes the federal funds rate to drop, banks will borrow more and, thus, lend more. In contrast, the chairman of the Fed may publicly state the opposite—that the Fed is causing the federal funds rate to rise. At the higher rate, banks will reduce their borrowing from other banks and raise the interest rates they charge their own customers. Economic activity may **contract.** (See **Figure 15.6** above.)

federal funds rate: interest rate that banks charge each other on loans (usually overnight)

Reading Check **Predicting Consequences** What happens to the money supply if the Fed raises the discount rate? Lowers it?

Open-Market Operations

Main Idea The Fed controls the money supply primarily through the purchase and sale of government securities.

Economics & You How long does it take for a change in the money supply to directly affect you? Read on to learn about delays in the effects of the Fed's monetary policy, as well as criticisms of the Fed.

open-market operations: buying and selling of United States securities by the Fed to affect the money supply

Buying and selling government securities, a practice known as **open-market operations,** is the major tool the Fed uses to control the money supply. An open market is one that is open to private businesses and not controlled or owned by the government.

Security dealers specialize in buying and selling government securities. When the Fed buys securities—such as Treasury bills, notes, and bonds—it pays for them by making a deposit in the dealer's bank. This deposit increases the bank's reserves, thus increasing the money supply. When the Fed adds even a relatively small amount of new reserves into the banking system, banks taken as a whole can create money by holding on to required reserves and loaning out the rest.

In contrast, when the Fed sells Treasury bills to a dealer, the dealer's bank must use its deposits to purchase the securities. This action means that banks have fewer reserves to support loans and must reduce their lending. The multiple expansion of money works in reverse by taking more money out of circulation than just the initial withdrawal.

How Much Money?

No matter what tool of monetary policy the Fed uses, the goal is to manipulate the supply of money in circulation.

Delays in the Effects of Monetary Policy No matter what tool of monetary policy the Fed uses, the effects are not felt immediately. Rather, after a monetary policy change, months may pass before the full effects make much change in the economy. Researchers believe that on average, 12 months go by before monetary policy changes are fully felt.

Criticisms of Fed Policies Throughout its history, the Fed's monetary policies have been criticized. In some instances of rising inflation, the Fed increased the amount of money in circulation, thereby worsening inflation. During other periods when the economy was slowing down and going into recession, the Fed decreased the money supply. This action made the recession worse. To prevent such misjudgments, some critics of the Fed have requested that the money supply simply be increased at the same rate every year. They recommend that the Fed *not* engage in monetary policy.

Although the Fed is protected from direct political pressure, it nonetheless still receives conflicting advice from many directions. In addition, the Fed is not the only force working to affect the economy. The spending and taxing policies of the federal government are also at work. The Fed's task is to consider all of these factors as it plots a course for the economy.

Reading Check **Examining** On average, how long does it take for a change in Fed monetary policy to affect the economy?

section 3 Review

Vocabulary
1. **Explain** the significance of: discount rate, prime rate, federal funds rate, open-market operations.

Main Ideas
2. **Summarizing** In a chart like the one below, insert the correct amount a bank can lend given the deposit amounts and reserve requirements listed.

Original Amount	% Reserved	Amount Banks Can Lend
$800	10%	
$800	20%	
$1,000	10%	
$1,000	20%	

3. **Explaining** Why does raising reserve requirements decrease the money supply?

Critical Thinking
4. **The BIG Idea** Explain why it is more expensive for everyone to borrow when the Fed raises the federal funds rate.
5. **Contrasting** What is the difference between the discount rate and the prime rate?

Applying Economics
6. **Government Policy** Construct a written argument that either supports or refutes having government strongly influence the economy. Find at least one quote from another source to defend your opinion.

INFLATION EXPECTATIONS

What you foresee is what you get.

Check It Out! In this chapter you learned that the Fed decides whether to raise or lower interest rates to control inflation. In this article, read to learn about a new economic indicator the Fed looks at when making this decision.

What the heck are inflation expectations, anyway? You won't find the term in any of the major economic data releases put out by the government. Yet whether inflation expectations are rising or falling may turn out to be a critical factor in determining how far and how fast the Federal Reserve raises interest rates.

That, at least, is the new line coming out of the Fed these days. Inflation expectations—a bit of a touchy-feely concept—represent the beliefs of consumers, investors, corporate execs, and economists about how fast prices will rise in the future. To Fed Chairman Ben S. Bernanke, inflation expectations are a key indicator. If people believe inflation will stay low, the Fed can afford to relax a bit. But if the masses start anticipating faster inflation, the odds are greater that the Fed will need to hit them with higher rates even if actual price hikes remain moderate.

. . . How are beliefs about future inflation measured? One way is to ask economists what they think is going to happen.

Another way to judge expectations is to look at the behavior of investors. . . .

The danger, of course, is that expectations about future prices might jump, forcing the Fed to raise rates sharply to

▲ Consumers' beliefs about whether prices will rise or fall are one measure of inflation expectations.

maintain its credibility as an inflation fighter. . . . [Today] the Fed has built credibility by both aggressively fighting inflation and communicating its commitment to price stability. As a result, even as energy prices skyrocketed in recent years, inflation expectations hardly budged, and non-energy inflation stayed relatively low.

—Reprinted from *BusinessWeek*

Think About It
1. **Defining** What are inflation expectations?
2. **Summarizing** How does the Fed plan to use inflation expectations as an economic indicator?

■ The primary **function of the Federal Reserve System** is to control the money supply, but it has other responsibilities as well.

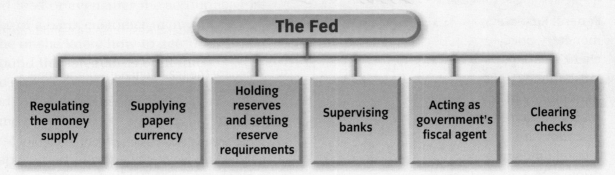

The Fed

| Regulating the money supply | Supplying paper currency | Holding reserves and setting reserve requirements | Supervising banks | Acting as government's fiscal agent | Clearing checks |

■ The Fed can implement either a **loose or tight money policy** to try to promote economic growth and employment.

Loose Money Policy

Tight Money Policy

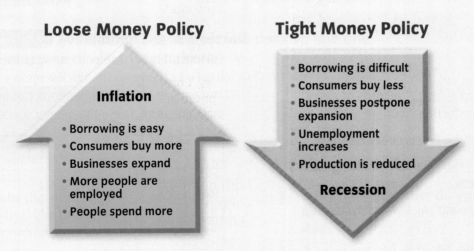

Inflation

- Borrowing is easy
- Consumers buy more
- Businesses expand
- More people are employed
- People spend more

- Borrowing is difficult
- Consumers buy less
- Businesses postpone expansion
- Unemployment increases
- Production is reduced

Recession

■ The Fed has several tools at its disposal to use to **regulate the money supply.**

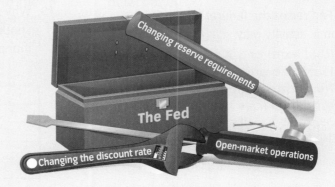

Changing reserve requirements

The Fed

Changing the discount rate

Open-market operations

Review Content Vocabulary

1. *Write a paragraph or two explaining the role of the Federal Reserve in the U.S. economy. Use all of the following terms.*

   Federal Reserve
   monetary policy
   check clearing
   loose money policy
   tight money policy
   reserve requirement
   discount rate
   federal funds rate
   prime rate
   open-market operations

Review Academic Vocabulary

Choose the letter of the term that best completes each sentence.

   a. assist   d. portion
   b. network   e. precise
   c. function   f. contract

2. Banks must keep _____ records of every account and transaction.

3. One _____ of the Fed is check clearing.

4. The Fed can _____ banks by holding excess reserves for them.

5. Banks operate as part of a linked system, or _____.

6. Banks can use the _____ of deposits that do not need to be reserved to make more loans.

7. If the Fed raises the federal funds rate, economic activity may _____ , or shrink.

Review the Main Ideas

Section 1 (pp. 391–396)
8. What does the Board of Governors do within the Fed?

9. How many Federal Reserve banks and branches are there?

10. What are the main functions of the Federal Reserve?

Section 2 (pp. 398–401)
11. What are the two basic types of monetary policies?

12. In a 10 percent fractional reserve banking system, what happens to the money supply when the Fed injects $100 of new money into the American economy?

13. Why do banks have to keep money in reserve accounts?

Section 3 (pp. 402–407)
14. Fill in a table like the one below to list methods the Fed can use to change the money supply, and explain how these methods can be used to increase or decrease the money supply.

Method	To Increase the Money Supply...	To Decrease the Money Supply...
Change reserve requirements	Lower reserve requirements to allow banks to lend more	

15. Why do some of the Fed's critics think the Fed should not engage in manipulating the nation's money supply?

Problem Solving

16. Look at **Figure 15.1** on page 393. Use the map to answer the following questions.

    a. In what federal district do you live?

    b. What is the Federal Reserve Bank city of district 9?

    c. What is the Federal Reserve Bank city of district 4? What are district 4's branch cities?

    d. What are the branch cities of district 11?

    e. To what district bank would checks written in Hawaii go first?

    f. Imagine that the population of district 12 grows very quickly and the district bank has trouble keeping up with the demand for services there. How might the Fed solve this problem?

    g. Suppose that there are suddenly many large withdrawals from banks in district 6, and these banks do not have enough in reserve to cover these withdrawals. How might the Fed solve this problem?

Economics ONLINE

Self-Check Quiz Visit the *Economics Today and Tomorrow* Web site at glencoe.com and click on *Chapter 15—Self-Check Quizzes* to assess your knowledge of chapter content.

Critical Thinking

17. **The BIG Idea** How do you think the Fed would operate differently if it were under the control of the executive branch?

18. **Contrasting** What is the advantage for banks to be members of the Federal Reserve today? How does this differ from the past?

19. **Understanding Cause and Effect** Create a flowchart like the one below to show how fractional reserve banking increases the money supply.

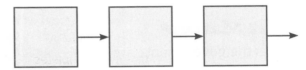

Analyzing Visuals

20. Study the cartoon on the right, and then answer the following questions.

    a. Who is the man holding the door, and what is his job?

    b. What does the dragon represent?

    c. Why does the man look unhappy about his welcome?

chapter # 16

Government Spends, Collects, and Owes

The **BIG Idea**

All levels of government use tax revenue to provide essential goods and services.

Why It Matters

How does the government impact your daily life? Highways and bridges, as well as the taxes you pay on gasoline, are just two examples of government involvement in your day-to-day activities. In this chapter, read to learn why the government collects taxes and what it spends those funds on.

Economics ONLINE

Chapter Overview Visit the *Economics Today and Tomorrow* Web site at glencoe.com and click on *Chapter 16—Chapter Overviews* to preview chapter information.

Growth in the Size of Government

GUIDE TO READING

Section Preview
In this section, you will learn how the size and spending of government at all levels have increased over the last century.

Content Vocabulary
- public-works projects *(p. 415)*
- Medicare *(p. 417)*

Academic Vocabulary
- exceed *(p. 416)*
- core *(p. 417)*

Reading Strategy
Sequencing As you read the section, complete a time line similar to the one below by listing key events and dates that led to increasing government size and spending.

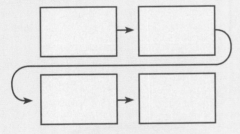

ISSUeS In ThE NeWS
—from *Reason*

CONTROL SHIFT Bill Clinton famously proclaimed that "the era of big government is over." He was wrong: it just moved to the suburbs. State and local governments now dwarf the national government. Fully 86 percent of civilian government employees work for state and local entities. That translates into 46 million Americans who either work for local governments or depend on someone who does.

By long-standing tradition, Americans prefer their government to be close to home, where . . . we can control it. We've got half our wish: most government is local, but it is out of control. Local governments are multiplying. . . at a rate of one new entity added each day. They operate the schools our children attend, determine the uses of our property, and tax us at a higher rate than the national government.

As you learned in Chapter 2, the United States is not a pure market economy. In addition to the market forces of supply and demand, other forces affect the use of resources throughout the economy. As you read this section, you'll learn that government at every level—local, state, and federal—is one of the most important of these forces.

Government Growth

Main Idea Government spending at all levels—federal, state, and local—has increased significantly over the years.

Economics & You How is the government involved in your day-to-day life? Read on to learn about how the government has grown and increased spending since the 1920s.

Government has grown considerably in the last 80 years or so. In 1929 government at all levels employed slightly more than 3 million civilian workers. During the Depression, however, there was a demand for more government services.

Today, about 2.7 million people work for the federal government alone. If you add local and state employees, the government employs over 22 million civilian workers. This figure represents more than a sevenfold increase during a period in which the population a little more than doubled.

The number of government workers has increased because the number of government functions has risen and the size of the population has grown. (See **Figure 16.1** below.)

Figure 16.1 | Government Involvement in the Economy

■ Government plays a major role in many aspects of our lives. Some individuals believe that government has grown too large and that the private sector should provide most goods and services without government intervention. Others argue that government should be even larger.

A. Transportation When you travel on a highway, you are using a resource financed by federal and state funds.

B. Education Your school probably receives some form of aid from the local, state, or federal government.

During the late 1960s, state and local governments spent less than the federal government. The federal government paid for national defense; the salaries of members of Congress, federal judges, and the employees of executive departments such as the State Department; and public-works projects. **Public-works projects** are publicly used facilities such as schools and highways that are built and paid for with tax dollars.

This situation continued until about 1970. Around that time, federal funds started diminishing, while state and local government spending for such items as sewers, roads, and schools increased rapidly. As you can see from the graph on the right, the different levels of government have grown at different rates over the past several years.

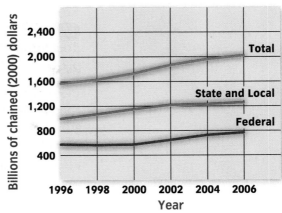

Government Purchases

Billions of chained (2000) dollars

2,400

2,000 — Total

1,600 — State and Local

1,200

800 — Federal

400

1996 1998 2000 2002 2004 2006

Year

Source: Economic Report of the President, 2006.

public-works projects: publicly used facilities, such as schools and highways, built by federal, state, or local governments with public money

✔ Reading Check **Explaining** Why has the number of government workers increased so drastically over the last 80 years?

C. Product Safety
Many goods that you buy are produced in accordance with local, state, and federal regulations.

E. Taxation
If you own property, buy goods, or earn income, you probably pay taxes that help pay for many government activities.

D. Worker Safety
If you have a job, government safety and other regulations often determine your working conditions.

Economic Analysis

Synthesizing *Why do you think government funds, rather than private funds, are used to build highways and bridges?*

Why Has Government Grown?

Main Idea The level of government spending reflects political decisions about how much goods and services should be provided by the public or private sectors.

Economics & You Do you think that a large, growing government is good or bad for society? Why? Read on to learn why the government has grown over the years and about the opportunity costs of this growth.

Economists have often tried to explain the huge growth in government spending. During the Great Depression, there appeared to be a need for more government services. In the 1940s, the government spent billions of dollars to pay for World War II. Why has the government continued to grow since then?

One theory is that as the nation became richer, especially in the late 1960s and early 1970s, people demanded more government services to even out certain income inequities. This goal relates to the economic question of who should share in what is produced.

Today, total government purchases represent about 19 percent of GDP. This figure does not include such items as interest payments on the national debt and transfer payments such as welfare programs. If you add these items, total government outlays easily **exceed** one-third of GDP.

The True Size of Government

The size of government cannot be measured merely by the cost of government spending. Any discussion of the government's size must include where government spends these funds.

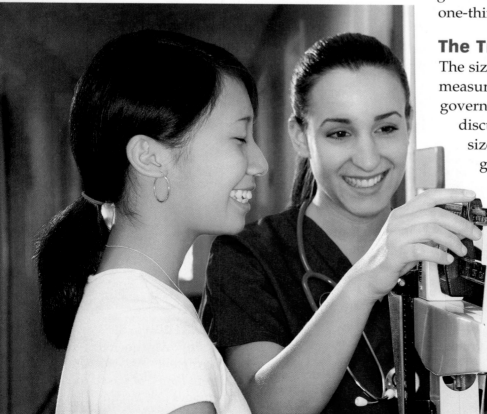

Health Care Controversy

Americans disagree about how much the government should be involved in social spending. For the past several decades, the question of whether the government should provide universal health care has been a topic of great debate.

When the government taxes you to provide you with a particular service, such as **Medicare** (health care for the aged), this cost of government is included in government spending. What if the government also requires that your employer provide that same service? State governments are doing just that. In Massachusetts, for example, employers with six or more employees must provide medical insurance for each employee. So, the federal government taxes employees to pay for government-provided health insurance, and a state government requires that employers provide health insurance directly. The true size of government, then, may be even greater than government estimates show because some "private sector" spending is required by law.

Medicare: government program that provides health care for the aged

The Growth of Government—Good or Bad? We know that government in the United States grew throughout the 1900s and even faster in the early 2000s. Although no one can know how much government is good for society, a general rule is that government taxing and spending have opportunity costs. Government activity displaces private economic decision making along the production possibilities curve, which you learned about in Chapter 1. This private decision making involved in buying and selling is at the **core** of wealth creation and a rising standard of living for all citizens.

Personal Finance Handbook
See pages R24–R27 to learn more about taxes.

✓ **Reading Check** **Explaining** How has the nation's increasing wealth affected the size of government?

---

section 1 Review

Vocabulary

1. **Explain** the significance of: public-works projects, Medicare.

Main Ideas

2. **Defending** In a chart like the one below, indicate whether you think the government should fund the items listed, and why. Also give a reason or reasons for your opinion.

Should Government Fund:	Yes/No	Reason
Medicare		
Highway construction		
Public schools		
Product safety information		
Worker safety information		

Critical Thinking

3. **The Big Idea** What political factors influence how much government spends on goods and services?

4. **Synthesizing** Why is it difficult to measure the true size of government?

Applying Economics

5. **Public Education** In recent years, there has been much debate about whether the public school system should be privatized. Do you think private schools would do a better job than public schools? Write a paragraph defending your view, and share your paragraph with the class.

The Functions of Government

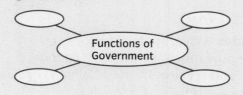
ISSUES IN THE NEWS
..
—from *Healthcare Financial Management*

A BROKEN SYSTEM? According to the U.S. Census Bureau's 2004 report, 45.8 million Americans have no health insurance at all. That's 15.7 percent of all Americans—almost one out of every six of us. . . .

Health care in America is an embarrassment for the world's most powerful nation. Undoubtedly, the United States has the highest-quality health care—for those who can afford it.

. . . Almost 16 percent of the United States' gross domestic product is consumed by health care. No other nation, save Switzerland, spends a double-digit percentage of its GDP on health care. And what are we getting for this $2+ trillion in annual spending? The 37th most "effective" health care system in the world, says the World Health Organization.

The general purpose of government in the United States is to protect individual rights, to promote a stable legal environment for economic activity, and to promote policies that support the general well-being of all citizens. In this section, you'll learn about how the government works toward accomplishing these goals.

Providing Public Goods

Main Idea Public goods are goods or services that many people can use at the same time.

Economics & You Have you ever visited a museum, library, or public park? Read on to learn about these and other public goods provided by the government.

Public goods are a special type of goods or services that government supplies to its citizens. Many people can use public goods—such as streetlights—at the same time, without reducing the benefit each person receives. Usually, different levels of government share responsibility for public goods, such as the legal system. Federal, state, and local governments **maintain** separate systems of courts, correctional institutions, and law-enforcement agencies. The most important public good that only government can provide is a sound system of property rights. In such a system, individuals have the right to own factors of production and to take entrepreneurial risks.

In any society, certain goods and services are considered to have special merit. A *merit good* is one that is deemed socially desirable by government leaders—museums, ballets, and classical music concerts, for example. The government may subsidize such goods by requiring all taxpayers to support them. This allows everyone to enjoy such goods for less than the full market price.

The opposite of merit goods are *demerit goods,* or goods which government officials have deemed socially undesirable, such as tobacco, alcohol, and gambling. The government exercises control over demerit goods by taxing, regulating, or prohibiting the manufacture, sale, and use of them. Taxes on these goods are sometimes called "sin taxes."

public goods: goods or services that can be used by many individuals at the same time without reducing the benefit each person receives

Skills Handbook

See page R41 to learn about Evaluating Information.

Reading Check Evaluating What is the most important public good that only the government can provide?

National Defense

National defense is one of the few public goods controlled solely by the federal government. Usually, state and local governments share the burden of providing public goods.

Promoting the General Welfare

Main Idea Government can use its power to tax and spend to alter market outcomes.

Economics & You Do you think that you have a responsibility to help out those less fortunate than yourself? Read on to learn about how the government redistributes income to the needy.

Some Americans do not have sufficient income for a tolerable level of living, placing them at the bottom of the distribution of income in this country. These people profit from another function of government: to provide for the public well-being by assisting specific groups. These groups include the aged, the ill, and the poor. Through their elected representatives, Americans have chosen to see that almost everyone in the nation is provided with a certain minimum level of support. This task is accomplished primarily through **income redistribution,** or using tax receipts to assist citizens in need. Tax dollars are used to subsidize two general categories of assistance: social-insurance programs and public-assistance programs.

Social-Insurance Programs When you receive a paycheck, you will notice that a portion of your pay has been withheld by various levels of government. Some of these taxes are earmarked for **social-insurance programs**—programs that pay benefits to retired and disabled workers, their families, and the unemployed. These benefits are financed by taxes that you, other workers, and employers pay into the programs. Examples of social-insurance programs include **Social Security,** a federal program that provides monthly payments to people who are retired or unable to work. Upon retirement, you are also eligible for Medicare, a federal program that provides low-cost health care for the elderly.

income redistribution: government activity that takes income from some people through taxation and uses it to help citizens in need

social-insurance programs: government programs that pay benefits to retired and disabled workers, their families, and the unemployed

Social Security: federal program that provides monthly payments to people who are retired or unable to work

Supplemental Security Income

Some American citizens with special needs receive assistance from this federally financed and administered aid program. The blind are one group that receives such benefits.

The federal Social Security program has always been intended to provide *supplemental*, or additional, income—sometimes referred to as a *safety net*—rather than serve as a retired person's primary source of income. Often, Social Security income alone is not enough for a retired person to live on comfortably.

Another social-insurance program is **workers' compensation,** a state program that provides payments for medical care to workers who have been injured on the job and are therefore unable to work for a period of time. People who have lost jobs altogether can receive payments through *unemployment insurance.* Unemployment insurance is intended to provide income temporarily to people who are unemployed through no fault of their own. People receiving such benefits are expected to actively seek employment.

Public-Assistance Programs

Often called **welfare, public-assistance programs** are different from social-insurance programs. Public-assistance programs make payments to individuals based on need, regardless of a person's age and whether or not the person has paid taxes into the program.

Supplemental Security Income is a federally financed and administered program that makes payments to the aged, blind, and disabled who have little or no income. It provides funds to meet basic needs for food, clothing, and shelter. Another program in this category is **Temporary Assistance for Needy Families,** a state-run program that provides assistance and work opportunities to needy families raising young children.

Medicaid, a state and federal program that helps pay health care costs for low-income and disabled persons, is another public-assistance program. Medicaid does not provide funds to individuals; instead, it sends payments directly to health care providers.

Reading Check **Contrasting** What is the difference between social-insurance and public-assistance programs?

workers' compensation: government program that extends payments for medical care to workers injured on the job

public-assistance programs/welfare: government programs that make payments to citizens based on need

Supplemental Security Income: federal programs that include food stamps and payments to the disabled and aged

Temporary Assistance for Needy Families: state-run program that provides assistance and work opportunities to needy families

Medicaid: state and federal public-assistance program that helps pay health care costs for low-income and disabled persons

LUCKY COW ▼Only serious, debilitating injuries qualify a person for workers' compensation.

Regulation and Economic Stability

Main Idea Stable growth, low unemployment, and low inflation are the primary economic goals of government.

Economics & You Should the government step in to protect citizens from pollution or unfair business practices? Read on to learn about ways that the government intervenes in economic activity.

Two other functions of government involve regulating economic activity and trying to ensure economic stability.

Regulating Economic Activity **Figure 16.2** below illustrates four ways in which the government **intervenes** in economic activity. One of the most important regulatory functions concerns the side effects of the production process—also called **externalities.** When a steel mill produces steel, for example, the resulting pollution from the smokestacks may cause health problems in the surrounding area. In the absence of legal rules that limit such pollution, the steel mill does not have to correct these negative externalities.

externalities: economic side effects or by-products that affect an uninvolved third party; can be negative or positive

Ensuring Economic Stability Ensuring economic stability has meant smoothing the ups and downs in the nation's overall business activity. Such intervention has been sought to shield citizens from the harmful effects of business fluctuations, including unemployment, high inflation, recessions, and even depressions. In Chapter 17, you'll learn more about the government's attempt to stabilize the economy.

Figure 16.2 | Government Regulation

■ Government under the American free-enterprise system regulates certain aspects of the economy.

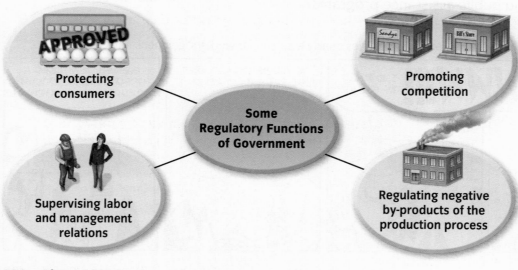

- Protecting consumers
- Promoting competition
- Supervising labor and management relations
- Regulating negative by-products of the production process

Some Regulatory Functions of Government

Economic Analysis

Analyzing *Why would the government be interested in promoting competition?*

Critics of Government Involvement

There are many critics of government involvement in the economy. They point out that merit goods, for example, should be provided by private organizations instead of being funded by taxpayer dollars. If people pay fewer taxes, they have more disposable income and can choose to fund parks, museums, arts programs, or other merit goods if they really want such services.

Opponents of redistribution programs think that most government assistance discourages personal initiative, affects incentives, and harms self-development. Critics of government regulations argue that most regulations raise the prices of goods and services. A better approach, these critics say, would be to encourage market solutions to such problems as pollution.

Let the Market Be?

Critics of government regulation argue that the market will take care of problems if left on its own. For example, they believe that consumers will stop buying cars that cause excessive pollution, and therefore, the government should not regulate car emission standards.

✓ Reading Check **Summarizing** What are three criticisms of government involvement in the economy?

---

section 2 Review

Vocabulary

1. **Explain** the significance of: public goods, income redistribution, social-insurance programs, Social Security, workers' compensation, public-assistance programs, welfare, Supplemental Security Income, Temporary Assistance for Needy Families, Medicaid, externalities.

Main Ideas

2. **Identifying** In diagrams like the ones below, provide examples of the kinds of assistance listed.

Critical Thinking

3. **The BIG Idea** The government regulates negative externalities of production. Explain what this means, and give one example.

4. **Comparing and Contrasting** What are two arguments supporting government intervention and two arguments opposing intervention in the economy?

Applying Economics

5. **Government Rules and You** Make a double-sided chart. On the left side of the chart, make a list of specific ways local, state, and national governments affect you. On the right side of each item, tell whether you do or do not support this policy.

ECONOMIST
(1883–1946)

John Maynard Keynes

- Author of *The General Theory of Employment, Interest and Money* (1936)

■ Long-time lecturer in economics at the University of Cambridge

■ Advisor to the British Treasury during World Wars I and II

■ Played a leading role in the creation of the International Monetary Fund

John Maynard Keynes was probably the most influential economist of the twentieth century. During the Great Depression of the 1930s, economic distress was widespread. Industrial output in the United States fell by over 30 percent, and unemployment rose to over 25 percent of the workforce. Capitalism appeared to be inherently unstable, and traditional laissez-faire economic theory seemed to offer few solutions other than waiting for free markets to readjust on their own.

In the midst of the suffering, Keynes's *General Theory of Employment, Interest and Money,* published in 1936, offered an alternative, arguing that government should actively stimulate the economy and reduce unemployment through its spending and taxing policies. According to Keynes, the assumptions of classical economic theory "are seldom or never satisfied, with the result that it cannot solve the economic problems of the actual world."

Ten years earlier, in an essay entitled *The End of Laissez-Faire,* Keynes had already made a case for greater government involvement:

"It is not true that individuals possess a prescriptive 'natural liberty' in their economic activities. There is no 'compact' conferring perpetual rights on those who Have or on those who Acquire. . . .

> **" The important thing for government is not to do things which individuals are doing already, and to do them a little better or a little worse; but to do those things which at present are not done at all. "**

The school of economic thought known as Keynesian economics grew out of these ideas that it is the duty of government to intervene in the economy to help the disadvantaged.

Checking for Understanding

1. **Explaining** According to Keynes, why couldn't classical economic theory solve the economic problems of the Great Depression?

2. **Synthesizing** What was Keynes's attitude toward Adam Smith's concepts of natural liberty and self-interest?

The Federal Budget and the National Debt

GUIDE TO READING

Section Preview
In this section, you will learn how the federal government prepares a budget and borrows funds.

Content Vocabulary
- fiscal year *(p. 427)*
- budget deficit *(p. 428)*
- deficit financing *(p. 428)*
- national debt *(p. 428)*
- budget surplus *(p. 429)*

Academic Vocabulary
- submit *(p. 427)*
- allocate *(p. 427)*

Reading Strategy
Listing As you read the section, complete a web diagram similar to the one below by listing the seven largest expenses for the federal government.

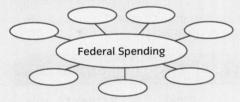

Federal Spending

ISSueS In ThE NeWS
—from CNN.com

TRACKING THE DEBT The plug was pulled on the [original] National Debt Clock, which has kept track of the federal government's red ink since the electronic billboard near Times Square [in New York City] was erected in 1989.

In its final moments . . . the sign read: "Our national debt: $5,676,989,914,887. Your family's share: $73,733."

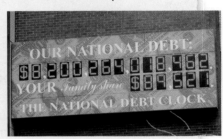

▲ **National Debt Clock in October 2005**

New York real estate developer Seymour Durst invented and bankrolled the clock to call attention to the then-skyrocketing national debt. . . . When it was first plugged in, the odometer-style clock whirred furiously as the national debt rose by $13,000 a second. Often the last few digits increased so fast they were just a blur. And at one point in the mid-1990s, the debt was rising so fast the clock's computer crashed.

[The National Debt Clock has since been replaced. In October 2005, the gross national debt surpassed eight trillion dollars.]

To carry out all of its functions, government must spend large sums. As a result, the federal budget is large and has numerous categories. Because all resources are scarce, an increase in spending in one area will cause a decrease in spending in some other area. As you read this section, you'll learn how the government prepares its budget and decides where to spend its funds.

The Budget-Making Process

Main Idea Congress and the president work together to prepare an annual budget showing the anticipated federal expenditures and revenues for the coming fiscal year.

Economics & You How do you decide how to spend your income? Read on to learn about the process the federal government goes through to plan its annual spending.

Considerable debate and compromise are necessary when lawmakers go about preparing an annual budget. (See **Figure 16.3** below.) A complicated budget-making process goes on every year, not just in Washington, D.C., but in every state and local government unit as well. State and local budgeting processes vary, but the federal government follows the same process every year. This process calls for the president and various congressional offices to work together.

Figure 16.3 | Federal Taxation and Spending

■ The goal of the budget-making process is to balance what the government takes in with what it spends. If the government takes in more than it spends, there is a budget surplus. If it spends more than it takes in, there is a budget deficit.

▼ **A. Federal Tax Receipts** This graph illustrates the sources from which the federal government collects taxes and the percentage it gets from each.

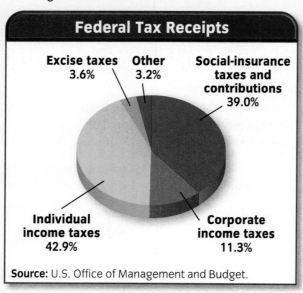

Federal Tax Receipts

Excise taxes 3.6%
Other 3.2%
Social-insurance taxes and contributions 39.0%
Individual income taxes 42.9%
Corporate income taxes 11.3%

Source: U.S. Office of Management and Budget.

▼ **B. Federal Spending** The federal budget is based on a fiscal year, rather than the calendar year. Spending is calculated from the beginning of the budget year on October 1 of one year to September 30 of the next year.

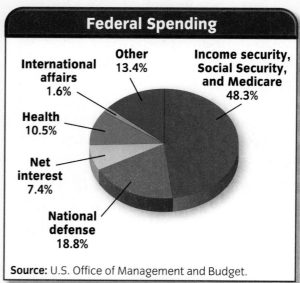

Federal Spending

Other 13.4%
International affairs 1.6%
Income security, Social Security, and Medicare 48.3%
Health 10.5%
Net interest 7.4%
National defense 18.8%

Source: U.S. Office of Management and Budget.

Economic Analysis

Using Graphs *Where does the largest chunk of federal spending go? The smallest?*

About 18 months before the **fiscal year** begins on October 1, the executive branch of the government begins to prepare a budget. Working with the president, the Office of Management and Budget (OMB) makes an outline of a tentative budget for the next fiscal year. The various departments and agencies receive this outline and usually start bargaining with the OMB for a larger allocation of federal funds.

The director of the OMB eventually puts together a set of figures and takes them to the president, along with the OMB's analysis of the nation's economic situation. At this point, the president and various advisers make key decisions about the potential impact of the budget on the nation's economic policy and goals. They discuss such issues as: Will the budget increase or reduce federal spending? Which federal programs will be cut back, and which will be expanded? Should taxes be raised or lowered?

Eventually, the president approves the budget plan. The budget is printed, and the president **submits** the budget to Congress by January. Then various committees and subcommittees of Congress examine the budget's proposals, while the Congressional Budget Office (CBO) advises the committees about different aspects of the budget. Throughout the year, each committee holds a series of discussions.

Congress is supposed to pass two budget resolutions that set binding limits on spending and taxes for the upcoming fiscal year. In practice, however, the required budget resolutions often do not get passed on time. Moreover, when they are passed, the resolutions are not always treated as binding. As a result, the fiscal year sometimes starts without a budget, and the government must operate on the basis of a continuing congressional resolution. Agencies that **allocate** funds can continue spending as they spent the year before until the new budget resolution is passed.

fiscal year: year by which accounts are kept; for the federal government, October 1 to September 30 of the next year

Steps in the Budget Process

February–September
Executive branch agencies develop requests for funds and submit them to the Office of Management and Budget (OMB).

September–December
The president and OMB review the requests and make the fiscal decisions on what goes in the budget. The budget is printed and formally sent to Congress.

January–September (of following year)
The House and Senate Budget Committees review the president's proposed budget. By April 15, these committees prepare an initial resolution for the budget that goes to the entire Congress for debate. By September 25, the congressional budget should be finalized and passed by the House of Representatives, which approves spending and revenue bills.

October 1
The fiscal year begins.

October 1–September 30
Agency program managers implement the budget and disburse funds.

October–November
Data on actual spending and receipts for the completed fiscal year become available, and the Government Accountability Office audits the fiscal-year outlays.

✔ Reading Check **Examining** What is the president's role in preparing the national budget?

The National Debt

Main Idea A budget deficit results when government expenditures exceed revenues collected, and the difference is financed through borrowing, which adds to the national debt.

Economics & You Have you ever run out of funds while waiting for your next paycheck? What did you do? Read on to learn about what happens when the federal government overspends its budget.

Skills Handbook

See page R53 to learn about Comparing Data.

budget deficit: situation when the amount of government spending exceeds its receipts during the fiscal year

deficit financing: government policy of spending more money than it is able to bring in through revenues

national debt: total amount of outstanding debt for the federal government

Federal government revenues are usually not equal to expenditures. Most years, the government spends more than it collects in taxes, causing a **budget deficit.** When a budget deficit occurs, the government must raise the extra funds through borrowing. This borrowing is similar to an individual overspending his or her income. The government's overspending is called **deficit financing.**

Government borrows to cover the deficit by selling government securities to individuals, businesses, and foreign governments. When you buy U.S. savings bonds, you are lending funds to the federal government. In addition, individual agencies of the federal government are authorized to sell bonds. State and local governments can borrow by selling bonds to finance some of their activities.

Each year the federal government creates new debt by issuing new securities. At the same time, it retires old debt by paying off bonds, notes, and bills as they come due. The total amount of outstanding debt for the federal government is called the **national debt,** or public debt. (See **Figure 16.4** below.)

Figure 16.4 | The National Debt

■ The U.S. net national debt (gross national debt minus intergovernmental borrowing) increased for many decades up to 1997, started to decline in 1998 as a result of annual budget surpluses, and then began to rise again in 2002 as budget deficits reappeared.

Graphs In Motion
See StudentWorks™ Plus or go to glencoe.com.

Economic Analysis

Using Graphs *By how much did the gross national debt exceed the net national debt in 2006?*

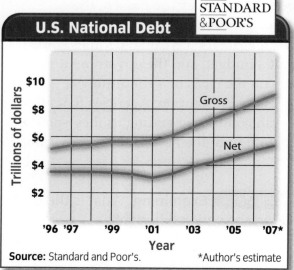

U.S. National Debt

STANDARD &POOR'S

Trillions of dollars

Gross

Net

'96 '97 '99 '01 '03 '05 '07*

Year

Source: Standard and Poor's.   *Author's estimate

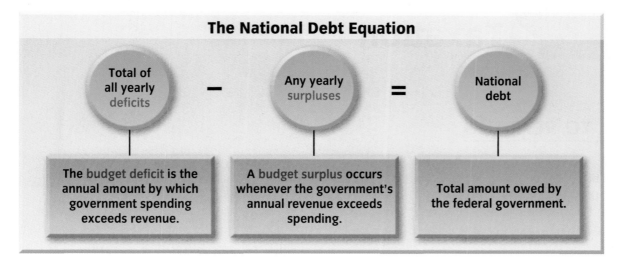

The National Debt Equation

| Total of all yearly **deficits** | — | Any yearly **surpluses** | = | National debt |

The budget deficit is the annual amount by which government spending exceeds revenue.

A budget surplus occurs whenever the government's annual revenue exceeds spending.

Total amount owed by the federal government.

In 1998, the government began to run a **budget surplus**— that is, government revenues exceeded expenditures during the fiscal year. When President George W. Bush took office in 2001, the government was projecting a 10-year budget surplus of $5.6 trillion. In less than three years, though, the government was projecting deficits totaling $4.4 trillion in the next ten years. What happened? After the terrorist attacks of September 11, 2001, the federal government began spending a great deal on terrorist-related activities. Also, Congress, with President Bush's approval, increased domestic spending at one of the fastest rates in U.S. history, while at the same time cutting taxes.

budget surplus: situation when the amount of government receipts is larger than its expenditures during the fiscal year

✔ Reading Check **Identifying** How does the federal government acquire funds to cover a deficit?

section **3** Review

Vocabulary

1. **Explain** the significance of: fiscal year, budget deficit, deficit financing, national debt, budget surplus.

Main Ideas

2. **Summarizing** Create a diagram like the one below, and describe the steps in the federal budget-making process.

☐ → ☐ → ☐

Critical Thinking

3. The **BIG Idea** What factors caused the large budget surplus in 2001 to turn into a large deficit by 2006?

4. **Determining Cause and Effect** How is the national debt affected by deficit financing?

Applying Economics

5. **The President and the Budget** The deficit can be reduced by cutting programs and/or increasing taxes. Make a list of cuts you would recommend and/or taxes you would recommend raising if you were president. Use graphics from this section or other sources to support your argument.

GUIDE TO READING

Section Preview
In this section, you will learn about the major principles and forms of taxation in the United States.

Content Vocabulary
- benefits-received principle *(p. 431)*
- ability-to-pay principle *(p. 431)*
- proportional tax *(p. 433)*
- progressive tax *(p. 433)*
- regressive tax *(p. 433)*

Academic Vocabulary
- major *(p. 430)*
- justify *(p. 431)*

Reading Strategy
Defining As you read, create a table like the one below by listing the two main principles of taxation and definitions and examples for each.

Principles of Taxation		
Principle	**Definition**	**Example**
Benefits-received principle		
Ability-to-pay principle		

ISSues In ThE NeWS
—from the *Tax Foundation Special Report*

PAID IN FULL What is Tax Freedom Day?

Tax Freedom Day is the day when Americans will finally have earned enough money to pay off their total tax bill for the year. Every dollar that's officially called income by the government is counted, and every payment to the government that is officially considered a tax is counted. Taxes at all levels of government are included, whether levied by Uncle Sam or state and local governments.

▲ Paying taxes

Tax Freedom Day gives Americans an easy way to gauge the overall tax take. . . . In effect, Tax Freedom Day provides taxpayers with a tax barometer that measures the total tax burden over time and by state.

The United States has traditionally been a low-tax country. From the founding of the republic until the early part of this century, total government spending at the federal, state, and local levels rarely exceeded 10 percent of national income, except during wartime.

You, the American taxpayer, are the source of most of the funds the government spends. Almost all federal, state, and local government revenue comes from taxes paid by individuals, small businesses, and corporations. In this section, you'll learn about the taxation process and the **major** kinds of taxes paid in this country.

Principles of Taxation

Main Idea Taxes are usually justified according to either one's ability to pay or the benefits received.

Economics & You Should you have to pay taxes for the upkeep of a public park or museum, even if you never visit these places? Why or why not? Read on to learn about the different principles of taxation.

The various levels of government use several different major taxes to raise revenue. Taxes are usually **justified** according to one of two major principles. Under the **benefits-received principle,** those who use a particular government service should support it with taxes in proportion to the benefit they receive. Those who do not use a service do not pay taxes for it. A gasoline tax to pay for highway construction and repair is based on the benefits-received principle. Frequent users of the highways often buy more gasoline and, therefore, pay more in gasoline taxes.

A tax based on the benefits-received principle is useful in raising funds to pay for a service only certain individuals use. Many government services—national defense, for example—benefit everyone equally, however. Also, those who most require services, such as the aged and poor, are the individuals least able to pay taxes.

Under the **ability-to-pay principle,** those with higher incomes pay more taxes than those with lower incomes, regardless of the number of government services they use. For example, in most cities all property owners, even those without school-aged children, must pay property taxes to support the local school system. Property taxes are calculated as a percentage of the value of a person's home. Thus, wealthier people with more expensive homes pay more property taxes.

benefits-received principle: system of taxation in which those who use a particular government service support it with taxes in proportion to the benefit they receive; those who do not use a service do not pay taxes for it

ability-to-pay principle: principle of taxation in which those with higher incomes pay more taxes than those with lower incomes, regardless of the number of government services they use

Reading Check **Analyzing** Why is national defense paid for according to the ability-to-pay principle?

Where Your Taxes Go

Ultimately, it is the American taxpayer who pays for military items such as ships, tanks, and submarines, as well as other government expenditures.

Forms of Taxation

Main Idea Taxes are classified as regressive, progressive, or proportional, depending on whether the tax as a percentage of income declines, increases, or remains the same as income increases.

Economics & You How much of your paycheck is taken out in taxes? Read on to learn how the government decides what proportion of a person's income should be spent on taxes.

Actual taxes are classified according to how they are set up and the effect they have on those who are taxed. In the United States today, these classifications include proportional, progressive, and regressive taxes.

Economics ONLINE

Student Web Activity
Visit the *Economics Today and Tomorrow* Web site at glencoe.com and click on *Chapter 16—Student Web Activities* to learn how the federal government spends your tax dollars.

Major Taxes

Tax	Description	Type
Personal income	Tax is a percentage of income and a major source of federal revenue; many state governments also levy	Progressive at the federal level, but sometimes proportional at the state level
Social insurance	Taxes covered by the Federal Insurance Contributions Act (FICA); the second-largest source of federal revenue	Proportional up to income of $94,200 in 2006, regressive above that
Corporate income	Federal tax as a percentage of corporate profits; some states also levy	Progressive up to $18.3 million at the federal level, proportional above that
Excise	Tax paid by the consumer on the manufacture, use, and consumption of certain goods	Regressive if people with higher incomes spend a lower proportion of income on taxed items
Estate	Federal tax on the property of someone who has died; some states also levy	Progressive; rate increases with the value of the estate
Inheritance	State tax paid by those who inherit property	Varies by state
Gift	Federal tax paid by the person who gives a large gift	Progressive; rate increases with the value of the gift
Sales	Tax paid on purchases; almost all states as well as many local governments levy; rate varies from state to state and within states; items taxed also vary	Regressive if people with higher incomes spend a lower proportion of income on taxed items
Property	State and local taxation of the value of both real and personal property	Proportional; rate is set by state and local governments
Customs duties	Tax on imports; paid by the importer	Proportional

Proportional Tax

Proportional Tax A **proportional tax** is the easiest type of tax to understand. The taxes you owe are simply a proportion of the money income you have earned. If there is a tax of 10 percent on all income and you earn $1,000, then you pay $100 in taxes. If you earn $10,000, you pay $1,000 in taxes, and so on.

proportional tax: tax that takes the same percentage of all incomes; as income rises, the amount of tax paid also rises

Progressive Tax With a **progressive tax,** when an individual earns a higher income, his or her taxes increase more than in proportion to the increase in money income. A good example of a progressive tax is our federal individual income tax system. As you make more reported income, you pay an increasingly higher percentage of that additional income in taxes to the federal government. A progressive income tax has often been justified on the basis of the ability-to-pay principle.

progressive tax: tax that takes a larger percentage of higher incomes than of lower incomes; justified on the basis of the ability-to-pay principle

Regressive Tax A **regressive tax** is the opposite of a progressive tax. The percentage that you pay in taxes actually goes down as you make more money income. Some economists believe that a good example of a regressive tax is the sales tax on food, because poorer families spend a larger proportion of their income on food than wealthier families do.

regressive tax: tax that takes a larger percentage of lower incomes than of higher incomes

Reading Check **Explaining** The federal individual income tax system is an example of what type of tax? Explain.

Skills Handbook

See page R45 to learn about Synthesizing Information.

section 4 Review

Vocabulary

1. **Explain** the significance of: benefits-received principal, ability-to-pay principle, proportional tax, progressive tax, regressive tax.

Main Ideas

2. **Describing** Copy the chart below, and for each form of taxation listed, provide a definition of how the tax works.

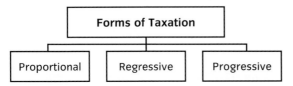

Critical Thinking

3. **The BIG Idea** Which of the three forms of taxation would likely bring in the most funds for the government, and why?

4. **Synthesizing** Create an argument a wealthy person might make against the progressive income tax.

Applying Economics

5. **Taxes and You** Look back at the chart you filled out listing the kinds of taxes people pay. Of these, which ones do you pay now? Which ones does your family pay now? List an example of each from your own experience.

THE **DEFICIT:**

A DANGER OR A BLESSING?

John Steele Gordon ▶

Good arguments can be made either way.

Check It Out! In this chapter you learned about budget deficits. In this article, the federal deficit and debt are looked at from both a positive and negative angle.

The federal government's fiscal stance is muddled. What's disturbing is how the ledger made a swing from a record surplus in 2000 to a record deficit now. How worried should Americans be about the red ink?

Some observers believe the administration's fiscal recklessness will end in catastrophe. Princeton University professor Paul Krugman is a harsh critic. Krugman argues that the gap between what America spends and what it takes in is so large that the nation will eventually careen into a major financial crisis.

Others aren't convinced. Take the perspective of historian John Steele Gordon.

As a general rule, Gordon dislikes deficits. Yet he notes that the current deficit is "a blessing because a national debt properly funded is a powerful tool that allows us to guard America's security, whether economic or military," Gordon says.

Whether you believe the deficit reflects irresponsible fiscal management or a rational response to crisis, one thing is clear: Better numbers are needed.

One suggestion Gordon puts forward is for the federal government to create an independent body. This watchdog's job would be to keep the books honest as well as easily understandable to the average citizen. At the same time, it might be a good idea to dust off an old idea: In the 1800s, governments could issue debt only to finance capital items like roads. As for everything else, the ordinary budget had to be paid when the bill came due.

—Adapted from *BusinessWeek*

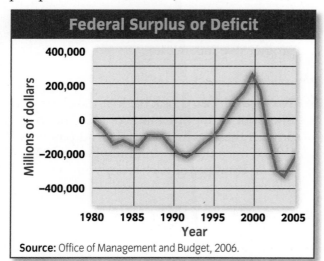

Federal Surplus or Deficit

Millions of dollars

400,000
200,000
0
−200,000
−400,000

1980 1985 1990 1995 2000 2005
Year

Source: Office of Management and Budget, 2006.

Think About It

1. **Summarizing** What are the arguments for and against a large federal deficit?

2. **Synthesizing** What suggestions are given in the article to help balance the budget?

chapter **16** **Visual Summary**

STUDY TO GO

Study anywhere, anytime! Download quizzes and flash cards to your PDA from glencoe.com.

■ **Government spending** at all levels—federal, state, and local—has increased significantly over the years.

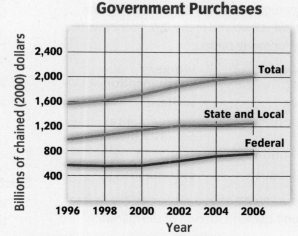

Government Purchases

Billions of chained (2000) dollars

Total

State and Local

Federal

Year: 1996 1998 2000 2002 2004 2006

Source: *The Economic Report of the President, 2006.*

■ Under the American free-enterprise system, the **government regulates** certain aspects of the economy.

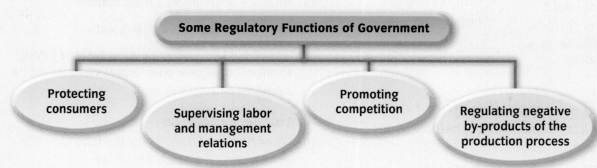

Some Regulatory Functions of Government

- Protecting consumers
- Supervising labor and management relations
- Promoting competition
- Regulating negative by-products of the production process

■ The goal of the government's **budget-making process** is to balance what the government takes in with what it spends.

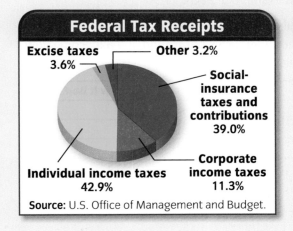

Federal Tax Receipts

Excise taxes 3.6%

Other 3.2%

Social-insurance taxes and contributions 39.0%

Corporate income taxes 11.3%

Individual income taxes 42.9%

Source: U.S. Office of Management and Budget.

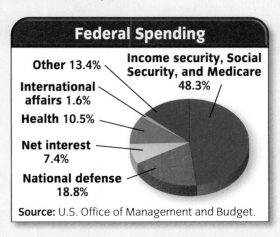

Federal Spending

Other 13.4%

Income security, Social Security, and Medicare 48.3%

International affairs 1.6%

Health 10.5%

Net interest 7.4%

National defense 18.8%

Source: U.S. Office of Management and Budget.

Review Content Vocabulary

1. *Write a paragraph or two explaining how the government is involved in the U.S. economy. Use all of the following terms.*

public-works projects	workers' compensation
Medicare	welfare
public goods	Supplemental Security Income
income redistribution	Medicaid
Social Security	externalities

2. *Write a paragraph or two explaining the federal budget and taxation. Use all of the following terms.*

fiscal year	ability-to-pay principle
budget deficit	proportional tax
deficit financing	progressive tax
national debt	regressive tax
budget surplus	
benefits-received principle	

Review Academic Vocabulary

Choose the letter of the term that best completes each sentence.

a. core	e. submit
b. exceed	f. allocate
c. maintain	g. major
d. intervene	h. justify

3. A national budget will _____ spending by dividing funds among government agencies.

4. Each agency must _____ its budget requests to the OMB months in advance.

5. Emergency spending often causes the government to _____ its budget.

6. A natural disaster is an example of something that would _____ emergency spending.

7. Decision making by private citizens is at the _____ of wealth creation.

8. Agencies must _____ records of their spending to help determine the next year's budget.

9. Changing the tax system would be a _____ undertaking for the federal government.

10. The government can _____ in economic activity in a variety of ways.

Review the Main Ideas

Section 1 (pp. 413–417)

11. In what ways has the government grown since the Great Depression?

12. What percentage of GDP is accounted for by total government purchases?

Section 2 (pp. 418–423)

13. What are government's main functions?

14. Give five examples of public goods.

15. What would be a negative externality of having an airport built near your home? What would be a positive externality?

Section 3 (pp. 425–429)

16. About how long does it take the federal government to prepare a budget?

17. What causes the nation's public debt?

Section 4 (pp. 430–433)

18. Identify the two principles of taxation and give an example of each.

19. Fill in a table like the one below by identifying the three forms of taxation and explaining how each works.

Form of Taxation	How It Works

Math Practice

20. The U.S. federal income tax is a progressive tax. This means that the more a person makes, the higher percentage of that income he or she pays in taxes. Look at the tax rate schedule below and answer the questions that follow.

2006 Tax Rate for Single Filers

Taxable income is over	But not over	The tax is	Plus	Of the amount over
$0	$7,550	$0.00	10%	$0
$7,550	$30,650	$755.00	15%	$7,550
$30,650	$74,200	$4,220.00	25%	$30,650
$74,200	$154,800	$15,107.00	28%	$74,200
$154,800	$336,550	$37,675.50	33%	$154,800
$336,550	no limit	$97,653.50	35%	$336,550

a. What is the range of tax rates that a single person might pay?

b. If Kim made $30,000 in 2006, how much did she pay in taxes?

Economics ONLINE

Self-Check Quiz Visit the *Economics Today and Tomorrow* Web site at glencoe.com and click on *Chapter 16—Self-Check Quizzes* to assess your knowledge of chapter content.

c. If Kim got a raise to $45,000 per year in 2007 and tax rates stayed the same, how much did she pay in taxes?

d. If Joe made $1 million in 2006, how much did he pay in taxes?

Critical Thinking

21. **The BIG Idea** In general, are you in favor of more or less government involvement in the economy? Explain your position.

22. **Explaining** IRS records show that in 2003, 96.5% of total federal income taxes were paid by the top 50% of earners. The bottom 50%, therefore, paid just 3.5% of all income taxes. Based on your understanding of the progressive tax system and the information in the tax schedule on this page, explain how half of the taxpayers can pay almost all of the total taxes.

Analyzing Visuals

23. Study the cartoon on the right, and then answer the following questions.

    a. What do the doors represent?

    b. What is humorous about the three doors?

    c. What point is the cartoonist making about government bureaucracy?

Should "junk food" be taxed?

For the first time in history, almost two-thirds of Americans are overweight or obese, including one in every five children. Healthful food costs more than junk food, and obesity rates are higher among poor people—50 percent higher for poor teens. Increases in the percentage of Americans living in poverty coupled with higher rates of obesity have caused the World Health Organization and others to propose taxing high-calorie, low-nutrition foods to discourage people from eating them. Is a "Twinkie tax" a good idea?

YES! The obesity epidemic is a national problem.

We live in a toxic food environment where high-calorie and high-fat foods are available at low cost. . . . The American food system is set up as if maximizing obesity were the aim. . . . you use the income from such a tax to subsidize the sale of healthy foods in order to reverse what is the unfortunate reality now: that it costs more to eat a healthier diet. The tax . . . would be a proactive response to a food industry and consumer culture that increasingly promotes high-fat/low-nutrition products as the cheapest, tastiest, most convenient and most available dietary options.

. . . The prevailing approach for dealing with obesity, which is to blame people who have the problem and hope the situation will disappear, is a fantasy. Something dramatic needs to be done to change the environment in order to prevent this problem from occurring in the first place. A 1-cent federal tax on each can or bottle of soda . . . could be used for a massive advertising and education program, especially aimed at children. . . . Once you are obese, it is very hard to treat, so prevention makes sense.

—Kelly Brownell, Ph.D., director, Yale Center for Eating and Weight Disorders and author, *Food Fight*

NO! It's the individual's problem, not the government's.

This proposal has a premise that there are somehow some good foods and bad foods, and if we could only tax the bad foods, then we wouldn't have an obesity problem. It doesn't work that way. We face an obesity problem in the United States because we consume too many calories for our needs and we don't exercise enough. It comes down to that. And, you know, there is room in life for potato chips and Twinkies and all these other maligned foods if you don't eat huge amounts of them. There is no good or bad food, there are only good and bad diets. And I know that's more complex than putting a tax on food. . . . It's just another way of trying to get revenue out of us. Obesity is a crisis in public health in America, but we need to have science-based attempts to solve it, not—not schemes of this sort of taxation.

—Elizabeth Whelan, M.D., president, American Council on Science and Health

Debating the Issue

1. **Explaining** Why is the idea of a "Twinkie tax" popular now?

2. **Choosing Sides** The two writers disagree on whether a tax on junk food is the best way to solve the increasing problem of obesity. With whom do you agree? Why?

Find Out More!

3. **Analyzing** Using the Internet or other resources, find out why junk food costs less than healthful foods.

Obesity Trends for U.S. Teenagers (Ages 12-19)

Y-axis: Percentage Obese (0, 5, 10, 15, 20)
X-axis: Year (1980, 1994, 2000, 2004)

Source: National Center for Health Statistics (NCHS).

The **BIG Idea**

Governments strive for a balance between the costs and benefits of their economic policies to promote economic stability and growth.

Why It Matters

In this chapter, read to learn about the factors that destabilize the economy and the actions that can be taken in response.

Economics ONLINE

Chapter Overview Visit the *Economics Today and Tomorrow* Web site at <u>glencoe.com</u> and click on *Chapter 17—Chapter Overviews* to preview chapter information.

Unemployment and Inflation

GUIDE TO READING

Section Preview
In this section, you will learn why unemployment and inflation are two major threats to a nation's economic stability.

Content Vocabulary
- stabilization policies *(p. 442)*
- unemployment rate *(p. 442)*
- full employment *(p. 443)*
- underground economy *(p. 443)*
- demand-pull inflation *(p. 444)*
- stagflation *(p. 445)*
- cost-push inflation *(p. 445)*

Academic Vocabulary
- expert *(p. 442)*
- survey *(p. 443)*
- adapt *(p. 444)*

Reading Strategy
Determining Cause and Effect As you read the section, complete a diagram like the one below by listing the main causes of demand-pull and cost-push inflation.

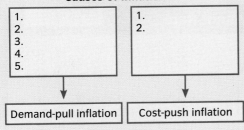

Causes of Inflation

1.	1.
2.	2.
3.	
4.	
5.	

| Demand-pull inflation | Cost-push inflation |

ISSUES IN THE NEWS

THE RETURN OF STAGFLATION? In the 1970s, soaring prices of oil and other commodities led to stagflation—a combination of high inflation and high unemployment, which left no good policy options. If the Fed cut interest rates to create jobs, it risked causing an inflationary spiral; if it raised interest rates to bring inflation down, it would further increase unemployment.

▲ Gas line in the 1970s

. . . [In April 2005,] fears of a return to stagflation sent stock prices to a five-month low. What few seem to have noticed, however, is that a mild form of stagflation has already arrived.

. . . [I]nflation is leading the Fed to tap on the brakes, even though this doesn't look or feel like a full-employment economy.

We shouldn't overstate the case: we're not back to the economic misery of the 1970s. But the fact that we're already experiencing mild stagflation means that there will be no good options if something else goes wrong.

—from the *New York Times*

When people are unemployed, they experience uncertainty. In the same way, unemployment in general causes uncertainty in the American economy. As you read this section, you'll learn that two of the biggest threats to a nation's economic stability are high unemployment and another issue—inflation.

Personal Finance Handbook

See pages R20–R23 to learn about getting a job.

stabilization policies: attempts by the federal government to keep the economy healthy; includes monetary and fiscal policies

unemployment rate: percentage of the civilian labor force that is unemployed but is actively looking for work

Measuring Unemployment

Main Idea Unemployment can be classified as cyclical, structural, seasonal, or frictional.

Economics & You Have you ever known someone who was out of work? Read on to learn about why unemployment is such a serious problem for workers and the national economy.

To keep the economy healthy and to make the future more predictable for planning, saving, and investing, the federal government uses monetary and fiscal policies. Together these are called **stabilization policies.**

Expert economists advise the president and Congress, but they often disagree about the causes and cures of the economic problems that the nation periodically faces. One statistic they all look at is the **unemployment rate**—the percentage of the civilian labor force that is without jobs but is actively looking for work. (See **Figure 17.1** below.) Note that not everyone is in the labor force. Students, retired people, and people in long-term hospital stays, for example, are not counted as part of the labor force.

High unemployment is usually a sign that all is not well with the economy. Moreover, the waste of human resources that unemployment causes is an extremely serious problem. As a result, maintaining a low unemployment rate is one of the major goals in stabilizing the economy.

Figure 17.1 Measuring Unemployment

■ Remember that the unemployment rate measures only the percentage of the labor force that is actively looking for work. Some people are unemployed voluntarily, and they are not included in this measurement.

Graphs In Motion
See StudentWorks™ Plus or go to glencoe.com.

Economic Analysis

Analyzing Graphs *During which year shown did unemployment peak?*

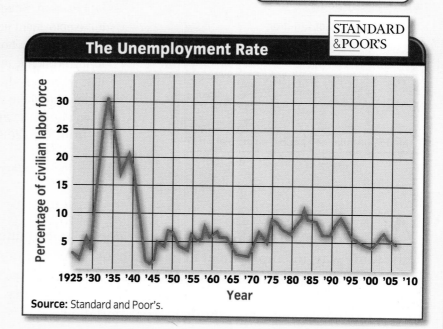

The Unemployment Rate

STANDARD &POOR'S

Source: Standard and Poor's.

Figure 17.2 **Reasons for Unemployment**

■ Unemployment can be caused by a variety of reasons. A certain amount of unemployment is natural in any economy, but too much of it can be a threat to economic stability.

Types of Unemployment

Type	Description	Characteristics
Cyclical	Unemployment associated with up or down fluctuations in the business cycle	Rises during recessions and depressions; falls during recoveries and booms
Structural	Unemployment caused by changes in the economy, such as technological advances or discoveries of natural resources	Can result when workers are replaced by computers or other machines or when cheaper natural resources are found elsewhere; often affects less-skilled workers
Seasonal	Unemployment caused by changes in the seasons or the weather	Affects construction workers, particularly in the Northeast and Midwest; also affects farmworkers needed only during certain months of the growing season
Frictional	Temporary unemployment between jobs because of firings, layoffs, voluntary searches for new jobs, or retraining	Always exists to some degree because of the time needed between jobs to find new work and the imperfect match between openings and applicants

Economic Analysis

Synthesizing *Which type of unemployment is most likely to affect highly skilled and experienced workers? Why?*

Many types of unemployment exist, as shown in **Figure 17.2** above. Some people work in seasonal jobs or jobs that are sensitive to technological advances or to changes in the marketplace. As a result, not all unemployment can or should be eliminated. Moreover, economists disagree over what the level of full employment should be. Economists today generally have come to consider the economy at **full employment** when the unemployment rate is around 5 percent.

It is important to remember that the unemployment rate is only an estimate. The unemployment rate does not include people who have stopped looking for work, nor does it include people who work in family businesses without receiving pay.

Unemployment is difficult to measure accurately because government statisticians cannot possibly interview every person in and out of the labor force. **Survey** results are also imperfect because of the existence of the **underground economy.** The underground economy consists of people who do not follow federal and state laws with respect to reporting earnings. Examples might include tax evaders, gamblers, and drug traffickers.

full employment: condition of the economy when the unemployment rate is lower than a certain percentage established by economists' studies

underground economy: transactions by people who do not follow federal and state laws with respect to reporting earnings

Reading Check **Analyzing** Why is it important to maintain a low unemployment rate?

Inflation

Main Idea Inflation is caused by excessive expansion of the money supply or government spending, according to the demand-pull theory.

Economics & You If you have a job, have you ever received a raise? Read on to learn why raises are important if workers are to maintain their standard of living in the face of rising prices.

A second major problem that may face any nation is inflation. The economy can usually **adapt** to gradually rising prices. If prices rise about 2 percent every year, for example, everyone comes to expect and understand that. Unpredictable inflation, however, has a destabilizing effect on the economy.

Inflation may affect consumers' standard of living. Suppose you receive a 5 percent pay raise in a year in which inflation was 8 percent. Your real (adjusted for inflation) income has decreased. Inflation is normally a serious problem only for people who live on *fixed incomes,* such as those who are retired.

Not all economists agree on a single explanation of why inflation occurs. Two competing ideas have developed: the demand-pull theory (prices are *pulled* up by high aggregate demand) and the cost-push theory (prices are *pushed* up by high production costs and wages).

demand-pull inflation: theory that prices rise as the result of excessive business and consumer demand; demand increases faster than total supply, resulting in shortages that lead to higher prices

Demand-Pull According to the theory of **demand-pull inflation,** prices rise as the result of excessive business and consumer demand. If economy-wide, or aggregate, demand increases faster than aggregate supply, the resulting shortage will lead to the bidding up of prices.

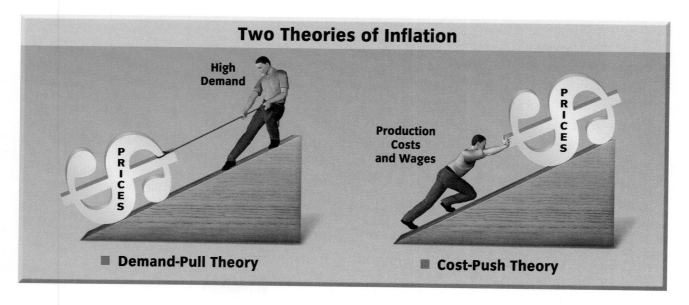

Two Theories of Inflation

High Demand

PRICES

■ **Demand-Pull Theory**

Production Costs and Wages

PRICES

■ **Cost-Push Theory**

Demand-pull inflation can occur for several reasons. If the Fed causes the money supply to grow too rapidly, individuals will spend the additional dollars on a limited supply of goods and services. Higher demand will cause prices to rise. Increases in government spending and in business investment can also increase overall demand. Aggregate demand can also increase if taxes are reduced or consumers begin saving less.

Cost-Push The demand-pull theory assumes that increased demand will increase output and reduce unemployment, but experience has shown that rising prices and unemployment can occur at the same time. This combination of inflation and stagnation (low economic activity) is sometimes called **stagflation.**

According to some economists, stagflation is a result of cost-push inflation at work in the economy. The theory of **cost-push inflation** states that the wage demands of labor unions push up prices. When businesses have to pay higher wages, their costs increase. To maintain their profit levels, businesses must raise the prices of the goods and services they produce.

During periods of cost-push inflation, unemployment can remain high. Prices are being adjusted for higher wages and profits—not because of increased aggregate demand. Without additional aggregate demand, producers have no reason to increase output by hiring new workers.

stagflation: combination of inflation and stagnation (low economic activity)

cost-push inflation: theory that higher wages push up prices

> **Reading Check** **Predicting Consequences** What group of people does inflation affect the most? Why?

section 1 Review

Vocabulary
1. **Explain** the significance of: stabilization policies, unemployment rate, full employment, underground economy, demand-pull inflation, stagflation, cost-push inflation.

Main Ideas
2. **Identifying** In a diagram like the one below, define each type of unemployment listed.

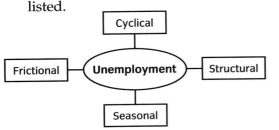

Critical Thinking
3. The **BIG Idea** When government tightens the money supply to slow inflation, what might happen to the unemployment rate? Why?
4. **Determining Cause and Effect** What is the relationship between fixed income and inflation?

Applying Economics
5. **Inflation** Create a chart with headings labeled *Weather, The Fed, Oil Shortage,* and *War.* Under each heading, list ways that this factor could lead to inflation.

WEB WORLD

There are dollar signs in the sky.

Check It Out! In this chapter you learned about the four kinds of unemployment. In this article, read to learn about a growing industry that may help to keep many people employed, and handsomely.

Mammas, let your babies grow up to get Web ad gigs. With the online ad business up 30% to $12.5 billion [in 2006], a labor crunch is raising salaries and recruitment efforts. . . . Pay for some jobs—such as creating ads or measuring their impact—has risen as much as 20% from 2005. And openings abound: Boston's Digitas, an online ad shop with a staff of 1,500, advertised to fill nearly 100 positions in April alone. T3, an Austin interactive-ad agency, is also struggling to fill openings. "I've kind of gulped at a few salaries, but I'm willing to pay," says President Gay Gaddis, who adds that not long ago, a freelancer turned down a creative director job at T3 paying $150,000 to $200,000 a year.

▲ Web advertising is big business.

One reason for the shortage is that making Web ads requires high-level tech know-how. Rich-media ads involving flash animation or video, for instance, call for math, programming, and design skills. Gaddis says she stopped by a cubicle recently where two employees were using calculus to program video game ads. "It's hard to do both—left-brain and right-brain," she notes.

. . . Beyond paying high salaries, agencies are responding by moving some jobs to where the talent is, by dropping some smaller clients, and by amping up training. "If you can find the people, you can find the revenue."

—Reprinted from *BusinessWeek*

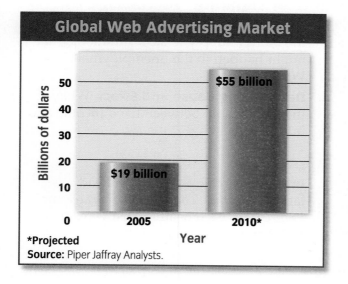

Global Web Advertising Market

Billions of dollars

- $19 billion (2005)
- $55 billion (2010*)

Year

*Projected
Source: Piper Jaffray Analysts.

Think About It

1. **Recalling** What types of skills are necessary to perform the job described in the article?
2. **Explaining** According to the article, why is there a shortage in this field?

The Fiscal Policy Approach to Stabilization

GUIDE TO READING

Section Preview
In this section, you will learn how government taxation and spending can be used to stimulate or slow the growth of the national economy.

Content Vocabulary
- fiscal policy *(p. 448)*
- circular flow of income and output *(p. 448)*

Academic Vocabulary
- remove *(p. 449)*
- offset *(p. 449)*

Reading Strategy
Explaining As you read, use a diagram like the one below to show how money moves around outside the circular flow of income.

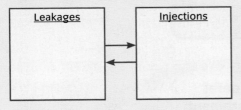

Leakages		Injections

ISSues In ThE NeWS
—from the *Washington Post*

GETTING PAST BUDGET BICKERING Our annual budget debates . . . have increasingly become exercises in political theater. They certainly aren't intended to bridge the gap between Americans' huge appetite for government services and their fierce distaste for taxes. Someone has to choose— higher taxes, lower spending, or some combination. But American politicians are loath to choose. . . .

▲ Discussing the budget

In the long run, tax levels reflect spending levels. There are practical and economic limits on budget deficits. Because [the president] has increased government spending, taxes will ultimately have to rise to cover the higher outlays. . . .

The political virtue of a balanced budget is that it compels choices. But choices are precisely what [the president] and congressional Republicans and Democrats dislike. . . .

Most economists belong to one of two groups on the question of stabilization. One group emphasizes the role of the Federal Reserve in stabilizing the economy, which you learned about in Chapter 15. In this section, you'll learn about the other group and what they believe concerning the issue of economic stabilization.

The Circular Flow of Income and Output

Careers Handbook

See pages R76–R80 to learn about becoming an economist.

fiscal policy: federal government's use of taxation and spending policies to affect overall business activity

circular flow of income and output: economic model that pictures income as flowing continuously between businesses and consumers

Main Idea Keynesian economists advocate the use of government spending to stimulate economic activity and reduce unemployment during recessions.

Economics & You When you spend your wages on a new outfit, computer game, or other purchase, you are putting your funds back into the economy. Read on to learn about this "circular flow" of income.

The term **fiscal policy** refers to the federal government's deliberate use of its taxation rates and expenditures to affect overall business activity. John Maynard Keynes developed fiscal policy theories during the Great Depression. Keynes believed that the forces of aggregate supply and demand operated too slowly in a serious recession, and that government should step in to stimulate aggregate demand.

To understand Keynesian theory, you must first understand what is known as the **circular flow of income and output.** (See **Figure 17.3** below.) You learned about this model in Chapter 2. The model pictures money income as flowing from businesses to households as wages, rents, interest, and profits. Money income flows from households to businesses as payments for consumer goods and services.

Figure 17.3 | Circular Flow of Income and Output

■ Government occupies a central position in the circular flow of income and output. By using fiscal policy, the federal government partially controls the levels of leakages and injections. This, in turn, may control the overall level of economic activity.

Purchases of goods and services

Federal Government

Taxes

Taxes

Government spending (purchases of goods & services, interest)

Government spending (wages, transfer payments, interest)

Government borrowing

Businesses

Consumers

Borrowing for Investment

Saving

Banks and Other Financial Institutions

Income (wages, rents, interest, profits)

■ Leakages
■ Injections

Economic Analysis

Using Charts *What are consumers' contributions to the circular flow of income and output?*

Figure 17.4 | Leakages and Injections

■ Outside the circular flow of income and output, we have leakages and injections.

A. Leakages When people deposit their income into savings accounts, this is considered a leakage from the circular flow. Government taxation is another form of leakage.

B. Injections Government spending on activities such as maintaining national parks is one form of income injection. Business investment is another form.

Economic Analysis

Defining *What is the term for the state in which leakages and injections are in balance?*

Not all income, however, follows this circular flow. Some of it is **removed** from the economy through consumer saving and government taxation. Economists use the term *leakage* to refer to this removal of money income.

Offsetting leakages of income are injections of income into the economy. Injections occur through business investment and government spending. (See **Figure 17.4** above.) The term *investment*, in this sense, means the purchase of new plants and equipment and increases in inventories. Much of the funds for investment comes from saving—a part of the leakage from circular flow.

Ideally, leakages and injections balance each other. In this state of equilibrium, the income that households save is reinjected through business investment. Income taken out through taxes is returned through government spending.

Reading Check **Evaluating** What is the federal government's role in the circular flow of income and output?

Fiscal Policy and Supply-Side Effects

Main Idea Supply-side economists advocate reductions in tax rates to stimulate private investment and employment.

Economics & You If your taxes went down, how would you use the additional spendable income? Read on to learn about how cutting taxes on a large scale can help stimulate the economy.

Many public officials and labor leaders have suggested starting jobs programs to reduce unemployment and stimulate the economy. Cuts in federal taxes are another way in which fiscal policy has been used in an attempt to speed up economic activity and fight unemployment. Giving businesses tax credits on investments allows them to deduct from their taxes some of the costs of new capital equipment. The goal is to encourage businesses to expand production and hire more workers.

Some argue that tax cuts lead to more work, saving, and investment. These are called *supply-side effects* because they affect the supply of key ingredients of economic growth. President Bush used this supply-side argument to promote his Jobs and Growth Tax Act of 2003.

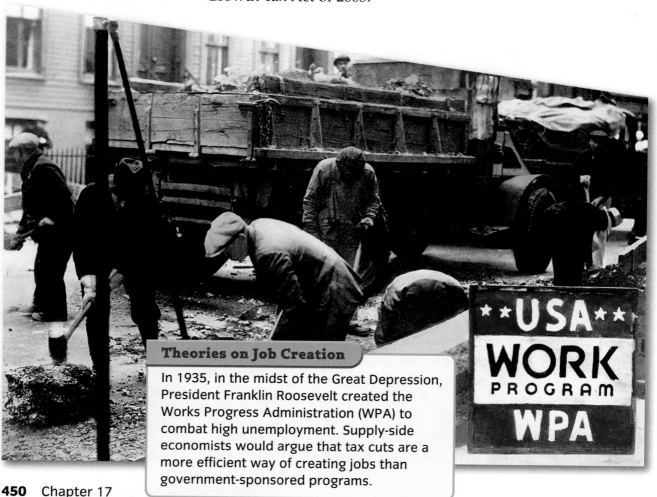

Theories on Job Creation

In 1935, in the midst of the Great Depression, President Franklin Roosevelt created the Works Progress Administration (WPA) to combat high unemployment. Supply-side economists would argue that tax cuts are a more efficient way of creating jobs than government-sponsored programs.

▲ Many people dislike paying taxes, even if they realize that some taxation is necessary.

Many features of this act were aimed at increasing economic growth. Tax rates that were to be phased in over several years instead became effective in January 2003. The highest tax rate fell from 39.6 percent to 35 percent. Investors got a big break, too. The tax rate applied to most dividends—income payments to shareholders of corporations—fell from as high as 39.9 percent to 15 percent. The tax rate on long-term capital gains (see Chapter 6) dropped from 20 percent to 15 percent. For some low-income earners, this rate fell to 5 percent.

✔ **Reading Check** **Identifying** What are two actions that the federal government can take to stimulate the economy? Which method has been used more frequently in recent years?

section **2** ▸ **Review**

Vocabulary

1. **Explain** the significance of: fiscal policy, circular flow of income and output.

Main Ideas

2. **Synthesis** In a diagram like the one below, list examples of fiscal policy leakages and injections.

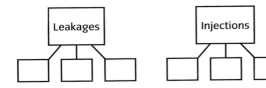

Critical Thinking

3. The **BIG Idea** Describe one positive aspect and one negative aspect of Keynesian economics.

4. **Analyzing** Briefly describe the characteristics of a stable economy.

Applying Economics

5. **Your Effect on the Economy** Make a list of the five most expensive items you or your family purchased this year. What industries would have suffered had you not bought these items?

Monetarism and the Economy

GUIDE TO READING

Section Preview

In this section, you will learn about the theory that the control of the money supply by the Federal Reserve, rather than fiscal policy, should be used to stabilize the economy.

Content Vocabulary

- monetarism *(p. 453)*
- monetarists *(p. 453)*
- monetary rule *(p. 455)*
- inflation targeting *(p. 455)*
- time lags *(p. 457)*

Academic Vocabulary

- guideline *(p. 455)*
- target *(p. 455)*

Reading Strategy

Organizing As you read, complete a web diagram similar to the one below by listing the reasons why monetarists oppose using fiscal policy to slow or stimulate the economy.

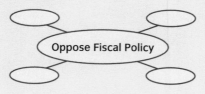

Oppose Fiscal Policy

ISSues In ThE NeWS

—from *CNNMoney.com*

THE U.S. MONEY SUPPLY How much money would you need to give everyone in the U.S. $1 million, and still have change left over?

. . . One way to do this would be to have the U.S. mint run off enough crisp new bills so that every one of the 296 million or so people in the U.S. comes away with a million bucks. But other than a monumental printing job—even if you went with $1,000 bills, you would need 296 billion of them— what would you have accomplished?

Such a jolt to the money supply would be a huge shock to the U.S. and the global economy, most likely revving up inflation and at the very least forcing a big re-adjustment in prices and currency values.

▲ **Bureau of Engraving and Printing in Ft. Worth, Texas**

Many economists do not believe that fiscal policy, which you learned about in the last section, plays a major role in stabilizing the U.S. economy. In this section, you'll learn about another theory that states that Federal Reserve monetary policy has a much greater impact on stabilization. You will also learn about the supporters of this alternative theory.

The Theory of Monetarism

Main Idea Monetarists favor monetary policy rather than fiscal policy to stabilize the economy.

Economics & You If your money income suddenly rose dramatically, chances are you would put it back into the economy by making purchases. Read on to learn about this theory on a larger scale: that putting more money into circulation may help to stimulate the economy.

Monetarism is the theory that deals with the relationship between the amount of money the Federal Reserve places in circulation and the level of activity in the national economy. The supporters of this theory are called **monetarists.**

Monetarism is often linked with economist Milton Friedman (see page 458). As you remember from Chapter 15, the Federal Reserve can change the growth rate of the money supply. Friedman and many other economists believe that the Fed should increase the money supply at a smooth, given percent each year. They argue that when the amount of money in circulation expands too rapidly, people borrow more and spend more. If the economy is operating below capacity, this extra demand will lead to a rise in output. To produce more, businesses will have to hire more workers, and unemployment will decrease. If there is already full employment, however, the increased aggregate demand will lead to a rise in prices—inflation.

monetarism: theory that deals with the relationship between the amount of money the Fed places in circulation and the level of activity in the economy

monetarists: supporters of the theory of monetarism, often associated with Milton Friedman

Reading Check **Determining Cause and Effect** According to monetarist theory, what will happen to a stable economy if too much money is put into circulation too quickly?

Too Much of a Good Thing

A major argument of monetarists is that when the money supply expands rapidly, people will spend more, especially on big-ticket items like cars. This situation could potentially lead to inflation.

Government Policy According to Monetarists

Main Idea Monetarists believe that the money supply should be increased at a steady rate of 3 to 5 percent per year for stable economic growth with low inflation.

Economics & You Should the federal government intervene to stabilize the economy in times of trouble, or is the economy better left on its own? Read on to learn about monetarists' criticism of government fiscal policies.

Friedman and his monetarist followers believe the economy is so complex and so poorly understood that government does more harm than good in trying to second-guess businesspeople and consumers. As a result, monetarists generally oppose using fiscal policy to stimulate or slow the economy.

Figure 17.5 | Changing Fed Policies

■ To monetarists, the reduction in the amount of money in circulation can mean only one thing—a reduction in aggregate demand. With less aggregate demand, fewer workers are needed and unemployment increases in the short run.

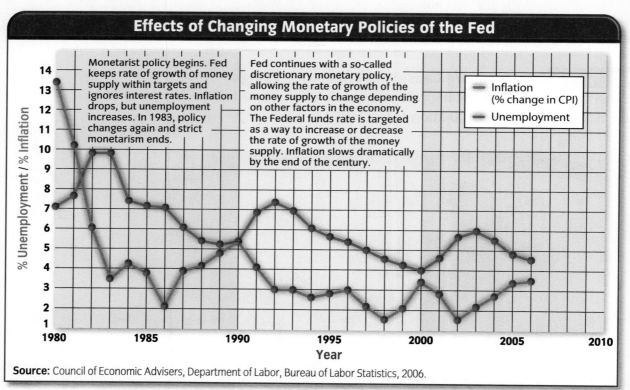

Effects of Changing Monetary Policies of the Fed

Monetarist policy begins. Fed keeps rate of growth of money supply within targets and ignores interest rates. Inflation drops, but unemployment increases. In 1983, policy changes again and strict monetarism ends.

Fed continues with a so-called discretionary monetary policy, allowing the rate of growth of the money supply to change depending on other factors in the economy. The Federal funds rate is targeted as a way to increase or decrease the rate of growth of the money supply. Inflation slows dramatically by the end of the century.

— Inflation (% change in CPI)
— Unemployment

% Unemployment / % Inflation

Source: Council of Economic Advisers, Department of Labor, Bureau of Labor Statistics, 2006.

Economic Analysis

Determining Cause and Effect *What happened to the unemployment rate when Fed policies began to lower inflation from 1980 to 1982?*

For example, they do not believe the government should operate with budget deficits each year in an attempt to stimulate the economy. Instead, monetarists believe that the government should balance the federal budget. This action would keep government from competing with private business in borrowing funds in the credit market.

Monetary Rule The Fed, according to monetarists, should also stop trying to smooth the ups and downs in the economy. Rather, the Fed should follow a **monetary rule,** or allow the money supply to grow smoothly and consistently at a rate of perhaps 3 to 5 percent per year. Monetarists believe that a steady growth in the money supply within strict **guidelines** (or **targets,** as they are called) is the best way to provide businesses and consumers with more certainty about the future. According to monetarism, this policy would result in a controlled expansion of the economy without rapid inflation or high unemployment.

The current chair of the Federal Reserve System, Ben S. Bernanke, has at times favored something similar to a monetary rule. He has said that the United States should target an inflation rate, such as 2 percent per year, and then steer inflation toward the target rate through the use of interest rate changes and other monetary tools. Some countries, such as the United Kingdom and New Zealand, already use **inflation targeting.**

Monetarist Theory and the Federal Reserve

Monetarist theory had a major influence on Fed policies in the 1980s. You can trace the effects of the changing monetary policies of the Fed in **Figure 17.5** on the previous page.

monetary rule: monetarists' belief that the Fed should allow the money supply to grow at a smooth, consistent rate per year and not use monetary policy to stimulate or slow the economy

inflation targeting: a possible central bank policy in which the head of the central bank is given a specified annual rate of inflation as a goal

Monetarists' Criticism of Fiscal Policy

Skills Handbook

See page **R48** to learn about **Problems and Solutions**.

Main Idea Monetarists believe that the main problem with fiscal policy is that it cannot be implemented effectively.

Economics & You Have you ever had an idea that sounded good at first but didn't work out in the long run? Read on to learn about what monetarists think the fundamental problems with fiscal policy are.

Monetarists believe that the theory of fiscal policy seldom matches the reality. Two main reasons account for this discrepancy.

The first reason concerns the political process involved in implementing fiscal policy. Monetarists point out that no single government body designs and implements fiscal policy. (See **Figure 17.6** below.) The president, with the aid of the director of the Office of Management and Budget (OMB), the secretary of the Treasury, and the Council of Economic Advisers, designs the desired mix of taxes and government expenditures, but then only recommends the policy to Congress. The president is not responsible for implementing the policy, nor does he determine exactly when the policy will be enacted.

Figure 17.6 | Implementing Fiscal Policy

■ As you can see from the chart, fiscal policy travels through many channels before reaching Congress and possibly being enacted. The complexity of the process is one of the main reasons monetarists criticize fiscal policy.

Implementing Fiscal Policy

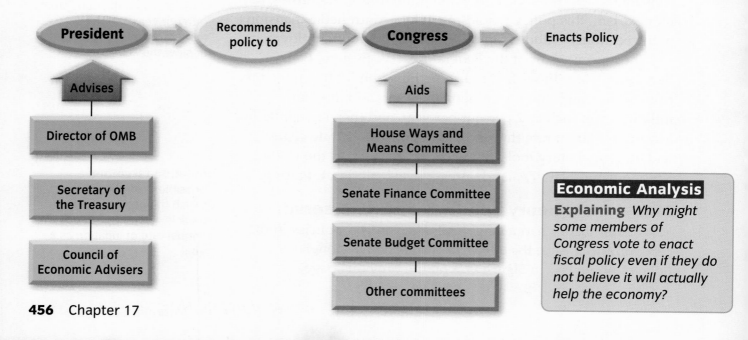

Economic Analysis

Explaining Why might some members of Congress vote to enact fiscal policy even if they do not believe it will actually help the economy?

Congress, with the aid of many committees (the House Ways and Means Committee, the Senate Finance Committee, and the Senate Budget Committee, to name a few), actually enacts fiscal policy. One built-in organizational problem is that the power to enact fiscal policy does not rest with a single government institution. Disagreement as to the proper fiscal policy emerges among members of Congress and between Congress and the president. Furthermore, being politicians, they have incentives to take actions that will look good today and help them get reelected, but which may hurt the economy in the long run.

Monetarists also point out that even if fiscal policy could be enacted when the president wanted, there are various **time lags** between when it is enacted and when it becomes effective. It takes many months, if not years, for fiscal policy stimuli to cause employment to rise in the economy. Consequently, a fiscal policy designed to combat a recession might not produce results until the economy is already experiencing inflation. In this event, the fiscal policy could worsen the situation.

time lags: periods between the time fiscal policy is enacted and the time it becomes effective

✔ **Reading Check** **Examining** According to monetarists, what should the federal government do in order to maintain a stable economy?

section 3 Review

Vocabulary
1. **Explain** the significance of: monetarism, monetarists, monetary rule, inflation targeting, time lags.

Main Ideas
2. **Determining Cause and Effect** Copy the arrows below. In the first arrow, list policies that monetarists would use to slow the economy. In the second arrow, list policies that monetarists would use to stimulate the economy.

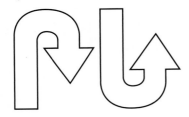

Critical Thinking
3. **The BIG Idea** What is the major difference between fiscal policy and monetary policy?
4. **Interpreting** What reasons does Milton Friedman have for wanting the government to follow a monetary rule?

Applying Economics
5. **Government Intervention** Find and bring to class one article that shows how government policies are influencing the economy. Write a paragraph explaining why you agree or disagree with the government's policies.

ECONOMIST
(1912–2006)

Milton Friedman

● Early and leading supporter of monetarism

■ Senior Research Fellow, Hoover Institution, Stanford University, and Professor Emeritus of Economics, University of Chicago

■ Recipient of the 1976 Nobel Prize for economics

■ Author of *A Monetary History of the United States, 1867–1960*, coauthored by Anna J. Schwartz (1963)

As a reminder that there is a price to pay for everything, including all government services, Milton Friedman entitled one of his books, *There's No Such Thing as a Free Lunch*. He was not the first to use the expression, but thanks to him, this phrase is now part of our everyday language, just as his ideas about competitive capitalism—once considered somewhat extreme—are an established part of current economic thinking.

Friedman was an early and forceful critic of the economic theories of John Maynard Keynes and his followers, especially the idea that government spending is necessary to counter the instability of free markets. Friedman examined the historical record and found that it is usually government policies—particularly monetary policy—rather than free markets that are most destabilizing. For example, the Federal Reserve allowed the money supply to fall by about a third during the Great Depression, with disastrous effects on output and employment. His research also led him to conclude that "inflation is always and everywhere a monetary phenomenon"—the result of excessive growth in the money supply.

Though he believed that the government that governs least governs best, Friedman was not an anarchist—that is to say, someone totally opposed to any government at all. Friedman once stated, "I believe we need government to enforce the rules of the game. . . . We need a government to maintain a system of courts . . . [and] to ensure the safety of its citizens—to provide police protection."

On the other hand, he had little faith in government as a source of solutions for economic problems.

> **Generally...I think the government solution to a problem is usually as bad as the problem and very often makes the problem worse.**

Checking for Understanding

1. **Defending** Name some government programs that you think are necessary and explain why.

2. **Theorizing** If someone who pays no taxes participates in a government program, why is the program still not really "free"?

Alpha has a comparative advantage in corn production. **Comparative advantage** is the ability of a country to produce a product at a lower opportunity cost than another country. Beta has a comparative advantage in soybean production. It can produce almost the same amount of soybeans as Alpha, but only half as much corn. By using its resources to grow only soybeans, Beta is just giving up the relatively inefficient production of corn. Beta, then, has a lower opportunity cost for soybean production than does Alpha. Beta should produce the maximum amount of soybeans, export soybeans to Alpha, and import corn. Both countries benefit when each country concentrates on that production for which it is relatively most efficient.

You should consider international trade as an economic activity just like any other. It is subject to the same economic principles. International trade can be looked at as a kind of production process that transforms exports into imports. For you and everyone else in the United States, the purpose of international trade is to obtain imports, not to export. What we gain as a country from international trade is the ability to import the things that we want. We have to export other things in order to pay for those imports.

comparative advantage: ability of a country to produce a product at a lower opportunity cost than another country

Skills Handbook
See page **R43** to learn about **Comparing and Contrasting.**

✓ **Reading Check** **Explaining** What does it usually mean when a country specializes in producing a particular product?

section 1 Review

Vocabulary
1. **Explain** the significance of: imports, exports, absolute advantage, specialization, comparative advantage.

Main Ideas
2. **Comparing** In a diagram like the one below, use the boxes to list an advantage each situation gives a country.

Advantages in Production	
Absolute	
Specialization	
Comparative	

Critical Thinking
3. The **BIG Idea** Explain why it is advantageous for a country to trade in order to specialize.
4. **Contrasting** What is the difference between an import and an export?

Applying Economics
5. **Comparative Advantage** List at least three activities in your daily life in which you have a comparative advantage (such as cooking or lawn maintenance). Describe how you and those who live at your house could use comparative advantage in order to "trade" to get more accomplished.

David Chu

● **Cofounder of Nautica**

■ CEO, president, and designer, Nautica International, 1984–2003

■ Founder of DC Designs International, 2004

David Chu came to the United States from Taiwan with his parents when he was 15 years old. After graduating from high school in New York, he planned to become an architect. Little did he realize when he enrolled in a drawing course at the Fashion Institute of Technology that he was taking the first step toward founding Nautica, a brand name that would become a billion-dollar global enterprise.

In 2003 Nautica was purchased by VF Corporation, a giant in the clothing industry whose brands include Lee and Wrangler. Chu made over $100 million in the transaction. Today Nautica Enterprises employs over 3,300 people and sells its products worldwide. Chu stayed on as CEO, but he retired in 2004. His retirement, however, didn't last long.

"After leaving Nautica in August, I played golf for eight or nine days, and then I realized that I needed to do something else. I'm passionate about this business and was ready to do something that I personally love."

In no time at all he was reestablishing the international relationships he'd built while at Nautica. His former colleagues there have nothing to fear from Chu as a competitor. The new line is very expensive: $185 shirts, $400 sweaters, $2,000 suits.

The time he spent building Nautica from scratch made his new venture much easier to get off the ground.

> **❝I didn't study business, but after a couple of years of experience I learned the business. . . . I think what's driving me is the stimulation. . . . It's not about the destination; it's about the journey.❞**

Checking for Understanding

1. **Applying** Like David Chu, do you have plans for a specific career? How do you plan to achieve your goals?

2. **Theorizing** Why do you think Chu chose to start another business even though he didn't need the money?

GUIDE TO READING

Section Preview
In this section, you will learn how nations convert their different currencies in order to trade more easily with one another.

Content Vocabulary
- exchange rate *(p. 472)*
- foreign exchange markets *(p. 472)*
- fixed rate of exchange *(p. 473)*
- International Monetary Fund (IMF) *(p. 473)*
- devaluation *(p. 473)*
- flexible exchange rate *(p. 474)*
- depreciation *(p. 474)*
- balance of trade *(p. 475)*

Academic Vocabulary
- affect *(p. 473)*
- benefit *(p. 476)*

Reading Strategy
Comparing and Contrasting As you read the section, complete a diagram like the one below by listing the advantages and disadvantages of a fixed rate of exchange.

Fixed Exchange Rates

Advantages   Disadvantages

ISSUES IN THE NEWS
···
—from *Money Magazine*

WHAT'S DRIVING DOLLAR PRICES? . . . [Americans] consume more stuff from the rest of the world than we sell back to them, resulting in an annual trade deficit set to top $600 billion. . . . We've racked up $2 trillion in consumer debt. . . .

What all this adds up to is that we've borrowed a lot of money from foreign investors—most notably China. About 40 percent of U.S. Treasuries, for example, are held by foreigners.

If investors start to think America is overextended, they may sell a lot of those assets, in the process selling dollars as they convert the money back into their own currency. . . .

▲ **Bank in China**

Investment flows into the U.S. have already begun to weaken, and the currency market may be driving dollar prices down in anticipation of more of the same.

T he United States uses the dollar as its medium of exchange; Mexico, the peso; India, the rupee; and Japan, the yen. As you read this section, you'll learn that to engage in world trade, people must have a way of knowing what the price of their currency is in terms of another nation's currency. They must also be able to exchange one type of currency for another.

Fixed Exchange Rates

Main Idea Under a system of fixed exchange rates, national governments set the value of their currencies relative to other currencies.

Economics & You What if your boss tried to pay you for a month's work in euros or in Japanese yen? These currencies would not be useful to you unless you exchanged them for U.S. dollars. Read on to learn about how countries must find a common way to pay one another for the goods they import and export.

exchange rate: the price of one nation's currency in terms of another nation's currency

The price of one nation's currency in terms of another nation's currency is known as the **exchange rate.** Why are exchange rates needed? A Chinese MP3 player manufacturer who exports MP3 players to the United States probably does not want American dollars in payment. The firm needs Chinese currency to pay its workers and suppliers.

Fortunately, international trade is organized so that individuals and businesses can easily and quickly convert one currency to another. **Foreign exchange markets** allow for these conversions. People in these markets deal in buying and selling foreign currency for businesses that want to import goods from other countries. Some of the currency trading also takes place through banks. **Figure 18.2** below gives examples of the information in a typical exchange rate list on any given day. You can find these rates in newspapers and on the Internet.

foreign exchange markets: markets dealing in buying and selling foreign currency for businesses that want to import goods from other countries

Figure 18.2 | Foreign Exchange Rate Listing

■ In the second column of this listing, on a particular day one British pound is worth 1.8228 American dollars. The third column shows that one United States dollar is worth .5486 British pounds.

Selected Exchange Rates

Country (currency)	U.S. Equivalent	Currency per U.S. $
Australia (dollar)	.7323	1.3655
Brazil (real)	.4488	2.2282
Britain (pound)	1.8228	.5486
Canada (dollar)	.8905	1.1173
China (yuan renminbi)	.1249	8.0064
European Union (euro)	1.2579	.7949
India (rupee)	.0215	46.5116
Japan (yen)	.0085	117.6470
Mexico (peso)	.0871	11.4810
South Africa (rand)	.1354	7.3855
Venezuela (bolivar)	.000466	2,145.9227

Economic Analysis

Using Tables *How many Venezuelan bolivars would you receive if you exchanged five U.S. dollars?*

Figure 18.3 Effects of Devaluation

■ This chart shows how devaluation of the Chinese yuan affects consumers in the United States.

Effects of Official Devaluation of Chinese Yuan

Before Devaluation	After Devaluation
Chinese MP3 player costs 800 yuan	Chinese MP3 player costs 800 yuan
Exchange rate: 8 yuan = $1 U.S.	Exchange rate: 10 yuan = $1 U.S.
MP3 player $= \dfrac{800 \text{ yuan}}{8 \text{ yuan per \$}} = \$100$	MP3 player $= \dfrac{800 \text{ yuan}}{10 \text{ yuan per \$}} = \$80$
An American would have to pay $100 for the Chinese MP3 player.	An American would have to pay $80 for the Chinese MP3 player.

TR 6 2:30:04

Economic Analysis

Calculating *How much would an American consumer pay for a Chinese MP3 player if the yuan was devalued to 14 per U.S. dollar?*

From 1945 to the early 1970s, the foreign exchange market operated with a **fixed rate of exchange.** Under this system, national governments set the value of their currency in relation to other currencies. With a fixed rate of exchange, a government could compare its currency to that of other countries. The **International Monetary Fund (IMF)** supported a fixed exchange rate system. Member governments of the IMF were obligated to keep their foreign exchange rates more or less fixed.

A fixed rate of exchange had some advantages for world trade. Importers and exporters knew exactly how much of a foreign currency they could purchase with their own nation's money. Also, the system allowed central banks to **affect** the level of exports and imports in their country by devaluing the currency. **Devaluation** means lowering a currency's value in relation to other currencies by government order. **Figure 18.3** above shows how the cost of a Chinese MP3 player would decrease if China devalues its currency.

This system of fixed exchange rates eventually proved impractical. The basic problem was that it was difficult to hold fixed exchange rates in an international economic climate that was constantly changing due to inflation and other factors. By the 1970s, many nations had begun to see the need to move to a more flexible system of exchange rates.

fixed rate of exchange: system under which a national government sets the value of its currency in relation to other currencies

International Monetary Fund (IMF): agency whose member governments once were obligated to keep their foreign exchange rates more or less fixed; today it offers monetary advice and provides loans to developing nations

devaluation: lowering a currency's value in relation to other currencies by government order

✓ **Reading Check** **Examining** What is devaluation? How does it affect a country's role in foreign trade?

Flexible Exchange Rates

Main Idea Under a system of flexible exchange rates, supply and demand determine currency values.

Economics & You How much is your American dollar worth in Canada? In Mexico? In Europe? Read on to learn about how flexible exchange rates mean that the value of the dollar in other nations is constantly changing.

flexible exchange rate: arrangement in which the forces of supply and demand are allowed to set the price of various currencies

depreciation: fall in the price of a currency through the action of supply and demand

On August 15, 1971, President Richard Nixon officially announced what would become the end of fixed American exchange rates. Most of the world's nations turned to a **flexible exchange rate** system. Under this arrangement, the forces of supply and demand are allowed to set the prices of various currencies. With flexible exchange rates, a currency's price may change, or float, up or down a little each day.

The forces actually determining exchange rates are the supply and demand of goods and services that can be bought with a particular currency. For example, suppose the amount of dollars wanted by Mexican exporters is greater than the quantity of dollars supplied by Americans who want to buy Mexican goods. Because the quantity demanded exceeds that supplied, the American dollar will become more expensive in relation to the peso. When the price of a currency falls through the action of supply and demand, it is termed **depreciation.** As with devaluation, depreciation of a country's currency improves its competitive edge in foreign trade.

Besides import-export transactions, political or economic instability within a country may encourage people to exchange their currency for a more stable currency, often the U.S. dollar. In that case, the value of the dollar would rise in relation to the other nation's currency. A country that is experiencing rapid inflation will find its currency falling in value in relation to other currencies.

Reading Check **Analyzing** Why might people want to exchange their own currency for a more stable currency?

Sticker Shock

Because of differences in currency values, goods priced in a foreign currency might seem to an American to cost much more than they actually do. A guitar that costs several thousand Japanese yen, for example, actually costs only a couple of hundred U.S. dollars.

Balance of Trade

Main Idea The United States has had a negative balance of trade since the 1970s.

Economics & You Traditionally, American video game systems do not sell well overseas, while Japanese consoles dominate the American market. Could this situation harm the American economy? Read on to learn about the delicate balance of trade between nations.

A currency's exchange rate can have an important effect on a nation's **balance of trade.** The balance of trade is the difference between the value of a nation's exports and the value of its imports. If a nation's currency depreciates, or becomes "weak," the nation will likely export more goods because its products will become cheaper for other nations to buy. Conversely, if a nation's currency increases in value, or becomes "strong," the amount of its exports will decline because its products will become more expensive abroad.

When the value of goods leaving a nation exceeds the value of those coming in, a positive balance of trade is said to exist. In this case, the nation is bringing in more funds as payments for goods than it is paying out. A negative balance of trade exists when the value of goods coming into a country is greater than the value of those going out. This situation is called a *trade deficit.* The United States has had a negative balance of trade, or trade deficit, for many years beginning in the 1970s and in fact, the trade deficit is growing, as you can see from the chart below.

balance of trade: difference between the value of a nation's exports and its imports

Economics ONLINE

Student Web Activity
Visit the *Economics Today and Tomorrow* Web site at glencoe.com and click on *Chapter 18—Student Web Activities* to learn about increased efficiency in international trade.

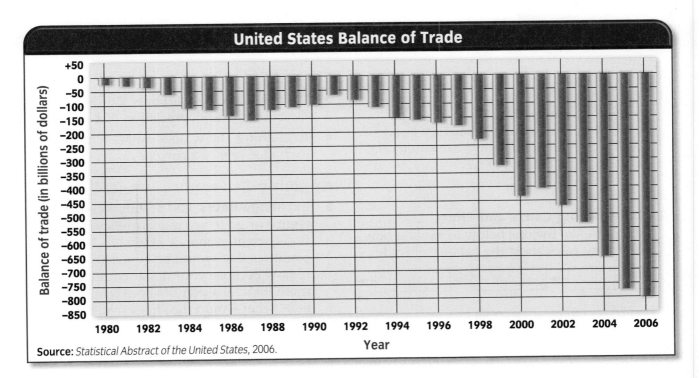

United States Balance of Trade

Balance of trade (in billions of dollars) vs. Year

Source: *Statistical Abstract of the United States,* 2006.

PRICKLY CITY

▲ Many American consumer products are made in China.

It is important to realize that a continued trade deficit is not necessarily a bad thing. A trade deficit continues because there are opportunities for foreigners to invest in the U.S. economy. For example, many Japanese automobile companies have built factories in the United States to satisfy the U.S. demand for Japanese cars. This creates supporting industries that **benefit** U.S. citizens by providing a great many domestic jobs.

Reading Check **Contrasting** Explain the difference between a positive and negative balance of trade.

section 2 Review

Vocabulary

1. **Explain** the significance of: exchange rate, foreign exchange markets, fixed rate of exchange, International Monetary Fund (IMF), devaluation, flexible exchange rate, depreciation, balance of trade.

Main Ideas

2. **Determining Cause and Effect** Use a diagram like the one below to explain how exchange rates affect the balance of trade.

Critical Thinking

3. **The BIG Idea** Explain how a drop in demand causes depreciation of a currency.

4. **Explaining** How does inflation affect the exchange rate of a currency?

Applying Economics

5. **Exchange Rates** Use an Internet search engine or go to www.gocurrency.com to find current exchange rates. List three countries that would be beneficial to travel to now because your dollar could buy more there. If a pair of shoes cost $100 here, what would the shoes cost in each country?

section 3 Restrictions on World Trade

GUIDE TO READING

Section Preview
In this section, you will learn about recent international trade agreements and restrictions.

Content Vocabulary
- tariff *(p. 478)*
- revenue tariff *(p. 478)*
- protective tariff *(p. 478)*
- import quota *(p. 479)*
- embargo *(p. 479)*
- protectionists *(p. 479)*
- World Trade Organization (WTO) *(p. 480)*
- North American Free Trade Agreement (NAFTA) *(p. 481)*
- Central American Free Trade Agreement (CAFTA) *(p. 481)*
- European Union (EU) *(p. 481)*

Academic Vocabulary
- restrict *(p. 477)*
- intense *(p. 479)*

Reading Strategy
Contrasting As you read, complete a table listing arguments for and against free trade.

For Free Trade	Against Free Trade

ISSUES IN ThE NeWS
—from *CNNMoney*

▲ Sneakers from China

QUOTAS REMOVED U.S. imports of Chinese-made clothing jumped sharply in January, the first month after the United States unshackled China and other countries from its long-standing quota restrictions.

...The U.S. eliminated apparel quotas on January 1, 2005. These barriers limited imports of sweaters, coats, shirts, and pants from countries such as China, India, Pakistan and Bangladesh.

Once the restriction was removed, industry watchers said they expected the "law of the jungle" to take over. Countries, in theory, will now have free access to the U.S. market, and they will compete globally on price for a greater chunk of the pie.

...Consumers could be the big winners as a greater influx of cheaper-priced clothes from China will help drive down prices since the long-standing quota had allowed retailers to inflate their sales prices.

To trade or not to trade? The difficulties that different currencies cause are only one problem of world trade. There are also natural barriers, which include the differences in languages and cultures between various trading partners. As you read this section, you'll learn that some nations may set **restrictions** to discourage or limit trade.

Three Ways to Restrict Imports

Main Idea Tariffs, quotas, and embargoes are three ways to restrict imports.

Economics & You Should the U.S. trade freely with nations that support communism or terrorism? Why or why not? Read on to learn about how embargoes are used to restrict trade with certain nations, often for political reasons.

Three major barriers to world trade are tariffs, quotas, and embargoes. The most commonly used barrier to free trade is the **tariff,** a tax on imports.

Tariffs Two types of tariffs can be applied to an import. A **revenue tariff** is used primarily to raise government revenue without restricting imports significantly. Although tariffs today account for less than 2 percent of the federal government's income, they were the major sources of federal funding until the early 1900s.

A **protective tariff** is one designed to raise the cost of imported goods and thereby protect domestic producers. As you learned from the law of demand, the quantity demanded of an item falls as the price rises. Higher prices for foreign goods because of tariffs mean that Americans will buy more domestic goods and fewer goods from abroad.

Some protective tariff rates have been as high as 62 percent of the value of the imported goods. Tariffs are much lower today, but they are still used to protect some industries from foreign competition.

tariff: tax placed on an imported product

revenue tariff: tax on imports used primarily to raise government revenue without restricting imports

protective tariff: tax on imports used to raise the cost of imported goods and thereby protect domestic producers

Figure 18.4 | The Free Trade Controversy

■ Free trade makes more products available to consumers at the best prices, but it also exposes domestic workers to greater foreign competition. Most Americans are neither completely for nor completely against free trade. They recognize that it carries both benefits and drawbacks, both for Americans and for citizens of countries we trade with.

Arguments Against Free Trade	
Job Security	Protectionists argue that many domestic workers will be unemployed if foreign competitors sell goods at lower prices than American firms. In the 1980s, for example, American steel mills laid off many workers because of foreign competition.
National Economic Security	Protectionists argue that certain industries are crucial to the economy of the United States. They believe that entire industries, such as oil, should be protected against foreign competition.
Infant Industries	Protectionists believe that tariffs and quotas are needed as temporary protection for new, infant industries. If foreign competition is restricted for a time, a young industry may become strong enough to compete in a world market.

Quotas An alternative method for restricting imports is the quota system. An **import quota** usually restricts the number of units of a particular good that can be brought into the country. At one time or another, the United States has placed quotas on imports of sugar, dairy products, various types of apparel, and cloth.

Embargoes An **embargo** is a complete restriction on the import or export of a particular good. Often embargoes are enacted for political reasons. For example, in 2003 an embargo was ordered against Syria for its support of terrorism.

The United States has also ordered embargoes on goods coming in *from* certain countries. For example, an embargo on trade with Cuba has been in place for more than four decades because the U.S. government does not agree with the political policies of Fidel Castro, Cuba's Communist dictator.

Arguments for and Against Free Trade The pros and cons of trade restrictions are still often the subject of **intense** public debate. **Protectionists** are those who argue *for* trade restrictions. They believe that certain restrictions are necessary to protect domestic industries. On the other side are free-trade supporters, who believe that exports and imports should not be restricted. There are three main arguments against and for free trade—see **Figure 18.4** below.

> ✓ Reading Check **Predicting Consequences** Explain how an embargo affects trade. What are two examples of embargoes ordered by the United States?

import quota: restriction imposed on the number of units of a particular good that can be brought into the country

embargo: complete restriction on the import or export of a particular good or goods going to or coming from a specific country

protectionists: people who argue for trade restrictions to protect domestic industries

Skills Handbook

See page *R47* to learn about *Making Predictions.*

Arguments for Free Trade	
Improved Products	Foreign competition encourages U.S. firms to improve their technology and production methods. Better technology increases the production and supply of goods and services available, which raises our standard of living.
Export Industries	American workers involved in export industries may become unemployed when trade restrictions are implemented. When the United States imports fewer goods, there is less American money available outside the United States to buy American exports. When the United States restricts imports, other nations may retaliate and restrict their own imports.
Specialization and Comparative Advantage	Those in favor of free trade admit that too much economic specialization puts the country at the mercy of world demand. However, some specialization benefits consumers because comparative advantage in production results in more goods at lower prices.

Economic Analysis

Evaluating *Would a recently unemployed American steel worker more likely be in favor of or against free trade policies? Why?*

International Trade Agreements

Main Idea International trade agreements are negotiated to reduce trade restrictions between countries.

Economics & You Have you ever visited Mexico or Canada? Why might the United States want to maintain good trade relations with its neighbors? Read on to learn about the importance of trade agreements between countries.

There have been continuing efforts worldwide to reduce tariffs and encourage more world trade.

The World Trade Organization The most important international trade organization is the **World Trade Organization (WTO).** As of 2007, the WTO had 147 member nations. The WTO has made decisions that affected the U.S. steel tariffs used in the early 2000s. As a result, the United States canceled its tariffs on steel imported from other countries.

The WTO is working hard at breaking down trade barriers in agriculture. The United States and the European Union, though, have not reached agreement on how to reduce their large government payments to domestic farmers. Some economists believe that if world agricultural trade were made freer, poor people in developing countries would be better off. Additionally, consumers both here and in Europe would not pay so much for food. Taxpayers would see fewer tax receipts go to support large agricultural businesses.

World Trade Organization (WTO): world's largest trade agreement, currently with more than 140 member nations

WTO Protests

Although the stated aim of the WTO is to promote free trade and stimulate economic growth, critics contend that it does not treat less-developed countries fairly. They also claim that the issues of health, safety, and the environment are ignored by the organization.

Regional Trade Agreements In many parts of the world, regional trade agreements have been reached in order to increase free trade. Certain nations in Southeast Asia as well as in Central and South America have such regional trade agreements. The United States formed one with Canada and Mexico called the **North American Free Trade Agreement (NAFTA).** The U.S. Congress approved NAFTA in 1993. Since then, trade has increased between the three nations to the general benefit of all.

The **Central American Free Trade Agreement (CAFTA)** was signed into law in the summer of 2005. This agreement covers most countries in Central America plus the Dominican Republic. CAFTA eliminated tariffs on more than 80 percent of U.S. exports to that geographic area.

Perhaps the most important regional trade agreement in the world today is the **European Union (EU).** Currently, the EU consists of 25 European countries. On January 1, 1993, the EU began eliminating most of its restrictions on trade between its member countries. Many European nations use a common currency, the euro. Eventually, the EU will have a common currency for over 400 million European consumers. It will rival the United States in market size.

North American Free Trade Agreement (NAFTA): trade agreement designed to reduce and gradually eliminate tariff barriers between Mexico, Canada, and the United States

Central American Free Trade Agreement (CAFTA): trade agreement designed to reduce tariff barriers between Costa Rica, El Salvador, Guatemala, Honduras, Nicaragua, the Dominican Republic, and the United States

European Union (EU): organization of European nations whose goal is to encourage economic integration as a single market

✓ **Reading Check** **Determining Cause and Effect** What is NAFTA? How has it affected U.S. trade?

section 3 Review

Vocabulary

1. **Explain** the significance of: tariff, revenue tariff, protective tariff, import quota, embargo, protectionists, World Trade Organization (WTO), North American Free Trade Agreement (NAFTA), Central American Free Trade Agreement (CAFTA), European Union (EU).

Main Ideas

2. **Examining** In a table like the one below, explain how each trade agreement listed helps U.S. exports.

NAFTA	
CAFTA	
EU	

Critical Thinking

3. **The BIG Idea** How does the WTO assist global trade?

4. **Interpreting** Explain why a protectionist would likely favor protective tariffs, import quotas, and embargoes.

Applying Economics

5. **Free Trade** Think of five foreign-made items you used or wore today. Where was each item made? How much did you pay for the items? Explain why you think each item might be cheaper or more expensive if made in the U.S.

A MAJOR SWIPE AT SWEATSHOPS

Working toward a living wage.

Check It Out! In this chapter you learned about regional trade agreements. In this article, read to learn about an agreement that could improve the lives of workers in sweatshops around the globe.

Remember sweatshop exposés? They haven't hit the headlines much in the past few years. In part that's because high-profile companies such as Nike Inc. and Gap Inc. now work regularly with labor rights groups to monitor their vast global networks of supplier factories. Still, only about 100 U.S. and European multinationals participate in such efforts to find and remedy abuses. . . . Perhaps the most troublesome absence has been that of the large retailers such as Wal-Mart Stores Inc. and Target Corp. These giants increasingly control the pricing power in overseas manufacturing that in turn dictates how much money factories can spend on improving labor conditions.

Now global labor monitoring may get a big leg up. Nike, Patagonia, Gap, and five other companies have joined forces with six leading anti-sweatshop groups to devise a single set of labor standards with a common factory-inspection system. The goal: to replace today's overlapping hodgepodge of approaches with something that's easier and

▲ Protesting sweatshops

cheaper to use—and that might gain traction with more companies. After two years of debate, the parties quietly signed an agreement to run a pilot project in several dozen Turkish factories that produce garments and other products for the eight companies.

. . . There may be little media attention paid to workers [in developing nations] these days, but human rights groups still routinely find abuses of every description.

—Reprinted from *BusinessWeek*

Workers in China's sweatshops make about $97 a month. → Boosting wages in sweatshops . . . . . .would increase the price of a $30 garment in the U.S. by only 25 cents.

Think About It

1. **Explaining** Why do we not hear as much about sweatshops today as we did in the past?

2. **Identifying Central Issues** Why is it a problem that giant retailers are not part of the joint project discussed in the article?

■ Countries benefit if they specialize in the production of goods for which they have a **comparative advantage** and then trade for other goods.

If country Alpha has a comparative advantage in corn production, it should produce only corn.

If country Beta has a comparative advantage in soybean production, it should produce only soybeans.

■ A nation has a **positive balance of trade** if the value of its exports is greater than the value of its imports. It has a **negative balance of trade** if the value of its imports is greater than the value of its exports.

| Balance of Trade | = | Value of Exports | − | Value of Imports |

■ As international trade continues to increase, intense debate goes on worldwide about the pros and cons of **trade agreements and restrictions.**

Protectionists	**Free-Trade Supporters**
Argue for trade restrictions. They feel that certain restrictions are necessary to protect domestic industries.	Argue against trade restrictions. They feel that the world market will take care of itself if left to operate with minimal restrictions.

Review Content Vocabulary

1. *Write a paragraph or two explaining the basics of world trade. Use all of the following terms.*

imports

exports

specialization

exchange rate

flexible exchange rate

depreciation

balance of trade

tariff

import quota

embargo

protectionists

World Trade Organization (WTO)

North American Free Trade Agreement (NAFTA)

European Union (EU)

Review Academic Vocabulary

Choose the letter of the term that best completes each sentence.

a. source

b. overseas

c. affect

d. benefit

e. restrict

f. intense

2. An import quota is meant to _____ the number of a particular good brought into the country.

3. The question of free trade versus protectionism is a _____ of heated debate in many countries.

4. The currency exchange rate can _____ a nation's balance of trade.

5. Many exports are sold _____ to consumers in countries across the oceans.

6. One _____ of free trade is that competition usually results in better products at lower prices.

7. Protectionists have a(n) _____ belief in trade restrictions to protect U.S. industries against foreign competition.

Review the Main Ideas

Section 1 (pp. 465–469)

8. How does a country determine whether it has a comparative advantage in the production of certain goods?

9. What does the United States gain from international trade?

10. "America can produce more DVDs per labor hour than can any other country in the world." Is this an example of an absolute advantage or a comparative advantage?

11. How does a nation benefit from specialization?

Section 2 (pp. 471–476)

12. Why are foreign exchange markets necessary?

13. In the past, why was it difficult to maintain a system of fixed rates of exchange?

14. What does it mean when a nation's currency devaluates?

15. How does a nation come to have a negative balance of trade?

Section 3 (pp. 477–481)

16. Fill in a graphic organizer like the one below to list three ways to restrict imports and explain how each one works.

Trade Restriction	How It Works

17. What is the difference between a revenue tariff and a protective tariff?

18. What are three arguments for free trade and three arguments against free trade?

Thinking Like an Economist

19. International trade affects all Americans. To understand how international trade affects you, describe what your world would be like if international trade were outlawed. You can do this by making a list of all the products you would not be able to purchase or whose price would go up dramatically without international trade. For example, the United States imports far more oil than it produces. If the United States stopped importing oil, it could not produce enough to meet current needs. Use a chart like the one below to record your thoughts, and then write a paragraph describing the impact of international trade on your life.

Product	Result

Economics ONLINE

Self-Check Quiz Visit the *Economics Today and Tomorrow* Web site at glencoe.com and click on *Chapter 18—Self-Check Quizzes* to assess your knowledge of chapter content.

Critical Thinking

20. **The BIG Idea** Are you in favor of free trade, protectionism, or some combination of the two? Explain your position.

21. **Understanding Cause and Effect** If the value of the dollar fell in relation to other currencies, what would you expect to happen to American exports?

22. **Synthesizing** The U.S. Constitution forbids restrictions on trade between the 50 states. What are two examples of problems that might have arisen if the Constitution had been silent on trade between the states?

Analyzing Visuals

23. Study the cartoon on the right, and then answer the following questions.

    a. The man's words are a play on a common saying. What is the original saying?

    b. What does the bull represent?

    c. What does the china shop represent?

    d. What is the cartoonist's message?

Global Economy

The European Union The European Union (EU) is an organization of 25 independent European nations whose goal is to create a unified and strong market. The map below shows the value of trade between the European Union and other regions of the world.

North America
Imports from EU = 224.9 billion dollars
Exports to EU = 335.3 billion dollars

South and Central America
Imports from EU = 67.5 billion dollars
Exports to EU = 47.3 billion dollars

The euro is the legal tender for more than 300 million people in Austria, Belgium, Finland, France, Germany, Greece, Italy, Ireland, Luxembourg, the Netherlands, Portugal, and Spain. Denmark, Sweden, and the United Kingdom are not currently using the euro. The 10 member states that joined the European Union in 2004 are committed to adopting the euro eventually.

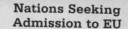

Current EU Members

France
Germany
Italy
Belgium
Netherlands
Luxembourg
Austria
Denmark
Finland
Greece
Ireland
Portugal
Spain
Sweden
Great Britain
Estonia
Latvia
Lithuania
Poland
Czech Republic
Slovakia
Slovenia
Hungary
Cyprus
Malta

Russia and Eastern Europe
Imports from EU = 112.4 billion dollars
Exports to EU = 80.8 billion dollars

Asia
Imports from EU = 451.0 billion dollars
Exports to EU = 274.1 billion dollars

dollars
dollars

Thinking Globally

1. **Listing** With which regions of the world does the EU have a trade surplus? A trade deficit?

2. **Identifying** Which region is the EU's biggest trade partner?

3. **Critical Thinking** Three EU countries—Great Britain, Denmark, and Sweden—do not use the euro. Why do you think this is so? Write down some possible reasons, and then conduct research on the Internet to find out whether your theories are correct.

487

Growth in Nations

The **BIG Idea**

Economists look at a variety of factors to assess the growth and performance of a nation's economy.

Why It Matters

What do you think it would take to improve economic conditions in less developed nations? In this chapter, read to learn how developing countries are working to become a bigger part of the global economy.

Economics ONLINE

Chapter Overview Visit the *Economics Today and Tomorrow* Web site at glencoe.com and click on *Chapter 19—Chapter Overviews* to preview chapter information.

Characteristics of Developing Nations

GUIDE TO READING

Section Preview
In this section, you will learn why many nations have less industrial development and a lower standard of living than the United States.

Content Vocabulary
- developed nations *(p. 490)*
- developing nations *(p. 490)*
- subsistence agriculture *(p. 492)*
- infant mortality rate *(p. 492)*

Academic Vocabulary
- technical *(p. 492)*
- fundamental *(p. 493)*

Reading Strategy
Explaining As you read, complete a diagram like the one below to explain why poorly defined property rights are a major cause of poverty in developing nations.

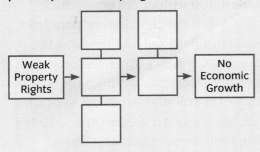

ISSUES IN THE NEWS
—from Sojourners Magazine

HELPING FARMERS AROUND THE WORLD Equal Exchange, a fair trade coffee importer in Massachusetts, works "to develop a more egalitarian, democratic model of trade." . . .

Equal Exchange provides security to farmers through loans given before the harvest, so that if crops are destroyed or damaged, members of the cooperatives will not lose their land or go hungry, as happens to many other

▲ **Equal Exchange Coffee**

small farmers. Fair trade buyers pay double the market price of 63 cents per pound and add a 5-cent-per-pound premium for development projects.

Such economic support provides everything from schools to health clinics in the communities. . . . After the earthquakes in El Salvador in 2001, pre-harvest financing received from Equal Exchange supported families in the cooperative.

. . . [T]he organization wants to form more trading relationships, but first the U.S. demand for fair trade coffee must increase.

Many Americans may not realize it, but even the poorest families in the United States usually have an income far above the average income in much of the rest of the world. About one-half of the world's population lives at or close to subsistence, with just enough to survive. As you read this section, you'll learn about the characteristics of these developing countries.

Developed and Developing Nations

Main Idea Developed nations have increased their standards of living by moving from agricultural to industrialized economies.

Economics & You Take a moment to think about the clothing, electronic goods, and other items that you own. People in many other countries cannot afford these luxuries. Read on to learn about the differences between the United States and other, less developed, nations.

developed nations: nations with relatively high standards of living and economies based more on industry than on agriculture

developing nations: nations with little industrial development and relatively low standards of living

Of the more than 190 nations in the world, only about 35 are considered **developed nations.** These nations include the United States, Canada, all European countries, Japan, Australia, and New Zealand.

The remaining people in the world live in **developing nations.** These are nations with less industrial development and a relatively low standard of living. Within this general definition, however, developing nations differ in many ways. The average income per person in Mexico, for example, is only about 24 percent that of the United States, but Mexico is much more developed and prosperous than almost all other developing nations.

Religion influences economic policies in some developing countries. This is not new. During the Middle Ages, the Church influenced many economic decisions throughout Europe. In colonial America, various churches influenced economics. Today some developing countries forbid lending money with interest. As a result, foreign investment in these countries is low.

✓ Reading Check **Describing** What is a developing nation?

Ahead of the Pack

Among developing nations, Mexico is one of the most modernized and prosperous. Its large cities, like Mexico City, for example, look very much like urban areas of the United States.

Figure 19.1 | Measuring GDP

Graphs In MOtion
See StudentWorks™ Plus or
go to glencoe.com.

■ As you can see from the graph, there is a huge difference in per capita GDP between developing and developed countries.

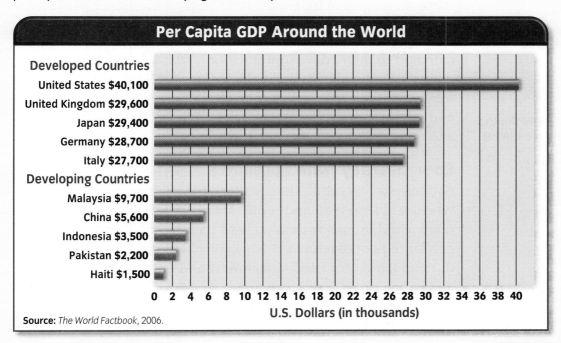

Per Capita GDP Around the World

Developed Countries
- United States $40,100
- United Kingdom $29,600
- Japan $29,400
- Germany $28,700
- Italy $27,700

Developing Countries
- Malaysia $9,700
- China $5,600
- Indonesia $3,500
- Pakistan $2,200
- Haiti $1,500

0 2 4 6 8 10 12 14 16 18 20 22 24 26 28 30 32 34 36 38 40
U.S. Dollars (in thousands)

Source: *The World Factbook,* 2006.

Economic Analysis

Contrasting *How does the GDP gap affect everyday life in developing and developed countries?*

Economic Characteristics

Main Idea Developing nations are usually characterized by low GDP per capita, emphasis on agriculture, poor health conditions, low literacy rates, and rapid population growth.

Economics & You How would your everyday life be different if you lived in a developing nation? Read on to learn about the economic characteristics that many developing nations have in common.

Skills Handbook

*See page **R37** to learn about **Making Generalizations.***

Economists often use per capita GDP as a rough measure of a nation's prosperity. Estimates of per capita GDP in the United States and other industrial nations range from $25,000 to about $40,000 per year.

Low GDP Per capita GDP in developing nations, in contrast, is considerably less, and in the world's poorest nations it is extremely low. Look at **Figure 19.1** above, which shows per capita GDP for a number of developing countries. While developing nations may have many natural and human resources, they lack the equipment, financing, and knowledge necessary to put those resources to use.

An Agricultural Economy

Agriculture is central to the economies of developing nations. Much of the population exists through **subsistence agriculture,** in which each family grows just enough to take care of its own needs. This means that no crops are available for export or to feed an industrial workforce.

Poor Health Conditions

Poor health conditions are also common in many developing nations. Many people die from malnutrition or illness due to lack of food. Developing nations may also suffer from a shortage of modern doctors, hospitals, and medicines. The result is often a high **infant mortality rate** and a low life expectancy among adults.

Low Literacy Rate

A fourth characteristic of developing nations is a low adult literacy rate—the percentage of people who are able to read and write. There are few schools, and many children miss school to help their families farm. The lack of a large pool of educated workers makes it difficult to train the population for needed **technical** and engineering jobs.

Rapid Population Growth

A fifth characteristic of developing nations—rapid population growth—is often the source of many other problems, such as lack of food and housing. The population in the United States grows at a rate of about 1 percent a year. The growth rate in many developing nations is three and sometimes four times this rate.

✔ **Reading Check** **Determining Cause and Effect** What conditions lead to high infant mortality rates?

Economic and Social Statistics for Selected Nations				
Country	Life expectancy at birth	Infant mortality (deaths per 1,000 live births)	Literacy (% of people who can read and write)	Population (in millions)
United States	78	6	97	295.7
Japan	81	3	99	127.4
Australia	80	5	100	20.1
Israel	79	7	97	6.3
Italy	80	6	99	58.0
China	72	24	91	1,306.3
Mexico	75	21	92	106.2
Brazil	72	30	86	186.1
India	64	56	60	1,080.3
Mozambique	40	131	48	19.4
Bangladesh	62	63	43	144.3
Ethiopia	49	95	43	73.1

Source: *The World Factbook*, 2006.

Weak Property Rights

Main Idea A weak system of legally protected property rights frequently undermines economic development.

Economics & You You probably know exactly where your property stops and your neighbors' property starts. This is not always so clear in developing nations. Read on to learn about how this lack of strong property rights causes problems in developing countries.

Economists have found that governments in developing countries generally do not support a system of strong, well-defined private-property rights. A good example is Peru. Only 20 percent of Peru's land is legally owned. Without specifically defined private-property rights, individuals cannot exchange land. As a result, no large-scale farming has occurred in Peru, and farmers have little incentive to improve the value of the property they farm.

Take another example. Many of the poorest countries in the world are on the African continent. A **fundamental** reason that there is little economic growth in Africa is that less than 10 percent of its land is formally owned. African residents who do not own the land or their houses cannot easily borrow against the values of those items. They cannot sell them, either.

✓ Reading Check **Speculating** Why might governments in developing countries not support private-property rights?

section 1 Review

Vocabulary

1. **Explain** the significance of: developed nations, developing nations, subsistence agriculture, infant mortality rate.

Main Ideas

2. **Explaining** Create a diagram like the one below to list and explain five economic characteristics of developing nations.

Characteristics of Developing Nations

Critical Thinking

3. **The BIG Idea** How does the lack of private-property rights keep some nations in poverty?

4. **Defending** Should developing nations be forced to develop? Explain your answer.

Applying Economics

5. **Political Economics** Draw up a plan to help a developing nation develop more quickly. List each negative economic characteristic you learned about in this section, and explain what you would propose to overcome that condition in your chosen country.

PUMPING OUT ENGINEERS

Mexico is swiftly upgrading its workforce.

Check It Out! In this chapter you learned about some factors that hinder development in some nations. In the following article, read to learn how Mexico is working toward a new trend.

▲ Engineering students in Mexico

For years, the Mexican workforce has meant one thing to multinationals: cheap, reliable labor, perfect for assembling cars, refrigerators, and other goods in the *maquiladoras* lining the border with America. But as *maquila*-syle assembly work migrated to cheaper locales, and India and China grabbed more sophisticated design and engineering assignments, Mexican officials knew they had to do something to stay in the global race. Quietly and steadily, they have. Over the past 10 years, the country's policymakers have been building up enrollment in four-year degree programs in engineering, developing a network of technical institutes that confer two-year degrees, and expanding advanced training programs with multinationals from the U.S. and elsewhere.

The result is a bumper crop of engineers. Currently, 451,000 Mexican students are enrolled in full-time undergraduate programs, vs. just over 370,000 in the U.S. The Mexican students benefit from high-tech equipment and materials donated to their schools by foreign companies, which help develop course content to fit their needs. . . .

Mexican officials hope that as more multinationals get hooked on the expertise of local technicians and engineers, they will keep sending more sophisticated work to Mexico, providing plenty of quality jobs for everyone and moving the country further up the ladder of development.

—Reprinted from *BusinessWeek*

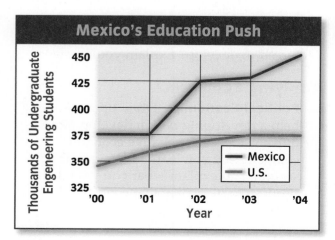

Mexico's Education Push

Chart: Thousands of Undergraduate Engineering Students (y-axis: 325, 350, 375, 400, 425, 450) vs. Year (x-axis: '00, '01, '02, '03, '04). Lines: Mexico, U.S.

Think About It

1. **Specifying** What led Mexican officials to increase the number of undergraduates in engineering?
2. **Synthesizing** How are multinationals helping Mexico's engineers?

The Process of Economic Development

GUIDE TO READING

Section Preview
In this section, you will learn how foreign investment and aid help nations to develop economically.

Content Vocabulary
- confiscation *(p. 497)*
- foreign aid *(p. 497)*
- economic assistance *(p. 497)*
- technical assistance *(p. 497)*
- military assistance *(p. 497)*

Academic Vocabulary
- devote *(p. 498)*
- enhance *(p. 500)*

Reading Strategy
Organizing As you read the section, complete a table similar to the one below by listing three types of foreign aid and a definition and example for each one.

Types of Foreign Aid

Type of Aid	Definition	Example

ISSUES IN THE NEWS
—from *CNNMoney*

WORLD BANK FOR SALE Don't like the policies of the World Bank? Then sell it on eBay.

The Center for Economic Justice tried to do just that.

The activist group, which aims to minimize the negative effects of globalization, initiated the eBay auction by posting a desktop globe last Friday with a coin slot cut in the top. The posting's headline read "World Bank— Antiquated (does not work)."

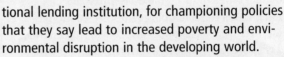

Social and environmental activists have long derided the World Bank, an international lending institution, for championing policies that they say lead to increased poverty and environmental disruption in the developing world.

The bank has argued that its loans for development projects are crucial to modernization and economic growth.

[The globe had a] starting bid of 30 cents, or, according to the product description, the hourly minimum wage under World Bank policies in Haiti. . . .

Most nations pass through three stages of economic development. The first is the agricultural stage, and the second is the manufacturing stage. In the third stage, many workers shift into the service sector—sales, food service, and technical services. As you read this section, you'll learn how developing nations use foreign investment and aid to move through the three stages of economic development.

Financing Economic Development

Main Idea The major outside sources of capital for developing nations are foreign investment and aid from developed nations.

Economics & You You have probably heard about controversial overseas labor practices of companies such as Nike and the Gap. Read on to learn about low wage rates and other reasons why developing countries are attractive to some American companies.

A basic problem for many developing nations is how to finance the equipment and training necessary to improve their standard of living. Domestic savings, which provide this financing in developed nations, are often limited or take a different form in developing nations. Therefore, many such nations must look to outside sources for investment capital. The two major outside sources of capital are investment by foreign businesses and foreign aid from developed nations.

Foreign Investment: Attractions and Risks

Investors are attracted to developing countries because of their low wage rates, few regulations, and abundant raw materials. Investment may include setting up branch offices and new companies, building new factories, or buying into companies already established.

Figure 19.2 | Foreign Aid

■ Three main types of foreign aid are provided by developed nations to developing nations—economic assistance, technical assistance, and military assistance. Such aid is provided by both governments and private organizations. Often, foreign aid plays an important role in economic development.

A. Economic Assistance This consists of loans and outright grants of funds or equipment to other nations. One use of such aid is to purchase basic producer goods, including machinery that will increase a nation's productivity.

Besides attractions, there are also risks to investing in developing countries. If the government is unstable, or if terrorist groups threaten stability, foreign businesses may lose their investment. In some cases, the governments in developing nations have taken over private firms—a practice called **confiscation**—forcing the firms' owners out of those countries.

Problems exist from the developing nation's viewpoint as well. In nations with heavy foreign investment, citizens often criticize the economic control these foreign companies have over their resources. What these critics may not realize is that factors of production will remain idle unless such firms organize the materials and skills of the country's inhabitants.

Foreign Aid A second type of financing available to nations is **foreign aid**—the funds, goods, and services given by governments and private organizations to help other nations. Types of foreign aid include **economic assistance, technical assistance,** and **military assistance.** (See **Figure 19.2.**) Emergency shipments of food, clothing, and medical supplies to victims of drought, earthquakes, floods, and other disasters are also considered foreign aid. This type of foreign aid, however, is not directed toward economic development.

Reading Check **Explaining** Name three reasons why foreign investors are attracted to developing countries.

confiscation: taking over industries by governments without paying for them

foreign aid: funds, goods, and services given by governments and private organizations to help other nations and their citizens

economic assistance: loans and outright grants of funds or equipment to other nations

technical assistance: aid in the form of engineers, teachers, and technicians to teach skills to individuals in other nations

military assistance: aid given to a nation's armed forces

▲ **B. Technical Assistance** This includes providing professionals such as engineers, teachers, technicians, and consultants to teach skills. This strengthens a nation's human resources in the same way economic assistance increases a nation's capital resources.

▲ **C. Military Assistance** This involves giving either economic or technical assistance to a nation's armed forces. Such assistance might include providing extensive training for a developing nation's military.

Economic Analysis

Extending *What might foreign aid be used for besides economic development?*

Who Supplies Foreign Aid?

Main Idea The United States devotes a smaller fraction of its GDP to foreign aid than many other countries.

Economics & You Do wealthy nations have a responsibility to help developing countries? Why or why not? Read on to learn about which nations supply the most foreign aid to developing countries.

Many developed nations offer some type of foreign aid to developing nations. After World War II, the United States **devoted** most of its foreign assistance to help rebuild Europe's war-torn economy. Today, most American foreign aid is sent to developing nations in the Middle East and Southeast Asia. Nations in Africa receive about 11 percent, Latin America about 14 percent, and East Asia and the Pacific about 5 percent.

Comparing Aid Many other major industrial nations also give foreign aid. France and Great Britain, for example, have concentrated most of their aid programs on their former colonies in Africa and Asia. Germany and Japan both began giving aid to developing nations after their own economies had recovered from World War II.

The dollar amount of American foreign aid may sound high—$27.5 billion in 2005. When viewed as a percentage of Gross National Income (GNI), however, that amount is just a fraction of what many other nations give in foreign aid. (See **Figure 19.3** below.) Norway's foreign aid, for example, is 0.9 percent of that nation's GNI. By comparison, foreign aid given by the United States is less than 0.25 percent of its GNI.

Skills Handbook

See page *R53* to learn about *Comparing Data.*

Figure 19.3 | Sources of Aid

■ Although the United States supplies more in foreign aid than any other developed country, as a percentage of GNI, it's not even in the top 10 giving nations. In 2005, the United States ranked 21st among developed nations in the amount it gave as a percentage of GNI.

Economic Analysis

Making Inferences *Most of the countries in the chart are in what part of the world? Why do you think this is so?*

Leading Suppliers of Foreign Aid

In Billions of U.S. Dollars		As Percentage of GNI*	
United States	$27.46	Norway	.93%
Japan	13.10	Sweden	.92%
United Kingdom	10.75	Luxembourg	.87%
France	10.06	Netherlands	.82%
Germany	9.92	Denmark	.81%
Netherlands	5.13	Belgium	.53%
Italy	5.06	Austria	.52%
Canada	3.73	United Kingdom	.48%
Sweden	3.28	France and Finland	.47% each
Spain	3.12	Switzerland	.44%

Source: Organization for Economic Cooperation and Development, 2006.

*gross national income

Channels of Aid The United States channels much of its foreign aid to other nations through the U.S. Agency for International Development (USAID). Funds are also channeled through United Nations agencies, including the International Bank for Reconstruction and Development—usually called the World Bank. Founded in 1944, the World Bank provides loans and other services to developing nations. Two affiliates of the bank are the International Development Association (IDA), which lends to nations that are the least able to obtain financing from other sources, and the International Finance Corporation (IFC), which encourages private investment in developing nations.

Recently, the International Monetary Fund (IMF) has become a major foreign aid agency. It has offered a variety of loans to Russia, Thailand, South Korea, Indonesia, Malaysia, Brazil, and Mexico.

These foreign aid agencies have grown increasingly alarmed as many developing nations find themselves unable to repay their foreign debts. By the late 1990s, the level of indebtedness had become extremely high, with about 40 of the most heavily indebted nations owing the IMF and the World Bank more than $127 billion. In 1999 the leaders of the major industrial nations proposed a plan that would cancel some of this debt. By 2006, 25 countries had received $83 billion in debt relief under this plan.

Economics ONLINE

Student Web Activity
Visit the *Economics Today and Tomorrow* Web site at glencoe.com and click on *Chapter 19—Student Web Activities* to learn about recent developments in foreign aid.

✔ **Reading Check** **Identifying** Where is most American foreign aid sent?

Reasons for Giving Foreign Aid

Main Idea Foreign aid is motivated by both humanitarian and political considerations.

Economics & You Have you ever donated money to a charity? Why or why not? Read on to learn the reasons why many nations supply foreign aid to developing countries.

Humanitarianism is the basis of some foreign aid, but other reasons are often given as well. The first reason involves economics. It is usually in the best interests of developed nations to encourage international trade. Foreign aid expands a nation's markets for exports and provides new opportunities for private investment.

Politics is another reason for giving foreign aid. From 1947 to 1991, an important objective of U.S. foreign aid was to **enhance** the appeal of democracy and stop communism. The United States has also used foreign aid to build political friends.

The final reason for providing foreign aid is to help protect a nation's own security. Economic aid is often a downpayment on a military alliance with a developing nation. Through alliances, the United States has gained overseas military bases and observation posts. This type of plan can backfire, however, if a friendly government loses power.

Reading Check **Analyzing** How has the United States benefited from military alliances formed as a result of overseas aid?

section 2 Review

Vocabulary

1. **Explain** the significance of: confiscation, foreign aid, economic assistance, technical assistance, military assistance.

Main Ideas

2. **Interpreting** In a chart like the one below, explain the reasons countries are willing to provide foreign aid to developing nations.

Reasons for Giving Foreign Aid	
Humanitarianism	
Politics	
National security	

Critical Thinking

3. **The BIG Idea** What risks exist for a country giving aid to another?

4. **Identifying** What two factors prevent some countries from becoming industrialized?

Applying Economics

5. **Monitoring Development** The United States is a developed country that has gone through the three stages explained in this section. Make a time line showing how the U.S. has gone from an agriculture-based economy through industrialization to service and technology.

Obstacles to Growth in Developing Nations

GUIDE TO READING

Section Preview
In this section, you will learn about the problems that developing nations face when trying to achieve economic growth.

Content Vocabulary
- bureaucracies *(p. 502)*
- capital flight *(p. 502)*

Academic Vocabulary
- regime *(p. 502)*
- substitute *(p. 502)*
- subsequent *(p. 503)*

Reading Strategy
Organizing As you read, complete a web diagram similar to the one below by listing obstacles to economic growth in Indonesia.

PLACES In ThE NeWS
—from the **Associated Press**

VIETNAM TODAY In the final days of the Vietnam War, Ly Ngoc Minh watched his friends pack their bags to flee [the country].
On April 30, 1975, as . . . tanks barreled into Saigon, he and his family decided to stay.

. . . [T]hree decades later, as Vietnam emerges from war, poverty, and isolation, and replaces crumbling Communist doctrines with free-market reforms, it turns out that he stayed long enough.

▲ **Vietnamese entrepreneur**

. . . In this reinvigorated nation of 82 million, Communist dogma blared daily over public loud-speakers has become background noise to the bustle of an army of new entrepreneurs. Vietnam's 7.7 percent annual growth rate is second only to China among Asian countries.

Ruling Communist Party leaders still struggle to define what economic model they are using—"socialism with market orientation" is borrowed from neighboring China. . . .

The successful rebuilding of Europe's economy following World War II convinced many economists that injections of money capital into a nation could achieve rapid economic growth. As a result, billions of dollars flowed into developing nations during the 1950s and 1960s. Aid to many of these nations, however, failed to produce the same growth as Europe experienced. In this section, you'll learn why this is so.

Four Obstacles to Growth

Main Idea Local traditions, rapid population growth, misuse of resources, and trade restrictions can all hinder economic development.

Economics & You Would the problem of American poverty be solved by simply giving money to every poor person? Probably not. Read on to learn about how many developing nations also face economic problems that are not so easy to fix.

Many developing nations face a number of obstacles to growth that are not immediately solved by injections of money capital. Europe after World War II already had skilled labor forces, corporations and trade groups, and experienced government **bureaucracies,** or specialized offices and agencies. This is not the case in developing nations.

One obstacle to economic growth resides in people's attitudes and beliefs. In many developing nations, people live and work much as their ancestors did hundreds of years ago. Innovation of any sort is often viewed with suspicion. Farmers, for example, may be reluctant to accept a new way of plowing, even though it means better soil conservation and a larger harvest.

A high population growth rate may also reduce the rate of growth of a nation's standard of living. Even if a nation's economy is growing, per capita GDP will decrease if its population is growing at a faster rate.

Development in some nations has furthermore been slowed by the misuse of resources. For example, government spending on the military could instead be directed toward agricultural development or training.

Corruption among government and military leaders also weakens the economies of many developing nations. Local currency may be legally exported or illegally sent from the country into leaders' private bank accounts, a practice known as **capital flight.** Even if new, honest leaders take over, they may have inherited crushing debts from previously corrupt **regimes.**

Finally, to develop domestic industries, many developing nations have used import restrictions such as quotas and tariffs. These trade restrictions prevent consumers from purchasing cheaper foreign **substitutes.**

bureaucracies: offices and agencies of the government that each deal with a specific area

capital flight: the legal or illegal export of currency or money capital from a nation by that nation's leaders

- Attitudes and beliefs
- Continued rapid population growth
- Four Obstacles to Growth
- Misuse of resources
- Trade restrictions

✓ **Reading Check** **Explaining** How can peoples' attitudes and beliefs inhibit a developing nation's economic growth?

Case Study: Indonesia

Main Idea The availability of natural resources or money for investment does not guarantee economic development if unstable conditions or other obstacles to growth are present.

Economics & You Do you own any clothing or other goods that were produced or assembled in Indonesia? Read on to learn about barriers to economic success in this nation, despite its large work force.

When Indonesia won independence from the Netherlands in 1949, it seemed well equipped for economic growth. It was rich in minerals and had vast oil reserves, as well as good farmland and rain forests. During his regime, President Sukarno obtained foreign aid totaling more than $2 billion from both capitalist and communist nations. Yet Indonesia's economy was a disaster.

The reasons behind this failure reveal some of the problems of trying to bring rapid growth to developing nations. One problem involved attitudes. Indonesians lacked a sense of national identity. The country had been formed from several former Dutch colonies, and its people were divided by nationality, religion, and politics. The major blame for economic failure, however, can be placed on Sukarno's economic policies.

Subsequent improvements in Indonesia's economy were credited to General Suharto, who assumed power in 1965. Suharto's initial economic policies made Indonesia one of the fastest-growing economies by the end of the 1970s.

Indonesia's Economy Under Sukarno and Suharto

President Sukarno's Regime (1949–1965)	General Suharto's Regime (1965–1998)
① Strong opposition to capitalism resulted in loss of foreign aid from the United States.	① Control of the money supply was tightened and confidence in government increased. Initially, corruption was reduced and bureaucracy decreased.
② Foreign aid from the former Soviet Union and others was often wasted on projects for the rich such as sports stadiums and department stores. Mineral resources were not developed, and decaying roads and rail lines went without repairs.	② Alliances with some Western nations were made.
	③ Foreign aid and investment increased, and resources were focused on improving agricultural output and oil production.
③ Nationalization of businesses placed them under government ownership, discouraging foreign investment.	④ Industry was developed. More funds could be spent on industry because fewer funds were needed to import food.
④ Heavy regulation of business, a huge government bureaucracy, and widespread corruption hurt the economy.	⑤ A system of "crony" capitalism developed— family members and close friends owned or controlled major businesses.
⑤ Inflation soared out of control. The nation's price index rose from 100 in 1953 to 3,000 only 10 years later. By the mid-1960s, the national debt was $2.5 billion.	⑥ The economy declined dramatically in 1998, forcing the resignation of General Suharto as the nation's leader. Currently presidential elections are held every five years.

Indonesia, like most Southeast Asian countries, suffered during the economic crisis that hit the region in the late 1990s. Its economy has stabilized somewhat since then. Major cities like Jakarta show signs of growing prosperity.

Unfortunately, Indonesia found that reliance on a few products could be dangerous. In the early 1980s, the world "oil glut" cut deeply into the nation's trade income. When an economic crisis hit Southeast Asia in 1997–1998, Indonesia's economy tumbled. Riots ensued and General Suharto resigned.

Indonesia's value as a case study lies in the variety of lessons it teaches about foreign aid. It illustrates that simply pouring money capital into a developing nation will not guarantee economic growth. Indonesia also shows that growth can occur if government restrictions on economic activity are reduced.

Foreign aid must be used wisely in combination with domestic savings, foreign investment, and government policies that ensure economic stability. Finally, the case study points out that growth of a developing nation's economy may prove temporary if it depends on only one or two products.

Reading Check **Examining** Why did Indonesia initially seem well equipped for economic growth after receiving its independence in 1949?

section 3 Review

Vocabulary

1. **Explain** the significance of: bureaucracies, capital flight.

Main Ideas

2. **Analyzing** Several obstacles prevent development in some countries. Copy the chart below, and for each example given, explain why it may slow growth.

Obstacles	Effects
Local traditions	
Rapid population growth	
Misuse of resources	
Corruption	
Trade restrictions	

Critical Thinking

3. **The BIG Idea** Why did providing finances for development help improve Europe after WWII but does not often work today?

4. **Contrasting** How is humanitarian aid different from foreign investment?

Applying Economics

5. **Foreign Aid Policy** Imagine you are asked by the president to develop guidelines for giving $2 billion in aid to a developing nation. Compose a list of guidelines, and provide an explanation for each of your recommendations.

Case Study: Indonesia

Main Idea The availability of natural resources or money for investment does not guarantee economic development if unstable conditions or other obstacles to growth are present.

Economics & You Do you own any clothing or other goods that were produced or assembled in Indonesia? Read on to learn about barriers to economic success in this nation, despite its large work force.

When Indonesia won independence from the Netherlands in 1949, it seemed well equipped for economic growth. It was rich in minerals and had vast oil reserves, as well as good farmland and rain forests. During his regime, President Sukarno obtained foreign aid totaling more than $2 billion from both capitalist and communist nations. Yet Indonesia's economy was a disaster.

The reasons behind this failure reveal some of the problems of trying to bring rapid growth to developing nations. One problem involved attitudes. Indonesians lacked a sense of national identity. The country had been formed from several former Dutch colonies, and its people were divided by nationality, religion, and politics. The major blame for economic failure, however, can be placed on Sukarno's economic policies.

Subsequent improvements in Indonesia's economy were credited to General Suharto, who assumed power in 1965. Suharto's initial economic policies made Indonesia one of the fastest-growing economies by the end of the 1970s.

Indonesia's Economy Under Sukarno and Suharto

President Sukarno's Regime (1949–1965)	General Suharto's Regime (1965–1998)
1 Strong opposition to capitalism resulted in loss of foreign aid from the United States.	**1** Control of the money supply was tightened and confidence in government increased. Initially, corruption was reduced and bureaucracy decreased.
2 Foreign aid from the former Soviet Union and others was often wasted on projects for the rich such as sports stadiums and department stores. Mineral resources were not developed, and decaying roads and rail lines went without repairs.	**2** Alliances with some Western nations were made.
	3 Foreign aid and investment increased, and resources were focused on improving agricultural output and oil production.
3 Nationalization of businesses placed them under government ownership, discouraging foreign investment.	**4** Industry was developed. More funds could be spent on industry because fewer funds were needed to import food.
4 Heavy regulation of business, a huge government bureaucracy, and widespread corruption hurt the economy.	**5** A system of "crony" capitalism developed—family members and close friends owned or controlled major businesses.
5 Inflation soared out of control. The nation's price index rose from 100 in 1953 to 3,000 only 10 years later. By the mid-1960s, the national debt was $2.5 billion.	**6** The economy declined dramatically in 1998, forcing the resignation of General Suharto as the nation's leader. Currently presidential elections are held every five years.

Unfortunately, Indonesia found that reliance on a few products could be dangerous. In the early 1980s, the world "oil glut" cut deeply into the nation's trade income. When an economic crisis hit Southeast Asia in 1997–1998, Indonesia's economy tumbled. Riots ensued and General Suharto resigned.

Indonesia's value as a case study lies in the variety of lessons it teaches about foreign aid. It illustrates that simply pouring money capital into a developing nation will not guarantee economic growth. Indonesia also shows that growth can occur if government restrictions on economic activity are reduced.

Foreign aid must be used wisely in combination with domestic savings, foreign investment, and government policies that ensure economic stability. Finally, the case study points out that growth of a developing nation's economy may prove temporary if it depends on only one or two products.

Reading Check **Examining** Why did Indonesia initially seem well equipped for economic growth after receiving its independence in 1949?

---

section 3 Review

Vocabulary
1. **Explain** the significance of: bureaucracies, capital flight.

Main Ideas
2. **Analyzing** Several obstacles prevent development in some countries. Copy the chart below, and for each example given, explain why it may slow growth.

Obstacles	Effects
Local traditions	
Rapid population growth	
Misuse of resources	
Corruption	
Trade restrictions	

Critical Thinking
3. **The BIG Idea** Why did providing finances for development help improve Europe after WWII but does not often work today?

4. **Contrasting** How is humanitarian aid different from foreign investment?

Applying Economics
5. **Foreign Aid Policy** Imagine you are asked by the president to develop guidelines for giving $2 billion in aid to a developing nation. Compose a list of guidelines, and provide an explanation for each of your recommendations.

Economic Development in China

GUIDE TO READING

Section Preview
In this section, you will learn about the reasons for the rapid growth of China's economy over the past several years.

Content Vocabulary
- five-year plans *(p. 506)*

Academic Vocabulary
- interval *(p. 507)*
- notion *(p. 508)*

Reading Strategy
Sequencing As you read the section, complete a time line similar to the one below by identifying key events in China's economic development from its Communist takeover to the present day.

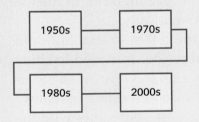

PLACES In ThE NeWS
—from *CNN.com*

GROWTH SPURT China is a sleeping giant, Napoleon once warned. "Let her sleep, for when she wakes she will shake the world."

Nearly two centuries later and China is well and truly awake.

. . . In the space of just 25 years, China has transformed from an inward-looking communist basket case to a nation fast becoming one of the most influential in the world.

▲ **Textile factory in China**

. . . [A]ccording to the World Trade Organization, China is expected to produce more than half the world's textiles by the end of the decade.

. . . "China is certainly growing fast, but it also has a very long way still to go," says [Dr. Linda Yueh of the London School of Economics]. "In terms of GDP per capita, it still ranks as an early developing country."

China is growing so fast, she says, because it can't afford not to. "China's overriding goal is to help its people develop and achieve a higher standard of living."

Not all developing countries stay poor forever. China is a case in point. It now has one of the fastest-growing economies in the world. Indeed, the United States and other Western nations may be overtaken economically in the next 30 years. The main reason is that China is developing a market economy.

Development of China's Economic System

Main Idea China's rapid economic growth is a result of recent free-market reforms.

Economics & You How many commonly used goods can you think of that bear the label "Made in China"? Read on to learn about how China has transformed itself from a controlled economy into one that more closely resembles a free-enterprise system.

five-year plans: centralized planning system that used to be the basis for China's economic system; eventually was transformed to a regional planning system leading to limited free enterprise

In 1953, the Chinese Communist government started an economic system based on **five-year plans,** which empasized central planning. However, in 1957 it reformed the system to give some decision-making powers to local government. The reforms did not transform the Chinese economy, however, because it was still not governed by capitalism's "three Ps"— prices, profits, and private property.

In 1978 Chinese leaders designed a reform to motivate people to work harder. Private individuals were permitted to rent land for up to 15 years. Each peasant household became responsible for its own plot of land. The household could keep whatever it produced in excess of a minimum amount required by the state. The results were impressive. Between 1979 and 1984, overall farm productivity increased dramatically.

During the 2000s, several hundred million rural residents moved to cities to work in factories and offices. Overseas companies started investing in many business ventures, sometimes with the Chinese government as a partner. Economic growth remains at 7 to 10 percent per year. China's economy may become the biggest in the world in the not-too-distant future.

Reading Check **Identifying** What are the "three Ps" of capitalism?

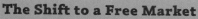

The Shift to a Free Market

China—after the failure of command economies throughout the world—has begun to allow free enterprise.

The Transition Toward a Mixed Economy

Main Idea The legal protection of some private property has encouraged the private investment necessary for China's transition to a mixed economy.

Economics & You Have you ever seen a "black market" DVD or video game? Read on to learn about the black market and other factors that challenge China's economic improvement.

As you may recall, one of the most important aspects of pure capitalism is well-defined private-property rights. In China, the state still owns large parts of the economy, especially urban industries. In the countryside, provincial governors are still held accountable for ensuring that each province grows as much grain as it consumes. The government still leases land for 15-year **intervals** to farmers. Without complete property rights, farmers are therefore not interested in investing in farm equipment and making improvements to the land. Private-property rights are, however, part of the Chinese constitution.

Establishing the Rule of Law Countries shifting from noncapitalist to capitalist systems all face the same problem—how to establish the rule of law. When no specific property rights exist, the unavoidable result is corruption. Throughout China there is an atmosphere of lawlessness and unpredictability for anyone in the business world. This is particularly true for foreign investors. Because army and government officials still control many resources, they continue to seek bribes. Thus, such individuals still influence the way business is conducted in China.

Careers Handbook

See pages R76–R80 to learn about becoming a lawyer.

Gradually China is becoming a nation of laws. The **notion** of property rights is slow to be accepted because communist dogma has for decades criticized private property as detrimental to the state. For example, compact disc factories in China routinely "pirate" CDs. The Chinese government supported this practice, but at one point shut down the factories because of international pressure. The pirates reopened a few years later, however. Chinese government officials ignored the fact that singers and musicians were being denied royalties.

Dealing With Increasing Pollution

In the middle of the first decade of the 2000s, the Chinese government made a prediction. Pollution levels could rise 400 percent in 15 years! Even today, China is the world's second biggest producer of undesirable gas emissions into the atmosphere. Acid rain affects a third of the country. China's air pollution even travels to far-off places, such as Los Angeles, and about 70 percent of China's rivers and lakes are polluted. Most city residents drink bottled water. In the countryside, people boil water before they drink it.

The question facing the government is not easy to answer. How does it change a booming, pollution-creating economy without slowing economic growth?

Reading Check **Determining Cause and Effect** Why has China been slow to accept the notion of private property rights?

Economics ONLINE

Student Web Activity
Visit the *Economics Today and Tomorrow* Web site at glencoe.com and click on *Chapter 19— Student Web Activities* to learn more about China's evolving economy.

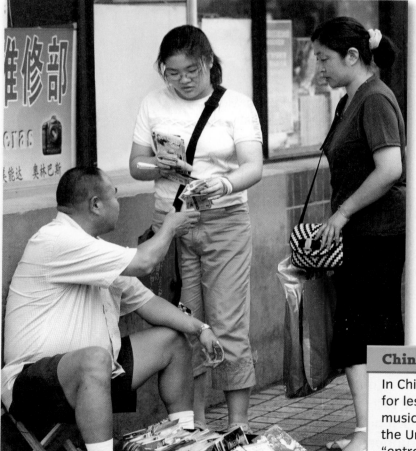

China's Black Market

In China, consumers can buy Nike T-shirts for less than $2, DVDs for under $3, and music CDs for a fraction of their cost in the United States. Many Chinese "entrepreneurs" produce and sell American brand-name products very inexpensively because they do not pay royalties on the brands they counterfeit.

Prospects for China's Economic Future

Main Idea China has encouraged foreign investment in its economy to promote growth and access to global markets.

Economics & You When you think of a Chinese city, what do you imagine? Many places in China are actually quite similar to the United States. Read on to learn about the expanding foreign presence in China.

A foreigner visiting Beijing or Shanghai or another large city in China would have difficulty knowing he or she was in the People's Republic of China. There are McDonald's restaurants, business executives with cellular phones and pagers, and advertisements for Levi's, 7Up, and Heinz products everywhere.

In 2000 that foreign presence began expanding when the United States agreed to allow China to join the World Trade Organization (WTO), which you read about in Chapter 18. This action had far-reaching effects for China and the rest of the world.

China is an enormous market for foreign companies eager to sell their products to the nation's 1.3 billion people. As a result of being admitted to the WTO, the inefficient state-owned industries draining China's economy were forced to face many economic reforms. WTO membership has increased the prospects for a more prosperous, democratic, and stable China.

Reading Check **Explaining** How has joining the World Trade Organization (WTO) affected the Chinese economy?

section 4 Review

Vocabulary

1. **Explain** the significance of: five-year plan.

Main Ideas

2. **Analyzing** How did the Chinese economic system develop following World War II?

3. **Determining Cause and Effect** Create a chart like the one below to explain two major problems China is facing in its move toward capitalism.

Problem	Cause	Effect

Critical Thinking

4. **The BIG Idea** In the past, China's government has been involved in setting production quotas for industries. This continues to a certain extent today. How could such a practice lead to surpluses and shortages of goods and services?

5. **Synthesizing** Why has the black market continued to thrive in China?

Applying Economics

6. **International Trade** Research the World Trade Organization on the Internet. Find and summarize the issues surrounding China's entry into the organization in 2000.

People and Perspectives

ECONOMIST
(1818–1883)

Karl Marx

- Coauthor of *The Communist Manifesto* and *Capital*

- Earned a doctorate in philosophy at the University of Jena, 1841
- Correspondent for the *New York Daily Tribune*, 1852–1862
- Helped found the International Working Men's Association, 1864

During the 1900s, Karl Marx's name was often associated with the Russian Revolution and, later, with the Soviet Union. In fact, though he traveled widely, Marx never set foot in Russia.

He was born into a respectable middle-class family in Germany and was descended, on both sides of his family, from generations of Jewish rabbis and scholars. His father converted to Christianity, and young Karl was baptized as a Lutheran in 1824.

Marx attended a local Jesuit high school, eventually earning a doctorate in 1841. It wasn't until he moved to Paris that he began to familiarize himself with the tenets of communism. While there he met many well-known socialists, including Friedrich Engels, who became his lifelong friend and collaborator and the person most responsible for converting him to the cause of communism. As the result of his advocacy of revolution, Marx was expelled from Paris. In time he was also expelled from Brussels and Prussia, finally immigrating to England, where he spent the remainder of his life.

His years in London with his wife and children were plagued by poverty, serious illnesses, and death. It was during this period that he wrote, in collaboration with Engels, one of his major works, *Capital: A Critique of Political Economy.*

Marx and Engels were prolific and insightful writers on many social and economic subjects. Their collected works run to 50 volumes. Yet today they are chiefly remembered for the prophetic, if now dated, sentences at the end of *The Communist Manifesto,* one of the most influential pieces of revolutionary propaganda ever written:

> **The proletarians have nothing to lose but their chains. They have a world to win. WORKING MEN OF ALL COUNTRIES, UNITE!**

Checking for Understanding

1. **Theorizing** What is it about the quote from *The Communist Manifesto* that makes it so memorable?

2. **Making Inferences** Why do you think so little of Marx's writings are known and quoted today?

■ Economists use **per capita GDP** as a measure of a nation's prosperity. There is a huge difference in per capita GDP between developed and developing nations.

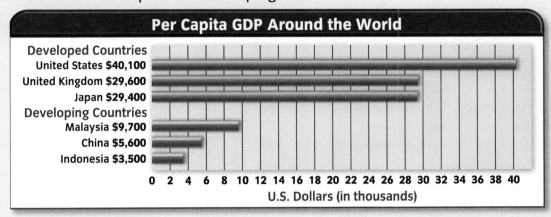

Per Capita GDP Around the World

Developed Countries
United States $40,100
United Kingdom $29,600
Japan $29,400
Developing Countries
Malaysia $9,700
China $5,600
Indonesia $3,500

0 2 4 6 8 10 12 14 16 18 20 22 24 26 28 30 32 34 36 38 40
U.S. Dollars (in thousands)

■ Although developing nations receive capital from developed nations in the form of foreign investment and aid, they still face **obstacles to growth**.

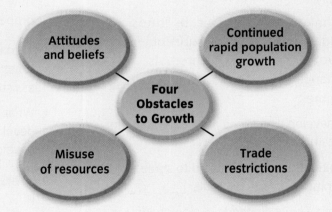

Attitudes and beliefs

Continued rapid population growth

Four Obstacles to Growth

Misuse of resources

Trade restrictions

■ China's **rapid economic growth** is a result of recent free-market reforms. An American visitor to Beijing would find that city to be very much like large cities in the United States.

▲ Beijing

Economic Growth in Developing Nations **511**

Review Content Vocabulary

1. *Write a paragraph or two explaining economic growth in developing nations. Use all of the following terms.*

developed nations
developing nations
subsistence agriculture
infant mortality rate
confiscation
foreign aid

economic assistance
technical assistance
military assistance
bureaucracies
capital flight
five-year plans

Review Academic Vocabulary

Choose the letter of the term that best completes each sentence.

a. technical
b. fundamental
c. devotes
d. enhance
e. regimes

f. substitutes
g. subsequent
h. intervals
i. notion

2. Many developing nations have been ruled for decades by corrupt _____.

3. The United States provides aid to some developing countries in regular _____.

4. The basic, _____ needs of many people in developing countries are not being met.

5. The _____ of property rights is a new idea to many countries.

6. The U.S. budget _____ billions of dollars to foreign aid each year.

7. Tariffs can help protect infant industries from having to compete with cheaper foreign _____.

8. Engineering and other _____ jobs require a highly educated workforce.

9. Aid from democratic countries can _____ the appeal of democracy in developing countries.

10. After receiving aid, developing countries often see _____ improvement in their economies.

Review the Main Ideas

Section 1 (pp. 489–493)

11. Fill in a graphic organizer like the one below to identify the five characteristics common to most developing nations.

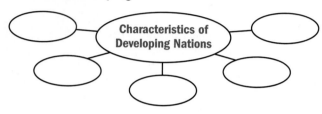

Characteristics of Developing Nations

12. How does a weak system of legally protected property rights affect economic development?

Section 2 (pp. 495–500)

13. What is the difference between military assistance and technical assistance?

14. What are the three stages of economic development? In what stage are most developing countries?

Section 3 (pp. 501–504)

15. How is rapid population growth an obstacle to economic development?

16. What is the danger of a nation relying too heavily on income from just a few products?

Section 4 (pp. 505–509)

17. Why has China been steadily shifting from a noncapitalist to a more capitalist system? What has been the result?

18. What are the main problems that China must still overcome?

Math Practice

In December 2004, a major earthquake caused a tsunami, or giant tidal wave, to hit parts of Asia and Africa. It caused terrible devastation and loss of life. Almost 200,000 people died, and many more lost their homes and their livelihoods. The United States immediately offered aid that included food and medical supplies, funds for rebuilding, experts to provide training, and programs to restore people's jobs and incomes. Look at the Tsunami Aid Summary below and answer the questions that follow.

Tsunami Aid Summary	
Country	**Amount of Aid**
India	$17.9 million
Indonesia	$400.1 million
Maldives	$12.0 million
Sri Lanka	$134.6 million
Thailand	$5.3 million
Other Countries	$33.4 million
Program Management	$21.4 million

Source: www.usaid.gov

Economics ONLINE

Self-Check Quiz Visit the *Economics Today and Tomorrow* Web site at glencoe.com and click on *Chapter 19—Self-Check Quizzes* to assess your knowledge of chapter content.

19. Based on the information in the table, which country was hardest hit by the tsunami?

20. How much more U.S. aid did India receive than Thailand?

21. What is the total tsunami aid budget as represented in this table?

22. What percentage of the tsunami aid budget was dedicated to program management?

Critical Thinking

23. **The BIG Idea** Why is per capita GDP a good way for economists to roughly measure a nation's relative prosperity?

24. **Analyzing** Is an abundance of natural resources required in order for a country to have economic growth and development? Explain.

25. **Synthesizing** What could other developing nations learn from China's example?

Analyzing Visuals

26. Study the cartoon on the right, and then answer the following questions.

    a. What does the speaker in this cartoon represent?

    b. What irony is the cartoon conveying?

    c. What do you think the cartoonist's attitude is about how developed nations treat developing ones?

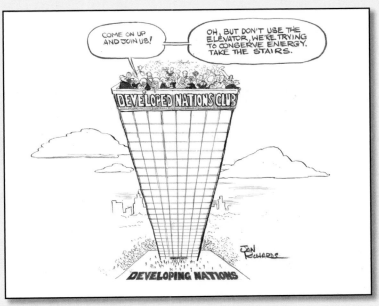

Jonathan Richards

Can developing countries improve local economies while conserving natural resources?

THE ISSUE

As developing countries struggle to expand their economies, some exhaust natural resources, like forests, in the process. Once the trees are gone, communities may lose their livelihood, and the animals that live there lose the habitat they need to survive. Dr. Jane Goodall, a primate scientist, ran headlong into this problem when she first tried to save endangered chimpanzees in Tanzania. In order to save the chimps, she and her team had to save the forests; to save the forests, they had to find better ways than logging for the Tanzanian people to earn a living. Is it possible for developing economies to advance their economies without damaging the environment?

THE FACTS

Forests convert toxic carbon dioxide given off by cars and factories into healthful oxygen. They are also home to millions of animals and medicinal plants. Forests once covered two-thirds of the Earth's surface (not counting Antarctica and Greenland). In the past few decades, forest loss has greatly accelerated. Today, half the world's forests are gone—32 million acres are lost each year. Forest loss can have a devastating environmental impact. However, the natural resources of developing nations are often the only foot in the door to the global economy that these nations have available to them.

Resource Capacity
Which countries use more or fewer total resources than they have available?

■ **Ecological Reserve:** Country has more land and water than it uses to produce what it consumes and absorb its wastes

■ **Ecological Deficit:** Country uses more land and water than it has to produce what it consumes and absorb its wastes

Source: Global Footprint Network, 2005

THE ECONOMIC CONNECTION: OPPORTUNITY COSTS

The main problem with the use of natural resources in many developing nations is that these resources are depleted for short-term economic gain only. In order to sustain populations and survive economically, nations must learn how to nurture and sustain their resources over the long term.

In Tanzania, for example, forests are lost because logging trees *seems* more profitable than conservation. In the case of the Tanzanian villages, the residents thought selling the trees and using the land to grow crops made sense. However, land left after forests are destroyed is less profitable and not fertile enough for long-term agriculture or grazing.

▼ Dr. Jane Goodall and friend in 2004

The strategy of the nonprofit Jane Goodall Institute (JGI) in Tanzania is to develop local economies by working with villagers to meet both short- and long-term community needs. So far, villagers have raised 2.4 million seedlings for firewood, built fuel-efficient stoves, planted 750,000 trees in 32 villages, and passed bylaws forbidding clear-cutting of trees. Village committees promote nontimber forest use, such as beekeeping and harvesting of herbal medicine. Farmers are trained in sustainable methods for growing coconut, coffee, and vegetables. More than 73 chapters of JGI's worldwide Roots & Shoots program involve Tanzanian youth in environmental projects. Other issues addressed are health, education, resource management, and small business loans.

CONCLUSION

Whenever short-term profit requires destruction of resources that cannot be replaced, it's important to weigh the opportunity cost. Although economic development often seems at odds with environmental protection, cooperation among communities, business, and government—combined with long-term vision—can find solutions. As the Jane Goodall Institute has shown in Africa, it is possible to meet human needs while promoting conservation values.

Analyzing the Impact

1. **Synthesizing:** Why do some land owners in developing countries log and burn forests? What are the results?

2. **Critical Thinking:** Name two ways in which your community could use sustainable practices to benefit the local economy.

The Global Economy

The **BIG Idea**

The study of economics helps us deal with global economic issues and global demand on resources.

Why It Matters

How are you personally affected by activities in the global economy? In this chapter, read to learn why global integration is now a fact of life.

Economics ONLINE

Chapter Overview Visit the *Economics Today and Tomorrow* Web site at glencoe.com and click on *Chapter 20—Chapter Overviews* to preview chapter information.

Reasons for and Results of Global Integration

GUIDE TO READING

Section Preview
In this section, you will learn about the technological developments that have led to the growth of the global market, as well as some of the outcomes of globalization.

Content Vocabulary
- global integration *(p. 518)*
- telecommunications *(p. 518)*

Academic Vocabulary
- transform *(p. 519)*
- transmit *(p. 519)*
- recover *(p. 521)*

Reading Strategy
Organizing As you read, complete a diagram similar to the one below by listing the inventions and factors that have led to rapid improvements in worldwide communications.

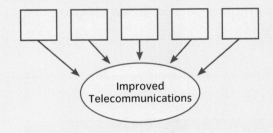

Improved Telecommunications

ISSues In ThE NeWS
—from *Current Issues in Economics and Finance*

CHOICES FROM ABROAD Over the last three decades, trade has more than tripled the variety of international goods available to U.S. consumers.

. . . The U.S. economy has advanced considerably since Henry Ford quipped that customers could have cars in "any color as long as it is black."

. . . One development that has significantly broadened consumers' choice of goods in recent decades is the growth of international trade. As trade with other nations has expanded, U.S. consumers have been able to acquire varieties of goods not available from domestic producers—Japanese cars, for example, and French wine.

In the United States, it is not unusual to ride on a bus that was made in Germany or drive a Japanese-made car. A Canadian may own a local restaurant. Some of the restaurant's food perhaps has been imported from Mexico, France, and Spain. Interest rates may fall because political upheavals in other countries have caused businesses there to invest their money capital in politically stable America. In this section, you'll learn that we now live not just as Americans, but as part of the global economy.

Improved Telecommunications

Main Idea Advances in telecommunications have significantly reduced the costs of business.

Economics & You Many of the technologies that you have access to every day, such as the Internet or satellite television, play an important role in worldwide communications as well. Read on to learn about how these innovations have affected the global economy.

global integration: interdependency among the countries of the world, especially within financial markets and telecommunications

telecommunications: long-distance communication, usually electronic, using communications satellites and fiber-optic cables

Skills Handbook

*See page **R45** to learn about **Synthesizing Information.***

Global integration—the interdependency among countries—has increased dramatically over the past several decades. Many reasons explain this increase. One reason is improved **telecommunications,** or long-distance electronic communication.

The first transatlantic telegraph cable was completed in 1866. Before then it took two weeks to find out the price of the dollar in London. The telegraph cable reduced that time to two minutes. With the invention of the semiconductor—the computer chip—telecommunications grew rapidly. Look at **Figure 20.1** below, which shows how much the price of computing power has fallen in just the last few decades.

Several other inventions and factors have influenced the rapid improvement in worldwide telecommunications. Communications satellites circle the Earth day and night. Radio and television waves, beamed up to them, are reflected down to other parts of the Earth. On the Earth's surface, fiber-optic cables are being placed throughout much of North America and already exist in parts of Europe. The rapid expansion of the Internet has also been an important aspect of the worldwide communications system.

Figure 20.1 | Decreasing Costs

■ The price per million units of computing power (expressed in millions of instructions per second, or MIPS) has fallen dramatically from 1978 to today.

Economic Analysis

Synthesizing *How does the falling cost of computing power affect the price of computers themselves?*

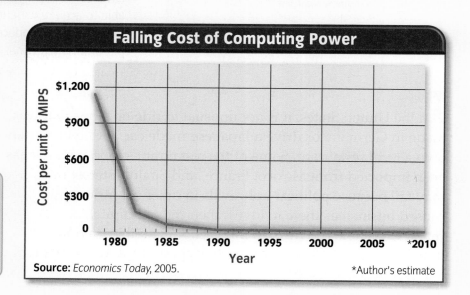

Falling Cost of Computing Power

Cost per unit of MIPS

$1,200
$900
$600
$300
0

1980   1985   1990   1995   2000   2005   *2010

Year

Source: *Economics Today,* 2005.

*Author's estimate

Consider some of the ways cheap and readily available satellite television has **transformed** the exchange of information between the Eastern Hemisphere and other parts of the world. Before the 1990s, virtually all of the television (and radio) available in the Eastern Hemisphere was both state-run and state-controlled. Viewers saw few programs and advertisements from other parts of the world. Today, people in Asia, Africa, and other regions of the world receive sports, music, soap operas, news, and advertisements via satellite, and much of this information is free of government control.

How does this increase in communications affect the rest of the world? Viewers in other nations are changing their cultural tastes and buying habits. In many countries, viewers buy copies of outfits worn by popular music, film, and television personalities from the United States and Europe. Viewers demand foreign products they see advertised on television, which increases exports from the originating nations. In addition, because many popular television programs are **transmitted** in English, more of the world's people want to learn English as a second language.

Reading Check **Predicting Consequences** How has the increased availability of satellite television impacted nations of the Eastern Hemisphere?

The Globalization of Financial Markets

....

Main Idea U.S. government securities, foreign exchange, and stocks are now traded continuously around the world.

Economics & You The September 11, 2001, terrorist attacks affected not only the American economy, but foreign stock markets as well. Read on to learn about what it means to have a global economy.

....

Because of the speed and power of computers and the affordability of telecommunications, the world has become one financial market. This globalization started in the 1970s and 1980s, when U.S. banks developed worldwide branch networks for loans and foreign exchange trading. Today money and financial capital markets are truly global, and many stocks and bonds are traded on them.

United States government securities (bonds that the U.S. government sells), foreign exchange, and shares of stocks are now traded continuously in vast quantities around the world. Trading in U.S. government securities is the world's fastest growing 24-hour market. Foreign exchange—the buying and selling of foreign currencies—became a 24-hour worldwide market in the 1970s. Markets also exist worldwide in commodities such as grains, gold and silver, and stocks. The worldwide stock market, started in the mid-1970s, however, has some problems.

Global Trading

Computers have transformed the world into one integrated financial market. Here, a man in Kuwait tracks stocks at the Kuwait Stock Exchange.

Problems With the Worldwide Stock Market The United States economy represents a major part of the world economy. So, when the U.S. stock market falters, so do the stock markets worldwide. For example, on October 19, 1987, the United States stock market suffered one of its worst days ever. The Dow Jones Industrial Average dropped over 500 points. It took two years for the United States stock market to **recover,** but many foreign stock markets took even longer.

On September 11, 2001, one of the most devastating acts of terrorism in history occurred. The World Trade Towers in New York City were destroyed, and thousands lost their lives. When the stock market reopened on September 17, the Dow fell by almost 700 points. In the meantime, stock markets worldwide had already fallen in response. Fortunately, stock markets at home and abroad started to recover within a few months.

Spreading Risks It's possible now to spread both banking and investment risks around the globe. Business conditions might be good in the United States but poor in another country, or vice versa. Banks and investors can spread their risks by lending and investing in a variety of countries. You could, for example, put some of your savings into a mutual fund that buys shares of stock or bonds in companies in different countries. In that way, you would be spreading your risk.

✓ Reading Check **Identifying** What is one problem with the worldwide stock market?

section 1 Review

Vocabulary
1. **Explain** the significance of: global integration, telecommunications.

Main Ideas
2. **Examining** In a diagram like the one below, list the transformations that satellite communication has brought to the world in recent years.

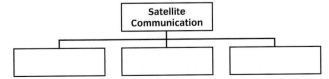

Critical Thinking
3. The **BIG Idea** What advantage has globalization brought to stock investors?
4. **Evaluating** Why is the U.S. stock market watched so closely?

Applying Economics
5. **Innovations** Make a list of the most important inventions you have seen come about in your lifetime. Then ask a grandparent or other older adult to tell you about important inventions they have seen in their lifetime. Compare the list and summarize the effect inventions have had in recent years.

ENTREPRENEUR
(1942–2007)

Anita Roddick

● **Founder of The Body Shop**

■ Recipient of many awards, including the 1993 National Audubon Society Medal and the 1999 British Environment and Media Award

■ In 2000 launched The Body Shop Human Rights Award, which sponsors grants to grassroots groups fighting for human rights

■ Involved in a campaign against the use of sweatshop labor by multinational corporations

On June 14, 2003, Anita Roddick was awarded the title of Dame Commander of the British Empire, an honor awarded to those who have provided valuable service to the United Kingdom. This was quite an achievement for the daughter of Italian immigrants. It was, in fact, just one of many honors and awards she has received over the years.

The source of Roddick's acclaim is The Body Shop, the cosmetic and toiletries company she founded in 1976 when she opened her first store in the seaside city of Brighton, England. Twenty-nine years later, The Body Shop was a global enterprise with 2,050 stores worldwide and sales of $1.2 billion.

The secret of Roddick's success has as much to do with operating in an ethical manner and with a dedication to environmentally sound practices as with her business skills. "The business of business," she wrote, "should not just be about money, it should be about responsibility. It should be about public good, not private greed." She opposed testing cosmetics on animals, refused to buy products manufactured by sweatshops, and insisted on using raw materials produced by sustainable methods. Apparently this approach appeals to her millions of customers.

"Today, it is impossible to separate the company values from the issues that I care passionately about—social responsibility, respect for human rights, the environment and animal protection. . . . "

Checking for Understanding

1. **Explaining** What type of people are The Body Shop customers likely to be? What issues might they care about?

2. **Analyzing** In what ways can operating in an ethically and environmentally sound manner help or hurt a business?

Direct Foreign Investment— Should We Be Worried?

GUIDE TO READING

Section Preview
In this section, you will learn about the advantages and drawbacks of foreign investment in the United States.

Content Vocabulary
- direct foreign investment (DFI) *(p. 524)*

Academic Vocabulary
- identical *(p. 524)*
- despite *(p. 526)*

Reading Strategy
Organizing As you read, complete a table like the one below by listing the fears that some Americans have about direct foreign investment, along with possible responses to these concerns.

Direct Foreign Investment

Fear	Response

ISSues In ThE NeWS
—from *BusinessWeek Online*

THE SHIFT IN OUTSOURCING These are anxious times for U.S. workers. Sure, the recovery seems to be getting under way. Yet hardly a week goes by without another report of a batch of high-paying, white-collar jobs getting exported to far cheaper locales such as India, China, or the Philippines. . . .

As white-collar jobs move away with increasing regularity, a debate that once focused on the loss of manufacturing to foreign outsourcing is once again raging: Just how serious for America, its workforce, and its economy is the shift? Two decades ago, the loss of auto jobs and other high-paying manufacturing jobs sparked fears of a hollowing-out of the U.S. economy. . . .

Now, the same process, many economists argue, is going on in services. . . . How worried should we be?

▲ U.S. production work is a common target of outsourcing.

Who owns whom? Nothing seems more American than Burger King or the Pillsbury Dough Boy, right? Not quite, for those companies are now owned by the British. In addition, the Japanese own about 20 percent of the office space in downtown Los Angeles, and a Thailand-based firm owns Chicken of the Sea tuna. Throughout the world, American companies have likewise purchased foreign firms. As you read this section, you'll learn that foreign investment has grown considerably in the past 20 years.

Foreign Investment, Then and Now

Main Idea Direct foreign investment in the United States has continued to grow as global integration of economic activity has progressed.

Economics & You Would you buy a foreign-made automobile? Why or why not? Read on to learn about some Americans' concerns about the role of foreign companies in the United States.

There is a long history of foreign investment in the United States. For example, Great Britain was the biggest foreign investor in American railroads in the late 1800s and early 1900s. At the beginning of World War I, the United States owed more to foreign lenders than any other country in the world.

direct foreign investment (DFI): the purchase by foreigners of real estate and businesses in another country

Direct Foreign Investment In the United States today, however, **direct foreign investment (DFI)**—the purchase of real estate and businesses by foreigners—has increased to the point where some Americans want to restrict it. In any single year, foreigners purchase billions of dollars of American real estate and businesses. Any time political upheaval strikes in another part of the world, foreign investment in the United States increases because we remain a politically stable country.

Foreign Control of American Companies Many people argue against foreign ownership of American companies because they worry about foreign control. Is foreign control important? Presumably, foreign investors purchase American assets in order to maximize profits. Foreigners' interests in running a corporation would seem to be **identical** to the interest of any domestic investor who owned the same corporation. The profit-making behavior of a corporation does not depend on the nationality of that corporation. If the British took over a hotel on Miami Beach, would the service necessarily be any different in the long run? Economists do not think so.

Visible Foreign Investment

Unlike Burger King or other companies that are not obviously owned by foreigners, some companies are clearly visible as being foreign-owned. Toyota is one of these.

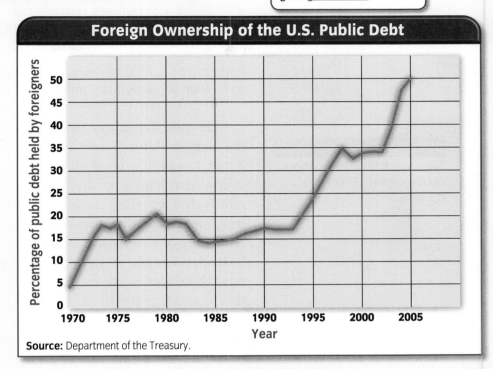

Figure 20.2 Foreign Ownership of Debt

Graphs In Motion
See StudentWorks™ Plus or go to glencoe.com.

■ Examine this graph carefully to see how foreign ownership of the public debt of the United States has changed over the past few decades.

Foreign Ownership of the U.S. Public Debt

Percentage of public debt held by foreigners

Year

Source: Department of the Treasury.

Economic Analysis

Analyzing *What has been the most recent trend in foreign ownership of debt? How do you explain this?*

What about the foreign investors' influence over the U.S. government? Foreigners own about 50 percent of all U.S. government securities that now exist. Can they use this to control American foreign policy? Probably not. Foreigners purchase U.S. government securities only when they think the rate of return is higher than they can get elsewhere.

In reality, the United States government has more control over foreigners. Because they own about 50 percent of the United States public debt, as you can see in **Figure 20.2,** foreign investors are subject to U.S. government policy. For example, the federal government, through its Federal Reserve System, could create tremendous inflation. In doing so, it would wipe out the real value of the United States government debt that foreigners own.

In a larger sense, foreign corporations may *indirectly* influence our government. Our government cannot make the business climate in America too difficult for these corporations or they will take their investments elsewhere. The positive side of this situation is that domestic corporations benefit from the hands-off approach of government toward foreign-owned businesses.

✔ **Reading Check** **Determining Cause and Effect** How is foreign investment in the United States affected by political upheaval in other nations? Why?

Investment Here and Abroad

Main Idea Consumers usually care more about the quality and price of a company's product than about the extent to which foreigners control that company.

Economics & You Have you ever traveled to another country? Read on to learn about how U.S. investments abroad influence other cultures.

Skills Handbook

See page *R38* to learn about *Distinguishing Fact from Opinion.*

Despite the concern some have about foreigners "owning" the United States, the total share of foreign ownership of American industries is about 10 percent. Although foreign investment here is readily visible, foreign investment is relatively low when compared to that of other nations. How much investing do American companies carry out abroad? The U.S. share of worldwide direct investment is more than 40 percent. Indeed, throughout the world many people fear that U.S. culture has taken over everyone else's culture. Some people have called this *economic imperialism.*

Most consumers, however, have little knowledge about who owns the companies that provide the goods or services they purchase—and they do not really care. Some even argue that we should *encourage* direct investment and debt purchases by foreigners. Foreigners then would have an increased incentive to want the American economy to remain strong and stable.

Reading Check **Explaining** What is economic imperialism?

---

section 2 Review

Vocabulary

1. **Explain** the significance of: direct foreign investment (DFI).

Main Ideas

2. **Determining Cause and Effect** In a diagram like the one below, list three effects of foreign investment in the U.S. and three effects of the U.S. investing elsewhere.

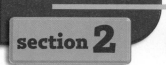

DFI into the U.S.   DFI by the U.S.

$$$$$ $$$$

_____   _____
_____   _____
_____   _____

Critical Thinking

3. **The BIG Idea** Why do Americans accept DFI from foreign countries?

4. **Synthesizing** What might encourage a foreign country to buy U.S. securities?

5. **Analyzing** What is the advantage to the U.S. when foreign countries buy our currency?

Applying Economics

6. **Foreign Investments** Use the Internet to find three foreign companies you might want to invest in. What country is the company in? What do they make or own? Why do you think the value of their stock might rise?

section 3 Multinationals and Economic Competition

GUIDE TO READING

Section Preview
In this section, you will learn why American firms do business in other countries and sometimes form alliances with foreign companies.

Content Vocabulary
- multinationals *(p. 528)*
- foreign affiliates *(p. 528)*

Academic Vocabulary
- manipulate *(p. 527)*
- appropriate *(p. 529)*
- ethnic *(p. 530)*

Reading Strategy
Listing As you read the section, complete a table similar to the one below by listing a definition and example of each type of international or cross-border business.

Type of Business	Definition	Example
Multinationals		
Alliances		

COMPANIES In ThE NeWS
—from *BusinessWeek Online*

WAL-MART HITS A WALL Global retail giant Wal-Mart is still bullish on India despite bearish signals from the Indian government.

. . . While the retail giant continues to explore market opportunities, government restrictions may keep it out.

. . . Wal-Mart

[is] feared by India's communist party as potentially putting mom-and-pop stores out of business by sheer virtue of its size. The retail behemoth rang up slightly more in retail sales for the year ending January, 2005, than the entire Asian subcontinent sold to its population of more than 1 billion, a quarter of whom live in poverty.

. . . The new India policy, while disallowing much foreign direct investment, does not prevent institutional investors from acquiring more than 51% of any Indian retail company.

Much international or cross-border investing is undertaken by firms that do business or have offices or factories in many countries. In the past, critics argued that because these firms are so large, they may come to dominate the world economy. Such firms were sometimes seen as ruthless companies that would exploit the poor and **manipulate** governments. In this section, you'll learn that these large firms usually set up operations on a regional basis, often forming alliances in the process.

The Size and Number of Multinationals

(Main Idea) **The top 100 multinational firms account for almost 50 percent of all cross-border assets.**

Economics & You Have you ever made a purchase from Wal-Mart, General Motors, or Microsoft? If so, then you were supporting a multinational company. Read on to learn how many of these multinationals exist today.

multinationals: firms that do business and have offices or factories in many countries

foreign affiliates: branches of multinational firms

Firms that do business and have offices or factories in many countries are known as **multinationals.** In the 1970s, many people predicted that a few hundred multinationals would control 80 percent of the world's production by the mid-1980s. By 2006, there were about 60,000 multinational corporations, with about 620,000 **foreign affiliates,** or branches of their firms. The foreign affiliates of the world's top nonfinancial companies accounted for about $2.9 trillion in assets.

Worldwide Ownership The top 100 multinationals are very important, accounting for almost 50 percent of all cross-border assets. This means nothing, however, without comparing these assets to the worldwide total. In 2006, the top 100 multinationals accounted for less than 20 percent of the world's productive assets—hardly an overwhelmingly dominant share. Today, the United States and Great Britain no longer dominate multinationals. Americans, Japanese, Germans, and the Swiss own only a little more than half of them. Numerous multinationals are based in the industrializing nations of Asia, such as China, Taiwan, South Korea, and Malaysia.

The Largest American Multinationals

Rank/Company	Revenue*	Net Income*	Assets*	Market Value*
1. Citigroup	120.32	24.64	1,494.04	230.93
2. General Electric	149.70	16.35	673.30	348.45
3. Bank of America	85.39	16.47	1,291.80	184.17
4. American International Group	106.98	11.90	843.40	172.24
5. ExxonMobil	328.21	36.13	208.34	362.53
6. JPMorgan Chase	79.90	8.48	1,198.94	144.13
7. Wal-Mart Stores	312.43	11.23	138.17	188.86
8. Chevron	184.92	14.10	124.81	126.80
9. Berkshire Hathaway	76.33	6.74	196.71	133.67
10. Procter & Gamble	61.68	7.79	136.52	197.12

Source: www.forbes.com

*All figures are in billions of dollars.
Rankings are based on a composite score for sales, profits, assets and market value.

Regional Cross-Border Investments

Although many of the biggest multinationals invest all over the world, most invest in regions that are closest to home. The European Union, for example, conducts more direct foreign investment in western Europe than anywhere else.

In a world in which borders matter less, the line separating sales at home and those abroad becomes less important. The most **appropriate** way to look at patterns of direct investment is to include direct domestic sales as a part of regional sales. European firms principally invest in western Europe. American firms principally invest in the United States, Canada, Mexico, and South America. Japanese firms principally invest in Japan, South Korea, China, and Southeast Asia.

Japan's Major Investment

Like most countries, Japan invests most heavily in itself. Downtown Tokyo shows evidence of how strongly Japanese companies dominate that nation's capital.

Beyond Multinationals—Alliances

In addition to multinational direct investments in other countries, firms in different countries are forming *alliances*. These may be joint ventures or licensing deals. Indeed, many foreign governments have insisted that multinationals enter their markets through joint ventures with local firms in the hope that locals will capture some of the profits.

Most alliances have been between firms from industrialized countries. Alliances are even popular within nations like the United States. International Business Machines (IBM), for example, developed its personal computer in alliance with Microsoft (for the software), Intel (for the central processing unit), and Lotus. In the late 1980s, IBM entered into an alliance with Siemens of Germany to work on memory chips. In the 1990s, IBM entered into an alliance with Apple Computer, once its archrival. (In late 2004, IBM sold its personal computer business to a Chinese company, Lenovo Group.)

Alliances can be seen as each firm's acceptance of its own limitations, whether they are financial, technological, or geographical. Alliances can be used to help a firm leapfrog its competitors or catch up to them. Such a strategy is particularly effective in industries that have seen rapid changes, such as software.

Economics ONLINE

Student Web Activity
Visit the *Economics Today and Tomorrow* Web site at glencoe.com and click on *Chapter 20—Student Web Activities* to see how one multinational corporation operates.

Reading Check **Summarizing** How has ownership of multinationals changed in the last three decades?

The Global Village and Tolerance

Main Idea Economic globalization has the potential to promote greater tolerance of diversity within society.

Economics & You Do you speak a foreign language, drive a foreign-made car, or have friends or classmates from ethnic, cultural, or racial backgrounds different from your own? Read on to learn why it is important to embrace diversity in today's globalized world.

One of the social results of the globalization of our world is increased immigration. America has become a truly multicultural society because of such immigration. In many cities the combined number of African Americans, Hispanics, Asians, and other minorities now constitutes a majority of the population.

In the 1980s, the Asian population in America increased more than 100 percent. In 2003, Hispanics became the largest minority group in the United States. With so many immigrants, public schools are more diverse. This diversity means that the need for tolerance and open-mindedness is more important today than it ever has been. For Americans, this includes learning one or more foreign languages and maintaining friendships with those of different **ethnic,** cultural, national, and/or religious backgrounds.

Globalization's Impact

Globalization has led to increased immigration into the United States and, as a result, more diverse public schools.

Globalization has also meant hiring firms from other countries to handle calls for customer service. For example, when you call with a computer problem, you may be connected with someone in India, Jamaica, or Scotland. In the same vein, many companies in Mexico send their financial information via the Internet to U.S. accounting firms for preparation of financial statements. Sometimes U.S. hospitals send digitized X-rays to physicians in India for quick diagnoses, especially during the middle of our night when it is daytime over there.

These continuing and increasing contacts with foreigners help U.S. residents understand that all global citizens have more in common than many people realize.

▲ Globalization has led to increased competition for jobs in some fields.

Reading Check **Identifying** What is the largest minority group in the United States today?

Skills Handbook

See page R58 to learn about Interpreting Political Cartoons.

section 3 Review

Vocabulary

1. **Explain** the significance of: multinationals, foreign affiliates.

Main Ideas

2. **Outlining** Copy the outline below, and list at least four pros and cons of multinationals.

Effects of Multinationals	
Pros	Cons
A.	A.
B.	B.
C.	C.
D.	D.

Critical Thinking

3. **The BIG Idea** Why might an economist support the formation of economic alliances between countries?

4. **Contrasting** What is the difference between a multinational and an affiliate?

Applying Economics

5. **Multinational Corporations** Use an Internet search engine to find five multinational corporations. Make a chart that shows where each company is based, where it has affiliates, and some of the products it produces.

FAR-FLUNG **WORKERS**

Geography is so twentieth century.

Check It Out! In this chapter you learned that globalization has increased dramatically over the past several decades. The following article proves that point.

When it comes to work, geography doesn't matter anymore. Even in smaller companies, a growing number of people now operate in teams spread across continents. They use standardized information technology platforms for laptop computers, e-mail addresses, mobile phones, and intranet access. Whether you're in Singapore or Sunnyvale, California, is irrelevant. With portable phone numbers and e-mail addresses, in fact, it can be tough to pinpoint where someone is on the planet. Meanwhile, two people on the same city block can be working in different time zones to serve a far-flung customer base. At 7 A.M.,

▲ The global economy continues to grow.

one could be ending the day while the other munches on cereal.

While the post-geographic world has made it possible for far-flung workers to collaborate like neighbors, there are challenges. Your Shanghai team members may be waking up just as the Chicago-based folks are going home—and London may need you online at 3 A.M. The result is a workday that could conceivably span 24 hours, if the limits of human biology didn't kick in. People must learn to work to the ebb and flow of their own schedule—and reach out in new ways. Though geography may have become less relevant, the need for community never goes away.

—Reprinted from *BusinessWeek*

Global Matters

If you do have to travel to another country, know your manners. One Web site offers this advice for doing business in Japan:

◆ Refrain from discussing business until after the first few minutes of any conversation.

◆ Avoid discussing World War II or making jokes.

◆ Wait to be invited before presuming to use first names.

◆ Gift-giving is an important part of Japanese protocol. Present your gifts with both hands.

◆ If you are invited to a Japanese home, bring flowers (an uneven number), cakes, or candy. Giving four or nine of anything is considered unlucky.

Think About It

1. **Identifying** What technologies make global teams possible?

2. **Defending** Do you believe global technologies make the ways in which people work more or less efficient? Why?

■ Developments in technology are strongly tied to the **growth of the global market**.

Improved Telecomunications

Global Integration

Globalization of Financial Markets

■ **Foreign investment** and **foreign ownership of U.S. debt** have grown significantly over the past few decades.

Source: Department of the Treasury.

■ **Multinationals** are firms that do business in many countries. Today, there are over 60,000 multinational corporations in the world.

Citigroup is the world's largest ▶ multinational corporation.

The Global Economy **533**

Review Content Vocabulary

1. *Write a paragraph or two explaining global integration. Use all of the following terms.*

   global integration   multinationals
   telecommunications   foreign affiliates
   direct foreign
   investment (DFI)

Review Academic Vocabulary

Choose the letter of the term that best completes each sentence.

   a. transform   e. despite
   b. transmit   f. manipulate
   c. recover   g. appropriate
   d. identical   h. ethnic

2. Global communication has the power to _____ traditional societies into more modern ones strongly influenced by Western cultures.

3. The profit-making motivation of foreign-owned companies is _____ to that of U.S.-owned companies.

4. The U.S. economy has continued to grow _____ concerns about direct foreign investment.

5. One result of globalization is that people have had to learn to be more tolerant of different cultural, _____, and religious backgrounds.

6. One can _____ messages around the world in an instant using satellite communications and the Internet.

7. Some are concerned that giant multinational companies might grow powerful enough to _____ governments into doing what they want.

8. Advising caution about foreign investment is _____, but it should not keep the United States from globalizing its economy.

9. When a stock market falls dramatically, it may take months or years for it to _____.

Review the Main Ideas

Section 1 (pp. 517–521)

10. Why has improved telecommunication led to increased global integration?

11. What happened elsewhere in the world economically when the U.S. stock market crashed in 1987?

12. Why is English a popular second language for many people around the world?

13. How did the terrorist attacks of September 11, 2001, affect the American economy?

Section 2 (pp. 523–526)

14. Why do foreigners purchase United States government securities?

15. In what ways do foreign corporations indirectly influence the U.S. government?

16. What is the United States's share of worldwide direct investment?

Section 3 (pp. 527–531)

17. People in what four countries own about half of the multinationals that exist today?

18. Why do firms in different countries form alliances with one another?

19. Fill in a graphic organizer like the one below to list some of the benefits of economic globalization for the United States.

Your Checking Account:
Check into independence

Are all banks alike? What if you bounce a check? Where do checks go?
Knowing the smart way to open and manage a checking account can help you avoid hassles—and save money.

How It Works

A checking account gives you a safer place to keep cash than a cookie jar while making it easy to pay bills and buy things.

Opening an Account To open an account, you need identification and usually a deposit (money you put into the account). Some banks offer student accounts requiring no initial deposit. The amount in your account at any given time is the balance. Putting money in or taking it out is a transaction.

To deposit a check, endorse (sign) it on the back. If you're depositing the entire check rather than keeping some cash, write "for deposit only" and your account number below your signature. When you open an account, you'll get a receipt for your deposit and, soon, numbered checks printed with your name, address, and account number; a check register; and a debit card. A debit card acts like an electronic check: money is taken out of your account immediately (a withdrawal or debit).

Making Withdrawals There are five ways to make withdrawals:
1. Write a paper check, or pay by check over the phone.
2. Get cash from a teller at a bank branch.
3. Use a debit card at a store or automated teller machine (ATM).
4. Use your bank's Web site to pay a bill.
5. Authorize the bank to automatically pay recurring bills.

Keeping Good Records Record all transactions in your check register. You'll get a monthly statement showing activity for the previous month. Compare it with your check register for errors and keep both in a file.

did you know? **Help!** *If your debit card is lost or stolen, your liability for an unauthorized withdrawal can vary. If you notify the financial institution within two business days after learning of the loss or theft, you're liable for only $50. If you don't report unauthorized use that appears on your statement within 60 days after its mailing date, you could lose all the money in your account.*

Financial Fitness: Money and Real Life

- **Can you afford a cool car?**
- **How can you avoid the credit trap?**
- **Is college for you?**
- **Can you become a millionaire?**

Only you can answer those questions—and thousands of others. Your life is ahead of you; it's up to you to decide how you'll live it. Whatever goals or dreams you may have, the way you live your life will be determined, at least in part, by your relationship to money: how you get it and how you use it.

The opportunities you create for yourself are greatly affected by the money habits you form when you're young. This handbook is designed to help you learn how to use money to meet your goals and to live the way you want to live. It can help you make intelligent decisions about money so you can get what you want and need—today and throughout your life.

Reference Section

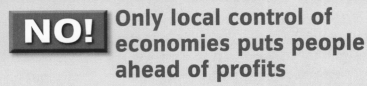

NO! Only local control of economies puts people ahead of profits

Globalization means control of world economies by giant corporations that don't have an allegiance to a community or to a particular country . . . as long as they can make more profit elsewhere. The essence of globalization is a subordination of human rights, labor rights, consumer rights, environmental rights, [and] democracy rights to . . . global trade and investment. . . . That is why, for example, globalization does not ban trade produced by child labor [or] by brutal working conditions.

Globalism is masqueraded by this phrase "free trade." And global trade and investment systems of governments . . . have nothing to do with free trade. This is *corporate-managed* trade. . . . The best way for an economy to prosper is from the ground up. It's from the community, the neighborhood, the farms, [and] the industry. Globalization is just the reverse.

—Ralph Nader, consumer advocate

The Big Picture

Number of school-age children working full time:	113 million
Number of people in the world living on less than $1 a day:	1.2 billion
Percentage of funds flowing into developing countries that come from private, foreign corporations:	80%
Number of manufacturing jobs moved out of the United States from 1994 to 2003:	2.5 million

Source: U.S. Agency for International Development; U.S. Bureau of Labor and Statistics

Debating the Issue

1. **Explaining** How does globalization help poor workers in developing countries? What are its disadvantages for these people?

2. **Choosing Sides** The two writers disagree about whether globalization helps everyone. Which writer do you agree with? Why?

Find Out More!

3. **Analyzing** After making jeans in America for 150 years, Levi Strauss closed its last U.S. factory in 2003 and moved its manufacturing plants overseas. Use the Internet to find other companies who have outsourced jobs. Then write a short essay explaining why you would or would not be willing to pay higher prices for goods if it meant saving American jobs.

Is Globalization Good for Everyone?

Whether you see globalization as an opportunity or a threat depends on who and where you are. Those in favor define globalization as the free flow of funds and products throughout the world—investment and marketing without borders. They believe it will lead to shared global values, political unity, reduced corruption, and increased wealth. Opponents say Western capitalists are forcing their economic system and consumer culture on other countries. They blame globalization for the loss of American jobs and the widening gap between the rich and the poor. Is globalization good for all?

YES! Globalization increases everyone's options

Under…"globalization"…our options and opportunities have multiplied. We don't have to shop at the big local company; we can turn to a foreign competitor. We don't have to work for the village's one and only employer; we can seek alternative opportunities. The world's culture is at our disposal. . . . Our ability to control our own lives is growing, and prosperity is growing with it.

Free markets and free trade and free choices transfer power to individuals at the expense of political institutions. . . . No company would import goods from abroad if we didn't buy them. If we did not send e-mails, order books, and download music every day, the Internet would wither and die. We eat bananas from Ecuador, order magazines from Britain, work for export companies selling to Germany and Russia, vacation in Thailand, and save money for retirement by investing in South America and Asia. These things are carried out by businesses only because we as individuals want them to.

—Johan Norberg, *The American Enterprise Online*

Thinking Like an Economist

20. Using a chart like the one below, make a list of reasons people give for why they are concerned about direct foreign investment in the United States or foreign ownership of U.S. debt. For each reason, present a counter-argument.

Reason for Concern About DFI	Counter-argument

Math Practice

21. Look back at the graph showing foreign ownership of the U.S. debt on page 525, and note what the percentage of ownership was in 2005. If that percentage decreased by 20%, what would the new percentage of ownership be?

Economics ONLINE

Self-Check Quiz Visit the *Economics Today and Tomorrow* Web site at glencoe.com and click on **Chapter 20—Self-Check Quizzes** to assess your knowledge of chapter content.

Critical Thinking

22. **The BIG Idea** Although cheap telecommunication is widespread in industrialized nations, it is not so widespread in developing nations. What will happen to global integration as developing nations catch up to the developed nations?

23. **Explaining** A foreign company buys an American company. Explain why that company might not necessarily be run any differently from other American companies.

24. **Evaluating** What are some possible advantages and disadvantages of multinationals and alliances?

Analyzing Visuals

25. Study the cartoon on the right, and then answer the following questions.

   a. What do the musicians represent?

   b. What does the word *synchronized* mean?

   c. What is about to happen to the musicians? What does this imply about the cartoonist's expectations for the global economy?

Which Bank, What Account?

Some banks offer better service or lower fees, or are conveniently located. Banks offer different types of accounts, some of which pay interest in exchange for having the use of your money. Before opening an account, savvy consumers ask if there's a minimum balance requirement, how many checks can be written per month, if there are fees for writing checks, and if the account will earn interest.

Choose a traditional bank that offers some services online or a bank that exists only on the Net. If you bank online, don't rely on the bank's system to protect you. Install a firewall and don't open suspicious e-mails or provide personal information to anyone who contacts you. Check your balance often to see if a thief has taken money from your account. You're liable for only the first $50 if you report it to the bank within two days. Find more tips at www.idtheftcenter.org.

Tip **Balancing Act** Be sure your balance is greater than the amount you withdraw. Otherwise, your check will bounce; that is, the recipient's bank will return it and you'll be charged a hefty fee by your bank—and usually theirs, too—for having an overdrawn account.

How to Write A Check

■ In this example, if you spelled out "Eleven fifty" instead of "Eleven hundred fifty," the bank would pay only $11.50—not $1,150.00. Be sure the numerals and longhand version are the same amount.

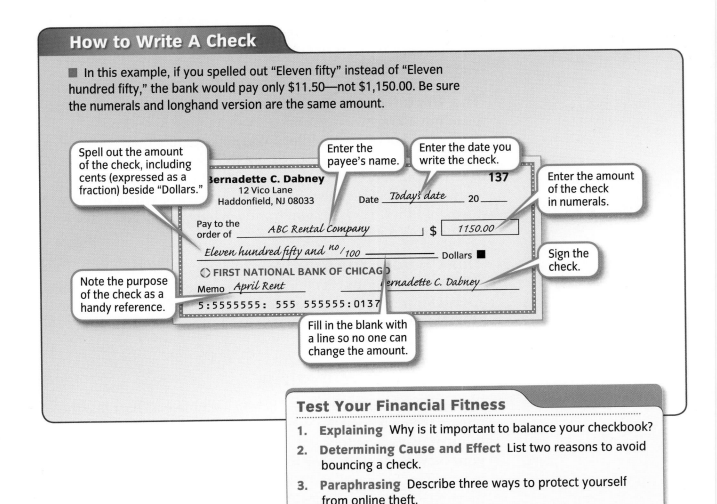

Spell out the amount of the check, including cents (expressed as a fraction) beside "Dollars."

Enter the payee's name.

Enter the date you write the check.

Enter the amount of the check in numerals.

Sign the check.

Note the purpose of the check as a handy reference.

Fill in the blank with a line so no one can change the amount.

Test Your Financial Fitness

1. **Explaining** Why is it important to balance your checkbook?

2. **Determining Cause and Effect** List two reasons to avoid bouncing a check.

3. **Paraphrasing** Describe three ways to protect yourself from online theft.

Budgeting:
Take control of your cash

Did you really need that cashmere sweater or those $200 sneakers? How did you get $5,000 in debt? Getting control of what you spend—budgeting—is a skill you'll need throughout your life.

Where Does Your Money Go?

Many people have no idea what happens to their money. It just seems to "disappear." Here's how to find out how where yours goes:

1. List the bills you pay every month.
2. For one month, jot down everything you buy and the price—no matter how little it costs.

At the end of the month, categorize the items you've listed: "Food," "Transportation," etc. Then break down each category; for example, "Food: School Lunches, Snacks, Restaurants." Now you know where your money goes.

The Urge to Splurge Advertising and peer pressure tempt us to buy things we don't need. Which of the items you categorized above were things you needed, like gym shoes or an ink cartridge? Which ones were things you just *wanted:* take-out pizza or that CD you played only once? Those are impulse purchases. They don't seem expensive when you buy them, but they can keep you from reaching larger goals like a vacation, a cool car, or college.

Think Before You Buy Before you buy an item, ask yourself whether the item is worth the time you'll have to work to pay for it. The better you get at saying "no" to unnecessary spending, the more money you'll have for what's important to you.

Creative Budgeting

Using the expenses you listed before, complete a chart like the one on the next page. Look at each expense in column 2 and think of ways to reduce it. Enter the lesser amount in column 3, your New Budget. Be sure to budget 10 to 30 percent of your income for "Savings." (To see why, go to Saving and Investing on page R6.) Total column 3 to see if your budget matches your income. If not, you'll need to keep trimming expenses until it does or find another source of income.

Building Your Budget

Part-time Job: $_____
Monthly allowance: $_____
Total income: $_____

Spending Category	Current Expenses	New Budget
Food: School lunches Restaurants & take-out Snacks		
Transportation: Car payment Insurance Gasoline Maintenance (estimate)		
Entertainment: Movies Music Games Sports and hobbies		
Personal care: Clothes Shoes Haircuts Accessories Cosmetics		
Savings (10–30% of income)		
Utilities: Phone Internet access		
Medical/dental		
Donations to charity		
Miscellaneous		
TOTAL		

did you know?

Autonomy According to the American Psychological Association, neither popularity, influence, money, nor luxury contributes the most to happiness. What does? Autonomy (feeling that your activities are self-chosen), feeling that you're effective in your activities, a sense of closeness with others, and self-esteem.

Advertising executive Gary Dahl became a millionaire by convincing people to pay $3.95 each for "Pet Rocks" in 1975. The product was simply a beach stone that cost him a penny, packaged in a box with a "Care and Training of a Pet Rock" manual.

Test Your Financial Fitness

1. **Listing** List five ways you can start saving money. How much could you save in a year by cutting these costs?
2. **Defining** What is an impulse purchase? What was the last one you made?
3. **Explaining** Why is it important to live on a budget?
4. **Applying** Make a list of three ways you can re-use things you usually throw away.

Saving and Investing:
Make your money grow

....

Want a faster computer or a great car? How about retiring at 40? You don't have to be old or rich to save and invest. People with ordinary jobs and moderate incomes can build wealth—and financial freedom—just by starting young.

....

In recent years, the average American family has earned about $40,000 per year but saved 0 percent of its income. The Chinese earn on average $1,500 per year—but save **23 percent** of their incomes. The worldwide average is about 20 percent.

Saving: The Frugal Habit

Frugality is the attempt to save money instead of spending it. Why save? Because saved money *grows*. Here's why it's worth it:

1. Savings are your only safety net in financial emergencies.
2. With an early start, you can amass huge amounts of money over time.
3. Having a savings account improves your credit rating (see **Credit and You** on page R10).

The Secret of Compounding Why save now? Because of a simple but very important concept: compounding. It's the process of interest earning interest. And it takes time to kick in. If a family saves $75 a month at 5 percent interest from the day a child is born, they'll have more than $24,000 by the time she's ready for college. More than $9,000 of it is interest—money their money earned. If they wait until the child is seven to start, they'll have to save almost $137 a month to get the same result. Two key concepts make compounding work: yield and time.

Yield: Different types of accounts offer different annual percentage rates (APR). That's the rate you'll get if the interest is compounded only once a year.

EXAMPLE: You deposit $10,000 in an account with an APR of 5 percent. At the end of the year, your money has earned $500 ($10,000 × 5% × one year = $500). So you have $10,500.

Interest for some accounts is compounded more often: semi-annually, quarterly, monthly, daily, or even continuously. The more frequently it's compounded, the more interest you get. That's because interest is added to your deposit periodically and the *entire amount* earns, or yields, interest—the annual percentage yield (or APY).

EXAMPLE: You deposit the same $10,000 at 5% APR, but interest is compounded *twice* a year. After six months, your money has earned half the annual interest ($10,000 x 5% x ½ year = $250). The bank adds that interest to your original deposit. Now the $250 also earns interest for six months. The APY is 5.0625%. So at the end of the year, you have $10,506.25 instead of $10,500. That may seem like a small change, but it can make a big difference as your balance grows over the years.

Time: The longer you leave your money in an account, the better compounding works—especially in an account with frequent compounding. If you left $10,000 in an account for *10 years*, with interest compounded *quarterly*, you'd have almost $16,500—without ever adding another cent!

Ways to Save Your goals should determine which savings methods you choose. A savings account is ideal for "emergency funds," since you have fast access to cash. But it also pays low interest, so you'll want to find other ways—including investments—to get enough interest to offset the taxes you'll pay on the interest, plus inflation.

Who Is Rich? Looking rich and being rich are not the same. Most millionaires drive used cars, live in modest houses, and don't wear expensive clothes. They save at least 15% of their earned income, and four out of five of them did not inherit their money.

SAVINGS VEHICLES AND RISKS

Savings account: Safe (FDIC-insured). Some student accounts offer no deposit requirement. Easy access to funds makes them good for emergencies, but interest is low.

Money market deposit account: Safe (FDIC-insured), with easy but infrequent withdrawals. These accounts pay slightly higher interest than savings accounts, with various deposit requirements.

Money market mutual fund: Relatively low risk because invested in a pool in short-term vehicles such as certificates of deposit and commercial paper. Terms are from 90 days to 13 months. Interest is comparable to money market deposit accounts.

Certificate of deposit (CD): FDIC-insured time deposit with slightly higher interest than savings accounts and opening requirements as low as $250. Terms are from 3 months to 5 years with varying interest and low penalties for early withdrawal.

U.S. savings bond: Safe (government-backed) and available for as little as $25. Terms vary, but after a waiting period bonds can be redeemed before maturity. Not taxed until redeemed. Most types offer interest higher than savings accounts.

Common Investments		
Type of investment	**Advantages**	**Disadvantages**
Stocks	High earnings potential	High risk Need broker to buy and sell
Stock mutual funds	Some risk, but less than buying stocks individually Professional investment manager	Need fund company or broker to buy and sell Minimum investment usually $1,000 or more
Bonds	Good earnings potential **Federal:** no default risk (see **Ways to Save** on page R7) **Municipal:** low risk, no federal tax **Corporate:** moderate risk	Federal tax on federal and corporate bond interest
Bond mutual funds	Professional investment manager Less risk than individual bonds	Need broker to buy and sell

Investing: Not Just for the Rich

About 19 percent of students in grades 8–12 own stocks or bonds. If you think you don't have enough money to invest now, remember the compounding principle: time is on your side. Even the spare change you keep in a jar every week, invested consistently and well, can reap big rewards in time. Investment advice can be confusing and, let's face it, boring. A good way to learn is to join—or start—an investment club. Get information at www.better-investing.org/youth/youth.html.

All investments involve two unknowns: the possibility of making money (the return), and the risk of losing it. In choosing investments, you're always balancing those two realities. Common investments include the following:

Stocks A stock is a share of a company's assets. Say you want to start a company that sells jewelry but can't afford to buy the beads. So you ask three friends for money. Now each of you owns one fourth of the company—one share. When you sell the jewelry, you each get a fourth of the profits. If it doesn't sell, you all lose money. That's the stock market, simplified.

Most investment professionals consider stocks the best way to get a fairly dependable, high return—but only if you keep them for more than ten years. Individual stocks and the stock market itself shoot up and down like a roller coaster. But over the last 50 years, the average return for stocks has been 10 percent—higher than savings vehicles and most other types of investments. Patience is the key to success.

You can buy stocks online, through a stockbroker or mutual fund company, or directly from companies that offer "Drip" (direct reinvestment) funds in which earnings are automatically reinvested in more of their stock.

The stock market crash of 1929 ushered in the Great Depression, which plunged one-third of Americans into poverty. By 1933, the market had lost 80% of its precrash value, and the unemployment rate had reached about 25%.

To reduce your risk, you can buy stocks through a mutual fund, a pool of money from many people invested in a variety of stocks or bonds by an investment manager.

There are two ways to make money with stocks. You can sell them when their value is high; the profit is called a capital gain and is taxed as income. Or you can keep them and receive regular payments (dividends), if the company pays dividends.

Bonds Governments (federal, state, and local) and corporations sell bonds to raise funds for projects like schools, bridges, or business expansion. They're borrowing your money. In return, you generally get periodic interest and a fixed amount of money at a specified time in the future (maturity date). Some types of federal bonds offer different payment plans. Maturity dates vary. Most bonds are considered less risky than stocks, and government bonds are less risky than corporate bonds, since companies sometimes lose money.

U.S. Treasury Instruments Treasury instruments are loans you make to the government. They include T-bills, T-notes, T-bonds, Treasury Inflation-Protected Securities (TIPS), and several series of savings bonds. (See the **Savings Vehicles** table on page R8). They offer various interest rates and maturity dates. Because they're issued by the government, treasury instruments offer low risk. They can be bought directly from the government online, or through banks or brokers. Minimum investments for most are $1,000–$10,000; some savings bond minimums are much lower.

Other Investments A home may be the largest investment you'll make. Real estate is considered a good investment because most properties increase in value—but *not all.* Other types of investments include precious metals (like gold and silver) and retirement plans.

Early Investing A 16-year-old who invests $2,000 a year at 10 percent APR will have more than $2 million at age 65. By waiting until you're 26 to begin, you'd have less than $803,000.

Test Your Financial Fitness

1. **Explaining** Look at the budget you prepared on page R5, and see if you can increase the amount you're saving. If so, what type of savings vehicle or investment will you use, and why?

2. **Defining** What is the difference between APR and APY?

3. **Summarizing** How can you make buying stocks less risky?

4. **Applying** In the library or on the Internet, research an investment you think you'd like to make. Write down your reasons.

Credit and You:
Use it, don't abuse it

How can you buy a hot new car if you don't have $25,000? Can you avoid the credit card trap? Whenever you buy something but don't have the cash, you're using credit. Mastering the wise use of credit gives you a head start on financial fitness.

Are You Creditworthy?

"Credit" means borrowing someone else's money. In exchange for the loan, you'll have to pay back more than you borrow. That's called interest. It's a percentage of the borrowed amount.

Who Decides? Lenders decide whether to lend you money and how much interest to charge by looking at three things:

1. **Can you pay them back?** Add your monthly income to your bank account balances to find your total assets. Then total your monthly expenses, including debts (obligations). Compare the two to see if you're able to take on more debt.

YOUR CAPACITY TO REPAY DEBT

Monthly income
+ Checking account
+ Savings account
= **Your assets**

Compared to

Monthly expenses
+ Total debt
= **Your obligations**

2. **Do you have a good credit rating?** Lenders want to know if you've repaid previous debts on time.
3. **Do you have collateral?** Collateral is used mostly to buy homes or cars. If you don't make the payments, the lender takes the property.

Your Credit Score Like your shadow, your credit score, or credit rating, follows you throughout your life. It's a number from 300 to 900 that shows how responsible you've been with your finances—recently and in the past. The higher your score is, the more likely you are to get credit and a low interest rate.

Credit scores are assigned by three credit bureaus— Equifax, Experion, and TransUnion—that track each person's financial history and create credit reports. Check yours at least once a year to be sure it contains no incorrect information.

Check Your Credit You can get one free report per year from each credit bureau. Call 877-322-8228; write to Annual Credit Report Request Service, P.O. Box 105281, Atlanta, GA 30348-5281; or go to www.annualcreditreport.com.

How Do You Score?

■ Paying on time raises your credit score; paying late lowers it. Here's how:

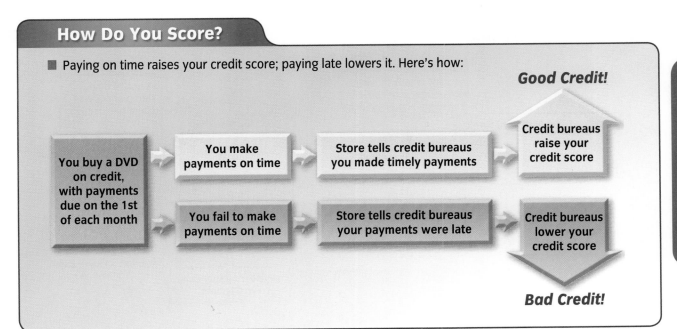

Good Credit!

You buy a DVD on credit, with payments due on the 1st of each month → You make payments on time → Store tells credit bureaus you made timely payments → Credit bureaus raise your credit score

You buy a DVD on credit, with payments due on the 1st of each month → You fail to make payments on time → Store tells credit bureaus your payments were late → Credit bureaus lower your credit score

Bad Credit!

Credit Cards

When you use a credit card, you're *borrowing* money that must be paid back—*plus interest*. Card issuers set a limit on the total amount you can spend. Smart borrowers avoid reaching that limit because it lowers their credit score.

Once you've established credit, you'll get offers for many cards. To avoid the temptation to rack up debt, keep no more than two or three. Choose those with the lowest annual percentage rates (APR)—not just low introductory rates that bounce up later. Be sure to read the fine print on the contracts—all of it.

did you know? *Endless Payments It will take you almost 22 years to pay off a $1,000 charge on an average credit card if you pay only a 2 percent minimum payment. The $1,000 purchase will wind up costing you $3,000— $2,000 of it in interest!*

The Price vs. the Real Cost The longer it takes you to pay off your credit card balance (the total amount you owe), the more the items you bought with the card actually cost. That's because card issuers make their profits by charging interest— from 1 to 25 percent or more—*on the amount still owed.*

EXAMPLE: If you pay cash for a pair of $100 sneakers, they cost $100. If you use a credit card at an interest rate of 18.9% and take a year to pay it off, they cost $118.90 or more, depending on how the interest is calculated.

The Credit Card Trap Every month, you'll get a statement listing everything you bought in the previous month, payments you made, and the balance. You are usually allowed to pay less than the total balance as long as you make at least the "minimum payment due" listed on the statement. This is how many people fall into the credit trap: they make only the minimum payment, racking up more debt month after month.

Sample Credit Card Statement

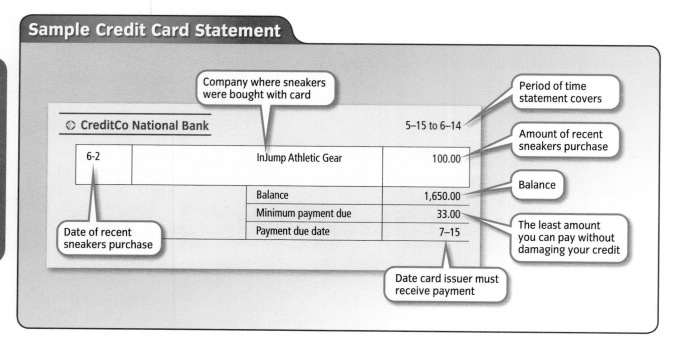

Company where sneakers were bought with card

Period of time statement covers

Amount of recent sneakers purchase

Balance

The least amount you can pay without damaging your credit

Date of recent sneakers purchase

Date card issuer must receive payment

○ CreditCo National Bank		5–15 to 6–14
6-2	InJump Athletic Gear	100.00
	Balance	1,650.00
	Minimum payment due	33.00
	Payment due date	7–15

Other Sources of Credit

There are a number of ways to borrow money besides credit cards. These include relatives and friends, as well as retail stores and financial institutions, such as banks, credit unions, and savings and loan associations.

Retail Stores Most department stores and other retailers let customers with good credit buy merchandise from their stores with one of three types of credit:

- *Installment sales credit:* Major items like refrigerators are often bought by making equal payments, which include interest and service charges, over a set period of time.
- *Regular charge accounts:* You can buy goods or services within a set dollar limit by agreeing to pay off the balance in the future. Interest is charged only if the balance is not paid in 30 days.
- *Revolving credit:* You usually make no deposit but can buy items on credit on an ongoing basis, up to a certain dollar limit. If you repay the balance by a certain date, some stores charge no interest; most charge interest on each month's unpaid balance. Credit cards are also a type of revolving, or open-ended, credit.

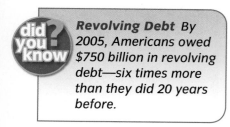

Revolving Debt *By 2005, Americans owed $750 billion in revolving debt—six times more than they did 20 years before.*

Service providers Your agreements with providers of services (electricity, cell phone, Internet, etc.) are credit arrangements. The history of your payments to them often appears on credit reports—especially if you pay late.

Financial Institutions Commercial banks, savings banks, credit unions, finance companies, and some insurance companies lend money, with varying interest rates and fees. Shop and compare costs before borrowing. Some loans require a single, lump-sum payment on a specific date; others accept monthly payments for either a set or indefinite period of time.

Comparing Costs

As with credit cards, the length of time it takes you to repay the balance of a loan from other creditors affects the total amount you pay. You can see in the table below that when you take longer to pay off a loan, you pay less each month, but your total cost is higher. That is because interest gets compounded over a longer period of time.

COSTS OF 3- AND 5-YEAR INSTALLMENT LOANS $10,000 loan at 12% interest compounded annnually		
	3-year loan	**5-year loan**
Number of monthly payments	36	60
Amount of each payment	$347	$231
Total interest paid	**$2492**	**$3770**

The annual percentage rate (APR) of the loan also affects the total amount you pay. Be sure to check it before signing any loan agreement.

APR COMPARISON 5-year Loan of $8,000		
	Lender A	**Lender B**
APR	11%	13%
Monthly payment	$174	$180
Total interest to be paid	$2,436	$2,921
Total cost	**$10,436**	**$10,921**

HOW TO ESTABLISH CREDIT

Paying cash for everything does not make you a good credit risk. To prove you're responsible enough to get credit, you have to establish a credit history.

About 15% of a credit score is based on *how long you've had credit.* So it's important to establish credit as soon as possible.

1. Apply for a "secured credit card" at a bank. You'll have to make a deposit—usually about $300—and you'll get a credit card you can use to make purchases up to the amount you deposited. Buy something each month with the card and be sure to make monthly payments on time. After about a year, if you've paid off the balance, you can get your deposit back and switch your secured credit card to an unsecured one.

2. Open an account at a major retail store. (They will probably ask for your current bank credit card number and expiration date.) Buy something on credit and make the payments on time.

3. Have someone with good credit co-sign a credit application. A co-signer agrees to pay your debt if you don't.

▲ Shredding old financial documents helps guard against identity theft.

Identity Theft

Criminals could steal your name, social security number, date of birth, and other private information—and use it to run up debts in your name: credit cards, wireless phone accounts, or loans. Here are some tips to help protect your identity; find more at www.idtheftcenter.org.

* Be careful who sees your personal information. Never provide it on the Internet or by phone to anyone who contacts *you*. Banks don't request private information by e-mail.
* Thieves sort through people's trash and mailboxes. Shred statements that include account numbers and any unused offers of credit cards you receive in the mail.
* Always know where your cards are. When you buy something with a card, watch to see that it's not copied and get it back as quickly as possible.
* Check your credit report periodically for accuracy.
* Report lost or stolen credit cards immediately to the fraud department of a credit bureau. You're liable for only the first $50 after your report.
* Do business only with companies that will provide their name, street address, and phone number.
* Don't use the links in an e-mail to get to any Web page. Type the Web address in your browser window. A secure site begins with "https://" rather than "http://".

CREDIT BASICS

Annual percentage rate (APR): The percentage of interest you are charged for every year you owe money. A fixed APR will stay the same; a variable APR will rise and fall with changes in national economic indicators.

Compounding: The process of charging interest on the amount of interest still owed. This interest is added to the stated interest rate because it's money you owe but have not yet paid.

EXAMPLE: If the stated APR on a $10,000 loan is 10%, you'd expect to pay $1,000 in interest per year (10% of $10,000). But since lenders compound interest, you may pay an extra $47 on the same $10,000 loan—for a total interest of $1,047. Some lenders compound interest more often—even daily. The more often interest is compounded, the more you will owe.

Delinquent payment: A payment that is 30 days or more past due. This is not the same as a late payment, which is one received after the due date but before it's 30 days past due. If a car payment due on the first of the month is received on the 20th, for example, it's late and you'll pay a late charge. But it's not delinquent and won't appear on your credit report.

Grace period: A period of time after you buy something on credit during which some creditors charge no interest if you pay the balance before the due date.

Finance charge: The total cost of credit. In addition to interest, some companies charge fees for annual membership, cash advances, services, transactions, and exceeding the credit limit.

Introductory rate: A lower rate of interest offered by some credit card companies to persuade consumers to apply for their card. After an initial period, the APR you're charged increases. It's important to read the fine print on the offer to find out when the APR increases and whether the low rate applies only to balances you transfer from another credit card, to new purchases, or to both. You also need to know how long you have to transfer balances; some cards feature a fixed APR on balance transfers for the life of the card; others for only 45 days to six months.

A Big Difference *Your credit score makes a big difference in the interest rates lenders charge. For example, a person with a credit score of 720 or above applying for a 3-year loan to buy an $18,000 car may pay 7.258% interest. The same dealer might charge a person with a credit score between 500 and 559 a rate of 15.294% for the same loan. At the end of the 3 years, the first applicant would have paid $2,085 in interest; the applicant with the low credit score would have paid $4,557.*

Test Your Financial Fitness

1. **Summarizing** Why is a good credit score important?
2. **Identifying** What are two ways to establish good credit?
3. **Listing** List two ways to avoid paying interest when you buy something.
4. **Applying** Analyze three credit card offers your family has received in the mail or that you have seen advertised. Which one offers the best deal? Why?

Your Education:
Jump-start your future

Is college for you? Which one? How can you pay for it? Whether you plan to attend college or enroll in vocational training after high school, don't let rising costs keep you from realizing your dreams.

Why Go to College?

A college education enriches a life in ways that can't be measured in dollars. But there's a practical reason to continue your education beyond high school, too: what you learn usually determines what you earn. Compared to workers with only high-school educations, those with bachelor's degrees have greater lifelong earning power and are less likely to be unemployed.

College-degreed workers earn an average of 62 percent more than those with high-school educations—roughly $2 million more overall during their working years.

Unemployment and Earnings			
Full-Time Workers Age 25 and Over by Educational Level			
Education Level	Unemployment Rate	Median Annual Earnings	
		Males	Females
No high school diploma	8.8%	$19,802	$10,613
High school diploma/GED	5.5%	$27,526	$15,972
Bachelor's degree (4 years)	3.3%	$55,188	$34,292
Source: *Statistical Abstract of the United States,* 2006.			

Choosing the Right School

Some schools are better at certain fields of study than others. Costs, too, vary widely from school to school. Consider these factors when choosing a college or vocational school:

How Much Is It? *A bachelor's degree can cost between $48,000 and $116,000, depending on the school. That's for tuition, fees, room, and board—but not transportation or living expenses.*

- *Your goals:* Can you get the educational experience you want at a public school? If not, don't rule out a private school because of cost; some are generous with financial aid. Another option is to start out at an inexpensive community college and transfer to a four-year school.
- *Income potential:* If you choose a career with high income potential—like medicine or computer engineering—you can afford to take on a higher debt at an expensive school.
- *Location:* Out-of-state students pay a surcharge—usually thousands of dollars a year—to attend public universities. Costs also vary in different parts of the country.

Comparative Costs and Financial Aid

4-Year Public and Private Colleges, Academic Year 2005–2006				
Type of Institution	Cost and tuition and fees	Total cost	Percentage of students qualifying for financial aid	Average aid amount (loans and grants)
Four-year private	$21,235	$29,026	76%	$11,600
Four-year public	$5,491	$12,127*	62%	$6,200
*Average annual costs at two-year public community colleges are about half those of four-year public colleges.				

Financial Aid Basics

Tuition is the amount a school charges for instruction. This does not include room, food, books, or other fees. In recent years, the cost of college tuition has risen faster than incomes or inflation. Few parents can afford the full cost of educating their children, and so most students need financial aid. The good news is that most students qualify for some type of financial aid. It takes research to find it, so the sooner you start looking, the better. How much aid you receive depends on these criteria:

- income—yours and your parents' or guardians'
- family assets and expenses
- number of college students in your family
- amount of aid available at the school
- number of students applying for aid and their financial need compared with yours

THE COST OF EDUCATION
Total Cost (tuition, board, books, fees, living expenses)
− **Total Aid**   (loans, scholarships, grants, work-study)
= **What you owe**

Types of Aid Available Apply for all types of financial aid for which you may be qualified, including:

Scholarships and grants: Both are outright gifts you don't have to pay back. Most scholarships are based on academic, athletic, or artistic ability. Many companies offer them to employees' children, and some states provide them to residents; for example, Georgia guarantees free tuition to drug-free students with at least a B average.

 Advanced Credit

You can lower college costs by taking advanced placement courses in high school and by scoring high on the College-Level Examination Program (CLEP) test. You'll get college credits for what you already know.

Some grants, such as federal Pell grants and Supplemental Educational Opportunity grants, are awarded for "exceptional financial need." Others are given to students belonging to a certain ethnic group, club, or civic organization. The armed forces offer aid in return for military service after graduation.

Work-study programs: Many colleges offer federally funded, on-campus jobs to students receiving financial aid.

Loans: More than half of all financial aid is in the form of loans—which *must* be repaid. Regardless of your income, you probably qualify for one of these loans:

- *Government loans:* The U.S. Department of Education (DOE) offers low-interest loans to students and parents. Some are subsidized (the government pays the interest until you're out of school) and are based on need; others are unsubsidized (interest accrues while you're in school) and are not need based. In order of desirability, they are
  - subsidized Perkins Loan
  - subsidized Stafford or Direct Loan
  - unsubsidized Stafford or Direct Loan
  - unsubsidized Parent Loans for Undergraduate Students (PLUS)
- *Private and college-sponsored loans:* Private loans are available from banks and other financial institutions. Interest rates are generally higher than those of federal loans.

Tip: Maximizing Aid

You'll be expected to contribute about one-third of your savings toward tuition, so if you have credit card debt, use your savings to pay down as much of it as possible before applying for financial aid.

Aid Application 1-2-3 Once you've been accepted at several schools, follow this loan application process:

1. *Gather up documents.* You'll need proof of income, such as tax returns, W-2 forms, pay stubs; mortgage statements; and proof of any unusual financial hardships in the family, such as high medical expenses or unemployment.

2. *Find aid sources.* Use the Internet to find grants and scholarships, then loans. Be sure to check deadlines.

3. *Fill out and send in applications.* The first form to complete is the Free Application for Federal Student Aid (FAFSA), available from your high school, library, or DOE's Web site. It's needed for any type of government aid. DOE will send you a number called an *Expected Family Contribution* (EFC), which is an amount computed according to a formula established by law. Colleges use it to determine the amounts of grants, loans, and work-study awards.

2006-2007
FAFSA ON THE WEB WORKSHEET
WWW.FAFSA.ED.GOV

FEDERAL STUDENT AID

DO NOT MAIL THIS WORKSHEET.

You must complete and submit a
(FAFSA) to apply for federal student financial aid and to apply for most state and college aid. Applying online with   at www.fafsa.ed.gov is faster and easier than using a paper FAFSA.

For state or college aid, the deadline may be as early as January 2006. See the table to the right for state deadlines. Check with your high school counselor or your college's financial aid administrator about other deadlines.

- Complete this Worksheet only if you plan to use *FAFSA on the Web* to apply for student financial aid.
- Sections in purple require parent information.
- **Submit your FAFSA early, but not before January 1, 2006.**

Apply Faster—Sign your FAFSA with a U.S. Department of Education PIN. If you do not have a PIN, you can apply for one at www.pin.ed.gov before beginning   . You will receive your PIN within a few days, and then you can electronically sign your FAFSA when you submit your information. If you are providing parent information, one parent must sign your FAFSA. To sign electronically, your parent can also apply for a PIN at www.pin.ed.gov.

You will need the following information to complete this Worksheet:

- Your Social Security Number and your parents' Social Security Numbers if you are providing parent information;
- Your driver's license number if you have one;
- Your Alien Registration Number if you are not a U.S. citizen;
- 2005 federal tax information or tax returns (including IRS W-2 information) for yourself and spouse if you are married, and for your parents if you are providing parent information. If you have not yet filed a 2005 income tax return, you can still submit your FAFSA but you must provide income and tax information.
- Records of untaxed income, such as Social Security benefits, welfare benefits (e.g., TANF), and veterans benefits, for yourself, and your parents if you are providing parent information; and
- Information on savings, investments, and business and farm assets for yourself, and your parents if you are providing parent information.

WARNING!
Be wary of organizations that charge a fee to submit your application or to find you money for school. In general, the help you pay for can be obtained for free from your school or from the U.S. Department of Education.

NOTE:
If you or your family has unusual circumstances (such as loss of employment), complete FAFSA on the Web to the extent you can, then submit the application and consult the financial aid office at the college you plan to attend.

STATE AID DEADLINES

AK	April 15, 2006
AR	For Academic Challenge - June 1, 2006 . For Workforce Grant - check with your financial aid administrator
AZ	June 30, 2007
* CA	For initial awards - March 2, 2006 For additional community college awards - September 2, 2006
# DC	June 30, 2006
DE	April 15, 2006
FL	May 15, 2006
IA	July 1, 2006
# IL	First-time applicants - September 30, 2006 Continuing applicants - August 15, 2006
IN	March 10, 2006
# *KS	April 1, 2006
# KY	March 15, 2006
# LA	May 1, 2006 Final deadline - July 1, 2006
# MA	May 1, 2006
MD	March 1, 2006
ME	May 1, 2006
MI	March 1, 2006
MN	30 days after term starts
MO	April 1, 2006
# MT	March 1, 2006
NC	March 15, 2006
ND	March 15, 2006
NH	May 1, 2006
NJ	June 1, 2006, if you received a Tuition Aid Grant in 2005-2006 All other applicants - October 1, 2006, for fall and spring terms; March 1, 2007, for spring term only
* NY	May 1, 2007
OH	October 1, 2006
# OK	April 15, 2006
# OR	March 1, 2006 . Final deadline - contact your financial aid administrator
* PA	All 2005-2006 State Grant recipients & all non-2005-2006 State Grant recipients in degree programs - May 1, 2006 All other applicants - August 1, 2006
# RI	March 1, 2006
SC	June 30, 2006
TN	For State Grant - May 1, 2006 For State Lottery–September 1, 2006
* WV	March 1, 2006

For priority consideration, submit application by date specified.
* Additional form may be required.

Check with the school's financial aid administrator for these states and territories: AL, *AS, CO, *CT, *FM, GA, *GU, *HI, ID, *MH, *MP, MS, *NE, *NM, *NV, PR, *PW, *SD, *TX, UT, *VA, *VI, *VT, WA, WI, and *WY

WWW.FAFSA.ED.GOV

2006-2007 FAFSA ON THE WEB WORKSHEET PAGE 1

Payback You don't begin repaying some government loans until after you're out of school. Other loans, such as PLUS loans, require you to begin making payments within 60 days after you receive the funds. Since unsubsidized loans accrue (accumulate) interest while you're still in school, you'll want to pay those off first. For some loans, you can repay just the interest for a period of time or start with smaller payments that increase as your income presumably increases. Some lenders even tie payment amounts to rises and drops in your income level.

Graduates who take teaching jobs in certain schools; who volunteer with the Peace Corps, Americorps, or VISTA; or who serve in the military may have their federal loans deferred, partially repaid, or even canceled.

It's important to repay your loan on schedule to avoid penalties and damage to your credit, as well as to reduce the amount of interest you pay. Some lenders lower the principal or the interest rate if you make on-time payments. Your lender or the school's financial aid office can help you establish a workable repayment plan.

> **did you know?**
>
> **Payback** *The average student graduates from a 4-year college with a debt of almost $19,000. About 60 percent of all students receive grants—averaging $3,300 at public, four-year schools in 2004–2005.*

Test Your Financial Fitness

1. **Stating** How much more money will the average college graduate earn per year than someone with only a high school diploma?

2. **Listing** List four things that are important to you in choosing a college or vocational school. Using the Internet or library resources, find three schools that meet your criteria.

3. **Applying** Choose one of the schools you identified above and calculate how much it would cost to attend that school for one year. Then find two types of financial aid for which you might qualify.

Getting a Job:
Make it work for you

Where are the jobs? What are your skills? Do you need a resume? Whether you're searching for a summer job or planning to enter the labor market right after high school, looking for work is hard work. Knowing where to look and how to present yourself can help you land a better job.

Eighty percent of jobs are never advertised in newspapers or online. Three-fourths of all employees find their jobs through networking.

Tip — Be the Boss

For ideas and advice for teen entrepreneurs (people who own their own businesses), check out the Web sites of the Small Business Administration (www.sba.org) and Junior Achievement (www.ja.org).

The Right Job

Besides earning money and learning good work habits, use your first few jobs to find out what tasks you like to do—and what you don't. Take the time to explore what interests you.

One good method is the "informational interview." Many businesspeople who may not have current job openings are willing to chat briefly with young job seekers. Call and ask if they have a few minutes to give you information about their field. Don't ask about job openings. Ask how they got their start in the field or what a typical day is like. Leave a resume and ask for names of others who might be helpful. You'll gain interviewing experience, contacts, and possibly a job lead. Always mail a handwritten thank-you note.

Finding Openings

The best way to find a job is to ask family, friends, and acquaintances for leads. It's called networking. Everyone you meet is a potential source of information about a job—now or in the future. Other resources include:

- *"Help Wanted" Signs:* Walk around town or the mall and apply in person. Dress appropriately and be ready for an on-the-spot interview and application.
- *Newspapers and the Internet:* Your local newspaper carries help-wanted ads every day. On the Internet, you can find job postings and post your resume.
- *Placement Agencies:* Free state-run employment services match qualifications with available jobs. Private placement companies charge applicants or employers; ask who pays before signing up.
- *Start Your Own Business:* Teenagers start businesses every day. Not all teen businesses are financially successful, but they all provide invaluable experience that impresses college admissions officers and potential employers.

Getting in the Door

For some jobs, like retail sales, you'll see a sign in the window and can simply walk in and complete an application. But most employers expect you to send a resume and cover letter first.

Your Resume: A resume is a document that summarizes your experience, skills, and education. Its purpose is to present you in the best possible light so that employers will contact you for an interview. You'll need more than one resume, since an effective one focuses on skills related to a *specific job*. These tips can help you get started:

1. Make a list of everything you've accomplished in your life. You can use it to identify skills that relate to various jobs, now and in the future.

For every job opening, employers receive about 500 resumes and spend about 5 seconds glancing at each one.

Your Resume

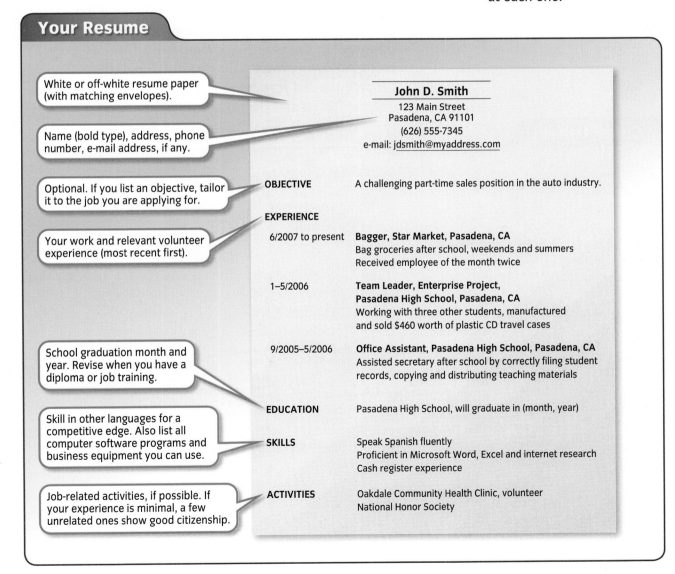

White or off-white resume paper (with matching envelopes).

Name (bold type), address, phone number, e-mail address, if any.

Optional. If you list an objective, tailor it to the job you are applying for.

Your work and relevant volunteer experience (most recent first).

School graduation month and year. Revise when you have a diploma or job training.

Skill in other languages for a competitive edge. Also list all computer software programs and business equipment you can use.

Job-related activities, if possible. If your experience is minimal, a few unrelated ones show good citizenship.

John D. Smith
123 Main Street
Pasadena, CA 91101
(626) 555-7345
e-mail: jdsmith@myaddress.com

OBJECTIVE   A challenging part-time sales position in the auto industry.

EXPERIENCE

6/2007 to present   **Bagger, Star Market, Pasadena, CA**
Bag groceries after school, weekends and summers
Received employee of the month twice

1–5/2006   **Team Leader, Enterprise Project, Pasadena High School, Pasadena, CA**
Working with three other students, manufactured and sold $460 worth of plastic CD travel cases

9/2005–5/2006   **Office Assistant, Pasadena High School, Pasadena, CA**
Assisted secretary after school by correctly filing student records, copying and distributing teaching materials

EDUCATION   Pasadena High School, will graduate in (month, year)

SKILLS   Speak Spanish fluently
Proficient in Microsoft Word, Excel and internet research
Cash register experience

ACTIVITIES   Oakdale Community Health Clinic, volunteer
National Honor Society

2. Get a description of the job you want from the company's Web site, ad, or human resources department. You can also check your local library for *The Dictionary of Occupational Titles* or the *Occupational Outlook Handbook* (also at http://stats.bls.gov/oco/oco1002.htm).

3. From your list of accomplishments, select those that match *this* job and list them in the "Experience" section of your resume (see the sample on the previous page for formatting). Be brief and use active verbs like *organized, developed,* or *implemented*. If you can truthfully claim results, do so: "raised $1,700" or "reduced filing errors by half."

4. Employers often toss resumes with typos or misspellings, so ask several people to proofread yours.

The Cover Letter: Your resume should be accompanied by a letter typed in a format similar to the sample below. First, state why you are interested in the company and where you heard about the opening. In the next two paragraphs (three at most), "sell" yourself: How will your skills be valuable to the employer? If an e-mailed resume was requested, type the cover letter in the e-mail itself.

Cover Letter

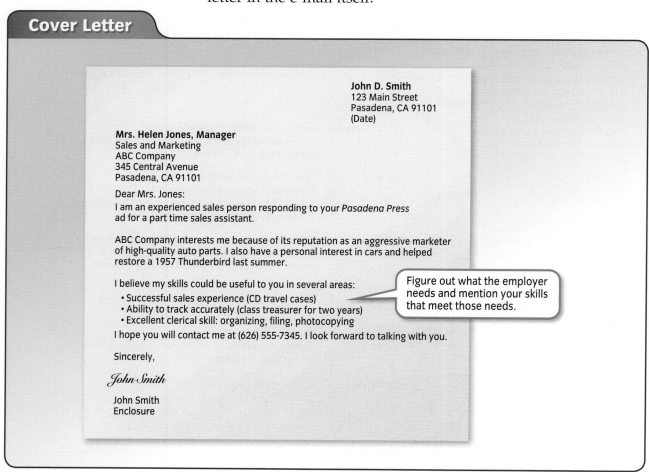

John D. Smith
123 Main Street
Pasadena, CA 91101
(Date)

Mrs. Helen Jones, Manager
Sales and Marketing
ABC Company
345 Central Avenue
Pasadena, CA 91101

Dear Mrs. Jones:

I am an experienced sales person responding to your *Pasadena Press* ad for a part time sales assistant.

ABC Company interests me because of its reputation as an aggressive marketer of high-quality auto parts. I also have a personal interest in cars and helped restore a 1957 Thunderbird last summer.

I believe my skills could be useful to you in several areas:

• Successful sales experience (CD travel cases)
• Ability to track accurately (class treasurer for two years)
• Excellent clerical skill: organizing, filing, photocopying

I hope you will contact me at (626) 555-7345. I look forward to talking with you.

Sincerely,

John Smith

John Smith
Enclosure

Figure out what the employer needs and mention your skills that meet those needs.

The Job Interview

Appearance is important, so dress appropriately for all interviews. Be prepared to answer questions like "Why do you want to work here?" Interviewers often ask this to see if you've researched the company's products, financial status, etc. You can request brochures from the company's human resource department or find this information on the Internet. Be ready to explain how your skills qualify you for the job.

EXAMPLE: "Although I don't have professional sales experience, I believe the skills I demonstrated selling school raffle tickets will be useful to you. According to the product vendor, my aggressive selling efforts increased sales by 22 percent."

Before you leave, hand the interviewer a typed sheet listing three references: names, titles, companies, and phone numbers. Send a brief thank-you letter; summarize why you're right for the job and include your daytime phone number.

Test Your Financial Fitness

1. **Summarizing** What is the purpose of a resumé?
2. **Listing** List ten of your accomplishments that you think demonstrate skills an employer might want.
3. **Applying** Write a resumé applying for a job you would like to have. In the "Experience" section, incorporate some of the accomplishments you listed.
4. **Analyzing** List four questions an employer might ask you during an interview and the answers you would give.

Paying Taxes:
Simplify the annual event

Who pays taxes? How do you file a return? If you have an income or buy anything, you'll pay taxes, regardless of your age. Being organized can make the process easier and maybe save you some money.

What Taxes?

The largest chunk of tax money goes to the federal government to fund programs such as the military, retirement security, space exploration, aid to foreign countries, and disaster recovery. When you see news reports about arguments in Congress over the budget, they're arguing about how to spend your tax dollars. States, cities, and other entities also assess taxes for various purposes.

Federal Income Tax Money you earn is taxable, including wages, tips, interest earned by bank accounts, and profits from the sale of property, like cars or stocks. Every year, the Internal Revenue Service (IRS) sets a taxable minimum income. If you earn more than that, it's taxed—even income from self-employment like babysitting or mowing lawns.

The IRS is the agency within the U.S. Treasury Department that administers tax laws and provides forms and advice. The IRS also has the power to ensure that people pay what they owe. It can assess penalties; charge interest on unpaid tax; confiscate wages, bank accounts, or property; and even imprison debtors for nonpayment. It's to your advantage to learn how to be a responsible taxpayer.

Other Taxes States, cities, and some school districts assess income taxes to pay for schools, fire protection, police, highways, and similar services. You'll file tax forms (returns) for those at the same time as you file your federal return. In most states, sales tax is added to the price of products sold in the state, including items bought online. Some states also assess this tax for online purchases when the seller does not have a "brick and mortar" store in that state. Then there are use (excise) taxes on things like gasoline, guns, gambling, tobacco, alcohol, and airline tickets. Finally, property owners pay taxes based on the value of their house or other real estate.

Notorious mafia boss Al "Scarface" Capone was never convicted of most of the violent crimes he allegedly committed—but he spent eight years in prison for not paying his taxes.

Withholding If you haven't received your first paycheck yet, it will be an eye-opener. Employers are required by law to deduct—or "withhold"—a certain percentage of wages for taxes and other payments. These are listed on your pay stubs and include:

- **Federal taxes:** Your employer will withhold a part of your pay based on a table from the IRS. The more you earn, the higher the amount withheld.
- **State and city taxes:** The amount varies from state to state and from city to city. If you live in one city and work in another, your employer will withhold the tax for the city where you work. You may have to pay a separate income tax to the city where you live.
- **Social Security:** The Social Security system provides a financial safety net for retirees and disabled citizens who contributed to the system throughout their working lives. Your employer matches your contribution.
- **Medicare:** Everyone who receives Social Security benefits automatically receives Medicare Part A benefits, which partially cover stays in hospitals and skilled nursing facilities. (Other Medicare benefits must be purchased after you reach age 65.) Your employer matches this contribution as well.
- **Optional withholdings:** You may decide to have your employer deduct more money. For example, you might get health insurance through your work. (See **Insurance Matters** on page R32.) Many employers also offer automatic savings plans and match a part of your contributions. (See **Saving and Investing** on page R6.)

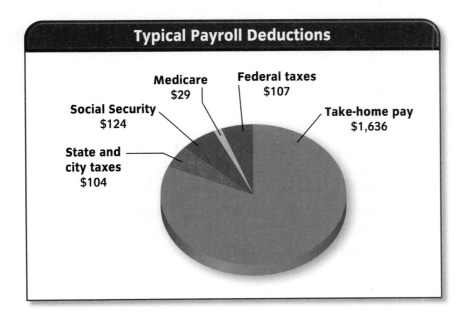

Typical Payroll Deductions

Medicare $29

Federal taxes $107

Social Security $124

Take-home pay $1,636

State and city taxes $104

Paperwork

Four kinds of paperwork are used in the tax process: a form you fill out when you're hired by a company (W-4), documentation of your income (W-2), your tax return, and records you'll need to complete the return.

W-4 Form When you start a job, you get a W-4 form on which you tell the employer how much money to withhold for federal income taxes. You choose the number of exemptions by asking yourself: Do I want to have the government keep the money for a year to make sure I don't spend it before tax time? Or, would I rather invest the money and make the payment in April? If more money is withheld than you owe, you'll get a refund, which makes tax season more pleasant. But your money is with the government instead of earning interest in a bank account or investment.

W-2 Form Every January, your employer(s) will send you a W-2 form listing your wages and withholdings for the previous year. If you don't receive yours by mid-February, call the employer. You'll attach this form to your tax return to prove your income.

Tax Return Every year, you'll complete a paper or online form telling the IRS how much tax you still owe or how much you believe should be refunded to you. If your income is below a certain level set annually by the IRS, you don't have to file a return, but you should anyway. It's the only way to get your refund. These guidelines may make it easier:

- *Forms:* The IRS will mail you a form and instructions. Free forms are also available at post offices, banks, libraries, and on the IRS Web site at www.irs.gov. Be sure your name and Social Security number are correct.
- *Deadline:* File any time between January 1 and April 15. If you file after April 15, you'll be charged a penalty and, if money is owed, interest on the amount owed.

Rock 'n' roll legend Jerry Lee Lewis's personal property was confiscated by the IRS twice for nonpayment of taxes. IRS agents took his cars, furniture, and piano and showed up at his concerts to collect gate receipts. Similar tax problems have sidetracked the finances of rapper M.C. Hammer and country singer Willie Nelson, among others.

INCOME TAX TERMS

Earned income: Wages, tips, and taxable scholarship and fellowship grants. You'll need to total these amounts to calculate your taxes.

Unearned income: Interest (from bank accounts, stocks, etc.) and dividends or capital gains from stocks.

Gross income: The total of earned and unearned income.

Adjusted gross income: Gross income minus deductions. This is the figure used to calculate the amount of your federal income tax.

- *Deductions:* The amount you pay is a percentage of your income minus any eligible deductions. These are expenses that meet IRS guidelines, like donations to charity and interest on college loans.
- *Preparing your return:* Whether you're filing a paper or electronic return, you'll have to decide several things:

1. What status to file under. For now, select "single."
2. Whether you want to take the standard deduction or list (itemize) your eligible deductions separately. If you choose the standard deduction, you can use a simple 1040EZ form. Or, you can try to lower the amount you owe by itemizing deductions on a 1040 form. (More complicated taxes use other forms.) With this form, you may need help from a tax preparer, because tax regulations are complicated and change frequently. The IRS offers free advice by phone at 800-829-1040 or on its Web site. Some nonprofit organizations also offer free services to low-income taxpayers.

Your Records You have two choices for tax recordkeeping: you can wait until tax time and search for documentation, or start a file in January and keep handy the papers you'll need to file a return the next year. Here's what tax experts recommend keeping for four to seven years:

TAX RECORDS

- Pay stubs and W-2 forms
- Bank statements
- Receipts for major purchases and charitable donations
- Records of insurance and medical payments
- Proof of any theft losses: value, date missing, proof of ownership

Test Your Financial Fitness

1. **Stating** Who is responsible for paying income taxes?
2. **Explaining** Why do young workers have to contribute to the Social Security system?
3. **Defining** What is "adjusted gross income"?
4. **Locating** How can you find out how much money was withheld from your pay?
5. **Listing** List three forms you need to file your income tax.

Renting an Apartment:
Know what to look for

How much rent should you pay? How do you find the best deal? What if your roommate moves out? Moving to a new apartment can be exciting. Finding and renting one takes work. Making good decisions and meeting your responsibilities as a tenant can make it easier—and avoid money problems later on.

The Rental Process

Before you begin searching for an apartment, first consider how you'll pay for it. Rent is only the beginning. Tenants usually pay for heat, air conditioning, and electricity, and sometimes water and garbage pick-up. Many landlords expect the first and last months' rent in advance, plus a security deposit they hold until tenants move. If you damage the property, your deposit pays for repairs. Any remainder should be returned to you, sometimes with interest, depending on local laws. If you own expensive items, you may want to add the cost of renter's insurance. Remember: rent plus utilities should generally equal no more than one-fourth of your monthly income.

Finding a Home Once you know how much you can afford, ask yourself:

- How close to school or a job do I want to live?
- Will I have roommates?
- How many rooms do I need?
- What else is important to me: Security? Noise level? Storage? Laundry facilities?

Begin your search with friends, newspaper ads, the Internet, bulletin boards, and/or rental agencies. Make appointments to view several apartments and be prepared to provide:

- identification
- social security number
- income amount and employer's name and phone number
- contact numbers for references (current or previous landlords, teachers, coaches, or employers) who can vouch for your character

Signing a Lease

You'll be required to sign a lease or a rental agreement. This is a binding legal contract, so read it—fine print and all—before signing. A lease requires the tenant to pay rent for the number of months listed—even if the tenant moves before the lease ends. Rental agreements are from month to month.

The Walk-Through Before signing anything, "walk through" the apartment with the landlord and note its condition. To safeguard your deposit, make sure any damages are listed on the lease. Take dated photos before you move in and when you move out.

The Right Roommates If you plan to share an apartment with roommates, be sure that they can afford the apartment and that they sign the lease to ensure equal legal responsibility. Make it clear that if they move before the lease ends, they're responsible for either paying their share of the rent until the lease ends or for finding replacement roommates. Agree on house rules up front: overnight guests, parties, chores, etc.

Rights and Responsibilities Your apartment is your home, but it belongs to the property owner. Landlords must keep it structurally safe and sanitary, and provide access to heat, water, and electricity. They can enter your apartment only to make repairs or show it to prospective tenants. In some states, they must give you advance notice. Prospective landlords can check references, employment, and credit, but it is against the law to discriminate on the basis of race, national origin, religion, gender, familial status, or disability. A local tenants' union can provide information and advice.

You're responsible for paying rent on time, keeping the apartment clean and in good condition, following the terms of the lease, and being considerate of neighbors. Remember: being a responsible tenant makes your new landlord a good reference for your next one.

WALK-THROUGH CHECKLIST

- ❑ Sturdy door and window locks
- ❑ Working smoke and carbon monoxide detectors
- ❑ Fire exits in front and back
- ❑ Enough rooms, closets, and storage space
- ❑ Damages such as:
  - ___ broken kitchen appliances or bathroom fixtures
  - ___ stains, loose tiles, or large scratches on floors
  - ___ cracks in windows or walls
  - ___ stained or peeling wallpaper, or garish paint colors

Test Your Financial Fitness

1. **Explaining** What are two reasons for taking good care of a landlord's property?

2. **Listing** What costs are involved in renting an apartment?

3. **Applying** List four factors that would affect your choice of an apartment, in order of importance to you. Then explain why they're important.

Buying a Car:
Drive a good deal

Is a cool car in your future? Where will you get the money? Picture yourself in the car of your dreams. Wait: Now picture yourself under a mountain of debt. Before you rush to a Ferrari dealer, do the homework that can help you get a good deal on a vehicle that meets your needs now—and down the road.

Choosing Your Car

The most important step in the car-buying process is figuring out how much you can afford. Do this *before* deciding which car you want. In general, car payments should be less than 15 percent of your monthly income.

Do the Research Check the Internet or consumer publications for comparisons of:

- *Safety:* Is the car likely to protect you in a crash or poor road conditions, and avoid rolling over? Also find unbiased reviews at www.nhtsa.dot.gov.
- *Performance:* The number of miles per gallon of gasoline (fuel efficiency) and the impact a car makes on the environment (emissions) vary with the type of car. You can check both at www.fueleconomy.gov. High gas prices alone make it essential to check mileage. Hybrid cars are designed to use less gas and pollute less by running on a combination of gas and electricity, but they cost more up front than gasoline-powered cars.
- *Repairs:* Consumer publications list which vehicles require fewer repairs and cost less to fix.

Compare Financing Dealers make most of their profit on loans, not car sales. Before discussing financing with a dealer, research loans at banks and other financial institutions. Also check your credit score, since it determines whether you'll get a loan and how much interest you'll pay. (See **Credit and You** on page R10.) If you're applying for credit at more than one place, do it within a 14-day period. Otherwise, your credit rating will drop because of "too many inquiries."

Every car has a "pink slip," or title—a document that proves ownership. You won't get the pink slip until you've made all the payments. Meanwhile, the seller gives you a receipt you'll need to register your car and buy license tags.

Getting a Deal

A new car is exciting, offers warranties, and requires fewer repairs. But a new car depreciates (loses value) the minute you drive it off the lot. Used cars depreciate more slowly and cost a lot less to begin with. Some even offer limited warranties.

New Cars A cool head and a game plan can save you thousands of dollars. Here are some tips:

1. *Take your time.* Don't let "special offers" or high-pressure sales tactics rush you into buying on your first visit.
2. *Find the fair price.* On the Internet, find the factory invoice price, which is the price the dealer paid for the car. This is not the "sticker" price on the car's window (a higher Manufacturer's Suggested Retail Price, or MSRP). Offer to pay that price plus a fair profit, usually 3 to 5 percent.
3. *Get bids.* Ask five dealers for written bids. Those bids are your bargaining edge.

High Cost of Driving *The average annual cost of driving a new car in the United States is more than 56 cents per mile, including gas, oil, maintenance, tires, insurance, licenses, registration, vehicle depreciation, and finance charges. That's $8,410 a year!*

Used Cars Check the Internet or newspapers for ads. If you're buying from a dealer, ask for names and phone numbers of previous customers. Contact them or the Better Business Bureau for any complaints against the dealer. Weed out the "lemons" with these tips:

- Drive the car, noticing odd noises and how it handles.
- Look at the title to see if the car was "salvaged." That means an insurer declared it a "total loss"; it probably has structural damage that could affect safety and performance.
- Have a mechanic you trust or the American Automobile Association (AAA) test the car. If the seller won't allow testing, don't buy the car.
- Ask to see receipts for recent repairs. Also get the vehicle identification number (VIN) (usually on the dash). At the CARFAX Web site, check the car's history.

Test Your Financial Fitness

1. **Explaining** What is the most important thing to consider when choosing a car? List three other important factors.
2. **Listing** List three things you can do to avoid getting a "lemon" when you buy a used car.
3. **Describing** Describe the process a smart car buyer would use before visiting a car dealer.
4. **Defining** What is the difference between the retail price and the factory invoice price?

Insurance Matters:
Protect yourself

Is your car legal? Who pays if you get sick or robbed? Nobody enjoys thinking about—or paying for—insurance. If you have an emergency, you'll be glad you did.

How It Works

Insurance is like a life raft. You pay an insurance company monthly or quarterly premiums. Then, if something bad happens, such as a traffic accident, an illness, or an apartment fire, insurance helps you stay afloat financially. If nothing bad happens, the company keeps the money.

A document detailing what your insurance covers is a policy. Most policies require a deductible, an amount you have to pay before the insurance kicks in.

EXAMPLE: You chose car insurance with a $1,000 deductible and you're involved in an accident. You'll have to pay the first $1,000 to fix the car. The insurance company will pay the rest, up to the amount you've purchased. If you had chosen a $500 deductible, you'd pay only the first $500, but your premiums would be higher.

TYPES OF CAR INSURANCE

Collision: Damage to your car, regardless of who caused the accident.

Comprehensive: Damage to your car not caused by an accident, such as theft, vandalism, and natural disasters.

Liability: Bodily injury and property damage to others, plus legal costs. State laws determine how much coverage you must have.

Medical: Medical expenses for everyone injured, regardless of fault.

Personal injury protection: Medical expenses for the insured driver, regardless of fault.

Uninsured motorist: Damage to your car in an accident caused by a driver with no liability insurance.

Underinsured motorist: Damage to your car in an accident caused by someone with insufficient liability insurance.

Rental reimbursement: Car rental if your vehicle cannot be driven after an accident.

Types of Insurance

Some types of insurance are useful to you now, but most can wait until you're out of school and have more responsibilities.

Auto It's illegal to drive in most states without basic liability insurance to cover property damage and injuries to others; some also require personal injury coverage for the driver. But you may want to buy more insurance than the law requires. Teenage drivers are involved in four times as many crashes as other age groups and are three times more likely to die in a traffic accident. Auto insurance helps pay the costs of injuries, car and property damage, and lawsuits.

Health Even if you're healthy, health insurance is a good idea at any age. It pays for hospitalization, surgery, exams, and other medical costs. Some employers pay part of the cost for employees and their families. Health insurance has deductibles and most plans require a small payment (co-payment, or "co-pay") whenever you visit a doctor's office.

Property What would it cost to replace everything you own: computer, TV, clothes, bicycle? If it's more than you could afford, it should be insured against theft, fire, and other dangers. *Renters insurance* covers the contents of rented property and injury to visitors. *Homeowners insurance* covers a house, its contents, and visitor injuries. Separate insurance is needed for flood or earthquake damage.

Other Insurance *Life insurance* provides financial support to loved ones when a person dies. Some types of life insurance offer lending or retirement income features. *Disability insurance* partially replaces income if you can't work because of illness or injury. *Long-term care insurance* pays for care in nursing homes, assisted living facilities, or private homes when an elderly or disabled person can't manage daily tasks.

INSURANCE TIPS

- Find out if the policy covers the amount it would cost you to replace the item (**replacement cost**), or only the amount the item was worth before it was damaged, lost, or stolen (**actual cash value**, or **ACV**).

- Read the fine print before signing a policy.

- Document your property with photos and keep receipts.

- To lower insurance costs:
  - Shop to get the lowest premium.
  - Maintain good credit.
  - Drive a low-profile car, not one that's flashy or expensive to repair.
  - Drive safely and ask about discounts for "good students," nonsmokers, nondrinkers, and good drivers.
  - Get an education: some insurers charge less to customers with higher educational levels.
  - If your car is worth less than $1,000, consider dropping collision and comprehensive coverage—but not liability.
  - Install safety and anti-theft devices (airbags, alarms).
  - Buy several types of insurance from the same company to qualify for a multiple-policy discount.

Test Yourself

1. **Stating** What type of insurance covers a stolen car?
2. **Determining Cause and Effect** Why do you think most states require drivers to have liability insurance, but not collision or comprehensive?
3. **Defining** What is a deductible?
4. **Listing** What two disasters are not covered by renters or homeowners insurance?
5. **Naming** Name three ways to cut the cost of car insurance.

CONTENTS

CRITICAL THINKING SKILLS

ECONOMICS SKILLS

Identifying the Main Idea

Why Learn This Skill?

Finding the main idea in a reading passage will help you see the "big picture" by organizing information and assessing the most important concepts to remember.

Learning the Skill

Follow these steps when trying to identify the main idea:

- Determine the setting of the passage.
- As you read the material, ask: What is the purpose of this passage?
- Skim the material to identify its general subject. Look at headings and subheadings.
- Identify any details that support a larger idea or issue.
- Identify the central issue. Ask: What part of the selection conveys the main idea?

▼ Industrial robot

Practicing the Skill

Read the excerpt below and answer the questions that follow.

Industrial robots can't speak English or Chinese, but they can communicate very well with their controllers—something they do 24/7, with no vacations and no health care. They don't receive a pension after they're retired, either. Instead, they get recycled or remanufactured and go to work again.

The average wage for a U.S. warehouse or distribution worker is around $15 per hour (plus benefits). The average wage for this same work in China is about $3 per hour. The average wage for a skilled UAW U.S. automobile worker is $25 to $30 per hour, plus the staggering costs of health care coverage and retirement.

The average cost per hour to operate an industrial robot is 30 cents per hour according to Ron Potter, director of robotic technologies of Factory Automation Systems.

—www.forbes.com, January 3, 2006

1. Where did this article appear?
2. When was it written?
3. What is the main idea of this article?
4. What additional details support the main idea?

Applying the Skill

Bring to class an article from a newspaper, magazine, real-estate buying guide, or other publication. Identify the main idea, and explain why it is important.

Determining Cause and Effect

Why Learn This Skill?

Determining cause and effect involves considering *why* an event occurred. A *cause* is the action or situation that produces an event. What happens as a result of a cause is an *effect*.

Learning the Skill

To identify cause-and-effect relationships, follow these steps:

- Identify two or more events or developments.
- Decide whether one event caused the other. Look for "clue words" such as *because, led to, brought about, produced, as a result of, so that, since,* and *therefore.*
- Look for logical relationships between events, such as "She overslept, and then she missed her bus."
- Identify the outcomes of events. Remember that some effects have more than one cause, and some causes lead to more than one effect. Also, an effect can become the cause of yet another effect.

Practicing the Skill

The classic cause-and-effect relationship in economics is between price and quantity demanded/quantity supplied. As a price for a good rises, the quantity demanded goes down and the quantity supplied rises.

1. Look at the photo above. What might cause a store to have a big sale on plasma televisions? What is the effect on consumers?

2. Now look at the demand curve for plasma televisions below. If the price is $5,000, how many will be demanded per year? If the price drops to $1,000, how many will be demanded per year?

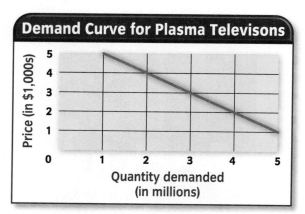

Demand Curve for Plasma Televisons

Price (in $1,000s)

Quantity demanded (in millions)

Applying the Skill

In your local newspaper, read an article describing a current event. Determine at least one cause and one effect of that event.

Making Generalizations

Why Learn This Skill?

Generalizations are judgments that are usually true, based on the facts at hand. If you say, "We have a great soccer team," you are making a generalization. If you also say that your team is undefeated, you are providing evidence to support your generalization. Generalizations are useful in the study of economics because they help economists see trends. Examples include the generalizations that men earn more than women and that prices go down when there is more competition. There are exceptions to both of these statements, but they are generally true.

Learning the Skill

To learn how to make a valid generalization, follow these steps:

- Identify the subject matter.
- Collect factual information and examples relevant to the topic.
- Identify similarities among these facts.
- Use these similarities to form some general ideas about the subject.

Practicing the Skill

Read the excerpt, then identify whether each generalization that follows is valid or invalid. Explain your answers.

Few times in a young person's life are as stressful as the first year out of college. If all goes well, you land a dream job in your chosen profession. But now everything hangs in the balance. Do well in your rookie job and it could put your career into overdrive. Your employer may shower you with promotions, pay raises, and increased responsibility, and you'll be able to leapfrog ahead of the competition in your next position. Do poorly, and you may be sent down to the minors.

The good news: Barring any serious infractions, relatively few people get completely sidetracked in their first year on the job, as most employers allow for a learning curve. The bad news is the reputation you make for yourself will be yours for a good long time—the corporate equivalent of your permanent academic record—coloring the way people see you for many years.

—*BusinessWeek Online,* September 18, 2006

1. The first year out of college is one of the most stressful times in a person's life.
2. All young workers who do well in their first year will have successful careers.
3. Most employers will tolerate a few rookie mistakes.
4. A young employee can never recover from a bad reputation.

Applying the Skill

Read at least three editorials in your local newspaper. Then make a generalization about each editorial.

Distinguishing Fact from Opinion

Why Learn This Skill?

Distinguishing fact from opinion can help you make reasonable judgments about what others say and write. Facts can be proved by evidence such as records, documents, or historical sources. Opinions are based on people's differing values and beliefs.

Learning the Skill

To learn how to identify facts and opinions, follow these steps:

- Read or listen to the information carefully. Identify the facts. Ask: Can these statements be proved? Where would I find information to verify them?
- If a statement can be proved by information from a reliable source, it is factual.
- Identify opinions by looking for statements of feelings or beliefs. They may contain words like *should, would, could, best, greatest, all, every,* or *always.*

Practicing the Skill

Read the excerpt and answer the questions that follow.

Office architects are envisioning improved cubicles—newbicles?—that feel private yet collegial, personal yet interchangeable, smaller yet somehow more spacious. Employing advanced materials, tomorrow's technology, and the fruits of sociological research, designers are fitting the future workplace to workers who are increasingly mobile and global. . . .

The father of the cubicle never meant to wreak such bleakness on the American office. We know this from the delightfully delusional name Robert Propst gave his invention: the Action Office. Back then, in 1968, most office workers toiled in open bull pens. Propst's pod offered at least as much privacy as they had in a toilet stall, albeit without the door. Corporate America, which is run by people whose offices have doors, has snapped up more than $5 billion worth of the units from maker Herman Miller. Today 70% of U.S. office workers sit in cubicles, which have long transcended mere office furniture to become a pop-cultural icon (thank you, Dilbert).

—*Time,* July 9, 2006

1. What are three factual statements in the passage?
2. Which statements are opinions? Explain.

Applying the Skill

Watch a television interview, and then list three facts and three opinions that you hear.

▼ A modern cubicle

Formulating Questions

Why Learn This Skill?

Asking questions helps you to process information and understand what you read.

Learning the Skill

Follow these steps to formulate questions as you read:

- Think about questions you have. Often you can find the answers in the next paragraph or section.
- Ask *who, what, when, where, why,* and *how* about the main ideas, people, places, and events.
- Reread to find answers to your questions.

Read the following excerpt, and then study the sample questions below.

A global fashion icon and megabrand, Hello Kitty is one of the most bizarre stories in modern-day marketing. After all, we are talking about a minimalist graphic rendering of a cat, one with a moon-shaped head and no mouth. Yet this simplistic image brings in a half-billion dollars annually in franchise fees for Tokyo-based corporate parent Sanrio. Licensees in Japan, the U.S., and Europe have plastered the cutesy image on 20,000-plus products world-wide—everything from waffle makers to diamond-studded luxury watches.

- Who or what is Hello Kitty?
- Why is Hello Kitty an interesting marketing story?
- Where is Hello Kitty popular?

Practicing the Skill

Read the second excerpt about Hello Kitty. Then, using a chart like the one below, ask questions about the excerpt and reread the selection to find the answers.

	Question	Answer
Who?		
What?		
Where?		
When?		
Why?		
How?		

The business mind behind [Hello Kitty] is Shintaro Tsuji, the founder, president, and CEO of Sanrio. In Japan, Tsuji is considered the closest thing the country has to a Walt Disney. He turned Sanrio, founded in 1960 as a small trinket maker, into a nearly $1 billion character-goods purveyor and theme park operator. Hello Kitty came on the scene in 1974 and appealed primarily to Japanese girls age 5 to 15.

Today, the fabulous feline is embraced by Parisian fashion houses, U.S. pop divas such as Mariah Carey and Christina Aguilera, and legions of fashion-conscious women in rich world markets.

—*BusinessWeek*, June 23, 2006

Applying the Skill

Select any section of this textbook to read or reread. Make a questioning chart to help you ask and answer five or more questions about the section as you read.

Analyzing Information

Why Learn This Skill?

The ability to analyze information is important in deciding what you think about a subject. For example, you need to analyze the effects of international free trade versus the effects of trade restrictions to decide where you stand on the issue of U.S. trade policy.

Learning the Skill

To analyze information, use the following steps:

- Identify the topic that is being discussed.

- Examine how the information is organized. What are the main points?

- Summarize the information in your own words, and then make a statement of your own based on your understanding of the topic and on what you already know.

Practicing the Skill

Read the excerpt and answer the questions that follow.

In May, the U.S. Mint informed Congress that the cost of making a penny and a nickel will soon exceed the actual value of each coin. . . . The U.S. mint estimates that by the end of the fiscal year, the cost of producing one penny will come to around 1.23 cents. . . . The news revived efforts to take the penny out of circulation. On July 18, Representative Jim Kolbe (R., Ariz.) introduced the Currency Overhaul for an Industrious Nation (COIN) Act that calls for the modernization of America's currency system. The bill includes implementing a rounding system for cash transactions that would eliminate the penny, increasing the production and circulation of the golden dollar while phasing out the dollar bill, and studying whether a change in the composition of coins to include less expensive metals would be worthwhile.

—*BusinessWeek*, July 19, 2006

1. What topic is being discussed?

2. What are the main points of this excerpt?

3. Summarize the information in this excerpt, and then provide your analysis based on this information and what you already know about the subject.

Applying the Skill

Select an issue in economics that is currently in the news, such as Social Security, oil prices, the national debt, or taxation. Read an article or watch a news segment about the issue. Analyze the information and make a brief statement of your own about the topic. Explain your thinking.

Evaluating Information

Why Learn This Skill?

We live in an information age. The amount of information available can be overwhelming, and it is sometimes difficult to know when information is true and useful. You need to evaluate what you read and hear to determine the reliability of the information presented.

Learning the Skill

When evaluating information to determine its reliability, ask yourself the following questions as you read:

- Is there bias? In other words, does the source unfairly present just one point of view, ignoring any arguments against it?
- Is the information published in a credible, reliable publication?
- Is the author or speaker identified? Is he or she an authority on the subject?
- Is the information up-to-date?
- Is the information backed up by facts and other sources? Does it seem to be accurate?
- Is it well-written and well-edited? Writing that has errors in spelling, grammar, and punctuation is likely to be careless in other ways as well.

Practicing the Skill

Look at the following statements about oil prices. Rank them in order of most reliable to least reliable, and then explain why you ranked them as you did.

"Oil prices are so high, becuz big oil companys are tryng to goug us. Greedy oil executives, are driven up prices to get richer."

—published on an individual's blog on the Internet

"It's certainly clear that high oil prices aren't dulling demand for energy products. According to the Energy Dept.'s Energy Information Administration (EIA), U.S. demand for gasoline in June was 9.5 million barrels per day, a record."

—*BusinessWeek*, July 7, 2006

"The single biggest factor in the inflation rate last year was from one cause: the skyrocketing prices of OPEC oil. We must take whatever actions are necessary to reduce our dependence on foreign oil—and at the same time reduce inflation."

—President Jimmy Carter, January 23, 1980

Applying the Skill

Find an advertisement that contains text and bring it to class. In a brief oral presentation, tell the class whether the information in the advertisement is reliable or unreliable and why.

Making Inferences

Why Learn This Skill?

To *infer* means to evaluate information and arrive at a conclusion. When you make inferences, you "read between the lines," or use clues to figure something out that is not stated directly in the text.

Learning the Skill

Follow these steps to make inferences:
- Read carefully for stated facts and ideas.
- Summarize the information and list important facts.
- Apply related information that you may already know.
- Use your knowledge and insight to develop some logical conclusions.

Practicing the Skill

Read the passage and answer the questions that follow.

Texans know their barbecue. But lots of them apparently don't know their Chinese food. The top question at the 10 Panda Express stores opened in Texas this year is "What's orange chicken?"

Andrew and Peggy Cherng, the husband-and-wife team who created Panda Express, know that answering that question and many others about their menu is part of the diner-education process that has turned a one-store eatery inside a California mall into an 820-store Chinese food empire. Orange chicken, a lightly sweetened fried chicken dish, is their best

seller but not as familiar in Texas as fajitas and hamburgers.

If they get their way, it will be. And not just on the coasts. The two are well on their way to cracking a frontier in fast food: creating a national Chinese fast-food chain.

—*USA Today*, September 11, 2006

1. What facts are presented in the passage?
2. What can you infer about the importance of educating Panda Express customers about Chinese food? Explain.
3. Can you also infer that there is currently no national Chinese fast-food chain? Explain.

Applying the Skill

Look over the headlines in today's Business and Finance section in your local newspaper. What can you infer about what economic issues are important in your community, the nation, and the world right now? Skim an article. Can you tell how the writer feels about the topic? How?

Comparing and Contrasting

Why Learn This Skill?

When you make comparisons, you determine similarities among ideas, objects, or events. When you contrast, you are noting differences between ideas, objects, or events. Comparing and contrasting are important skills because they help you choose among several possible alternatives.

Learning the Skill

To learn how to compare and contrast, follow these steps:

- Identify or decide what two or more items will be compared and/or contrasted.
- To compare, determine a common area or areas in which comparisons can be drawn. Look for similarities within these areas.
- To contrast, look for areas that are different. These areas set the items apart from each other.

Practicing the Skill

Study the advertisements for two computers at the bottom of the page, and then answer the questions that follow.

1. How are these products similar?
2. How are they different?
3. Which of these two computers would you choose? Why?

Applying the Skill

Survey your classmates about an issue in the news. Summarize the opinions and write a paragraph or two comparing and contrasting the different opinions.

The BasicBox XL is a reliable and versatile entry-level computer system designed especially for students.

Priced at a tidy $550, the BasicBox XL features:

- 3.06 GHz processor
- 512 MB of memory
- 160 GB hard drive
- 16X CD/DVD burner
- multiple USB ports
- keyboard and mouse

BasicBox XL

You can add a 15-inch flat panel monitor for a small extra charge.

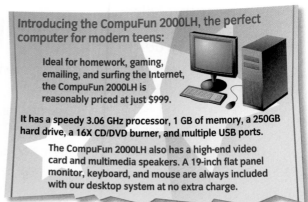

Introducing the CompuFun 2000LH, the perfect computer for modern teens:

Ideal for homework, gaming, emailing, and surfing the Internet, the CompuFun 2000LH is reasonably priced at just $999.

It has a speedy 3.06 GHz processor, 1 GB of memory, a 250GB hard drive, a 16X CD/DVD burner, and multiple USB ports.

The CompuFun 2000LH also has a high-end video card and multimedia speakers. A 19-inch flat panel monitor, keyboard, and mouse are always included with our desktop system at no extra charge.

Detecting Bias

Why Learn This Skill?

Most people have a point of view, or bias. This bias influences the way they interpret and write about events. Recognizing bias helps you judge the accuracy of what you hear or read.

Learning the Skill

Follow these steps to learn how to recognize bias:

- Examine the author's identity, especially his or her views and particular interests.
- Identify statements of fact.
- Identify any expressions of opinion or emotion. Look for words that have positive or negative overtones for clues about the author's feelings on a topic.
- Determine the author's point of view.
- Determine how the author's point of view is reflected in the work.

Practicing the Skill

Read the passage and answer the questions that follow.

Sometime in October the U.S. will join China and India in the very small club of countries with at least 300 million residents. This really is a big deal, like hitting 700 home runs in baseball. No other country is expected to reach the 300 million mark for at least 30 more years. . . .

But here are a couple of questions for you to ponder as the U.S. gets closer to the big 300: Is it coincidence that the three countries with the largest populations also have the most dynamic economies in the world? And is it coincidence that the most innovative major industrialized country, the U.S., also has the fastest growing population and the most young people?

No coincidence at all, as it turns out.

—*BusinessWeek,* September 5, 2006

1. What statements of fact are presented in this passage?
2. What opinions are stated?
3. What is the purpose of this passage?
4. What evidence of bias do you find? Does the author think it is a good thing or a bad thing that the United States is hitting this population milestone?

Applying the Skill

Find an editorial in the newspaper that deals with a topic of specific interest to you. Apply the steps for recognizing bias to the editorial. Write a paragraph summarizing your findings.

Synthesizing Information

Why Learn This Skill?

Synthesizing information involves combining information from two or more sources. Information gained from one source often sheds new light upon other information.

Learning the Skill

Follow these steps to learn how to synthesize information:

- Analyze each source separately to understand its meaning.
- Determine what information each source adds to the subject.
- Identify points of agreement and disagreement between the sources. Ask: Can Source A give me new information or new ways of thinking about Source B?
- Find relationships between the information in the sources.

Practicing the Skill

Read the passages and answer the questions that follow.

Source A "The flat tax. In the eyes of many fiscal conservatives, it's the Holy Grail of public policy: One low income tax rate paid by all but the poorest wage-earners, who are exempt. No loopholes for the rich to exploit. No graduated rates that take a higher percentage of income from people who work hard to earn more. No need for a huge bureaucracy to police fiendishly complex tax laws."

—*BusinessWeek,* September 26, 2005

Source B "Under Steve Forbes' plan the flat [income tax] rate would be 17%. All families would get generous personal exemptions, so that a family of four would not pay taxes until its income exceeded $46,000. To encourage growth, the Forbes plan exempts income that is saved and invested. Which means that the Forbes plan is really a consumption tax. It taxes people based on what they take out of the system, not on what they put in."

—*Forbes,* September 29, 2005

1. What is the main subject of each source?
2. Does Source B support or contradict Source A? Explain.
3. Summarize what you learned from both sources.

Applying the Skill

Find two sources of information on banking practices. What are the main ideas in each? How does each add to your understanding of the topic?

▼ Steve Forbes

Drawing Conclusions

Why Learn This Skill?

A conclusion is a logical understanding that you reach based on details or facts that you read or hear. When you draw conclusions, you use stated information to figure out ideas that are unstated.

Learning the Skill

Follow these steps to draw conclusions:
- Read carefully for stated facts and ideas.
- Summarize the information and list important facts.
- Apply related information that you may already know.
- Use your knowledge and insight to develop some logical conclusions.

Practicing the Skill

Read the passage and answer the questions that follow.

In the automotive business these days, big is out and small is in. Sales of large sport-utility vehicles are down 45%. Small-car sales have increased 70%. Of course, having suffered from $3-plus-a-gallon gasoline for longer, the rest of the world has been thinking small for years. And there is no production car smaller than the Smart Car from DaimlerChrysler.

But can a car that is just slightly more than 8 feet long and 5 feet high with 15-inch wheels co-exist with the mastodons that rule the American road? . . . Only time will tell.

—*BusinessWeek*, August 24, 2006

1. What topic is the writer describing?
2. What facts are given in the selection?
3. What do you already know about the subject?
4. What conclusion can you draw about why small-car sales are increasing while sales of large sport-utility vehicles are decreasing?

Applying the Skill

Read one of the "People & Perspectives" features about a prominent economist or entrepreneur in this text. Using the information in the profile, what can you figure out about the life of the person described? Draw three conclusions about this famous person's life and ideas.

▼ DaimlerChrysler's Smart Car

Making Predictions

Why Learn This Skill?

Predicting future events can be difficult and sometimes risky. The more information you have, however, the more accurate your predictions will be. Making good predictions will help you understand what you read.

Learning the Skill

To help you make predictions, follow these steps:

- Gather information about the decision or action.
- Use your knowledge of history and human behavior to identify what consequences could result.
- Analyze each of the consequences by asking: How likely is it that this will occur?

Practicing the Skill

Read the passage and answer the questions that follow.

Google and Yahoo! have been raking in the cash for years, as large advertisers shift more spending to online media. But judging by recent earnings figures from the Internet leaders, the trend is just hitting its stride. . . .

Driving this breakneck growth [in Internet advertising] is the companies' ability to draw advertising dollars onto the Internet—and away from other media. In 2002, 2.5% of U.S. ad dollars were spent online. The figure is expected to reach 4.6% this year [2005] and 7.5% by 2009, according to researcher eMarketer.

—*BusinessWeek,* October 21, 2005

1. What trend does the passage describe?
2. Do you think this trend is likely to continue?
3. On what do you base this prediction?
4. What are three possible consequences of this trend?

Applying the Skill

Analyze three articles in the business section of a newspaper. Predict three consequences of the actions in the articles. On what do you base your predictions?

Problems and Solutions

Why Learn This Skill?

Suppose you are not doing well in basketball. You wonder why you cannot do better since you always go to practice, try your best, and pay attention to the coach's instructions. In order to improve a situation such as this one, you need to identify a specific problem and then take actions to solve it.

Learning the Skill

Follow these steps to help you through the problem-solving process:
- Identify the problem.
- Gather information.
- List possible solutions.
- Consider the advantages and disadvantages of each solution.
- Choose the best solution to your problem and carry it out.
- Evaluate the effectiveness of the solution.

Practicing the Skill

Read the selection and answer the questions that follow.

The soaring price of cement is having a disproportionate effect on lower-middle to middle-income families. Why? Because the denser housing that tends to get built for them uses lots of concrete, which is made from cement, sand, gravel, and water. Designs with lots of concrete are becoming so expensive to build that they're getting out of the potential buyers' price range, says Tim Sullivan, president of Sullivan Group Real Estate Advisors. . . .

[Sullivan says] that because of the high price of cement and concrete products, builders are putting more of their efforts into homes that are built primarily of lumber. These are single-family homes or town homes that tend to be aimed at higher-income families. Tall condo and apartment buildings made of concrete are so expensive to build that these days they're aimed almost exclusively at wealthier buyers. . . .

—*BusinessWeek Online*, June 9, 2006

1. What problem does the writer present in this selection?
2. What options are available to solve this problem? Can you think of any other options?
3. Explain the solution that was implemented according to the selection.
4. Evaluate the solution described in the passage. Was it successful? How do you determine this?

Applying the Skill

Select an economic problem that needs to be solved. The problem can be anything from how you plan to pay for an upcoming expense to how the United States might solve the problem of funding Social Security long-term. Create a simple presentation in which you identify the problem, list options with their advantages and disadvantages, choose a solution, and evaluate the chosen solution.

Using Line Graphs

Why Learn This Skill?

A graph, like a picture, may present information in a more concise way than words. Line graphs are drawings that compare numerical values. They often are used to compare changes over time or differences between places, groups of items, or other related events.

Learning the Skill

Follow these steps to learn how to understand and use line graphs. Then answer the questions below.

1. Read the title of the graph. This should tell you what to expect or look for.

2. Note the information on the left side of the graph—the vertical axis. The information being compared usually appears on this axis.

3. Note the information along the bottom of the graph—the horizontal axis. Time often appears along this axis.

4. Determine what the line(s) or curve(s) symbolizes.

5. Select a point on the line, then note the date below this point on the horizontal axis and the quantity measured on the vertical axis.

6. Analyze the movement of the line (whether increasing or decreasing over time) or compare lines (if more than one is on the graph) to determine the point being made.

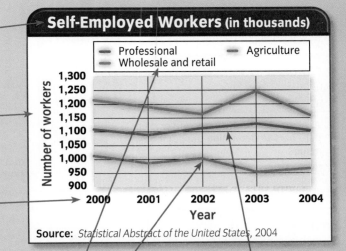

Self-Employed Workers (in thousands)

Professional   Agriculture
Wholesale and retail

Number of workers: 1,300 1,250 1,200 1,150 1,100 1,050 1,000 950 900

Year: 2000 2001 2002 2003 2004

Source: *Statistical Abstract of the United States*, 2004

Practicing the Skill

1. About how many people in wholesale and retail businesses were self-employed in 2003? In 2004?

2. How many more people were self-employed professionals in 2003 than in 2001?

Applying the Skill to Economics

1. What trends are shown on the graph?

2. What economic forces might have influenced the changes shown on the graph?

3. What kinds of jobs do you think are represented in each category shown?

Using Bar and Circle Graphs

Why Learn This Skill?

Bar graphs are often used to show changes over time or to compare quantities between similar categories of information. Circle graphs usually show the relationship of parts to a whole.

Learning the Skill

Follow these steps to learn how to understand and use bar graphs.

> 1. Read the title and labels. They tell you the topic, what is being compared, and how it is counted or measured.

> 2. Examine a bar on the graph. Note the date below the bar on the horizontal axis and the quantity measured on the vertical axis.

> 3. Analyze the change over time or compare bars to determine the point being made.

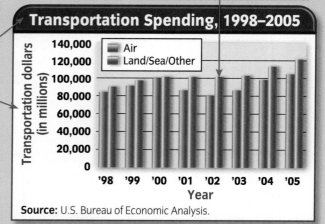

Transportation Spending, 1998–2005

Source: U.S. Bureau of Economic Analysis.

Learning the Skill

Follow these steps to learn how to understand and use circle graphs.

> 1. Examine the title to determine the subject.

> 2. Read the legend to see what each segment represents.

> 3. Compare the relative sizes of the circle segments, thus analyzing the relationship of the parts to the whole.

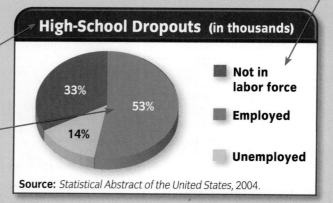

High-School Dropouts (in thousands)

Source: *Statistical Abstract of the United States,* 2004.

Practicing the Skill

1. In the bar graph, what year had the lowest spending on air travel?
2. According to the circle graph, what percentage of high school dropouts are employed?

Applying the Skill to Economics

1. Using the bar graph, what projection could you make about the future of air transportation?
2. Based on the circle graph, what can you tell about the employment chances of high-school dropouts?

Comparing Data

Why Learn This Skill?

Economists compare data in order to identify economic trends, draw conclusions about the relationships of sets of economic information, analyze the effectiveness of economic programs, or perform other types of analysis. It is often easiest to compare data that is organized in charts, tables, or graphs.

Learning the Skill

Follow these steps to compare and contrast data:

- Look at each set of data separately to understand what each one means on its own.
- Look for relationships among the sets of data. Ask yourself: How are these sets of information connected to each other?
- Note similarities and differences among the sets of data.
- Draw conclusions about what the sets of data, taken together, might mean.

Practicing the Skill

Compare the data in the charts at the bottom of the page, and then answer the questions below.

1. Look at the left graph. What was the overall trend in manufacturing employment from 1996 to 2005?
2. Look at the right graph. What was the overall trend in professional and business employment during the same period?
3. How are the data in the two charts related?
4. What conclusions can you draw about the two areas of employment?

Applying the Skill to Economics

Look in a world almanac or on the Internet to find two sets of data about an economic topic of your choice. Compare the data and draw at least two conclusions based on your analysis. Share your conclusions with a partner.

Employment in Manufacturing

Source: U.S. Bureau of Labor Statistics.

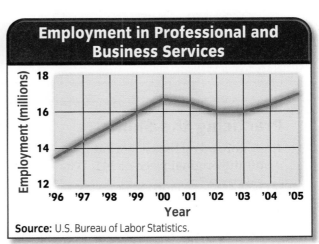

Employment in Professional and Business Services

Source: U.S. Bureau of Labor Statistics.

Understanding Percentages

Why Learn This Skill?

If you shop, you probably like seeing the word *percent,* as in "30 percent off." Stores often advertise sale prices as a percent of regular prices. *Percent* means "parts per hundred." So, 30 percent means the same thing as 30/100 or 0.30. Expressing change as a percentage allows you to analyze the relative size of the change.

Learning the Skill

Follow these steps to learn how to calculate and use percentages. Then answer the questions below.

1. Suppose a pair of shoes is on sale for 30 percent off the regular price. Calculate the discount by multiplying the original price by the sale percentage. Change percent to a decimal before you multiply.

2. Find the sale price by subtracting the discount from the regular price.

Calculating Percent

Regular price of shoes	$57.00	Regular price	$57.00		$57.00
30%	× .30	Discount	− 17.10	OR	× .70
Discount	$17.10	Sale price	$39.90		$39.90

3. Or, figure the sale price by multiplying the regular price by the percent you *will* pay. (Subtract the sale percentage from 100 to get the percent you will pay.) Change percent to a decimal before you multiply.

Arithmetic Change vs. Percentage Change

4. Calculate an increase in sales by subtracting the quantity sold last year from the quantity sold this year.

Arithmetic change   1.6 billion pounds of butter sold this year
     −1.5 billion pounds of butter sold last year
     .1 billion pounds

Percentage change $\frac{0.1}{1.5} = .067 \times 100 = 6.7$ percent

5. Determine the percentage change by dividing the arithmetic difference by the original quantity. Multiply by 100 to change the decimal to percent.

Practicing the Skill

1. A store advertises a shirt at 25 percent off the original price of $44. What is the sale price?

2. What is the percentage increase in high school enrollment from 1,165 students to 1,320?

Applying the Skill to Economics

The total number of digital single music tracks downloaded online or to mobile phones rose to 470 million units in 2005, up from 160 million in 2004. What was the percentage change of single-track downloads from 2004 to 2005?

Determining Averages

Why Learn This Skill?

The most commonly used summary statistic is the average. There are two ways to compute the average: by using the mean or the median. The *mean* is the average of a series of items. When your teacher computes the class average, he or she is really computing the mean. Sometimes using the mean to interpret statistics is misleading, however. This is especially true if one or two numbers in the series are much higher or lower than the others. The median can be more accurate. The *median* is the midpoint in any series of numbers arranged in order.

Learning the Skill

Follow these steps to learn how to determine and use averages.

1. Suppose you want to find the mean weekly salary for a group of teenagers. First, add all the earnings together.

3. Locate the median by finding the midpoint in the series ($41). Compare the mean with the median. Determine which is the more useful statistic.

Students' Weekly Earnings From After-School Jobs

$ 20
32
34
41
53
65
175
―――
$420

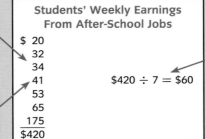

$420 ÷ 7 = $60

2. Divide the sum by the number of students to find the mean.

Median Weekly Income of the Four Highest-Paid Students

$ 41	$ 53
53	+ 65
65	$ 118
175	

$118 ÷ 2 = $59

5. When an even number of figures is in the series, the median is the mean of the two middle numbers. Follow steps 1 and 2 to find the mean.

4. Suppose you want to calculate the median for the four highest-paid students. First, arrange the numbers in order, from least to greatest.

Practicing the Skill

1. What is the mean salary for the four lowest-paid students?
2. What is the median salary for the four lowest-paid students?

Applying the Skill to Economics

Average Monthly Rent: 2005

| Miami, FL | $ 971 | Dallas, TX | $ 709 |
| Boston, MA | $1,216 | Los Angeles, CA | $1,330 |

1. What is the mean monthly rent for these four cities?
2. What is the median monthly rent?

Skills Handbook

Understanding Nominal and Real Values

Why Learn This Skill?

The rise in the economy's average price level is called inflation. To make comparisons between the prices of things in the past and those of today, you have to make the distinction between *nominal*, or current, and *real*, or adjusted for inflation, values. You can use the consumer price index (CPI), an index of average prices for consumer goods, to calculate real values. Then you can accurately compare changes in income and prices over time.

Learning the Skill

Follow these steps to learn how to calculate nominal and approximate real values when price changes are small.

1. Suppose a family sells a house after living there for 10 years. To calculate whether they made any profit from the sale, they need to know the real sale price of their house. First, find the nominal price increase.

4. Determine the percentage increase in real price. Subtract the percentage increase in CPI from the percentage increase in nominal price. Evaluate the sales in real values.

Purchase price of house in 1995: $75,000
Sale price of house in 2005: $150,000

CPI in 1995: 100
CPI in 2005: 200

$$\begin{array}{r} \$\ 150{,}000 \\ -\ \ 75{,}000 \\ \hline \$\ \ \ 75{,}000 \end{array}$$

$$\frac{\$75{,}000}{\$75{,}000} = 1 \times 100 = 100\%$$

$$\begin{array}{r} 200 \\ -100 \\ \hline 100 \end{array}$$

$$\frac{100}{100} = 1 \times 100 = 100\%$$

$$\begin{array}{r} 100\% \\ -100\% \\ \hline 0\% \end{array}$$

2. Calculate the nominal percentage increase in price. Divide the amount of increase by the original price and multiply by 100 to express the answer as a percent.

3. Determine the percentage increase in the consumer price index. First find the actual change in CPI. Then divide the amount of increase by the original CPI and multiply by 100.

5. Suppose that last year you earned $10 per hour. You receive a 5 percent raise. The CPI is 3 percent higher than last year's CPI, which means there is a 3 percent inflation rate.

Earnings: $10 per hour
Raise: 5%
Inflation Rate: 3%

$$\begin{array}{r} 5\% \\ -\ 3\% \\ \hline 2\% \end{array}$$

6. Calculate the real salary increase by subtracting the inflation rate from the nominal raise.

Practicing the Skill

1. What was the nominal price increase on the sale of the house?
2. How much money, in real dollars, was made on the house?
3. How much was the real value of the raise?

Applying the Skill to Economics

From 2004 to 2005, the cost of employer health insurance premiums increased by 9.2 percent—nearly three times the rate of inflation. Based on this information, what was the inflation rate that year? How could you adjust the cost of health insurance for inflation?

Skills Handbook

Understanding Interest Rates

Why Learn This Skill?

When you deposit money in a savings account, the bank pays you interest for the use of your money. The amount of interest is expressed as a percent, such as 6 percent, for a time period, such as per year. Two types of interest exist: simple and compound. *Simple interest* is figured only on the principal, or original deposit, not on any interest earned. *Compound interest* is paid on the principal plus any interest that has been earned.

Learning the Skill

Follow these steps to learn how to understand and calculate interest rates.

1. Suppose you deposit $100 in a savings account that earns 6 percent simple interest per year. Get ready to figure your earnings by converting 6 percent to a decimal.

2. To calculate the simple interest earned, multiply the principal by the interest rate.

3. Calculate the account balance for the first two years, assuming the bank pays the same interest rate each year. Add the principal, the first year's interest, and the second year's interest.

Simple Interest

```
6% = .06        $ 100      $ 100
                × .06      +   6
                $6.00         6
                           $ 112
```

4. Suppose you deposit $100 in a savings account that earns 6 percent compound interest per year. Calculate the interest earned the first year.

5. Find the bank balance for the end of the first year. Add the principal and first year's interest.

6. Determine the interest earned in the second year. Multiply the new balance by the interest rate.

7. Figure the total bank balance after two years. Add the second year's interest to the first year's balance.

Compound Interest

```
$ 100      $100     $ 106     $106.00
× .06      +  6     × .06     +  6.36
$6.00      $106     $6.36     $112.36
```

Practicing the Skill

1. What would be the difference in earnings between simple and compound interest if your initial balance was $1,000 rather than $100?

2. What would be the difference in earnings between simple and compound interest on your $100 savings after five years?

Applying the Skill to Economics

1. What would be the impact of compounding interest on a daily basis rather than an annual basis?

2. Banks often pay higher rates of interest on money you agree to keep in the bank for longer periods of time. Explain why this might be.

Interpreting Political Cartoons

Why Learn This Skill?

Political cartoonists use art to express opinions. Their work appears in newspapers, magazines, books, and on the Internet. Political cartoons usually focus on public figures, political events, or economic or social conditions. They can give you a summary of an event or circumstance and the artist's opinion in a quick, entertaining manner.

Learning the Skill

To interpret a political cartoon, follow these steps:

1. Read the title, caption, or conversation balloons. They help you identify the subject of the cartoon.

3. Identify any symbols shown. Symbols are things that stand for something else. Commonly recognized symbols may not be labeled. Unusual symbolism will be labeled.

5. Identify the cartoonist's purpose. What statement or idea is he or she trying to get across? Decide if the cartoonist wants to persuade, criticize or just make people think.

2. Identify the characters or people shown. They may be caricatures, or unrealistic drawings that exaggerate the characters' physical features.

4. Examine the actions in the cartoon—what is happening and why?

Practicing the Skill

1. What is "cow tipping"? What does this imply about the U.S. economy as it is pictured in the cartoon?

2. What does the rhinoceros represent? Why might the cartoonist have chosen this particular symbol?

3. What overall message do you think the cartoonist is trying to send?

Applying the Skill to Economics

Bring a newspaper or business magazine to class. With a partner, analyze the message in each political cartoon that you find.

Skills Handbook

Reading Stock Market Reports

Why Learn This Skill?

A stock market report alphabetically lists stocks and provides information about stock prices and trades. Every business day, shares of stock are bought and sold. At the beginning of each trading day, stocks open at the same prices they closed at the day before. Prices generally go up and down throughout the day as the conditions of supply and demand change. At the end of the day, each stock's closing price is recorded.

Learning the Skill

Follow these steps to learn how to understand and use the financial page.

1. Locate the stock in the alphabetical list. Names are abbreviated.

3. Note the ticker symbol, or computer code, for the stock.

5. Review the yield. The yield is the return on investment per share of stock. It is calculated by dividing the dividend by the closing price.

7. Note the volume, or number of shares of stock, traded that day. The number given represents hundreds of shares.

9. Examine how the day's closing stock price compares with the prior business day's closing price. Positive numbers indicate a price increase. Negative numbers mean a price drop.

Stock Quotations

52 Weeks Hi	52 Weeks Lo	Stock	Sym	Div	Yld %	PE	Vol 100s	Hi	Lo	Close	Net Chg
86.40	47.87	AppleComp	AAPL	2.22	2.9	34.96	391290	77.78	76.10	77.74	+ 1.86
475.11	290.69	Google	GOOG	6.82	1.7	59.68	51928	407.68	401.77	406.99	+ 3.01
27.49	16.75	Intel	INTC	1.10	5.5	18.15	939098	19.98	19.32	19.96	+ 0.55

2. Examine the stock's history over the last 52 weeks. The high and low prices for one share of stock appear.

4. Evaluate the annual dividend. Stockholders receive this dividend, or payment, for each share of stock they own.

6. Read the price/earnings ratio. Lower price/earnings ratios generally mean more earnings per share.

8. Examine the day's high, low, and closing stock price.

Practicing the Skill

1. How many shares of Google stock were traded on the day shown?
2. What was the day's highest price for a share of Apple Computer stock?
3. Which stock had the greatest increase in closing price from the previous day?

Applying the Skill to Economics

If you had purchased 100 shares of Intel stock at its lowest 52-week price and sold it at this day's closing price, how much money would you have made?

The data and forecasts for the graphs, tables, and charts in the Databank are based on information from Standard & Poor's.

U.S. Population Projections, 2000–2050

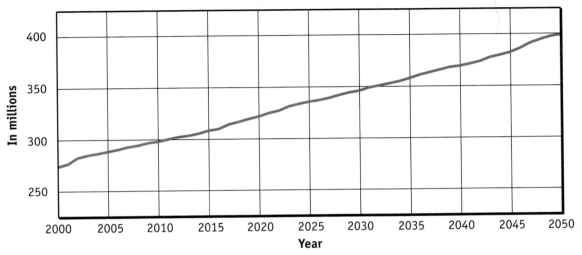

Source: U.S. Bureau of the Census

Civilian Labor Force, 1950–2010

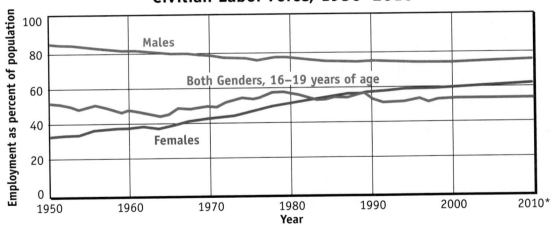

Source: Department of Labor, Bureau of Labor Statistics
*Estimate

Standard & Poor's Databank

Hours and Earnings in Private Industries, 1960–2006

A **Average Weekly Hours of Production Workers**

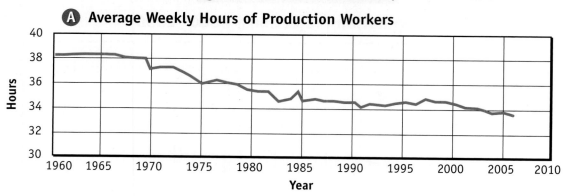

B **Average Weekly Earnings of Production Workers, Current Dollars**

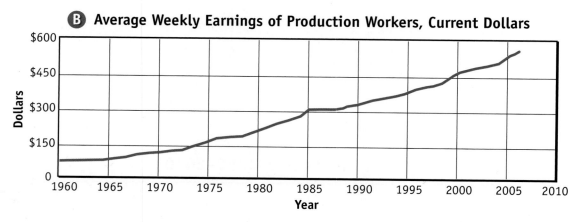

C **Average Weekly Earnings, 1982 Dollars**

Source: Bureau of Labor Statistics

Gross Domestic Product, 1950–2005

Source: U.S. Department of Commerce, Bureau of Economic Analysis

A Look at Stock Market History

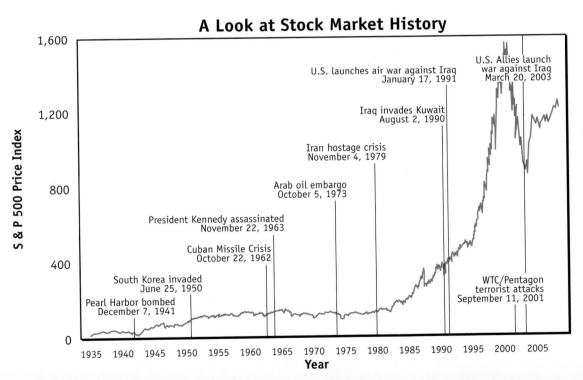

Source: Standard & Poor's

Standard & Poor's Databank

The U.S. Economy

Real Personal Consumption Expenditures, 1990–2005

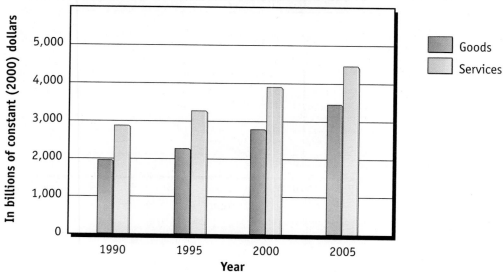

Source: Department of Commerce, Bureau of Economic Analysis

Personal Consumption Expenditures, 1960–2005

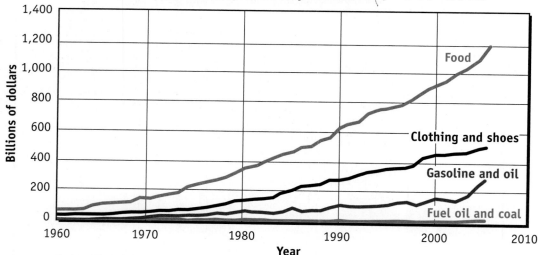

Source: Department of Commerce, Bureau of Economic Analysis

Average Prices of Selected Goods, 1990–2006

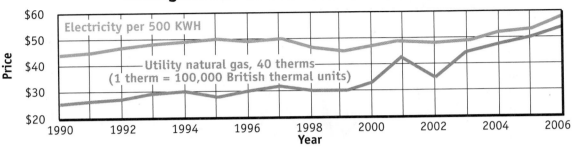

Electricity per 500 KWH

Utility natural gas, 40 therms
(1 therm = 100,000 British thermal units)

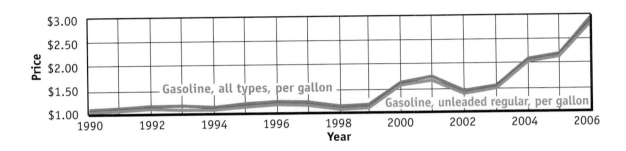

Gasoline, all types, per gallon

Gasoline, unleaded regular, per gallon

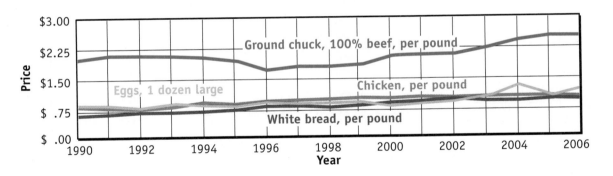

Ground chuck, 100% beef, per pound

Eggs, 1 dozen large

Chicken, per pound

White bread, per pound

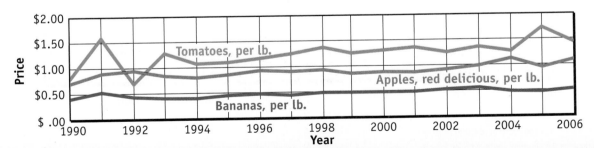

Tomatoes, per lb.

Apples, red delicious, per lb.

Bananas, per lb.

Source: Bureau of Labor Statistics; U.S. city average prices for July

Standard & Poor's Databank

Annual Changes in Consumer Price Indexes, 1950–2006

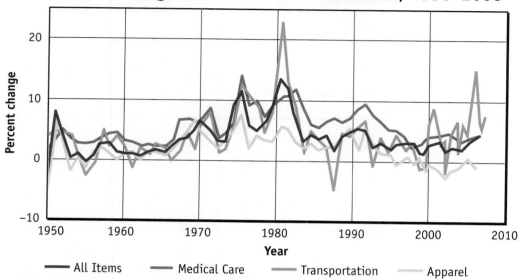

All Items   Medical Care   Transportation   Apparel

Inflation in Consumer Prices, 1950–2006

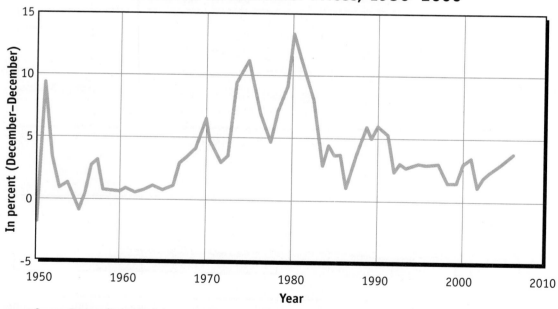

Source: Bureau of Labor Statistics

Federal Government Expenditures, 1950–2010

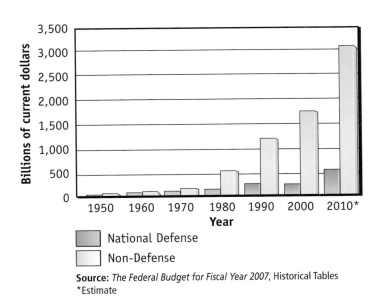

Source: *The Federal Budget for Fiscal Year 2007*, Historical Tables
*Estimate

Total Government Expenditures, 1965–2005

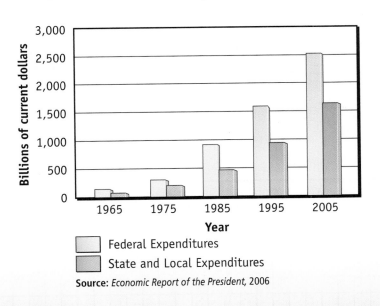

Source: *Economic Report of the President,* 2006

Standard & Poor's Databank

The Government Sector

Federal Government Total Receipts and Total Outlays, 1950–2007

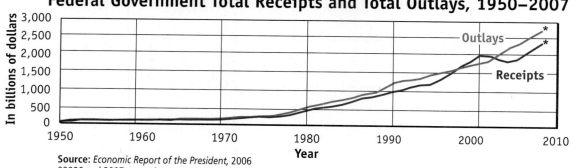

In billions of dollars

Outlays*
Receipts*

Year

Source: *Economic Report of the President,* 2006
*2006 and 2007 are estimates

Federal Debt Held by the Public, 1950–2007

In billions of dollars

Year

Source: *Economic Report of the President,* 2006
*2006 and 2007 are estimates

Federal Debt Held by the Public Per Capita, 1950–2007

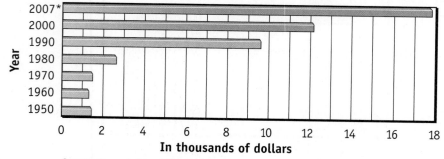

Year

In thousands of dollars

Source: *Economic Report of the President,* 2006
*Estimate

Federal Budget Receipts, 1990–2010

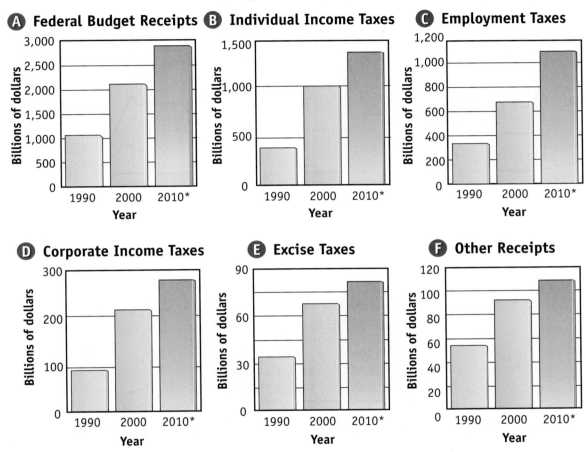

A Federal Budget Receipts

B Individual Income Taxes

C Employment Taxes

D Corporate Income Taxes

E Excise Taxes

F Other Receipts

Percentage of Total Receipts

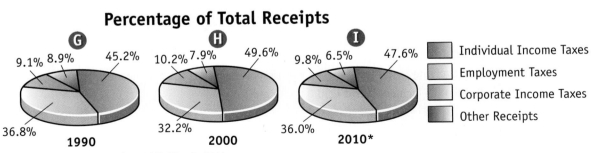

G 1990

9.1% 8.9% 45.2% 36.8%

H 2000

10.2% 7.9% 49.6% 32.2%

I 2010*

9.8% 6.5% 47.6% 36.0%

- Individual Income Taxes
- Employment Taxes
- Corporate Income Taxes
- Other Receipts

Source: *Federal Budget for FY 2007,* Historical Tables
*Estimates

The Financial Sector

Interest Rates, 1960–2005

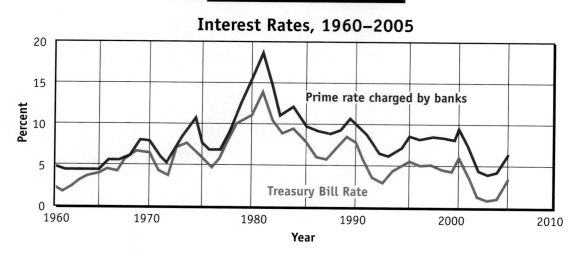

Prime rate charged by banks

Treasury Bill Rate

Percent / Year

Consumer Credit Outstanding, 1985–2005

Total Consumer Credit	
1985	$599.7 billion
1995	$1,141.4 billion
2005	$2,147.9 billion

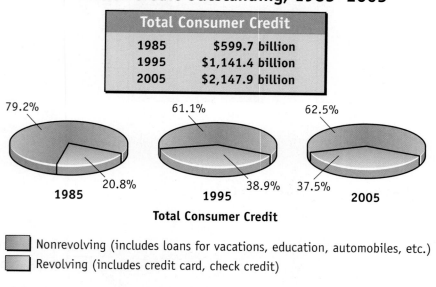

79.2% — 20.8% — **1985**
61.1% — 38.9% — **1995**
62.5% — 37.5% — **2005**

Total Consumer Credit

Nonrevolving (includes loans for vacations, education, automobiles, etc.)
Revolving (includes credit card, check credit)

Source: Board of Governors of the Federal Reserve System

Personal Saving, 1960–2006

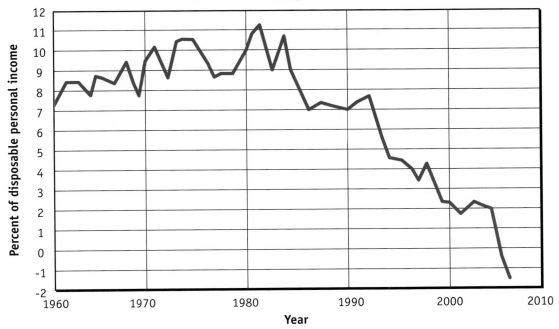

Source: U.S. Department of Commerce, Bureau of Economic Analysis

Money Stock, 1975–2005

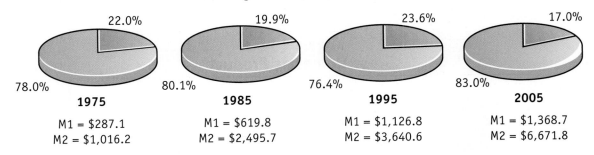

22.0%	19.9%	23.6%	17.0%
78.0%	80.1%	76.4%	83.0%
1975	**1985**	**1995**	**2005**
M1 = $287.1	M1 = $619.8	M1 = $1,126.8	M1 = $1,368.7
M2 = $1,016.2	M2 = $2,495.7	M2 = $3,640.6	M2 = $6,671.8

In billions of dollars

M1 consists of all currency and checkable deposits.

M2 consists of M1 plus noncheckable savings accounts, money market deposit accounts, time deposits, and money market mutual funds.

Source: Board of Governors of the Federal Reserve System

Standard & Poor's Databank

Population

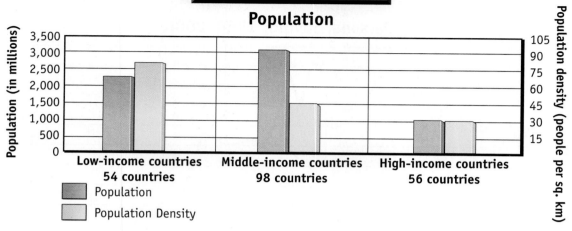

Population (in millions)

Population density (people per sq. km)

| Low-income countries 54 countries | Middle-income countries 98 countries | High-income countries 56 countries |

Population

Population Density

Gross National Income

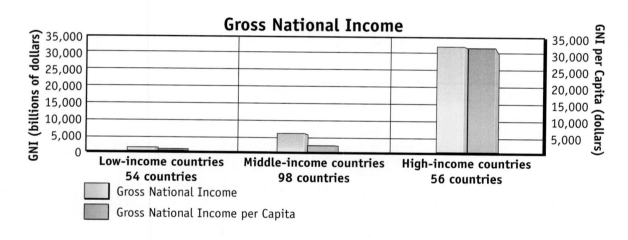

GNI (billions of dollars)

GNI per Capita (dollars)

| Low-income countries 54 countries | Middle-income countries 98 countries | High-income countries 56 countries |

Gross National Income

Gross National Income per Capita

Gross Domestic Product

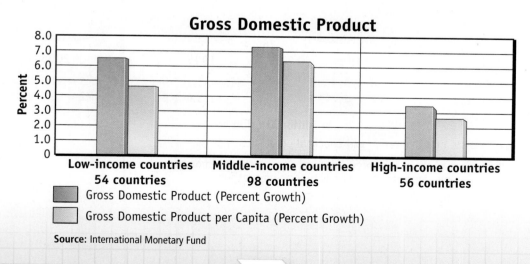

Percent

| Low-income countries 54 countries | Middle-income countries 98 countries | High-income countries 56 countries |

Gross Domestic Product (Percent Growth)

Gross Domestic Product per Capita (Percent Growth)

Source: International Monetary Fund

World Population by Age, 2000–2050

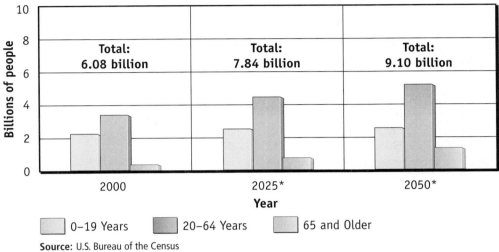

Source: U.S. Bureau of the Census
*Estimate

Countries Ranked by Population, 2000 and 2050

Country	Year 2000		Year 2050*	
	Population (in millions)	Rank	Population (in millions)	Rank
China	1,261	1	1,470	(2)
India	1,014	2	1,620	(1)
United States	276	3	404	(3)
Indonesia	224	4	338	(4)
Brazil	173	5	207	(7)
Russia	146	6	118	(14)
Pakistan	142	7	268	(6)
Bangladesh	129	8	205	(8)
Japan	127	9	101	(16)
Nigeria	123	10	304	(5)
Mexico	100	11	153	(12)

Source: U.S. Bureau of the Census
*Estimate

Aging Index in Selected Nations of the Americas, 2000 and 2025

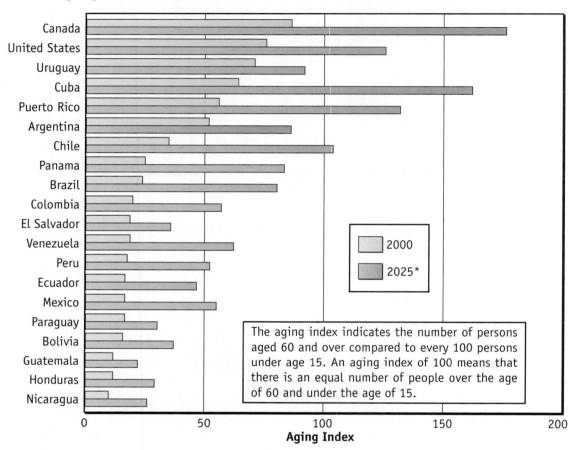

Canada
United States
Uruguay
Cuba
Puerto Rico
Argentina
Chile
Panama
Brazil
Colombia
El Salvador
Venezuela
Peru
Ecuador
Mexico
Paraguay
Bolivia
Guatemala
Honduras
Nicaragua

2000
2025*

The aging index indicates the number of persons aged 60 and over compared to every 100 persons under age 15. An aging index of 100 means that there is an equal number of people over the age of 60 and under the age of 15.

0   50   100   150   200
Aging Index

Median Age, World, 1975–2025

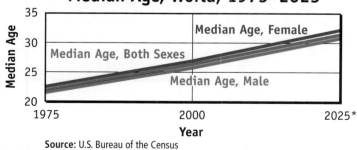

Median Age, Female
Median Age, Both Sexes
Median Age, Male

Median Age

35
30
25
20

1975   2000   2025*
Year

Source: U.S. Bureau of the Census
*Estimate

Standard & Poor's Databank

U.S. Exports and Imports, 1960–2005

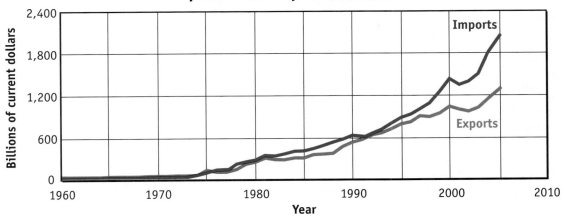

Inflation and Unemployment, Selected Economies 1990–2005

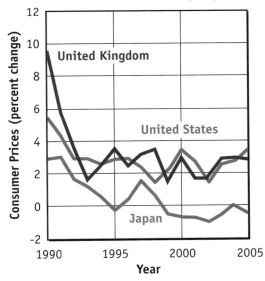

Source: *Economic Report of the President,* 2006

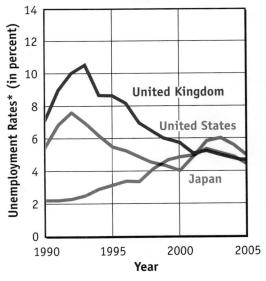

Source: International Monetary Fund
*Based on national definitions

Standard & Poor's Databank

Career Name	Job Description	Qualifications	Median Salary	Job Outlook
Advertising Manager	• Oversee the development of advertisements • Manage the creative services and media services departments	• Bachelor's degree in liberal arts, advertising, or journalism • Knowledge of marketing and consumer behavior	$57,130	Above Average
Aerospace Engineer	• Design, develop, and test aircraft, spacecraft, and missiles • Specialize in areas such as structural design, guidance, navigation and control, instrumentation and communication, or production methods	• Bachelor's degree in engineering • Graduate training is essential for engineering faculty positions and many research and development programs	$50,993	Below Average
Air Traffic Controller	• Coordinate the movement of air traffic • Direct planes efficiently to minimize delays	• FAA-approved education program • Regular medical exams and drug screenings required	$103,030	Average
Anesthesiologist	• Care of surgical patients and pain relief • Responsible for maintenance of the patient's vital life functions	• Undergraduate degree • 4 years of medical school • 3 to 8 years of internship and residency	$259,948	Above Average
Buyer	• Determine which products a company will sell • Buy the finished goods for resale to the public	• 4-year college degree in business • Ability to accurately predict demand, or what will appeal to consumers	$40,780	Below Average

Careers

Career Name	Job Description	Qualifications	Median Salary	Job Outlook
Consumer Loan Officer	• Analyze loan applications • Make decisions regarding the extension of credit	• Bachelor's degree in finance, economics, or a related field	$43,980	Average
Dentist	• Diagnose, prevent, and treat problems with teeth or mouth tissue • Perform corrective surgery on gums and supporting bones • Remove decay, fill cavities, examine x-rays, straighten and repair teeth	• Minimum 2 years college-level pre-dental education • Dental school	$129,920	Average
Dispatcher	• Schedule and dispatch workers, equipment, or service vehicles to carry materials or passengers • Keep records, logs, and schedules of all calls and vehicles	• High-school diploma for entry level position • Typing, filing, and record-keeping skills	$30,920	Average
Economist	• Research, collect, and analyze economic data • Monitor economic trends and develop forecasts • Advise businesses, government, and other organizations on economic policy	• Master's degree in economics • Experience gathering and analyzing data for economic models	$68,550	Average
Editor	• Review, rewrite, and edit the work of writers • Decide what material will appeal to readers • Offer comments to improve the work	• Undergraduate degree in communications, journalism, or English	$43,890	Average

Career Name	Job Description	Qualifications	Median Salary	Job Outlook
Electrician	• Install, connect, test, and maintain electrical systems • Install wiring systems into new homes, businesses, and factories	• High-school diploma • Usually a 4-year apprenticeship program	$40,660	Average
Emergency Medical Technician/ Paramedic	• Respond to patients in emergency situations; determine the nature of their condition and extent of injuries • Give appropriate emergency care and, when necessary, transport the patient	• High-school diploma • Formal EMT training	$25,310	Excellent
Fashion Designer	• Study fashion trends, sketch designs of clothing and accessories, select colors and fabrics, and oversee the final production of designs	• 2- or 4-year degree • Experience in textiles, sewing, pattern-making, computer-aided design	$55,840	Below Average
Financial Manager	• Prepare financial reports • Assess the risk of transactions, raise capital, and analyze investments • Communicate with investors	• Master's degree in business administration, economics, finance, or risk management	$73,340	Average
Information Technology (IT) Specialist	• Work in areas ranging from complexity theory to hardware to programming-language design • Web page development	• Bachelor's degree in Computer Science, Information Science, or Management Information Systems	$85,190	Excellent

Career Name	Job Description	Qualifications	Median Salary	Job Outlook
Landscape Architect	• Plan the location of buildings, roads, and walkways, and the arrangement of flowers, shrubs, and trees around structures • Design landscaping of residential areas, public parks and playgrounds, college campuses, shopping centers, golf courses, parkways, and industrial parks	• Bachelor's and/or Master's degree in landscape architecture	$53,120	Above Average
Lawyer	• Represent parties in criminal and civil cases • Counsel clients concerning legal rights and obligations and suggest particular courses of action	• Undergraduate degree • 3 years of law school • Must pass a written bar examination	$94,930	Average
Market Research Analyst	• Analyze data on past sales to predict future sales • Design market surveys • Analyze competitors' prices and methods of marketing	• Graduate degree in economics, business administration, marketing, or statistics • Strong background in mathematics and consumer behavior	$53,810	Above Average
Meteorologist	• Study the atmosphere's physical characteristics, motions, and processes, and the way in which these factors affect the rest of the environment • Forecast the weather	• Bachelor's degree in atmospheric science • Master's degree preferred	$70,100	Average
Occupational Therapist	• Help physically challenged people improve their ability to perform day-to-day tasks in their living and working environments • Help clients have independent, productive, and satisfying lives	• Bachelor's degree in occupational therapy • Starting in 2007, Master's degree in occupational therapy	$54,660	Excellent

Careers

Career Name	Job Description	Qualifications	Median Salary	Job Outlook
Pharmacist	• Distribute drugs prescribed by physicians • Provide information to patients about medications and their use • Advise physicians and other health practitioners on the selection, dosages, interactions, and side effects of medications	• Undergraduate degree • Doctor of Pharmacy Degree • Pass the North American Pharmacist Licensure Exam	$84,900	Above Average
Pilot	• Fly airplanes or helicopters • Transport passengers and cargo • Thoroughly check aircraft to make sure that the engines, controls, instruments, and other systems are functioning properly	• 250 hours of flight experience • Commercial pilot's license	$53,870	Average
Real Estate Agent	• Help home buyers find a house to purchase • Help home sellers find a buyer for their property	• Knowledge of neighborhoods, local zoning and tax laws, and where to obtain financing • High school graduate, licensed real estate agent	$30,930	Below Average
Registered Nurse	• Treat patients and educate them and the public about various medical conditions • Provide advice and emotional support to patients' family members	• One or more of the following: • Bachelor of Science in nursing • Associate degree in nursing • Nursing diploma	$52,330	Excellent
Stockbroker	• Relay investors' stock orders to the floor of a securities exchange, or process them over the Internet • Offer financial counseling and advice on the purchase or sale of particular securities	• College degree • Must pass a state licensing exam and the General Securities Registered Representative Exam	$60,990	Average

Careers

REFERENCE ATLAS

NATIONAL GEOGRAPHIC

ATLAS KEY

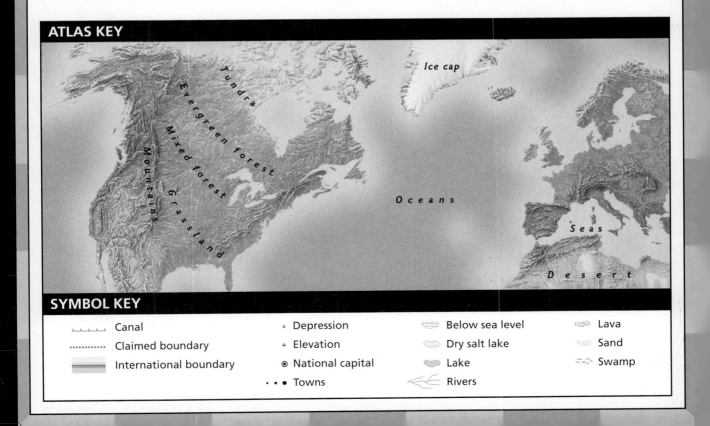

SYMBOL KEY

Canal	∘ Depression	Below sea level	Lava
Claimed boundary	+ Elevation	Dry salt lake	Sand
International boundary	⊛ National capital	Lake	Swamp
• • ● Towns		Rivers	

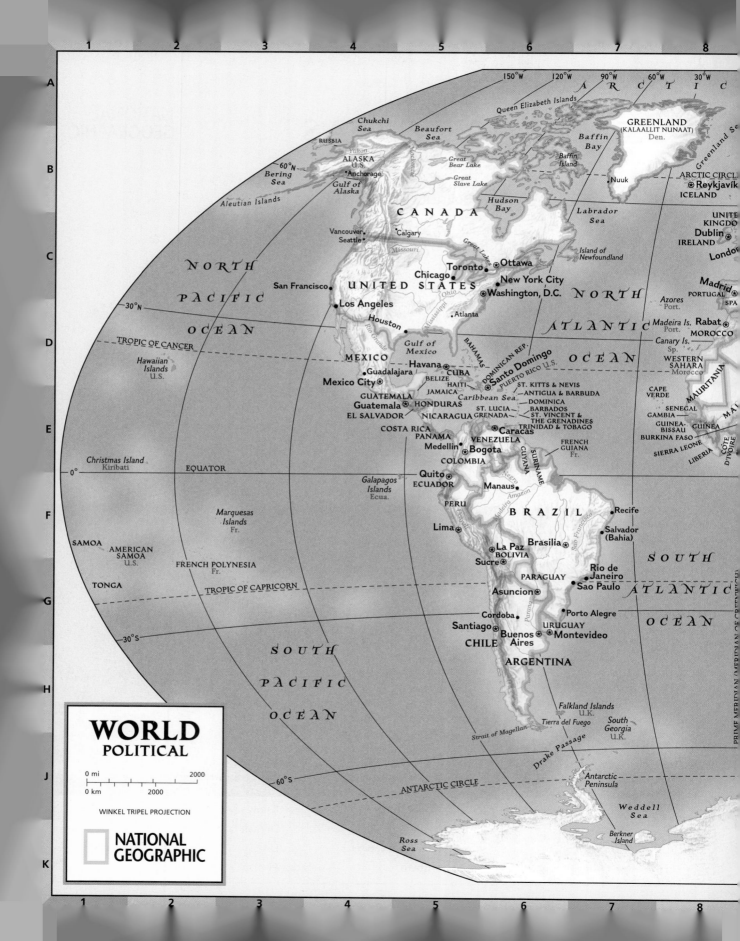

150°W   120°W   90°W   60°W   30°W

A R C T I C

Queen Elizabeth Islands

GREENLAND
(KALAALLIT NUNAAT)
Den.

Chukchi
Sea

Beaufort
Sea

Baffin
Bay

Greenland Sea

RUSSIA

60°N
Bering
Sea

ALASKA
U.S.

•Anchorage

Gulf of
Alaska

Yukon

Mackenzie

Great
Bear Lake

Baffin
Island

•Nuuk

ARCTIC CIRCLE
⊛ Reykjavík
ICELAND

Aleutian Islands

Great
Slave Lake

C A N A D A

Hudson
Bay

Labrador
Sea

UNITED
KINGDO
Dublin ⊛
IRELAND
London

N O R T H

P A C I F I C

Vancouver•
Seattle•

•Calgary

Missouri

Great Lakes

Island of
Newfoundland

San Francisco•

U N I T E D   S T A T E S

Toronto •
Chicago ●
● Ottawa
● New York City

N O R T H

Madrid ⊛
PORTUGAL   SPA

30°N

Los Angeles•

Houston•

Ohio

●Atlanta

● Washington, D.C.

A T L A N T I C

Azores
Port.

TROPIC OF CANCER

O C E A N

Mississippi

Rio Grande

Gulf of
Mexico

BAHAMAS

O C E A N

Madeira Is. Rabat ⊛
Port.   MOROCCO
Canary Is.
Sp.

Hawaiian
Islands
U.S.

M E X I C O

•Havana ⊛
CUBA

DOMINICAN REP.
⊛ Santo Domingo
PUERTO RICO U.S.

WESTERN
SAHARA
Morocco

•Guadalajara
Mexico City ⊛

BELIZE
HAITI
JAMAICA

ST. KITTS & NEVIS
ANTIGUA & BARBUDA
DOMINICA
BARBADOS

CAPE
VERDE

MAURITANIA

GUATEMALA

Guatemala ⊛ HONDURAS
EL SALVADOR   NICARAGUA

Caribbean Sea

ST. LUCIA
ST. VINCENT &
THE GRENADINES
GRENADA   TRINIDAD & TOBAGO

SENEGAL
GAMBIA
GUINEA-
BISSAU   GUINEA

MA

COSTA RICA
PANAMA

⊛ Caracas
VENEZUELA

FRENCH
GUIANA
Fr.

BURKINA FASO
SIERRA LEONE
LIBERIA

CÔTE
D'IVOIRE

E

Christmas Island
Kiribati

0°

EQUATOR

Galapagos
Islands
Ecua.

Medellin•
● Bogota
COLOMBIA

Quito ⊛
ECUADOR
Manaus•

GUYANA

SURINAME

Negro

Amazon

Marquesas
Islands
Fr.

PERU

Lima•

Madeira

B R A Z I L

•Recife

Purus

F

SAMOA
AMERICAN
SAMOA
U.S.

FRENCH POLYNESIA
Fr.

⊛ La Paz
BOLIVIA
Sucre•

Brasilia •

São Francisco

•Salvador
(Bahia)

S O U T H

TONGA

TROPIC OF CAPRICORN

PARAGUAY

Asuncion ⊛

Rio de
Janeiro
●São Paulo

A T L A N T I C

G

30°S

Cordoba•

•Porto Alegre

O C E A N

S O U T H

Santiago ⊛
CHILE

Buenos
Aires ⊛

URUGUAY
⊛ Montevideo

P A C I F I C

ARGENTINA

H

O C E A N

Falkland Islands
U.K.

Tierra del Fuego

South
Georgia
U.K.

PRIME MERIDIAN (MERIDIAN OF GREENWICH)

Strait of Magellan

Drake Passage

60°S

ANTARCTIC CIRCLE

Antarctic
Peninsula

Ross
Sea

Weddell
Sea

Berkner
Island

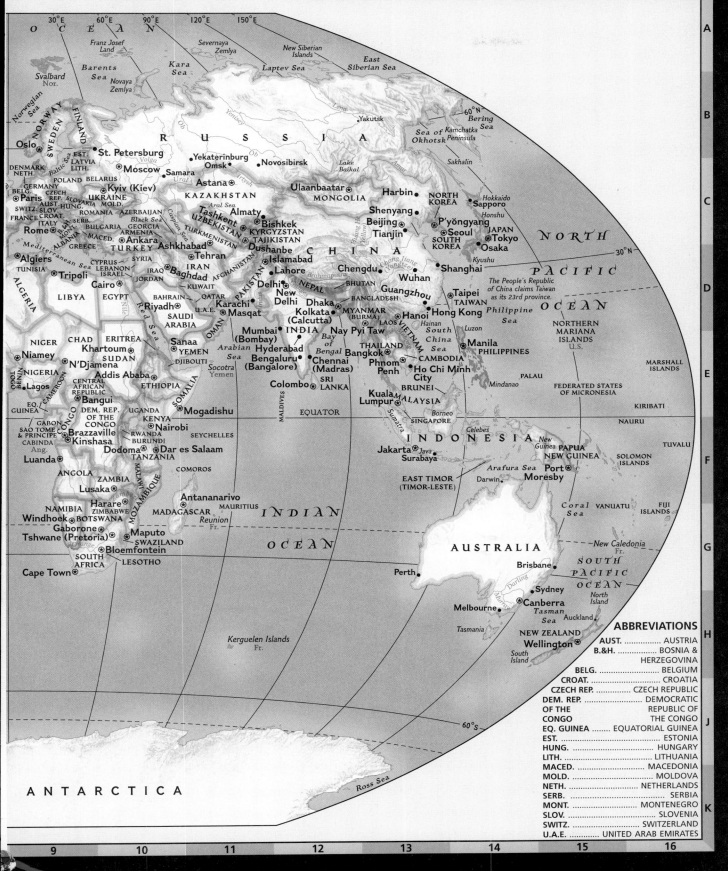

9 10 11 12 13 14 15 16

A

30°E 60°E 90°E 120°E 150°E

O C E A N

Franz Josef
Land

Barents
Sea

Novaya
Zemlya

Severnaya
Zemlya

New Siberian
Islands

Laptev Sea

East
Siberian Sea

Svalbard
Nor.

Norwegian
Sea

Kara
Sea

B

Yakutsk

60°N

Bering
Sea

NORWAY FINLAND

SWEDEN

Ob

Yenisey

Lena

Sea of
Okhotsk

Kamchatka
Peninsula

Oslo

St. Petersburg

Yekaterinburg
Omsk
Novosibirsk

Sakhalin

C

DENMARK
NETH.

EST.
LATVIA
LITH.

Moscow
Samara

R U S S I A

Lake
Baikal

Amur

Harbin

NORTH
KOREA

Hokkaido
Sapporo

GERMANY
BELG.
POLAND BELARUS
CZECH

Astana

KAZAKHSTAN

Irtysh

Ural

Volga

Ulaanbaatar

MONGOLIA

Shenyang

P'yŏngyang

Honshu

JAPAN

Paris
SWITZ.
AUST. HUNG.
FRANCE CROAT.

SLOVAKIA MOLD.

Kyiv (Kiev)
UKRAINE

ROMANIA AZERBAIJAN

Tashkent
UZBEKISTAN

Almaty
Bishkek
KYRGYZSTAN

Beijing
Tianjin

Seoul
SOUTH
KOREA

Tokyo
Osaka

ITALY SLOV.
Rome
ALBANIA
GREECE

BULGARIA GEORGIA
ARMENIA
MACED.
TURKEY

Aral Sea

Caspian Sea

Black Sea

TURKMENISTAN
TAJIKISTAN

Dushanbe

Hwang He
(Yellow)

C H I N A

Chang Jiang
(Yangtze)

Shanghai

Kyushu

The People's Republic
of China claims Taiwan
as its 23rd province.

N O R T H

P A C I F I C

30°N

Algiers
TUNISIA
Tripoli

Mediterranean Sea
CYPRUS
SYRIA

Ankara
Ashkhabad

IRAN

Tehran

AFGHANISTAN

Islamabad

Lahore

Chengdu

Wuhan

Guangzhou

Taipei
TAIWAN

O C E A N

LEBANON
ISRAEL
JORDAN

Baghdad

PAKISTAN

Delhi
New
Delhi

NEPAL

Brahmaputra

BHUTAN

Hanoi
Hong Kong

Philippine
Sea

NORTHERN
MARIANA
ISLANDS
U.S.

D

ALGERIA
LIBYA
EGYPT

Cairo

KUWAIT
IRAQ
BAHRAIN
QATAR
Riyadh
U.A.E.

SAUDI
ARABIA

OMAN

Karachi
Masqat

Indus

Dhaka
Kolkata
(Calcutta)

BANGLADESH
MYANMAR
(BURMA)

LAOS

VIETNAM

South
China
Sea

Hainan

Luzon

Manila
PHILIPPINES

MARSHALL
ISLANDS

NIGER
CHAD

Khartoum

ERITREA

Sanaa

Mumbai
(Bombay)
Hyderabad

I N D I A
Nay Pyi Taw

Bay
of
Bengal

THAILAND

Bangkok

CAMBODIA

Mindanao

PALAU

E

NIGERIA

Niamey

N'Djamena

SUDAN

Addis Ababa

YEMEN

DJIBOUTI

Arabian
Sea

Socotra
Yemen

Bengaluru
(Bangalore)

Chennai
(Madras)

SRI
LANKA

Phnom
Penh

Ho Chi Minh
City

BRUNEI

FEDERATED STATES
OF MICRONESIA

KIRIBATI

TOGO
BENIN
EQ.
GUINEA
Lagos

CENTRAL
AFRICAN
REPUBLIC

CAMEROON

Bangui

ETHIOPIA

SOMALIA

Colombo

MALDIVES

EQUATOR

Kuala
Lumpur
MALAYSIA

SINGAPORE

Borneo

Sumatra

NAURU

GABON
SAO TOME
& PRINCIPE
CABINDA
Ang.

Brazzaville
Kinshasa

DEM. REP.
OF THE
CONGO

Congo

UGANDA

RWANDA
BURUNDI

KENYA

Nairobi

Mogadishu

SEYCHELLES

Celebes
Sea

I N D O N E S I A

Java

New
Guinea

PAPUA
NEW GUINEA

SOLOMON
ISLANDS

TUVALU

F

Luanda

ANGOLA

ZAMBIA

Dodoma
Dar es Salaam

TANZANIA

MALAWI

COMOROS

Jakarta
Surabaya

EAST TIMOR
(TIMOR-LESTE)

Arafura Sea

Darwin

Port
Moresby

Lusaka

Harare

NAMIBIA
Windhoek
Gaborone

ZIMBABWE

BOTSWANA

MOZAMBIQUE

Antananarivo

MADAGASCAR

MAURITIUS

Reunion
Fr.

I N D I A N

Coral
Sea

VANUATU

FIJI
ISLANDS

G

Tshwane (Pretoria)
Maputo
SWAZILAND
Bloemfontein

O C E A N

New Caledonia
Fr.

Cape Town

SOUTH
AFRICA

LESOTHO

A U S T R A L I A

Perth

Darling

Brisbane

Sydney

S O U T H

P A C I F I C

O C E A N

North
Island

H

Kerguelen Islands
Fr.

Melbourne

Murray

Canberra

Tasman
Sea

Auckland

ABBREVIATIONS

Tasmania

NEW ZEALAND

Wellington

South
Island

AUST. .... AUSTRIA
B.&H. .... BOSNIA &
HERZEGOVINA

BELG. .... BELGIUM
CROAT. .... CROATIA
CZECH REP. .... CZECH REPUBLIC
DEM. REP. .... DEMOCRATIC
OF THE   REPUBLIC OF
CONGO   THE CONGO

J

60°S

EQ. GUINEA .... EQUATORIAL GUINEA
EST. .... ESTONIA
HUNG. .... HUNGARY
LITH. .... LITHUANIA
MACED. .... MACEDONIA
MOLD. .... MOLDOVA
NETH. .... NETHERLANDS
SERB. .... SERBIA
MONT. .... MONTENEGRO
SLOV. .... SLOVENIA
SWITZ. .... SWITZERLAND
U.A.E. .... UNITED ARAB EMIRATES

K

A N T A R C T I C A

Ross Sea

9 10 11 12 13 14 15 16

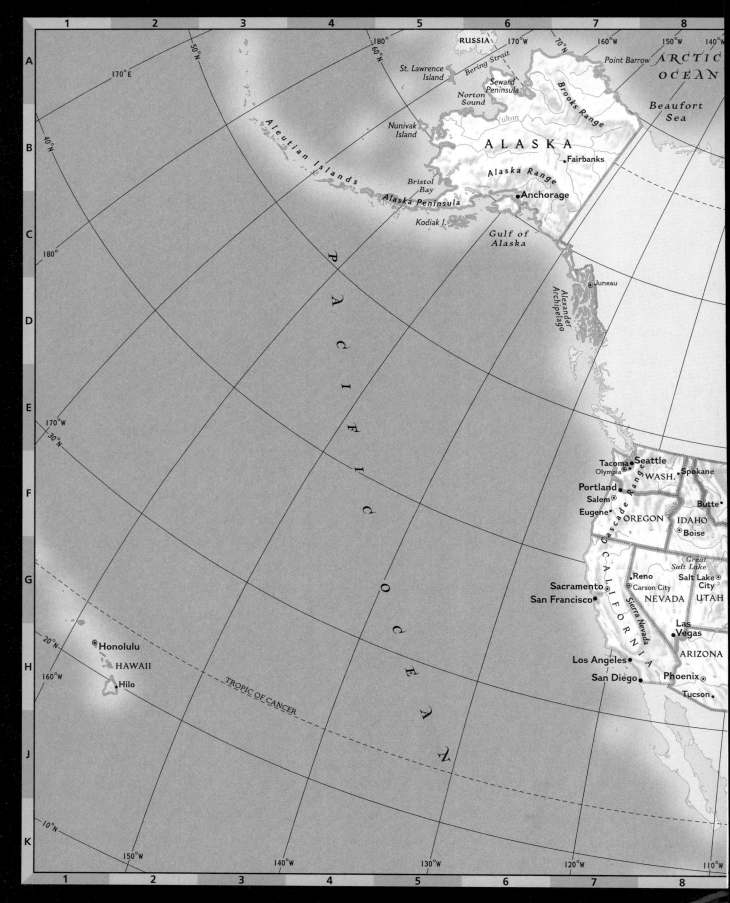

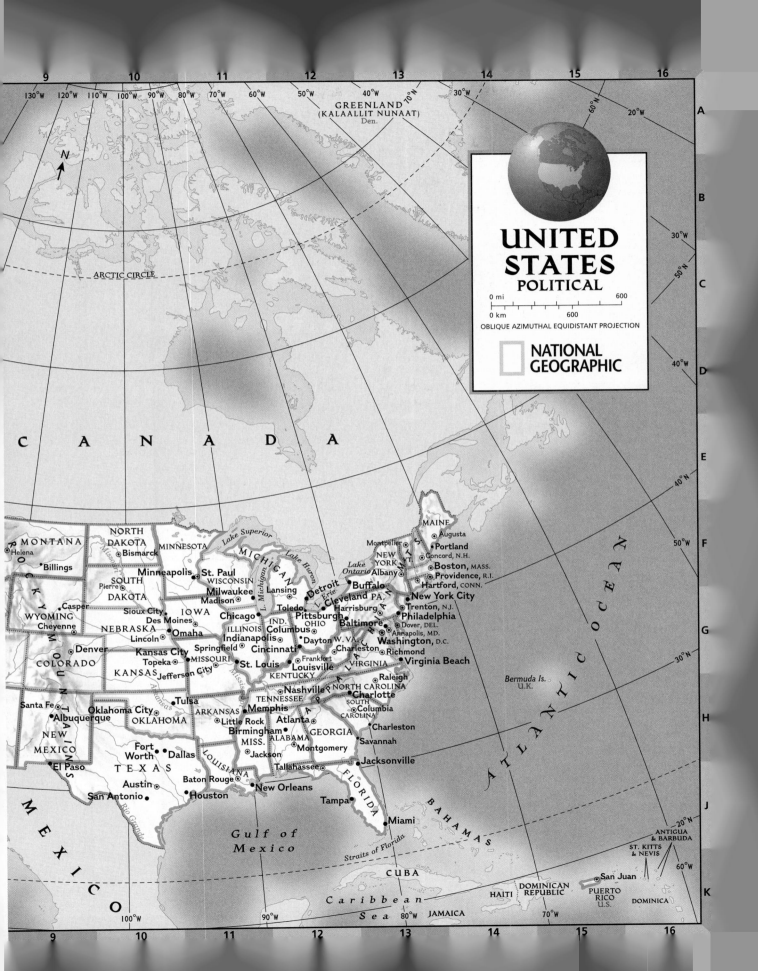

UNITED
STATES
POLITICAL

0 mi   600
0 km   600
OBLIQUE AZIMUTHAL EQUIDISTANT PROJECTION

NATIONAL
GEOGRAPHIC

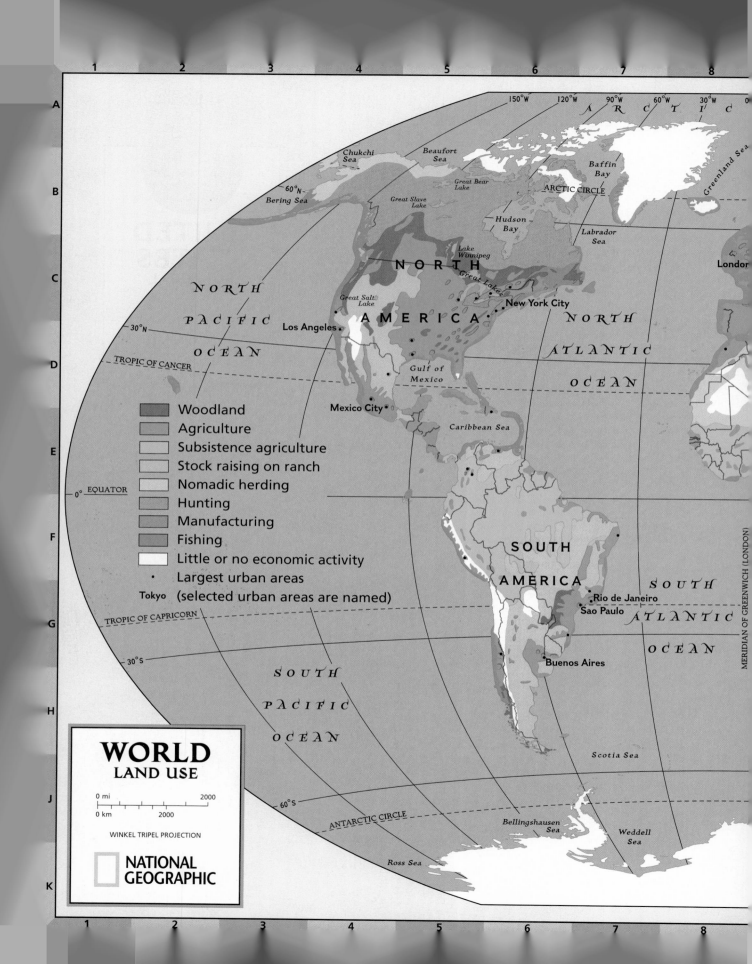

WORLD
LAND USE

Legend:
- Woodland
- Agriculture
- Subsistence agriculture
- Stock raising on ranch
- Nomadic herding
- Hunting
- Manufacturing
- Fishing
- Little or no economic activity
- • Largest urban areas
- Tokyo (selected urban areas are named)

0 mi — 2000
0 km — 2000

WINKEL TRIPEL PROJECTION

NATIONAL GEOGRAPHIC

ARCTIC

150°W 120°W 90°W 60°W 30°W 0

Chukchi Sea
Beaufort Sea
Baffin Bay
Greenland Sea
60°N
Bering Sea
Great Bear Lake
ARCTIC CIRCLE
Great Slave Lake
Hudson Bay
Labrador Sea
Lake Winnipeg
NORTH
Great Lakes
London
NORTH PACIFIC
Great Salt Lake
AMERICA
New York City
NORTH
30°N
Los Angeles
ATLANTIC
OCEAN
TROPIC OF CANCER
Gulf of Mexico
OCEAN
Mexico City
Caribbean Sea
EQUATOR 0°

SOUTH
AMERICA
SOUTH
Rio de Janeiro
Sao Paulo
ATLANTIC
TROPIC OF CAPRICORN
OCEAN
30°S
SOUTH
Buenos Aires
PACIFIC
OCEAN
60°S
Scotia Sea
ANTARCTIC CIRCLE
Bellingshausen Sea
Weddell Sea
Ross Sea

MERIDIAN OF GREENWICH (LONDON)

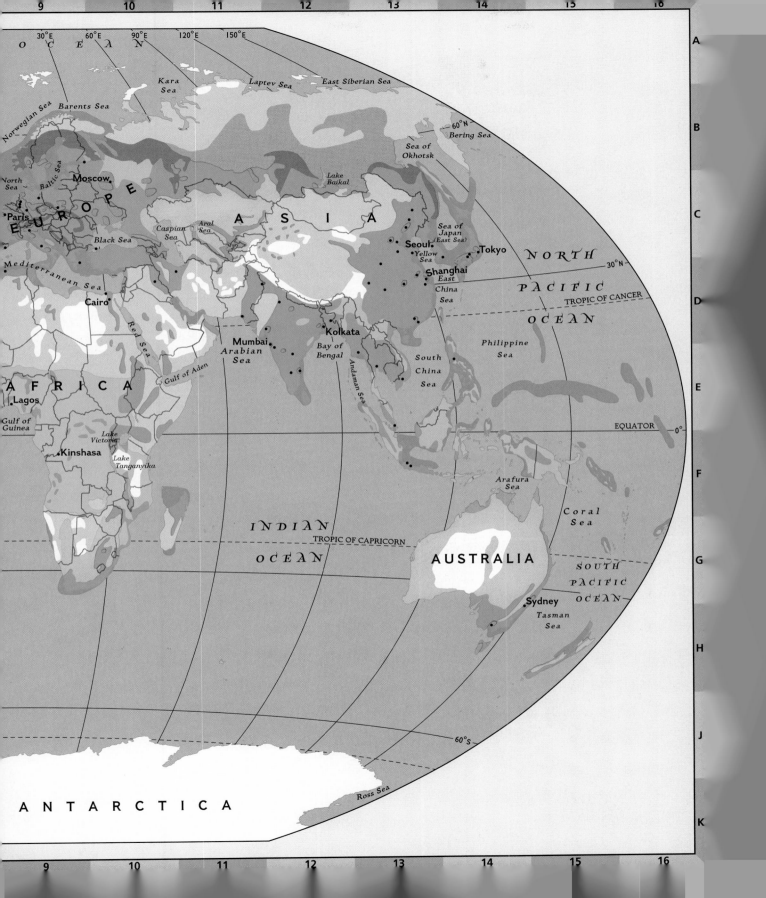

9   10   11   12   13   14   15   16

30°E 60°E 90°E 120°E 150°E

O C E A N

Kara
Sea

Laptev Sea

East Siberian Sea

Norwegian Sea

Barents Sea

60°N

Bering Sea

Sea of
Okhotsk

North
Sea

Baltic Sea

Moscow

Lake
Baikal

E U R O P E

A S I A

Paris

Caspian
Sea

Aral
Sea

Sea of
Japan
(East Sea)

Black Sea

Seoul

Tokyo

Mediterranean Sea

Yellow
Sea

N O R T H

Shanghai

30°N

Cairo

East
China
Sea

P A C I F I C

TROPIC OF CANCER

O C E A N

Red Sea

Kolkata

Philippine
Sea

A F R I C A

Mumbai
Arabian
Sea

Bay of
Bengal

South
China
Sea

Gulf of Aden

Andaman Sea

Lagos

Gulf of
Guinea

Lake
Victoria

Kinshasa

Lake
Tanganyika

EQUATOR   0°

Arafura
Sea

I N D I A N

Coral
Sea

TROPIC OF CAPRICORN

O C E A N

AUSTRALIA

S O U T H

P A C I F I C

O C E A N

Sydney

Tasman
Sea

60°S

A N T A R C T I C A

Ross Sea

9   10   11   12   13   14   15   16

A B C D E F G H J K

Legend:

- Woodland
- Agriculture
- Woodland and Agriculture
- Stock raising on ranch
- Wetlands
- Urban land
- Fishing
- Tundra
- Little or no economic activity

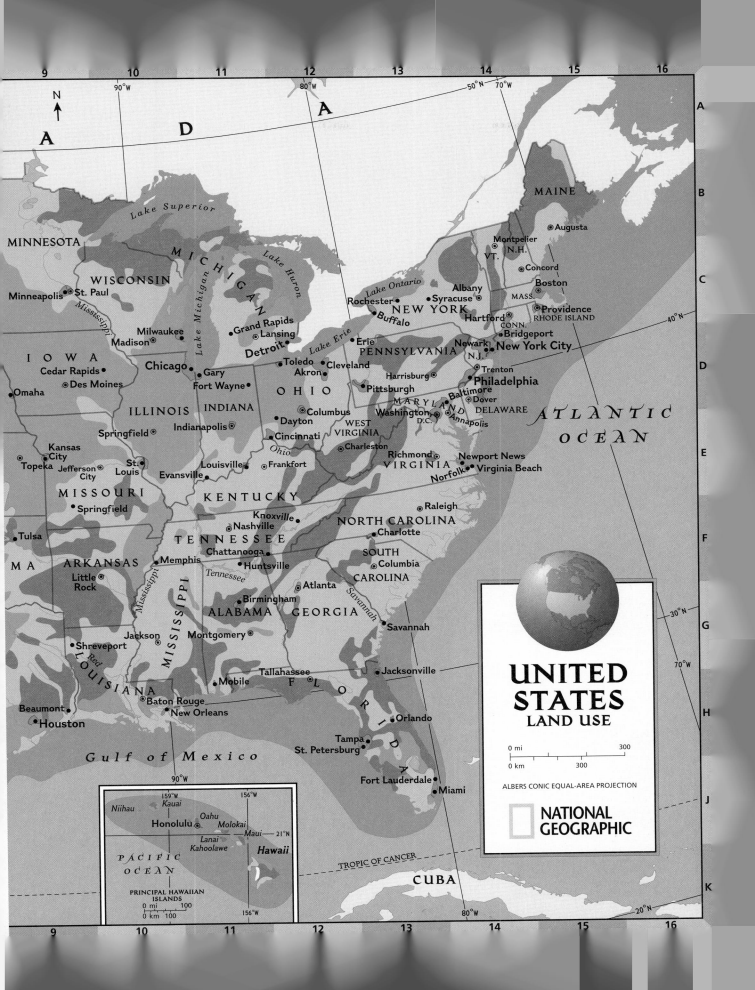

UNITED STATES
STATES
LAND USE

0 mi   300
0 km   300

ALBERS CONIC EQUAL-AREA PROJECTION

NATIONAL GEOGRAPHIC

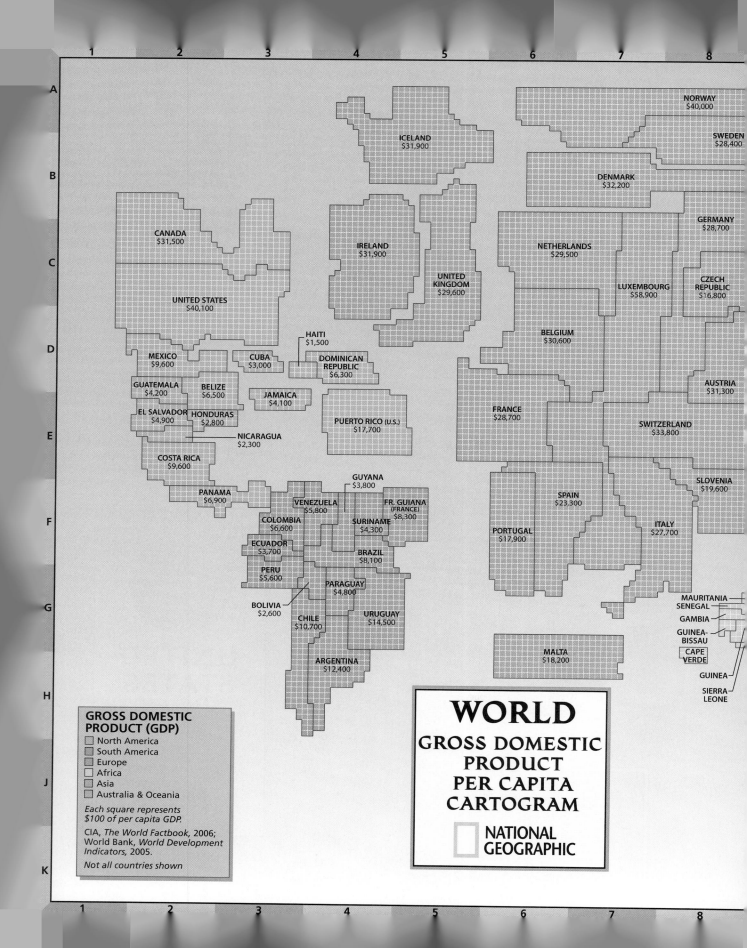

WORLD
GROSS DOMESTIC PRODUCT PER CAPITA CARTOGRAM

NATIONAL GEOGRAPHIC

GROSS DOMESTIC PRODUCT (GDP)
- North America
- South America
- Europe
- Africa
- Asia
- Australia & Oceania

Each square represents $100 of per capita GDP.

CIA, *The World Factbook,* 2006; World Bank, *World Development Indicators,* 2005.

Not all countries shown

NORWAY $40,000
SWEDEN $28,400
ICELAND $31,900
DENMARK $32,200
GERMANY $28,700
CANADA $31,500
IRELAND $31,900
NETHERLANDS $29,500
LUXEMBOURG $58,900
CZECH REPUBLIC $16,800
UNITED KINGDOM $29,600
UNITED STATES $40,100
BELGIUM $30,600
HAITI $1,500
MEXICO $9,600
CUBA $3,000
DOMINICAN REPUBLIC $6,300
AUSTRIA $31,300
GUATEMALA $4,200
BELIZE $6,500
JAMAICA $4,100
FRANCE $28,700
SWITZERLAND $33,800
EL SALVADOR $4,900
HONDURAS $2,800
PUERTO RICO (U.S.) $17,700
NICARAGUA $2,300
COSTA RICA $9,600
SLOVENIA $19,600
GUYANA $3,800
PANAMA $6,900
VENEZUELA $5,800
FR. GUIANA (FRANCE) $8,300
SPAIN $23,300
ITALY $27,700
COLOMBIA $6,600
SURINAME $4,300
ECUADOR $3,700
BRAZIL $8,100
PORTUGAL $17,900
PERU $5,600
PARAGUAY $4,800
MAURITANIA
BOLIVIA $2,600
URUGUAY $14,500
SENEGAL
CHILE $10,700
GAMBIA
GUINEA-BISSAU
CAPE VERDE
MALTA $18,200
ARGENTINA $12,400
GUINEA
SIERRA LEONE

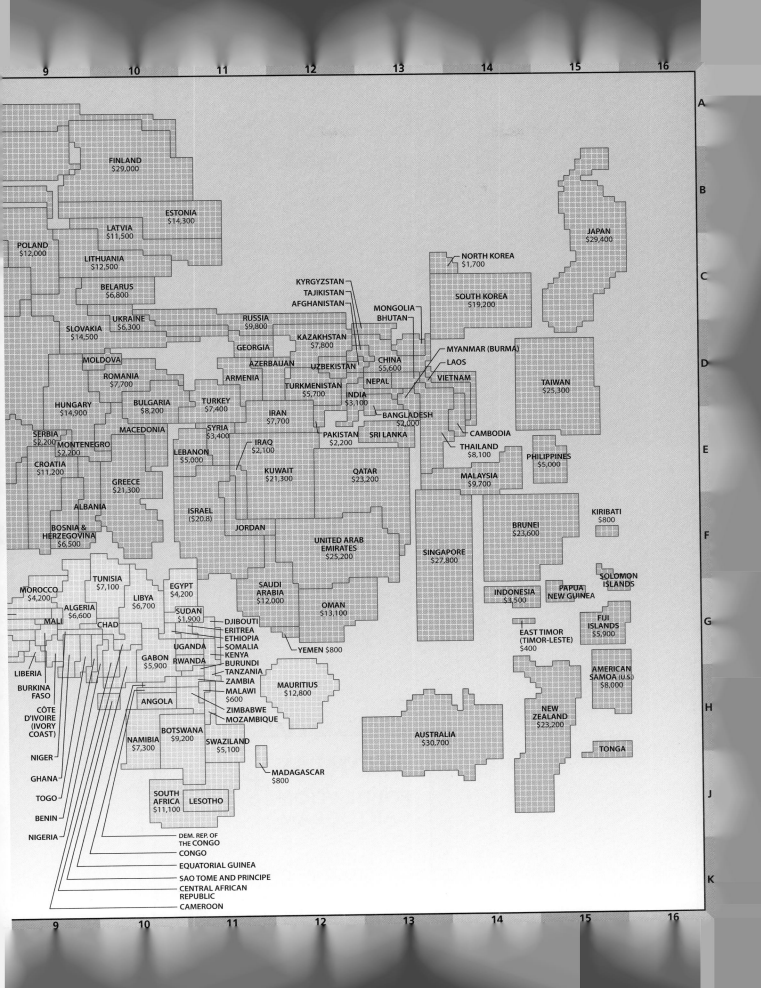

9	10	11	12	13	14	15	16

A

FINLAND
$29,000

B

ESTONIA
$14,300

LATVIA
$11,500

POLAND
$12,000

LITHUANIA
$12,500

JAPAN
$29,400

C

BELARUS
$6,800

NORTH KOREA
$1,700

KYRGYZSTAN
TAJIKISTAN
AFGHANISTAN

SOUTH KOREA
$19,200

UKRAINE
$6,300

RUSSIA
$9,800

MONGOLIA
BHUTAN

SLOVAKIA
$14,500

KAZAKHSTAN
$7,800

GEORGIA

MYANMAR (BURMA)

D

MOLDOVA

AZERBAIJAN

UZBEKISTAN

CHINA
$5,600

LAOS

TAIWAN
$25,300

ROMANIA
$7,700

ARMENIA

NEPAL

VIETNAM

HUNGARY
$14,900

BULGARIA
$8,200

TURKEY
$7,400

TURKMENISTAN
$5,700

INDIA
$3,100

SERBIA
$2,200

MACEDONIA

SYRIA
$3,400

IRAN
$7,700

BANGLADESH
$2,000

MONTENEGRO
$2,200

PAKISTAN
$2,200

SRI LANKA

CAMBODIA

E

CROATIA
$11,200

LEBANON
$5,000

IRAQ
$2,100

THAILAND
$8,100

PHILIPPINES
$5,000

GREECE
$21,300

KUWAIT
$21,300

QATAR
$23,200

MALAYSIA
$9,700

ALBANIA

KIRIBATI
$800

F

BOSNIA &
HERZEGOVINA
$6,500

ISRAEL
($20.8)

JORDAN

BRUNEI
$23,600

UNITED ARAB
EMIRATES
$25,200

SINGAPORE
$27,800

SOLOMON
ISLANDS

G

MOROCCO
$4,200

TUNISIA
$7,100

EGYPT
$4,200

SAUDI
ARABIA
$12,000

INDONESIA
$3,500

PAPUA
NEW GUINEA

FIJI
ISLANDS
$5,900

ALGERIA
$6,600

LIBYA
$6,700

OMAN
$13,100

MALI

CHAD

SUDAN
$1,900

EAST TIMOR
(TIMOR-LESTE)
$400

DJIBOUTI
ERITREA
ETHIOPIA
SOMALIA
KENYA
BURUNDI
TANZANIA
ZAMBIA
MALAWI
$600
ZIMBABWE
MOZAMBIQUE

YEMEN $800

LIBERIA

UGANDA
RWANDA

GABON
$5,900

AMERICAN
SAMOA (U.S.)
$8,000

BURKINA
FASO

MAURITIUS
$12,800

H

CÔTE
D'IVOIRE
(IVORY
COAST)

ANGOLA

BOTSWANA
$9,200

SWAZILAND
$5,100

NEW
ZEALAND
$23,200

NIGER

NAMIBIA
$7,300

AUSTRALIA
$30,700

TONGA

GHANA

MADAGASCAR
$800

J

TOGO

SOUTH
AFRICA
$11,100

LESOTHO

BENIN

NIGERIA

DEM. REP. OF
THE CONGO

K

CONGO

EQUATORIAL GUINEA

SAO TOME AND PRINCIPE

CENTRAL AFRICAN
REPUBLIC

CAMEROON

9	10	11	12	13	14	15	16

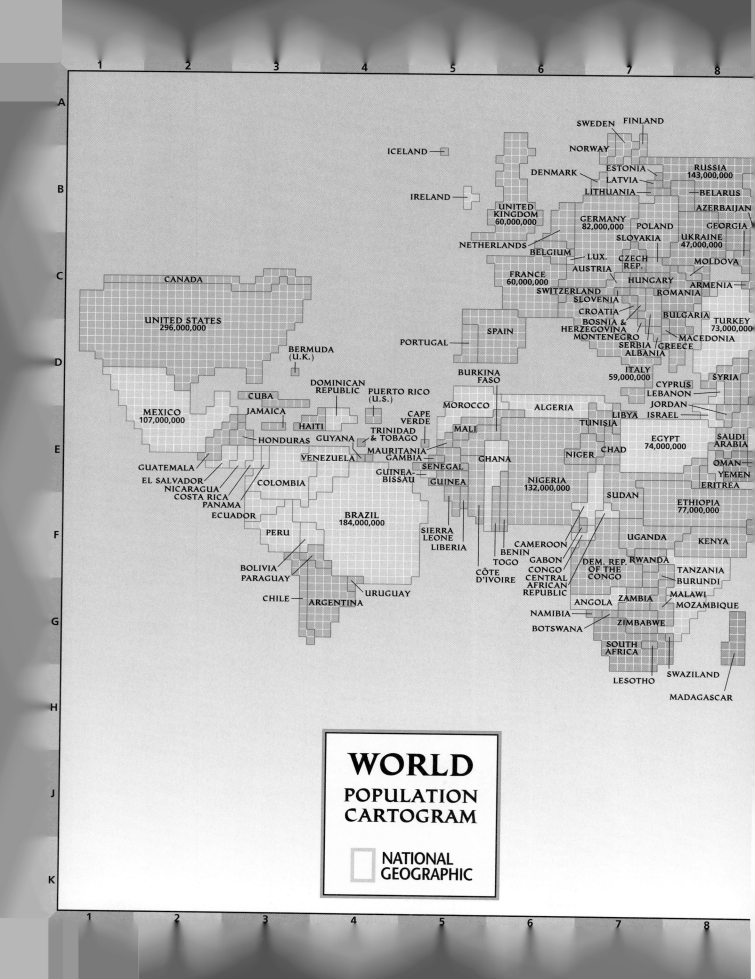

WORLD
POPULATION
CARTOGRAM

NATIONAL
GEOGRAPHIC

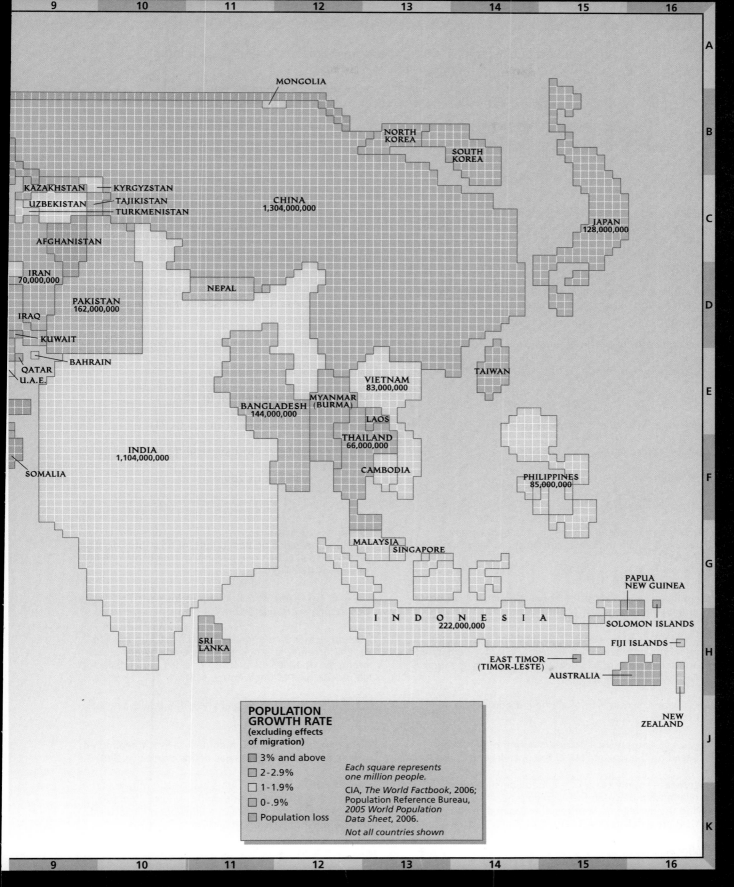

9 10 11 12 13 14 15 16

A
B
C
D
E
F
G
H
J
K

MONGOLIA

NORTH
KOREA

SOUTH
KOREA

JAPAN
128,000,000

KAZAKHSTAN — KYRGYZSTAN
UZBEKISTAN ——— TAJIKISTAN
TURKMENISTAN

CHINA
1,304,000,000

AFGHANISTAN

IRAN
70,000,000

NEPAL

PAKISTAN
162,000,000

IRAQ

KUWAIT

BAHRAIN

QATAR
U.A.E.

TAIWAN

VIETNAM
83,000,000

MYANMAR
(BURMA)

BANGLADESH
144,000,000

LAOS

THAILAND
66,000,000

CAMBODIA

SOMALIA

INDIA
1,104,000,000

PHILIPPINES
85,000,000

MALAYSIA
SINGAPORE

PAPUA
NEW GUINEA

I N D O N E S I A
222,000,000

SOLOMON ISLANDS

FIJI ISLANDS

SRI
LANKA

EAST TIMOR
(TIMOR-LESTE)

AUSTRALIA

NEW
ZEALAND

**POPULATION
GROWTH RATE**
(excluding effects
of migration)

3% and above

2-2.9%

1-1.9%

0-.9%

Population loss

*Each square represents
one million people.*

CIA, *The World Factbook*, 2006;
Population Reference Bureau,
*2005 World Population
Data Sheet*, 2006.

Not all countries shown

9 10 11 12 13 14 15 16

Glossary/Glosario

- Content vocabulary terms in this glossary are words that relate to economics content. They are **highlighted** yellow in your text.
- Words below that have an asterisk (*) are academic vocabulary terms. They help you understand your school subjects and are **boldfaced** in your text.

ENGLISH | **ESPAÑOL**

Ⓐ

ability-to-pay principle: principle of taxation in which those with higher incomes pay more taxes than those with lower incomes, regardless of the number of government services they use (p. 431)

principio de la capacidad de pago: principio de tributación que propone que los que tienen más ingresos deben pagar más impuestos que los que tienen menos, sin tomar en cuenta la cantidad de servicios gubernamentales que usan (p. 431)

absolute advantage: ability of one country to produce more output per unit of input than can another country (p. 467)

ventaja absoluta: capacidad de un país de producir más salidas por cada unidad de insumos que otros países (p. 467)

*access: ability to obtain or make use of (p. 96)

*acceso: habilidad de obtener o usar (p. 96)

*accompany: go with (p. 290)

*acompañar: ir con otro (p. 290)

*accumulate: build up (p. 100)

*acumular: juntar y amontonar (p. 100)

*accurate: exact; free from errors (p. 71)

*preciso: exacto; fiel; libre de errores (p. 71)

*adapt: adjust; get used to (p. 444)

*adaptarse: ajustarse; acostumbrarse (p. 444)

*adequate: enough (p. 266)

*adecuado: suficiente (p. 266)

*affect: influence (p. 473)

*afectar: influir (p. 473)

agency shop: company in which employees are not required to join the union, but must pay union dues (p. 318)

fábrica con cuota por agencia sindical: compañía en que los empleados no tienen que ser miembros del sindicato, pero sí tienen que pagar la misma cuota que los miembros (p. 318)

aggregate demand: the total of all planned expenditures in the entire economy (p. 348)

demanda agregada: el total de todos los gastos planeados de una economía entera (p. 348)

aggregate demand curve: a graphed line showing the relationship between the aggregate quantity demanded and the average of all prices as measured by the implicit GDP price deflator (p. 348)

curva de demanda agregada: línea gráfica que muestra la relación entre la cantidad de demanda agregada y el promedio de todos los precios, medidos por el deflactor de precios del PIB implícito (p. 348)

aggregates: summation of all the individual parts in the economy (p. 348)

agregado: suma de todas las partes individuales de una economía (p. 348)

aggregate supply: real domestic output of producers based on the rise and fall of the price level (p. 349)

oferta agregada: producción doméstica real, tomando en cuenta los aumentos y rebajas de los precios (p. 349)

aggregate supply curve: a graphed line showing the relationship between the aggregate quantity supplied and the average of all prices as measured by the implicit GDP price deflator (p. 349)

curva de oferta agregada: línea gráfica que muestra la relación entre la cantidad de oferta agregada y el promedio de todos los precios, medidos por el deflactor de precios del PIB implícito (p. 349)

*allocate: assign; give out (p. 427)

*asignar: repartir; adjudicar (p. 427)

Glossary/Glosario

ENGLISH	ESPAÑOL
*alternate: the other choice in a situation (p. 173)	*suplente: otra poción en una situación (p. 173)
*alternative: something else to be chosen (p. 16)	*alternativa: otra cosa que se puede escoger (p. 16)
*analysis: examination (p. 171)	*análisis: examen (p. 171)
*analyze: examine in detail (p. 20)	*analizar: examinar detenidamente (p. 20)
*annual: yearly (p. 221)	*anual: que se repite cada año (p. 221)
annual percentage rate (APR): cost of credit expressed as a yearly percentage (p. 98)	tasa de interés anual: costo del crédito expresado como porcentaje anual (p. 98)
*anticipate: expect (p. 357)	*prever: esperar (p. 357)
antitrust legislation: federal and state laws passed to prevent new monopolies from forming and to break up those that already exist (p. 246)	legislación antimonopolista: leyes federal y estatales aprobadas para evitar que se formen nuevos monopolios o para deshacer los que ya existen (p. 246)
*appropriate: suitable; proper (p. 529)	*apropiado: adecuado; indicado; correcto (p. 529)
arbitration: union and management submit the issues they cannot agree on to a third party for a final decision (p. 321)	arbitraje: el sindicato y los gerentes entregan los asuntos que no pueden resolver a un tercero para que tome una decisión final (p. 321)
articles of incorporation: document listing basic information about a corporation that is filed with the state where the corporation will be headquartered (p. 220)	escritura de constitución: documento que contiene información básica acerca de una sociedad anónima que se presenta al estado donde tendrá su oficina principal (p. 220)
assembly line: production system in which the good being produced moves on a conveyor belt past workers who perform individual tasks in assembling it (p. 274)	línea de montaje: sistema de producción en que el artículo producido es trasladado por una correa transportadora a distintos obreros que, por turnos, hacen labores particulares para ensamblarlo (p. 274)
assets: all items to which a business or household holds legal claim (p. 214)	activos: todos los bienes que son la propiedad legal de un negocio o persona (p. 214)
*assist: help (p. 392)	*asistir: ayudar (p. 392)
*assume: to take for granted; suppose (p. 77)	*suponer: dar por cierto una cosa (p. 77)
authoritarian socialism: system that supports revolution as a means to overthrow capitalism and bring about socialist goals; the entire economy is controlled by a central government; also called communism (p. 53)	socialismo autoritario: sistema que apoya la revolución como modo de derrocar el capitalismo y realizar metas socialistas; la economía entera es controlada por el gobierno central; también se llama comunismo (p. 53)
automated teller machine (ATM): unit that allows consumers to do their banking without the help of a teller (p. 376)	cajero automático: máquina que permite a los consumidores hacer sus transacciones bancarias sin la ayuda de un cajero (p. 376)
automation: production process in which machines do the work and people oversee them (p. 275)	automatización: proceso de producción en que máquinas hacen el trabajo y personas las supervisan (p. 275)
*available: to be had or used (p. 34)	*disponible: fácil de conseguir o usar (p. 34)

Glossary/Glosario

ENGLISH	ESPAÑOL

B

bait and switch: ad that attracts consumers with a low-priced product, then tries to sell them a higher-priced product (p. 72)

engatusar: anuncio que atrae a los consumidores con un producto a precio bajo para después tratar de venderles otro producto más caro (p. 72)

balance of trade: difference between the value of a nation's exports and its imports (p. 475)

balanza comercial: diferencia entre el valor de las exportaciones e importaciones de una nación (p. 475)

bankruptcy: the state of legally having been declared unable to pay off debts owed with available income (p. 106)

bancarrota: haber sido legalmente declarado incapaz de pagar las deudas con los ingresos que se tienen (p. 106)

barriers to entry: obstacles to competition that prevent others from entering a market (p. 237)

barreras al mercado: obstáculos que impiden que competidores entren en un mercado (p. 237)

barter: exchange of goods and services for other goods and services (p. 368)

trueque: intercambio de bienes y servicios por otros bienes y servicios (p. 368)

base year: year used as a point of comparison for other years in a series of statistics (p. 343)

año base: año que se usa como punto de comparación con otros años en una series de estudios estadísticos (p. 343)

*benefit: help (p. 476)

*beneficiar: ayudar (p. 476)

benefits-received principle: system of taxation in which those who use a particular government service support it with taxes in proportion to the benefit they receive; those who do not use a service do not pay taxes for it (p. 431)

principio de beneficio obtenido: sistema de tributación en que los que usan un servicio gubernamental pagan impuestos por él en proporción al beneficio que reciben; los que no usan el servicio no pagan impuestos por él (p. 431)

black market: "underground" or illegal market in which goods are traded at prices above their legal maximum prices or in which illegal goods are sold (p. 199)

mercado negro: mercado ilegal en que se venden bienes a precios más altos de los que permite la ley o en que se venden productos ilegales (p. 199)

blue-collar workers: category of workers employed in crafts, manufacturing, and nonfarm labor (p. 309)

obreros: clasificación de trabajadores empleados en artesanías, manufactura y labores no agrícolas (p. 309)

boom: same as *peak* (p. 352)

auge: véase *peak/auge* (p. 352)

boycott: economic pressure exerted by unions urging the public not to purchase the goods or services produced by a company (p. 322)

boicot: presión económica que ejerce un sindicato, animando al público a que no compre los bienes o servicios producidos por una compañía (p. 322)

brand name: word, picture, or logo on a product that helps consumers distinguish it from similar products (p. 74)

marca de fábrica: palabra, imagen o logotipo que lleva un producto para ayudar a los consumidores a distinguirlo de otros productos similares (p. 74)

broker: person who acts as a go-between for buyers and sellers of stocks and bonds (p. 150)

corredor de bolsa: persona que sirve de intermediario entre los vendedores y compradores de acciones y bonos (p. 150)

budget deficit: situation when the amount of government spending exceeds its receipts during the fiscal year (p. 428)

déficit presupuestario: situación en que la cantidad de dinero que el gobierno gasta es mayor que sus ingresos durante el año fiscal (p. 428)

ENGLISH	ESPAÑOL
budget surplus: situation when the amount of government receipts is larger than its expenditures during the fiscal year (p. 429)	**superávit presupuestario:** situación en que los ingresos del gobierno son mayores que los gastos durante el año fiscal (p. 429)
bureaucracies: offices and agencies of the government that each deal with a specific area (p. 502)	**burocracias:** oficinas y agencias del gobierno que se ocupan de asuntos particulares (p. 502)
business cycle: irregular changes in the level of total output measured by real GDP (p. 352)	**ciclo económico:** cambios irregulares en el nivel de producción total, medidos por el PIB real (p. 352)
business fluctuations: ups and downs in an economy (p. 352)	**fluctuaciones comerciales:** alzas y bajas en una economía (p. 352)
bylaws: a set of rules describing how stock will be sold and dividends paid (p. 221)	**reglamentos:** reglas que detallan cómo se van a vender acciones y a pagar dividendos (p. 221)

ENGLISH	ESPAÑOL
***capacity:** ability (p. 352)	***capacidad:** habilidad (p. 352)
capital: previously manufactured goods used to make other goods and services (p. 9)	**capital:** bienes manufacturados que se usan para producir otros bienes y servicios; el dinero es capital financiero (p. 9)
capital flight: the legal or illegal export of currency or money capital from a nation by that nation's leaders (p. 502)	**fuga de capital al extranjero:** exportación legal o ilegal de divisas o del capital financiero de una nación por los líderes del mismo país (p. 502)
capital gain: increase in value of an asset from the time it was bought to the time it was sold (p. 147)	**ganancia de capital:** aumento en el valor de un activo en el tiempo que transcurre entre su compra y su venta (p. 147)
capitalism: economic system in which private individuals own the factors of production (p. 43)	**capitalismo:** sistema económico en que individuos son dueños de los factores de producción (p. 43)
capital loss: decrease in value of an asset from the time it was bought to the time it was sold (p. 147)	**pérdida de capital:** disminución en el valor de un activo entre el momento en que se compra y el momento en que se vende (p. 147)
cartel: arrangement among groups of industrial businesses to reduce international competition by controlling the price, production, and distribution of goods (p. 241)	**cártel:** arreglos entre grupos de negocios industriales para controlar el precio, producción y distribución de bienes y así reducir la competencia internacional (p. 241)
***category:** group (p. 338)	***categoría:** grupo (p. 338)
Central American Free Trade Agreement (CAFTA): trade agreement designed to reduce tariff barriers between Costa Rica, El Salvador, Guatemala, Honduras, Nicaragua, the Dominican Republic and the United States (p. 481)	**Tratado de Libre Comercio entre Centroamérica y Estados Unidos:** acuerdo comercial diseñado para reducir las barreras arancelarias entre Costa Rica, El Salvador, Guatemala, Honduras, Nicaragua, la República Dominicana y Estados Unidos (p. 481)
certificates of deposit: time deposits that state the amount of the deposit, maturity, and rate of interest being paid (p. 144)	**certificados de depósito:** depósitos a plazos que especifican la cantidad del depósito, la fecha de vencimiento y el tipo de interés que se paga (p. 144)

channels of distribution • commmand economy

channels of distribution: routes by which goods are moved from producers to consumers (p. 297)

canales de distribución: vías por las cuales se mueven los bienes de los fabricantes a los consumidores (p. 297)

charge account: credit extended to a consumer allowing the consumer to buy goods or services from a particular company and to pay for them later (p. 95)

cuenta de crédito: crédito que se le extiende a un consumidor, que le permite comprar bienes y servicios de una compañía en particular y pagar por ellos más adelante (p. 95)

checkable deposits: funds deposited in a bank that can be withdrawn at any time by presenting a check (p. 380)

depósitos a la vista: fondos depositados en un banco que se pueden sacar en cualquier momento con sólo presentar un cheque (p. 380)

check clearing: method by which a check that has been deposited in one institution is transferred to the issuer's depository institution (p. 395)

compensación de cheques: método de pagar y transferir cheques de la institución en que se depositan a la institución depositaria de la persona que los emite (p. 395)

checking account: account in which deposited funds can be withdrawn at any time by writing a check (p. 380)

cuenta corriente: cuenta de la cual se pueden sacar fondos depositados por medio de un cheque (p. 380)

circular flow of income and output: economic model that pictures income as flowing continuously between businesses and consumers (pp. 39, 448)

flujo circular de ingresos y produccion: modelo económico que representa a los ingresos circulando continuamente entre negocios y consumidores (pp. 39, 448)

civilian labor force: total number of people 16 years old or older who are either employed or actively seeking work (p. 308)

fuerza laboral civil: número total de personas mayores de 16 años que tienen empleo o lo están buscando (p. 308)

closed shop: company in which only union members could be hired (p. 318)

fábrica cerrada: compañía en que sólo se puede dar empleo a miembros del sindicato (p. 318)

closing costs: fees involved in arranging for a mortgage or in transferring ownership of property (p. 128)

costos de cierre: cuotas que se pagan para obtener una hipoteca o transferir una propiedad a un dueño nuevo (p. 128)

club warehouse store: store that carries a limited number of brands and items in large quantities and is less expensive than grocery stores (p. 115)

club almacén: tienda que tiene un surtido limitado de marcas y artículos que vende en grandes cantidades; es más barato que las tiendas de comestibles (p. 115)

coincident indicators: economic indicators that usually change at the same time as changes in overall business activity (p. 359)

indicadores coincidentes: indicadores económicos que cambian a la misma vez que la actividad comercial en general (p. 359)

collateral: something of value that a borrower lets the lender claim if a loan is not repaid (p. 100)

garantía: algo de valor que el prestatario se compromete a darle al prestamista si no le devuelve el dinero (p. 100)

collective bargaining: process by which unions and employers negotiate the conditions of employment (p. 321)

negociación colectiva: proceso mediante el cual los sindicatos y gerentes acuerdan las condiciones de trabajo (p. 321)

command economy: system in which the government controls the factors of production and makes all decisions about their use (p. 37)

economía dirigida: sistema en que el gobierno controla los factores de producción y toma todas las decisiones sobre su uso (p. 37)

ENGLISH	ESPAÑOL
commercial bank: bank whose main functions are to accept deposits, lend funds, and transfer funds among banks, individuals, and businesses (p. 93)	**banco comercial:** banco cuyas funciones principales son aceptar depósitos, prestar fondos y transferir fondos entre bancos, individuos y negocios (p. 93)
commodity money: a medium of exchange such as cattle or gems that has value as a commodity or good aside from its value as money (p. 371)	**dinero material:** medios de cambio, como el ganado o las joyas, que tienen valor propio como mercancías además de su valor como dinero (p. 371)
common stock: shares of ownership in a corporation that give stockholders voting rights and a portion of future profits (after holders of preferred stock are paid) (p. 221)	**acciones ordinarias:** tipo de participaciones en una sociedad anónima que da a los accionistas el derecho al voto y una porción de las futuras ganancias (después de que se haya pagado a los accionistas con acciones preferentes); también se llaman acciones comunes (p. 221)
communism: term used by Karl Marx for his idealized society in which no government is necessary (p. 53)	**comunismo:** término usado por Carlos Marx para referirse a su sociedad idealizada en que no hace falta gobierno (p. 53)
comparative advantage: ability of a country to produce a product at a lower opportunity cost than another country (p. 469)	**ventaja comparativa:** capacidad de un país de producir un producto por un costo de oportunidad más bajo que otro país (p. 469)
comparison shopping: getting information on the types and prices of products available from different stores and companies (p. 73)	**comparar antes de comprar:** obtener información sobre los tipos de productos y los precios de éstos en distintas tiendas y compañías (p. 73)
competition: rivalry among producers or sellers of similar goods and services to win more business (p. 45)	**competencia:** rivalidad entre los productores o vendedores de bienes y servicios semejantes para tener más clientes (p. 45)
competitive advertising: advertising that attempts to persuade consumers that a product is different from and superior to any other (p. 72)	**publicidad competitiva:** anuncios que tratan de convencer al consumidor que un producto es distinto o mejor que los demás (p. 72)
***compile:** gather (p. 358)	***compilar:** reunir; recopilar (p. 358)
complementary good: a product often used with another product (p. 181)	**bienes complementarios:** productos que se usan en conjunto (p. 181)
***complex:** complicated (p. 22)	***complejo:** complicado (p. 22)
***concentrate:** focus (p. 102)	***concentrarse:** enfocarse; fijar la atención (p. 102)
***concept:** an idea or thought (p. 178)	***concepto:** una idea o pensamiento (p. 178)
confiscation: taking over industries by governments without paying for them (p. 497)	**confiscación:** toma de posesión de industrias por un gobierno sin pagar por ellas (p. 497)
conglomerate: large corporation made up of smaller corporations dealing in unrelated businesses (p. 247)	**conglomerado:** gran corporación compuesta de empresas más pequeñas cuyos negocios no están relacionados (p. 247)
***consist:** to be made of (p. 379)	***consistir:** estar compuesto de (p. 379)
consumer: any person or group that buys or uses goods and services to satisfy personal needs and wants (p. 66)	**consumidor:** cualquier persona o grupo que compra o utiliza bienes y servicios para satisfacer sus necesidades o deseos personales (p. 66)

Glossary/Glosario

Glossary/Glosario

ENGLISH	ESPAÑOL
consumer goods: goods produced for individuals and sold directly to the public to be used as they are (p. 272)	**bienes de consumo:** bienes producidos para individuos y vendidos directamente al público para usarse tal y como son (p. 272)
consumerism: movement to educate buyers about the purchases they make and to demand better and safer products from manufacturers (p. 77)	**protección al consumidor:** movimiento dedicado a informar al consumidor sobre las compras que hace y a exigirles productos mejores y más seguros a los fabricantes (p. 77)
consumer price index (CPI): a statistical measure of the average of prices of a specified set of goods and services purchased by typical consumers in city areas (p. 343)	**índice de precios al consumidor:** medida estadística de los precios promedios de un grupo de bienes y servicios comprados pro consumidores típicos de un área urbana (p. 343)
consumer sovereignty: the role of the consumer as ruler of the market when determining the types of goods and services produced (p. 284)	**soberanía del consumidor:** manera en que el consumidor gobierna el mercado cuando determina los tipos de bienes y servicios que se producen (p. 284)
*continual: repetitive (p. 52)	***continuo:** repetitivo (p. 52)
*contract: grow smaller (p. 405)	***contraerse:** hacerse más pequeño (p. 405)
contraction: part of the business cycle during which economic activity is slowing down (p. 352)	**contracción:** parte del ciclo económico en que la actividad económica disminuye (p. 352)
*contrast: a striking difference in things being compared (p. 105)	***contraste:** gran diferencia entre dos cosas que se comparan (p. 105)
*contribute: give (p. 157)	***contribuir:** dar (p. 157)
convenience store: store open 16 to 24 hours a day, carrying a limited selection of relatively higher-priced items (p. 115)	**tiendas de artículos de consumo frecuente:** tienda que se mantiene abierta de 16 a 24 horas al día con un surtido limitado de artículos a precios más altos (p. 115)
*convert: change; switch (p. 371)	***convertir:** cambiar (p. 371)
copyright: exclusive right to sell, publish, or reproduce creative works for a specified number of years (p. 238)	**copyright:** el derecho exclusivo de vender, publicar o reproducir obras creativas por un determinado número de años; también se llama derechos de autor (p. 238)
*core: center (p. 417)	***corazón:** centro (p. 417)
corporate charter: license to operate granted to a corporation by the state where it is established (p. 220)	**licencia para negociar:** permiso para operar una sociedad anónima que da el estado en que se establece una compañía (p. 220)
corporation: type of business organization owned by many people but treated by law as though it were a person; it can own property, pay taxes, make contracts, and so on (p. 219)	**sociedad anónima:** tipo de empresa de la cual muchas personas son dueñas, pero la ley la trata como si fuera una persona; puede tener propiedad, pagar impuestos, entrar en contratos, etc.; también se llama corporación (p. 219)
cost-benefit analysis: a financial process in which a business estimates the cost of any action and compares it with the estimated benefits of that action (p. 261)	**análisis de costo-beneficios:** proceso financiero en que un negocio calcula el costo de emprender una actividad y los beneficios de ésta para compararlos (p. 261)

ENGLISH	ESPAÑOL
cost-of-living adjustment (COLA): provision calling for a wage increase each year if the general level of prices rises (p. 321)	**ajuste por el costo de la vida:** provisión que requiere un aumento de sueldo anual si el nivel general de los precios sube (p. 321)
cost-push inflation: theory that higher wages push up prices (p. 445)	**inflación de costos:** teoría que los salarios más altos fuerzan los precios hacia arriba (p. 445)
craft union: union made up of skilled workers in a specific trade or industry (p. 317)	**sindicato de artesanos:** asociación de trabajadores especializados en un oficio o industria en particular (p. 317)
*****create:** make (p. 381)	*****crear:** hacer (p. 381)
credit: receipt of funds either directly or indirectly to buy goods and services in the present with the promise to pay for them in the future (p. 88)	**crédito:** recibir fondos directa o indirectamente para comprar bienes y servicios en el presente bajo promesa de pagar por ellos en el futuro (p. 88)
credit bureau: private business that investigates a person to determine the risk involved in lending to that person (p. 100)	**oficina de crédito:** negocio privado que investiga a individuos para determinar el riesgo de hacerles préstamos (p. 100)
credit card: credit device that allows a person to make purchases at many kinds of stores, restaurants, and other businesses without paying cash (p. 96)	**tarjeta de crédito:** instrumento de crédito que le permite a una persona hacer compras en muchas clases distintas de tiendas, restaurantes y negocios sin tener que pagar con dinero en efectivo (p. 96)
credit check: investigation of a person's income, current debts, personal life, and past history of borrowing and repaying debts (p. 100)	**investigación de crédito:** investigación de los ingresos, deudas actuales, vida privada e historial de préstamos pedidos y deudas pagadas de una persona (p. 100)
credit rating: rating of the risk involved in lending to a specific person or business (p. 100)	**clasificación de crédito:** evaluación del riesgo de hacer un préstamo a una persona o negocio en particular (p. 100)
credit union: depository institution owned and operated by its members to provide savings accounts and low-interest loans only to its members (p. 94)	**cooperativa de crédito:** institución de depósitos que es propiedad de sus miembros, que es administrada por ellos y que proporciona cuentas de ahorro y préstamos a intereses bajos exclusivamente a sus miembros; también se llama unión crediticia (p. 94)
*****crucial:** important; critical (p. 285)	*****crucial:** importante; crítico (p. 285)

debit card: device used to make cashless purchases; money is electronically withdrawn from the consumer's checkable account and transferred directly to the store's bank account (p. 381)	**tarjeta de débito:** utensilio que se usa para hacer compras sin dinero en efectivo; el dinero se retira electrónicamente de la cuenta de cheques del comprador y se transfiere directamente a la cuenta de banco de la tienda (p. 381)
debt financing: raising funds for a business through borrowing (p. 265)	**financiamiento mediante deudas:** recaudar fondos para un negocio por medio de préstamos (p. 265)
deficit financing: government policy of spending more money than it is able to bring in through revenues (p. 428)	**financiamiento del déficit:** política gubernamental de gastar más dinero de los ingresos que tiene y obtener préstamos para cubrir los gastos adicionales (p. 428)

deflation • devote

ENGLISH	ESPAÑOL
deflation: prolonged decline in the general price level of goods and services (p. 342)	**deflación:** caída prolongada en el nivel general de los precios de bienes y servicios (p. 342)
demand: the amount of a good or service that consumers are able and willing to buy at various possible prices during a specified time period (p. 170)	**demanda:** cantidad de un producto o servicio que los consumidores pueden o están dispuestos a comprar a varios precios posibles durante un período de tiempo determinado (p. 170)
demand curve: downward-sloping line that shows in graph form the quantities demanded at each possible price (p. 179)	**curva de demanda:** línea descendiente en una gráfica cuya inclinación muestra la cantidad de demanda a cada precio posible (p. 179)
demand-pull inflation: theory that prices rise as the result of excessive business and consumer demand; demand increases faster than total supply, resulting in shortages that lead to higher prices (p. 444)	**inflación de demanda:** teoría que los precios suben como consecuencia de la demanda excesiva de los negocios y consumidores; la demanda aumenta más rápido que la oferta total, ocasionando una escasez que conduce a precios más altos (p. 444)
demand schedule: table showing quantities demanded at different possible prices (p. 179)	**lista de demanda:** tabla que muestra la cantidad de demandada a distintos precios (p. 179)
democratic socialism: system that works within the constitutional framework of a nation to elect socialists to office; the government usually controls only some areas of the economy (p. 53)	**socialismo democrático:** sistema que obra dentro del marco de la constitución de una nación para elegir socialistas a cargos públicos; el gobierno generalmente controla solamente algunos sectores de la economía (p. 53)
depreciation: loss of value because of wear and tear to durable goods and capital goods (p. 338); fall in the price of a currency through the action of supply and demand (p. 474)	**depreciación:** pérdida de valor de los bienes duraderos y bienes capitales por causa del uso constante (p. 338); rebaja en el valor de una moneda a través de la acción de la oferta y la demanda (p. 474)
depression: major slowdown of economic activity (p. 352)	**depresión:** disminución significativa en la actividad económica (p. 352)
deregulation: reduction of government regulation and control over business activity (p. 248)	**desregulación:** reducción en el número de regulaciones y controles gubernamentales sobre las actividades comerciales (p. 248)
***design:** plan (p. 153)	***diseño:** plan (p. 153)
***despite:** even though (p. 526)	***a pesar de:** contra la voluntad de (p. 526)
devaluation: lowering a currency's value in relation to other currencies by government order (p. 473)	**devaluación:** rebajar el valor de una moneda con relación a otras divisas (monedas extranjeras) por orden gubernamental (p. 473)
developed nations: nations with relatively high standards of living and economies based more on industry than on agriculture (p. 490)	**naciones desarrolladas:** naciones con niveles de vida relativamente altos y economías basadas en la industria más que en la agricultura (p. 490)
developing nations: nations with little industrial development and relatively low standards of living (p. 490)	**naciones en vías de desarrollo:** naciones con poco desarrollo industrial y niveles de vida relativamente bajos (p. 490)
***devote:** dedicate (p. 498)	***dedicar:** aplicar, destinar (p. 498)

ENGLISH	ESPAÑOL
direct foreign investment (DFI): the purchase by foreigners of real estate and businesses in another country (p. 524)	**inversión extranjera directa:** compra de bienes inmuebles (terrenos y edificios) y negocios en un país por extranjeros (p. 524)
direct-mail advertising: type of promotion using a mailer that usually includes a letter describing the product or service and an order blank or application form (p. 293)	**publicidad por correo directo:** tipo de promoción por correo que generalmente incluye una carta describiendo el producto o servicio y un formulario para encargar o solicitarlo (p. 293)
discount rate: interest rate that the Fed charges on loans to commercial banks and other depository institutions (p. 404)	**tasa de descuento:** tipo de interés que el Sistema de Reserva Federal les cobra por préstamos a los bancos comerciales y otras instituciones depositantes (p. 404)
discretionary income: money income a person has left to spend on extras after necessities have been bought (p. 66)	**ingresos discrecionales:** dinero que le queda a una persona de sus ingresos después de cubrir lo imprescindible (p. 66)
*displace: relocate (p. 309)	***desplazar:** trasladar (p. 309)
disposable income: income remaining for a person to spend or save after all taxes have been paid (p. 66)	**ingresos disponibles:** ingresos que le quedan a una persona para ahorrar o gastar después de pagar los impuestos; también se llama renta disponible (p. 66)
disposable personal income (DPI): same as *disposable income* (p. 340)	**ingresos personales disponibles:** véase *disposable income/ingresos disponibles* (p. 340)
*distinct: different (p. 219)	***distinto:** bien diferenciado (p. 219)
*distribute: to give out in shares (p. 35)	***distribuir:** repartir en partes (p. 35)
diversification: spreading of investments among several different types to lower overall risk (p. 159)	**diversificación:** hacer varios tipos de inversiones distintas para disminuir el riesgo total (p. 159)
dividend: portion of a corporation's profits paid to its stockholders (p. 221)	**dividendo:** porción de las ganancias de una sociedad anónima que se paga a los accionistas (p. 221)
division of labor: the breaking down of a job into small tasks performed by different workers (p. 275)	**división del trabajo:** partición un trabajo en pequeñas tareas desempeñadas por distintos obreros (p. 275)
*document: record (p. 212)	***documento:** registro o escritura (p. 212)
*dominate: control (p. 240)	***dominar:** controlar (p. 240)
durability: ability of an item to last a long time (p. 121)	**durabilidad:** cualidad de poder aguantar mucho tiempo sin estropearse o romperse (p. 121)
durable goods: manufactured items that have a life span longer than three years (p. 88)	**bienes duraderos:** artículos manufacturados con una vida de más de tres años (p. 88)
*duration: the time that a thing continues or lasts (p. 359)	***duración:** el tiempo que algo dura o continúa (p. 359)

ENGLISH	ESPAÑOL
e-commerce: business transactions conducted over the Internet (p. 298)	**comercio electrónico:** llevar a cabo transacciones de negocio a través de Internet (p. 298)

Glossary/Glosario

economic assistance • enhance

ENGLISH	ESPAÑOL
economic assistance: loans and outright grants of money or equipment to other nations (p. 497)	**asistencia económica:** préstamos y subsidios de dinero o maquinaria a otras naciones (p. 497)
economic efficiency: wise use of available resources so as to obtain the greatest benefits possible (p. 48)	**eficiencia económica:** buen uso de los recursos disponibles para obtener los mayores beneficios posibles (p. 48)
economic equity: the attempt to balance an economic policy so that everyone benefits fairly (p. 49)	**equidad económica:** una política económica gubernamental que trata de lograr que todos se beneficien de manera justa (p. 49)
economic growth: expansion of the economy to produce more goods, jobs, and wealth (p. 49)	**crecimiento económico:** expansión de la economía para producir más bienes, trabajos y riqueza (p. 49)
economic indicators: statistics that measure variables in the economy (p. 358)	**indicadores económicos:** estadísticas que miden muchas variables en la economía (p. 358)
economic model: a theory or simplified representation that helps explain and predict economic behavior in the real world (p. 21)	**modelo económico:** teoría o representación simplificada que ayuda a explicar y prever la conducta económica en el mundo real (p. 21)
economics: the study of how people make choices about ways to use limited resources to fulfill their wants (p. 6)	**economía:** estudio de cómo la gente decide en qué manera va a usar recursos limitados para satisfacer sus deseos (p. 6)
economic system: way in which a nation uses its resources to satisfy its people's needs and wants (p. 34)	**sistema económico:** manera en que una nación usa sus recursos para satisfacer las necesidades y deseos de su pueblo (p. 34)
economies of scale: low production costs resulting from the large size of output (p. 238)	**economías de escala:** bajos costos de producción que resultan de la producción en gran cantidad (p. 238)
economy: the production and distribution of goods and services in a society (p. 21)	**economía:** producción y distribución de bienes y servicios en una sociedad (p. 21)
elastic demand: situation in which a given rise or fall in a product's price greatly affects the amount that people are willing to buy (p. 183)	**demanda elástica:** situación en que una rebaja o aumento dado en el precio de un producto tiene gran efecto en la cantidad de ese producto que los consumidores están dispuestos a comprar (p. 183)
elasticity: economic concept dealing with consumers' responsiveness to an increase or decrease in the price of a product (p. 182)	**elasticidad:** concepto económico que se refiere a la reacción de los consumidores al aumento o rebaja de precio de un producto (p. 182)
electronic funds transfer (EFT): system of transferring funds from one bank account directly to another without any paper money changing hands (p. 376)	**transferencia electrónica de fondos:** sistema para transferir fondos de una cuenta bancaria directamente a otra sin traspasar papel moneda (p. 376)
***element:** basic quality (p. 48)	***elemento:** qualidad básica (p. 48)
***eliminate:** to get rid of (p. 197)	***eliminar:** veshacerse de (p. 197)
embargo: complete restriction on the import or export of a particular good or goods going to or coming from a specific country (p. 479)	**embargo:** prohibición total de la importación o exportación de un producto o de productos que entran o salen de un país en particular (p. 479)
***enhance:** improve (p. 500)	***realzar:** mejorar, aumentar (p. 500)

ENGLISH	ESPAÑOL

*enormous: huge (p. 87)

*enorme: muy grande (p. 87)

entrepreneur: person who organizes, manages, and assumes the risks of a business in order to gain profits (p. 208)

empresario: persona que organiza, administra y acepta los riesgos de un negocio para sacarle ganancias (p. 208)

entrepreneurship: when individuals take risks to develop new products and start new businesses in order to make profits (p. 9)

empresarismo: cuando individuos toman riegos al desarrollar nuevos productos y empezar nuevos negocios para sacarles ganancias (p. 9)

equilibrium price: the price at which the amount producers are willing to supply is equal to the amount consumers are willing to buy (p. 195)

precio de equilibrio: precio al que la cantidad de un producto que los fabricantes están dispuestos a ofrecer es igual a la cantidad que los consumidores están dispuestos a comprar (p. 195)

*equivalent: equal (p. 122)

*equivalente: igual (p. 122)

*estimate: guess (p. 284)

*estimación: cálculo aproximado (p. 284)

ethical behavior: acting in accordance with moral convictions about right and wrong (p. 79)

comportamiento ético: actuar de acuerdo con convicciones morales acerca del bien y el mal (p. 79)

*ethnic: relating to a grouping of people according to race, region of origin, or other characteristics (p. 530)

*étnico: relacionado con un grupo de personas de acuerdo con su raza, lugar de origen, u otras características (p. 530)

European Union (EU): organization of European nations whose goal is to encourage economic integration as a single market (p. 481)

Unión Europea: organización de naciones europeas cuyo objetivo es promover su integración económica para formar un solo mercado (p. 481)

*exceed: go beyond (p. 416)

*exceder: sobrepasar (p. 416)

exchange rate: the price of one nation's currency in terms of another nation's currency (p. 472)

tipo de cambio: valor de la moneda de una nación comparado con la moneda de otra (p. 472)

*expand: extend beyond the prior state (p. 49)

*expandir: extenderse más allá de su estado anterior (p. 49)

expansion: part of the business cycle in which economic activity slowly increases (p. 352)

expansión: parte del ciclo económico en que la actividad económica aumenta lentamente (p. 352)

*expert: specialist (p. 442)

*experto: especialista (p. 442)

exports: goods sold to other countries (p. 466)

exportaciones: bienes que se venden a otros países (p. 466)

externalities: economic side effects or by-products that affect an uninvolved third party; can be negative or positive (p. 422)

factores externos: consecuencias indirectas de actividades económicas que afectan a terceras personas que no tomaron parte en ellas; pueden ser negativas o positivas (p. 422)

*factor: thing to be considered (p. 119)

*factor: cosa que hay que tomar en cuenta (p. 119)

Glossary/Glosario

Glossary/Glosario

ENGLISH	ESPAÑOL
factors of production: resources of land, labor, capital, and entrepreneurship used to produce goods and services (p. 8)	**factores de producción:** recursos de tierra, trabajo, capital y espíritu empresarial que se usan para producir bienes y servicios (p. 8)
Fed: the Federal Reserve System created by Congress in 1913 as the nation's central banking organization (p. 392)	**Sistema de Reserva Federal:** sistema creado por el Congreso en 1913 para servir de organización bancaria central de la nación; conocido como "Fed" (p. 392)
federal funds rate: interest rate that banks charge each other on loans (usually overnight) (p. 405)	**tasa federal por fondos prestados:** tipo de interés que se cobran los bancos unos a otros (generalmente por menos de 1 día) (p. 405)
Federal Open Market Committee (FOMC): 12-member committee in the Federal Reserve System that meets 8 times a year to decide the course of action that the Fed should take to control the money supply (p. 393)	**Comité Federal del Mercado Libre:** comisión de 12 personas, parte del Sistema de Reserva Federal, que se reúne 8 veces al año para determinar lo que debe hacer la Reserva Federal para controlar la oferta monetaria; también se llama Comité Controlador del Dinero (p. 393)
fiat money: money that has value because a government fiat, or order, has established it as acceptable for payment of debts (p. 371)	**dinero fiduciario:** dinero que tiene valor porque un decreto gubernamental ha establecido que se puede aceptar como pago por deudas (p. 371)
finance charge: cost of credit expressed monthly in dollars and cents (p. 97)	**cargo de financiamiento:** costo mensual del crédito expresado en dólares y centavos (p. 97)
finance company: company that takes over contracts for installment debts from stores and adds a fee for collecting the debt; a *consumer finance company* makes loans directly to consumers at high rates of interest (p. 94)	**compañía financiera:** compañía que asume los contratos de deudas a plazos de tiendas y les añade una cuota por cobrar la deuda; las *compañías de financiamiento directo al consumidor* hacen préstamos directamente a los consumidores a intereses altos (p. 94)
financing: obtaining funds or money capital for business expansion (p. 260)	**financiamiento:** obtener fondos o capital financiero para la expansión de un negocio; también se llama financiación (p. 260)
fiscal policy: federal government's use of taxation and spending policies to affect overall business activity (p. 448)	**política fiscal:** uso por el gobierno federal de tributación (impuestos) y gastos para afectar la actividad comercial general (p. 448)
fiscal year: year by which accounts are kept; for the federal government, October 1 to September 30 of the next year (p. 427)	**año fiscal:** período de un año en que se llevan las cuentas; para el gobierno federal, empieza octubre 1 y termina septiembre 30 del próximo año (p. 427)
five-year plans: centralized planning system that used to be the basis for China's economic system; eventually was transformed to a regional planning system leading to limited free enterprise (p. 506)	**planes quinquenales:** sistema de planificación central que formaba la base del sistema económico chino; fue transformado en un sistema de planificación regional que ha conducido a la libre empresa limitada (p. 506)
fixed rate of exchange: system under which a national government sets the value of its currency in relation to a single standard (p. 473)	**tipo de cambio fijo:** sistema bajo el cual un gobierno nacional establece el valor de su moneda en relación con un patrón único (p. 473)
flexible exchange rate: arrangement in which the forces of supply and demand are allowed to set the price of various currencies (p. 474)	**tipo de cambio flexible:** arreglo bajo el cual la oferta y la demanda determinan el valor de varias monedas (p. 474)
*****focus:** the center of attention (p. 6)	*****enfoque:** centro de atención (p. 6)

ENGLISH	ESPAÑOL
foreign affiliates: branches of multinational firms (p. 528)	**sucursales extranjeras:** establecimientos que forman parte de empresas multinacionales (p. 528)
foreign aid: money, goods, and services given by governments and private organizations to help other nations and their citizens (p. 497)	**ayuda al exterior:** dinero, bienes y servicios que gobiernos y organizaciones privadas donan para ayudar a otras naciones y sus ciudadanos (p. 497)
foreign exchange markets: markets dealing in buying and selling foreign currency for businesses that want to import goods from other countries (p. 472)	**mercados de divisas:** mercados donde negocios que desean importar bienes de otros países compran y venden divisas (monedas extranjeras) (p. 472)
fractional reserve banking: system in which only a fraction of the deposits in a bank is kept on hand, or in reserve; the remainder is available to lend (p. 400)	**reserva bancaria parcial:** sistema que permite que los bancos tengan sólo un porcentaje de sus depósitos a mano o en reserva; el resto lo pueden usar para hacer préstamos (p. 400)
franchise: contract in which one business (the franchisor) sells to another business (the franchisee) the right to use the franchisor's name and sell its products (p. 222)	**franquicia:** contrato mediante el cual un negocio (el franquiciante) vende a otro (el franquiciatario) el derecho de usar su nombre y vender sus productos; también se llama licencia (p. 222)
free-enterprise system: economic system in which individuals own the factors of production and decide how to use them within legal limits; same as *capitalism* (p. 44)	**sistema de libre empresa:** sistema económico en que los individuos son dueños de los factores de producción y deciden cómo los van a usar dentro de los límites legales; lo mismo que *capitalismo* (p. 44)
full employment: condition of the economy when the unemployment rate is lower than a certain percentage established by economists' studies (p. 443)	**pleno empleo:** condición económica en que el índice de desempleo está por debajo de un porcentaje establecido por estudios económicos (p. 443)
*function: job; task (p. 398)	***función:** labor; tarea (p. 398)
*fundamental: basic (p. 493)	***fundamental:** básico (p. 493)

GDP: see *gross domestic product (GDP)*	**GDP:** véase *gross domestic product (GDP)*
GDP price deflator: price index that removes the effect of inflation from GDP so that the overall economy in one year can be compared to another year (p. 344)	**deflactor de precios del PIB:** índice de precios que sustrae del PIB los efectos de la inflación para poder comparar el estado de la economía en un año con el estado económico en otro (p. 344)
*generate: make; produce (p. 209)	***generar:** hacer; producir (p. 209)
generic brand: general name for a product rather than a specific brand name given by the manufacturer (p. 74)	**nombre genérico:** nombre común de un producto en vez de la marca de fábrica que le da el fabricante (p. 74)
global integration: interdependency among the countries of the world, especially within financial markets and telecommunications (p. 518)	**integración global:** dependencia mutua entre los países del mundo, en especial con respecto a los mercados financieros y las telecomunicaciones; también se llama integración mundial (p. 518)
goods: tangible objects that can satisfy people's wants or needs (p. 8)	**bienes:** objetos materiales que pueden satisfacer los deseos o necesidades del público (p. 8)

Glossary/Glosario

ENGLISH   **ESPAÑOL**

gross domestic product (GDP): total dollar value of all final goods and services produced in a nation in a single year (p. 337)

producto interior bruto (PIB): valor total en dólares de todos los bienes y servicios producidos por una nación en un año (p. 337)

*guarantee: a promise to replace something if it is not as represented (p. 77)

*garantía: la promesa de reemplazar algo si no es como se presentó (p. 77)

*guideline: pattern (p. 455)

*directriz: pauta (p. 455)

hypothesis: an assumption involving two or more variables that must be tested for validity (p. 22)

hipótesis: suposición que tiene dos o más variables y que se tiene que comprobar para ver si es válida (p. 22)

*identical: exactly the same (p. 524)

*idéntico: exactamente igual (p. 524)

import quota: restriction imposed on the number of units of a particular good that can be brought into the country (p. 479)

cuota de importación: restricción en el número de unidades de un producto que se puede traer a un país (p. 479)

imports: goods bought from other countries for domestic use (p. 466)

importaciones: bienes traídos de otro país para el uso doméstico (p. 466)

*impose: to establish or apply by authority (p. 191)

*imponer: ser establecido o aplicado por una autoridad (p. 191)

*incentive: stimulus; motive (p. 37)

*incentivo: estímulo; aliciente; motivo (p. 37)

income redistribution: government activity that takes income from some people through taxation and uses it to help citizens in need (p. 420)

redistribución de rentas: actividad gubernamental que toma los ingresos de algunas personas a través de impuestos y los usa para ayudar a otras personas necesitadas (p. 420)

*indicate: to be a sign of; signify (p. 369)

*indicar: señalar; revelar (p. 369)

*individual: one person (p. 287)

*individuo: una persona (p. 287)

individual retirement account (IRA): private retirement plan that allows individuals or married couples to save a certain amount of untaxed earnings per year with the interest being tax-deferred (p. 157)

cuentas de retiro individuales: planes de jubilación privados que permiten que individuos o matrimonios ahorren cierta porción de sus ingresos anuales sin pagar impuestos y que posponen el impuesto sobre los intereses (p. 157)

industrial union: union made up of all the workers in an industry regardless of job or skill level (p. 317)

sindicato industrial: asociación de todos los obreros de una industria, que no toma en cuenta el tipo de trabajo ni el nivel de especialización (p. 317)

inelastic demand: situation in which a product's price change has little impact on the quantity demanded by consumers (p. 183)

demanda inelástica: situación en que el precio de un producto tiene poco efecto en la cantidad demandada por los consumidores (p. 183)

ENGLISH	ESPAÑOL
infant mortality rate: death rate of infants who die during the first year of life (p. 492)	**índice de mortalidad infantil:** porcentaje de muertes de niños en el primer año de vida (p. 492)
inflation: prolonged rise in the general price level of final goods and services (p. 342)	**inflación:** aumento prolongado en el nivel general de los precios de bienes y servicios finales (p. 342)
inflation targeting: a possible central bank policy in which the head of the central bank is given a specified annual rate of inflation as a goal (p. 455)	**objetivo inflacionario:** posible política de un banco central que le da al director del banco central una tasa de inflación anual específica como meta (p. 455)
informative advertising: advertising that benefits consumers by providing useful information about a product (p. 72)	**publicidad informativa:** anuncios que benefician a los consumidores al darles información útil sobre un producto (p. 72)
***initial:** first (p. 233)	***inicial:** primero, al principio (p. 233)
***initiative:** ability to originate new ideas (p. 54)	***iniciativa:** habilidad de originar ideas nuevas (p. 54)
injunction: court order preventing some activity (p. 323)	**prohibición judicial:** orden de un juez que impide alguna actividad (p. 323)
innovation: transforming an invention into something useful to humans (p. 357)	**innovación:** transformar un invento en algo útil para la humanidad (p. 357)
installment debt: type of loan repaid with equal payments, or installments, over a specific period of time (p. 88)	**deudas pagadas a plazos:** tipo de préstamo que se paga en cantidades iguales durante un período determinado de tiempo (p. 88)
***instance:** case; example (p. 263)	***instancia:** caso; ejemplo (p. 263)
***integral:** essential; basic (p. 260)	***integral:** esencial; básico (p. 260)
***intense:** strong (p. 479)	***intenso:** fuerte; profundo (p. 479)
***interact:** work together (p. 233)	***interactuar:** trabajar juntos (p. 233)
interest: amount the borrower must pay for the use of someone else's funds (p. 88)	**interés:** cantidad que un prestatario tiene que pagar por usar los fondos de otro (p. 88)
interlocking directorate: a board of directors, the majority of whose members also serve as the board of directors of a competing corporation (p. 246)	**directorio entrelazado:** junta directiva de una compañía cuya mayoría también sirve en la junta directiva de otra sociedad anónima que compite en el mismo mercado (p. 246)
intermediate-term financing: funds borrowed by a business for 1 to 10 years (p. 266)	**financiamiento a mediano plazo:** fondos prestados que un negocio tiene entre 1 y 10 años para pagar (p. 266)
International Monetary Fund (IMF): agency whose member governments once were obligated to keep their foreign exchange rates more or less fixed; today it offers monetary advice and provides loans to developing nations (p. 473)	**Fondo Monetario Internacional (FMI):** agencia que antes obligaba a los gobiernos de países miembros a mantener sus tipos de cambio más o menos fijos; hoy ofrece asesoramiento monetario y proporciona préstamos a países en desarrollo (p. 473)
***interval:** period of time (p. 507)	***intervalo:** período de tiempo (p. 507)
inventory: extra supply of the items used in a business, such as raw materials or goods for sale (p. 210)	**inventario:** artículos que un negocio tiene almacenados, como materias primas o mercancía para vender (p. 210)

Glossary/Glosario

Glossary/Glosario

ENGLISH	ESPAÑOL
*involve: concerned with (p. 128)	***involucrar:** comprender; abarcar (p. 128)
*issue: give out; distribute (p. 375)	***emitir:** repartir; distribuir (p. 375)

joint venture: partnership set up for a specific purpose for a short period of time (p. 216)	**negocio en participación:** sociedad establecida por un corto período de tiempo con un propósito determinado (p. 216)
*justify: give reason for (p. 431)	***justificar:** dar una razón (p. 431)

Keogh plan: retirement plan that allows self-employed individuals to save a maximum of 15 percent of their income up to a specified amount each year, and to deduct that amount from their yearly taxable income (p. 156)	**plan Keogh:** plan de jubilación que le permite al que trabaja por su cuenta ahorrar un máximo del 15 por ciento de sus ingresos anuales hasta llegar a una cantidad determinada y descontar la cantidad ahorrada de sus ingresos anuales gravables (p. 156)

labor: human effort directed toward producing goods and services (p. 8)	**trabajo:** esfuerzo humano dirigido a la producción de bienes y servicios (p. 8)
labor union: association of workers organized to improve wages and working conditions for its members (p. 316)	**sindicato de obreros:** asociación de trabajadores organizados para mejorar los salarios y condiciones de trabajo de sus miembros; también se llama sindicato laboral y gremio de obreros (p. 316)
lagging indicators: indicators that seem to lag behind changes in overall business activity (p. 359)	**indicadores de rezaga:** indicadores que ocurren después de los cambios en las actividades comerciales (p. 359)
laissez-faire: economic system in which the government minimizes its interference with the economy (p. 43)	**laissez-faire:** sistema económico en que el gobierno interfiere lo menos posible en la economía (p. 43)
land: natural resources and surface land and water (p. 8)	**tierra:** recursos naturales, la superficie terrestre y el agua (p. 8)
law of demand: economic rule stating that the quantity demanded and price move in opposite directions (p. 172)	**ley de la demanda:** regla económica que dice que al cambiar el precio, la cantidad demandada cambia en sentido contrario (p. 172)
law of diminishing marginal utility: rule stating that the additional satisfaction a consumer gets from purchasing one more unit of a product will lessen with each additional unit purchased (p. 174)	**ley de utilidad marginal decreciente:** regla que dice que el consumidor recibe menos satisfacción adicional cada vez que compra una unidad más de un producto (p. 174)
law of diminishing returns: economic rule that says as more units of a factor of production are added to other factors of production, after some point total output continues to increase but at a diminishing rate (p. 193)	**ley de los rendimientos decrecientes:** regla económica que dice que al añadir más unidades de un solo factor económico a los otros factores económicos, después de cierto punto el aumento en la producción será menos y menos significativo (p. 193)

ENGLISH	ESPAÑOL
law of supply: economic rule stating that price and quantity supplied move in the same direction (p. 187)	**ley de la oferta:** regla económica que dice que al cambiar el precio, la cantidad ofrecida cambia en el mismo sentido (p. 187)
leading indicators: statistics that point to what will happen in the economy (p. 358)	**indicadores anticipados:** estadísticas que pronostican lo que va a suceder en la economía (p. 358)
lease: long-term agreement describing the terms under which property is rented (p. 126)	**contrato de alquiler:** acuerdo a largo plazo que describe los términos bajo los cuales se alquila o arrienda una propiedad (p. 126)
legal tender: money that by law must be accepted for payment of public and private debts (p. 371)	**medios de curso legal:** moneda que, por ley, se tiene que aceptar en pago de deudas públicas y privadas (p. 371)
liability insurance: insurance that pays for bodily injury and property damage (p. 133)	**seguro de responsabilidad civil:** seguro que paga por lesiones corporales y daños a propiedad (p. 133)
*license: a permit (p. 45)	***licencia:** un permiso (p. 45)
limited liability: requirement in which an owner's responsibility for a company's debts is limited to the size of the owner's investment in the firm (p. 220)	**responsabilidad limitada:** requisito que limita la responsabilidad de cada dueño por las deudas de una compañía al tamaño de su inversión en la firma (p. 220)
limited liability company: type of business enterprise that protects members against losing all of their personal wealth; members are taxed as if they were in a partnership (p. 216)	**compañía de responsabilidad limitada:** tipo de negocio que protege a sus miembros contra la pérdida de toda su riqueza personal; los miembros pagan impuestos como si estuviesen en una sociedad (p. 216)
limited partnership: special form of partnership in which one or more partners have limited liability but no voice in management (p. 216)	**sociedad limitada:** tipo de sociedad en que uno o más socios tienen responsabilidad limitada, pero no pueden participar en la administración del negocio (p. 216)
local union: members of a union in a particular factory, company, or geographic area (p. 318)	**sección sindical:** miembros de un sindicato en una fábrica, compañía o área geográfica en particular (p. 318)
*location: site; place (p. 272)	***ubicación:** sitio; lugar (p. 272)
lockout: situation that occurs when management prevents workers from returning to work until they agree to a new contract (p. 323)	**cierre patronal:** situación en que los gerentes impiden que los trabajadores regresen al trabajo hasta que acepten un nuevo contrato; también se llama paro forzoso o paro patronal (p. 323)
long-term financing: funds borrowed by a business for a period of more than 10 years or funds raised by issuing stock (p. 267)	**financiamiento a largo plazo:** préstamo de fondos que un negocio tiene por más de 10 años o fondos que recauda por medio de la venta de acciones (p. 267)
loose money policy: monetary policy that makes credit inexpensive and abundant, possibly leading to inflation (p. 399)	**política monetaria expansiva:** política monetaria que resulta en crédito barato y abundante; puede conducir a la inflación (p. 399)

Glossary/Glosario

Glossary/Glosario

ENGLISH	ESPAÑOL

M1: narrowest definition of the money supply; consists of moneys that can be spent immediately and against which checks can be written (p. 383)

M1: definición más estricta de la oferta monetaria; comprende el dinero que se puede gastar inmediatamente y contra el cual se pueden emitir cheques (p. 383)

M2: broader definition of the money supply; includes all of M1, plus such near moneys as savings deposits, small-denomination time deposits, money market deposit accounts, and retail money market mutual fund balances (p. 383)

M2: definición más general de la oferta monetaria; incluye la M1 más cuasi-dinero como depósitos de ahorro, depósitos a plazo de pequeña denominación, cuentas de depósito de mercado monetario y balances de fondos mutualistas del mercado monetario al por menor (p. 383)

macroeconomics: the branch of economic theory dealing with the economy as a whole and decision making by large units such as governments (p. 6)

macroeconomía: rama de la teoría económica que trata de la economía en su totalidad y de los modos en que grandes organismos, como los gobiernos, toman decisiones (p. 6)

*maintain: keep (p. 420)

*mantener: preservar; continuar (p. 420)

*major: main (p. 430)

*importante: principal (p. 430)

*manipulate: influence; control (p. 527)

*manipular: influir; controlar (p. 527)

marginal utility: an additional amount of satisfaction (p. 174)

utilidad marginal: una cantidad adicional de satisfacción o provecho (p. 174)

market: the process of freely exchanging goods and services between buyers and sellers (pp. 38, 170)

mercado: el proceso de intercambio libre de bienes y servicios entre compradores y vendedores (pp. 38, 170)

market basket: representative group of goods and services used to compile the consumer price index (p. 343)

canasta de compras: grupo representativo de bienes y servicios usado para calcular el índice de precios al consumidor (p. 343)

market economy: system in which individuals own the factors of production and make economic decisions through free interaction while looking out for their own and their families' best interests (p. 38)

economía de mercado: sistema en que particulares son los dueños de los factores de producción y toman decisiones económicas, relacionándose libremente con otros, para el mayor beneficio de sus familias y sí mismos (p. 38)

marketing: all the activities needed to generate consumer demand and to move goods and services from the producer to the consumer (p. 284)

mercadotecnia: todas las actividades necesarias para generar demanda y mover bienes y servicios de los productores a los consumidores; también se llama marketing (p. 284)

market research: gathering, recording, and analyzing data about the types of goods and services that people want (p. 285)

investigación de mercados: reunir, anotar y analizar datos acerca de los tipos de bienes y servicios que desea el público (p. 285)

market structure: the extent to which competition prevails in particular markets (p. 232)

estructura del mercado: punto hasta el cual la competencia predomina en un mercado (p. 232)

market survey: information gathered by researchers about possible users of a product based on such characteristics as age, sex, income, education, and geographic location (p. 287)

estudio del mercado: información obtenida por investigadores sobre los posibles usuarios de un producto, como su edad, sexo, ingresos, estudios y ubicación geográfica (p. 287)

maturity: period of time at the end of which time deposits will pay a stated rate of interest (p. 144)

plazo de vencimiento: período de tiempo al final del cual los depósitos a plazos pagan una tasa de interés establecida (p. 144)

mechanization: combined labor of people and machines (p. 274)

mecanización: esfuerzo combinado de personas y máquinas (p. 274)

mediation: a neutral person tries to get both sides to reach an agreement during negotiations (p. 321)

mediación: una persona neutral trata de hacer que ambas partes lleguen a un acuerdo durante una negociación (p. 321)

Medicaid: state and federal public-assistance program that helps pay health care costs for low-income and disabled persons (p. 421)

Medicaid: programa de asistencia público estatal y federal que provee apoyo financiero para los gastos médicos de personas de bajos ingresos y personas incapacitadas (p. 421)

Medicare: government program that provides health care for the aged (p. 417)

Medicare: programa gubernamental que proporciona cuidado de la salud para personas de la tercera edad (p. 417)

medium of exchange: use of money for exchange for goods or services (p. 368)

medio de cambio: uso del dinero a cambio de bienes y servicios (p. 368)

merger: the legal combination of two or more companies that become one corporation (p. 247)

fusión: combinación legal de compañías en una sola sociedad anónima (p. 247)

*method: system; mode (p. 298)

*método: sistema; modo (p. 298)

microeconomics: the branch of economic theory that deals with behavior and decision making by small units such as individuals and firms (p. 6)

microeconomía: rama de la teoría económica que estudia la conducta y modos de tomar decisiones de unidades pequeñas, como individuos y empresas (p. 6)

military assistance: aid given to a nation's armed forces (p. 497)

asistencia militar: ayuda dada a las fuerzas armadas de una nación (p. 497)

*minimum: smallest possible amount (p. 142)

*mínimo: cantidad menor posible (p. 142)

minimum wage law: federal law that sets the lowest legal hourly wage rate that may be paid to certain types of workers (p. 313)

ley del salario mínimo: ley federal que establece el sueldo por hora más bajo que se puede pagar legalmente a ciertos tipos de trabajadores (p. 313)

mixed economy: system combining characteristics of more than one type of economy (p. 40)

economía mixta: sistema que combina las características de más de un tipo de economía (p. 40)

monetarism: theory that deals with the relationship between the amount of money the Fed places in circulation and the level of activity in the economy (p. 453)

monetarismo: teoría que relaciona la cantidad de dinero que el Sistema de Reserva Federal pone en circulación con el nivel de actividad en la economía (p. 453)

monetarists: supporters of the theory of monetarism, often linked with Milton Friedman (p. 453)

monetaristas: partidarios de la teoría del monetarismo, a menudo conectada con Milton Friedman (p. 453)

monetary policy: policy that involves changing the rate of growth of the supply of money in circulation in order to affect the cost and availability of credit (p. 392)

política monetaria: política que controla el crecimiento de la cantidad de dinero en circulación para afectar el costo y la facilidad de obtener crédito (p. 392)

Glossary/Glosario

Glossary/Glosario

ENGLISH	ESPAÑOL
monetary rule: monetarists' belief that the Fed should allow the money supply to grow at a smooth, consistent rate per year and not use monetary policy to stimulate or slow the economy (p. 455)	**norma monetaria:** creencia de los monetaristas que el Sistema de Reserva Federal debe permitir que la oferta monetaria crezca a un ritmo anual constante y no usar la política monetaria para estimular o reducir la actividad económica (p. 455)
money: anything customarily used as a medium of exchange, a unit of accounting, and a store of value (p. 368)	**moneda:** cualquier cosa que se acostumbra usar como medio de cambio, unidad de contabilidad y reserva de valor; también se llama dinero (p. 368)
money market deposit account: account that pays relatively high rates of interest, requires a minimum balance, and allows immediate access to funds (p. 143)	**cuenta de depósito de mercado monetario:** cuenta que paga interés relativamente alto, requiere un saldo mínimo y mantiene los fondos disponibles en cualquier momento (p. 143)
money market fund: type of mutual fund that uses investors' funds to make short-term loans to businesses and banks (p. 152)	**fondo de mercado monetario:** tipo de fondo mutualista que utiliza los fondos de los inversionistas para hacer préstamos a corto plazo a empresas y bancos (p. 152)
monopolistic competition: market situation in which a large number of sellers offer similar but slightly different products and in which each has some control over price (p. 242)	**competencia monopolística:** mercado en que un gran número de vendedores ofrecen productos parecidos aunque algo distintos y en que cada vendedor tiene algún control sobre el precio (p. 242)
monopoly: market situation in which a single supplier makes up an entire industry for a good or service with no close substitutes (p. 237)	**monopolio:** mercado en que hay sólo un proveedor que comprende la industria entera de un producto o servicio sin verdaderos sustitutos (p. 237)
mortgage: installment debt owed on houses, buildings, or land (p. 89)	**hipoteca:** tipo de deuda pagada a plazos por casas, edificios o terrenos (p. 89)
multinationals: firms that do business and have offices or factories in many countries (p. 528)	**corporaciones multinacionales:** firmas que hacen negocio y tienen oficinas y fábricas en muchos países; también se llaman empresas transnacionales o internacionales (p. 528)
mutual fund: investment company that pools the funds of many individuals to buy stocks, bonds, or other investments (p. 152)	**fondo mutualista:** compañía inversionista que reúne los fondos de muchos individuos para comprar acciones, bonos y otros tipos de inversiones (p. 152)

national debt: total amount of outstanding debt for the federal government (p. 428)	**deuda pública:** cantidad de deuda que tiene el gobierno federal (p. 428)
national income (NI): total income earned by everyone in the economy (p. 339)	**renta nacional:** ingresos totales de todas las personas que forman parte de una economía (p. 339)
national income accounting: measurement of the national economy's performance, dealing with the overall economy's output and income (p. 336)	**cálculo de la renta nacional:** medida del rendimiento económico de una nación, tomando en cuenta la producción y los ingresos totales (p. 336)
near moneys: assets, such as savings accounts, that can be turned into money relatively easily and without the risk of loss of value (p. 382)	**cuasi-dinero:** activos, como las cuentas de ahorro, que se pueden convertir en dinero con bastante facilidad sin correr el riesgo de que pierdan valor (p. 382)

ENGLISH	ESPAÑOL
net domestic product (NDP): value of the nation's total output (GDP) minus the total value lost through depreciation on equipment (p. 338)	**producto interior neto:** valor de la producción total de un país (PIB) menos el valor total perdido por la depreciación de equipos (p. 338)
net exports: difference between what the nation sells to other countries and what it buys from other countries (p. 338)	**exportaciones netas:** diferencia entre lo que una nación le vende a otros países y lo que compra de ellos (p. 338)
*network: system (p. 392)	*red: sistema (p. 392)
*neutral: unbiased; not taking sides (p. 321)	*neutral: imparcial; que no se adhiere a un partido (p. 321)
North American Free Trade Agreement (NAFTA): trade agreement designed to reduce and gradually eliminate tariff barriers between Mexico, Canada, and the United States (p. 481)	**Tratado de Libre Comercio Norteamericano:** acuerdo comercial diseñado para disminuir y eliminar gradualmente las barreras arancelarias entre México, Canadá y Estados Unidos (p. 481)
*notion: idea (p. 508)	*noción: idea (p. 508)

ENGLISH	ESPAÑOL
*obtain: get (p. 128)	*obtener: conseguir (p. 128)
*obvious: clear; apparent (p. 292)	*obvio: claro, evidente (p. 292)
*offset: counteract; make up for (p. 449)	*contrarrestar: resistir; compensar (p. 449)
oligopoly: industry dominated by a few suppliers who exercise some control over price (p. 240)	**oligopolio:** industria dominada por pocos proveedores que ejercen algún control sobre los precios (p. 240)
open-market operations: buying and selling of United States securities by the Fed to affect the money supply (p. 406)	**operaciones del mercado abierto:** compra y venta de valores de los Estados Unidos por el Sistema de Reserva Federal para afectar la oferta monetaria (p. 406)
opportunity cost: value of the next best alternative given up for the alternative that was chosen (p. 16)	**costo de oportunidad:** valor de la mejor opción a la que se renuncia al escoger otra opción (p. 16)
*output: production; yield (p. 348)	*rendimiento: producción; provecho (p. 348)
*overall: total (p. 159)	*total: general; en su totalidad (p. 159)
overdraft checking: checking account that allows a customer to write a check for more money than exists in his or her account (p. 376)	**cuenta corriente con descubierto:** cuenta corriente que le permite al cliente escribir cheques por más dinero del que tiene en la cuenta; también se llama cuenta corriente con sobregiro (p. 376)
*overseas: abroad; out of the country (p. 466)	*extranjero: fuera del país (p. 466)
over-the-counter market: electronic purchase and sale of stocks and bonds, often of smaller companies, which often takes place outside the organized stock exchanges (p. 151)	**mercado extrabursátil:** compra y venta electrónica de acciones y bonos, a menudo de compañías pequeñas, que a menudo se realiza fuera de las bolsas de valores organizadas (p. 151)

Glossary/Glosario

Glossary/Glosario

ENGLISH	ESPAÑOL

P

partnership: business that two or more individuals own and operate (p. 215)

sociedad: negocio operado por dos o más individuos que son los dueños (p. 215)

patent: exclusive right to make, use, or sell an invention for a specified number of years (p. 238)

patente: derecho exclusivo de fabricar, usar o vender su invento por un determinado número de años (p. 238)

peak: period of prosperity in a business cycle in which economic activity is at its highest point (p. 352)

auge: período de prosperidad en el ciclo económico en que la actividad económica ha llegado a su nivel más alto (p. 352)

penetration pricing: selling a new product at a low price to attract customers away from an established product (p. 291)

fijar un precio de penetración: vender un producto nuevo a precio bajo para atraer a los compradores de un producto establecido (p. 291)

pension plans: company plans that provide retirement income for their workers (p. 156)

planes de pensiones: planes que empresas tienen para proporcionar ingresos a sus trabajadores jubilados (p. 156)

*perceived: apparent or obvious (p. 69)

*percibido: aparente (p. 69)

perfect competition: market situation in which there are numerous buyers and sellers, and no single buyer or seller can affect price (p. 232)

competencia perfecta: mercado en que hay muchos vendedores y compradores y ninguno puede afectar el precio independientemente (p. 232)

*period: a portion of time (p. 88)

*periodo: espacio de tiempo (p. 88)

personal income (PI): total income that individuals receive before personal taxes are paid (p. 339)

ingresos personales: ingresos totales que recibe una persona antes de pagar sus impuestos personales; también se llama renta personal (p. 339)

*physical: material (p. 342)

*físico: material (p. 342)

picketing: action of strikers who walk in front of a workplace carrying signs that state their disagreement with the company (p. 322)

piquetear: acción de trabajadores en huelga que se pasean delante del lugar de trabajo con letreros que declaran sus desacuerdos con la compañía (p. 322)

points: fees paid to a lender and computed as a percentage of a loan (p. 129)

puntos: suma que se le paga a un prestamista y se calcula como un porcentaje del préstamo (p. 129)

*portion: a part (pp. 156, 401)

*porción: una parte (pp. 156, 401)

*potential: possible (p. 115)

*potencial: posible (p. 115)

*precede: come before (p. 353)

*preceder: anteceder; venir primero (p. 353)

*precise: accurate (p. 403)

*preciso: exacto; fiel (p. 403)

preferred stock: shares of ownership in a corporation that give stockholders a portion of future profits (before any profits go to holders of common stock), but no voting rights (p. 221)

acciones preferentes: participaciones en una sociedad anónima que dan a los accionistas una porción de las ganancias futuras (antes de pagar a dueños de acciones ordinarias), pero sin el derecho al voto; también se llaman acciones preferidas (p. 221)

*previous: occurring before; prior (p. 95)

*previo: que ocurre primero; anterior (p. 95)

Glossary/Glosario

ENGLISH	ESPAÑOL
price ceiling: a legal maximum price that may be charged for a particular good or service (p. 198)	**precio máximo:** precio más alto que la ley permite que se cobre por un producto o servicio en particular (p. 198)
price elasticity of demand: economic concept that deals with *how much* demand varies according to changes in price (p. 182)	**efecto del precio en la elasticidad de la demanda:** concepto económico que trata de *cómo* la demanda varía de acuerdo con los cambios en el precio (p. 182)
price floor: a legal minimum price below which a good or service may not be sold (p. 199)	**precio mínimo:** precio más bajo que la ley permite que se cobre por un producto o servicio (p. 199)
price leadership: a practice in some industries in which the largest firm publishes its price list ahead of its competitors, who then match those announced prices (p. 291)	**liderazgo en la fijación de precios:** práctica en algunas industrias en que la compañía más grande publica sus precios antes de sus competidores que entonces tratan de igualarlos (p. 291)
prime rate: rate of interest that banks charge on loans to their best business customers (p. 404)	**tasa preferencial:** tipo de interés que los bancos cobran por préstamos a sus mejores clientes comerciales (p. 404)
principal: amount originally borrowed in a loan (p. 88)	**principal:** cantidad original de un préstamo; también se llama capital (p. 88)
*principle: a rule of conduct (p. 70)	***principio:** regla de comportamiento (p. 70)
private-labeled products: lower-priced store-brand products carried by some supermarket chains and club warehouse chains (p. 116)	**productos de marca privada:** productos a precios más bajos que llevan la marca de la tienda en que se venden y son vendidos por cadenas de supermercados y de clubes almacenes (p. 116)
private property: whatever is owned by individuals rather than by government (p. 46)	**propiedad privada:** todo lo que pertenece a particulares y no al gobierno (p. 46)
*process: method; procedure (p. 271)	***proceso:** método; procedimiento (p. 271)
producer price index (PPI): measure of the change in price over time that U.S. producers charge for their goods and services (p. 344)	**índice de precios de productores:** medida, a través del tiempo, de los cambios en los precios que los productores estadounidenses cobran por sus bienes y servicios (p. 344)
product differentiation: manufacturers' use of minor differences in quality and features to try to differentiate between similar goods and services (p. 241)	**diferenciación de productos:** uso de pequeñas diferencias en calidad y características por parte de los fabricantes para tratar de diferenciar bienes y servicios parecidos (p. 241)
production: process of changing resources into goods that satisfy the needs and wants of individuals and businesses (p. 272)	**producción:** proceso de convertir recursos en bienes que satisfacen las necesidades y deseos de individuos y negocios (p. 272)
production possibilities curve: graph showing the maximum combinations of goods and services that can be produced from a fixed amount of resources in a given period of time (p. 17)	**curva de posibilidades de producción:** gráfica que muestra la mayor combinación de bienes y servicios que se pueden producir con una cantidad fija de recursos en un período de tiempo determinado (p. 17)
productivity: the amount of output (goods and services) that results from a given level of inputs (land, labor, capital, and entrepreneurship) (p. 9)	**productividad:** producción final (cantidad de bienes y servicios) que rinde una cantidad determinada de insumos (tierra, trabajo, capital y empresa) (p. 9)

Glossary/Glosario

Glossary/Glosario

ENGLISH	ESPAÑOL
product life cycle: series of stages that a product goes through from first introduction to complete withdrawal from the market (p. 294)	**ciclo de vida de un producto:** etapas por las que pasa un producto desde que se introduce hasta que se retira del mercado (p. 294)
professionals: highly educated individuals with college degrees and usually additional education or training (p. 310)	**profesionales:** personas muy preparadas, que han cursado por lo menos cuatro años al nivel universitario y generalmente tienen educación o preparación adicional (p. 310)
profit: amount earned after a business subtracts its costs from its revenues (pp. 45, 261)	**ganancias:** dinero que le queda a un negocio después de restar los costos de las entradas; también se llama lucro, beneficios y utilidad (pp. 45, 261)
profit incentive: desire to make money that motivates people to produce and sell goods and services (p. 45)	**afán de lucro:** deseo de ganar dinero que alienta a las personas a producir y vender bienes y servicios (p. 45)
progressive tax: tax that takes a larger percentage of higher incomes than of lower incomes; justified on the basis of the ability-to-pay principle (p. 433)	**impuesto progresivo:** impuesto que grava un porcentaje mayor a los que tienen más ingresos y menor a los que tienen menos; se justifica con el principio de la capacidad de pago (p. 433)
*prohibit: forbid; disallow (p. 246)	***prohibir:** vedar; desautorizar (p. 246)
proletariat: term Karl Marx used to refer to workers (p. 52)	**proletariado:** término que Carlos Marx usó para referirse a los obreros (p. 52)
*promote: endorse; help (p. 248)	***promover:** apoyar; impulsar; ayudar (p. 248)
promotion: use of advertising to inform consumers that a new or improved product or service is available and to persuade them to purchase it (p. 293)	**promoción:** uso de la publicidad para informar a los consumidores que un producto o servicio nuevo o mejorado está en venta y para convencerlos a que lo compren (p. 293)
proportional tax: tax that takes the same percentage of all incomes; as income rises, the amount of tax paid also rises (p. 433)	**impuesto proporcional:** impuesto que grava el mismo porcentaje a todos los ingresos; al subir los ingresos, la cantidad de impuestos que hay que pagar también sube (p. 433)
proprietor: owner of a business (p. 214)	**propietario:** dueño de un negocio (p. 214)
protectionists: people who argue for trade restrictions to protect domestic industries (p. 479)	**proteccionistas:** personas que abogan en favor de restricciones comerciales para proteger las industrias domésticas (p. 479)
protective tariff: tax on imports used to raise the cost of imported goods and thereby protect domestic producers (p. 478)	**aranceles proteccionistas:** impuestos sobre las importaciones usados para subir el precio de bienes importados y proteger a los productores domésticos (p. 478)
public-assistance programs: government programs that make payments to citizens based on need (p. 421)	**programas de asistencia pública:** programas gubernamentales que hacen pagos a personas necesitadas (p. 421)
public goods: goods or services that can be used by many individuals at the same time without reducing the benefit each person receives (p. 419)	**bienes públicos:** bienes y servicios que pueden ser usados por muchas personas a la misma vez sin reducir el beneficio que obtiene cada una (p. 419)

ENGLISH	ESPAÑOL
public-works projects: publicly used facilities, such as schools and highways, built by federal, state, or local governments with public money (p. 415)	**proyectos de obras públicas:** edificaciones e instalaciones para el uso público, como escuelas y carreteras, construidas por el gobierno federal, estatal o local con dinero público (p. 415)
purchasing power: the real goods and services that money can buy; determines the value of money (p. 342)	**poder adquisitivo:** cantidad real de bienes y servicios que se pueden comprar con el dinero; determina el valor del dinero (p. 342)

Q

quantity demanded: the amount of a good or service that a consumer is willing and able to purchase at a specific price (p. 172)	**cantidad demandada:** cantidad de un producto o servicio que los consumidores están dispuestos y pueden comprar a un precio dado (p. 172)
quantity supplied: the amount of a good or service that a producer is willing and able to supply at a specific price (p. 187)	**cantidad ofrecida:** cantidad de un producto o servicio que un productor está dispuesto y puede ofrecer a un precio dado (p. 187)

R

rational choice: choosing the alternative that has the greatest value from among comparable-quality products (p. 69)	**selección racional:** escoger la alternativa de mayor valor entre productos de la misma calidad (p. 69)
rationing: the distribution of goods and services based on something other than price (p. 199)	**racionamiento:** basar la distribución de bienes y servicios en razones que no incluyen el precio (p. 199)
real GDP: GDP that has been adjusted for inflation by applying the price deflator (p. 344)	**PIB real:** PIB al que se le ha aplicado el deflactor de precios para corregir los efectos de la inflación (p. 344)
real income effect: economic rule stating that individuals cannot keep buying the same quantity of a product if its price rises while their income stays the same (p. 173)	**efecto de ingresos reales:** regla económica que dice que los consumidores no pueden continuar comprando la misma cantidad de un producto si el precio de éste sube mientras que sus ingresos se mantienen iguales (p. 173)
receipts: income received from the sale of goods and/or services; also, slips of paper documenting a purchase (p. 211)	**entradas:** ingresos recibidos de la venta de bienes o servicios; recibos escritos que comprueban que se han hecho ciertas compras (p. 211)
recession: part of the business cycle in which the nation's output (real GDP) declines for at least six months (p. 352)	**recesión:** parte del ciclo económico en que el rendimiento nacional (PIB real) baja por seis meses al menos (p. 352)
***recover:** to regain strength, get better (p. 521)	***recuperar:** recobrar fuerzas; mejorarse (p. 521)
recovery: same as *expansion* (p. 352)	**recuperación:** lo mismo que *expansion/expansión* (p. 352)
***regime:** political system (p. 502)	***régimen:** sistema político (p. 502)
***region:** any division or part of a geographical area (p. 66)	***región:** cualquier división o parte de un área geográfica (p. 66)

Glossary/Glosario

Glossary/Glosario

ENGLISH	ESPAÑOL
*regional: local (p. 116)	*regional: local (p. 116)
registration fee: licensing fee, usually annual, paid to a state for the right to use a car (p. 131)	cuota por la matrícula: suma, generalmente anual, que se paga a un estado por el derecho de usar un automóvil (p. 131)
regressive tax: tax that takes a larger percentage of lower incomes than of higher incomes (p. 433)	impuesto regresivo: impuesto que toma un mayor porcentaje de ingresos más bajos que de ingresos más altos (p. 433)
*regulate: to control according to a rule or principle (p. 43)	*regular: controlar de acuerdo con una regla o principio (p. 43)
*relevant: important (p. 208)	*relevante: pertinente; importante (p. 208)
*remove: take away (p. 449)	*quitar: sacar; eliminar (p. 449)
representative money: money that is backed by an item of value, such as gold or silver (p. 371)	dinero crediticio: dinero que está respaldado por algo de valor, como el oro o la plata (p. 371)
*require: need (p. 142)	*requiere: necesita (p. 142)
reserve requirements: regulations set by the Fed requiring banks to keep a certain percentage of their checkable deposits as cash in their own vaults or as deposits in their Federal Reserve district bank (p. 400)	reserva obligatoria: regulación establecida por el Sistema de Reserva Federal que requiere que los bancos mantengan un porcentaje de sus depósitos a la vista en efectivo en sus propias bóvedas de seguridad o en el banco de la Reserva Federal de su distrito (p. 400)
*resolve: decide; solve (p. 321)	*resolver: decidir; arreglar (p. 321)
*resource: supply (p. 307)	*recurso: suministro disponible de algo (p. 307)
*restrict: limit (p. 477)	*restringir: limitar (p. 477)
retailers: businesses that sell consumer goods directly to the public (p. 298)	tiendas al por menor: negocios que venden bienes directamente al consumidor (p. 298)
*reveal: make known (p. 17)	*revelar: hacer que se sepa algo (p. 17)
revenues: total income from sales of output (p. 261)	ingresos: total de las ganancias provenientes de la venta de la producción de una compañía (p. 261)
revenue tariff: tax on imports used primarily to raise government revenue without restricting imports (p. 478)	derechos aduaneros: impuesto sobre las importaciones usado principalmente para recaudar ingresos gubernamentales sin restringir las importaciones; también se llaman impuestos aduaneros o derechos arancelarios (p. 478)
*reverse: opposite (p. 349)	*contrario: opuesto (p. 349)
*revolution: uprising (p. 239)	*revolución: levantamiento (p. 239)
right-to-work laws: state laws forbidding unions from forcing workers to join and pay union dues (p. 318)	leyes de derecho al trabajo: leyes estatales que prohíben que los sindicatos fuercen a los trabajadores a afiliarse y a pagar cuotas sindicales (p. 318)

ENGLISH	ESPAÑOL
robotics: sophisticated computer-controlled machinery that operates an assembly line (p. 275)	**robótica:** maquinaria compleja, controlada por computadoras, que opera una línea de montaje (p. 275)
Roth IRA: private retirement plan that taxes income before it is saved, but which does not tax interest on that income when funds are used upon retirement (p. 157)	**cuenta de retiro individual Roth:** plan de jubilación privado en que se gravan los ingresos antes de ser ahorrados, pero no se gravan los intereses por los ahorros cuando se usan esos fondos después de jubilarse (p. 157)

S

saving: setting aside income for a period of time so that it can be used later (p. 142)	**ahorrar:** guardar ingresos por un período de tiempo para poder usarlos más adelante (p. 142)
savings account: account that pays interest, has no maturity date, and from which funds can be withdrawn at any time without penalty (p. 143)	**cuenta de ahorro:** cuenta que paga interés, no tiene fecha de vencimiento y de la cual se pueden sacar fondos en cualquier momento sin tarifas (p. 143)
savings and loan association (S&L): depository institution that accepts deposits and lends funds (p. 93)	**sociedad de ahorro y préstamos:** institución que acepta depósitos y presta fondos (p. 93)
savings bank: depository institution originally set up to serve small savers overlooked by commercial banks (p. 93)	**banco de ahorro:** tipo de institución depositaria establecida originalmente para servir a personas que ahorraban pequeñas cantidades y eran ignorados por los bancos comerciales (p. 93)
savings bonds: bonds issued by the federal government as a way of borrowing money; they are purchased at half the face value and increase every 6 months until full face value is reached (p. 149)	**bonos de ahorro:** bonos emitidos por el gobierno federal para obtener dinero prestado; se compran a la mitad de su valor nominal, y cada 6 meses aumentan en valor hasta llegar al valor nominal completo (p. 149)
scarcity: basic economic problem that results from a combination of limited resources and unlimited wants (p. 7)	**escasez:** problema que resulta de la combinación de recursos limitados y deseos sin límite (p. 7)
***scheme:** a secret plan (p. 153)	***confabulación:** un plan secreto (p. 153)
secured loan: loan that is backed up by collateral (p. 101)	**préstamo garantizado:** préstamo que está asegurado por propiedad (p. 101)
security deposit: funds a renter lets an owner hold in case the rent is not paid or the apartment is damaged (p. 126)	**depósito de garantía:** fondos que un inquilino pone en manos del dueño en caso de que no pague el alquiler o deje el apartamento dañado (p. 126)
semiskilled workers: people whose jobs require some training, often using modern technology (p. 310)	**obreros semicalificados:** personas cuyos trabajos requieren un poco de preparación, a menudo en el uso de la tecnología moderna; también se llaman obreros semiespecializados (p. 310)
***series:** a number of things coming one after another (p. 105)	***serie:** un número de cosas que suceden una después de la otra (p. 105)
service flow: amount of use a person gets from an item over time and the value a person places on this use (p. 121)	**servicio útil:** cantidad de uso que una persona le saca a un artículo a través del tiempo y el valor que le da a su uso (p. 121)

Glossary/Glosario

ENGLISH	ESPAÑOL
services: actions that can satisfy people's wants or needs (p. 8)	**servicios:** actividades económicas que pueden satisfacer los deseos o necesidades del público (p. 8)
service workers: people who provide services directly to individuals (p. 309)	**trabajadores en el área de servicio:** personas que proporcionan servicios directamente al público (p. 309)
shortage: situation in which the quantity demanded is greater than the quantity supplied at the current price (p. 197)	**escasez:** situación en que la cantidad demandada al precio actual es mayor que la cantidad ofrecida; falta de un producto (p. 197)
short-term financing: funds borrowed by a business for any period of time less than a year (p. 265)	**financiamiento a corto plazo:** préstamo de fondos que un negocio tiene que pagar en menos de un año (p. 265)
***significant:** noteworthy (p. 317)	***significativo:** notable (p. 317)
***similar:** nearly but not exactly the same (p. 74)	***similar:** muy parecido pero no exactamente igual (p. 74)
skilled workers: people who have learned a trade or craft either through a vocational school or as an apprentice to an experienced worker (p. 310)	**obreros calificados:** personas que han aprendido un oficio o artesanía en una escuela de artes y oficios o como aprendices de obreros maestros; también se llaman obreros especializados (p. 310)
small-business incubator: private- or government-funded agency that assists new businesses by providing advice or low-rent buildings and supplies (p. 209)	**incubadora de pequeños negocios:** agencia privada o financiada por el gobierno que asiste a nuevos negocios, proporcionando asesoramiento, locales con alquileres bajos y artículos de uso diario (p. 209)
social-insurance programs: government programs that pay benefits to retired and disabled workers, their families, and the unemployed (p. 420)	**programas de seguridad social:** programas gubernamentales que pagan prestaciones a trabajadores retirados o inválidos, a sus familias y a los desempleados (p. 420)
Social Security: federal program that provides monthly payments to people who are retired or unable to work (p. 420)	**Seguro Social:** programa federal que proporciona pagos mensuales a personas que están jubiladas o no pueden trabajar (p. 420)
socialism: a system in which the government owns the major factors of production and attempts to manage output and the distribution of goods (p. 52)	**socialismo:** sistema en que el gobierno es dueño de todos los factores de producción importantes y trata de dirigir la producción y distribución de bienes (p. 52)
sole proprietorship: business owned and operated by one person (p. 214)	**propiedad individual:** negocio operado por un solo dueño, el propietario único (p. 214)
***source:** place from which something comes (p. 466)	***fuente:** sitio de donde proviene algo (p. 466)
specialization: concept that a nation should produce and export a limited assortment of goods for which it is particularly suited in order to use its resources most efficiently (p. 468)	**especialización:** concepto de que una nación debe limitarse a producir y exportar una selección de aquellos bienes que son más apropiados para ser producidos en ella, para usar sus recursos lo más eficientemente posible (p. 468)
***specific:** particular (p. 180)	***específico:** particular (p. 180)
stabilization policies: attempts by the federal government to keep the economy healthy; includes monetary and fiscal policies (p. 442)	**políticas de estabilización:** intentos por parte del gobierno federal de mantener sana la economía; incluyen las políticas monetaria y fiscal (p. 442)

Glossary/Glosario

ENGLISH	ESPAÑOL
stagflation: combination of inflation and stagnation (low economic activity) (p. 445)	**estagflación:** combinación de inflación con estancamiento (poca actividad económica); también se llama estanflación (p. 445)
standard of living: the material well-being of an individual, group, or nation, measured by how well their necessities and luxuries are satisfied (p. 49)	**nivel de vida:** bienestar material de un individuo, grupo o nación, en forma de cálculo de lo bien que puede satisfacer sus necesidades y obtener lujos (p. 49)
startup: a beginning business enterprise (p. 209)	**negocio nuevo:** empresa nueva (p. 209)
*statistic: numerical data collected to show information (p. 336)	***estadística:** datos numéricos recolectados para mostrar información (p. 336)
*status: legal condition (p. 133)	***condición jurídica:** situación legal (p. 133)
stock: share of ownership in a corporation that entitles the buyer to a certain part of the future profits and assets of the corporation (p. 219)	**acciones:** participaciones en una sociedad anónima que hacen al comprador uno de sus propietarios con derecho a recibir parte de las ganancias y activos de la sociedad (p. 219)
stockholders: people who have invested in a corporation and own some of its shares of stock (p. 147)	**accionistas:** personas que han invertido en una sociedad anónima y son dueños de un número de acciones (p. 147)
stock market indexes: measures of what is happening to a given set of stock prices for a specified list of companies; the most well known is the Dow Jones Industrial Average (p. 151)	**índices del mercado de acciones:** medidas de lo que está sucediendo a los precios de un grupo determinado de acciones de una lista de compañías en particular; el mejor conocido es el Dow Jones Industrial Average (p. 151)
store of value: use of money to store purchasing power for later use (p. 369)	**reserva de valor:** uso del dinero como almacén del poder adquisitivo que una persona recibe como pago, a cambio de su trabajo o de un artículo vendido, y que puede usar en el futuro (p. 369)
*strategy: plan (p. 289)	***estrategia:** plan (p. 289)
strike: deliberate work stoppage by workers to force an employer to give in to their demands (p. 317)	**huelga:** paro de trabajo intencional por parte de los trabajadores para forzar a los patronos a que ceden a sus demandas (p. 317)
*submit: present (p. 427)	***someter:** presentar (p. 427)
*subsequent: coming after; following (p. 503)	***subsiguiente:** posterior; que sigue (p. 503)
subsistence agriculture: growing of just enough food by a family to take care of its own needs; no crops are available for export or to feed an industrial workforce (p. 492)	**agricultura de subsistencia:** cultivar alimentos suficientes para satisfacer las necesidades de una familia solamente; la cosecha no alcanza para exportar o alimentar a la fuerza laboral industrial (p. 492)
*substitute: replacement (p. 502)	***sustituto:** reemplazo; suplente (p. 502)
substitution effect: economic rule stating that if two items satisfy the same need and the price of one rises, people will buy more of the other (p. 173)	**efecto de sustitución:** regla económica que dice que si dos artículos satisfacen la misma necesidad y el precio de uno sube, el público comprará más del otro (p. 173)
*sufficient: enough (p. 259)	***suficiente:** bastante (p. 259)

Glossary/Glosario

Glossary/Glosario

Supplemental Security Income • Temporary Assistance for Needy Families

ENGLISH	ESPAÑOL
Supplemental Security Income: federal programs that include food stamps and payments to the disabled and aged (p. 421)	**Ingresos Suplementarios de Seguridad:** programa federal que provee beneficios que incluyen cupones de alimentos y apoyo financiero a personas ancianas y personas incapacitadas (p. 421)
supply: the amount of a good or service that producers are able and willing to sell at various prices during a specified time period (p. 170)	**oferta:** cantidad de un producto o servicio que los productores pueden y están dispuestos a vender a varios precios durante un período de tiempo determinado (p. 170)
supply curve: upward-sloping line that shows in graph form the quantities supplied at each possible price (p. 189)	**curva de oferta:** línea ascendiente en una gráfica cuya inclinación muestra la cantidad ofrecida a cada precio posible (p. 189)
supply schedule: table showing quantities supplied at different possible prices (p. 188)	**lista de oferta:** tabla que muestra las cantidades que se ofrecen a distintos precios (p. 188)
surplus: situation in which quantity supplied is greater than quantity demanded at the current price (p. 197)	**superávit:** situación en que la cantidad ofrecida es mayor que la cantidad demandada al precio actual (p. 197)
***survey:** a detailed study, as by gathering and analyzing information (p. 443)	***encuesta:** estudio detallado, por medio de recoger y analizar información (p. 443)

ENGLISH	ESPAÑOL
***target:** a goal (p. 455)	***blanco:** meta; objetivo (p. 455)
tariff: tax placed on an imported product (p. 478)	**arancel:** impuesto que grava un producto importado (p. 478)
tax-exempt bonds: bonds sold by local and state governments; interest paid on the bond is not taxed by the federal government (p. 148)	**bonos exentos de impuestos:** bonos emitidos por los gobiernos locales y estatales; los intereses que pagan no son gravados por el gobierno federal (p. 148)
***technical:** of a specific science, art, or craft (p. 492)	***técnico:** que tiene que ver con una ciencia, arte, o artesanía en particular (p. 492)
technical assistance: aid in the form of engineers, teachers, and technicians to teach skills to individuals in other nations (p. 497)	**asistencia técnica:** ayuda proporcionada por ingenieros, maestros y técnicos para enseñar técnicas a personas de otros países (p. 497)
technology: the use of science to develop new products and new methods for producing and distributing goods and services (pp. 10, 191)	**tecnología:** el uso de la ciencia para desarrollar nuevos productos y nuevos métodos de producción y distribución de bienes y servicios (pp. 10, 191)
telecommunications: long-distance communication, usually electronic, using communications satellites and fiber-optic cables (p. 518)	**telecomunicaciones:** comunicaciones a larga distancia, generalmente electrónicas, que usan satélites de comunicación y cables de fibra óptica (p. 518)
***temporary:** impermanent; not lasting (p. 216)	***temporario:** temporal; pasajero; no duradero (p. 216)
Temporary Assistance for Needy Families: state-run program that provides assistance and work opportunities to needy families (p. 421)	**Asistencia Temporal para Familias Necesitadas:** programa administrado por los estados que ofrece servicios de apoyo y oportunidades de empleo a familias necesitadas (p. 421)

ENGLISH	ESPAÑOL
test-marketing: offering a product for sale in a small area for a limited period of time to see how well it sells before offering it nationally (p. 287)	**hacer una prueba de mercado:** poner un producto en venta en un área pequeña por un período de tiempo limitado para ver lo bien que se vende antes de ofrecerlo en todo el país (p. 287)
***theory:** a model that explains observations (p. 22)	***teoría:** un modelo que explica observaciones (p. 22)
thrift institutions: mutual savings banks, S&Ls, and credit unions that offer many of the same services as commercial banks (p. 380)	**instituciones de ahorro:** bancos de ahorro mutuos, sociedades de ahorro y préstamos y cooperativas de crédito que ofrecen los mismos servicios que los bancos comerciales (p. 380)
tight money policy: monetary policy that makes credit expensive and in short supply in an effort to slow the economy (p. 399)	**política monetaria restrictiva:** política monetaria que hace que el crédito sea caro y difícil de obtener para tratar de reducir la actividad económica (p. 399)
time deposits: savings plans that require savers to leave their funds on deposit for certain periods of time (p. 144)	**depósitos a plazos:** planes de ahorro que obligan al ahorrador a dejar sus fondos en depósito por períodos de tiempo determinados (p. 144)
time lags: periods between the time fiscal policy is enacted and the time it becomes effective (p. 457)	**demoras:** período entre el momento en que se aprueba una política fiscal y el momento en que entra en vigor (p. 457)
trade-off: sacrificing one good or service to purchase or produce another (p. 15)	**compensación:** renunciar a un producto o servicio para comprar o producir otro (p. 15)
traditional economy: system in which economic decisions are based on customs and beliefs that have been handed down from generation to generation (p. 36)	**economía tradicional:** sistema en que las decisiones económicas se basan en las costumbres y creencias que se han pasado de generación en generación (p. 36)
transfer payments: welfare and other supplementary payments that a state or the federal government makes to individuals (p. 340)	**transferencias:** pagos de asistencia social y otros pagos suplementarios que el gobierno estatal o federal le hace a individuos (p. 340)
***transform:** change (p. 519)	***transformar:** cambiar (p. 519)
***transmit:** broadcast (p. 519)	***transmitir:** emitir (p. 519)
***transport:** move; transfer (p. 370)	***transportar:** mover; transferir (p. 370)
Treasury bills: certificates issued by the U.S. Treasury in exchange for a minimum amount of $1,000 and maturing in a few days up to 26 weeks (p. 149)	**letras del Tesoro:** certificados emitidos por el Tesoro de los EE.UU. que requieren una inversión mínima de $1,000 y se vencen entre varios días y 26 semanas después (p. 149)
Treasury bonds: certificates issued by the U.S. Treasury in exchange for minimum amounts of $1,000 and maturing in 30 years (p. 149)	**bonos del Tesoro:** certificados emitidos por el Tesoro de los EE.UU. a cambio de inversiones mínimas de $1,000 con fechas de vencimiento de 30 años en el futuro (p. 149)
Treasury notes: certificates issued by the U.S. Treasury in exchange for minimum amounts of $1,000 and maturing in 2 to 10 years (p. 149)	**pagarés del Tesoro:** certificados emitidos por el Tesoro de los EE.UU. a cambio de inversiones mínimas de $1,000 con fechas de vencimiento de 2 a 10 años después (p. 149)

Glossary/Glosario

Glossary/Glosario

trough • vary

ENGLISH	ESPAÑOL

trough: lowest part of the business cycle in which the downward spiral of the economy levels off (p. 352)

punto bajo: parte del ciclo económico en que la actividad económica en disminución se nivela; también se llama depresión (p. 352)

*undergo: go through (p. 264)

*experimentar: pasar por (p. 264)

underground economy: transactions by people who do not follow federal and state laws with respect to reporting earnings (p. 443)

economía sumergida: transacciones hechas por personas que no obedecen las leyes federales y estatales que requieren que se de parte al gobierno sobre los ingresos (p. 443)

unemployment rate: percentage of the civilian labor force that is unemployed but is actively looking for work (p. 442)

índice de desempleo: porcentaje de la fuerza laboral civil que no tiene empleo pero está buscando trabajo (p. 442)

union: see *labor union*

sindicato: véase *labor union/sindicato de obreros*

union shop: company that requires new employees to join a union after a specific period of time (p. 318)

fábrica sindical: compañía que obliga a nuevos empleados a hacerse miembros del sindicato después de un período de tiempo determinado (p. 318)

*unique: only one of its kind (p. 234)

*único: que no hay otro de su tipo (p. 234)

unit of accounting: use of money as a yardstick for comparing the values of goods and services in relation to one another (p. 369)

unidad de contabilidad: uso del dinero como medida del valor de distintos bienes y servicios que se puede usar de criterio para compararlos (p. 369)

unlimited liability: requirement that an owner is personally and fully responsible for all losses and debts of a business (p. 214)

responsabilidad sin límite: requisito que hace a un dueño total y personalmente responsable de todas las pérdidas y deudas de su negocio (p. 214)

unsecured loan: loan guaranteed only by a promise to repay it (p. 101)

préstamo no garantizado: préstamo hecho sin obtener una garantía, sólo la promesa de devolver el dinero (p. 101)

unskilled workers: people whose jobs require no specialized training (p. 310)

trabajadores no calificados: personas cuyos trabajos no requieren preparación especial (p. 310)

usury law: law restricting the amount of interest that can be charged for credit (p. 105)

ley contra la usura: ley que limita la cantidad de interés que se puede cobrar por el crédito (p. 105)

utility: the ability of any good or service to satisfy consumer wants (p. 174)

utilidad: capacidad de un producto o servicio de satisfacer los deseos de los consumidores (p. 174)

*utilize: to make use of (p. 6)

*utilizar: hacer uso de (p. 6)

*valid: legitimate (p. 299)

*válido: legítimo (p. 299)

*vary: differ (p. 376)

*variar: ser diferente (p. 376)

Glossary/Glosario

ENGLISH	ESPAÑOL
*visible: able to be seen (p. 219)	***visible:** que se puede ver (p. 219)
*visual: that can be seen (p. 178)	***visual:** que tiene que ver con lo que se puede ver (p. 178)
voluntary exchange: a transaction in which a buyer and a seller exercise their economic freedom by working out their own terms of exchange (p. 171)	**intercambio voluntario:** transacción en que el comprador y el vendedor ejercen su libertad económica al llegar a un acuerdo sobre las condiciones del intercambio (p. 171)

warranty: promise made by a manufacturer or a seller to repair or replace a product within a certain time period if it is found to be faulty (p. 74)	**garantía:** promesa de un fabricante o vendedor de reparar o reemplazar un producto defectuoso dentro de un plazo de tiempo determinado (p. 74)
welfare: same as *public-assistance programs* (p. 421)	**bienestar social:** lo mismo que *public-assistance programs/programas de asistencia pública* (p. 421)
white-collar workers: category of workers employed in offices, sales, or professional positions (p. 309)	**empleados en trabajos no manuales:** categoría de trabajadores empleados en oficinas, ventas o puestos profesionales (p. 309)
wholesalers: businesses that purchase large quantities of goods from producers for resale to other businesses (p. 297)	**mayoristas:** negocios que compran grandes cantidades de bienes de los fabricantes para vendérselas a otros negocios (p. 297)
workers' compensation: government program that extends payments for medical care to workers injured on the job (p. 421)	**compensación a trabajadores accidentados:** programas gubernamentales que hacen pagos para asistencia médica a trabajadores que se lesionan en el trabajo (p. 421)
World Trade Organization (WTO): world's largest trade agreement currently with more than 140 nations (p. 480)	**Organización Mundial del Comercio:** acuerdo comercial más extenso del mundo, actualmente entre más que 140 naciones (p. 480)

Glossary/Glosario

Index

The following abbreviations are used in the index: *crt* = cartoon; *fig* = figure, chart, graph; *p* = photograph

Abate, Joe, 92

ability-to-pay principle, 431

absolute advantage, 467–68, *p468*

accounts receivable, *fig265*

Adams, William, 315

Adar, Nir, 113

adjustable-rate mortgages, 92

adjusted balance, 97, *fig97*

advantage: absolute, 467–68, *p468;* comparative, 468–69

advertising: children as target of, 283, 304–5; competitive, 72, *fig72, p243;* direct-mail, 293; as element of business operation, 211, *fig210;* goal of, 70; informative, 72, *fig73;* on Internet, 70, *p70;* in monopolistic competition, 243, *p243;* in oligopoly, *fig240;* persuasive, *fig72;* for teenagers, 283, *p283;* wise use of, 72, *fig72–73*

AFL-CIO, 315, 317, 319

Africa: property rights in, 493; telecommunications in, 519

agency shop, 318

aggregate(s), 348

aggregate demand, 348–49, 350, *fig348*

aggregate demand curve, 348, *fig348*

aggregate supply, 349, 350, *fig349*

aggregate supply curve, 349, *fig349*

agriculture: absolute and comparative advantage in, 467–69, *p468;* in developing nations, 489, 492; and displaced farmers, 309; as example of perfect competition, 234–35, *fig234, p233;* financing of, 265, *p266;*

during Great Depression, 351; labor unions in, 326; subsistence, 492; supply in, *p235*

Agriculture, U.S. Department of (USDA), *p77*

airline bailouts, 245

Allen, Paul, 244

alliances, 529

American companies, foreign control of, 524–25, 526, *p524*

American economy: characteristics of, 42–46, 57, *fig46, p44, p45;* competition in, 45, *p45;* credit in, 87–91, 92, *fig88, fig89, fig90, p87, p91, p92;* defined, 57; freedom of choice in, 44–45, 48, *p44;* free enterprise in, 44; goals of, 48–49, *fig49;* limited role of government in, 43, *crt43;* planning in, 55, *fig54;* private property in, 46; profit incentive in, 45; rights and responsibilities of individuals in, 50

American Exchange Bond Market, 151

American Federation of Labor (AFL), 317, 319, 324

American Fire Safety Council, 76

American International Group, *fig528*

American Telephone & Telegraph (AT&T), 246

annual percentage rate (APR), 98

antitrust legislation, 246

Apple Computer, 529

APR (annual percentage rate), 98

arbitrary clauses, 127

arbitration, 321

articles of incorporation, 220

assembly line, 274, *fig274*

assets, 214

ATMs (automated teller machines), 376, *crt377, fig375, p376*

Australia: dollar equivalent of currency, *fig472;* economic and social statistics for, *fig492;* economy of, 37

authoritarian socialism, 53

automated teller machines (ATMs), 376, *crt377, fig375, p376*

automation, 275

automobiles, 130–33; buying, 131, 135, *crt29, crt131;* depreciation of, 133; extended warranty coverage for, 131; and gas prices, 341, *crt137;* insuring, 133, *fig132;* maintaining, 132–33; operating, 132–33; registering, 131; safety of, 130; trade-offs in buying, 135

average daily balance, 97, *fig97*

bait and switch, 72

balance: adjusted, 97, *fig97;* minimum, 142; past due, 97, *fig97*

balanced budget, 447

balance of trade, 475–76, *fig475*

Bangladesh, economic and social statistics for, *fig492*

bank(s): commercial, 93, 142, 380, *p93;* Federal Reserve, 392, 394, *fig392, p393;* during Great Depression, *fig375;* savings, 93; World Bank, 495, 499

banking: electronic, 373, 376–77, *crt377, fig375, p373, p376;* fractional reserve, 400–401; history of, 373–77, 391, *fig374–75, p391;* laws on, 375, 377, *fig375;* reforms in, *fig375;* reserve requirements in, 400, 403, *fig400, fig403;* services in, 376–77, *crt377, p376*

Bank of America, *fig528*

bankruptcy, 106–7, *crt107, p106*

Barreto, Hector, 372, *p372*

barriers to entry: and competition, 45; defined, 237; in

Index

Index

Index

Index

Index

Index

Index

Acknowledgments

Graphic elements for unit and chapter openers and People & Perspectives pages, icon images for section openers, figure and summary numbers, Case Studies, Global Economy, Careers, Technology Activity and Skills features, and icons for Critical Thinking, Technology, and Study & Writing Skills: PhotoDisc, Inc.

Type design element for Study & Writing Skills pages: Tony Cordoza/Photonica.

Gear design element for Critical Thinking Skills pages: Allen Wallace/Photonica.

Cover i (tl) Wei Yan/Masterfile, (tc) Tim Kiusalaas/Masterfile, (tr) Jean Miele/Corbis, (cl) Blend Images Photography/Veer, (cr) Steve Craft/Masterfile, (bl) G. Biss/Masterfile, (bc) Yellow Dog Productions/Getty Images; **iv** Ryan McVay/Getty Images; **v** Michael Newman/PhotoEdit; **vi** Andersen Ross/Getty Image; **vii** Mario Tama/Getty Images; **viii** The McGraw-Hill Companies; **ix** Alain Evrard/Lonely Planet Images; **x** George Tiedemann/Corbis; **xi** James Wells/Getty Images; **xvi–xvii** Ryan McVay/Getty Images; **xviii** The McGraw-Hill Companies; **xix** Getty Images; **xx** (t) Getty Images, (b) Jim Craigmyle/CORBIS; **2–3** Bill Aron/PhotoEdit; **4** Ryan McVay/Getty Images; **5** John Gress/Reuters/CORBIS; **6** Zits Partnership. Reprinted with Permission of King Feature Syndicate; **7** (l) Najlah Feanny/CORBIS, (r) Peter Horree/Alamy Images; **8** (l) Corbis, (r) Ariel Skelley/CORBIS; **9** (l) Keith Brofsky/Getty Images, (r) Michael Newman/PhotoEdit; **11** North Wind/North Wind Picture Archives; **12** Getty Images; **14** Alan Schein Photography/CORBIS; **15** Chuck Savage/CORBIS; **19** FOXTROT ©1996 Bill Amend. Reprinted with permission of UNIVERSAL PRESS SYNDICATE. All rights reserved; **20** Ariel Skelley/Masterfile; **21** Tim Fuller; **22** Getty Images; **24** (l) Chuck Kennedy/Getty Images, (r) Pablo Martinez Monsivais/Pool/Consolidated News Photos/CNP/CORBIS; **26** George Tiedemann/Corbis; **29** The New Yorker Collection 2004 Mick Stevens from cartoonbank.com All rights reserved; **30–31** Tim Fuller; **32** Jeff Christensen/Reuters/CORBIS; **33** Sherwin Crasto/Reuters/CORBIS; **34** (l) Jeremy Horner/Alamy Images, (r) Danny Lehman/CORBIS; **35** Jeff Zelevansky/Reuters/CORBIS; **36** Wendy Stone/CORBIS; **37** Gerald Bourke/EPA/Landov; **38** Mike Mergen/Bloomberg News/Landov; **41** Library of Congress; **42** Corbis; **43** CLOSE TO HOME © 2006 John McPherson. Reprinted with permis-

sion of UNIVERSAL PRESS SYNDICATE. All rights reserved; **44** David Young-Wolff/PhotoEdit; **45** Scott Olson/Getty Images; **47** Jeff Haynes/AFP/Getty Images; **48** By permission of Entrepreneur Press; **49** (l) Frances Roberts/Alamy Images, (r) Joel Stettenheim/CORBIS; **51** Igor Kostin/Corbis; **53** akg-images; **54** (l) Shiva Twin/Getty Images, (r) Christopher Morris/VII/AP/Wide World Photos; **55** Jose Luis Pelaez, Inc./CORBIS; **56** Dima Korotayev/Epsilon; **59** Harley Schwadron/CartoonStock; **60–61** Alexander Ruesche/dpa /Landov; **62–63** Brand X Pictures/Alamy; **64** David Young-Wolff/PhotoEdit; **65** Jed Jacobsohn/Getty Images; **66** Bryan Mitchell/Getty Images; **69** Bob Daemmrich/PhotoEdit; **70** Susan Van Etten/PhotoEdit; **71** David Young-Wolff/PhotoEdit; **72–73** Mark Steinmetz; **74** CLOSE TO HOME © 1996 John McPherson. Reprinted with permission of UNIVERSAL PRESS SYNDICATE. All rights reserved; **75** Dima Gavrysh /AP/Wide World Photos; **76** Jose Luis Pelaez, Inc./CORBIS; **77** Montes De Oca Art/Getty Images; **79** Kayte M. Deioma/PhotoEdit; **80** Ellis Nadler/Getty Images; **83** Zits Partnership. King Features Syndicate; **84** Dinodia; **84–85** Tim Flach/Tony Stone Images; **86** Andersen Ross/Getty Images; **87** Stephen Chernin/Getty Images; **89** Zack Seckler/Bloomberg News /Landov; **91** Michelle D. Bridwell/PhotoEdit; **92** VStock/Alamy Images; **93** Mark Lennihan/AP/Wide World Photos; **94** John Meyer; **95** Paul Collis/Alamy Images; **96** (l) Purestock/SuperStock, (tr) StudiOhio, (br) StudiOhio; **98** Michael Newman/PhotoEdit; **99** Keith Brofsky/Getty Image, **101** Tim Fuller; **103** Corbis; **104** (l) TransUnion, (tr) Equifax, (br) Experian; **105** Bob Daemmrich/The Image Works; **106** Richard Drew/AP/Wide World Photos; **107** FOXTROT ©1996 Bill Amend. Reprinted with permission of UNIVERSAL PRESS SYNDICATE. All rights reserved; **108** Mark Humphrey/AP/Wide World Photos; **112** Eric Glenn/Getty Images; **113** Courtesy of crispycones; **115** (l) Ric Francis/AP/Wide World Photos, (r) Tim Boyle/Getty Images; **116** (l) The McGraw-hill Companies, (r) David Young-Wolff/PhotoEdit; **117** Doug Martin; **118** Anders Krusburg/Reuters/CORBIS; **119** littlemismatched.com; **120** Grace/zefa/CORBIS; **121** (l) Grace/zefa/CORBIS, (r) Tom & Dee Ann McCarthy/CORBIS; **122** Ryan McVay/Getty Images; **124** David Young-Wolff/PhotoEdit; **125** Frank Siteman/Getty Images; **126** Ryan Donnell/Getty Images;

129 Ariel Skelley/CORBIS; **130** Carol T. Powers/Bloomberg News/Landov; **131** CORNERED © 2004 Mike Baldwin. Reprinted with permission of UNIVERSAL PRESS SYNDICATE. All rights reserved; **134** Courtesy of Colorful Harvest, LLC; **135** (l) Carol T. Powers/Bloomberg News/Landov, (r) Dick Reed/CORBIS; **137** TOLES © 2000 The Washington Post. Reprinted with permission of UNIVERSAL PRESS SYNDICATE. All rights reserved; **138–139** Aneal Vohra/Index Stock Imagery; **140** Getty Images; **141** Don Farrall/Getty Images; **142** King Features Syndicate, Inc; **145** Owaki-Kulla/CORBIS; **146** Doug Benc/Getty Images; **147** William Thomas Cain/Getty Images; **148** Comstock Images/Alamy; **149** Comstock Images/Alamy Images; **150** Ramin Talaie/CORBIS; **151** Ryan McVay/Getty Images; **152** Mandel Ngan/AFP/Getty Images; **154** Marianne Barcellona//Time Life Pictures/Getty Images; **155** Kwame Zikomo/SuperStock; **157** Noel Hendrickson/Masterfile; **159** Digital Vision/Getty Images; **160** TIm Fuller; **163** Toles © 1991 John McPherson. Reprinted with permission of UNIVERSAL PRESS SYNDICATE. All rights reserved; **164–165** Spencer Grant/PhotoEdit; **165** Geoff Butler; **166** Ron Fehling/Masterfile; **168** Tim Boyle/Getty Images; **169** Bernard Weil/Toronto Star/ZUMA Press; **170** (l) David Young-Wolff/Getty Images, (r) Hugh Sitton/Getty Images; **171** (l) GDT/Getty Images; (r) These materials have been reproduced with the permission of eBay Inc. COPYRIGHT © 2006 EBAY INC. ALL RIGHTS RESERVED; **173** DiMaggio/Kalish/CORBIS; **174** Andrew D. Bernstein/Getty Images; **175** Zits Partnership. Reprinted with Permission of King Feature Syndicate; **176** (t) Jeff Minton/Time & Life Pictures/Getty Images, (b) Jim Craigmyle/CORBIS; **177** Ted Soqui/CORBIS; **186** Yoshikazu Tsuno/AFP/Getty Images; **191** Bettmann/CORBIS; **193** Vittoriano Rastelli/CORBIS; **194** David Young/PhotoEdit; **197** (l) John F. Martin/AP/Wide World Photos, (r) CORBIS; **199** Robin Nelson/PhotoEdit; **200** AP Photo/Charles Rex Arbogast; **203** Rogers © 2005 Pittsburgh Post-Gazette/Dist. by United Features Syndicate; **204–205** Paul J. Sutton/Duomo/CORBIS; **206** Andersen Ross/Getty Images; **207** James Leynse/Corbis; **208** Ulf Wallin/Getty Images; **209** Comstock Images/Alamy; **210** (l) BananaStock/Alamy Images, (r) Martucci Studios; **211** (l) Glencoe Photo, (r) Jim Craigmyle/CORBIS; **212** FARCUS® is

Acknowledgments

Acknowledgments

437 NON SEQUITUR ©2004 Wiley Miller. Dist. By UNIVERSAL PRESS SYNDICATE. Reprinted with permission. All rights reserved; **438–439** Vincent Besnault/Getty Images; **440** REUTERS/Henny Ray Abrams/Landov; **441** AP/Wide World Photos; **447** Ron Edmonds/ AP/Wide World Photos; **449** (l) Arnold Gold/New Haven Register/The Image Works, (r) Richard Price/Getty Images; **450** Bettmann/CORBIS; **451** BALDO © 2005 Baldo Partnership. Dist. By UNIVERSAL PRESS SYNDICATE. Reprinted with permission. All rights reserved; **452** Robbin Weiner/Newswire/The Image Works; **453** David Young-Wolff/Getty Images; **455** TIM SLOAN/AFP/Getty Images; **458** Roger Ressmeyer/CORBIS; **461** FOXTROT © 2000 Bill Amend. Reprinted with permission of UNIVERSAL PRESS SYNDICATE. All rights reserved; **462–463** Jeremy Horner/Corbis; **464** Getty Images; **465** Vladimir Dubrovsky/Pressphotos; **466** Courtesy Boeing Co., Ed Turner/AP/Wide World Photo; **468** Rickey Rogers/Reuters/CORBIS; **470** Zack Seckler/Corbis; **471** AP/Wide World Photos; **474** Iain Masterton/Alamy; **476** Prickly City ©2005 Scott Stantis. Reprinted with permission of UNIVERSAL PRESS SYNDICATE. All rights reserved. Email: PRICKLYCITY@GMAIL.COM; **477** Dwayne Newton/Photo Edit; **480** REUTERS/Fred Greaves/Landov; **482** Tim Boyle/Getty Images; **485** Toles © 2005 The Washington Post, Reprint with permission of Universal Press Syndicate. All rights Reserved; **486** Vincenzo Lombardo/Getty Images; **488** Andrew Marshall & Leanne Walker/Lonely Planet Images; **489** Courtesy of Equal Exchange Trading Ltd.; **490** HIRB/Index Stock; **494** Keith Dannemiller/Corbis; **495** RUBIN STEVEN/CORBIS SYGMA; **496** Juan Silva/Getty Images; **497** (l) Courtesy of the Peace Corps, (r) Robert A. Sabo/Getty Images; **499** KAZUHIRO NOGI/AFP/Getty Images; **501** Alain Evrard/Lonely Planet Images; **504** Mark Lewis / Getty Images; **505** China Photos/Getty Images; **506** FREDERIC J. BROWN/AFP/Getty Images; **507** Phil Weymouth/Lonely Planet Images; **508** AP Photo/Ng Han Guan; **510** Bettmann/CORBIS; **511** Redlink/Corbis; **513** Jonathan Richards; **514–515** JENS SCHLUETER/AFP/Getty Images; **516** James Wells / Getty Images; **517** Tim Boyle/Getty Images; **519** Josef Polleross/The Image Works; **520** STEPHANIE MCGEHEE/Reuters/Landov; **522** Jon Santa Cruz/Rex USA; **523** Mika/zefa/Corbis; **524** ROBERTO SCHMIDT/AFP/Getty Images;

527 © TIM SLOAN/AFP/Getty Images; **529** Robert Holmes/CORBIS; **530** Will Hart/PhotoEdit; **531** CARLSON © Milwaukee Sentinel. Reprinted with permission of UNIVERSAL PRESS SYNDICATE. All rights reserved; **532** John Hersey; **533** (t) STEPHANIE MCGEHEE/Reuters/Landov, (b) Zhu gang/Imaginechina/ZUMA Press; **535** TOLES © 2001 The Washington Post. Reprinted with permission of UNIVERSAL PRESS SYNDICATE. All rights reserved; **536–537** Bob Daemmrich/Corbis; **R35** AP Photo/Kai-Uwe Knoth; **R36** AP Photo/Steve Helber; **R38** Kayte M. Deioma/PhotoEdit; **R39** YOSHIKAZU TSUNO/AFP/Getty Images; **R40** Jan Cobb Photography Ltd/Getty Images; **R42** The McGraw-Hill Companies; **R45** Munshi Ahmed/Bloomberg News /Landov; **R46** Bill Pugliano/Getty Images; **R47** (l) Scott Barbour/Getty Images, (r) Scott Barbour/Getty Images; **R58** Scott Stantis/Copley News Service; **R76** (t) TRBfoto/Getty Images, (tc) Keith Brofsky/Getty Images, (c) PhotoLink/Getty Images, (b) Keith Brofsky/Getty Images, (bc) Ryan McVay/Getty Images, **R77** (t) Getty Images, (tc) Keith Brofsky/Getty Images, (c) John A Rizzo/Getty Images, (b) Getty Images, (bc) Keith Brofsky/Getty Images; **R78** (t) Arthur S Aubry/Getty Images, (tc) Don Tremain/Getty Images, (c) TRBfoto/Getty Images, (b) Ryan McVay/Getty Images, (bc) John A Rizzo/Getty Images; **R79** (t) Keith Brofsky/Getty Images, (tc) Jacobs Stock Photography/Getty Images, (c) PhotoLink/Getty Images, (b) CORBIS, (bc) George Doyle/Getty Images, **R80** (t) CORBIS, (tc) PhotoLink/Getty Images, (c) Ryan McVay/Getty Images, (b) Ryan McVay/Getty Images, (bc) Ryan McVay/Getty Images.

The following articles have been reprinted or adapted from *BusinessWeek* by special permission by The McGraw-Hill Companies:

26 "The Grease Pits of Academia," March 13, 2006; **56** "Here Comes Lunar Power," March 6, 2006; **80** "Revenge of the Irate Shopper," April 17, 2006; **103** "Breaking the Cycle of Bad Credit," February 23, 2006; **134** "Eat Your Hybrid Veggies," June 24, 2006; **160** "Follow My Money," March 6, 2006; **176** "It's a What?" July 18, 2005; **224** "Panera Bread," April 17, 2006; **250** "A Window Into Microsoft's Battle," April 24, 2006; **276** "What Great Wall?" April 3, 2006; **295** "Shaping Shopper's Emotions," December 19, 2005; **314** "iPod'ing at Work?" April 24, 2006; **346** "GDP: What's Counted, What's Not," February 13, 2006; **384** "Banks: 'Protection' Racket?" May 2, 2005; **408** "Inflation 'Expectations,'"

April 3, 2006; **434** "The Deficit: A Danger or a Blessing?" June 16, 2004; **446** "Web World," May 29, 2006; **482** "A Major Swipe at Sweatshops," May 23, 2005; **494** "Pumping Out Engineers," May 22, 2006; **532** "Far-Flung Workers," December 19, 2005

"I won't accept that."

Jamie sat up straighter and looked at him. "Yes, Daniel, you will have to accept that. There are some things in this world that your money can't buy, and I'm one of them."

"Did I say anything about money?"

"It's implied. You're so used to getting your way that you forget other people have free will."

"Let me rephrase, then. I don't accept that you don't want to find the man who took two lives and ruined two others... That doesn't excite you?"

She took her time answering. "I would be pleased to prosecute that man as part of my job. But for me, it's not personal."

"So this case is nothing personal? Just business?"

She nodded curtly.

"What was that kiss all about, then?"

Her gaze locked with his. Jamie licked her lips and swallowed. "Th-that kiss is immaterial to this discussion. We were talking about the justice system. Our work."

"You're right. Immaterial. Completely out of line for me to even bring it up." With that, he leaned in and kissed her again.

Dear Reader,

Revenge is an ugly thing. I guess that's why it works so well as a motivation in a novel—it creates instant internal conflict. If the author does her job, the reader will share the character's outrage and totally understand the desire to strike back; at the same time, the reader knows that taking the law into your own hands is wrong.

Creating that inner conflict is why I write novels. I find it delicious!

In this story, my hero, Daniel, feels a strong desire to strike back at the person who framed him for murder, causing him to spend six miserable years on death row. What better heroine to give him than a law-and-order prosecutor? I hope you enjoy the long journey each of them has to make before they can be together for the long haul.

Best,

Kara Lennox

A Score to Settle
Kara Lennox

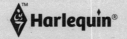

TORONTO NEW YORK LONDON
AMSTERDAM PARIS SYDNEY HAMBURG
STOCKHOLM ATHENS TOKYO MILAN MADRID
PRAGUE WARSAW BUDAPEST AUCKLAND

Recycling programs
for this product may
not exist in your area.

ISBN-13: 978-0-373-78446-2

A SCORE TO SETTLE

www.eHarlequin.com

Printed in U.S.A.

ABOUT THE AUTHOR

Kara Lennox has earned her living at various times as an art director, typesetter, textbook editor and reporter. She's worked in a boutique, a health club and an ad agency. She's been an antiques dealer, an artist and even a blackjack dealer. But no work has ever made her happier than writing romance novels. To date, she has written more than sixty books. Kara is a recent transplant to Southern California. When not writing, she indulges in an ever-changing array of hobbies. Her latest passions are bird-watching, long-distance bicycling, vintage jewelry and, by necessity, do-it-yourself home renovation. She loves to hear from readers; you can find her at www.karalennox.com.

Books by Kara Lennox

For my sister Pat.

You are so good at everything.
I wouldn't be the person I am today if I hadn't
tried so hard to keep up with you.

CHAPTER ONE

JAMIE MCNAIR FUMED SILENTLY as she crawled along a traffic-clogged Houston freeway. Who did Daniel Logan think he was, summoning her as if she was one of his lackeys? When she'd heard that the billionaire wanted to overturn one of *her* verdicts, she'd been anxious to talk to him and set him straight. But on her terms, not his.

Unfortunately, he'd gone over her head, which tweaked her all the more. Now, because her boss was scared of Daniel and his charitable foundation, she had to make a command performance.

A meeting at the Project Justice office would have been tolerable. But no, Logan had decided he wanted to meet her at his home.

She hated being manipulated. But since Logan had forced her into this meeting, she intended to make it count. In her briefcase she had every piece of information she needed to convince Logan that Christopher Gables was right where he belonged—on death row for brutally killing his business partner.

She had far better things to do than cater to the whims of a spoiled, supposedly do-gooder billionaire. Logan might be wealthy and powerful, but he was also a convicted murderer himself. Her own father had prosecuted Daniel many years ago, and her dad hadn't been one to make mistakes.

To prepare for the meeting, she had learned everything she could about Logan. She'd found lots of data about his arrest and trial, as well as his family's oil company. Unfortunately, personal information was in short supply.

The most recent picture she had found was a blurry wire-service photo of him the day he was released from prison six years ago. Back then, he'd been a tall, thin, pale man with a bad haircut. In photos from his trial—more than twelve years ago—he'd looked like a handsome but scared frat boy.

A few minutes later she pulled up to a set of ornate wrought-iron gates in tony River Oaks, one of the richest zip codes in America.

She was steamed, but she couldn't deny a certain curiosity to see the inside of this place. From the outside, it looked like a nineteenth-century English estate home, something that might be found in a Jane Austen novel, complete with ivy-covered walls and worn cobbles forming the driveway.

Jamie was about to get out of her car and walk up to the intercom when the gates opened quietly on well-oiled hinges. She pulled her car—an aging Subaru that must have looked as out of place as a donkey in church—down the cobbled driveway toward the house.

When she got out, one of her heels caught in the cobbles and she turned her ankle. *Good night.* Who made their driveway out of real cobblestones? Limping slightly and silently cursing at the added annoyance, she made her way to the front door; two huge panels of carved oak that looked as if they belonged on an ancient castle.

She reached for the bell, but before she could press it the door opened.

"Ms. McNair, please come in."

Standing in the doorway was a beautiful young woman with a sleek, blond bob.

She wore a snug lavender cashmere sweater, skinny black pants and pointy-toed boots. Though Jamie wasn't exactly a clotheshorse, she knew quality when she saw it.

Even Daniel's servants were well-to-do.

"Thank you. You must be Jillian." Jamie had recognized the slight British accent as belonging to Daniel Logan's personal assistant.

Inside, the foyer was no less impressive than the outside, soaring three stories to a peaked roof with stained-glass windows that shot beams of colorful light to the white marble floor below. At the center of the foyer was a fountain in the shape of a boy riding a sea horse, like something one might find in ancient Greece. On the walls were oil paintings in gilt frames, museum-quality portraits and landscapes.

Holy mother of…was that a Van Gogh?

"You're a few minutes late," Jillian said matter-of-factly.

"Yes. The traffic…" Jamie was damned if she was going to apologize for being twenty minutes late when Logan was the one who had insisted she meet him here, rather than at his downtown office, which was within walking distance of her own workplace at the Criminal Justice Center.

"Unfortunately, Mr. Logan had another appointment. He should be free in about an hour. In the meanwhile, I'm sure you'd like some lunch."

Jamie was starved, but she wasn't going to let Logan's underling lead her around by the nose. "Unfortunately," Jamie said, enunciating every word, "my time is limited as well, and the traffic jam tightened my schedule. If Mr. Logan can't see me right now, perhaps he can come by my office when it's convenient for him."

Jillian's eyes widened slightly. Probably she was so used to people bowing and scraping, eager to please her high-and-mighty boss, that Jamie's behavior came as a surprise.

"Give me a minute and I'll see what can be arranged." Her tone had gone a bit frosty.

Jillian stepped out of the foyer, leaving Jamie alone and steaming. Just because she was a public servant didn't mean Logan could treat her as if she were insignificant. She would walk right out of here and see how he liked it.

Jamie turned toward a noise she heard in

the doorway, thinking Jillian had returned, but instead it was a large golden retriever. Tongue lolling, tail wagging, he accelerated toward her, and for a moment she thought he was going to jump up on her. But he skidded to a stop mere inches from her and stared up at her with big chocolate-brown eyes.

"Oh. Hello, there." She reached out cautiously to pat his head. He looked friendly, but you could never tell with dogs. This one wagged half his body, obviously thrilled by her scant attention. He leaned into her, and she scratched him behind the ear.

Jillian finally reappeared. "Tucker. Behave."

The dog obediently abandoned Jamie and trotted to Jillian, sitting at her heel, and she gave him an absent pat on the head. He was obviously well trained.

"Mr. Logan will see you now. But he apologizes for his rather, um, casual attire."

He could be dressed in a potato sack for all Jamie cared. She just wanted to get this meeting over with. Having tangled with Project Justice before, she knew that the foundation often took on cases that had merit.

This wasn't one of them.

With the dog following them, Jillian led

Jamie through an opulent living room, a strange study in contrasts—ancient-looking tapestries and modernist furniture; cold marble and a warm sandstone fireplace; an antique, ivory-inlaid table here and a modern one of polished limestone there.

She got only a quick impression. Soon they were walking down a long hallway lined with more paintings, and finally down a flight of stairs.

He had a basement?

This just didn't seem normal. What had she gotten herself into? Logan might be a refined gentleman, but he was also a convicted murderer. The governor had pardoned him, but the conviction had never been overturned—a distinction that made Jamie feel edgy about meeting him in an underground bunker.

Finally, they ended up in an enormous workout room with fancy machines worthy of any upscale health club. But what drew her eye was the naked man lying on a massage table, getting worked over by a busty blonde in a pink velour tracksuit.

Jamie sucked in a long breath. He had only a small towel over his hips to preserve his modesty.

"Daniel, Ms. McNair is here." Jillian sounded faintly disapproving.

"Ow, Greta, have a heart," said the naked man, who Jamie assumed was Daniel Logan.

He was still tall, but no longer skinny or pale. In fact, the large expanse of skin on his muscular back was an even golden color, and for a moment she wished with all her heart that she was Greta, digging her fingers into those firm-looking muscles.

Daniel turned his head and caught sight of Jamie for the first time. Their eyes locked and held for several seconds.

He was arrestingly gorgeous, and he looked nothing like the stereotypical Texas billionaire in the oil bidness. No boots, no hat, no cigar and no Texas twang. His voice was cultured, educated.

"I'm afraid you've caught me at my worst, Ms. McNair," he said. "But I got a muscle spasm in my back just before you arrived, and Greta is the only person who can get rid of it."

Yeah, and he probably got *lots* of muscle spasms.

"Mr. Logan," Jamie said succinctly. "We

can't have an intelligent discussion under these conditions. I suggest that if this meeting is important to you, we reschedule. Or even speak on the phone. You can call my office—"

"No, wait, please." Daniel pushed himself up on his strong-looking arms and swung his legs over the massage table, somehow managing to wrap the towel around himself in the process so that he didn't flash the three women surrounding him. "I can meet with you now."

Greta handed him a silk robe, which he donned as he hopped off the table, letting the towel drop to the carpet. He shrugged experimentally, stretched his neck side to side and smiled. "I think you did it, Greta. Now, if you don't mind giving us a bit of privacy?" He included Jillian in his request.

Greta melted away as quietly as an icicle in the hot sun, but Jillian hesitated. "Are you sure you don't need me to take notes? Or bring you a file?"

"That won't be necessary for this meeting, thanks." He leaned down to scratch the dog, which had been waiting patiently for some attention from him. "Hey, Tucker."

With one last warning scowl toward Jamie, Jillian walked away.

"My office is this way," Daniel said. "Thank you for coming. It won't be a waste of your time—I think you'll be interested in what I have to say."

Jamie was dumbfounded by the luxury she saw all around her. In a basement, no less. Though they were underground, what appeared to be natural light surrounded them, pouring in from windows and skylights covered with frosted glass or translucent shades. But the most impressive sight was Daniel Logan himself.

He literally made her mouth go dry. No sign of a bad haircut now. As soon as he'd moved to an upright position, his silky brown hair had fallen into place perfectly. The hair was a medium length on top and short over his ears, where he had a sprinkling of premature gray.

Her research had told her he was in his mid-thirties, but he looked slightly older. Not that that was a bad thing. He was still handsome as sin. Perhaps prison had aged him.

She stopped herself before she started feeling sorry for him. He was a convicted murderer who belonged behind bars. Because of his money and influence, he was free to enjoy all this luxury.

His victim, Andreas Musto, would never enjoy anything again.

Daniel's office was another surprise. She'd expected a commanding antique walnut desk or maybe a workspace carved from a solid piece of granite, and walls decorated with more original art, perhaps a giant, saltwater fish tank or a bearskin rug—something masculine. Instead, she found herself in a high-tech cave.

She'd never seen so much electronic equipment in one place outside a Best Buy. A huge U-shaped desk dominated the room, littered with gadgets of every description: multiple phones, keyboards, printers, three computers, each of which appeared to be in use. One of them had a monitor the size of a movie-theater screen.

Mounted on the walls above them were four TVs, each tuned to a different news channel.

Daniel indicated that Jamie should sit in one of the silk-covered wingback chairs facing the desk. He moved around the room to take his place in the giant rolling chair inside the U. Tucker settled onto a big pillow where he could watch his master with adoring eyes.

For all its high-tech feel, the room was still beautiful. More faux windows covered with black, wooden shutters lined one wall. A fine Oriental carpet topped the wood floor, and above them, two stained-glass chandeliers bathed them in warm light.

"Perhaps we can just cut to the chase here," Jamie said, wanting to get in the first word. "You have some wild idea that Christopher Gables is innocent. I don't know what might have led you down that garden path, but I can assure you, the facts speak for themselves. Gables and his victim argued. A couple of hours later, the victim was found dead with a slashed throat, a bloody knife lying nearby. Gables's prints—and only his prints—were found on the knife.

"Gables, who was normally in the restaurant until closing, could not account for his whereabouts at the time of the murder.

"That, Mr. Logan, is what we in the prosecution business call a slam dunk. The jury reached a verdict in less than an hour."

Daniel Logan seemed to be listening intently. He kept his gaze firmly focused on her as she spoke, his expression grave, nodding every so often. It unnerved her, having that laser beam of attention pointed at her, and she got the impression he was not only listening to her words, but observing every nuance of her face, her gestures—and learning more than she wanted him to know.

"So what do you have to wow me with, Mr. Logan?" she asked, struggling to keep from sounding smug. "If it's that little bit of unidentified DNA found on Sissom's apron, you should know that fingerprints trump DNA any day. Four separate fingerprint experts identified the prints on the knife as belonging to Gables—even the defense's own expert witness. The DNA could have come from anywhere."

Logan nodded again. "It was a solid case. You did an excellent job prosecuting."

Yes, she had. It had been the first big case in which she'd led the prosecution. After the verdict, for the first time in her life, she'd felt sure her father was proud of her. Not that she would ever know for sure, since he had died while she was in law school.

She did not thank Logan for the compliment. Flattery wouldn't sway her. "So, what's your point?"

"Ms. McNair, how would you like to prosecute a serial killer?"

DANIEL COULD SEE HE'D GOTTEN Jamie's attention. His initial salvo was a shock tactic, sure; he'd have to have the facts to back up his claim. But at least she'd dropped that infuriating smugness. Her pouty lips were open slightly in surprise, her eyes wide and attentive.

He hadn't expected her to be so beautiful in person. But the photos and video he'd seen didn't do her justice. The glossy, fudge-brown hair had depth and texture no camera could pick up; the unusual shade of blue-green in her eyes defied description. And her skin— like the smoothest stone—somehow also looked warm to the touch.

He told himself it was best for him not to think about her lips too much.

All that was above the neck. He didn't dare study her anywhere else until her attention was diverted.

Finally she spoke. "You think Christopher

Gables has killed before?" She barely whispered the possibility.

"No. I think whoever killed Frank Sissom—and framed Christopher—has killed before. He's the same man who framed me."

At last Jamie found her voice. "You have got to be kidding. You brought me all the way here, disrupted my whole day's schedule, so you could hit me with this...this *ridiculous* fairy tale about a serial killer?"

"It's still an unproven theory, I'll admit. But aren't you the least bit curious as to why I'm trying to convince you it's true?"

"Because you like manipulating people, and you have the money and influence to do it?"

He bit the inside of his lower lip to hold on to his temper. Typical prosecutor. She was so sure she was right, that the almighty justice system was infallible. "You seem a bit cranky this morning. You probably haven't had enough protein. Let me guess—you skipped breakfast."

"My diet is no concern of yours. Are we done here?" She started to rise from her chair.

"Metal shavings. Were any metal shavings found on Frank Sissom's body?" It was one of two anomalies brought to light during Daniel's own murder trial. The prosecution never successfully explained where those shavings had come from, but Daniel had always believed they'd come from the murderer's own clothing during a struggle.

These days, metal shavings could be analyzed every which way right down to their atoms. Every metal object had a distinct signature, so shavings could be matched to their source. It wasn't perfect, not like DNA or fingerprints. But cases had been won and lost based on similar trace evidence.

The other anomaly was, in fact, a bit of unidentified DNA found on Andreas's clothing. Another similarity to the Gables/Sissom case, which Jamie herself had just mentioned.

"I don't recall hearing about any metal shavings," Jamie said.

Daniel tried not to be too disappointed. It was a long shot. "Let me go over the facts, then, as I see them."

Jamie glanced at her watch. "I have other appointments today. You can put your so-called facts in an email."

Just then someone tapped on Daniel's office door. He knew that tap. Everyone knocked on doors differently. It was one of those patterns that Daniel had picked up without trying.

"Come in, Jillian."

She entered, holding a plate with a metal warming lid over it in one hand, and a tall glass of iced tea in the other. "I am so sorry to interrupt, but Claude insists this chicken will go bad if it's not eaten immediately. Something about the sauce coagulating."

It was past Daniel's usual lunchtime; the muscle spasm—and Jamie's tardiness—had put a kink in his schedule. Jillian knew he put great stock in eating well and often to fuel the brain. But she also knew not to interrupt an important meeting.

He accepted the plate from her. "Thank you, Jillian, but it would be excessively rude for me to eat in front of my guest. Especially since she hasn't had breakfast."

"I never said I skipped breakfast," Jamie objected.

"But you did." He knew he was right just by the slight shade of defensiveness in her tone.

"Of course I brought a plate for Ms. McNair."

Jillian quickly produced another covered dish from a rolling cart she'd left in the hallway.

"I'm not staying," Jamie said.

"Give me fifteen minutes to convince you." Daniel stood and came out from behind his desk. "Share a meal with me. You've got to eat at some point, and this will save you time." *And probably improve your temperament.* Also, sharing food was a bonding activity. He needed to convince Jamie that he was not the enemy. If things went his way, they would soon become allies, fighting to save an innocent man's life. As the prosecutor of this case, she was uniquely able to handle some tasks he would find difficult to do himself.

Jamie inhaled deeply; she probably had gotten a whiff of whatever genius concoction Claude, his chef, had whipped up today, because something convinced her.

"Fine, if you insist, I'll have some lunch. But keep in mind you can't soften me up with a gourmet meal."

No, but good food could make her more open to his suggestions.

Jillian set up their lunch in the small room adjacent to Daniel's office, where he sometimes took his meals when he was deep into a project and didn't want to go all the way upstairs to the dining room or patio. He'd had it specially designed to relieve stress.

Although it had no windows, he'd had lights installed that replicated the electromagnetic spectrum of sunlight. The limestone floor and running-water feature helped to ionize the air, and all the plants, of course, provided an oxygen-rich environment.

"Good night!" Jamie paused at the doorway, her jaw about to hit the floor.

CHAPTER TWO

"SOMETHING WRONG?" Daniel asked innocently as Jillian placed napkins and silverware on the wrought-iron umbrella table.

Jamie shook her head in obvious amazement. "Oh, nothing, just that I thought for a moment I'd walked through a wormhole and was transported to an outdoor café in Tuscany. This is incredible!"

"I'm glad you like it." Daniel enjoyed surprising people.

"Are those...grapes?" Jamie looked above them at the grape arbor, which did, indeed, have a few clusters of fruit growing on it.

"Yes, they are. I had some of our grapevines transplanted to this room. I wasn't sure they'd survive—grapes are tricky. But they seem to love it here."

"Where did you get that fountain?" she asked suspiciously.

"From an antiquities dealer. Legal, I assure

you. It was recovered in pieces from an Italian farmer's field. The restoration cost more than the fountain did. Shall we eat?"

Daniel pulled out a chair for Jamie, then took his own. He did love this room. Already, he could feel some of the tension leaving his body. He shrugged, testing his back, but the muscle spasm appeared to be gone for good.

Sometimes he took for granted what his wealth could create.

Jillian took Tucker and departed, leaving Daniel and Jamie alone.

Daniel lifted the lid on his plate and inhaled. His mouth watered. "I'll have to find out the name of this dish so I can request it again."

"It does smell good," Jamie said cautiously as she examined her own plate. It was a small portion of chicken with a light dousing of creamy sauce, along with a generous helping of fresh asparagus and some rosemary new potatoes.

Daniel cut a piece off the chicken, but his attention was focused more closely on Jamie than his meat. He wanted her to enjoy the food.

She took a bite, chewed thoughtfully, swallowed. "Your fifteen minutes are running."

"Right." Damn, he'd almost forgotten the reason she was here. Who cared if she liked Claude's cooking? It was more important that she like his facts.

"Are you familiar with the Andreas Musto murder case?"

"The one for which you stood trial. I'm somewhat well versed," she said cautiously. Which probably meant that what she knew, she'd absorbed from the media. It had been one of those crimes that reporters loved to sensationalize—a billionaire's son accused of a gruesome slaying.

"I'll quickly refresh your memory. Andreas Musto was my business partner. We owned a restaurant together. He was found at the restaurant with his throat cut, the murder weapon—a wickedly sharp butcher knife— lying nearby. The knife had my fingerprints on it. I did not have an alibi. Does this sound at all familiar?"

Jamie, who had been devouring her rosemary potatoes during his speech, made a show of chewing, swallowing, taking a sip of iced tea and delicately blotting her mouth with her napkin.

"I'll admit, the circumstances are similar to those of the Frank Sissom murder. But lots of crimes sound alike. There are only so many ways to kill people—shooting, stabbing, poisoning, strangling, drowning or blunt-force trauma."

"But how many killers—seemingly intelligent young men like myself and Christopher Gables—leave behind the murder weapon with their prints on it?"

"Criminals often act without logic. In the heat of the moment, a person can lose their ability to reason. Take the bank robber who wrote the demand note on his own deposit slip. Or the man who, hours after a murder, goes on a spending spree with the victim's credit cards."

"And just how many murder victims have their throats slashed with a butcher knife? In a restaurant?"

"Murders often take place in restaurants. They're open late at night, they deal in cash—"

"Robbery wasn't the motive in either case."

"The crimes took place many years apart,"

Jamie said sensibly. "The locations were twenty, maybe thirty miles from each other. I'm sorry, but the facts do not scream 'serial killer' to me."

He was losing her. He could see it in her eyes.

"So this is why Project Justice took on Christopher Gables as a client?" she asked. "The crime reminded you of the one that landed you in prison?"

"Partly." He'd rather not tell Jamie about Theresa Chavez until he interviewed the woman himself. But he had to do something to make an impression.

"The similarities in the crimes are one reason I took the case," he admitted. His decision had shocked his staff; he'd never personally led an investigation before. "It was easy for me to put myself in Christopher's place. But what really swayed me was the witness."

"Witness? There was no witness."

"Ah, but there was. A young woman who bussed tables at the restaurant, El Toreador. She called the police, babbling incoherently in Spanish, then fled the scene before she could be interviewed."

Jamie leaned back in her chair. "Theresa Chavez. She was the one we think found the body," Jamie said. "That's not the same as a witness to the murder."

"So you know about her." Damn, he'd been hoping to take Jamie by surprise.

"She was considered briefly as a suspect, but dismissed because she was hardly more than a teenager and weighed a hundred pounds soaking wet. Frank Sissom was six foot and two-twenty. No way she could have overpowered him."

"But she was never questioned."

"Unfortunately, Theresa was an illegal alien. Apparently she was scared of being deported, so she went into hiding. We never found her."

"How hard did you look?"

"The police made a concerted effort to locate her." Jamie didn't conceal her defensiveness very well. "But a person with no credit cards, no social security number or driver's license—she disappeared. Completely."

"But not forever. Theresa has recently come forward. Her conscience was bothering her. She says she spotted a stranger in the restaurant kitchen only minutes before Frank was killed. It certainly wasn't Christopher Gables, whom she knew quite well."

His news did not have the desired effect. Jamie did not look shocked or even surprised. She raised one skeptical eyebrow. "After what, six years? Her conscience is bothering her?"

He supposed he couldn't blame Jamie for her skepticism. Her job put her in daily contact with criminals of the worst order, most of whom would do or say anything to get them off the hook.

"It's more like a change of circumstances," Daniel said, noting with some satisfaction that Jamie was well on the way to cleaning her plate. "Her conscience has always bothered her. But she recently got a green card. She doesn't have to fear deportation. Her English has also improved a great deal in the last seven years."

"Well. If she has something to say, I'd like to hear it." Jamie's tone indicated she didn't want to hear it at all, but didn't want to be considered unreasonable. "Have her contact my office. I will at least listen to what she has to say."

"Will you really?"

"If I say I will, then I will. But keep in mind, eyewitness testimony isn't the gold standard it once was. So many things can taint a person's memories—the passage of time, the influence of the media or others' recollections, even a fervent wish to have seen something different. And, of course, the promise of a load of cash can improve a person's memory in sudden and dramatic ways."

This was the height of rudeness. "You think I would pay someone to— You're actually accusing me of—"

"I am not accusing anyone," she said hastily. "Just stating a few well-known facts about witness testimony in general. I'm willing to hear the woman's statement. But I will accept hard, physical evidence over witness testimony any day."

"Are you saying an eyewitness to the crime wouldn't convince you to reopen a case?"

"I won't know until I actually talk to this Theresa. I mean, how will I know she's even the same person, since she had no documentation back then?"

"We'll cross that bridge, trust me."

"That's just the problem. I don't trust you. I don't trust anyone with an ax to grind."

At least he and Jamie had that in common. Daniel didn't trust anyone, either, at least not beyond his senior staff at Project Justice and in his own home. He wouldn't begrudge Jamie that mistrust. "All I ask is that you give the woman a chance to speak."

"If she'll call my office and make an appointment, I'll meet with her." Jamie popped the last bit of asparagus into her mouth, chewing with a satisfied expression.

This was the best Daniel could expect. Having reached the terms he'd hoped for, it was time to end this meeting. He had learned long ago that once someone agreed with him, the best course of action was to get the hell away from them before he said or did something to change their mind.

But he was loath to send Jamie away. When was the last time he had shared a meal with a beautiful woman? He often grabbed a bite to eat with Jillian when they were on a tight schedule and she was helping him with some project or another, but that was different. She was practically a little sister. He'd known her forever and didn't think of her in sexual terms.

It was hard to look at Jamie and *not* think of sex. She had a strangely strong effect on him.

One of the worst things about being in prison had been the lack of female companionship of any kind, and he'd always imagined that the first thing he would do if he regained his freedom was find a beautiful, willing woman and have sex for days on end.

It hadn't happened like that, of course. Once he got out, he'd had to rebuild himself, physically and mentally, before he could even think about bringing another person into the mix. Then he'd had to deal with the deaths of his parents, one right after the other, all while building his fledgling foundation and handling crisis after crisis at Logan Oil & Gas.

Jamie was the first flesh-and-blood woman to arouse him in a very long time.

"I hope you left room for dessert," he found himself saying against his better judgment.

Jamie seemed to rouse herself from the

pleasure induced by a superior meal. "Oh, no, I don't have time for that."

Daniel reached for the hardwired phone that was nestled in a stone niche near their table. "Cora, we're ready for dessert," he told Claude's assistant when she answered. "What's on the menu today?"

"Tiramisu," Cora said. "I'll get a couple of slices right down to you."

"Tiramisu," he repeated for Jamie's benefit.

"I really have to go."

"Another few minutes won't—"

"No, I really *have* to go." She was much firmer this time as she scooted her chair out and found her feet.

Daniel was tempted to try to cajole her into staying for dessert. But he risked making her angry, and she'd only just recently lost that tense, mulish expression and begun to speak to him as an intelligent human being, rather than a bug on the sidewalk she'd like to squish.

"I'll show you out, then," he said amicably. He picked up the phone again and pushed the Jillian button—every phone in the house had a Jillian button. After speaking briefly to his assistant, he showed Jamie back through his office where she grabbed her all-but-forgotten briefcase. They continued up the stairs and down the long hall that led to the front door.

"Who are all these people?" Jamie asked, nodding toward the portraits that lined the walls. "Logan ancestors?"

"Good heavens, no. Most of my ancestors were Scottish peasants, not the kind who were immortalized by great artists. My grandfather bought most of these paintings as investments."

"Your grandfather was a self-made man?"

"If you call discovering oil on your little piece of hardscrabble farm *made* and not *lucky*."

"I imagine it takes a bit more than luck to build an empire the size of this one."

"Some hard work," Daniel agreed. "My father was never home for dinner. Worked himself to an early grave."

"I take it that's not your philosophy."

"Make no mistake, Jamie, I work hard. But I also take care of myself, and I insist my employees do, too. What's the point of working yourself to a frazzle—even for something you care deeply about—if you're not around to appreciate the fruits of your labor?"

"I guess people do it so their children will have the kind of life they didn't," Jamie said, rather philosophically.

"Is that what your father did?"

"Oh, no. My father wanted me to live exactly the same life he did." An edge in her voice suggested disapproval.

"He was a lawyer, too, I take it. A prosecutor?" His research had told him Jamie was born out of wedlock and the father was out of the picture.

She didn't answer, and Daniel thought better of pursuing the subject. They'd arrived in the foyer, and Jillian was there, clipboard in hand as well as a small, white cardboard box, which she handed to Jamie with a brittle smile.

"What's this?"

"Tiramisu. Something to nosh on if you get stuck in traffic again. Daniel didn't want you to miss it. Although our chef, Claude, is French, not Italian, he does an incredible job."

"Thank you," Jamie said uncertainly.

"No, thank you," Daniel said, meaning it.

"I know it was an imposition, driving out to River Oaks, but I appreciate you taking the time to meet with me. I believe in the end you'll be glad you did."

She turned to face him, and that mulish expression had returned to her face. "Mr. Logan. Best-case scenario for me is that you've wasted some of my time. Worst case, you make me look like an incompetent fool and possibly cost me my job."

"I hope it won't come to that."

"If you're right, that is exactly what would happen. Believe it or not, I would be willing to accept unemployment if you could prove I'd made such a heinous mistake. But I'm not willing to be made a fool simply because you have the money, and the clout, and the patience to get your way. I will not give in simply to be done with this. I will fight you every step of the way, no matter how good your freaking tiramisu is."

On that note, Jillian opened the front door for her, and Jamie stepped out into the blustery fall day toward her car.

Jillian closed the front door with a bit more force than necessary. "She's a real piece of work."

"I thought she was fantastic! Intelligent, outspoken, passionate about her work…"

"And drop-dead gorgeous," Jillian observed drily. "I don't suppose you're crushing on her, are you?"

"Jillian, please. I'm well out of adolescence. I don't get crushes."

"Whatever you call it, I hope you won't let it get in the way of what you have to do. Because to free Christopher Gables, you might very well have to *crush* one passionate, over-zealous prosecutor."

WHAT JUST HAPPENED BACK THERE?

Jamie's hands actually trembled as she put the car in gear and headed toward the gates that were, even now, opening for her. She'd walked into Daniel Logan's home practically breathing fire, ready to dazzle him with her facts and her smart-ass wit. Instead, she'd found herself ogling a half-naked man, sharing one of the best meals she could remember while the same man wore nothing but a bathrobe, and saying yes to something she never should have agreed to.

Now she was committed to giving Theresa Chavez an audience. And if the woman convincingly claimed to have witnessed someone other than Christopher Gables killing Frank Sissom, Jamie could not, in good conscience, dismiss the woman's statement.

She would have to investigate. She would have to find out if it really was the same woman who discovered the body, then fled, and then determine if the woman was credible.

None of which would change the fact that Christopher Gables's fingerprints, and only his prints, were found on the murder weapon. But if she didn't perform due diligence, Daniel Logan would never leave her alone.

She knew how Project Justice operated, because quite a few cases prosecuted by her office had been overturned due to the persistence of the foundation's people. Daniel— who believed in this case so strongly that he had taken it on personally—would not give up until he was convinced beyond any reasonable doubt that his client really was guilty.

God, what a nightmare. Winston Chubb, the district attorney, wasn't going to be happy with this turn of events. And he would find a way to blame Jamie for it, she was sure.

Winston always managed to grab the credit for anything good that happened, and passed the buck regarding anything bad.

On top of everything else, she could smell the tiramisu, faint threads of chocolate, vanilla and coffee. She ought to just throw the little white box—tied with a satin ribbon, for God's sake—into the first trash can she saw. The dessert was a symbol of everything that had gone wrong with that meeting, including her completely inappropriate physical reaction to the billionaire.

Imagine her, Jamie McNair, attracted to a convicted killer! But she was.

It was hard to visualize Daniel Logan killing anyone. Even knowing the facts, she hadn't felt the least bit uncomfortable alone in his presence, other than having to hammer down her libido.

But then, people had said that about Ted Bundy.

THIRTY MINUTES LATER, Jamie was back into her office and the little white box was empty, damn it.

Her day was shot. A pile of cases sat on her desk—mostly routine plea-bargain requests from defense attorneys. She went through as many as she could, signing off on the reasonable ones, rejecting the more outrageous requests for repeat felons and violent offenders.

She spent an hour returning phone calls, talked to three different detectives regarding a felony assault case, then checked her schedule for the following day.

Jury selection for a drunk hit-and-run case in the morning; three appointments in the afternoon.

With fifteen minutes left of her official workday, Jamie did what she'd known she would do all along. She opened the Gables/Sissom murder file and dug through a mountain of reports until she found the one from the crime lab regarding the evidence they'd processed—bloodstains, fingerprints, the knife and, finally, the victim's clothing.

Most of the details regarding the clothing had to do with bloodstains—including one tiny biological stain on the apron that hadn't belonged to the victim and had remained unidentified. But there was also a list of substances other than blood found on the victim's shirt, which included olive oil, tomato juice, salt—all the things once might expect to find on someone who spent time in a restaurant kitchen.

One finding, though, made Jamie stop: "a black, powdery substance assumed to be from a laser printer or copy machine."

Assumed to be? Since when did crime-scene analysts assume anything? Probably the restaurant had a printer or copy machine, and since Frank Sissom was one of the owners, she had every reason to believe he'd been in the office and changed a printer cartridge.

But a black, powdery substance could also be metal shavings. Damn it.

She called the guy who'd signed the report, Eddie Goddard. He'd been working at the crime lab since Jamie was in high school, and though he was normally thorough and dependable, he still was not her favorite person. A card-carrying member of the Good Ol' Boys Club, he didn't like women telling him what to do.

"Eddie. I see you're working late like me." It was now well after five.

"I was just heading out, actually. What can I do for you?" He did not sound enthusiastic about adding any tasks to his To Do list.

"I won't stop you from getting home in time for dinner," she promised, hoping to earn brownie points. "But tomorrow morning, I'm going to bring you a piece of clothing from the Frank Sissom case. I need some additional analysis on a certain stain."

"You're joking, right? That case is ancient."

"Wish I was. But I need to shut somebody up before he goes to the press and makes our lives more miserable than they already are. A quick look-see under a microscope will probably do the trick." She hoped.

"Okay, sure," he agreed in monotone.

Tomorrow morning, she would retrieve the actual physical evidence from the police, hand the victim's shirt over to Eddie and pray that Theresa Chavez didn't call.

CHAPTER THREE

"DANIEL, SORRY TO disturb you, but Jamie McNair is on line two."

The four men and two women seated in Daniel's conference room looked surprised by the interruption, and it was no wonder; his staff knew not to disturb him during a Logan Oil & Gas board meeting. The company was largely responsible for maintaining Daniel's personal wealth, and Daniel remained involved in the overall direction and philosophy of the company his grandfather had started.

The meeting was important, but Jamie took priority.

"I have to take this call," Daniel said to the board as he rose. "Shouldn't last more than five minutes."

When Jamie had left his home two days ago, Daniel hadn't been sure how, or even if, she would follow up. So he was a bit surprised and pleased that she'd called him.

He stepped down the hall and into his private office, then picked up the phone.

"Jamie. Good to hear from you."

"Mr. Logan."

Damn, she didn't sound nearly as warm as he'd hoped. "Did Theresa get in touch with you?" He already knew she had; he'd personally seen to it. He'd even hired a car and driver to take her to the district attorney's office for an interview.

"She did. And I'll be honest with you, she piqued my interest."

"Then you'll reopen the case," he said confidently.

"Don't get your hopes up. She seemed genuine, but I still haven't verified she was at the scene of the crime. For all I know, she's an actress you hired."

Daniel bit his tongue to stifle a snide retort. After spending six years hitting brick wall after brick wall trying to overturn his own conviction, he shouldn't be a bit surprised by Jamie's attitude.

"I can provide the documentation you need—"

"I'll provide my own, thanks very much. And if I find out she's lying, I'll personally see to it she's prosecuted. And if I find you paid her to lie, I'll prosecute you."

Daniel was livid. He was so tired of this attitude. Of course, the Harris County D.A.'s office would be doubly motivated to prevent another overturned conviction; Project Justice had recently gained freedom for a mobster's son convicted of killing his girlfriend, and the case had caused some major embarrassment for the D.A.

"It sounds as if you simply don't like me very much. Are you going to let personal feelings stand in the way of justice?"

"Please stop being so simplistic. I'm convinced I did a good job convicting Christopher Gables. Naturally, it's going to take a solid argument to persuade me I made a mistake."

"We're talking about a man's life here."

"Yes, the life of Frank Sissom, Gables's victim. Do you have anything else to show me? If so, bring it on."

"What about that unidentified DNA?"

"If you have a theory about where it came from—or any other evidence—I'm willing to talk. Contrary to what you might believe, I do not have a closed mind. In fact, I'm having one of our evidence analysts reexamine Frank Sissom's apron."

"Really?" She'd succeeded in surprising him.

"I should have results tomorrow."

"Then by all means, we should talk again. When can you get here? I can free up my schedule anytime—"

"I'm glad to hear that, because mine is packed. I can spare you an hour tomorrow afternoon or Monday morning, here at my office."

Daniel's heart clutched, and he forced himself to breathe deeply. "I can't possibly drive downtown."

"Afraid you'd miss your afternoon massage? Exactly how serious are you about wanting to free your client? I disrupted my whole schedule to drive to River Oaks. If you want my cooperation, you can meet me halfway. Besides, we might need to talk to people in the crime lab or the investigating officers involved in the case—all of whom can be found downtown."

"I can send one of my best people." And admit to his staff—already skeptical—that he was not up to handling a case on his own. That would be a bitter pill to swallow.

"Okay. Your assistant can meet with my assistant."

Now she was playing hardball. "Ms. McNair. Jamie. This matter is too serious for us to play games."

"Don't talk to me about games. You're the one who made me cool my heels while you got your massage and sent me home with tiramisu, trying to butter me up."

Maybe she had a point. "Did you like it, by the way? Chef Claude is a genius."

"That is immaterial. I've got a lot on my plate and I really don't have time to chase after every hard-luck and if-only story I hear. You believe he's innocent? Fair enough. Show me the commitment that says you mean it. I'm willing to listen, but I'm not going to deal with layer upon layer of assistants and bodyguards. You started this, and I think you should be the one to finish it. Personally."

His awareness of her primed his body for action, even over the phone. She wanted to deal with him personally, did she? Her reasons sounded plausible, but he didn't completely buy them. Perhaps she wanted to see more of him, just as he wanted to see more of her. He would have been pleased, if not for the massive logistic problem her ultimatum caused.

"What's it going to be?" she prompted. "I'm due in court in ten minutes."

"Name your time," he finally said. "I'll be there, so long as you keep our meeting discreet. Being out in public can cause difficulties for me."

"Believe me, I'm as anxious as you to keep this thing under wraps. Two o'clock tomorrow? I can reserve the conference room."

"I'll be there." Come hell or high water. He hadn't heard any flooding forecasts for South Texas, but hell was a definite possibility.

The board meeting broke up at close to noon. After seeing everyone out to their cars, Jillian returned to Daniel's office to go over his afternoon schedule.

"It's nice poolside, if you'd like to take your lunch there. You haven't breathed any fresh air in a couple of days."

He resisted the urge to remind Jillian that the filtered air in his home was nine times cleaner than the smog-infused air of Houston. "Good suggestion." Dirty air or not, he liked sitting outside when he could, looking out over his swimming pool and listening to birds and wind in the trees. It helped him think, and he had a lot of thinking to do. And it reminded him he was a free man.

"Also, Jillian, please have the limo ready tomorrow at 1:30—no, 1:15. I'm going downtown to meet with Jamie McNair... What?"

The unflappable Jillian's mouth gaped open. "You're going downtown?" she repeated.

"Yes. Maybe not in the limo, I don't want to draw attention. The Bentley might be better."

"You are going downtown," she said again.

"It's the Christopher Gables case. Ms. McNair is willing to talk, which is frankly more than I expected at this stage."

"But...*you're* going to a meeting? Personally?"

"Jillian, have you gone hard of hearing? I'm perfectly capable of attending a meeting off-site. I'll admit, I usually choose not to, but this is important."

"With all due respect, sir, you haven't left the estate in three years."

That stopped him. "Three— Oh, surely you're mistaken."

"Your grandmother's funeral in Miami. October 3, two thousand—"

"It doesn't matter. I'm going. I have to go."

Jillian's face softened. "Do you want me to come with you?"

The tightness in his chest eased slightly as he pictured Jillian sitting next to him, dealing with pesky details. But when he pictured himself meeting with Jamie, he saw the two of them alone.

Hell, he didn't need Jillian to hover and fuss over him. He could handle this mission on his own. He had taken on the responsibility of being Christopher Gables's champion, and he needed to see it through.

"No, thank you, Jillian. I'll bring Randall for security. That should be sufficient."

Jillian looked as if she wanted to argue, but in the end she nodded her head and turned. "Yes, sir."

THE FOLLOWING DAY, Daniel sucked up a monumental case of nerves and strode to his limo parked in the driveway. He'd opted for the larger, more ostentatious car after all; it seemed safer.

He had a briefcase full of information about the Sissom/Gables case as well as the Andreas Musto murder—the parallels between the two cases simply could not be coincidence. He'd even drawn up a chart, with graphics, showing similarities. And if there was a remote chance that he could find the person who'd stolen six years of his life…

Daniel wasn't a violent man, as his lawyers had so tirelessly reminded the jury. But if he ever came face-to-face with the man who'd framed him, he could easily kill with his bare hands. That thought had provided comfort during many sleepless nights.

His special-order Mercedes limousine was familiar and comforting, and he breathed in the scent of well-tended leather. But the car must be at least four years old now.

"Randall," he said just before his driver and bodyguard closed his door, "order a new limousine."

"Is something wrong with the car?" Randall asked, concerned. He was the one who insisted on personally keeping the vehicle in perfect condition, mechanically and cosmetically.

"No, it's just time." Keeping up appearances

didn't really matter much to him, but others depended on his maintaining a certain image. The slightest show of weakness—financial or otherwise—could give rise to rumors that could affect Logan Oil & Gas stock prices, and the well-being of countless investors who'd risked their retirement to his care.

Moments later, the car eased down the driveway and the wrought-iron gates opened noiselessly.

And Daniel felt sick to his stomach.

The car was as safe as any presidential limo, with triple-thick steel doors and bulletproof tinted glass. Randall was a former Secret Service agent, an expert in every sort of bodyguard skill on the planet, including evasive driving, marksmanship and hand-to-hand combat. But that didn't stop Daniel from envisioning everything that could go wrong—car accidents, breakdown, traffic snarls, Randall suddenly falling ill...

Daniel told himself it was because he was nervous about meeting Jamie. She'd opened the door a crack; if he was late, she might slam it shut again, making his job more difficult. But the truth was, he just wanted to turn around. Behind the brick wall and iron gates, Daniel dictated everything that happened around him.

Away from that cocoon, anything could happen.

What had gone wrong with him? He'd once loved adventure. He'd traveled, embarked on business ventures, tried every sport he could manage. He'd climbed mountains, dated movie stars and earned a business degree from Harvard.

Now, just leaving the house took a monumental dose of courage.

Yes, being falsely accused of a murder he didn't commit, then going through the trial and six years of incarceration on death row, was bound to change a man. Once he'd been freed, he'd come home and, for the first time in a very long time, he'd felt safe and loved.

But even back then, he hadn't been housebound. He'd made periodic trips to Logan Oil and to Project Justice after his father's death to keep things running. He'd attended funerals and visited doctors.

But the past few years he'd ventured forth less and less as the people he'd hired to run his empire had competently taken over.

I'm fine, damn it.

There was nothing wrong with how he'd chosen to live. After what he'd been through—having a good chunk of his youth stolen away—he ought to be allowed to enjoy his every hour of freedom on his own terms. Thanks to his father and grandfather, plus a few smart decisions he'd made, he had the money to do that, and he refused to feel guilty about it.

Focus on the prize, he told himself. He had to think about Christopher. Succeeding with his mission to find justice for Christopher meant giving a man back his life, and Daniel knew what a huge gift that was. Succeeding also meant more favorable publicity for Project Justice, which was important to all those other men and women the foundation could help.

Then there was the little matter of showing smug Jamie she didn't know everything. Somehow, though, that thought didn't fill him with the pleasure he thought it would.

Finally, there was the satisfaction vengeance would bring.

Daniel cracked a tinted window, immediately aware of how different the breeze from outside felt. It smelled wild. Unsafe.

"Nice day for a drive," Randall said. Daniel had left the glass partition open. "Sometimes I miss the old days, just you and me out and about in the Jaguar."

"We were a pair, weren't we? Tearing through town like we didn't have a care in the world." That was back when Daniel thought he was invincible.

The bodyguard's presence reassured Daniel. Randall was the best—discreet and potentially deadly. He looked ordinary enough, harmless even with his light brown skin, round face and close-cropped, salt-and-pepper hair.

But appearances could be deceiving.

Daniel considered Randall a friend. He was good company—educated, intelligent, funny. And they'd once spent countless hours together.

But they'd had little face-to-face contact in recent years.

Daniel spent the short drive toward downtown looking over papers in his briefcase, information he already knew by heart. He had an almost photographic memory. But he wanted to have answers right at hand for any questions Jamie might pose—and the hard data to back him up.

Jamie. Seeing her again was worth all this trouble. She was the first person in a very long time to challenge him—or excite him. Though of course he couldn't know her on anything but a professional level, the undeniable electricity that charged the air around them when they were in the same room added an element of interest to this case.

Daniel didn't "date." He could not envision himself in a real romantic relationship. Sharing with anyone the world he'd so carefully crafted would ruin it. But that didn't stop him from the occasional fantasy, and lately Jamie McNair had taken a starring role in his daydreams. He'd also lost a bit of sleep over her, as she'd appeared in his night dreams, too.

He'd best not get too attached to his fantasy. When he put the prosecutor in her place, firmly convinced she wasn't infallible, she wouldn't gratefully fall into his arms.

Traffic was light, and soon they were wending through downtown streets. Crowded. Noisy.

Abruptly, Daniel shut his window, sealing the noise outside. But that didn't stop the panic that suddenly rose in his chest.

He could stop now. Turn around. Cancel the meeting, hand the whole thing over to Ford or Raleigh, his top lieutenants. There was time. Although Christopher's appeals had run out, his execution hadn't yet been scheduled.

The urge to run was so strong, it made Daniel light-headed.

"Do you know the suite number of Ms. McNair's office?" Randall asked.

Daniel turned to Jillian, realized she wasn't there, and his panic increased. "I wrote it down somewhere... Hell." It was a simple detail, but his mind was suddenly blank. "I'll look it up."

He checked his schedule on his phone. Yes, there it was, on the sixth floor.

He cast his mind ahead to the coming meeting with Jamie, but now he had trouble visualizing it. Was that because he was about to enter an unknown building with unfamiliar elevators and strangers within inches of him? Perhaps.

Or maybe it was the unpredictable woman herself. For the first time in a long time, he would not be in control of every detail around him. It was both exciting and terrifying.

He shook his head. Billions of people could walk into a strange building without thinking twice. He was being ridiculous. If Jamie perceived any nervousness or weakness, she could gain an advantage. Especially on her home turf.

As they turned onto Franklin Street, Daniel couldn't believe his eyes. Three TV news vans, bristling with antennae and satellite dishes, were parked at odd angles in front of the Harris County Criminal Justice Center. Reporters with microphones and cameramen and -women crawled the sidewalks and steps to the contemporary skyscraper, along with a crowd of at least a hundred curious onlookers.

The limo pulled to a stop, and lots of heads turned to gawk. Cameras swiveled in Daniel's direction.

"What the hell...?" If Jamie had engineered this welcome wagon, he would wring her neck. Hadn't he emphasized how important privacy and discretion were? Had she done this to deliberately sabotage his efforts?

"Any idea what's going on?" Randall asked.

"None." He quickly dialed in the internet on his phone and checked the local headlines. "Ah. Judge John Harlow was caught in the backseat of his car with a fifteen-year-old. Story broke this morning."

"You can't get out here," Randall said firmly. "If the press gets wind that you're out and about, it'll ruin any chance you have of conducting normal business."

"Is it really a front-page story? I mean, come on."

"Yes, Daniel. You driving downtown to meet with a prosecutor about Christopher Gables would be front-page material."

Daniel thought he had a pretty good grip on the media and their opinion of him. After all, he watched every news channel all day in his office. Did he have a blind spot where he, personally, was concerned?

More important, what was he going to do now? He wished he'd brought Jillian. She could contact Jamie, smooth things over, re-schedule the meeting—

Hell, what was he thinking? He could call Jamie himself. He had the fanciest cell phone on the planet, which Jillian programmed with any number he might need.

Moments later he was dialing Jamie's direct number, and a rush of sweet anticipation coursed through him as he waited for her to answer.

JAMIE WAS AS PREPARED for her meeting with Daniel Logan as she could be. She had reserved the conference room, and had even sprung for a snack tray from the deli around the corner out of her own pocket. Daniel had fed her lavishly, so she felt obligated to at least see that he didn't go hungry while on her turf.

Frankly, she was surprised—and flush with inappropriate pleasure—that he had agreed to her terms. As she assembled her stack of papers she intended to present, she couldn't deny a certain eagerness. But behind it was a dark cloud of impending doom she couldn't shake.

If Daniel succeeded in his quest, her job was in danger. Certainly her chances of rising to any level of prominence in the district attorney's office would be quashed. Winston Chubb had been livid when she'd told him what Daniel Logan was up to. Though he feared the man, Chubb had instructed her to neutralize Logan and his do-gooder efforts using any means at her disposal.

Any means.

As she returned to her desk to check messages one last time before the meeting, the phone rang. The number on caller ID was blocked and she considered letting it go to voice mail. But at the last minute she picked it up. If it was Daniel, telling her he was delayed, she would politely remind him she couldn't rearrange her schedule—just as he'd done to her.

"McNair." Her voice came out a bit sharper than she'd intended.

"It's Daniel. I'm in front of your building now, but I'm trapped. There's a media frenzy going on out here, and if I step out of my car I'll become a part of the uproar."

"Oh, for the love of—" She tried mightily to hold on to her patience as she moved to the window and looked down. From her sixth-floor office she had a perfect view of the front entrance, and it was exactly as Daniel had described.

"It's the Judge Harlow thing, I imagine," Daniel said.

Jamie sighed in frustration. She hadn't yet

read her newspaper today, but she'd heard about the judge. The whole office buzzed with the news. Just what the city needed, another scandal.

"Is there a back entrance?" Daniel asked.

"I'm afraid not. With our heightened security, everyone has to come and go through the front doors. You'll just have to cope."

"I can't." His voice held a note of panic. "It's highly unlikely I would make it into the building unobserved. And I don't think either of us wants to see our business splashed on the front page until we're ready."

He did have a point. "What do you suggest? My time is extremely limited. I'm awaiting a jury verdict, and I could be called back into court at any minute."

"We can meet in my car. There's a big backseat—it's private, it's roomy and very secure."

Jamie didn't like it. Not at all. Was he simply manipulating her, forcing her to abandon her plans and conduct the meeting on his turf—again?

But she couldn't deny that a security problem existed. That crowd outside looked hungry, and if they couldn't get a glimpse of the judge or at least get a statement from someone in Public Relations about the situation, they would take what they could get.

And they would have a heyday with the juicy combination of Daniel Logan trying to free Christopher Gables. They would grab on to the surface similarities between the cases, and she would have to spend all of her time chasing down rumors and denying, denying, denying.

"All right, we can meet in your car," she said, barely able to part her jaws to get the words out. "Give me a few minutes to gather my materials." And her wits.

She was about to get in the backseat of a car with a man who had the ability to short-circuit her rational mind and possibly tank her whole career.

"Thank you," he said, sounding like he meant it. His relief was almost palpable. "It's the black Mercedes limo parked near the corner."

Five minutes later, she was wending her way past reporters and cameras on the walkway leading from the criminal justice building to the street. Despite her efforts to appear insignificant and ignorant, one reporter jumped into her path and stuck a microphone in her face.

"Ms. McNair, can you comment on the situation with Judge—"

"Even if I knew anything, which I don't, I wouldn't comment. Excuse me." She stepped around the microphone, hoping the reporter holding it would focus on someone else.

A few more steps, and she reached the longest, blackest, shiniest vehicle she'd ever seen. A uniformed driver popped out to open the back door and she slid in as quickly as possible, praying no one noticed. The only time she'd been at the center of media attention—during the Christopher Gables trial—she hadn't liked it. It was something she needed to get comfortable with, though, if she wanted to advance in her chosen profession.

Jamie kept her eyes focused down on herself as she smoothed her skirt and gathered her thoughts. Only then did she look up and face Daniel Logan.

At least he had clothes on this time. But the effect of Daniel in a well-tailored gray suit and silk tie was no less devastating to her hormones. Her heart gave a little jump, and she sucked in her breath.

He held out his hand. "Jamie. Sorry for the inconvenience."

She took his hand. "Daniel. Thank you for coming."

It was the first time she'd called him by his given name. She'd been avoiding it, because it seemed a bit too chummy. Too intimate, given their adversarial relationship.

But it seemed positively Victorian to keep calling him Mr. Logan.

As soon as she could do so politely, she eased her hand away from the warmth of his. His handshake absolutely oozed confidence. How did he do that? And what did hers communicate? Shivering nerves?

"How was the traffic?" she asked, because that was what everyone in Houston asked first thing in any meeting.

"I wasn't really paying attention," he admitted. "I was going over my notes. But I guess it was okay. We got here quickly."

Of course he didn't have to concern himself with mundane matters like traffic. He had a chauffeur and a limousine the size of a battleship. She tried to imagine living like him—hot and cold running servants, mostly hot from what she'd seen—a three-story mansion, polo ponies and tennis courts. She couldn't even wrap her mind around it. She couldn't imagine what it would be like to not work like a dog every day, watch her spending, save for retirement.

She resented the ease of his life. Yeah, six years on death row wouldn't have been a picnic. But he'd been convicted of murder. And here he was, flaunting his wealth and dabbling in "charitable" work, helping others like himself escape retribution for their crimes.

"So," she said crisply, imagining a clear shell around her that would make her immune to the handsome billionaire's physical proximity. "The driver can't hear us, can he?" She glanced at the glass partition that separated the driver from the passenger seating.

"Not a word. We could scream at the tops of our lungs and he wouldn't hear us."

That thought didn't particularly cheer her.

"Yes, well. Since I called this meeting, and we have limited time, let's get started."

"All right. Tell me about Theresa."

That was a good place to start. "She was credible. Sincere. My investigation leaves me certain she is the same Theresa who made the 9-1-1 call, bringing the police to El Toreador. And her statement about seeing a stranger in the restaurant kitchen sounds plausible."

"Only plausible? You don't think it rings with truth?"

"Plausible," she said firmly.

Daniel's eyes almost twinkled as he listened attentively with his whole body. She liked that about him, even if she disapproved of everything else. So many people—men especially—might appear to be listening, but they were actually waiting for their turn to speak.

"I'm very glad to hear you say that," he said. "Can you show her mug shots? Have her work with a sketch artist? I have an artist on call for Project Justice that does excellent work."

Now came the hard part. "As I've explained before, one eyewitness statement, delivered all these years after the crime, will not trump the physical evidence. All Theresa gave me was a vague description. She saw an unfamiliar man in the kitchen talking to the victim. Minutes later, as she was bussing tables, she heard a loud crash in the kitchen and went to investigate. She found the victim dead."

"But she gave *some* description, right? Male Caucasian in his thirties, medium build…"

"Wearing a baseball cap, so she couldn't even get a hair color. It's too general."

"But she told you it was positively *not* Christopher Gables. Correct?"

"Yes," Jamie admitted. "But if we press her for details at this point…well, it's easy for the mind to play tricks. Her subconscious could provide details just to please me."

Daniel opened his mouth to object, but she cut him off.

"Not that she would deceive me on purpose, but memory is a strange and unreliable beast. Considering your experience with Project Justice, I'm sure you understand that."

Daniel seemed to deflate slightly. "Still, it seems likely to me that if this stranger was the last person seen talking to Frank before he died, he is a more probable suspect than Christopher."

"Except that his prints weren't found on the murder weapon."

Daniel pressed his lips together, and Jamie

tasted victory. At last, she just might have convinced him he was on a fool's errand.

She tried to press her advantage. "I brought the case file with me. I'm ready to go step-by-step through the thinking process that led me to prosecute this case."

"I'd like that."

Jamie opened her briefcase just as her phone rang. It was rude to take a call during a meeting, but she was still waiting for that verdict.

"I'm sorry, this might be important." She quickly looked at the caller ID. "Oh. You may actually be interested in this." It was Eddie, the evidence tech whom she'd bullied into taking another look at Frank Sissom's clothing. "Yes, Eddie?"

"I got the results on those stains. Put it through the spectrometer. It's not toner powder at all."

Her stomach sank. *Let it be dirt. Charcoal. Cigarette ash.* "Well, what is it?"

"Very fine metal filings. Ferrous."

This could not be happening to her. Metal filings? As in exactly what Daniel had predicted she would find?

"Thanks, Eddie, I'll get back to you."

"Well?" Daniel said. Then his face softened. "Jamie, what's wrong? You're pale. Did he say something to upset you?"

Her lips felt suddenly cold, and she could barely form the words. "You said something about a s-serial killer?"

CHAPTER FOUR

"WHO WAS THAT ON THE PHONE?" Daniel asked sharply. Whoever it was, he'd sure said something to shake up Jamie.

"My evidence tech, the one reexamining Frank Sissom's clothes. He found something no one else did—very fine metal shavings."

Daniel could hardly believe what he was hearing. His long shot had paid off. "Jamie, this is huge. Do you realize what this means?" In his exuberance, he threw his arms around the lawyer and hugged her. Finally, someone had listened to him about those damn metal shavings.

"Um, do you always get this happy at the prospect of helping a client?"

Suddenly self-conscious, he released her and scooted back a few inches on the enormous bench seat. "Sorry." Had he been out of the social scene so long, he'd forgotten how to behave appropriately with someone he barely knew?

Only, he felt as if he knew her. Over the past twenty-four hours, he had delved deeply into Jamie McNair's background, and his admiration for her had only grown.

Her roots had come from anything but privilege. Her single mother had raised her in a one-bedroom apartment with a series of low-paying jobs. Her father was completely absent—Daniel hadn't even been able to learn his identity.

Yet Jamie had gotten herself an education with a lot of hard work, scholarships and student loans. Still not rolling in dough, judging from her off-the-rack plum-colored suit and a pair of slightly scuffed black pumps—recently polished, but in need of new soles.

Not that she didn't look stunning in that color. She would look stunning in just about anything.

Daniel forced himself to focus. "You don't share my optimism, I take it."

"Frankly, I'm too shocked to know what I feel. The black, powdery substance on Frank Sissom's shirt was written off as copier or printer toner. No one ever questioned it or analyzed it until now. It didn't seem relevant."

"I've learned it's those tiny, overlooked elements that can make or break a case. So, are we on the same page now? Same offender?"

"It warrants looking into," she said with some degree of resignation. "One thing I can't help but notice—Frank Sissom was murdered a scant two months after you were released from prison. If we have a serial offender, who's to say it isn't you?"

Daniel felt a prickling of fear. He'd never even considered that he could become a suspect. But he grabbed a bottled water and took a sip to relieve his suddenly dry mouth.

"Why would I push to exonerate Christopher and find the real murderer, if the real murderer was me?" he asked sensibly.

She shrugged. "I'll put that possibility on the back burner. For now. But that leaves me with Gables as a two-time murderer."

Daniel curbed his impatience. "Gables was a college kid at the time of the first crime."

"College kids are adults, perfectly capable of homicide."

One inch at a time. Daniel had more now

than he did last time he'd met with Jamie. He just had to keep building.

"Back to the metal shavings. Was your guy able to distinguish the type of metal, or where it might have come from?"

"Well, it's ferrous, which means iron or nickel, or an alloy of either. We haven't gotten beyond that yet. The type of close analysis you're talking about takes time... and money."

"I'll give you the name of a lab. They do photo-chemical spectography, which can give us the exact— What?"

Her expression was closed again, guarded. "It's not just a question of time or money. My boss is going to throw a fit."

"Does he have to know?"

"Of course he does! If you're right, if Christopher Gables was involved in two murders—"

"Wait. Stop right there. You can't seriously think Gables is a serial killer."

"How can you know it's *not* Gables? Look at it from my perspective, Daniel. I am as sure as I've ever been that Christopher Gables committed the murder of Frank Sissom. You can't argue away those fingerprints. If trace evidence links this murder to another, then Christopher might well be involved in the previous murder, as well. It only makes sense."

It made no sense at all.

"Would you like me to give you an explanation for the fingerprints?" Daniel asked.

"Oh, this I've got to hear."

Daniel had given this a lot of thought. Because, unlike Jamie, he knew beyond any shadow of a doubt that he hadn't killed anyone, yet his prints had been found on a murder weapon.

"Christopher used the knife for something else—hours, days, even months prior to the murder. So long as no one else touches the knife, the prints remain intact.

"The real murderer then uses an identical knife to commit the crime. Wearing gloves, he smears some blood on the knife bearing Christopher's prints and places it near the body. Voilà, a perfect frame-up."

"The medical examiner matched the knife to the wound," she argued.

Daniel opened his briefcase, rifled through it until he came up with a page of the trial transcript with some testimony highlighted in yellow.

"'The wound on Mr. Sissom's neck is consistent with a Messermeister Meridian Elite eight-inch chef's knife—the knife found near his body.' Do you recognize that testimony, Jamie?"

She closed her eyes for a moment. "Yes."

"'...is consistent with...' doesn't mean the same as 'exact match,' does it?"

"Please, I'm not on trial here. You've made your point. The murder could have been committed with an identical knife."

"You have no idea how many nights I lie awake, thinking about how my prints ended up on a murder weapon. I had no conscious memory of using the knife that killed my partner. I'm not a chef, and I spent little time in the kitchen."

"So how do you explain it?"

"I tried to think of the things I might use a knife for. And here's what I came up with. I might have used a knife to open a package. Not the day of the murder, but perhaps weeks earlier. I had a penknife I kept in my pocket for such things, because the restaurant received packages all the time. But I could have mislaid it and picked up whatever was handy."

Daniel could almost see the gears turning in Jamie's head as she mulled over his theory.

"Christopher wasn't a chef, either," she finally said. "Our theory was that Christopher confronted Frank in the kitchen, knowing ahead of time he would have his choice of murder weapons."

"I'd like to talk to him," Daniel said. "See if he has any memory of touching that knife for an innocent purpose."

"I can answer that for you. He said he used it to cut up an apple for lunch that day. Which was an obvious lie, because he always ate something off the menu for his lunch, and at least three witnesses saw him eating fajitas."

"It was a lie, I'll grant you that. Probably concocted on the spur of the moment out of fear and desperation. Have you ever been interrogated, Jamie?"

"No, but I've witnessed many police interviews and watched loads of video."

"That's not the same. Until you're locked in that room with a couple of mean-eyed cops, pointing fingers at you, shouting at you, playing head games with you—you have no idea what it's like. You are tempted to say anything, no matter how untrue, just to get those guys to leave you alone."

"Did you?" Jamie asked, not without compassion.

"I didn't. But I was still secure in the belief that my father and his influence and money would straighten everything out. Christopher didn't have that to fall back on.

"I submit that he told that lie because he was terrified. And his lawyer coached him to continue the lie rather than admit to it."

Jamie digested the story some more.

Daniel gave her a few moments of silence before he pressed his argument. "Raleigh, our chief legal counsel, has put in the paperwork for a face-to-face interview with Christopher. I'd like you to go with her to the prison."

"Raleigh? Why not you?"

"Prison officials have to grant an interview for a death-row inmate with his attorney of record. I'm not an attorney."

"Daniel, I know how Project Justice operates. Your people conduct interviews with prisoners on death row all the time, often without an attorney present."

"It wouldn't work this time."

"I submit," she said, reflecting his own verbiage back to him, "that you are not the best person to argue on Christopher's behalf. Not only are you seriously biased because of the similarities between the crimes, but your high profile—by your own admission—makes it difficult for you to move about comfortably in public situations.

"So why don't you assign this case to one of your people. Full-time. It will be easier on everyone."

"My 'serious bias,' as you put it, makes me uniquely qualified to fight passionately for Christopher's freedom."

"Then don't you think you're the best one to interview him?"

She was right. And yet…the thought of walking into that prison—the very same prison where Daniel had been incarcerated—was abhorrent to him.

"If I agree, will you go with me? Because, as the prosecutor of this case, you also are uniquely qualified to shoot down any half-baked theories. You know what will and won't fly in a courtroom before a judge."

"I'll have to clear it with my boss."

And she'd already told him: her boss hated the idea of reopening this case.

"I'll set something up for next week. That should give you a chance to clear your schedule."

"I'll send the metal shavings for further analysis. What's the name of your lab?"

"PrakTech Laboratories. They're certified by the county, so that shouldn't be a problem. Of course, Project Justice will pick up the bill."

She shook her head, firmed her lips. "I can't believe I'm doing this. I can't believe I've let you talk me into this. In the end, I'll probably trash my career, and for what? Christopher Gables isn't going to walk unless another suspect turns himself in and confesses."

He felt for her. He really did. "You're doing this because a man's life is at stake. You're a good person, and you don't like the thought of prosecuting an innocent man any more than I do."

"Or maybe you're just one persuasive man."

"That, too." He smiled at her for the first time since she'd gotten in the car, and she smiled back.

"I *will* be checking into Christopher Gables's whereabouts at the time of the Andreas Musto murder."

"You would be remiss in your duties if you didn't. Jamie...I want you to know that I'm grateful."

"Because you've backed me into a corner?"

"For doing the right thing. The man who prosecuted my case—Chet Dotie, as I'm sure you know—he stonewalled every effort I made to exonerate myself. He considered my effort a personal affront, and he threw every barrier into my path he could think of, ethical or not."

"I'm sure it looked that way..." She trailed off and looked away, less composed, suddenly. "Prosecutors invest a lot of time and money into an important case. I mean, it's not just about that. Most of them believe... they fight passionately..."

"Dotie didn't believe in it, though," Daniel informed her. "He looked me straight in the eye and told me he didn't care if I'd done it or not, he wasn't going to let some snot-nosed rich kid get out of jail just because his daddy had money."

Jamie's eyebrows shot up and her nostrils flared.

"I'm not telling you this simply to malign one of your own. It's just that the contrast of your open mind is refreshing."

She didn't seem to appreciate the compliment. "We'll see how refreshed you feel when this is all over." Her phone rang, and she answered it without apology this time. "McNair...okay, on my way."

"Verdict's in?"

"I assume I'll hear from you when you have new information."

"And I assume the same."

She shot out of his car like the hounds of hell were chasing her. A few enterprising reporters tried to thwart her progress, but she put her briefcase in front of her like a battering ram and they got out of her way.

He didn't blame them. She seemed soft and sweet sometimes, but then she could turn around and breathe fire at him. The contrast was interesting.

She was interesting. The reporters eyeing

his limo were just plain scary. Daniel opened the glass partition. "Let's get out of here."

"You got it."

AS SHE PRACTICALLY SPRINTED UP the stairs toward the justice center, Jamie felt like she couldn't get enough air. Those things he'd said about her father—were they true? Or had he just made up a story to manipulate her emotions?

Daniel might be manipulative, but she hadn't caught him in a lie yet. What little she'd read about his arrest and trial indicated that his story had never changed. He hadn't made up anything to explain away facts, as Christopher had.

Which left her wondering—was her father not the man she believed he'd been?

She and Chet Dotie had never enjoyed a warm relationship. Although she'd always known his name, her mother had forbid mention of it and had refused to allow her daughter any contact with the man who had sired her.

Apparently her father had sent money from time to time. Although he'd never made any concerted effort to see his daughter, he hadn't completely forgotten her.

That knowledge had led her to seek him out when she was in college, when her mother couldn't stop her. He'd been surprised, confused and not altogether welcoming of her intrusion into his life. But gradually he'd come around when he realized she wasn't going to publicize their relationship and possibly taint his reputation.

He started taking a keen interest in her studies, even paying her tuition on occasion, provided she took the classes he specified. Though she'd been drawn to art and literature, he had pointed out to her that she couldn't afford that indulgence. She needed a career that would provide a solid, regular income. Law school it was. Period.

She had bristled at his high-handedness at first, but she'd soon discovered she was well suited to the legal profession and had settled in to be the best law student she could be.

Chet took for granted her good grades and the prestigious internship she'd earned. She'd thought he was reserving his praise for when she graduated. But then he died suddenly, just before she got her juris doctorate.

She could have gone into private practice, but she'd wanted to follow in his footsteps. Prosecuting crimes had seemed noble. Her father had been well respected, and she thought it a worthy goal to emulate him.

Had it all been a lie? The thought of him telling a man on death row that he didn't care about guilt or innocence turned her stomach.

She should have told Daniel that Chet was her father. But such an emotional bombshell would likely derail the tenuous alliance they'd formed. She needed to stay on friendly terms with him, she reasoned. If this "serial killer" thing panned out, she wanted some say in how the situation was handled.

If Christopher Gables had killed before, and she broke the news, it would be a feather in her cap that she'd been the one to send him to prison.

If, on the other hand, the killings were linked and someone other than Christopher was responsible... No, she didn't want to think about that. It couldn't be true. Daniel had spun a pretty story about the knife and the fingerprints, but it was improbable at best, like something out of an Agatha Christie novel.

She had to stop allowing him to get through her defenses!

Jamie operated on automatic pilot as the verdict for her drunk-driving case was announced. Guilty. Judge sentenced the defendant to five years. She considered that a victory.

Next stop: the D.A.'s office. Her heart thudded inside her chest as she contemplated how Winston Chubb would take the latest developments she and Daniel had just discussed. The first time she'd brought up the Gables case, he'd nearly blown a gasket.

Winston's admin squeezed her in between appointments. When Jamie tapped on his door, he beckoned her inside with no welcoming smile.

Winston Chubb was tall, angular, almost emaciated, an image that didn't jibe with his name at all. He had sparse black hair and deep-set, probing eyes. He scared the hell out of people in the courtroom.

"Please tell me you got a guilty verdict with the Mosely case," he said.

"Yes. He got five years."

"Okay, then. Good job. Why are you here?"

He didn't waste words, this guy.

"It's the Christopher Gables case."

His face turned to thunder. "Thought I told you to leave that one alone."

"I'd like to. But the witness I told you about was credible. And some evidence has been reanalyzed—"

"Who authorized that?"

He was trying to intimidate her, and she refused to let him. "I did," she said boldly. "I was curious. It turns out the Gables case might be linked to another, earlier murder. The, um, Andreas Musto case."

Winston's bushy eyebrows flew up. "Are you joking?"

"I wouldn't joke about something like this. The surface similarities are enough to intrigue me."

"Please, Jamie, let it drop. When I sent you to talk to Logan, I assumed you would quietly talk him out of this nonsense. I can't afford another scandal. I'm still taking crap from the Anthony Simonetti case. And you—your career is really taking off. You can't afford it, either." This last, he delivered as a warning.

"I feel we don't have a choice. Daniel

Logan has made it his personal mission to free Christopher Gables."

"Free him? I thought you said Gables was a possible two-time offender, not that he might be innocent."

"Mr. Logan and I have a difference of opinion as to what the new evidence means. I feel it's important to pursue this so we'll know the truth."

"The truth? God, Jamie, surely you're not that naive. There's no room for truth in the court system, only different interpretations of events and evidence."

Did he really believe that? Was she the only lawyer left who cared about true guilt or innocence?

"If we drop the ball, Logan's going to put his own spin on this. And it won't be pretty."

"Read my lips, Jamie. No. My budget has been cut to the bone, and you know as well as I do every assistant D.A. in this office is overworked. I can't have you gallivanting around on some fool's errand, trying to scare up evidence that will convict a man who's already in jail or exonerate one who's already been pardoned."

"And what if we convicted the wrong man?" she asked. "We can't let Christopher Gables be executed if it's possible we got things wrong."

"If you help Daniel Logan spin the evidence that way, it would be a very, *very* bad development for everyone involved."

Not for Christopher.

It would be easy for Jamie to slink out of her boss's office and tell Daniel she was sorry, but she couldn't cooperate with him anymore unless she wanted to lose her job.

But that was a coward's way out.

"Jamie. You're one of my brightest stars. Keep your nose clean, get a few more showy convictions and in a couple more years you might be sitting in this chair."

"Me? District attorney?" She almost fell over.

"Why not you? You're attractive, smart, hard as an unripe pumpkin and you get the job done. I'm not running for reelection. Someone has to replace me, and it might as well be you."

Winston made a shooing gesture with his hands. "Go, Jamie. Earn your paycheck. And don't lead with your heart."

Dazed, Jamie backed out of the office and closed the door. District attorney? She didn't appreciate that he'd mentioned her looks first, or that he'd compared her to a vegetable, but if he really meant what he'd said…

No chance of her advancing if it turned out she'd convicted an innocent man in her biggest, most publicized case.

Still, her conscience would not let her walk away from Daniel Logan and his quest. If the D.A. wouldn't authorize her to cooperate, she would do what she could nights, weekends and on her lunch break. To do otherwise would be wrong.

A conscience could be a real inconvenience, sometimes.

CHAPTER FIVE

DANIEL'S FAVORITE HORSE, Laramie, thundered down the polo field as Daniel focused on the ball, leaning over the horse's neck, becoming one with the surging animal.

He swung his mallet up, and with the perfect timing that happens so rarely, gave the ball a resounding thwack, launching it straight into the opposing team's goal.

A cheer went up and he brought Laramie up and swiveled him around, feeling a momentary wash of elation at seeing his teammates congratulate him.

He often invited a local polo team to play on his field, just so he could keep his hand in the sport he'd enjoyed in college and give his two ponies some exercise. He also found that the strenuous mental and physical exertion that went with playing polo helped to sweep his mind of extraneous thoughts so that he could focus more clearly on the challenges of his Project Justice work.

Today, especially, he'd needed the stress relief of a good workout. His attempts over the weekend to gather evidence he would need to free Christopher Gables had met with only limited success. Any day now, the state would set the date for Christopher's execution, and time seemed to be slipping away.

He hadn't heard from Jamie over the weekend, and it was all he could do not to call her at home or on her cell. But she had to be handled delicately. Somehow, Daniel had to juggle the urgency of his quest with his desire not to push Jamie so hard that she walked away.

The chukker was over, and it was time to change horses, give Laramie a well-deserved rest. He had just dismounted, handing Laramie off to a groom, when he spotted Jillian approaching with a determined stride and a distinct frown.

Normally she didn't let any aspects of her duties bother her on an emotional level. She was always upbeat, so a frown was out of character.

When she reached him, she handed over

a cell phone to him. "Jamie McNair. You told me to put her calls through under any circumstances."

"And I meant it." He took the phone. "Yes, Jamie."

"Took you long enough."

"Jillian had to hunt me down. Sometimes I get away from all communications, just to clear my head."

"She said you were playing polo."

Jillian knew better than to give someone more information about him than they absolutely needed. "Yes, I was. Clears my head, like I said."

"Hmm. Best I can do is a little deep breathing."

"I'd be happy to teach you how to play polo," he said cheerfully, refusing to let her put him down because he had money. He'd learned long ago not to apologize for his wealth.

"No time for that, I'm afraid. I'll be over after work—around six. I hope you're free."

He smiled slightly at her high-handed tone. She was determined to prove to him he couldn't push her around because of his money and position, and she probably secretly wanted to rankle him, too. If there was one thing Jamie feared, it was that someone would view her as soft.

He suspected she had a soft side. He'd get to it eventually.

"If I'm not free, I'll rearrange my schedule. For you. We'll have dinner."

"That's not necessary."

"Yes, it is. Our brains will work much more efficiently if we—"

"Yes, yes, I've heard it before. We have to refuel our bodies."

"You don't disagree, do you?"

"I just… It seems frivolous, enjoying the sort of meals you routinely eat."

This wasn't the first time he'd run into this attitude. Some people, particularly those raised in poverty, felt guilty for treating themselves.

"I'll see if Chef Claude can rustle up some gruel and moldy bread, if you'd rather."

She actually laughed. "I'll see you at six."

"Is there a reason you're coming, or will you leave me in suspense?"

She almost whispered her next words. "Can't talk here. Have to go."

Well, that was sufficiently mysterious.

He handed the phone to a still-scowling Jillian. "What?" he asked.

"I just don't like that woman. She's high-handed and snooty."

"She's insecure, and trying to establish her authority. Cut her some slack. As you pointed out, my actions might cost her her job, and she deserves some credit for at least keeping the lines of communication open."

"But she thinks Christopher Gables is a serial killer. That's nuts...isn't it?"

"She thinks that only because she can't stomach the alternative—that she put the wrong man on death row. Eventually she'll turn around if I handle things just right."

"You like her, don't you?"

"Like her? I suppose I do." More to the point, he wanted her in his bed, but though he shared a lot with Jillian, his sexual appetite wasn't a subject he ever broached with her.

"You get all sparkly whenever you talk to her, or when her name comes up."

"Do I?"

"Maybe this is none of my business, Daniel, but if you're ready to get...romantic with someone, you can do better than her. Aside from the fact her profession is diametrically opposed to yours, she could be dangerous. People get crazy when their livelihoods, their very identities, are threatened."

Daniel took a deep breath, held it, then let it out slowly. "You're right, Jillian. It *is* none of your business."

Jamie, dangerous? To his control, yes. But she wasn't going to try to kill him.

He turned his back on Jillian to thank the guys from the polo club, but not before he saw the flash of hurt in her eyes.

Damn it, he didn't want to hurt her. She was like a kid sister to him. Their fathers had been friends, and she'd been working for his family since her teenage years.

But neither was he willing to take dating advice from her. Although he wasn't certain what she did on her days off, he didn't think she dated, either. She was as socially isolated as he was.

Maybe he should encourage Jillian to take a different job within the Logan organization. His CEO was always trying to steal her. If she worked at Logan Oil and lived away from his estate, her life would be more normal.

He made a mental note to consider the

possibility further. For the first time in years, he really didn't want Jillian around, not if she was going to judge what he did—or didn't do—with Jamie McNair.

JAMIE WAS SURPRISED, and not quite prepared, when Daniel himself answered the door with Tucker at his heel.

"Come in, Jamie." He offered a brief smile, but his eyes were solemn.

"Thank you. Did your butler take the day off?"

"You know, you're going to have to get that boulder-size chip off your shoulder if we're going to work together."

"Sorry?"

"Your resentment of my wealth. Would you like me better if I gave it all away and lived in a cardboard box under a bridge?"

She stepped past him over the threshold, her heels clicking on the marble floor. "You aren't going to tell me your money is a curse, are you?"

"Far from it. I am grateful every day of my life for the circumstances I was born into. My parents gave me every opportunity, every advantage. If not for money, frankly, I'd be dead right now. Because legal skills alone would not have gotten me a pardon. It took money, too—for publicity, for lawyers, for scientific tests. My father made it his full-time job to exonerate me."

Jamie took a mental step back. When she'd fired off her crack about the butler, she hadn't expected this impassioned speech.

Did she resent his wealth? Maybe a little. As a prosecutor, she had a limited budget and limited resources. Maybe she did bristle at the fact he had unlimited supplies of both.

"The extent of your wealth overwhelms me," she said in all honesty. "I can't wrap my mind around it. But I didn't intentionally malign your father." She squatted down to greet Tucker and give him a little scratch behind the ears. It was easier to look into his sweet brown eyes than face Daniel's challenging gaze.

"No, you didn't. And maybe I overreacted. Let's go sit down. Dinner should be ready in about an hour, is that okay?"

"That's…that's fabulous." Whatever he served was sure to beat the dinner she would have had on her own—probably something frozen popped into the microwave.

She thought he'd take her down to the basement again. Instead, he led her down the same hallway as before, stopping before reaching the stairs where he entered a different room. It was a large library, probably larger than the public library she'd checked out books from as a child. The room was a symphony of warm wood and leather and stone, very masculine yet somehow cozy and inviting. An enormous stone fireplace dominated the room, smack in the center and open on two sides. Though it was only in the sixties outside, a low flame burned, giving the room more intimacy than it otherwise would have had.

Tucker headed straight to the fireplace and flopped onto a rug in front of the raised hearth.

The walls were lined with floor-to-ceiling shelves stuffed with all manner of books, from ancient-looking leather-bound volumes to current bestselling novels. At the opposite end of the room was a carved oak bar, which appeared fully stocked with bottles and bottles of liquor lined up on mirrored shelves.

Jamie was drawn, though, to a Christmas

tree. The thing had to be fifteen feet tall, a lovely, lacy cedar whose top brushed the vaulted wood-beamed ceiling.

She looked up at a string of lights, only half strung. The tree was in progress. "I'd almost forgotten that the holidays were coming."

"They're not my thing, either, but Jillian always makes a big deal about the decorating. She seems to enjoy it."

"Maybe if I had a place like this to decorate, I'd get more excited." She could almost picture a Christmas morning here, stockings hung on that enormous hearth stuffed with goodies, shiny packages under the tree, a cheerful fire—never mind that Houston Christmases were often downright balmy.

Then she imagined children squealing in delight as they discovered the presents Santa had brought, the smell of hot cocoa...

She shook her head, alarmed by the fanciful turn of her imagination. The only things she knew of squealing children on Christmas morning were what she'd seen on TV. Her mother had always worked on Christmas because she could get double time, and presents had been a foreign concept.

One time, Toys for Tots had stopped by,

wanting to give Jamie a shiny wrapped package. Her mother had tartly told them she didn't accept charity.

"Jamie?"

She snapped back to reality. "Sorry. I'm curious—how do you celebrate? Do you hand out BMWs and diamond necklaces? Buy the biggest goose in town and stuff it with caviar?"

"You're doing it again."

"I am. Sorry."

"My Christmas is always low-key. I give my employees bonuses, usually a few days before the holidays so they can do something nice for themselves. Then I let them celebrate with their families."

"So you hang out here by yourself? I know your parents have passed away, but don't you have any family?"

"I like the solitude. And no, no family. Oh, some cousins in Philadelphia. I invite them to visit every year, but they haven't come since... Well, it was awkward. Small children involved, and all that."

His relatives were afraid to expose their children to him? Because they thought he was a murderer?

That thought made Jamie unbearably sad. Though she'd believed he was a killer at one time, possibly even a serial offender, she had a hard time reconciling that possibility with the man she was coming to know.

"Christmas is hardly a blip on my radar screen," she said. "No family here, either. Christmas is so overdone, anyway."

"So that's one thing we have in common," Daniel observed. "We don't get all caught up in the holiday baloney. Probably suits you just fine, am I right?"

"Absolutely. People go crazy. They spend money they can't afford. They buy toys their kids will get tired of in a week."

"They gain weight and spend all of January feeling guilty for their excesses."

"They cut down trees that'll just end up in the landfill." She glanced at the behemoth of a cedar.

"I turn mine into mulch and use it for the gardens."

"Well, all right, then. You're excused for the ginormous tree."

Daniel smiled at her, and something inside her that was hard and tight loosened just a bit. Maybe she did have a chip on her shoulder where money and privilege were concerned. She'd hated those snotty rich kids she'd gone to law school with who'd looked down on her because she didn't drive the right car and wear the right labels.

Daniel did some good things with his money. Logan Oil was one of the most ecologically conscious fuel companies on the planet. The company donated massive amounts of money to clean up oceans, and Daniel personally gave away lots of money to worthy causes, not to mention all he did with Project Justice.

Maybe she would never relate to his lifestyle, but that didn't mean she had to condemn him for it.

Condemn. Funny she should use that word.

"Maybe we should get down to business," she said, hoping to reel her mind in from its errant path.

"Good idea. We can work over here." He led her to a large walnut gaming table where they had plenty of room to spread out. The moment they got settled, a servant entered with a platter of hors d'oeuvres, small plates, napkins and wineglasses.

Daniel held up a hand when the servant would have poured them wine. "Not tonight, Manuel. We're working."

"Yes, sir."

Jamie's stomach was rumbling, so she availed herself of the nibbles—water chestnuts wrapped in crispy bacon, mushrooms stuffed with a wild-rice concoction, Brie and some of the tastiest crackers she'd ever sampled.

"So, Jamie, can I ask why you're here?" Daniel asked, also diving into the food. "And with a large, fully stuffed briefcase?"

Right. She'd almost forgotten the reason she'd come. "First, you have to give me your word you won't divulge what I'm about to tell you to anyone."

"If it will help free Christopher—"

"It won't."

"Okay, I give you my word."

"Good, because if it suited you, you could easily get me fired. I'm here because I want to find out what, if any, real connection exists between the Frank Sissom and Andreas Musto murders. Unfortunately, the district attorney doesn't agree that this research is necessary or appropriate. He forbade me to assist you. In fact, he ordered me to throw every possible roadblock at you."

Daniel set down the mushroom he'd been about to pop into his mouth. "Wow."

"He's my boss, and I'm supposed to support his policies. But I can't walk away. I may not agree with you about Christopher's innocence, but I want to find out what really happened. Who was the man Theresa saw in the kitchen? Where did those metal shavings come from? And who belongs to that DNA?"

"We may not want the same outcome," Daniel said. "But we both want the truth, and we can help each other."

"But I can't do this on the county's dime. My assistance is limited to evenings and weekends. And my part in this is to be kept in strictest confidence—unless and until we're prepared to take some kind of legal action, such as filing charges or making a motion to have Christopher's verdict overturned."

"Of course. Believe me, I don't want you to get fired. It's not in my best interest."

"So what about your servants? Jillian and Manuel and…the chef? Claude?"

"You can trust them. I don't allow anyone

to work on the estate who hasn't been vetted six ways to Sunday. Jillian has been working for my family since before I was released from prison. Manuel's father is the head gardener here—he was raised on the estate. And Claude—I've known Claude since high school. In fact, he was a part of my first restaurant venture right out of college."

Daniel lowered his voice. "It was a colossal failure, I'm afraid. That's when I learned that a fancy business degree and a talented chef don't add up to a successful restaurant."

"You owned a business that failed?" That surprised Jamie.

"Most restaurants fail. We made a lot of bad calls. My dad could have bailed us out, but he wanted me to learn from my mistakes. Otherwise, I'd just keep making them."

"That must have been a painful lesson. I mean, your father was a legend in business. Was it hard to live up to that?"

"Sometimes. He lived and breathed Logan Oil. I think he was disappointed when I wanted to go into the restaurant business, but he supported me. That's what I remember about him the most. He let me make my own decisions and supported me, no matter what.

"When I was arrested, he never once believed, even for a second, that I could have committed a violent crime."

Daniel's face clouded over. "The strain of those years is what killed him. My mom, too."

Jamie couldn't help but feel bad for a man who'd lost both of his parents just when he'd finally regained his freedom. "They both died within a year of your release...is that right?"

"Yeah. Dad had a massive coronary. Mom had cancer—she was already sick by the time I came home. It wasn't as happy a time as it might have been."

It struck Jamie suddenly that Daniel wasn't a happy man. He put on a good show, but deep down, he must have been very lonely. Maybe all that money *was* a curse. Especially when he didn't trust anyone, didn't let anyone close unless they were "vetted," as he put it.

"Anyway, back to work." Daniel seemed to shake off his melancholy. "I've set up a tentative appointment on Wednesday to meet with Christopher Gables. Unfortunately, it's smack in the middle of the day. If you can't make it, that's unfortunate, but I'll try to be flexible, given your new constraints."

"I could take a personal day off." She was treading in dangerous territory. If Winston found out… But she was entitled to a day off once in a blue moon, right?

THE UPCOMING VISIT to Christopher Gables became the focus of the evening. Though the work was somber in nature, Daniel actually enjoyed using his wits and collaborating with someone as bright as Jamie.

She'd brought a transcript with her of Christopher's original interrogation, which she'd already read and highlighted—she must have stayed up all night doing it. They picked apart various statements he'd made, making lists of follow-up questions and clarifications they wanted.

Sometimes, though, Daniel found his focus drifting to Jamie's hair, and how it fell across her cheek every time she looked down to read something. She would impatiently shove it behind her ear, only to have it fall again within a few minutes.

He could smell her, too.

In prison, he used to dream about the way

women smelled. Whether it was baby powder, expensive perfume or flour and sugar and yeast, women smelled like nothing else in the world, and he'd sorely missed that olfactory stimulation when he'd been locked up.

Then, one day, he couldn't call it up in his imagination. Couldn't fantasize about it as he lay in his bunk. And he'd felt a panic all out of proportion. His memories, his imagination, those were all he'd had in prison to comfort him. He'd been afraid of losing his ability to think at all. Afraid of going stark-raving mad.

Was it Jamie's skin that smelled like vanilla? Her hair? Did he detect a faint scent of lipstick?

Would she taste as good as she smelled?

"So here, he says he noticed the time he got home," Jamie was saying, and Daniel snapped his attention back to her words. "Yet fifteen minutes later, he says he didn't look at the clock and didn't wear a watch. Why the discrepancy?"

"Could be a number of things. He might have turned on the TV and noticed a particular show was starting. He might have noticed the time on his car clock right before coming in. He might have seen the time on a VCR or a coffeemaker or a microwave or even his cell phone. He might have seen how high the moon was—it was a full moon that night."

Jamie made notes. "I want to ask him."

"We'll have limited time. Are you sure it's relevant?"

"It's relevant because I can catch him lying."

They already knew Christopher was apt to make stuff up. Even if they did catch him in a lie, it wouldn't necessarily speak to his guilt or innocence. But Daniel didn't argue. He had Jamie on his side—sort of—and he didn't want to blow it.

"We have a psychologist on call—Claudia Ellison. Have you heard of her?"

"Sure. She testifies as an expert witness all the time."

"She's an expert on body language. She has watched video of Christopher Gables and feels certain he's telling the truth—about the important stuff."

"I disagree. I remember thinking, when I watched the interrogation, that he was lying."

"But you had a vested interest in his guilt."

"Which is why I want to ask him certain questions."

"With an open mind?"

"Yes, Daniel."

He sighed. "It's after seven. Claude will have dinner on the table. Let's take a break."

"Okay." She picked up a stack of papers. "I can read you this part of the transcript—"

He touched her hand and his awareness went off like a firecracker.

"We need to give our minds a break, too. If we come back fresh after dinner, we'll get more done."

"But—"

"Trust me on this. I've studied the research. Working harder doesn't necessarily mean working smarter."

She laughed. He loved the sound of her laughter, so rare and unexpected. "You sound like one of those inspirational speakers they bring in to professional development seminars."

"Busted. Once upon a time, I attended those types of seminars on a monthly basis.

It was right after college, when I was intent on the success of my own business. I felt like a sponge, wanting to soak up every piece of advice anyone had to offer."

"Aren't those seminars just gimmicks? Do they really help?"

"If there's one thing I took away from that part of my education," he said as he stood, then went to pull out her chair for her, "it's that the best thing you can do for any kind of challenging mental or physical activity is take care of your body."

"That's easier to do when you have someone preparing your food."

"I'll grant you that. But I didn't always have Claude to cook for me. I lived on my own at one time."

"By yourself? No servants? No live-in administrative assistant?"

"Hard as you find it to believe that, yes. Right after college I worked for Logan Oil in the marketing department, earned a paycheck, paid rent on a condo. Provided my own meals."

"Sounds like you lived pretty normally."

"Different from now, huh?"

He took her hand—pretty, soft, with her

natural fingernails painted in clear polish—and placed it firmly on his arm. His mother had taught him that when called to dinner, all ladies must be escorted to the table.

She didn't resist, but she smiled wryly. "Very courtly. Did they teach you that at finishing school?"

"Girls go to finishing school. Boys take comportment classes."

"Did you really?"

"In seventh grade I did. My mother was from Savannah, Georgia, and she insisted her only son have manners. I learned more from her, though, than any class."

Daniel led Jamie to the main dining room. Predictably, she gasped when she saw it.

"Good night! You could give a dinner here and invite the entire Texas legislature. Where do you buy a table that big? They don't sell them at the local IKEA."

Now it was his turn to laugh. "The table came from some castle in Spain."

"And the chandeliers?"

He shrugged. "Not sure. My father wanted his house to be like the homes of the well-to-do in Great Britain and Europe. He was pretentious, I'll admit it. My mother made it her job to hunt down furniture and carpets and chandeliers that would make him happy."

"I could easily believe I was in an ancient castle somewhere. But please tell me we won't be sitting at opposite ends of the table. We'll be shouting to hear each other."

She was probably just teasing, because clearly there were two places set at one end.

But Jillian hadn't used the good china, as he'd asked. He had wanted to create an oasis of comfort and beauty, so that for a few tranquil minutes they could forget about the grisly deaths they had immersed themselves in.

The ordinary stoneware and stainless cutlery were what he usually ate with outside, on the patio, where it wouldn't matter if they got broken or misplaced. And there was no tablecloth, only some brown cloth place mats.

Jillian had certainly been acting strangely. Normally she followed his wishes to a T, sometimes anticipating his wants and needs before he even spoke them. Maybe Manuel or Cora had set the table, and there'd been a miscommunication somehow.

"You're frowning."

"Oh, it's nothing." If he made a big deal about their place settings, it would only add to Jamie's opinion that he was a rich snob who didn't occupy the same earthly plane as she did.

He seated her on the side of the table, then grabbed a candelabra from the buffet and lit it, setting it nearby. Candlelight could make anything look better.

"Do you always eat dinner here?"

"Usually." He spoke briefly into the phone, alerting the kitchen staff that they were ready, then took his own chair. "When my parents were alive, they always ate a formal dinner. And they dressed for dinner, too—my mother wouldn't have dreamed of coming to the table without stockings and heels and proper jewelry."

"Daniel, I don't mean this as criticism, but your life is about as strange as it gets. You spend your days in the Batcave, analyzing TV broadcasts and going over data your people send to you, and in the evening…this. You never leave the house."

"Not never," he reminded her. "I did go downtown to see you."

"And you couldn't exit your limousine. It's not normal, even for someone with your wealth."

He didn't argue with her, because she was only telling it like she saw it. He knew he wasn't like most people. He preferred to think of it as living life on his own terms, something most people didn't have the means to do.

But Jamie thought he was weird.

The realization disturbed him. He didn't want her to see him that way. It shouldn't matter; Jamie McNair was a means to an end. He was using her position and her fine brain to help him save a man's life.

But it was impossible to remember that when he saw Jamie not as an adversary or reluctant ally, but as a beautiful, vibrant woman he would very much like to invite into his bed.

Romantic conquests had once come easily to him, and he told himself that his celibacy since prison was a choice. But the truth was, he hadn't tried to woo any woman since he'd been granted his freedom. Despite his persistent prison fantasies of willing women and nonstop bedroom acrobatics, romance and sex had fallen way down on his priority list.

His sex drive had chosen an inconvenient moment to wake up.

Not now. For the first time, he believed he stood a chance of finding the man who'd framed him for the murder of his friend. Once he did, he fully intended to dispense justice his way. And Jamie, thoroughly disillusioned, wouldn't find him at all attractive. She would try to put him behind bars.

CHAPTER SIX

JAMIE FORCED HERSELF TO RELAX. If a wealthy millionaire—some said billionaire—was determined to serve her another excellent meal, why should she argue? As he'd pointed out before, she had to eat.

But this was like something out of a movie about the Tudors or the Bourbons. At least the dishes were ordinary, though the ornate porcelain candelabra looked as if it belonged in a museum somewhere.

The door to the dining room opened, and a portly man in white entered pushing a cart filled with bowls and jars of mysterious ingredients. In his late thirties, he wore his blond hair very short. His face was flushed and jowly, and his tall chef's hat didn't quite disguise a receding hairline.

"Claude." Daniel sounded surprised. "What brings you out of the kitchen?"

Ah, so this was the mysterious Claude who concocted the brilliant food.

"I hear you have a guest," Claude said, beaming. "So I wanted to make sure things were done right." He looked over the table, then frowned. "Bah, what are those dishes?"

"A misunderstanding," Daniel said in a voice that indicated he didn't want to pursue the issue. What was that about?

"You can't eat my beef tips à la Bourgogne on such common dishes. It's heresy. I'll have them replaced with—"

"No, Claude, really, it's not necessary," Jamie interrupted. "We have a lot to get done tonight. These dishes are just fine.

"My associate, Jamie McNair," Daniel said by way of introduction. She supposed "associate" was as good a term as any.

"It is very nice to meet you, Mademoiselle Jamie. I come to make a Caesar salad fresh for you." He had a lovely French accent. "I apologize for the place setting. A beautiful lady such as yourself should only eat from the finest china."

Jamie found herself charmed. "It's all right, believe me. I usually eat my dinner out of a paper microwave box, so this is an improvement."

Claude looked pained. "Microwave. Bah."

He proceeded to make a show of sharpening a knife, then mincing several cloves of garlic so quickly his fingers blurred. Eggs, anchovies, Worcestershire sauce, mustard, olive oil, all were tossed into the dressing mix with the grace of a circus juggler, and Jamie found herself relaxing. The troubles of the day—her conflict with Winston, her growing doubts about the Christopher Gables verdict—receded into the background as she once again allowed Daniel to delight her senses.

She applauded as Claude served her salad and added grated Parmesan and freshly sautéed crispy croutons.

The dinner was, as expected, incredible. The beef was so tender it didn't need a knife, the flavors in the rice pilaf so delicate and aromatic she wanted to linger over it. Even the string beans—normally an uninspiring vegetable—were elevated to a new level just by virtue of their freshness and simple preparation.

As Manuel cleared the table, Jillian made

an appearance, dressed to the nines once again in form-fitting leather pants and a gauzy shirt, through which her black bra was clearly visible. She nodded at Jamie through slitted eyes, then turned her back and focused solely on her boss.

"I'm working on the office holiday party, and I thought it might be nice to just have it here."

"Here?"

"It's not like we don't have plenty of room for entertaining, and Claude could prepare the food. It would be cost-effective."

"I don't care about—" He stopped himself, probably not wanting to admit in front of Jamie that he didn't care about the cost. "Why don't we have it at the Windsor Hotel, like always?"

"They're booked already. And we can't change the date—we've already told everybody to save December 5."

And why was Jillian hitting him with this particular problem now, at 7:45 in the evening? Jamie wondered. It wasn't as if she could do anything about the venue tonight. But Jamie was pretty sure she knew the answer.

"Filling the house with people—it just can't be done. The security, for one thing, would be a nightmare."

"Daniel, these are your people. Your hand-picked employees. You don't trust them?"

"I trust them. But their spouses, their kids—"

"We'll put them through a metal detector," Jillian said practically, and Jamie couldn't tell if she was kidding or not. "Before and after the party, so they won't be tempted to make off with the silver."

"Let me sleep on it. Jillian, really, I don't have time for something so trivial. I'm working on a case."

"Oh. I thought you were having dinner."

"A working dinner. We'll discuss this later."

Clearly she was being dismissed, and just as clearly, she didn't like it. With one last hostile glance at Jamie, Jillian left.

Dessert consisted of a thin slice of pound cake with fresh strawberries and whipped cream. Jamie longed to clean her plate, but an overfull stomach would only make her sleepy, and there was much more work to do.

She took a couple of bites, barely refraining from moaning in gustatory pleasure, then pushed the plate aside.

"No good?" Daniel asked just before forking a strawberry into his mouth.

"No room. Daniel, are you aware that your administrative assistant is in love with you?"

DANIEL STOPPED MIDCHEW, almost spewing a half-eaten strawberry across the table. "Excuse me?"

"Jillian. She's in love with you."

Daniel swallowed painfully and took a sip of water as he recovered his composure. "That's ridiculous. She's like a sister to me. I've known her since she was a kid—she worked for my mother as a summer job when she was still in high school."

"She might be a sister to you, but you're not a brother to her," Jamie said, looking faintly amused. "At first, I wondered why she disliked me so intensely."

"She doesn't dislike you, I'm sure. She doesn't even know you."

"She knows that I'm a single woman spending a great deal of time with you. How often do you bring women here to the estate?"

"It's not that rare. I bring the Logan Oil board of directors here, I conduct meetings—"

"How often do you share intimate meals with your female guests? One-on-one?"

She had him there. "Pretty much never."

"Jillian is threatened by my presence. Although we know that your interest in me is purely professional, she worries that it's something else."

"Are you sure?" If Jamie was right, he had a big problem.

"I'm positive. She already does everything a wife does—she runs your house, handles your schedule, sees to every detail of your needs. I'll bet she even buys your clothes for you."

Damn it, Jamie was right. "She doesn't do *everything* a wife does," he pointed out.

"No, but she wants to. She wants to have the Christmas party here, because then she could act as your hostess, the queen bee. She figures all she has to do is seduce you, and once you're sleeping together, all she lacks is a wedding ring."

"How long has this been going on?" he asked aloud. It was meant as a rhetorical question, but Jamie answered anyway.

"Probably since she first met you. Think about it. She's the young, impressionable girl, you're the older, sophisticated heir apparent to all this." Jamie swung her arms wide, encompassing his whole estate, he supposed. "It probably started out as a case of hero worship. While you were in prison, she waited for you."

"She went to college," he objected.

"And wrote you letters once a week, I'll bet."

Daniel winced. "Yes. One of the few people who did. Her loyalty impressed me."

"Did you write back to her?"

"Yes. What else did I have to do? Her letters cheered me up, and it would have been rude not to acknowledge them."

"She saw it as an intimate connection, a secret you two shared, in a way. You were a romantic figure. And when you came home, she probably made it her mission to make up for what you suffered. Did she sign on as your personal assistant then?"

"Yes."

"Has she had a boyfriend in all those years?"

"Not that I know of. Jamie, you're interrogating me."

She'd been leaning across the corner of the table, almost in his face. Now she slumped back into her chair. "Sorry. It's a habit. Probably the reason I haven't had a relationship that lasted more than five minutes."

Daniel tucked that bit of information away to dissect later. Right now, he had more pressing problems. "Damn it, you're right. What am I going to do?"

"If you don't return her feelings—"

"Of course I don't. I value her and trust her as a friend, but not…" He shuddered. That would be so wrong.

"Then you should confront her and tell her. Tell her there is no chance the two of you will ever be together. You can't let her keep mooning over you."

He considered Jamie's advice. "Or," he said after a moment, "I relocate her to a different job. To Logan Oil…or, with her organizational skills, she could do wonders at Project Justice. I'll move her to her own apartment.

Once she's not around me every day, she'll meet other men, develop other interests."

"That is the coward's way out."

"I never said I was brave. Oh, God, how will I function without her?"

"She's made you dependent on her, just by being so damned efficient. Cutting the ties will be good for both of you."

He really didn't like that Jamie could see things so clearly. She was an outsider. How could she know the things she knew?

Manuel entered to clear their dishes, and Daniel realized he'd forgotten completely about why Jamie was here. Time to get back to business.

"Thanks, Manuel. Say, Manuel, is Jillian in love with me?" He expected his question to evoke a laugh and a quick denial. Instead, Manuel bit his lower lip and looked away.

"It's not my place to say, sir. You always say how you don't like gossip." He grabbed some dishes and hightailed it out of the dining room.

Jamie flashed him an I-told-you-so smirk.

"I'll see about transferring her—right after the holiday party. She really does love planning events, and I don't want to ruin that for her. Now, let's get back to work."

"I'm ready."

They worked until almost midnight, mostly arguing over what to ask Christopher, and when. The way they approached this interview reflected their vastly different agendas. Once they agreed that Daniel's friendlier questions should come first, followed by Jamie's more confrontational approach, they made quick progress.

Finally, though, Jamie had to throw in the towel. "I've got an early appearance in court tomorrow," she said. "Much as I've become fascinated by these murders, I still have a job, and I owe it to the good people of Harris County to show up with some semblance of a clear mind."

"Understood. We made good progress. Tomorrow, you'll send the metal-shavings evidence to PrakTech Labs?"

"Yes." She'd been trying to figure out how to accomplish that task without Winston finding out. But he probably wouldn't. He was so busy worrying about his public image, and whether his suits were tailored correctly, that he seldom observed anything that didn't get thrust right in front of his face.

"Then I'll walk you out."

Daniel was nothing if not a gentleman. His courtliness was refreshing, if a bit archaic, in this age of supposed equality between the sexes. She found herself charmed and leery all at the same time, wondering if he was buttering her up, manipulating her for the next big thing he was going to ask of her.

"Tomorrow, I'm going to track down the mystery DNA results from both cases and send them off for comparison. I'll also submit them both to the database again. Neither could be matched years ago. It's a long shot, but the database grows every day."

"Excellent idea. And you are going to make it on Wednesday, right?"

She'd been telling herself all evening that she would have to think about it some more before committing to calling in sick on Wednesday. She'd never missed a day of work in her life, and certainly not for something so subversive.

But she never would have prepared so thoroughly for the meeting if she hadn't intended to be there.

"Yes. How will we get to Wichita Falls? It's a long drive."

"We'll fly, of course."

Of course. When money was no object, you flew wherever you wanted to go. "I'll pay for my own ticket." She didn't want her acceptance of free air travel to come back later and bite her in the butt.

"I'll send you a bill." He smiled crookedly at her, and she got the feeling she'd never see that bill.

Funny, a few days ago she never would have considered flying to a strange town with Daniel and not telling anyone. But the more time she spent with him, the harder it was to view him as a murderer. If her father had gotten to know Daniel, would he still have prosecuted the case?

Daniel held her leather jacket while she slid her arms into it, then opened the massive front door and walked her to her Subaru, which looked even smaller and shabbier than usual in these overblown surroundings. She had to admit, though, the place was beautiful at night—artfully lit. The fountain in the center of the circular driveway gurgled softly.

In any other circumstances, she might have described the surroundings as romantic. Girl, boy, alone…

No. *Keep your mind on business.*

"Jamie, thank you for coming—for everything. I know you're taking a tremendous risk for me, and I appreciate it."

"It's not for you."

"For Christopher, then."

"And for me. If I was wrong about Christopher…well, it shakes my faith in the whole justice system."

"The justice system isn't perfect, because it relies on the feelings and opinions of human beings, who are also not perfect. People make mistakes, perfectly natural mistakes. It's no reason to doubt yourself, or to think you're not good at your job."

Oh, but it did. It would change everything about how she saw her work. She still clung to the possibility that Christopher was responsible for both murders, but she kept that fact to herself.

"Let's touch base tomorrow." She needed to get home and regroup. Spending so much time in this fantasyland Daniel called home was messing with her brain.

She opened her car and climbed in, stuck her key in the ignition, twisted and…nothing. The engine was deader than a doornail.

"Oh, God, not now," she grumbled. Of all times and places to have car trouble. This was going to be awkward.

As she opened her door again, Daniel stopped on his way inside and turned. "Problem?"

"Dead battery." She pulled her phone out of her purse. "I'll just call my auto club. They'll come in a jiffy and give me a charge. If you can just make sure they can get through the front gate, I'll wait here for them."

"You'll do no such thing. It's late, and you need your sleep. I have a guest room waiting, and by morning your car will be ready to drive. I'll have Randall take care of it."

It must be nice to be rich! This time, though, she refrained from ribbing Daniel about his easy life.

She tried one more time. "Really, you don't have to."

"Look." He strode purposefully toward her. "I'm not going to leave you sitting out here in the cold waiting for Triple A, because I won't be able to sleep. And I value my sleep. So come inside, make both of our lives easier."

"All right. Thanks," she added reluctantly. She hated depending on him.

What if he'd tampered with her car? Now he would lure her to his den and turn her into a sex slave.

She grinned, realizing that such a fate didn't appall her as much as it should have. Daniel was definitely getting under her skin.

WHEN JAMIE AWOKE the next morning, she felt like a storybook princess. The room certainly befitted royalty, with a bed made up of pale blue satin linens and carpet she could lose her feet in.

Though she wasn't ready to face the day, she forced herself to slide out from under the feather comforter, put her feet on that fantastic carpet and head into the ridiculous bathroom.

The bathroom featured a huge shower and a whirlpool bath, both big enough for two. Her traitorous mind couldn't help but conjure an image of herself with Daniel, naked, bodies slick with melon-scented soap as they writhed—

Damn. She had to get her mind back on business, and fast. Better make her shower water cold.

But when she turned the shower handle, the faucet didn't come on. Frowning, she tried the faucet to the whirlpool tub. Water gushed out. Oh, well, she'd take a bath instead of a shower. She used some of the vanilla-scented bath crystals sitting on a shelf above the toilet, sprinkling them into the water and creating mountains of bubbles.

The bathtub had its own flat-screen TV mounted on the wall. Perfect, she could multitask. Seeing no remote control, she pushed the power button and was about to sink into the warm, softly scented water when she remembered her washcloth. She stepped out of the water.

That was when the entire TV pulled loose from the wall and crashed into the tub, complete with sparking, smoking wires. Jamie could actually feel the electricity in the air. The bathroom lights flickered and went out.

Her heart thudding, Jamie sank to the floor as her knees would no longer support her.

She'd just come within an inch of electrocution.

Once the immediate reaction of fear and relief wore off, anger took its place. Who would put a TV over a bathtub anyway? That was ridiculous. And if they did, why wouldn't they make sure it was securely mounted?

Gingerly, she turned off the running water, then grabbed her robe, stuffed her arms into the sleeves and cinched it closed with a tug, ready to march downstairs, find Daniel and give him a piece of her mind.

Turned out that wasn't necessary. As she plowed through the bathroom door, Daniel was rushing into her bedroom calling her name. An agitated Tucker was right behind him.

"Jamie. Oh, thank God you're okay. Security reported a huge power surge in this part of the house. I called several times and you didn't answer." To her dismay he put his arms around her and hugged her. And here she was, with only a robe on, one that was gaping at the neck.

Suddenly the anger went out of her and she got all wobbly-kneed again. "Daniel, I almost died. The TV…fell in the bath…"

"What?" He gently disengaged from the hug and led her to the edge of the bed, so she could sit down. She tugged her robe more securely closed.

"I was running a bath. I went to turn on the TV and it fell right into the water."

Daniel marched into the bathroom and cursed colorfully. "How could this have happened? The TV shouldn't have been loose. I have one in my bathroom, too, and a jackhammer couldn't get it free from the tile."

Tucker, calmer now, sat next to Jamie and placed one big paw in her lap, as if checking to make sure she was really okay. Jamie petted him absently.

Daniel exited the bathroom, looking shaken. "Jamie, I'm so sorry. When these TVs were installed, I questioned the safety, but the company assured me they weren't a danger, even if you touched them with wet hands."

"You'd better report this to the company, then. It's a product-liability lawsuit waiting to happen, if it hasn't already."

He smiled at her. "I guess you're okay, if you're thinking like a lawyer."

"I'm okay." She picked up her cell phone,

which she'd left on the nightstand. "I really need to get dressed and get going."

"Breakfast is ready whenever you are. We're eating in the breakfast room off the kitchen today."

"I don't have time. I still have to go home and change clothes." She stood and shooed him out of the room. "What about my car?"

"It's fine. A loose battery cable. Oh, and check the closet. There's probably something appropriate in your size. The dresser drawers will have, um, intimate apparel, too."

Of course they would.

As soon as he left the bedroom, the lights came back on. No way was Jamie getting near that bathtub again. She settled for a quick scrub-down with a wet washcloth, then opened the closet and found several clothing selections, including a delicious gray wool suit in a size 8, designer label, that still had the tags. Everything he'd promised was there—including new undies still in the package.

Amazing. She could skip a trip home and eat breakfast instead. The fact that she wanted to share breakfast with Daniel, almost more than anything right now, surprised her.

THAT WAS THE SECOND TIME Daniel had spontaneously hugged Jamie McNair. He'd never been a hugger.

As he headed down the stairs, Tucker trotting ahead of him, Daniel pondered the meaning of his recent behavior. The first time he'd hugged her, he'd been grateful. This time, he'd been overwhelmed with relief that Jamie was okay.

Having spent so much time with her lately, both physically and in his mind, he felt strangely close to her. But close enough for his arguably inappropriate physical contact?

Jillian met him in the sunny breakfast room, a large, glass-walled enclosure filled with plants. The floor had been crafted from antique Mexican tiles. The room always felt good to him, warm and cheerful.

Jillian looked a crisp, wintry contrast in ice-blue wool and cashmere.

"Daniel, what's going on? A power surge?"

"A TV in the blue guest room fell in the bath. Almost fried Jamie McNair to a crisp. Jillian, I want you to call the company that installed those TVs—"

"Wait. Jamie McNair is…here?" Her face turned icy, like her outfit.

"She had car trouble last night. Seemed easier to just let her stay over."

"Car trouble. And then she almost died from a TV in the bath? And you don't see through her act?"

"Jillian," he said sternly.

"Daniel." She lowered her voice, too. "I know you think this woman is the cat's pajamas, but have you gone crazy? She probably sabotaged her own car, then rigged the TV to fall in the water. Think about it. Those TVs don't just fall off the walls."

"This one did. And you're wrong to insinuate that Jamie is to blame." Although, now that he thought about it, it was odd that he hadn't immediately suspected some nefarious plot on Jamie's part.

She could have easily disconnected a battery cable on her car. But if she did, it would be on his security video. What if she'd instigated some plan to blame him for her near-death, to distract him enough that he would be forced to give up the Christopher Gables case?

"You see it now, don't you?" Jillian said, a note of triumph in her voice.

He refused to give Jillian the point. "Just make the call. I'll deal with Jamie. And let Tucker outside, please."

As Jillian stalked out of the room, dragging a reluctant Tucker by the collar, he picked up the phone and pushed the button that would instantly connect him to his on-site security office. "Doug?"

"Brandon, sir."

"Oh, right. I need you to review some video. I had a guest arrive last night in a blue Subaru. Check the video from the driveway cam and see if she opened the hood of her car when she got out, or if she came straight to the front door. Then check to see if anyone tampered with the car while she was inside," he added as an afterthought.

"Yes, sir."

"Let me know ASAP."

There. He'd done his due diligence, and he would be pleased to prove Jillian wrong.

Why wasn't he more suspicious of Jamie? But the thought that she might have a malicious agenda hadn't crossed his mind until… well, frankly, until Jillian brought up the possibility.

Then, a terrible thought occurred to him.

What if *Jillian* was somehow responsible? Jamie claimed his personal assistant was in love with him. What if she was jealous of Jamie and wanted to get rid of her somehow?

No. In the first place, he couldn't see her putting her hands into a car engine, or doing a complex sabotage of a TV. He knew Jillian. She could be stubborn, and she liked things a certain way, but she wasn't devious, and no way was she homicidal.

This was just a series of unfortunate accidents, nothing more.

CHAPTER SEVEN

A FEW MINUTES LATER, Jamie joined Daniel in the breakfast room. She'd obviously found appropriate clothing in her closet, because she definitely hadn't been wearing the gray suit and hot-pink blouse yesterday. The suit's snug, short skirt hugged her bottom, and Daniel had to force himself not to stare.

"You look nice," he said.

"I ought to. A prosecutor's salary couldn't begin to pay for this suit. But I'm grateful for it. I'll have everything cleaned and returned to you as soon as possible."

He waved away her concerns. "Keep it. It looks good on you."

"I'm not allowed to accept gifts from constituents. I'll have a hard enough time explaining why I'm wearing such an expensive suit."

It definitely was a nice suit. He recognized

the quality, but would her coworkers? He didn't think so.

Cora brought in a cart with their breakfast choices—eggs, toast, bacon and sausage, fresh fruit and yogurt, and his favorite Kona coffee.

Jamie eyed the choices with a troubled expression. "I don't usually eat breakfast."

"Now that is a terrible mistake."

"I've always heard you shouldn't skip it, but then I get to running late…" She chose fruit, yogurt and one slice of whole-wheat toast, dry.

He put an almost identical choice on his plate. "Have you made a decision about tomorrow?"

"Yes. After putting in all this preparation, I want to go to Wichita Falls. I'll take a personal day."

"Good." A wave of pleasure washed over him at the knowledge he would likely spend the whole day with Jamie. But then he remembered exactly where they were going, and his pleasure diminished. When he'd walked out of the Conklin Unit six years ago, he never in a million years imagined he would ever willingly return, even as a visitor.

"I'll pick you up at seven tomorrow morning."

His phone rang, and Jamie nodded. "Go ahead."

"Brandon?"

"Yes, sir. The subject came straight to the front door, and no one got near the car."

Daniel's spirits lifted, as if a lead weight had been lifted from his stomach. "Thank God."

"Pardon?"

"Thank you, Brandon."

THE NEXT MORNING, as Jamie rifled through her closet, looking for something prison chic, her gaze fell upon the gray suit and pink blouse, which she'd neatly folded last night in anticipation of taking them to the cleaner's.

That suit had caused her no end to problems. She'd known it was a high-quality piece of clothing, but she didn't pay attention to which designers were hot or how much their stuff cost. She usually bought her clothes at outlets or department stores on sale. She bought whatever looked professional, fit well, felt comfortable and didn't break her bank account.

Some of her associates, however, took a keen interest in clothing. She hadn't been at the office ten minutes before someone asked her where she'd gotten the Tonio Cucci suit and how she'd been able to afford it.

She hadn't dared mention Daniel. Put on the spot, she'd finally choked out something about borrowing it from a friend. Then, first chance she got, she performed a Google search on Tonio Cucci and discovered her suit retailed for over a thousand dollars.

Daniel bought thousand-dollar ladies' suits to hang randomly in his guest-room closets, on the off chance some female guest would need such a thing?

The depth of his wealth once again boggled her mind. She might go as far as putting a new toothbrush in her guest room, not that she often had sleepover guests. But a selection of designer outfits in various sizes for every occasion…no.

That was crazy.

Last night, she'd started to feel something kind of warm and squiggly inside of her whenever Daniel innocently touched her arm or her shoulder, or when he became passionate about a point he was trying to make, and even when he alluded to the trial that convicted him.

She'd stopped thinking of him as a convicted murderer who'd gotten out on a technicality, and started thinking of him as a man, one with whom she actually had things in common. Someone she could talk to and never run out of conversation. Someone who challenged her on every level.

Yes, all right, she might have even spun a little romantic fantasy about him. That they could somehow become...involved. That once they'd finished with this Christopher Gables thing, they could watch a movie together or...or...

Play polo?

C'mon, Jamie. He was so far out of her league, operating in a completely different universe than she did, and the suit proved it. Once they were done with Chris Gables, they would have nothing else in common.

And, more to the point, once they were done, one of them was likely to be very disappointed in the outcome. If Project Justice freed Gables, she would feel that the system had failed. And if she succeeded in tying Christopher to the Andreas Musto murder, Daniel wasn't just going to be disappointed, he was going to feel a whole range of emotions.

It was almost seven. Jamie quickly made a decision, grabbing a pair of loose black pants with a rather boxy jacket, a high-necked blouse and low heels. Early in her career, she'd once made the mistake of wearing a skirt to a prison. When she'd had to walk past the exercise yard she'd heard so many catcalls, wolf whistles and disgusting suggestions she'd wanted to run away and take a bath.

She caught herself wondering what Daniel would think of her choice, then censored herself. Did she want to be like one of those pathetic women who sent Daniel love letters and stood outside the gate to his home, hoping for a glimpse of him?

She grabbed her briefcase and tape recorder, then at the last minute, a coat, because Wichita Falls was farther north and it might actually be cold there in November.

As she stepped out onto the porch of her town house, a gorgeous black Bentley—not the limo—pulled up in front. How many luxury cars did Daniel own?

As luck would have it, her neighbor Frances was just coming out to get her paper. She stopped and gawked at the Bentley.

Jamie groaned inwardly. Why couldn't he have sent a normal car? Why did everything with Daniel have to be a grand gesture?

"Is that gorgeous vehicle for you?" Frances asked in awe.

"Um, yeah." How did she explain this? "I'm doing some pro bono work for a charitable foundation. The car belongs to the man who runs it." That was all true.

"I'm gonna start volunteering more," Frances said wistfully.

Jamie didn't have time to worry about what Frances thought. The driver, a muscular man in a uniform, had just gotten out and was coming around to open her car door.

"Good morning, Ms. McNair," the man said with a friendly smile. "I'm Randall, your driver."

"I'd be more comfortable riding in the front." She wasn't the type of woman who rode in the backseat like some pampered princess.

"If that's your preference," Randall said, and opened the door for her.

"I can open my own doors, you know."

"Yes, you look very strong to me," Randall said with a perfectly straight face. "But opening your door is my job. You don't want to get me fired, do you?"

She rolled her eyes and got in.

Randall was fast on his feet, and moments later he was behind the wheel and putting the big vehicle in motion, whistling a little tune.

"How long have you worked for Daniel?" she asked.

"Oh, a long time. Since his college days."

"Is he nice to work for?"

"The best, ma'am. His daddy, too. The Logans are good people. Most of the senior staff has been around since before the, um, incident."

"Since before Daniel's arrest."

"Yes. Even though I was no longer needed to drive Daniel around or protect him, Mr. Logan, Sr., kept me on, found other duties for me. He was always sure Daniel was coming home. Everybody felt that way. We all knew he couldn't have done what they said, that it was just a terrible mistake."

"Eventually, you were proven right." About him coming home, at least.

"Yes, ma'am."

"Are we going to Intercontinental or Hobby?" Jamie asked. She hadn't thought to find out which airport they were using.

"Neither. Mr. Logan keeps his plane at a private airport just north of town."

"His… He has a plane?"

"It belongs to Logan Oil, but Daniel can use it anytime he needs."

"Does he, um, fly it himself?"

"He has a pilot's license, and he used to fly the Piper Cub quite a bit. But he doesn't fly jets."

Jets. They were flying a private jet to Wichita Falls.

She couldn't help herself. She felt a little thrill wiggle up her spine at the idea that she, Jamie McNair, the poor girl in the thrift-store clothes who never had enough money to go to the movies with her friends, was in a Bentley, on her way to a private airport, so that she could ride in a private jet with an oil billionaire.

She couldn't even tell anyone!

Once she had resolved Christopher's guilt

or innocence, she might be forced to go public with her Project Justice work. Until then, she didn't want anyone to know, not if she wanted to keep earning a paycheck.

What she was doing wasn't unethical. She'd taken a personal day, and she hadn't specified what she would be doing. But Chubb would flip his wig if he found out she had not severed herself from Daniel and his problematic quest for justice.

The small airport was just outside town, and Randall drove the limo right up to the runway, where a sleek, gleaming jet with the Logan Oil logo on the side sat waiting.

"Let me get the door," Randall said, and for some reason, she let him. She could play the princess for a short while. No one was here but Daniel's own people, and she gathered they were discreet or he wouldn't allow them near.

The hatch was already open, providing steps into the cabin. Randall walked her the few feet toward the stairs, then followed her as she ascended, ducked her head and entered the aircraft.

Good night.

The cabin smelled of new carpeting and

leather, and it looked less like an aircraft and more like the living room of a luxury home. Sofas and chairs upholstered in buttery suede were arranged here and there around tables of various sizes that were antique mahogany, or at least disguised to look that way. The furniture, of course, was bolted to the floor—the only concession to aircraft decor. Expensive-looking curtains hung over the windows.

Finally, Jamie's gaze zeroed in on Daniel, who sat in the center of it all like king of all he surveyed.

He stood to greet her. "Nice day for flying."

Her mouth automatically went dry. She'd thought her borrowed suit was nice, but the one he was wearing…it was just wool and thread and buttons, but somehow it made him look like the billionaire he was.

"So tell me again why we couldn't just take a commercial flight?"

"Because I don't fly common carriers," he said easily, though something in his eyes told her he was uncomfortable with her question. "It's a security issue. Because of my position with Logan Oil, my life is insured for an unusually large sum, and my insurance company has certain mandates about how I travel."

"But statistically a private plane is less safe than a commercial jet," she pointed out.

"Yes, but my plane doesn't allow any nutcases on board. There are lots of people who don't like me. Disgruntled former employees, antioil fanatics and a host of people who don't like the work of Project Justice. Trust me, a private plane is safer—not to mention more comfortable. Have a seat."

"Anywhere?"

"Anywhere you like. No assigned seating on Logan Air."

She chose a love-seat-size sofa at random, still amazed that this living room would soon be airborne.

"Good morning, Randall," Daniel greeted his chauffeur.

"Good morning, sir."

"Randall's coming with us?" Jamie asked.

"In addition to being a fantastic chauffeur, Randall is the best bodyguard in the world. He's former Secret Service on the presidential detail. I figure if the president trusted him, that's good enough for me."

Jamie eyed Randall curiously from the corner of her eye. He looked ordinary enough, harmless even, with his cherubic face and eyes full of humor.

But she knew appearances could be deceiving. She had prosecuted murderers who looked like innocent kids who shouldn't even be shaving yet, much less killing someone.

"I'm sure you'll be interested to hear that I've solved the mystery of the falling TV. The company that originally installed it rushed out when I told them of the accident. Apparently, the cement they used hadn't cured properly, and they took complete responsibility. So rare these days. They'll be sending you a letter of apology and offering you a free TV."

"Really. You're not going to sue them?"

"Are you?" he countered.

She shook her head. "Despite my profession, I'm not the litigious kind. I spend enough hours in the courtroom."

"I hope to never see the inside of another courtroom as long as I live."

The jet was under way quickly, and Cora—the nice woman who had served them breakfast yesterday—brought out coffee and a tray of fresh Danishes.

Since Jamie had skipped breakfast, she availed herself of the refreshments, which she knew would be excellent. But Daniel, for the first time since she'd met him, didn't seem interested in eating.

"Have you had breakfast already?" she asked.

"What? Oh. Um, no, but I can't eat right now."

"You wouldn't let me get away with that. You'd give me a speech about how we need to fuel our bodies for the tough work ahead."

"Yeah, well, that only applies if you don't have a thousand hyperactive gremlins in your stomach."

She immediately felt contrite for ribbing him. "Oh, Daniel, I'm sorry, I didn't mean to tease a man when he's not feeling well. Are you a nervous flier?" No, that couldn't be it. He had a pilot's license.

"Today I'm a nervous flier. Do you know this is the first time I've been out of Houston in three years?"

"Really? I would assume with this jet at

your disposal, along with almost unlimited disposable income, you'd be jetting all over the place. I would."

"You like to travel?"

"I don't know. I've never done much of it. But if I had your resources...yes, I think I'd travel the world."

"I've done my share of that," Daniel said. The distraction of having a conversation seemed to relax him slightly. "But it gets old."

"Traveling? Strange hotels, living out of a suitcase?"

"I don't mind that so much. But it's the spending money that gets old. I've always known that I would work, like my father, doing something I enjoyed, doing something that mattered to people."

"Is that why you opened a restaurant?"

"That was a start. I thought providing high-quality food at a moderate price so everyone could afford it was a noble idea. I had a lot of ideas about things I wanted to accomplish, changes I wanted to make in the world with my money."

"You are making a difference in the world,"

she pointed out. "I'm a prosecutor and I'm supposed to hate you, but realistically, I know you do sometimes correct mistakes that people in my profession make."

"So you don't hate me?"

"Of course not. I'm still not convinced I'm wrong about Christopher Gables, but I'm keeping an open mind."

"That's a lot more than most D.A.s will do. You're okay, Jamie McNair."

She felt ridiculously pleased by his approval. Automatically, she wondered whether he was buttering her up for some kind of manipulation. But then she decided to just take the compliment at face value.

"You're not bad yourself, Daniel Logan."

He flashed her a genuine, warm smile, and she found herself smiling back, almost wanting to giggle with giddiness. She had found a friend in the most unlikely place, and her fantasies about becoming more than friends returned to life.

When they were close to their destination, they did a quick review of how they would approach Christopher, but Jamie could tell

Daniel's heart wasn't in it, and soon they lapsed into silence. The closer they got to Wichita Falls, the more tense Daniel became—drumming his fingers on the table, getting up and walking around in circles like a cooped-up cat that longed to be free.

She wasn't used to seeing him like this. He was normally so composed, so in control.

"Is something wrong?"

"No," he said brusquely.

Well, okay, then.

They finally touched down at some other small airport. Basically it was an airstrip in the middle of a soybean field. As soon as the jet came to a stop, a limousine cruised up to within a few feet.

Randall appeared to open the hatch and lower the stairs. He was quite the multi-talented man. He descended the steps first, apparently checking things out, because it was only when he called up to them that it was safe to deplane that Daniel felt ready to descend.

"Ladies first."

She smiled at his gallantry. When was the

last time anyone had referred to her as a lady? Certainly no one she faced in a courtroom, where she enjoyed a good verbal brawl with the best of 'em.

As she reached the bottom of the steps, Daniel himself offered his hand to steady her for the last, bigger step to the tarmac. The electricity that shot through her with the physical contact was more likely to make her fall than anything. But somehow she managed to alight without any ungainly sprawls onto the blacktop.

It felt good, his protectiveness. No one ever worried about her or treated her like a fragile flower. "Thanks," she said as he continued to hold her hand.

Finally he let it go.

Randall ushered them into a rented limo. Jamie scooted to the far side, clutching her briefcase in front of her like a shield against the sudden, potent attraction for this unlikely man. If she could flush it out of her system somehow, she would. Getting ambushed by it every time she turned around was wearing her down.

"Here goes nothing," she murmured as the car got under way.

Daniel still didn't appear his usual, exuberant self. He stared out the tinted window, looking pale and a little green, and she was starting to get worried about him.

"Sure you're okay?" she asked again.

"I'm fine." His tone indicated he was anything but.

It took almost no time at all for the limo to reach the James T. Conklin Unit. It was in the middle of empty, treeless agricultural lands, surrounded by soybean and sorghum fields. A long driveway led up to a series of nondescript, one-story buildings.

Conklin was one of the newer Texas correctional facilities, a maximum-security unit that had been housing death-row inmates for about fifteen years. The prison's security and reputation were very good, but that didn't make Jamie any more eager to enter the gate.

Randall pulled their car up to a guardhouse, where he exchanged a hushed conversation with a uniformed woman who apparently had been prepared for their arrival. Soon they were ushered into a visitor's lot. A warden was waiting for them, ready to personally escort them into the cell block where Christopher resided.

Visits like this to prisoners whose appeals had run out were rare enough that the prison personnel took special notice, she supposed.

Randall opened her door first, so she was first to greet the warden.

"Good morning." She read the name tag identifying him as Bill Palusky and extended her hand. "I'm Jamie McNair."

"The Houston prosecutor."

"Yes, but today I'm visiting in an unofficial capacity. Thank you for seeing us."

"It's not every day someone like Daniel Logan visits our facility," the jovial Palusky replied, shaking her hand vigorously. But his eyes looked past her, into the limo, where Randall patiently held Daniel's door.

Finally Daniel emerged with a pasted-on, polite smile, and he shook the warden's hand, too, with a barely audible greeting.

"We'll go this way." Palusky indicated a

concrete sidewalk. A row of dead pansies lined the walkway, as if someone had made a futile effort to cheer the place up.

Nothing could cheer this place up.

When she successfully prosecuted a case and sent a man or woman to prison, she usually felt good about getting a dangerous person off the streets. But she tried not to think too hard about exactly where they went, or what happened to them once they arrived.

As they made their way toward the building, Palusky chatted happily about the prison band he'd started up. His whole demeanor seemed such a stark contrast to the place he worked. But she supposed you had to have rose-colored glasses to enjoy working here.

She noticed that Daniel and Randall lagged behind her and Palusky, engaged in a hushed conversation. The warden stopped, looking back uneasily.

"I'm sorry, Mr. Logan, but your group needs to stay together."

Daniel skidded to a stop, and when he looked up, Jamie realized he truly was ill. Every bit of color had drained from his face.

"Daniel!" She strode back to his side in two seconds. "What's wrong?"

"Give me a minute…" He closed his eyes, and his Adam's apple bobbed up and down as he swallowed several times.

Jamie cast a questioning look at Randall, but the chauffeur's attention was firmly on his employer. "You okay, Daniel?"

Daniel shook his head slightly and opened his eyes. "I'm sorry, Jamie."

CHAPTER EIGHT

GOD, JAMIE THOUGHT, she'd been so stupid. This was the same prison Daniel had been sent to. Of course he would feel sick at the thought of returning to the place where he'd spent six no-doubt miserable years of his life, believing he was going to die.

"It's...it's the smell." Daniel shook his head again, as if trying to rid himself of something.

"You don't have to explain," she said, all businesslike. "We'll reschedule—"

"No, Jamie. I'm not going to make Christopher wait because I'm feeling...squeamish. Who knows how much time he has left. I can do this."

Randall, who'd surreptitiously grabbed Daniel's wrist to check his pulse, looked grave. "Not a good idea, boss. Your heart is beating so fast you're about to stroke out."

"I'll conduct the interview by myself,"

Jamie said decisively. "We went over our questions so many times, I know the information you're seeking. I'll be fine. I've done lots of prison interviews."

Never mind that they'd spent hours talking about the dynamic of having both of them there, playing off each other. She wouldn't be responsible for Daniel having a stroke.

"Go," she said to Randall. "I've got this covered."

Daniel cursed softly, but he didn't fight Randall when the other man urged him to retreat.

"Just a minute, you can't—" Palusky, no longer quite as jovial, pulled a radio from his pocket and spoke briefly into it. Moments later a guard appeared. "See Mr. Logan to his car," Palusky instructed, pointing toward the rapidly receding figures of Daniel and Randall. "Make sure he's okay."

Palusky looked dubiously at Jamie. "That didn't go as planned."

"It's not what Daniel planned, either, I assure you," she said. "He hasn't been feeling well all day. But I'd still like to see Mr. Gables."

The warden nodded. "I'll take you."

She was escorted to a rather strange room. It was about the size of a large walk-in closet with a partition running right down the center. On her side, two surprisingly attractive upholstered chairs and an oak table. She could see the other half of the room through a large, thick glass window. Its furnishings were much more basic, industrial-looking and probably indestructible. A metal grate just under the window allowed visitors and inmates to hear each other.

She waited about five minutes; finally a noise on the other side alerted her to Christopher's presence. She stood, ready with her polite greeting, but she didn't get the chance to use it.

"What the hell are you doing here?"

"Good morning, Mr. Gables. I'm Jamie McNair—"

"I know who you are!"

"I'm not here as a prosecutor," she said quickly. "I'm consulting with Project Justice on your—"

"Oh, that's just rich! *You're* working on my case, the bitch that screwed me over and sent me to this hellhole?"

Preoccupied as she'd been with worries

about Daniel, Jamie hadn't thought through how Christopher Gables would react to seeing her, and her alone, waiting on the other side of the glass partition.

"Please, Mr. Gables, if you'll hear me out—"

"Where's Daniel Logan? I don't want to talk to you. He's supposed to be here."

Gables looked awful. During the trial, he'd had glistening blond hair and a clean-shaven, childish face. Now his hair was buzzed short, his cheeks lean, his body thin, and he sported a scraggly goatee.

"Unfortunately Mr. Logan has been detained," Jamie said. "Can we just start over here?"

"Like hell. I'm not talking to you. You're the devil. The devil's concubine." He hit the glass with his fist, and Jamie jumped back, her heart pumping wildly. "If you're consorting with my last hope, then I best get my affairs in order 'cause I'm about to meet my maker."

"Listen to me, Christopher. Things have changed. We have new evidence, and I'm no longer convinced of your guilt." At least not one hundred percent. "Think what it could mean, having your former prosecutor pulling for your innocence." Not that she was there yet. Looking at the man now, it was quite easy to believe he could kill. His eyes had a slightly crazed look, and he'd lost a tooth.

"Forget it. I'm not talking to you, with your tricky questions and the way you twist words and make people believe stuff that you just made up out of thin air. You don't fool me. You're here to make sure I get the needle, aren't you?"

He turned his back on her and pushed a buzzer, and moments later a guard opened the door. Christopher, suddenly meek, offered up his wrists to be cuffed.

"Christopher, please wait. Please talk to me."

He ignored her. The guard looked at her, shrugged and escorted Christopher out of the room.

Suddenly Jamie wanted out of this place. It reeked of hopelessness. And she was behind a locked door. What if they didn't let her out?

For one crazy moment, she understood Daniel's fear. This moment, she was completely under the prison guards' power. No one but Daniel and his staff even knew she was here. What if she just disappeared, never came out?

She pushed the buzzer. Pushed it multiple times as an irrational panic threatened to overcome her.

Then the door opened, and Palusky was waiting for her. "What happened?"

She took a deep breath to calm herself. "He won't talk to me. Not without Daniel."

"I'm sorry you came all this way for nothing. Perhaps you can reschedule when Mr. Logan is, um, feeling better."

"Sure." But Jamie didn't see that happening. Daniel would have to turn this case over to one of his people, someone who could meet Gables face-to-face.

Damn, she needed answers from Gables. But he didn't have to talk to anyone if he didn't want to. They had no way to pressure him, no way to entice him since he'd obviously lost hope that anyone could save him.

Palusky escorted her to the parking lot, but the limousine was nowhere to be seen. Hmm. Daniel wouldn't leave her stranded here. She realized her cell phone was turned off—she hadn't wanted any interruptions during the interview. When she switched it on, she had a text from Daniel, short and sweet:

limo returning 4U shortly

"The car is on its way," she told Palusky. "You don't have to wait here with me."

Palusky shook his head. "Forgive me for saying so, but this entire episode has been odd. I think I'd like to wait with you."

He probably wanted to personally see her off the property and make sure they weren't trying to smuggle weapons or aid in an escape. Stranger things had happened, so she couldn't blame him.

An awkward fifteen minutes later, the limo finally reappeared. She was relieved to see Randall hop out from behind the wheel.

"I'm sorry to have kept you waiting, Ms. McNair. Are you ready to go?" He opened the back door for her.

She nodded and climbed into the car's luxurious interior. She didn't expect to see Daniel, so she wasn't surprised to find herself alone.

As soon as Randall climbed behind the

wheel, Jamie lowered the glass partition. "Is Daniel okay?"

"He's waiting for you at the airport."

"You didn't answer my question."

"'Okay' is a term that calls for speculation."

So, in other words, no, he wasn't okay. "I'm sorry I fell into lawyer mode there for a minute."

"It's all right. Sometimes Daniel's behavior can try the most patient of souls."

She wouldn't call it trying. Scary, more like it.

"Did the interview go okay?" Randall asked. "It didn't last very long."

"'Okay' is a term that calls for speculation." Although she trusted Randall because Daniel did, she didn't think it appropriate to report to anyone but Daniel himself about this latest catastrophe.

As soon as the car pulled up close to the plane, she didn't wait for Randall to open her door. She got out, hooked her briefcase over her shoulder and climbed the stairs toward the open hatch.

Daniel was pacing the cabin as she stepped inside. When he caught sight of her he stopped, looked at his watch, then looked back at her.

"What the hell happened? You're not supposed to be back yet."

As if this was her fault? She got in his face, surprised at the anger that welled up inside her. "What happened, Daniel, is that Christopher Gables refused to talk to me. He was expecting you. He got me—the woman who put him behind bars."

"Did you explain—"

"I tried. He was not in any mood to listen." She wrestled with the briefcase until she was free of it and tossed it onto one of the recliners.

"So we have nothing?"

"We have nothing." She slumped onto the sofa, dejected. "I've risked my job, my whole career, to get cursed at and threatened by a guy who really doesn't seem to want anybody's help."

Daniel shook his head. "I was afraid of that."

She looked at him suspiciously. "What do you mean?"

"From what the warden told me, Christopher wasn't too keen about this meeting.

Said he'd been screwed over by the system so many times, had his hopes raised only to have them dashed, that he didn't believe anyone could help him."

"And you didn't see fit to warn me?"

Daniel rubbed his temples as if he had a headache. "I thought I'd be able to relate to him. I thought…"

"You thought he'd be so impressed with the big-shot billionaire oilman that you could weasel past his hostility."

"Yeah, something like that." He looked at her squarely. "I've hosed this up, haven't I?"

"I'd wager we won't get another chance to talk to Christopher Gables. Even that smiley-faced warden was unhappy with us by the time I left."

"It takes a lot of time and effort to move around a prisoner who's in isolation."

"Isolation?"

"Death-row inmates are always isolated from the other prisoners. Surely you knew that."

"I guess I don't think about it much."

"I do."

Damn. She'd been so focused on how

today's events had inconvenienced and frustrated her that she'd forgotten how Daniel must feel. She wasn't exactly a ten on the warm-fuzzy scale, but today she'd reached a new level of heartlessness.

Randall chose that moment to come through the hatch and close it behind him. "Back home?"

Daniel nodded. "Nothing else we can do here, that's for sure."

Perhaps sensing his boss's black mood, Randall disappeared into the cockpit, where the company might be better.

Daniel walked over to a fold-out, self-service bar and selected a highball glass. "Drink? I have some thirty-year-old single-malt McClelland's on board."

"The kind that costs, like, $10,000 a bottle?"

He shrugged. "I just know it tastes good."

Jamie glanced at her watch. It wasn't even noon. What the hell. She didn't like Scotch, but she'd never tried the best. "Might as well drown our sorrows."

Daniel made a production out of putting ice in the glasses with a pair of fancy silver tongs, then measuring out exactly one dram and adding water.

He'd taken off his jacket and tie, opened his shirt and rolled up his sleeves, though the cabin felt quite cool to Jamie. As she watched him work, some of her irritation washed away. He was such a gorgeous man. Observing him was like looking at a magnificent painting in a museum. Except this painting walked and talked—and hurt.

She could see the pain in his every gesture now. Maybe it was always there, and she'd missed it before. Maybe he was only now dropping his guard enough to show her how he felt.

All she knew for sure was that she shouldn't have bitten his head off like that.

He took an experimental sip of his drink, nodded with satisfaction and brought the other drink to her.

"Mr. Logan, we're cleared for takeoff," the pilot's voice said from the overhead speaker. A seat-belt sign simultaneously lit up.

Daniel sat next to her, rather than across the way. She set her drink in the armrest cup holder and fastened her seat belt. Once they were both strapped in, Daniel held his glass aloft. She grabbed hers and joined him in a toast.

"I can't even think of anything to make a toast to," he said glumly. "I might have just cost a man his life."

Jamie drew back her glass before it came into contact with his. "No. It's not your fault."

"Whose fault do you suggest it is?"

"In the first place, this was just one step in the process. We've had a setback, but it's not insurmountable. I'm not sure Gables would have told us anything useful, anyway."

"Part of my reason for wanting you here was so you could gauge his sincerity. Now you think even less of him than you did before."

"I'm not abandoning the case, Daniel."

"Really?" He seemed genuinely surprised. "I wouldn't blame you if you did."

"Nothing that happened here erased the questions I have about these two crimes."

"Then maybe I have something to drink to after all." He took another sip of his Scotch, and she felt obligated to taste the expensive liquor herself, given that her glass probably held at least $500 worth of the stuff.

Oh, God. It was horrible. She only barely managed not to spit her mouthful out onto the plush carpet. It burned all the way down her throat, and she wasn't able to stifle a cough.

"Not good?"

"I've heard it's an acquired taste, but I don't think I'm sufficiently motivated to cultivate a Scotch-friendly palate." She set the glass aside.

"Don't worry, I'll drink it."

"Daniel…what happened back at the prison?"

"Aside from me turning into a gibbering idiot and nearly tossing my cookies in a parking lot? Nothing much."

"I *know* what happened. I mean, I was there, I saw. Was it a flashback? Do you have post-traumatic stress disorder?"

"Aren't you the curious one all of a sudden."

"I'm not asking out of morbid curiosity. I need to know. Remember that first day we met? You said you made it a priority to learn as much as possible about the people you worked with. Well, that goes for me, too. If we're going to continue to work together, I need to know what's going on. I don't want to put you in another situation—"

"Jamie. We won't be working together. It should be obvious to you that I'm not capable of handling a case of this caliber on my own. I'll reassign it to Ford or Raleigh. I should have done it in the first place. But I thought…"

"You thought because of all you and Gables had in common, you'd be the most effective investigator."

"Exactly. But clearly I was wrong. I'm fine in a research or advisory capacity—which I can do from the safety of my home. But I'm not fit to… I'm broken, Jamie."

She longed to tell him that no, there was nothing wrong with him. Every person you passed in the street had problems, phobias, dark pasts, bad dreams, whatever. But she couldn't deny that Daniel's problems were a little darker than average.

Jamie had no brave words of wisdom, no advice, no comforting sentiments. The one thing she could possibly offer was compassion, an emotion she wasn't exactly famous for.

But she did feel something for Daniel. She'd

seen the clever, funny persona he showed to the world, she'd seen the intense, intelligent side of him, the part of him that cared deeply. And now she'd seen his pain.

Something inside of her awakened and responded to all of him. She laid a hand on his bare arm just as the jet began its acceleration down the runway. His muscles tensed beneath her hand, as if he didn't want her comfort or her lame attempt at understanding him.

But he didn't pull away.

"I know I can't come close to imagining how bad it was for you. I wish I could help."

"The best therapists money could buy all took a crack at me." His voice held a touch of bitter humor. "What could you do that they couldn't?"

I could be with you. I could love you.

The thought came out of left field. Love him?

Oh, no. Her mother didn't teach her much worth remembering, but one lesson Jamie had learned well was that you never fell in love with a man who needed fixing. You never fell in love with "a project." You never fell in love with a man's potential or assumed that your love could heal them.

Every man her mother was with—and there were a lot—needed fixing. They were either alcoholics or drug users, unemployed, uneducated or undermotivated, had physical and mental disabilities or were just plain lazy or crazy.

She was not falling into that trap. Much as she was drawn to Daniel, as crazy hot as their chemistry appeared to be, she was most certainly not going down that road.

Thank God she hadn't said anything stupid out loud.

There was one thing she could do for him, and she was willing. "You're right, I can't undo the damage of six years on death row. But that doesn't mean I give up on you. I don't want you to turn over this case to an associate. I don't want to start over with someone new. We can move forward, with or without Gables's cooperation."

"You really want that?"

"I wouldn't say it just to make you feel better. I'm not that nice."

He smiled at her, a real smile that actually reached his eyes. "I think you're very nice."

Her hand was still on his arm, and he placed his own over it, then traced his fingers up her arm toward her shoulder. Even through the wool of her suit jacket she felt the electricity of his touch clear down to the bone.

Her heart was the clapper inside the large bell of her rib cage, thunking back and forth until she was positively dizzy. And yet she couldn't move, couldn't pull away. His eyes mesmerized her, his touch rooted her to the spot, a frozen statue waiting for something to bring her to life.

That something was a kiss.

Most everything Daniel Logan did was calculated down to the last raise of his eyebrows. But this...this was so spontaneous and real, so *not* calculated, that she fell right in line, tilting her head, parting her lips slightly as she tried to suck in a bit more oxygen.

The first contact produced an explosion of sensation. It was a mere brush of his lips on hers, but suddenly her whole body felt alive in a way that was entirely new to her. She could feel every ridge of those oh-so-notorious fingerprints against her skin, feel the course of blood through the veins and arteries of his fingertips.

They shared a breath, and for one insane moment she wondered if she was about to become the newest member of the mile-high club.

She wanted him. Despite everything she'd just told herself about staying away from "projects," despite the precarious nature of their professional association, despite that she was a prosecutor and he was a bleeding-heart do-gooder, she wanted him.

For a moment it seemed as if he might pull away. She sensed a split second of hesitation, a thread of reasoned thought wrapped in the craziness.

Instead, he kissed her again, less gently this time. His mouth was hot and insistent on hers now, demanding response, demanding surrender.

She wanted to fight the longing that seeped into her every pore, but it was so much easier to give in to feelings, to live in the moment, drowning in sensation and desire and the intimate connection with this dynamic and complex man.

She leaned her head back against the

headrest as he took full command of the kiss. He unfastened her seat belt so he could move her closer, then pulled the clip out of her hair so he could dig his fingers into her scalp.

He caressed her ears with his thumbs, sending violent shivers all the way down to her toes.

His tongue darted into her mouth, and Jamie sensed the taste of the fine Scotch, which had somehow transmuted to a pleasant flavor when mingled with Daniel's unique essence. His soap or aftershave—something that smelled like a fresh spring morning after a rain—teased her nose.

Jamie was dimly aware of a noise toward the front of the plane.

"Whoa. Excuse me."

Daniel pulled away abruptly, and Jamie felt as if she'd just come to the surface of a very deep and dark pool. Gasping for breath, she glanced over her shoulder just in time to see Cora retreating into the galley.

She huffed out a nervous laugh as Daniel stared first at the door where Cora had disappeared, then at her, his expression impossible to read. Irritation? Relief? Embarrassment?

Looking for something to do with her

suddenly empty hands, she went to work repairing the damage to her hair, finding the discarded clip and finger-combing the unruly strands. "Why do I suddenly feel like a teenager who got caught necking in the backseat of a car?"

"Possibly because we've just done something idiotic, in front of a witness?" Daniel grabbed his forgotten drink and drained it.

Idiotic? How about *earth-moving? Life-altering?* She'd never known any simple kiss to completely shatter her like that one did, but apparently it meant little to Daniel.

Women probably threw themselves at him all the time. Had she thrown herself at him? No, but she certainly hadn't played hard to get.

The way she felt now—it was untenable. She wouldn't be able to endure his company without thinking about what happened just now.

"Maybe," she said carefully, "it *would* be better if I dealt with one of your associates from now on."

CHAPTER NINE

DANIEL STOOD AND RESUMED his pacing. "Jamie, I apologize. That was totally out of line."

How could he have let go of his control like that? A man's life was at stake, and he *knew* a personal involvement with the prosecutor could jeopardize the fragile common ground they'd found.

"It's all right, Daniel. I'm to blame as much as you." She'd dug a small zippered bag from her briefcase and was busy repairing the damage he'd done to her lipstick. She wouldn't look at him.

He probably had her makeup all over his face, too. He grabbed a paper napkin from the bar and wiped his face. It came back streaked with the rusty-pink shade she wore. It smelled slightly of her teasing scent, too. He folded it carefully and tucked it into his shirt pocket.

"Maybe you're right. Raleigh is very good

at negotiating her way around prisons. She can probably smooth over what happened today and arrange another meeting."

Failure didn't sit well with him. In his youth, everything he'd touched had turned golden. Grades and sports came easily. Any woman he wanted was his for the asking. With the exception of his first restaurant, his businesses thrived.

Even after Andreas's murder, all through incarceration and trial, the guilty verdict and the failed appeals, he'd somehow known he would triumph.

True, he wasn't the same man he'd been before prison. But he hadn't lost his drive, and when he was passionate about something, he applied himself and made it happen.

Though his father had died when Project Justice was in its infancy, Daniel had single-handedly molded it into the vision they'd shared, as a tribute to the man who had never lost faith in him. He was accustomed to winning, even if he had lost the feeling of joy he used to have.

This business of failure didn't feel good.

"I'll still be involved," he said. Because if he wasn't involved, how else was he going to make sure the person who framed him paid the price for his crime? "But day to day, you'll be dealing with Raleigh. I'll bring her up to speed as quickly as possible."

"Whatever you think is best." She didn't sound any happier than he felt about it.

Daniel made his way forward and tapped on the galley door. Cora opened it. "Yes?"

"Coast is clear."

Cora smiled nervously and followed him into the main cabin. "I was just going to ask if you folks wanted a snack."

"I'm not really very hungry, thank you, Cora. Jamie?"

"I'm starving," she admitted.

Hmm. Usually he had to force-feed her.

Cora disappeared once again into the galley, which Daniel knew was fully equipped to facilitate the preparation of gourmet meals for up to ten people.

But Cora, who was fully capable of said gourmet meal, instead produced two fancy cloth bags that bore the logo of AirKitchens, handing one to each of them.

Daniel gave Cora a questioning look. "Airline food?"

"Jillian said for such a short flight, I shouldn't

go to the bother of cooking. Did I do the wrong thing?"

"No, this is fine, Cora," he said soothingly.

Jillian again. If she didn't curb this jealous streak of hers, she was going to end up unemployed, never mind her long history with the family.

"Are you set for beverages?" Cora asked.

"Yes. Thanks again."

She quietly retreated.

Daniel sat across from Jamie, pulled out a tray table and examined the contents of the bag. Some kind of sandwich, bag of chips, a brownie and apple juice.

Jamie dumped out her bag and went straight for the brownie. She ate it as if she hadn't had chocolate in years. Bolting down a brownie was so unlike her usual behavior that he had to laugh.

"You might think a lot of Chef Claude's tiramisu," she said between bites, "but this brownie is the best thing I've ever eaten."

Maybe it was the aftereffect of being inside the prison walls. Everyone tended to take freedom for granted until they were forced to consider what the lack of it meant.

Or maybe she was substituting chocolate for sex.

He pulled at the cellophane around the brownie and stuffed some of the dessert into his mouth. Not bad for airplane food. But certainly no substitute for having Jamie naked and writhing beneath him.

God, he would miss her.

JAMIE MANAGED TO HOLD HERSELF together throughout the rest of the short flight. She kept herself busy gobbling down every single bite of the prefab lunch, despite the fact she'd eaten a Danish only a short time earlier. Her sudden ravenous appetite was as baffling as it was impossible to ignore.

She wondered what prisoners on death row got to eat. Like hospital food, she imagined, only worse. Christopher would eat alone, she imagined, just as he did everything else.

After they landed, Jamie was surprised to find two cars waiting to shuttle them off to their separate destinations. Her heart sank; she'd been counting on those last few minutes, riding in the limo together, to mentally say her goodbyes to Daniel.

Working on this case with him had stimulated her in every way—physically, intellectually, emotionally. She hadn't realized what she'd been missing, slaving away in her little cubicle at the D.A.'s office, methodically clearing cases, pleading them out when she could, going to trial when she had to.

Most of them were cut-and-paste cases. An intriguing murder, like ones Daniel and Christopher had been charged with, came along very rarely in a prosecutor's life.

She didn't want Daniel to hand the case over to someone else. But she also didn't want to subject him to any more of the emotional trauma he'd gone through today.

At some point, Daniel might actually be required to testify before a judge, depending on what they found and how they found it—especially if she managed to conclusively tie the two cases together.

"I've enjoyed getting to know you, Jamie," Daniel said. "We'll talk again soon. Meanwhile, expect to hear from Raleigh."

"All right. I've enjoyed getting to know you, too." At least those parts of him he was willing to show her. He kept a lot of himself hidden away.

He took her hand and clasped it between his. "Take care, okay?"

"Yeah. You, too." Her voice cracked, giving her away.

"This way, Ms. McNair." Randall led her toward the Bentley. "Celeste will drive you home."

"Celeste? Who is she?"

"One of Daniel's most trusted employees. Don't let appearances fool you. You'll be safe with her."

What was that supposed to mean?

Though Randall tried to open the Bentley's back door, Jamie climbed into the passenger seat. "I've had enough *Lifestyles of the Rich and Famous* today, so don't argue with me."

"Wouldn't dream of it."

He made sure she was safely inside and closed her door. Only then did she look over at her new driver.

Good night. The woman was well into her seventies, judging from all the creases in her face and the wild, gray hair, which she'd tried and failed to tame with a series of little-girl barrettes. She wore a blousy top splashed with loud red poinsettias and green leggings tucked into black boots that reached above her knees.

"Hello, dear. I'm Celeste Boggs, office manager and head of security at Project Justice." With that, one of those amazing boots hit the gas, and the Bentley shot forward like a rocket. "Woo-hoo, always wanted to drive me one of these."

Jamie grabbed on to the door handle. "It sounds like you have a lot of responsibility at Project Justice."

"The place would fall apart without me."

"I'm sorry to have taken you away from your normal job, then."

"It's no problem. In fact, I volunteered. I wanted to see firsthand the woman who got Daniel off his estate. Twice in a week's time."

Jamie wasn't sure if Celeste approved or not. She drove 70 mph down the farm-to-market road that led from the airport to the freeway and whooped every time the Bentley hit a bump and nearly became airborne.

"Tell the truth now," Celeste said. "Are you and Daniel doin' the horizontal mambo?"

"What? No! In fact, I probably won't be seeing him again."

"Really." Celeste sounded as if she didn't believe Jamie.

"He's handing over our project to another person, so we won't be working together anymore. It wasn't working out."

"So you're dropping him like a hot rock?"

Jamie was startled by Celeste's hostility. "I'm not 'dropping' him. It was his decision to pull back." Well, a mutual decision, anyway.

"So you're not working together anymore. Does that mean you can't see him anymore?"

"Celeste, we aren't personally involved."

"Huh, you might not think you are. But these last couple of weeks, Daniel's been a completely different man."

"Different...how?" she felt compelled to ask.

"Alive. Oh, technically he was alive before. Walking, talking, breathing, letting Skeletor move him around like a piece on a chessboard."

"Skeletor?"

"Jillian, I mean. Girl could use some meat on her bones, that's all," Celeste muttered.

"But he was more like a walking corpse. Just going through the motions of living.

"But since he met you—he's a different man. He *cares* about stuff now. He smiles, he's excited, he's like the old Daniel. You walk out of his life, he'll go back to being corpse man again."

Jamie was flabbergasted. Surely Celeste was exaggerating. How much did she even see of Daniel?

"I think it's working on the case that has, er, exhilarated him," Jamie said carefully. "He'll still be involved, just not running the show."

"I beg to disagree. It's you. He needs a real woman in his life. Why not you?"

Jamie screamed as Celeste swerved to avoid a rabbit that dashed across the road. "Would you like to hear the reasons alphabetically or in order of importance?"

"A lot of women would kill to be in your position."

"That's not a good enough reason to want a relationship." She softened when she recognized the look of worry and concern on Celeste's face. "Look, it's not that I don't think Daniel is a good man. But for many reasons,

pursuing a relationship with him would be…
unwise. What if it didn't work out?"

"That's the risk in any relationship, isn't
it?" Celeste sounded quite sane all of a
sudden.

"But the fallout…with Daniel…" She
stopped short of pointing out that Celeste's
boss had issues. And she didn't want to
become one of them.

"Do you consider him a friend?" Celeste
asked.

"Yes." She'd realized that just today.

"If you don't want to date him, he could use
a friend. He doesn't have many, you know.
It's hard for someone in his position to make
friends. Everybody wants something from
him. Or they're afraid of offending him."

"He has you. And Randall, and Cora and
Claude, and all the people at Project Justice.
He holds you all in such high esteem."

"I do count Daniel as a friend. But I'm
also his employee. We're not equals. You see
yourself as his equal, and that's rare."

She didn't want to come out and tell
Celeste that after such a mind-bending kiss,
she didn't think she could be "just friends"
with Daniel.

"It's not my decision to make. If Daniel wants any further dealings with me, he has my phone number."

"And he'll be too proud to dial it."

DANIEL HAD NEVER APPRECIATED his home as much as he did that day, as Randall drove him through the wrought-iron gate into the safety of his estate.

"You look awful," Jillian said bluntly as he entered through the garage door. "I know you can't reveal too much about an open case, but did it go well?"

Surely she'd been able to tell by his demeanor that things hadn't gone well. "No, I'm afraid it was a spectacular failure."

"I'm sorry to hear that."

"No, you're not."

She looked at him sharply. "Excuse me? Of course I'm sorry. Why would I want you to fail?"

"Maybe so you can prove you were right and I was wrong? That I shouldn't have left the estate, especially without you, because I wasn't ready."

He yanked off his jacket and handed it to her out of habit.

"Are you going to tell me what happened?"

"I had a....a panic attack." Might as well call a spade a spade. "I never saw my client because I couldn't walk into the prison."

"Oh, Daniel. I'm sorry."

"I've put the whole case in jeopardy."

"I'm sure you're exaggerating. Have you had lunch? Claude has been working on something *très mystérieuse* this morning, and it smells divine."

"I had a sandwich on the plane." He couldn't remember much about the lunch. His mind was too full of kissing Jamie.

"Then why don't I schedule a massage this afternoon."

It was tempting to let Jillian take over. But Jillian's overfunctioning had been his crutch for too long. If today had taught him one lesson, it was that he needed to take back control of his life.

"I have work to do."

"Work. That reminds me—someone called from Project Justice. Lab results or something—she said it was important."

"*Someone* called? You didn't happen to catch a name?" What was wrong with

Jillian? Normally she could quote verbatim from memory any message she'd taken for him.

"I wrote it down. It's on your desk."

It could be a call from one of his people, just giving him a progress report on another case. Jamie had sent everything to PrakTech Labs. They would report any results directly to her. But Beth McClelland, head of the Project Justice lab, had a mole at PrakTech who would report directly to her.

Why hadn't Jillian immediately forwarded the information to his phone? He could have returned the call during the drive. Unless she was trying to shield him from unhappy news?

Now that he knew, or at least suspected, that Jillian had feelings for him, he questioned her motives in everything. All the more reason to transfer her away from the estate.

As Daniel passed through the kitchen, he caught the scent of Claude's creations—onion and garlic and delicate spices he couldn't even identify floated lightly in the air. Claude was in full regalia today, with apron and tall hat, a dishcloth draped over each shoulder.

"What are you up to?" Daniel asked.

"Trying new recipes for the Christmas party. Jillian says we are having it here. My reputation is at stake. I have to wow your guests."

Daniel didn't want to burst Claude's bubble, but his Project Justice parties were only a bunch of ex-cops and lawyers. He could serve most of them day-old burritos and Mountain Dew and they'd be happy.

"I'm sure whatever you serve, everyone will be impressed," Daniel said, because Claude's ego needed stroking on a regular basis. When they'd worked together at their restaurant, Le Bistro, nothing made him happier than when a diner made the special effort to personally compliment him on the dishes he prepared. When they'd gotten a good write-up in *Food* magazine, he'd been nearly apoplectic with joy.

It had to be a little bit different working in a private home. Though Claude was compensated well, this was a much more private life. Maybe Daniel could ask Griffin Benedict, his newest agent and a former journalist, to write up a story about the office party—with special emphasis on the food—and submit it to the local society rag. The magazine had asked numerous times to do a feature story on him or his home—anything—and he'd always declined.

Both Claude and Jillian would get a kick out of that.

"Smells great. Carry on."

Claude, his hands busy separating thin sheets of phyllo dough, nodded, and Daniel headed straight down to his office, Jillian following him with a rundown of his afternoon schedule.

She had, indeed, left a sticky note on his desk. Very old-school of her. He had a complex schedule software program that she normally used to coordinate phone calls and messages.

He shook his head.

"Jillian," Daniel said, "call Raleigh and make an appointment with her. Set aside at least an hour. Tell her I'm handing over the Christopher Gables case to her."

"You are? Really? Why?"

"Just do it, okay?" She knew why. He'd just told her a few minutes ago. His reaction to being near a prison had jeopardized the case, and Jillian knew as well as anyone how important these wrongly imprisoned men and women were to him.

Did she want him to go over it again? So she could comfort him?

The message was indeed from Beth.

He donned his Bluetooth earpiece, then clicked the link on his computer that would put in a call directly to the lab.

"Beth. What's up?"

"We've got a match."

His blood pounded inside his ears. "Between the two crime scenes? Andreas Musto and Frank Sissom?" he clarified, just to be sure.

"Yes. An unidentified body-fluid sample found on Musto's shirt matched an unidentified saliva sample found on Sissom's apron."

Daniel came out of his chair. "But no matches in the database?"

"Those results aren't in yet."

"Okay. Thanks, Beth."

Still, this was huge. The two cases were definitely connected.

Christopher Gables had been a twenty-one-year-old college senior at Kansas State University at the time of Andreas's murder. He had no conceivable connection to that case.

Finally, they had a viable suspect for both murders. As yet unidentified, but that would come.

If there was a match, Daniel would finally have the name of the man who had brutally murdered his friend and framed Daniel. They could present their evidence to the Harris County sheriff's department and pressure them to reopen the case.

But Daniel had much swifter justice in mind.

The next thing he did, as soon as he disconnected from talking with Beth, was to dial Jamie's number.

Of all the people in the world, she was the one he wanted to share the news with.

"Daniel?"

"Jamie. Could you come over right away?"

"I just got home."

"This is important. I have news. I can call Celeste, have her turn around—"

"Good God, no, that woman is a menace to drivers everywhere. I can take my own car."

He didn't understand the reason for the

sharpness he heard in her voice, but just now he didn't care. He would straighten everything out when she got here.

He hadn't ruined the case after all. They now had a strong piece of physical evidence that would reopen both cases.

He picked up the framed portrait of his parents, the only nonfunctional object he allowed on his desk. "Dad, we're on our way. I'm going to find the animal who derailed my life. And I'm going to personally see that justice is done this time."

His office door opened a crack and Jillian poked her head in. "Oh. I thought you were on the phone."

Daniel set the picture down. "What is it?"

"Raleigh is in court, and she'll be there all day. Soonest she can get you in is probably tomorrow."

"That's okay, never mind." He wasn't going to let go of this case, not now. Not when victory was so close. If he handed it over to Raleigh, he would have no more reason to see Jamie.

And he wanted reasons—lots of reasons—to see her.

He might have miscalculated, summoning her as if she had no choice in the matter. Old habits were hard to break. But he had to stop thinking of Jamie as someone he could manipulate or use for his own purposes.

"Jamie is on her way over," he told Jillian. "Send her into the library when she arrives."

"You just spent all morning with her."

"Yeah, so...?"

"Doesn't she have a job?"

"She has the day off. Jillian, I know you don't like her, but I don't appreciate your questioning me every time I schedule an appointment with her. She is a crucial part of the puzzle with the case I'm working on."

"Mmm. Sorry."

"How are the plans for the holiday party coming along?" he asked, hoping to distract her from her negative thoughts.

She smiled. "Fabulous. The decorations are arriving today, everything except the ice sculptures. By Friday, this place is going to look like a winter wonderland. We're going to have a snow machine and sleigh rides."

Ice sculptures? Sleigh rides? Oh, God help him. Well, maybe his people would like the novelty. They all worked so hard. One evening of fantasy might be appreciated.

By the time Jamie arrived, Daniel was waiting in the library. Anxious to be out of the suit and tie—which still, in his mind, smelled like prison—he'd changed into a pair of worn jeans and a sweater. He'd built a fire—the temperature outside was down in the fifties, cold enough to justify a warm blaze, he figured—and Claude had sent a plate full of appetizers for him to sample and approve for the party.

Not that he really cared; they would all be good. But the party had become a big deal to his staff, so he would humor them.

He tossed a stuffed mushroom to Tucker, who was watching intently but was too well trained to beg.

When the door opened and Jillian ushered Jamie in, he shot out of his chair.

She really had just gotten home when he called, apparently, because she hadn't even changed out of her suit. He felt a little underdressed.

"Do you need anything, Daniel?" Jillian asked sweetly.

"No, thanks. In fact, take the rest of the

day off." Her hovering had become a bit tiresome.

"Thank you." She didn't sound grateful at all.

"Daniel, what's this about?" Jamie asked when they were alone. "I don't like games."

He frowned. "I didn't mean for it to be a game. But it's good news. Too good for the phone."

"What?"

"The lab found a DNA match between the two murders. They're definitely linked."

For a moment, she stood there looking stunned. "So we're back to the serial-killer idea?" she asked dubiously.

"All I know is, the two cases are definitely linked, and by more than the coincidence of metal shavings. Gables was a college kid halfway across the country at the time of the first murder, and I can prove it. He was sitting for a final exam in a Shakespeare class. He has no possible connection. Someone else committed both crimes."

"Holy crap."

This wasn't the reaction he'd hoped for. "I thought you'd be happy."

"Happy that the client I prosecuted and put

on death row is innocent?" She collapsed into the sofa and idly petted Tucker, who looked worried. The dog was amazingly attuned to the feelings of people around him.

"You've known this was a possibility for a long time. You said you wanted answers."

"I did want answers. I thought they'd be different. I wanted proof that I did the right thing."

Daniel realized he hadn't thought this through. He'd been so focused on the outcome *he* wanted, he'd forgotten the implications for Jamie.

He sat down beside her on the sofa. "Listen, Jamie. You've done an enormously courageous thing. Yes, you prosecuted the wrong man. But that's because someone framed Christopher. Someone planted evidence. You can't be blamed—"

"Of course I can be blamed. You don't think Chubb will make me the sacrificial lamb? I'll lose my job. By the time he's done with me, I won't be able to get work as a prosecutor anywhere in the country."

"Let's look at the bigger picture. We are going to right a cruel injustice. We're going to save a man's life. And we are perilously close to finding the actual murderer in two high-profile, now-unsolved cases."

"How do you figure that?"

"We've got his DNA. If we have to get samples from every person in the country, we'll find a match. You don't think Chubb would like that? If you brought him a person who'd almost gotten away with two brutal murders?"

"Daniel, you're forgetting. I won't be a part of that. Once we show that Christopher didn't kill anyone, my role in this is over."

"No. I won't accept that."

She sat up straighter and looked at him, suddenly steely-eyed. "Yes, Daniel, you will have to accept that. There are some things in this world that your money can't buy, and I'm one of them."

"Did I say anything about money?"

"It's implied. You're so used to getting your way, and everyone in our life is so eager to please you that you forget other people have free will."

"Let me rephrase, then. I don't accept that you don't *want* to keep going. To find the man who took two lives and ruined two others… That doesn't excite you?"

She took her time answering. "I would be pleased to prosecute that man as part of my job. But, for me, it's not personal."

Daniel had a hard time understanding how these life-or-death issues could *not* be personal. But he had to tread carefully here. If Jamie figured out what his true intent was, she would find a way to stop him.

"So this case is nothing personal? Just business?"

She nodded curtly.

"What was that kiss all about then?" Just saying the word *kiss* caused every part of Daniel's body to tighten. They were in the middle of an argument, and all he wanted to do was kiss her again. And again.

Jamie, her gaze locked with his, licked her lips and swallowed. "Th-that kiss is immaterial to this discussion. We were talking about the justice system. Our work."

She made perfect sense. Yet somehow Daniel had gotten the whole thing mixed up in his mind. If he could find closure, check this one item off his list, he could move on to other things.

To Jamie.

The news about the DNA had given him

real hope for the first time in a very long time. For Jamie, the stakes were professional. For him, they were very, very personal. And she didn't get it.

"You're right. Immaterial. Completely out of line for me to even bring it up." With that, he leaned in and kissed her again.

CHAPTER TEN

THOUGH EVERY PART OF HER BODY wanted to melt into a pool of surrender, she pulled back. "Daniel…"

"I want you, Jamie. You want the same thing. I can see it in your eyes. I can feel it on your lips."

"That doesn't make it…"

He kissed her again, harder this time, placing his hands on her shoulders and pressing her against the back of the sofa. A delicious lethargy stole over her body as the kiss intoxicated her.

Yes, he was right, she did want him.

After a few moments, or maybe it was a few minutes, he came up for air. "You were saying?"

She had to search her beleaguered brain for her argument. "Mutual desire…doesn't justify…"

"We're both single…" *Kiss* "…unattached…" *Kiss* "…consenting…" *Kiss*.

Why not? She sensed there was a good reason to resist Daniel's appeal, but she couldn't come up with it.

"Jamie." He whispered against her ear. "I haven't felt this good about anything in years. It feels *right*. I want to celebrate. I want to make love to you."

Jamie's cynical side clamored for attention. He was manipulating her again. Like most men when they wanted something, they said whatever it took to get their way.

But somehow none of that seemed to matter. She wanted to be with him at least as badly as he wanted her.

She didn't kid herself that he was serious about her. Lowly county prosecutors from the wrong side of the tracks didn't become the girlfriends of billionaire oil tycoons except in fairy tales.

But as Daniel nibbled on her earlobe, waiting for a yes or no from her, she didn't care much what the future held. She'd been attracted to Daniel from the first time she'd seen him lying naked on that massage table, and her hunger for the man had done nothing but build.

It *did* feel right. For this moment, anyway.

"Daniel?"

He stilled, tense, waiting for her to reject him. "Yes?"

"Is the door locked?"

"My staff knows better than to walk in here when I'm in a meeting. Not unless the house is on fire."

"I don't care. Lock it."

"Happy to." Tucker followed him, and he nudged the dog out the door before locking it. Then he returned to Jamie and put his arms around her. "Is that a yes, dear Jamie?"

"It is." Something still nagged at her, but she shoved it aside. Daniel Logan was going to make love to her, and she was damn well going to enjoy it.

He kissed her neck and she wiggled with anticipation. Committed, now, she was downright eager.

"Are you protected?" he asked almost casually as he deftly unbuttoned her blouse with one hand and she slid farther and farther down until she was nearly horizontal on the buttery-soft leather sofa.

Of course he would have to ask. A man in his position didn't risk paying astronomical child support to some enterprising young lady.

"Yes." At the urging of her father years ago, she'd gotten an IUD so she didn't have to worry about birth control.

One careless moment could derail your whole career.

She'd never been sure why he felt that way, since her conception hadn't been even a speed bump in his career, unless an occasional birthday gift... *Damn.*

Her father. That was the thing that was bothering her. Daniel still didn't know her relationship to the man who had sent him to death row.

Daniel had her shirt all the way unbuttoned and was working on the front clasp of her bra.

"Daniel. Daniel, wait. I have to tell you something."

His fingers went still. "It can wait. Can't it?"

He was right. If she brought up the subject

of her father right now, it would kill the mood completely. "Never mind. It's not important." At least, it didn't seem very important in this context.

What difference did it really make that her father had prosecuted Daniel? She'd never been close to her father. She'd had only a handful of face-to-face meetings with him, during which he preached and she absorbed what she perceived as his wisdom. She was in no way directly connected to the miscarriage of justice that had put Daniel away.

She smiled, made herself relax again.

Why was she fighting this so hard? As Daniel said, they were two consenting adults and there was no ethical or moral reason they couldn't make love.

She sat up and stripped off her blouse and jacket at the same time. Her bra followed. Daniel stared at her with hungry eyes, like a kid who'd just won the biggest stuffed animal at the carnival.

"Can I touch?" he asked almost shyly.

She wondered if she was his first since prison. If so, he'd hardly been more than a kid the last time he'd been with a woman. She took his hand and guided it to her breast.

The muscles of her abdomen spasmed as he touched her.

"You're so beautiful," he said reverently.

A deer head mounted over the fireplace seemed to be looking at her accusingly. She closed her eyes and shut out all distractions, focusing on the feel of his hand on her breast, his thumb caressing her nipple.

For the second time that day, he pulled the clip out of her hair and dug his fingers through it, massaging her scalp as he massaged her breast.

Jamie slid her feet out of her shoes and reached for the side zipper of her pants. She wanted to be naked, to open herself completely. She wanted to feel the texture of his skin, feel the heat of it touching her.

"I don't want to let go of you long enough to get undressed," he said. "Isn't that insane? But I'm afraid you'll evaporate."

"I'm here, Daniel, and I'm not going anywhere."

He let go of her to quickly unbutton his shirt and peel it off, revealing a chest that was tanned to a golden brown. The skin was smooth, with just a light dusting of hair at the center.

His jeans came next. Her mouth went dry as he shoved them down his legs, revealing a pair of navy boxer briefs that showed every inch of the extent of his desire for her.

Then the underwear was gone, too, and she couldn't take her eyes off his beautiful male anatomy, standing proudly, ripe for her taking.

Suddenly, more than anything, she wanted to take him in her mouth and shower her attention on him. She'd heard men preferred the activity over all others, because it was the only time a woman's attention was focused solely on his pleasure, forsaking her own.

She wouldn't be forsaking anything. Without any conscious decision she sat up straighter, reached for him, placed her hands on his hip bones and urge him to stand in front of her.

"What… Oh."

Jamie took him into her mouth, exploring him from the base of his shaft to the tip with her eager, curious tongue and lips while he filled his hands with handfuls of her hair.

"Um, Jamie…" The words came out on a groan and she realized he was fighting for control. "I want to be inside…"

She released him. "Yes. Yes, I want that, too." Their first time, perhaps their only time, she wanted him to climax inside her.

Jamie raised her hips from the sofa just long enough to shuck her pants and panties, kicking them out of the way as she grabbed Daniel's wrist and pulled him down on top of her.

His weight crushed her and she loved it, feeling pinned and helpless for a few seconds as he adjusted their positions, insinuating himself between her legs.

"I'm not hurting you…?"

"No. Oh, Daniel, please. Now."

Even before he entered her, heat pooled between her legs and her skin tingled all over, forecasting what she knew was going to be an explosive orgasm.

She threw one leg over the back of the sofa, opening herself to him. She was wet and ready for him, her whole body throbbing with need. Reaching between their bodies, she grasped his erection. They both groaned as she guided him into her. But it wasn't as if he couldn't find her on his own. He pushed inside, paused, pushed deeper, paused.

She was hyperventilating, and she forced

herself to clamp her mouth shut, breathing through her nose as he took possession of her, sheathing himself even more deeply, and she spread her legs wider to give him full access.

He was nearly nose to nose with her, and he looked deeply into her eyes. "Jamie."

That one word was a powerful aphrodisiac. It said he knew to whom he was making love, that she wasn't some interchangeable collection of female body parts.

He withdrew almost all the way until she whimpered, then plunged inside again, his stroke hard and swift this time. After a few moments, unless she'd lost track of time altogether, he paused again, still struggling for control and driving her to the brink of insanity.

She deliberately moved against him.

"No wiggling."

"Do that again, Daniel."

"Only if you want this to end way too soon."

She never wanted it to end. "Then take your time." Still, he repeated the long withdraw, and again plunged inside until it felt as if he were reaching down into her core and touching parts of her psyche that had lain dormant her whole life until now. Frothy emotions bubbled up inside her, uncontrollable yet strangely pleasant.

Eventually he found the control he'd been striving for and began to stroke her in earnest, working her into a frenzy.

This wasn't sex. It was a slow stairway to heaven, not even on the same plane as any encounters in her past.

Daniel's strokes intensified, and what had started as a leisurely stroll turned into an Olympic sprint. When she finally couldn't take the tension a moment longer she relaxed her body with a whimper, giving over complete control.

The pleasure was the most intense she'd ever felt as tingles rippled from her core outward in wave after crashing wave.

Daniel released the grip on his self-control and tensed, his whole body rigid. Jamie wrapped her arms and legs around him, practically absorbing his climax along with him.

Gradually she became aware of their physical surroundings again—the feel of the leather against her naked bottom, the afternoon's winter light spilling through the blinds and that blasted deer head looking down on her.

Idiot. What have you done?

Their bodies were slick with sweat, as if they'd just run a marathon. Physically she was exhausted, spent down to the last penny. She wondered how in the world she would put her clothes on and stroll out of this room as if nothing had happened.

But she would. Gossip about her and Daniel would get back to her office like wildfire and kill her career. If anything was left of her career.

Daniel eased himself off her, swinging her legs over the side of the sofa, sitting down, then pulling her against him.

Cuddling. Nice touch.

"You wanted to tell me something?"

Of course he would remember. "It was good for me, too."

He laughed. "Sorry. But I was rude to put you off so abruptly. It seemed like it was important to you and my lust got the better of my manners."

Now wasn't the time. "It wasn't important."

Maybe he didn't have to know. If she didn't tell him, no one else would. No one knew.

"Would you mind if I dressed?" she asked. "I feel really odd, knowing your house is crawling with servants. I mean, what if the house really does catch fire and someone has to run in here to save our lives?"

"You get used to servants. But go ahead. As long as I can watch."

She felt slightly self-conscious—which was ridiculous, given what they'd just shared—as she pulled on panties and bra, pants, shirt, all while Daniel observed appreciatively.

"Not *quite* as interesting going on as they were coming off, but not bad."

When she was dressed, he quickly donned his own clothes, his movements graceful and economical. He was right, it was fun to watch.

"Now what?" she asked. She had no expectations. Really, none.

"I have a luxurious apartment on the third floor where I install all my lovers. You'll have everything you need, and your only responsibility will be to please me."

The shock must have showed on her face, because he laughed. "Jamie. God, what you must think of me. I'm kidding. You act like I have all the answers, and I haven't got a clue. I was hoping you'd tell me."

"Unfortunately, I think we have to pretend this never happened. We're professionally involved." Why was she saying this? Was she making a preemptive strike so he couldn't reject her first? She didn't want to go back to their previous amicable but strained way of being around each other.

But lying down in the path of a herd of runaway cattle wasn't her style, either.

The look he gave her was inscrutable. "Fine. Once you get official word of the DNA results, we'll decide together how to proceed."

"Okay, but keep in mind, if you want me publicly connected to this thing, I'll soon be a disgraced and jobless former prosecutor."

He shook his head. "Don't be so sure. If there's anything I can do to shore up your professional reputation, I'll do it. But presented in the right light, I think you can come up smelling like roses. You took the courageous step to right an injustice, and you'll catch a serial killer in the bargain."

It sounded good when he put it that way.

"I'll wait to hear from you."

Jamie went into the half bath off the library to repair her appearance. Thank God she'd tucked a hairbrush and her travel makeup bag into her purse.

She could fix the wild-looking hair and the smeared lipstick and straighten her clothes, but she couldn't take the roses out of her cheeks. Try as she might, when she looked in the mirror, she still looked like a woman who'd just enjoyed an afternoon of passion.

"One more thing," Daniel said when she rejoined him. He was still barefoot and his hair was mussed from her digging her fingers through it.

In fact, he looked so good that she could easily have jumped him again—if she'd been a woman of little self-control.

"Yes, what is it?"

"Can you come to the holiday party?"

"Isn't it just for the Project Justice employees?"

"And their families, close friends and a few key associates. You qualify."

As a friend or key associate?

"If it's important to you. Jillian won't like your adding me to the guest list. She's probably planned a sit-down dinner with seat-ing arrangements."

"Jillian is my employee. She'll deal with it."

Jamie smiled. "All right. I'll come, then." It might be difficult and slightly awkward, but how could she say no to the man who had just pleasured her so fiercely?

JAMIE GOT TO WORK EARLY the next day, hoping to make some sense of her in-box and her phone messages before her official work-day began. But the first thing she saw was a note smack in the middle of her desk. It was written in angry capital letters on Winston Chubb's personal notepaper: SEE ME.

That really didn't sound good.

He wasn't in yet, so Jamie had a few min-utes to get worked up about what he wanted. Had he found out about her consorting with Daniel?

I've done nothing wrong. She'd investigated on her own time, off the county payroll, and she'd taken no official action.

But she'd gone directly against what her boss had told her to do. Winston would see it as a frontal assault to his authority, and it would not be pretty.

When she heard his voice from the hallway, floating over the partitions into her tiny cubicle office, her stomach flipped. She had to get this over with.

She made sure her clothes were straight and she didn't have lipstick on her teeth. Then she charged off to his office, ready to defend her actions.

"He wanted to see me right away," she explained to Alice, Winston's admin.

"Go on back," Alice said with an uncharacteristic smile and wink, as if she knew something Jamie didn't know.

Jamie tapped on Winston's door, and he summoned her inside.

"Ah, Jamie. Just who I wanted to see. Have a seat."

He was smiling. Why was he smiling? Surely he wouldn't take that much pleasure in firing her.

"As you know, Jamie, this is my last term as Harris County district attorney. I'll be retiring in May."

"In May? Your term isn't up until September."

"I have personal reasons for leaving office early, but that's immaterial. The county already has a special election scheduled for April, and the people are going to vote in a new D.A. I'm thinking that person should be you."

Oh, boy. This really wasn't what she'd expected.

"You look surprised."

"To say the least. When you mentioned the possibility before, I assumed you meant far into the future."

"With my endorsement, you'd be a shoo-in. You're a little young for the job, I'll admit, and you and I have had our run-ins, but when I look around this office, you're the one who's most capable of doing the job."

"I'm flattered." For a few seconds, she let herself fantasize about it. Harris County District Attorney Jamie McNair. Her father would be so proud...

No, her father wouldn't give a rat's ass. It was time for her to concede that the man had been a narcissist, and anything that didn't directly concern him didn't make a blip on his personal radar screen. His only reason for giving her career advice was so that she could be a reflection of him, a "mini-me" he could someday brag about to his big-shot friends, if she distinguished herself.

"Good. I've set up a meeting with my campaign people—they're ready to gear up the 'Jamie McNair for District Attorney' machine as soon as you sign on the dotted line. Are you free on Friday after work?"

Friday evening was Daniel's party. Oh, who was she kidding? She couldn't even consider running for D.A., not when a big fat PR nightmare was about to hit the fan.

"Winston, I'm honored, really. But there's something you need to know, and you won't like it."

His eyebrows flew up. "What? Is there a skeleton in your closet I don't know about? Child out of wedlock? Illicit affair with the county sheriff?"

He was kidding, because he believed her to be of sterling character. She was about to change his mind.

"I prosecuted an innocent man and sent him to death row."

"Oh, God, not the Christopher Gables thing. Is Project Justice actually pursuing that case?"

"Yes, and I'm afraid they've come up with some definitive evidence. DNA links the murder of Frank Sissom with another similar crime for which Gables is in no way connected, and for which he has an ironclad alibi."

"And you know this...how?" he asked suspiciously.

"I've been working with Project Justice during my off hours. I had to know, Winston. I had to know if Gables was innocent. And I firmly believe he is."

"You're going to trash the reputation of this office—*my* reputation—because you were curious? Is that how you want me to leave office? Disgraced?"

"It's my reputation. I take full responsibility."

"You certainly better." He stood up, and for one insane moment she thought he was going to leap across his desk and go for her throat.

"We could take a courageous stand," she said in one last-ditch effort to get him to understand. "We made a mistake. We're taking responsibility for it and righting an injustice.

And we may actually be able to bring the real killer—in two murder cases—to justice."

"*You* made a mistake," he corrected her. "I told you to block Project Justice, and you've assisted them instead. I'll expect your letter of resignation on my desk by noon."

"You don't even want to see how this plays out?"

"I already know. We're going to look bad, the media is going to have a field day and my last days in office are going to be a living hell. Thank you, Ms. McNair."

Fine, if that was how he wanted to view the situation.

She stood. "I've done nothing wrong and I won't resign. You'll have to fire me."

"Yes, that would look better. Consider it done."

CHAPTER ELEVEN

DANIEL HAD SO MUCH ENERGY, he couldn't stay inside. Giving the briefest of excuses to Jillian, he set off for the stables, intending to give Laramie as well as himself some exercise.

Usually he grabbed a golf cart for transportation to the stables, but today he walked—partly to discourage Jillian from following him, which she was inclined to do if she felt he was neglecting some portion of the schedule she arranged for him.

She wouldn't be able to negotiate the wet grass in the high-heeled shoes she perpetually wore.

He was only now beginning to see the degree to which he had allowed Jillian to dictate his life. He'd thought of it as a convenience—one of the privileges his money afforded him. But it had become a weakness.

He had imagined that his lifestyle gave him

complete control. But he'd turned over control to everybody else. Even his meals were planned by Claude. Oh, sure, he could request something, but when it came right down to it, Claude cooked what Claude wanted to cook.

Things needed to change, and watching Jamie walk out his front door had convinced him of that. She had used their professional association as an excuse for pulling back. But that wasn't why she couldn't embrace the idea of the two of them together. He'd asked her point-blank what she wanted to happen next, and she'd backed away as quickly as she could.

His theory was, she couldn't see herself fitting into his life, as it currently stood. He never left the estate—well, very rarely, and only if sorely pressed. He had servants doing everything for him. He had polo ponies for pets. He had no social life, no friends except the ones on his payroll.

He had panic attacks when he couldn't control things around him, like at the prison. He hadn't wanted to put a name on what had happened at the Conklin Unit, but that's what it was.

He was *paranoid*.

Well, no more. Things were going to change. He was going to start living a more normal life. And somehow, he was going to convince Jamie McNair that she ought to be a part of it.

He knew it would be difficult. After his disastrous trip to north Texas, the very idea of getting in a car and driving off the estate made him queasy. But whatever it took—therapy or hiring a coach, maybe convincing Randall to push him—he'd do it.

Laramie was grazing in a small paddock off the stable. Daniel grabbed a handful of oats and lured the animal to him, then looped a halter around his head and led him into the barn. He bridled the gelding, but didn't bother with a saddle.

When he'd been a kid, he'd had a pony that he loved to ride bareback all over the estate.

He jumped onto Laramie's back with no saddle, and the horse just stood there and turned his head as if to say, *What are you doing?* But Daniel nudged him with the lightest of kicks to the horse's flanks, and he moved forward, obedient beast that he was.

They rode around the estate, walking at first, then cantering and finally at a full-out gallop, dodging trees and jumping walls, and—though not on purpose—trampling a flower bed. Daniel hugged the horse's barrel-shaped body with his knees and leaned low over his neck, guiding him more with his thoughts than the bridle.

He felt truly free.

Daniel rode hard until he was gasping with exhilaration and the horse was lathered with sweat. After cooling him down with a few minutes of walking he returned to the barn, intending to give the horse a rubdown himself rather than turn him over to a groom.

Instead, he found…Jillian. She'd taken the golf cart and followed him after all.

"Have you gone insane?" she asked.

"What? I can't ride my own horse?"

"He's a polo pony. You were riding him like he was a wild mustang."

"And it was a helluva lot of fun, too, wasn't it, fella?" He gave the horse a pat and led him into his stall, placing a blanket over him so he wouldn't get chilled.

Luis, his groom, appeared out of nowhere. Sometimes Daniel didn't appreciate how truly skilled his staff was—there when he needed them, invisible when he didn't.

"I'll take him," Luis offered.

"No, that's all right. I got him all sweaty, I'll rub him down. But give him an extra measure of oats tonight, okay?"

"Yes, sir."

"Call me Daniel. Please?"

Luis raised one eyebrow. "Okay...Daniel."

"You *have* gone insane," Jillian persisted. "Your crazy horseback riding around the estate is just one symptom. Asking the servants to address you by your first name is another. But what I was really talking about was Jamie McNair. You had sex with her, didn't you?"

Now how the hell did she know? He'd thought Jamie's concern about the servants was unnecessary, but it appeared he was wrong. He removed Laramie's blanket and began going over his slick coat with a dandy brush.

"Whether I did or didn't, it's none of your concern, Jillian," he said sharply.

She stood staring at him, unconvinced and silently disapproving, as he worked. He grabbed a hoof pick and went to work on one muddy hoof while the horse munched some hay.

Jillian leaned her head and shoulders over the stall door. "You *did* have sex with her. God, Daniel, what were you thinking? And to shut me out as if I mean nothing to you. Who wrote to you practically every day when you were in prison? Did she?"

"Jillian. I want you to stop and listen to yourself. You are a valued and trusted employee, one I've relied on heavily for years. Relied on too much, apparently. But you're off the deep end here. I like Jamie. I like her very much, and I intend to keep seeing her. Stop acting like my mother."

"Your mother?" Jillian looked downright shocked.

Daniel had a hard time remembering that Jillian had a crush on him. He wanted to come down hard on her inappropriate behavior, but he didn't want to hurt her.

He finished off Laramie's grooming with a quick rubdown.

"Speaking of Jamie, I invited her to the party."

Jillian sighed. "Okay, Daniel. I didn't want

to do this. But how much do you truly know about your new girlfriend?"

"Quite a bit, actually. I had her investigated pretty thoroughly before I decided to ask for her cooperation. I found nothing in her background to suggest she is anything but what she claims to be."

"Did you happen to look at her birth certificate?"

"Did you?" he shot back, looking at his assistant over the horse's neck. How would she get access to such a thing?

"I haven't been doing work for you and Project Justice without learning anything about investigation," she explained.

"No, I haven't seen her birth certificate. But yes, I know she was born out of wedlock. Please. Who cares? Her mother was a cleaning lady, and look how far Jamie has come."

"It's her father I'm concerned about."

Her father. Something had bothered Jamie whenever the subject of her father came up.

"What about her father?"

"His name is Chet Dotie. Ring any bells?"

Daniel dropped the cloth he was holding. Chet Dotie. The son-of-a-bitch Harris

County assistant district attorney who had prosecuted him for Andreas's murder.

Dear God. Jamie's father had sent Daniel to death row.

ON FRIDAY EVENING, Jamie stared into her closet, looking over the grim wardrobe possibilities. She had nothing appropriate for a glittery affair at Daniel's estate, and in truth she didn't feel very festive.

She'd been fired. She'd never lost a job before, and even though she'd considered the possibility ever since she first spoke to Daniel, it felt a lot worse than she'd imagined it would.

Her whole identity was wrapped up in her work as a prosecutor. Although sometimes the work was dreary, she'd always felt she was performing a necessary function in society—getting violent offenders off the street, or at least demanding a price from those who didn't follow the rules.

Without her job, who was she?

For two days she'd wandered around her apartment like a ghost, living on peanut butter and microwave popcorn, watching Oprah and

Dr. Phil and Dr. Oz, all of which only served to make her feel worse.

She would have to look for another job soon. But where else could she go with her background?

She could probably get a job with a criminal-defense firm—they were always looking for former prosecutors who were ready to switch sides, since they knew the ins and outs of the system already.

But that life wasn't for her.

Depending on how this thing with Gables played out—and how vindictive Winston Chubb was—her job options could be very limited.

The same thoughts had been chasing around in her head for two days now, and she was sick of them. Maybe the party would do her good. At least the food and drink would be better than what she'd been subsisting on.

Since new clothes weren't materializing in her closet, she grabbed a plain black dress. She could jazz it up with some jewelry, her highest heels and a pair of textured stockings. If she put her hair up and wore dark lipstick, she'd pass.

As she dressed, she wondered what fantastic, stylish creation of a dress Jillian would wear. Jamie bet it would be flashy and sexy.

It didn't matter. Jamie wasn't in competition with Jillian. As spectacular as the lovemaking between Jamie and Daniel had been, she knew it wasn't to be repeated. She didn't belong in his world and would never feel comfortable there. Daniel wasn't ready to be an equal partner to any woman. Those control issues of his weren't going to disappear overnight; he wouldn't magically be "cured" by the love of a good woman.

She was happy, though, that he thought enough of her to invite her to his party. He didn't think of her as merely a conquest or a means to an end. She genuinely believed he liked her, which had to mean she was better than the zero she'd felt like since losing her job.

When she'd finished her toilette, she inspected herself in the mirror and decided she looked pretty good. The glittering vintage rhinestones at her ears and around her neck— about the only thing of her mother's she'd kept—elevated the outfit to evening wear.

She looked somber...but elegant.

When she arrived at Daniel's estate, she got into a long queue of cars waiting to be let inside the gates. A guard was checking the credentials of each potential guest, apparently, making sure they were on the list.

This was a far cry from the parties she was used to, the kind where someone in the office shouted they were watching a game on their wide-screen TV that evening, and whoever was in earshot was welcome as long as they brought beer.

When she pulled up to the guard, he smiled. "Evening, ma'am. Can I see your invitation?"

"I didn't get one. Daniel invited me personally."

"Oh, right. You're Jamie. Sorry for the misunderstanding. You can go right in."

A valet was set up in the driveway. Jamie was happy to surrender her humble car and step into fantasyland, pretending she was someone else for a few hours.

And it was a fantasyland. Daniel's foyer—already impressive without any added effects—had been transformed into a glittering gallery of ice sculptures depicting trees and snowflakes, a full-size ice sled, a candy cane with a ribbon. Every once in a while, a handful of Hollywood-style snow would fall, sprinkling down on the guests who had paused to ooh and aah over the ice.

A uniformed man asked to take Jamie's coat, which she gladly surrendered. The wool tweed didn't go with her hastily assembled cocktail attire.

As she handed off the garment she spotted Jillian standing near the fountain—now a frozen waterfall—greeting the guests like a queen-bee hostess, just as Jamie had predicted. She wore a deep red satin dress, cut low, and a string of what were no doubt real diamonds around her long neck. Tall black heels and elbow-length gloves completed the picture.

When Jillian spotted Jamie, her smile fell away. But then, consummate little actress that she was, she pasted on a pleasant expression. "Jamie. So glad you could make it on short notice." She took Jamie's hand in both of hers, gave it a quick squeeze, then released her and moved on to the next guest.

Poor Jillian. She probably had no idea the ax was about to fall on her world. Jamie would try to think charitably of her, now that she knew what it felt like to have the rug pulled out from under her.

Jamie followed a designated path that led into the living room. Although *living room* seemed much too tame of a term for such a huge space. The Christmas tree in here dwarfed the one in the library. It had to be twenty feet tall, lightly flocked and decorated with blue-green lights and silver balls.

She'd gotten only a swift impression of this room on earlier visits here. Now she couldn't help but admire the strange assortment of time periods that, against all logic, blended seamlessly—an Oriental rug here, a modern geometric one in complementary colors there. A chilly but sophisticated marble table was softened by a tapestry table runner and brass candlesticks; a warm sandstone fireplace was the backdrop for a modern brushed-nickel sculpture.

Daniel's interior designer must have a split personality. The final effect was impressive, but she much preferred the traditional warmth of his library.

A trio of musicians had set up in one corner, playing soft jazz. Another servant was passing around a tray of appetizers. It was Manuel, who'd brought in their snack the first night she was here.

"This one is a Grand Marnier crème puff," he was telling one of the guests. "And this, a marzipan truffle."

"I wonder how Daniel stays so trim," the woman guest enthused after taking a bite of one of the bite-size desserts. "Mmm, outstanding."

"I'll tell Chef Claude you said so."

Another server practically shoved a glass of champagne into Jamie's hand. She wasn't much of a champagne drinker, but it would at least give her something to do. She gave the golden liquid an experimental taste and was surprised at how smooth it went down. This was probably an expensive brand, something that normally wouldn't have touched her tongue.

She was so out of her element, and she didn't know anyone here except Daniel—if he was even here.

He'd said he didn't like crowds, and this definitely qualified. She wouldn't be surprised if he was hiding out somewhere—in the library or his Batcave-like basement, perhaps watching the festivities on a computer monitor. He would make a quick appearance, greet his guests and wish them a happy holiday season, then vanish like smoke.

An older woman in a floor-length blue sequined gown, her silver hair pointing every which way, was making the rounds holding a piece of mistletoe, kissing any man who would stand still long enough. Jamie suddenly recognized her and realized she did know one of the party guests.

Celeste, her forthright chauffeur.

Celeste whirled around and paused in front of Jamie. It took a moment for the light of recognition to glow from behind her thick glasses. "Jamie!"

"It's me, all right."

She handed Jamie a piece of mistletoe, then snatched it back. "Wait a minute. You don't need that. I understand you got all the kisses you can handle."

Good heavens. Just as she'd feared, she and Daniel had become the center of gossip among his employees.

"I can't imagine what you're talking about," she said primly.

A good-looking younger man—one of

several Jamie had spotted among the guests—
put an arm around Celeste and led her away.
"Celeste, Daniel will have your hide if he finds
out you're harassing an esteemed member of
the district attorney's office."

Guess he hadn't gotten the memo.

"Oops," Celeste said as she allowed herself to be led away. "Forgot about that." She
laughed loudly and teetered precariously on
her four-inch heels.

Someone tapped Jamie on the shoulder and
she turned, not knowing what to expect. But
it certainly wasn't Daniel in a tuxedo that
molded to his body like black paint flowing
over granite—and an expression on his face
like a pot about to boil over.

"Daniel." Any further words froze in her
throat. He looked so good and...so angry.

"I thought about telling the front gate not
to let you in. But then I realized I wanted to
see you."

"What are you talking about?"

Jillian chose that moment to interrupt, bub-
bling over with enthusiasm. She had a tall
flute full of a ruby-red liquid clasped between
her hands.

"Daniel. Claude asked me to personally

give this to you. It's cranberry juice and rasp-
berry liqueur. He said you requested something without much alcohol."

"Not now, Jillian."

The dismissal caused his assistant to flinch,
but she didn't give up. "He was quite insistent. You know how he can be."

Daniel seemed to be struggling to get hold
of his temper. He took the flute from Jillian.
"Fine, you've given it to me." He immediately
set the drink down on the nearest table.

Jamie wanted to make her escape. This
wasn't what she'd come here for. She'd wanted
a few hours of escape and maybe, just maybe,
she'd fantasized about another stolen tryst, or
at least a kiss, with Daniel.

But now that he'd gone on the attack, she
had to know what she'd done to infuriate him
so.

Daniel gave Jillian a withering glare, and
finally she got the message and skulked
away.

"When did you plan to tell me that it was
your father who put me in a cage for six long
years?"

Oh, no. Somehow, he'd found out.

And now, *everyone* would know. Because

all conversation in the room had ceased, and everyone was staring at them.

"Could...could we continue this conversation someplace more private?" she asked, mortified that he would purposely air their conflict so publicly.

"What, you don't want everyone to know that your father is the man who worked so tirelessly so that I could die? It was the case that made his whole career, you know."

"He has nothing to do with this, with *us*," she said desperately.

"Then why didn't you mention it? 'Oh, by the way, Daniel, funny coincidence. My father prosecuted your trial.' It wasn't because you had some ulterior motive, was it? Like defending dear old Dad's reputation even as you were trying to save yours?"

"Daniel, stop."

"Were you hoping I'd slip up and admit I was guilty after all? They can't re-try me for the same crime, but you could have restored the image of the man you so looked up to, the man you emulated to a T."

Jamie had no arguments left. He was right about her belief that he was guilty—at least, at first. Before she got to know him.

A handsome man with short, dark hair and a military bearing insinuated himself between her and Daniel. "Don't you think that's enough, Daniel? Or would you like to have her publicly flogged?"

"She'll get a public flogging, all right. Just wait till the media gets hold of this story. And Jamie, you can forget about me sugarcoating your errors and omissions. You're going down."

It was too late for that. Had he not learned about her dismissal? She thought he knew everything.

The man between then deftly guided Daniel away. "Leave her be, Daniel. It's over."

Almost as if it was planned, everyone in the room looked away and went back to their hushed conversations. Even Celeste spoke in an undertone. And Jamie was left standing there like an idiot.

Her mouth was as dry as a musty old book. She grabbed the drink Daniel had abandoned and downed several swallows. But nothing—not even Claude's special drink—was going to wash away this scene from her mind. Ever.

She'd drained the glass before it registered

that the stuff tasted awful. But then, she'd thought expensive Scotch was awful, too. She had no taste, apparently.

She should just leave. But instead she wandered out the back door onto the patio, where a number of heaters kept the area comfortable. The crowd parted, giving her a wide berth. Beyond the patio on the vast grounds was a snow machine creating a winter wonderland and...yes, a horse-drawn sleigh filled mostly with screaming kids.

"I'll escort you off the estate now." Jillian had appeared out of nowhere, looking as if she could hardly contain her glee.

Jamie felt the pressure building behind her eyes. She wanted to cry, but she wouldn't do it here in front of all these people. Especially not in front of Jillian. So she imagined she was one of Daniel's ice sculptures, her feelings frozen inside a block of ice.

"I'll need my coat," she said curtly.

Jillian herded her through the house and back to the foyer. "I'll get your coat. Stay right there."

Jamie felt as if she'd been flattened by a steamroller. Even if a relationship with Daniel was impossible, she hadn't wanted to lose his respect. She should have been honest with him from the very beginning. But a good lawyer didn't show all her cards until necessary.

Standing alone, forlorn, she began to shiver. Her teeth were chattering. Was it that cold? She felt light-headed, and her eyes started to swim.

She'd drunk only a half glass of champagne and those few gulps of the cranberry concoction, which was supposedly non-alcoholic. Such a small amount of alcohol wouldn't cause any noticeable impairment. Could strong emotion cause physiological symptoms?

Jillian returned and thrust Jamie's tweed coat at her. "Where's your valet ticket?"

"In m-my p-pocket, I th-think." It took her three tries to shove her arm through her coat sleeve.

Jillian put her hands on her hips. "Are you a drunk on top of everything else?" Abruptly her combative attitude changed to one of concern. "Do I need to call you a cab?"

Jamie couldn't seem to formulate a coherent answer. The surrealistic ice sculptures began to spin around her like some crazy

North Pole carousel. Then the floor tipped and the lights went out.

"DON'T YOU THINK you were a little hard on her?"

Daniel had retreated to his library, which was off-limits to the partygoers. He sat at his carved oak bar, rescued from a London pub that had been slated for destruction, nursing a Scotch that he didn't really want.

The person interrogating him was Ford Hyatt, who had followed him in here. If Ford hadn't been his most trusted investigator, he would have kicked him out.

"Her father sent me to death row."

"Her father was a prosecutor doing his job. He was set up, given phony evidence just like Jamie was."

"The man was a monster with no heart."

"So, maybe he was. Jamie had no control over what her father did."

"She should have told me. It was an important fact, given the nature of our business together. Now it will look like she had an ax to grind—that she wanted to somehow prove her father did the right thing. She's no longer impartial. We won't be able to call her to testify."

"She was never impartial. But let's just say you're right. She did you wrong by keeping the facts of her parentage from you. Did you have to publicly humiliate her? You might have succeeded in putting her down, but your behavior didn't reflect well on you. Very few of those people in there really know you. For some of them, this is their first real contact with you. And you showed them a ranting maniac."

"I'll send out a memo, apologizing for my behavior."

Ford shook his head and poured himself some Wild Turkey.

"It's not like you. There's something going on with you and Jamie McNair besides a business relationship."

"What have you heard?"

"Nothing. But I know what I see. You wanted to hurt her, and that's not like you."

"Maybe you don't know me as well as you think. There are people out there I sincerely would like to hurt."

"But is Jamie really one of them? Or did

you unload on her because you can't do anything to a man who's in his grave?"

Now that the adrenaline from his confrontation with Jamie was dissipating, Daniel could think more clearly. Maybe he'd gone overboard. He should have at least asked her why she hadn't told him about her father. And he should have talked to her in private.

He pulled a paper napkin out of his pocket and brought it to his nose. Faint traces of a lipstick scent teased him. He'd been carrying it around with him like a security blanket ever since he'd wiped Jamie's lipstick from his face the day they flew to Wichita Falls. It reminded him of everything he'd just thrown away.

"I didn't intend to do what I did," he said at last. "It's just that when I saw her, a lot of old buried feelings came surging to the surface."

He'd lost control. And he didn't like that one bit.

"Jamie gave me hope," he continued. "She made me want to rejoin the human race, to be a better person than I've been in the past. I trusted her, and you know that doesn't come easy for me."

"So you have feelings for her."

"I did. But now I see how impossible the situation is. She's a prosecutor. And it's not just her job, it's her heritage. She chose her profession because she wanted to be just like Daddy. She told me that much."

Ford shrugged and took a gulp of his drink. "You're forgetting, it's not her job anymore."

"What do you mean?" Daniel asked sharply.

"You didn't know? I thought Raleigh would have told you."

Damn. He had a message from Raleigh on his phone, but with Jillian pestering him every five minutes about some damn detail having to do with the party, he'd neglected to call her back.

"What happened?"

The phone on the bar rang, but Daniel ignored it.

"Jamie's no longer with the prosecutor's office," Ford informed him. "She's gone, as of two days ago. Raleigh tried to call her— she had a question pertaining to the Gables case, some small thing—and she was told Jamie no longer worked there."

"And Jamie didn't let me know?" Had

she been fired, or had she resigned? "If I'd known she lost her job I might not have…" Oh, who was he kidding? He hadn't planned his strategy based on anything other than raw, unfettered emotion.

It was a bad way to run his life. Everything good that had happened to him—including getting pardoned by the governor—had involved a cool head and logical, organized actions.

"I should talk to her. Apologize—at least for the way I dressed her down in a social situation."

"It's gonna have to be a mighty big apology."

Just then someone banged insistently on the door. "Daniel, are you in there?"

Jillian again. Would the woman not leave him alone?

Ford went to the door and opened it. "What is it, Jillian? This isn't a good time to disturb him."

Jillian pushed past Ford into the room. "Daniel. Jamie just collapsed in the foyer."

CHAPTER TWELVE

DANIEL'S VISION CLOSED in until all he could see was a pinprick of light. Jamie, passed out?

"I've called for an ambulance," Jillian continued, "but I thought you should know."

In a fraction of a second, Daniel's vision cleared and he was off his bar stool and striding for the door, heart pumping furiously.

His habitual mistrust forced him to ask, "Any chance she's faking?"

"I thought so at first. But when she fell she hit her head on the floor and she's bleeding everywhere. She's definitely unconscious."

A crowd of his guests had assembled in the foyer, murmuring in hushed voices. But they parted like the Red Sea as Daniel moved through them.

Jamie lay on the floor, arms and limbs at odd angles. His first thought was to go to her, draw her into his arms and breathe life and vitality into her like some mythical Prince Charming. But she was no sleeping beauty, under a magic spell, and he was sure as hell no Prince Charming.

Randall was there. Thank God. Randall had all kinds of CPR certification.

Daniel went down to one knee.

"Careful of the blood, sir," Randall said.

Daniel didn't care about any damn blood. "How is she?"

"Breathing, but unresponsive. Her pulse is slow."

Daniel lightly slapped her cheek. "Jamie, honey, wake up." If he could see some response from her, a flutter of eyelash, even, he would feel better.

He took her hand in his. "Jamie, if you can hear me, squeeze my hand."

There! He'd felt it, just the slightest tension in her fingers.

"You're going to be okay, Jamie," he said all in a rush, somehow feeling responsible for her condition. Maybe he'd only verbally assaulted her, and normally chewing someone out with words didn't produce unconsciousness, but he couldn't help feeling the two were connected.

Now her eyelashes did flutter. She could definitely hear him.

"Help's on the way. Hang in there. Please, Jamie, try to hold on, okay? I'm sorry for losing my temper with you. It was the wrong thing to do." God, he didn't want those harsh words to be the last exchange between them.

What had he been thinking? He cared about Jamie. Yes, she'd done something he didn't like, and if she were an employee he would be justified in abruptly terminating her.

But she wasn't his employee. He'd come to see her as a friend—no, clearly more than a friend, since he'd made love to her. When someone you cared about did something you didn't care for, the appropriate thing to do was talk about it, not cut them out of your life in the cruelest way possible.

The paramedics arrived. As they checked Jamie's vital signs, one of them asked questions and Jillian was there to answer them, since she was the one who'd witnessed Jamie's collapse.

"Did she have too much to drink?"

"She was only here a few minutes, and she

didn't seem tipsy until right before it happened," Jillian said.

"Is she diabetic?"

"I don't know."

"She's not diabetic," Daniel supplied. "At least, I've never seen her take insulin. She hasn't mentioned any health problems."

"On any medications?"

"Not that I know of, but…truthfully, I don't know that much about her." She'd hidden her parentage from him. What else might she be hiding? She hadn't shared a lot of personal information with him.

"Has her next of kin been notified?"

"I don't think she has any family," Daniel said.

"A friend, then. Someone should go to the hospital with her."

Daniel wanted to go with her. He didn't want her to wake up alone in a strange place with no one at her side. But he didn't trust himself in that environment. What if he freaked out, like he did at the prison? That wouldn't help Jamie at all.

"Want us to go with her?" Ford asked, his fiancée, Robyn, by his side.

"Would you mind?"

"Of course we'll go," Robyn said. "I'll get our coats."

"Whatever she needs—make sure she has it," Daniel said to Ford. "I'll take financial responsibility."

"We'll make sure she gets the best of care."

"And tell her...tell her I'm sorry."

"You should tell her yourself."

"I can't go to a hospital." Too many unpleasant memories. He'd spent way too much time in hospitals after he'd gotten out of prison—first, to restore his own health. Then, watching his parents die.

"You could," Ford said. "Sometimes, Daniel, I think you use your unfortunate past as an excuse so you don't have to do anything the least bit tough or uncomfortable."

Wow. Nobody ever talked to him like that.

Ford shrugged, looking a big guilty. "There, I said it."

Daniel tried one last time to cling to his philosophy. "You don't think I've earned the right to live life on my own terms?"

"I guess if you've got the resources to do that...but you didn't corner the market on unpleasant circumstances. Raleigh witnessed her husband die in a terrible car accident. Robyn..." He lowered his voice. "Hell, Robyn lost eight years of her son's life to kidnappers. But she never felt sorry for herself."

Robyn returned with their coats. The paramedics had loaded Jamie onto a stretcher, and Daniel managed to touch her hand one last time before she was wheeled away.

Ford and Robyn followed the stretcher out the door.

He didn't feel sorry for himself, damn it. He did what he had to do, that was all.

JAMIE'S HEAD WEIGHED at least two hundred pounds, and someone was whacking at it repeatedly with a machete. Her throat felt raw, and the rest of her didn't feel much better.

Worst hangover on earth?

But she hadn't had that much to drink at Daniel's party...

Daniel. He'd found out about her father. She remembered that much, at least, and the terrible fight they'd had. But after that, events were hazy.

Had she gotten drunk? That wasn't like

her. She'd never been the type to drink excessively, not even in college.

She forced her eyes open a crack, saw bright fluorescent lights, and that was when the panic hit. She wasn't at home, in her own bed.

Her eyes flew open and she gave a strange, hoarse little shriek as she tried to sit up, but a hand on her shoulder stopped her.

"Easy, it's okay, Jamie. You're safe."

Jamie's bleary eyes focused on the person leaning over her bed. A woman…

"I'm Robyn Hyatt. My husband works at Project Justice, and we were at the party."

Jamie must have looked at her blankly.

"You were at Daniel's house and you passed out suddenly. You hit your head. You were taken to Johnson-Perrone Medical Center."

"I…I don't remember." Her voice was strangely raspy. She remembered Jillian wanting to eject her from the party, and then…nothing. "Why are you here?" The question came out sounding ungrateful, so she quickly revised it. "I mean, thank you for being here… Oh. You're here to…to talk me out of suing Daniel? Don't worry, I'm not the lawsuit-happy type."

"It's not that," Robyn said emphatically. "Daniel was very worried about you. In fact, he wanted to come here himself, but…well, you know Daniel doesn't get out much."

Daniel, worried? "He didn't seem too worried about me when he chewed me out in front of a zillion people. He hates me."

"That's not true. If you could have seen him when he learned you'd fallen ill…"

"Whatever." Jamie didn't want to discuss Daniel with Robyn or anyone else. Her feelings felt as raw as her throat. "Why is my throat so sore?"

"I don't know. They won't tell me anything, since I'm not family."

Jamie opened her eyes again and looked around, taking in a few more details. "I'm in the E.R." She had an IV in one arm and various straps, patches and clamps on and around her, probably measuring her vital signs.

"Yes."

"Get me a doctor, then. Please." She didn't intend to be rude to Robyn. It was kind of her to come to the hospital and watch over her. Or maybe she was just following Daniel's orders. But this situation wasn't Robyn's fault.

"Yes, of course."

As Robyn left the cubicle, Jamie again tried to remember getting sick. But her last memory was of Jillian, announcing she would escort Jamie off the premises.

A woman in a white coat entered the cubicle. She had a round, cherubic face and a sweet smile. "Ah, you've come back to us."

"Are you my doctor?" Jamie asked, to be sure.

The woman came forward and took Jamie's hand. "I'm Dr. Novak. You gave us a scare. How do you feel?"

"On a scale of one to ten? A negative five. What happened to me?"

"You don't remember?"

"Not a thing."

"Do you remember taking any pills?"

"I don't remember what the paramedics or doctors did—"

"I mean, before you passed out."

Jamie shook her head. "No idea what you're talking about."

"Ms. McNair, you had enough barbiturates and alcohol in your blood to take down a rhinoceros."

Barbiturates?

"Secobarbital Sodium, to be exact. You might know it as Immenoctal, Novoseco-barb, Seconal. Mixed with alcohol it can be deadly—"

"No. I don't take pills."

"No one is going to blame you or punish you," the doctor said gently. "You've been under a tremendous amount of stress. You lost your job, you had an argument with your boyfriend—"

Jamie jerked her hand away from the doctor's grip. "Look, let's get one thing straight. I don't know who you've been talking to, but I do not, and never have, taken any kind of tranquilizer or sleeping pills or whatever the hell you're talking about, with or without alcohol."

The doctor looked at her with cloying sympathy, and Jamie wanted to smack her.

"You think I tried to kill myself?"

"When a patient presents themselves with that amount of prescription tranqs in their blood, along with alcohol, it's usually not an accident."

"Not an accident..." Oh, God. Could

someone have drugged her? Stuck her with a syringe, put the drugs in her drink? She didn't remember what happened.

At least she knew what the sore throat was about. They'd probably pumped her stomach.

"Is there someone I can call?" Dr. Novak said. "A friend, relative…"

This was a nightmare. The doctor didn't believe her. "Never mind. How soon can I get out of here?"

"I'll want to keep you overnight for observation," Dr. Novak said, now all business. "In addition to the drug overdose, you got a pretty good thump on the head. After that… we'll have to see."

Oh, good night. The doctor still didn't believe her, and Jamie was going to end up in the psych ward if she didn't do something fast.

But she couldn't think of a single person she wanted to call, someone she trusted to share this mess with, someone who would stand up and say, "Lord, no, Jamie wasn't suicidal and she most certainly would not take an overdose of tranquilizers."

Funny, Jamie hadn't really noticed the lack of close friends in her life. She had associates at her job—her former job, she amended—people she sometimes shared lunch or coffee with. She got invited to their weekend barbecues and socialized with them easily enough, talking shop, usually.

But she wasn't close to any of them. None of them had called after she'd been fired. She couldn't trust any of them, now that she was no longer one of them.

"I need to speak with a detective from the Houston police," Jamie said with as much authority as she could muster. "There's been a crime, and as we speak, someone could be destroying evidence."

"You just rest now, Jamie. I'll get the paperwork started for your admission."

Jamie spied a white garbage bag that looked as if it contained her clothes, shoes and purse. Thank God. She leaned back on her pillow and pretended to be meek and submissive. "All right. I'm resting."

Dr. Novak gave her one more worried look before leaving the room.

Once alone, Jamie sat up. She climbed down from the gurney and tested her legs. Wobbly. And she was dizzy as hell. She had to pull her IV drip bag with her, but she finally managed to reach the white garbage bag.

Settled back on the gurney, she reached inside and found the small black leather clutch she'd taken to the party. Her cell phone was inside.

"Please, dear God," she murmured, "let me get a signal in here."

Yes! She dialed the major crimes unit of the Houston P.D.

"Major Crimes, this is Sergeant Comstock."

"Abe. It's Jamie McNair."

"Jamie? I heard you got fired."

"I did, but that has nothing to do with anything right now. Someone tried to kill me, or at least make me very, very sick. I'm in the emergency room at Johnson-Perrone. Can you come? Please?"

"Did you say someone tried to kill you?"

"I was at a party. They slipped me drugs somehow."

"You mean like date rape drugs?"

"I don't know, exactly. Tranquilizers."

"I'll be there in a few minutes."

DANIEL PACED HIS DARKENED living room like a caged animal, waiting to hear from Ford. If Jamie didn't recover, he would never forgive himself. He wasn't sure how he could be responsible—he hadn't touched her—but she'd taken ill under his roof, right after he'd verbally assaulted her.

Maybe she'd eaten or drunk something she was allergic to and gone into anaphylactic shock. Maybe she'd been so upset, she'd had a stroke or a heart attack. He'd assumed she was a young, healthy woman in the prime of her life, but maybe she had some illness she hadn't mentioned.

His party guests were all gone; the festivities had broken up pretty quickly after Jamie's collapse. His ever-efficient servants had already cleaned everything up. Even the melting ice sculptures had been set outside and the paper snow put into recycling.

The place felt strangely large and empty to him, unusually quiet.

He could go to her. He could wake up

Randall and have him drive…or he could drive himself, like a normal human being. But the last time he'd gone out had been such a disaster. He still tightened up inside just thinking about his visit to the prison. A hospital wouldn't be much better.

Finally the phone rang, and Daniel snatched up the receiver. "Ford?"

"Yeah. It's me. Jamie's conscious. Looks like she's gonna be okay."

Thank God. "So what happened to her?"

"You're not gonna like this."

"I already don't like it. What, for God's sake?"

"She overdosed on barbiturates and alcohol."

"She tried to…to…"

"Well, that's what everyone thought. But right now, a Houston P.D. detective is on his way over to talk to her. She claims she didn't take anything, and that someone must have slipped her the drugs somehow."

The news just got worse and worse.

"You know her better than us, Daniel," Ford said. "Did she take pills? For pain or whatever?"

"Absolutely not. Jamie wouldn't try to kill

herself. That's preposterous. She was level-headed, smart, well-grounded."

"She'd lost her job."

"She knew that was a possibility from the beginning, and it was a risk she was willing to take. She wouldn't have been happy about it, but she wouldn't be suicidal."

"Which leaves us with a pretty uncomfortable alternative. Someone at the party tried to kill her. Has she had trouble with anyone? Any conflicts with the staff?"

A painful possibility occurred to him. He hesitated to say anything; the last thing he wanted to do was falsely accuse someone. How much of a hypocrite that would make him!

"Jillian. She formed an irrational dislike for Jamie from the moment they met. But Jillian would never... I mean, I've known her since she was a kid. No way."

"There was the incident with the TV in the bathroom."

"That was an accident. A...a glue failure. Jillian couldn't be responsible for that."

"It's an awful coincidence, then. Jamie almost dying twice at your place. As a former cop, I can tell you, cops don't like coincidence."

"There's nothing I can do about that. Will you be there when Jamie talks to the detective?"

"She's asked us to be present for the interview, so we can back up her statements whenever we can."

"Try to keep a lid on things."

"I will."

"And please tell Jamie, if there's anything I can do, all she has to do is ask. She could recuperate here. I could hire a staff of twenty-four-hour nurses, her own private doctor, whatever she needs."

"I'll tell her. But Daniel, don't hold your breath. You weren't exactly the most gracious host last time she was there. And considering she almost got killed at your place twice, she won't be too anxious to spend time under your roof."

All of which meant, if he wanted to see her and repair the damage he'd done, he was going to have to go to her.

Maybe he could. For Jamie, maybe he could do the impossible.

Tomorrow. Would tomorrow be too late?

"JAMIE, HAVE ANY OTHER attempts been made to harm you?" Lieutenant Abe Comstock asked. He was a handsome man with dark skin and the beginnings of gray at his temples. At this hour of the night, his shirt, which stretched over wide shoulders and muscular arms, was wrinkled and his tie askew.

Jamie liked Abe. He was smart and no-nonsense, and she was glad to be able to tell her story to someone who knew she wasn't a crackpot—*if* the D.A.'s office hadn't poisoned his mind against her already.

She'd asked Robyn and Ford Hyatt to stay with her during the interview. They were all crammed into Jamie's hospital room—she'd finally been admitted sometime around 2:00 a.m.

She started to say no, that no one had tried to harm her before the previous evening. But then she remembered the TV incident. "When I was staying at Daniel's, I was about to take a bath when a TV fell off the wall where it was mounted, into the tub. I could have been electrocuted. I thought it was just a freak accident."

"It was an accident," Ford put in. "The

company that put the TV in admitted it was their fault. Something about the wrong kind of glue."

Abe looked at Ford. "And you know this… how?"

"Daniel told me."

Abe made a few scratches in his notebook, then returned his attention to Jamie. "You say you and Daniel had a very public argument a few minutes prior to your getting sick. What did you argue about?"

Jamie saw no way out of this. "He'd just found out the prosecutor who sent him to death row was my father."

Abe's eyes widened and Robyn gasped, but Ford obviously already knew.

"I should have told him, and he had a right to be angry," Jamie said.

"Do you think he was angry enough to harm you?"

"He was very angry," Jamie said. "But honestly? He would never hurt me physically. I just can't see it."

"Who else would want you dead?" Abe asked. "Because without another viable suspect, Daniel Logan is looking very suspicious."

This wasn't the direction she wanted Abe to go in. "There's something else. I've been working to prove that a man I prosecuted is actually innocent," Jamie said. "We now have the DNA of an alternate suspect. Maybe…"

"Project Justice does make plenty of people angry," Ford said. "When someone is falsely convicted, the real perpetrator gets away with his crime. Then we come along with new evidence, and the perp gets nervous. Just a few months ago, my wife was assaulted by one such person."

"And then there was Raleigh," Robyn said. "Our chief legal counsel almost got pushed off a rooftop—"

"That one, I remember," Abe said. "And I thought my work was dangerous. But how would this as-yet-unnamed murderer be at Daniel's office party? Doesn't make sense."

Jamie sagged in defeat.

"There is one other possibility we haven't mentioned," Ford said, sounding supremely uncomfortable. "One other person at the party who doesn't like you, Jamie."

Jamie looked at him questioningly. "I don't think— Oh."

"Who?" Abe prodded.

Jamie sighed. "Jillian, Daniel's assistant. She was jealous of me. Mistakenly," Jamie added quickly, hoping it didn't come to light that she and Daniel had had sex. "She's rather territorial about Daniel, and I think she saw me as an invader—coming into his home, spending time with him, sharing meals with him. We were working very closely on this case and she resented me."

"Everybody knows Jillian has a...a thing for her boss," Ford added.

"Jillian wouldn't hurt anyone," Robyn argued.

"She might not have intended to kill any-body," Ford said. "Maybe she just wanted Jamie to act drunk...make a fool of her-self."

Abe made more notes. "I've always wanted to see Daniel Logan's house. Now, I guess I have a reason to drop by."

"Jillian has the guest list, too," Jamie said, feeling the first stirrings of unease about bringing this mess down on Daniel. If only this was some huge mistake. But blood tests don't lie, and she *was* drugged. And it *did* happen at the party, there was no question.

Abe finally left. He didn't offer her any

protection, citing budget cuts and a lack of evidence suggesting she was in urgent mortal danger.

She didn't argue with him. She was too exhausted.

"I'll keep an eye on things," Ford offered. "Daniel would want that. He's offered to let you recuperate in his home. He said he would hire a staff of private nurses to watch over you every minute."

"No."

"I told him you probably wouldn't be too keen on the idea. But he feels bad, Jamie."

If he felt all that bad, wouldn't he be here? If he cared about her at all... But instead he'd sent his soldiers, two of the hundreds of people who went out into the world to live his life for him.

"Some things his money can't fix," she said to no one in particular, "no matter how many nurses he can hire."

Robyn looked as if she wanted to argue, but she kept quiet.

"I appreciate everything you two have done for me tonight. Really. But tomorrow I'll get out of this place. I just need to go home and forget tonight ever happened."

"Good luck with that," Ford said. "If someone truly tried to kill you, the ordeal is just beginning."

CHAPTER THIRTEEN

DANIEL HAD MANAGED TO CATCH a couple of hours' sleep. But by the time he received word that the police had arrived, he was awake, showered, shaved and dressed. He'd checked in with Ford; Jamie was safe and sleeping normally. He'd sent Randall to relieve Ford and Robyn, who were probably beyond exhausted by now.

He met Lieutenant Abe Comstock in the foyer and showed him into the library.

"You had a party here last night?" Comstock began conversationally, looking around with obvious curiosity.

"Yes, that's right."

It had been a long time since Daniel had last been interrogated, but he knew the routine. Abe would act like a pal, try to get him to relax, ease into the subject gradually. But Daniel already knew he would be considered a suspect. He had argued with Jamie, loudly and publicly, just minutes before her collapse.

He had a motive—revenge. He couldn't kill the man who had wrongly prosecuted him, but he could kill that man's daughter. That was exactly what Abe Comstock must be thinking right now.

"Place sure is clean."

"My staff is very efficient."

"Do you always clean this thoroughly right after a party? 'Cause it always takes me and the missus days to find all the half-empty beer cans."

"This is the first party I've had in this house since my parents died. Please, sit down."

Comstock parked himself in a red leather armchair, and Daniel sat on the leather sofa— the one he and Jamie had made love on. He probably should have chosen a different locale, one that wouldn't remind him of her—and what he'd lost—in such a visceral way.

Daniel decided to go on the offensive. "I've already spoken with Ford Hyatt this morning. He says I'm suspect number one in the attempted murder of Jamie McNair."

"You don't seem too surprised."

"I was plenty surprised—and horrified—

when I learned Jamie had been drugged. I also understand exactly why you think I did it. I'm willing to cooperate in every way possible so that you can find out who's responsible. You can search anywhere on the estate. I'll give you a complete list of everyone who was here.

"I'll do anything in my power to make you see that I would never hurt Jamie."

"Are you involved with her?"

"Yes." It was true, and if there was one thing his work with Project Justice had taught him, it was that you never lied during an interrogation, even if your answer seemingly had nothing to do with the crime. It would come back to bite you.

"I felt betrayed when I found out she hadn't been completely truthful with me. I did lose my temper. I said some things intended to be hurtful. But that was as far as it went."

Comstock asked a lot more questions; he wanted a minute-by-minute timeline of Daniel's whereabouts. He had Daniel walk him through the various locations involved.

Then he asked to see Jillian.

"She didn't do it," Daniel said. "From the beginning she didn't like or trust Jamie. But she was the one who found out about Jamie's father and told me. That was her revenge. She wanted me to cut Jamie out of my life, and I did. She wouldn't have any reason to act."

"Unless she knew you and Jamie had…"

"I don't think she knew."

"Women always know. They just do." It sounded like Comstock knew from personal experience.

"I'll call Jillian."

But before he could, Jillian walked into the room. Maybe she'd been eavesdropping. Wearing a pair of wrinkled jeans and a plain blue T-shirt, she didn't look quite as well put together as usual. Her hair looked as if she'd just gotten out of bed, and she wore no makeup.

She'd probably been up late last night, he reasoned, seeing to the cleanup.

"I was just getting ready to call you," Daniel said. "This is Lieutenant— Jillian, what's wrong?" Her eyes were filled with tears, and his first thought was that she'd heard something from the hospital and Jamie had taken a turn for the worse. "Is it Jamie?"

"It's Chef Claude. He was in a car accident

this morning, on his way to work. His mother just called. He's got a broken leg, a bruised kidney…and he's…he's lost an eye."

"Oh, dear God. Is he going to live?"

"She said yes. But she doesn't know if he'll ever be able to work again."

"Of course he will. We'll get him the best doctors, the best physical therapists. Call his mother back. Tell her we'll spare no expense."

"This Claude is your employee?" Comstock asked.

"He's much more than that," Daniel replied, wanting to crawl into a hole and forget the last twenty-four hours had ever happened. "I've known him since he was a kid. He was an assistant in the kitchen when I was growing up. While I was away at college, my dad sent Claude to the Cordon Bleu school in Paris. He was my first business partner."

"I didn't know that," Jillian said.

"We opened a restaurant. It's not something I mention much, seeing as it was a crashing failure."

"You had a business failure?" Comstock asked, seemingly fascinated. "Was the food that bad?"

"Claude's cooking wasn't the problem. His ambition was. He wanted to expand too much, too fast, when we didn't have enough cash flow. We went our separate ways after that. But when I got out of prison, my father tracked him down and hired him to work here—for me. He's been here ever since."

"Who should I put in charge of the kitchen?" Jillian asked.

"Cora. But wait a minute," Daniel said. "Lieutenant Comstock wants to talk to you."

"Me?"

"Someone tried to kill Jamie McNair," Daniel said.

Jillian took a step backward and blinked. "You think I had something to do with it?" she shrieked.

"Jillian. Calm down. Just answer Lieutenant Comstock's questions. I urge you to answer truthfully."

"What do you want to know?"

"You were there when Jamie and your employer argued," Comstock said. "I want to know what you saw, what you heard. For instance, was she eating or drinking anything at the time?"

"She was poisoned?"

Comstock said nothing, just waited for her to answer the question.

"Oh, my God." Jillian turned the color of grits. She grabbed on to the nearest table as she swayed on her feet, then sank onto a footstool. "Daniel, do you remember why I interrupted you and Jamie?"

"Frankly, no. Your timing was very bad, and I was focused on Jamie."

"I was trying to give you a drink. Claude made it special. For you."

Daniel strained his brain. "I do remember something...about cranberries?"

"Yes. You took the drink from me, but you didn't taste it. You set it aside."

"Yeah..."

"After you walked away from Jamie, she picked up that drink and chugged down the whole thing. Oh, my God. I'm the one who poisoned her."

"Wait. So you were trying to poison *me*?"

Her eyes widened in horror. "Oh, Daniel, of course not. I would never hurt you. I lo—" She caught herself. "I think you're a wonderful person."

Comstock hadn't missed the slip.

"But if that drink was poisoned..." Comstock's voice trailed off.

"Claude gave it to me. To give to Daniel. Jamie wasn't the target. You were."

"RED ROSES, HUH?" Robyn plucked the card from the bouquet sitting on a shelf near Jamie's hospital bed. Jamie already knew what was written on the card by heart: *Dearest Jamie, please be well soon. Daniel.* When Robyn read it she looked at Jamie with a speculative gleam in her eye.

"He's been very kind," Jamie said.

Jamie spent two days in the hospital. Since Daniel had told them to spare no expense, he would pay for everything, they'd run every test imaginable on her. They'd tested her kidneys and liver, they'd looked at her stomach lining, they'd done an MRI on her head because of the concussion.

She'd been moved to a larger room, and instead of hospital food, she'd been offered meal choices from nearby restaurants. She'd also had fresh flowers delivered to her room both days. Her TV had offered all the premium channels.

She'd had no idea a hospital would have VIP suites.

She'd even agreed to a psych evaluation—just to put to rest any lingering suspicion that she might have tried to kill herself.

At first, she'd been irritated by Daniel's high-handed ways. Didn't he get the message? She wasn't impressed by his money and power. Other women might swoon over the fact that he could get the chef at the hottest restaurant in town to personally prepare chicken Kiev for her.

But that wasn't what she wanted from Daniel.

She wanted him. All of him. Not just the parts that were convenient for him to show her. She wanted him to get out into the world and live. She wanted him to admit he needed help, and get it.

She wanted him to let go of the past, because until he did, he couldn't move forward toward the future—with her.

But as it stood, he was just another project like all those men her mother tried to fix. Granted, he was a rich, handsome, charismatic project. But she'd made the mistake of falling in love with his potential—the well-adjusted Daniel Logan who didn't exist and probably never would.

"Red roses don't say 'kind,'" Robyn said. "Men don't send red roses to associates or friends or relatives."

"He probably didn't even pick them out."

"Well, it wasn't Jillian. She'd have sent you dead flowers."

At the mention of Jillian's name, Jamie sobered. "They haven't arrested anyone, have they?"

"Not that I've heard."

Jamie hadn't heard any updates on the investigation, either, but that wasn't surprising. Often the crime victim was the last one to know.

Dr. Novak paid Jamie one last visit before she was discharged. "I see you have someone here to drive you home."

"Yes." Robyn and Ford had offered to let Jamie stay at their house for a few days, and she had reluctantly agreed that it might not be a good idea to stay alone.

"Have they caught the person who drugged you?" the doctor asked.

"Not that I know of."

Dr. Novak lowered her voice. "So what's

it like, having a boyfriend who could buy a foreign country, if he wanted to?"

Jamie laughed. "He's not my boyfriend."

"Honey, a man doesn't send flowers like that—" she pointed to a vase containing two dozen red roses "—to a friend."

"What did I tell you?" Robyn said.

"Daniel doesn't do anything small, that's all."

But maybe the roses did mean something, if two people had pointed out the significance in the span of five minutes.

Jamie signed a seemingly endless stack of paperwork. Then finally she was rolled downstairs in a wheelchair to the front door.

Robyn led her to a gorgeous silver Jaguar parked at the curb. Either teachers were getting paid more than they used to, or ex-cops turned investigators for Project Justice earned a darn good living.

Jamie stuffed her cute rolling train case— courtesy of Daniel—and the flowers into the backseat. She jumped when a golden retriever occupying the far seat leaned over to sniff the flowers.

Oh, no. Someone was already behind the wheel, and it wasn't Robyn.

"Daniel." Her heart began a staccato rhythm behind her ribs and her stomach fluttered madly. No wonder Robyn had insisted she put on lipstick and comb her hair before leaving the hospital.

Seeing no way out of this, she climbed into the passenger seat, sending Robyn a withering look.

"Bye-bye, now," Robyn said as she closed the car door and sauntered away.

Jamie felt the urge to leap out of the car and flee to the safety of the hospital. She wasn't ready to face Daniel. He'd been so angry with her during their last face-to-face conversation, and...

"Daniel," she said again, blinking stupidly at him. "You're driving a car."

"Did you think I couldn't drive?"

"I thought you preferred limousines with bulletproof glass, and drivers and bodyguards." She still wondered if she was dreaming. She'd longed for Daniel to show her that he cared. She'd wanted him to come to her. And he'd done it—though not without a manipulative twist in the mix.

"So, this is something new for me," he said casually.

"How do you like it so far?"

"Well, I haven't turned into a pumpkin yet. I imagined this horde of reporters following me wherever I went, like they did after I got out of prison. But you know what? No one's interested. They've moved on."

"Don't underestimate the media. It's possible they simply haven't noticed you yet." And when news got out about an attempted murder at his mansion, interest would be revived.

So far, though, the press hadn't caught on.

"How are you, Jamie?" he asked. "You look much better than you did last time I saw you."

"I would have to. I was unconscious and bleeding last time you saw me."

"Are you okay? I had no trouble providing you with roses and four-star meals, but the one thing I couldn't buy was information about your health. Hospitals take privacy very seriously."

"I'm fine. The doctor said no lasting damage from the tranquilizers."

He expelled a breath he'd been holding. "Thank God. I was so worried about you."

"Um, maybe we should go." A couple of people had stopped on the sidewalk to gawk at the gorgeous, expensive car. And though the tinted windows prevented them from seeing inside, they were curious.

"Right. Away we go." He put the car in gear and smoothly pulled away from the curb, then accelerated toward the hospital exit.

Daniel couldn't believe he was actually out driving a car with a beautiful woman beside him. Inside, he was a lot shakier than he let on. But it was thrilling, too. All this time he'd imagined he was in complete control of his life, when in reality he'd been turning over control to everybody else—Jillian, Randall, even Claude.

Claude. Thinking about his old friend made his heart constrict.

"You're taking me to the Hyatts' house, right?" Jamie asked.

"I thought we'd go for a drive. If you're not too tired."

"I'm exhausted. You'd think lying around for two days, I'd be raring to go. But getting poked and prodded nonstop—thanks for that, by the way—wore me out. Couldn't sleep, either."

"A hospital isn't like staying in the penthouse at the St. Regis," Daniel said. "But I'm sure Ford and Robyn have a nice, quiet guest room." He sounded disappointed.

"We don't have to go straight there," Jamie said suddenly. "It's actually nice, sitting in this comfy leather seat, watching the world go by."

The weather was perfect—sunny and in the sixties. Hot, muggy Houston summers might not be the envy of everyone in the world, but the balmy winters made up for it.

"Do you even have a driver's license?" Jamie asked.

"I've kept it current, even though I wasn't actually driving."

"Did the DMV come to you?"

He grinned but didn't answer, because she was absolutely right. He couldn't remember the last time he stood in line anywhere.

He merged onto the freeway, amazed at how quickly the skills required for driving in the kamikaze Houston traffic came back to him. Maybe his grip on the steering wheel was a bit tight, but that was more due to his nearness to Jamie than the cars swerving lane to lane all around him.

Jamie was being civil, but that didn't mean she'd forgiven him. Or forgotten. He could never take those harsh words back.

"Have the police reached any conclusions?" she asked.

"They haven't told you anything?"

"Not a word. It's awful, being out of the loop."

"Actually, there is a suspect."

"Is it Jillian? Daniel, I did give the police her name. But I told them in no uncertain terms I didn't believe she would stoop that low."

"It's not Jillian, although they're still looking at her. It's someone we never considered, and frankly, I'm a bit skeptical. Are you hungry?"

"Starving, but don't leave me in suspense like that. Who?"

"Claude. My chef."

Daniel's revelation was met with thundering silence.

He didn't rush to explain. He wanted to hear her take on it, without any preconceived notions. So while he let her absorb what he'd just said, he got off the freeway and, prompted by his GPS, drove to a little-known urban park, a small slice of green grass and ancient live oak trees that had been spared the bulldozer for over a hundred years.

"Why are we stopping?" Jamie asked as Daniel pulled up to a parking meter, then realized he didn't have change. Such an ordinary thing, pocket change. Everybody had it but him.

"Picnic."

"Are you kidding?"

"No. I packed the basket myself. It's not as fancy as Claude would have made, but you'll like it."

"Claude. Are you going to tell me why you think he tried to kill me? 'Cause I don't have a clue."

"I will. If you'll loan me all the quarters in your purse. I'll pay you back with interest."

Jamie laughed. God, it was good to hear her laugh. "There's something ironic about the unemployed government employee loaning the billionaire a few quarters."

"I'm not a billionaire, you know. After

the last stock-market crash, it's down to only about seven hundred million."

"The funny thing is, I think you're serious." She grabbed the small bag he'd had sent to the hospital, along with a change of clothes he'd retrieved from one of the guest-room closets and a few toiletries. Inside she found her small, black clutch purse, the one she'd brought to his party, and fished around.

"You're in luck. Three quarters."

"Perfect."

"Why don't you just risk the ticket? It's not like thirty-five bucks is going to bankrupt you."

"True. But that was the old Daniel, the one who thought he didn't have to follow the rules of ordinary people. I've changed, Jamie. Or at least, I'm trying to change. You've made me see my life for what it was, and I didn't care for it too much."

He got out, tipped his seat forward, snapped a leash on Tucker's collar. The dog clamored out of the backseat. Daniel stuffed the borrowed quarters into the meter as Jamie climbed out, looking around curiously.

Daniel pressed a button on his keychain and the trunk popped open. He grabbed a basket and an old quilt from the trunk.

"You're serious? We're going on a picnic?"

"You don't want to?"

"I'm too hungry to turn down food."

They set out to walk the two blocks to the park.

His park.

It was a little triangle of green space at a nondescript intersection in a not-so-great part of downtown. But despite the blowing trash and graffiti that marred the blocks on all sides, this park was pristine. It was surrounded by a wrought-iron fence, but the gate was always open.

A sign over the gate proclaimed the park's name.

"Logan Park," Jamie read. "Coincidence? I think not."

"See that building right there?" He pointed to an old redbrick office building. "That was the first location of Logan Oil. My grandfather gave this land to the city, with the provision that it always be kept a public park. He set up a trust for the perpetual care of the land and improvements."

"He was ahead of his time, your grand-father." She stepped through the gate. "It's beautiful. I've worked downtown my whole adult life and I never knew this was here."

"Most people don't."

They had their choice of picnic spots—a couple of old stone tables and benches, a stucco pavilion with a red tiled roof made to look like an old Spanish mission or a sunny spot on a patch of soft green grass.

"Do you mind sitting on the ground?"

"No, I don't mind."

Daniel let Tucker off the leash, since no one else was around. The retriever set about sniffing every tree, bush and bench, probably happy for a new space to explore where other dogs had been.

Jamie helped Daniel spread out the old quilt. They sat down on it and Daniel opened the basket. He plucked out a block of cheddar cheese, already cut into slices, some crack-ers, sliced apples and green grapes, and two bottles of mineral water.

"I was expecting some gourmet concoction," Jamie said. "But I love crackers and cheese."

"The police confiscated almost everything from my kitchen. This was about all that was left."

"Claude," she said, as if suddenly remembering. "Tell me again why you think he tried to kill me. His name certainly never came up in the Christopher Gables investigation."

Tucker, apparently satisfied that the park was free of marauding squirrels and enemy dogs, flopped down on the grass near the quilt with a contented sigh.

Daniel scratched the dog's belly. "Not you. Me. You just got in the way. Do you remember the drink Jillian tried to give me when we were arguing?"

Jamie tried. She had a vague memory of something red, but that was it. She shook her head.

"You drank it. The whole thing, according to several witnesses. A few minutes later you passed out suddenly. You'd drunk some champagne earlier, which only magnified the effects of the tranquilizer."

"I do remember the champagne. Oh,

Daniel, why would Claude want to kill you? That doesn't make sense, either."

"I didn't think so. But Claude was supposedly in a car accident early on the morning after the party. Now, he can't be found. The police are looking for him."

"It does seem suspicious that he would disappear," Jamie agreed.

What no one else knew was that his own people were investigating Claude, too. In addition to trying to determine his whereabouts, they were searching for any possible connection Claude had to either of the two murders.

"We have only Jillian's word that Claude gave her the tainted drink that was meant for me," Daniel said.

"So it could have been Jillian herself who doctored the drink."

"It's another scenario the police are considering. Frankly, I don't like either one. All those years I insulated myself from the outside world, surrounding myself with only the most trusted people, thinking I was safe. To discover a lethal threat coming from my inner circle—it's life-changing."

Jamie said nothing. She threw a grape to Tucker, who snapped it up in midair.

"I'd like to apologize for the way I treated you at the party. It was horrible. I was horrible."

A shadow crossed her face. "It certainly took me off guard. Not the Daniel I thought I knew."

"That angry man isn't someone I often show the world. But he's there, inside me. The fact I was so out of control—that was another revelation for me. Again, I thought I had control of my life. But not everything. Can you ever find it in your heart to forgive me?"

She gave him a wry smile. "Can you ever forgive me for not telling you who my father was? I meant to. I planned to. But it never seemed the right time.

"At first, it didn't matter. I assumed my association with you would be brief. By the time I realized you'd become—" she stopped and took a sip of mineral water "—more than a friend to me, it was too late to tell you without some fallout. So I took the easy way out, and didn't say anything. I didn't think you'd find out until I was ready. Who told you?"

"Jillian, at her most scarily efficient. She knows more about investigating than I thought. She got hold of your birth certificate."

"I'm sure she enjoyed telling you all about it."

"She thought she was protecting me. I spoke to her this morning. I told her things were going to change, and that there would always be a place for her on my staff—but not as my assistant."

"Ouch. How'd that go?"

"Not well, but it needed to be said."

"You've really put yourself outside your comfort zone today, Daniel. I'm amazed."

"And impressed?" he asked.

"Daniel, you don't have to impress me. You just have to be yourself. You once told me you were broken, but I don't believe that. Not anymore. You've showed me today that you're capable of change. You see yourself clearly, and you're willing to fix the things in your life that aren't working. That's extraordinarily healthy."

"So you are impressed?" he asked with a grin.

"Yes. Clearly you have more work ahead of you," she teased. "But I am impressed."

"A lot of things in my life weren't working. For instance, I wasn't the kind of man you could fall in love with. Could that change?"

She reached up and touched his face. "Yes, Daniel, it could." She raised up on her knees, leaned in and touched her lips to his.

It was the sweetest kiss Daniel had ever experienced, filled with so much promise it took his breath away.

He reached for her, but she pulled away and sat back down on the quilt, looking guilty. "Probably not the best decision I ever made."

"Why not? I can't think of a better occasion than a picnic for two people to make out."

"I don't want to rush things, Daniel. With all that's going on, I have so much to think about."

"Nothing's ever perfect. When I was in prison, I spent a lot of time regretting the things I didn't do, the chances I didn't take."

"The women you didn't bed."

"That, too," he admitted.

"You aren't going to prison again," Jamie stated emphatically. "Not unless the police think that you mixed the drink Jillian gave you, intending to murder yourself."

"The police have come to stupider conclusions." Daniel pushed himself to his feet, then offered Jamie his hand. "Come with me. I want to show you something."

She willingly placed her hand in his and pulled herself up. He was amazed she trusted him so easily. The Jamie he'd first met two weeks ago trusted no one.

He led her to the pavilion, then to the wooden slat door that was part of the miniature mission-style building. Grateful that he'd thought to bring the key, he opened it.

It was just a large storage room where the man who took care of the park left his lawn equipment and paint. Everything was clean and well cared for, and the room smelled faintly of earth and freshly mown grass.

"What's in here?"

Daniel closed the door behind them.

"You, me and some privacy."

She laughed nervously. "You're kidding, right?"

He took her hand and guided it toward his zipper. He wanted her to feel just exactly how serious he was. "I've said in so many words how sorry I am for heaping blame on you where it wasn't warranted, for making you the scapegoat for anger that had nowhere else to go. But words don't really cut it, do they? Let me show you, Jamie."

"You want to have sex in a garden shed?"

CHAPTER FOURTEEN

DANIEL PUSHED JAMIE up against the wall and kissed her, hard. "You mean the smell of fertilizer doesn't turn you on?" he murmured in her ear.

"I don't smell fertilizer." Her voice was hoarse with need, and her eyes had gone all smoky. "I smell fertile earth and grass and… machine oil." And never had there been a more potent aphrodisiac.

"You can say no. You did just get out of the hospital."

She didn't answer with words. Instead, she peeled her thin cashmere sweater over her head and tossed it aside, allowing him to admire her in a wispy, barely-there bra.

Amazing what a tiny scrap of lace could do to a man's brain, sending hormones and neurotransmitters racing all over his body, hooking up with receptors everywhere in an instant, causing his erection to surge forward, begging for freedom.

The delicate skin of her breasts blushed pink as he gazed at them.

"Your first time out of the house on your own in months—"

"Years," he corrected her.

"—and you go completely berserk."

He got busy unbuttoning his shirt, pulling it out from his jeans. "The freedom has gone to my head."

"I'd say it's gone somewhere else in your body." She unfastened his jeans and pulled them down, along with his boxers. His erection sprang forward, and she immediately leaned over and took him into her mouth.

She'd done the same thing the last time they'd had sex. She must like it, he thought hazily. It was a good quality in a woman. But he wanted to be inside her.

It took a monumental amount of willpower, but he put his hands on her shoulders and pushed her away. "Too much."

"No, it's not. It's just enough." She drew him inside her mouth again, and again he pulled away. "I want to make love to you, Jamie."

"I'm not sure that's possible in here."

"Of course it is." *Where there's a will, there's a way.* He spied a stack of bagged garden soil, stacked four deep and two wide, that would make a dandy bed.

She saw it too and shook her head. "I'm not having sex on a pile of manure."

"It's not manure. It's good clean dirt in nice plastic bags."

"Works for me." She kicked off her loafers and shucked her jeans. They piled their clothes on the plastic bags and fell onto the impromptu bed, both of them naked and hungry.

He spotted the bruise on the inside of her elbow, where her IV had been, which prompted a stab of guilt. "I shouldn't be ravishing a woman who just got out of the hospital."

She wrapped her arms around his neck and pulled him on top of her. "You are the only medicine I need, Daniel Logan." She kissed him as if she meant business, and he forgot everything except how much he wanted to be inside her. He wanted them to be one. He was crazy about her. Somehow, she'd brought him back to life when he didn't even realize he'd been numb, almost dead, inside.

His awakening was both painful and thrilling.

He ran his hands lightly up and down her body as if he'd never felt a woman's body before. Everything felt new, fresh, exciting—her hip bone under his thumb, the soft swell of her breasts. He kissed the inside of her elbow where the bruise was, then her wrists. He placed his mouth over one nipple and sucked gently, and she whimpered and wiggled in response.

"Daniel." Her name on his lips was a caress, stoking his desire more fiercely than any stroke of her hands or her mouth could. She was so alive, so vital, and yet he knew now that he could lose her with careless words and actions.

The first time he'd made love to her was mind-blowing, but now it meant so much more.

"Daniel," she said, more insistently this time.

"Are you sure you're ready?" He reached between their bodies and touched her soft mound. His fingers sought the warmth between her legs. She was slick and hot, but suddenly she clamped her legs closed.

"Stop being so freaking concerned about me. You, inside me. Now."

No one ever dared speak to him like that. It was a turn-on.

"Yes, ma'am."

She opened her legs again and he poised himself above her. She wrapped her hand around him and guided him inside her. The outside world slipped away. The universe contracted until all that was left were Jamie and himself, joined as one, soaring together. Each stroke brought him closer to paradise as she alternately encouraged him and cursed him for prolonging her climax.

It wasn't deliberate. But the fates intervened so that when he finally reached that peak from which he could not return, she did, too. Their cries mingled as he released himself into her, waves of ecstasy washing over them in violent crescendos that gradually calmed to ripples in a pond. Their surroundings came back, and Jamie gave one last shiver.

"Well," she said.

"Exactly." He laughed in pure delight. "I

think I'm going to like rejoining the human race."

Just then, Tucker started barking.

"Oh, hell, someone's out there," Daniel said, reluctantly separating himself from Jamie.

"Great, just great!" She moved faster than he'd ever seen her move, grabbing her clothes and wiggling into them in a fast-forward, reverse striptease that he cataloged in his memory for review later.

"The door's locked," he reminded her.

"Don't other people have keys? Like the gardener?"

Tucker's barking grew more frenzied just as the knob turned. Daniel thrust Jamie behind him, ready to face the intruder.

But the middle-aged man who entered hardly looked threatening in his overalls and worn denim jacket. In fact, he was the one who looked surprised and a little scared when he spotted them.

He unleashed a stream of frantic Spanish. To his surprise, Jamie replied—in what sounded like pretty competent Spanish to him—while nudging Daniel toward the door.

The man stood aside and allowed them to make their escape.

Tucker greeted Daniel enthusiastically, tail wagging, and Daniel gave him a quick scratch behind the ears without pausing. "Good boy. Thanks for the warning." The dog would never bite anyone, but Daniel was grateful the gardener hadn't hurt his dog or called animal control.

He and Jamie quickly packed up the picnic and made a hasty exit from Logan Park.

"What did you say to him?" Daniel asked.

"Just that we meant him no harm and we were leaving. He thought we were trespassers."

"He didn't recognize me?"

"Apparently not."

"Good." Daniel laughed as he started the car. He was about to pull away from the curb when his phone rang.

Ordinarily he would have let it go to voice mail: bad manners to take phone calls when he was entertaining a lady. But given that he was expecting all kinds of urgent news, he felt compelled to answer.

"Go ahead," Jamie said.

Daniel checked the caller ID. The call came from Project Justice. "Daniel Logan."

"Daniel. It's Mitch. I hope you're sitting down."

"Spill it."

"I've been doing deep background on Claude Morel. At first, he didn't appear to be connected to the Frank Sissom murder. But it turns out that while you were in prison, he was in business with...wait for it... Christopher Gables."

"Are you kidding me?" Daniel's mind struggled back into its habitual pathways, analyzing data, finding the patterns. But this one wasn't difficult. In each murder case, Claude had been the former business partner of the man accused of the crime.

"They opened a French restaurant about ten years ago. The business filed for bankruptcy after only nine months."

"Then it's him. That's the connection we've been missing."

"Theoretically, he might have tried to kill you—or at least put you out of commission and buy himself some time—because you were getting too close to the truth."

"We have his DNA. He must have known that."

"I have more. Flight reservations for two, in the names of Claude Morel and Marie Morel, departing Houston Intercontinental at 4:17 p.m. this afternoon headed for Paris. Marie is his mother, right?"

"Yes." And a sweet little lady, at least in his memory. "Call Abe Comstock at the Houston P.D. Fill him in. If Claude boards that plane we've lost him, and probably any chance for a DNA match."

"Is there time?" Mitch asked.

"We have to try. Without knowing his current location—"

"Wait, I have an address. From Marie's credit card."

"Give it to me."

"Seventeen-oh-three Templeton."

Daniel punched the address into his on-board GPS. It took him a couple of tries to get the unfamiliar gadget to respond, but finally he had a map.

"I'm about nine miles away. I can go there and…" And what? "See if he's there."

"Will you…send Randall?"

"I'm in my car. I can drive there."

"Wait, you're...*where?*"

Daniel didn't have time to explain his sudden metamorphosis from recluse to man-about-town. "Send Randall as backup. Call him after you call the police. Quickly."

Daniel disconnected, set the phone on the console and pulled out into the street, very nearly colliding with a Toyota approaching from behind.

"Watch out!" Jamie yelled, but Daniel had already put on the brakes, and the car swerved around them.

"Sorry."

"What's going on?" she asked urgently.

"Claude murdered both Andreas and Frank Sissom, that's what. Mitch found the link." He pulled into traffic, then cut across to the left turn lane.

"Where? How?" She knew the name of every person connected to Sissom. She'd been studying this case for weeks.

"Claude and Christopher once owned a restaurant together. But he knows we're on to him—that's why he tried to kill me. He's trying to leave the country and I'm not about to let that happen."

"So, call the police!"

"Mitch is handling that. But convincing takes time. Comstock might not be available. He might be off duty. Mitch will have to explain how he got the information he has, which could be dicey."

"He got it by hacking?"

"I don't ask how Mitch gets his information. We can't wait for all this to filter through the proper channels. Claude is probably packing as we speak. He might already be on his way to the airport."

She looked at the GPS screen, then back at Daniel as he pulled a U-turn. "Wait—we're going to Claude's house?"

"His mother's house, I think. Claude lives in Montrose."

"But if you're right, he's a cold-blooded murderer! What are we going to do? We're not cops, we don't have guns or badges or any kind of authority."

"You're right. I wasn't planning to confront him, but it could be dangerous. I'll drop you off someplace safe on the way."

"You will not. Daniel, *I'll* call Comstock. He'll listen to me." Maybe. She dug into her purse for her cell phone. But after two days in the hospital without a charge, it was dead.

"Mitch is already doing that. Anyway, Comstock would just tell us to go home and lock the door."

Which would be very good advice. Just exactly when had Daniel gone from agoraphobic to action hero?

"Hang tight, Jamie. All we're going to do is drive by the house. See if it looks occupied. See if Claude's car is in the driveway."

"All right. Okay." Jamie took a few deep, calming breaths. That didn't sound too dangerous. "He won't know this car?"

"This car is brand-new. Just drove it off the lot this morning."

"And it goes from zero to sixty in five seconds, I see. Daniel, seriously, you haven't driven in years. Don't you think this is a bit much for your first outing?"

"It's all coming back to me. Like riding a bicycle. You never forget."

"Fine, but if we get pulled over for speeding—"

"I could outrun a cop."

"Daniel, listen to yourself! What about the new Daniel who insisted on putting quarters in a parking meter because he intended to follow the rules like an ordinary person? Was that all a lie? Do you believe you're above the law? Are you still trying to impress me?"

He was impressing her, all right. His tone, his manner and that determined gleam in his eye impressed her as being just a little bit crazy.

Something she'd said must have gotten through to him, because he did ease off the accelerator. They were still above the speed limit, but not excessively so.

"I just… I've never been this close to finally catching the man who stole six years of my life. My parents' lives. Every waking minute of their last good years was spent trying to prove my innocence. Trying to save my life.

"Claude. Of all people. He was my friend. I brought him into my house, gave him a great job, paid him well, gave him complete freedom to set up the kitchen with the latest equipment, buy the most exotic ingredients, cook anything he could dream up. It's all he ever wanted. Why would he do this?"

Jamie, who had seen all kinds of people commit all kinds of crimes for all kinds of bizarre reasons, had an idea.

"Jealousy. He started a restaurant with you.

It failed. Then you went on to own a successful restaurant with Andreas. What better revenge than to kill one partner and frame the other?

"Then, he and Christopher Gables owned a restaurant. It went bankrupt, I'm guessing. Christopher then partnered with Sissom. Their restaurant was a success. It was like slapping Claude in the face with the proof of his inadequacy."

"If he hated me, why did he come to work with me?"

"Maybe as a chance to redeem himself, to show the world that he really was the best chef around? Maybe he was happy. Maybe he didn't hate you, and never would have tried to hurt you...if we hadn't started digging around."

"Exit right," the computerized GPS voice instructed.

Jamie's stomach swooped. They really were going to drive past a house where a murderer resided. A man who wanted Daniel dead, and had very nearly killed her.

"If you're right—if Claude's our man—the metal shavings make sense. He made a big production out of sharpening his knife when he made us Caesar salad."

"He's obsessive about sharpening his knives. Can't believe I didn't see the connection earlier. Listen, there's no reason for you to go anywhere near Claude. I'll drop you off at that Starbucks up ahead."

"No way. I'm not letting you go there alone." She might be the only voice of reason in this car. She had to stop him if he got any crazy notions about confronting his enemy.

Claude's house was just outside the tony Bellaire neighborhood. Lots of trees, upscale shopping and restaurants. As Daniel prepared to turn left onto Templeton Avenue, they had to wait for a tow truck coming the other way, turning right. On the bed of the truck was a blue Renault sedan, crunched in on one side.

As the truck turned, Daniel's jaw dropped. "That's Claude's car. It looks like he really was in a wreck. I thought that was just a cover story to explain why he hadn't come in to work."

"He was in a wreck?"

"His mother called this morning and talked

to Jillian. Said he was in a bad accident. Broke his leg, lost an eye—"

"Good Lord."

"I'd already begun to suspect him, and when he couldn't be located, I thought the accident was just a cover story."

They followed the truck at a discreet distance. Templeton Avenue was a street of cute little bungalows that had transformed themselves to upscale. Mature trees, neatly manicured lawns, expensive SUVs and sports cars parked in the driveways all indicated this was a neighborhood that had gone up in value.

The truck stopped in front of a little white cottage with a picket fence and pansies planted around the bright red front door.

Daniel drove by slowly.

"Destination on the right," the GPS lady told them.

He switched it off. "That's the place." He pulled past the house, turned around and parked near the curb a couple of houses down.

"We've seen the house," Jamie said as the tow truck maneuvered into the driveway. "Can we go now?"

"In a minute." Daniel looked alert, like

a hunting dog who'd just gotten a whiff of deer.

As the truck's driver got out and began unhitching the Renault, the front door opened and a tiny, white-haired woman tottered outside, leaning heavily on a cane.

"Oh, my God," Daniel said. "Is that Marie? What I wouldn't give for a good pair of binoculars."

"She looks kind of old to be Claude's mother."

"She was near forty when he was born. Anyway, I think she's been sick. If I could see her up close, I would know for sure."

"You've met her?"

"A few times, years ago, when Claude and I had the restaurant. Lots of our recipes were hers. She came into the restaurant on a regular basis to keep an eye on things, make sure her boy was doing everything right."

"Seriously?"

"She was a sweet lady. Harmless. I'm going to talk to her," Daniel said. "I need to figure out what's going on."

"Daniel. Let the police handle this."

"You know, Jamie, the police did not do such a bang-up job investigating Andreas's murder before. You might trust them to take care of things as they should, but sometimes a man has to take matters into his own hands."

Jamie didn't like this. Not at all. "I'm going with you." If Claude had been seriously injured in a car accident, he wouldn't be here, she reasoned. He would be in the hospital. And the frail little old lady didn't look capable of hurting anybody.

Daniel reached into the backseat and grabbed the vase of roses he'd sent to her in the hospital. "Tucker, you stay in the car." He fixed Jamie with his laserlike stare. "You, too. I'll only be a minute." He turned the Jaguar's ignition long enough to crack a window for Tucker. Then he opened his door and climbed out.

"That's bullshit." She quickly exited and walked around the front of the car to join him, whether he wanted her there or not. "You're giving Claude *my* flowers?"

"I'll buy you more."

"You can't solve everything with money. And you can't order me around like one of your house staff."

"I apologize. I'm a little keyed up."

"Ya think? Okay, is it safe or not? If it is, I'm going with you. If not, we should wait in the car for the police to arrive. Which is it?"

"Just get back in the car. Please," he added.

She didn't, of course. She waited until he'd walked several purposeful steps toward the old woman, who was talking to the truck driver. Then she followed him.

He stopped, turned and stared daggers at her. She stared right back. If not for the situation they were in it would have been comical. Daniel simply wasn't used to people not following his orders.

"Fine," he ground out. "Follow my lead." He took her hand, and they walked together up to the yard.

The woman finally saw them when they were almost upon her. "Mrs. Morel?" Daniel said.

"Yes?" she asked guardedly. Then the light of recognition came into her eyes. "Oh, *mon Dieu,* is it really you, Daniel? It has been so many years." Her voice carried a heavy French accent.

"It's me."

"And you brought such beautiful flowers. But you never... Not since... Claude said you do not leave the estate."

"I heard Claude was injured. He's been a friend for so many years, I had to come see him. I want to be sure he has the care he needs to get better. He's staying here with you, isn't he?"

"He needs someone to take care of him." Mrs. Morel turned her eyes, which were sharp and shrewd despite how frail the rest of her looked, toward Jamie. "And who might this pretty *mademoiselle* be?"

Daniel still held on to Jamie's hand. He raised it and kissed the knuckles. "This is my girlfriend, Jamie."

"I didn't know you had a girlfriend. Not that Claude tells me everything..."

"It's a recent development. Can we see Claude?"

"He is..." Mrs. Morel shook her head sadly. "Not in a good condition for visitors."

Jamie let out a pent-up breath. He was here. But was he truly injured? Or would Claude and his mother bolt for the airport the moment she and Daniel left?

"It's a terrible shame this happened right before your trip to France," Daniel said.

Mrs. Morel blinked in surprise, but quickly schooled her features. "Yes, we were so looking forward to seeing our family. My parents—Claude's grandparents—might not have many years left. And Claude was looking forward to seeing many cousins. We have postponed the trip, of course."

Oh, she was good. Unless...the trip really had been planned in advance, and she didn't realize that Claude had never told Daniel about it. Maybe she had no idea what her son had done. It did seem that the accident, at least, was real.

"Please, Mrs. Morel, I need to see Claude," Daniel said. "I want to personally reassure him that I'll provide the best medical care, rehabilitation, whatever it takes. And that he will always have a position in my household, whenever he's ready to come back."

"That's very kind of you, but..." Finally she relented. "I'll check. He takes many pain pills. He might be asleep, and I wouldn't want to disturb him."

Mrs. Morel quickly concluded her business

with the truck driver, then led the way toward her front door, pausing to stoop down and pinch a dead pansy blossom from a large pot on the front porch.

Jamie squeezed Daniel's hand hard. This wasn't part of the plan.

He leaned down and whispered in her ear. "I just want to see if he's really injured. Ten to one she won't let us see him."

She had a bad feeling about this. Recalling how Daniel's temper had suddenly flared when he'd seen her at the party, she mentally winced. How much worse would it be when he faced the man who'd murdered his friend and set him up to take the rap?

DANIEL'S HEART POUNDED as he crossed the threshold. The man he had hated for so many years, the man he'd vowed to punish, one way or another, was here. So close.

What Daniel chose to do in the next few minutes would dictate Claude Morel's future, as well as his own. Was he up to making that decision?

Certainly Jamie's presence put a kink in the fantasy he'd nurtured, the one-on-one showdown he'd lived over and over in his dreams. Then there was Marie. He couldn't very well assault a critically injured man in front of his mother.

But he was going to do something besides meekly slink away and wait for the police and the lawyers to muck everything up. He would have his day with the man who had stolen his youth, stolen his parents' golden years and sentenced him to six years of hell on earth.

Mrs. Morel's house smelled faintly of garlic and onions, the remnant of the lunch she'd prepared, perhaps. Otherwise, it was neat as a convent, with dainty, elegant furnishings, pastel-pink carpets, bookcases displaying glass figurines. Needlepoint pillows and embroidery samplers were everywhere.

In the living room, where she asked them to wait, was an ancient armchair and a large needlework basket next to it, a half-finished crochet project sitting on top. The TV was on, tuned to a daytime talk show, the volume turned down.

When Mrs. Morel left the room, Jamie nearly came unglued. "Daniel, we shouldn't be here," she whispered. "From a prosecutor's standpoint, I'm telling you this is bad. We could ruin the case against him if we talk to him before the police interrogate him."

"So long as he doesn't know we suspect him, we'll be safe," Daniel reasoned, still not sure where this was going. But he didn't want Jamie making the decisions. This was his fight. "We're here to visit a sick friend, nothing more."

A few minutes passed. Daniel paced, looking out the window. Now that the adrenaline of discovery was wearing off, he began to feel the first faint stirrings of unease. "Maybe you're right. Maybe this wasn't such a good idea."

"Let's leave, then," Jamie said. "Just shout down the hallway that we have to go and we'll get the hell out of here."

Just then, Mrs. Morel reappeared, bearing a tray of cheeses, crackers and sliced apples. "I was just fixing a snack for Claude. Even with all of the fancy dishes he cooks, he still enjoys simple foods—*les frommages, les fruits.*" She set the tray down on the coffee table.

"How is Claude?" Jamie asked, wondering if he was here at all, or if the woman was stalling them for a reason.

"You can ask me. I'm right here." A wheelchair stood poised at the entrance to the living room. Seated in it was Claude—once Daniel's friend, now his enemy—in a checkered flannel bathrobe. His leg extended along the footrest, encased in a metal brace. A huge wad of gauze was taped over his right eye, and his face was bruised and peppered with small cuts.

"Claude. Here, let me help you." His mother rushed to get behind his chair and maneuver it into place in the center of the room.

"Daniel? I couldn't believe it when Mama said you were here." Claude's speech was slurred, probably from pain medication.

Daniel wasn't prepared for the intensity of the emotion welling up inside him. His jaw clenched, and his hands balled themselves into fists. His vision seemed to blur, and for a few seconds he viewed Claude's broken body through a reddish haze. Then his vision cleared and he saw everything with crystal clarity. The clock on the fireplace mantel ticked loud enough to cause an earthquake. His own breathing roared in his ears.

"I'll leave you young people alone to talk," Mrs. Morel said.

"No, please, stay," Jamie said, sounding slightly desperate. "We'll only be a minute. How are you feeling, Claude? It must have been a terrible accident. Look, we brought you some flowers." She picked up the vase from where Daniel had set it down and more or less shoved it at him.

"That's nice. Red roses, Daniel? I didn't know you cared quite that much."

"I'll read the card," Mrs. Morel said, plucking the small florist's envelope from the depths of the bouquet, where it had been hiding.

"No!" Daniel and Jamie said together, realizing their mistake. But the elderly woman was faster than she looked, and she danced away from them as she pulled the card from the envelope.

"Dearest Jamie…"

"I was in a hurry," Daniel said unconvincingly.

"We should go, Daniel," Jamie said. "Claude obviously needs his rest."

"I don't think so." It was Mrs. Morel who spoke. She no longer had the envelope in her hand. She had a handgun almost bigger than she was, and it was pointed straight at Daniel's heart.

CHAPTER FIFTEEN

THE FIRST THING DANIEL DID was shove Jamie behind him. But then he went very still as he considered his options. Claude's mother was a frail old woman, but she was probably strong enough to pull that trigger, and that gun had enough firepower to kill both himself and Jamie with one bullet.

God, what had he gotten them into?

"Mama!" Claude sat up straight in his wheelchair, suddenly much more alert than he'd been before. "What are you doing? I'll handle this."

"But he knows, Claude. Whatever it is you've done that's caused the trouble, he knows about it. I see it in his eyes. He has such a look of hatred." She took a menacing step forward. "You two leave. Now."

"Sure, no problem," Jamie said, taking Daniel's arm and trying to drag him toward the door.

But he was rooted to the floor. "Why, Claude? Just tell me why you would kill a man and let me take the fall."

"I didn't just *let* you take the fall. I made sure you did." Claude worked furiously at the brace on his leg, unfastening buckles and loosening straps. "You were at my apartment, remember? I asked you to carve the roast. Then when no one was looking, I carefully placed the knife in a plastic bag."

"My God, that was months before the murder."

"I planned it for a long time. When I heard you were going into business with Andreas Musto, that untalented fry cook, I couldn't believe it. We could have made it, you and I, Le Bistro. If you'd just been more patient and given my ideas time to come to fruition—"

"You were bleeding us dry, Claude. You seemed to think I had an endless supply of cash, and I didn't."

"Of course you did! Your father was a billionaire."

"My father, not me. He loaned us the money to open the restaurant. I had to pay him back. We had to close the doors because we'd run out of operating capital."

"No. You plotted behind my back with Andreas."

"So why didn't you just kill me?" Daniel asked.

"Because the police would have figured it out. I had a motive. But if I killed Andreas and framed you…it was perfect. I didn't even know the bastard."

"But you left DNA at the scene," Jamie said. "At both scenes. Because you killed Frank Sissom, too."

"You two must be crazy," Mrs. Morel said. "My Claude could never kill anyone."

"Then why were you helping him leave the country?" Daniel demanded.

"He said he'd gotten into some trouble. The car accident—he said he'd crashed with the car of a powerful, angry man. So I make up a little story, that he'd been hurt much worse than he was to buy him a little time so he could get away for a while. He would never hurt anyone on purpose."

The woman sounded on the verge of tears, but the gun never wavered. It was still pointed directly at Daniel.

Claude finally worked the brace free of his leg, which apparently was not injured at all.

In one swift move he hoisted himself up and out of the wheelchair, swung the brace over his head, and crashed it into Daniel's head.

The unexpected salvo was enough to stun Daniel, driving him down to one knee.

"Claude, what are you doing?" his mother objected.

"I know what I'm doing, Mama." He ripped the gauze off his perfectly good eye, then grabbed the sharp cheese knife from the tray and hauled Jamie up by her hair. Before Daniel could react, Claude had the knife at Jamie's throat.

"Don't even think of trying anything clever," Claude said. "This knife might be small, but Mama keeps her knives very sharp, just like I do.

"Here's how this is going to work. Daniel, you're going to lie down on the floor. Mama, you're going to tie him up."

"With what?" Mrs. Morel sounded completely lost.

"Use the belt to my robe," Claude said curtly.

Daniel's wits were returning. He had a cut on his cheekbone where the sharp metal from the leg brace had made contact. Blood dripped onto his shirt, and his head throbbed, but otherwise he was okay.

He glanced up. Seeing Jamie's terrified eyes and Claude holding that knife at her throat was almost too much to bear. He wanted to launch himself at Claude and rip his heart out with his bare hands.

But one false move could cost Jamie her life. And God knew whether Mrs. Morel would shoot. A mother's love for her son sometimes transcended sanity.

"What do I do with the gun?" Mrs. Morel said.

"Put it down," Claude answered impatiently. "I've got them covered. The interfering D.A. can't move without getting a sliced jugular. And Daniel—he won't risk her life by disobeying orders. Isn't that right, Daniel?"

"Right," Daniel managed, still crouched, holding his head in his hands, feigning an injury far greater than the reality. Why not use a chapter from Claude's book against him?

Mrs. Morel laid the gun down on the mantel and, moving hesitantly, went to her son and untied the belt of his robe. Daniel knew if he was going to do something, it had to be fast. Once he was tied up, it would be a simple matter for Claude to neutralize Jamie.

But he soon discovered he'd underestimated the woman he loved.

"What are you going to do with us?" Jamie asked.

"I won't kill you unless I have to," Claude said. "Not in my mother's home. Clearly you haven't gone to the police, or they'd be here. If I can slow you down long enough, I'll be away safely."

"To Paris," Jamie said. "We know about the reservations."

While she talked, Daniel moved subtly until he had one shoulder under the coffee table.

"Well, go on, Mama," Claude said. "Tie him up."

Mrs. Morel came up behind him, leaned over and grabbed one of Daniel's wrists. Her grip was surprisingly strong.

Jamie picked that moment to make her move. She grabbed Claude's knife hand and pulled it away from her neck. She was only able to get a couple of inches clearance, but that enabled her to circle-step one foot behind his and unbalance him. As he stumbled, the tip of his knife sliced through Jamie's sweater and into her arm. She screamed as a splash of crimson stained her clothing.

With a roar of fury Daniel rose, bringing the whole coffee table with him, cheese plate, glass figurines and all. He threw all of his weight behind it, smashing it down on Claude, finishing the job Jamie had started.

Daniel lurched to his feet and tossed the upturned table aside with the strength of outrage fueling him. Jamie lunged toward the fireplace, perhaps trying to get her hands on the gun, but Mrs. Morel extended her cane and hooked Jamie's ankle with it.

With a cry of frustration Jamie fell to her knees.

Daniel was on top of Claude now, one hand clamped over Claude's wrist and beating it against the pink carpet, trying to get him to drop the knife. But the rug beneath them was soft, and Claude stubbornly refused to let go.

Daniel placed a knee in Claude's gut, grabbed half of a broken glass dog, and banged the sharp edge into Claude's knife hand.

Finally the chef released the knife. "All

right, all right! For God's sake, man, you've won!"

"I've got the gun, Daniel!" Jamie shouted. "It's over."

But it wasn't, not for Daniel. His fantasy was coming true. He tossed the knife well away, then fitted his hands around Claude's neck. "This is for the six years of hell you put me through." He squeezed. "This is for ruining the last years my parents had on earth." Claude choked as Daniel squeezed harder. "For killing my friend, and for Christopher Gables and Frank Sissom and everyone else whose lives you ruined."

"Daniel, stop! I've got the gun."

He didn't want to stop. He wanted to choke the life out of the bastard.

"Daniel!" she said again, pleading this time. Someone pounded on the door. Mrs. Morel sobbed, pleading for the life of her son.

Daniel looked over his shoulder at Jamie. She had blood all over her. What was he doing? Letting the woman he loved bleed to death so he could get his revenge? How many lives had *he* been about to destroy, just so he could settle a score?

He loosened his hands. Claude gasped for breath.

"Police. We need to talk to you!" It was Abe Comstock on the front porch, bellowing through the door.

Daniel raised himself on one knee. "Jamie, how bad are you hurt?"

"It's not that bad."

"You know how to handle a firearm?"

"Yes. Go get the door."

That turned out to be unnecessary. The front door flew open and a crowd of blue uniforms pushed inside, guns drawn.

Comstock pushed his way to the front and looked around the living room. "Holy mother of— What the hell is going on in here? Jamie, put the gun down!"

She slowly lowered it. "Mrs. Morel pulled a gun on us," Jamie said, sounding ridiculously calm. "Then Claude assaulted Daniel with his leg brace and put a knife to my throat, and Daniel fought back, and I got the gun and here we are."

"If you'd waited ten minutes," Comstock said, "you could have saved yourself a lot of trouble. I had a warrant to arrest Claude

Morel. This him?" He pointed to the bleeding man on the floor.

"That's him."

"Somebody call for paramedics." Comstock knelt down, helped Claude to sit up, then promptly snapped handcuffs on him.

Daniel went to Jamie and led her to a chair, urging her into it. "You're not okay. You're bleeding all over the place." The blood had soaked through her sweater halfway down her arm and in a half circle over her torso. He pulled apart the sweater where the knife had cut it, then ripped the sleeve apart.

"Daniel!"

"Honey, you're gushing blood like a geyser." He grabbed one of Mrs. Morel's needlepoint pillows and pressed it against the cut. "Lean back." He'd never seen so much blood. If he didn't stop it, she might bleed out before the paramedics even arrived.

"Thank you, Daniel." She stroked his hair with her free hand.

"Don't thank me yet. This is dicey first aid."

"No, I mean, thank you for not killing Claude. I know you wanted to."

"Part of me wanted to," he admitted.

"When I saw that he'd hurt you, everything came rushing back all at once—the pain he'd inflicted on me and my family. I wanted him to feel that pain. But that was the old Daniel, the one who was angry and bitter and wanted an eye for an eye. But the part of me that wants to live—that part was stronger."

"Thank you," she said again.

"You saved me. I heard your voice calling my name, and it brought me back from the brink. I knew if I killed Claude, my life was over, too. If I killed him—even if it was ruled self-defense—I would have lost you. And that was something I couldn't give up, my chance with you, a future with you by my side."

Daniel heard the sirens approaching and knew he had limited time to say what he wanted to say. Once the paramedics came they would take Jamie away, and then the police would have their day, dissecting today's events second by second, trying to decide who was guilty of what.

For all he knew, they might throw him in jail for attempted murder.

That thought didn't upset him as much as it would have only yesterday. If he could just get one thing settled.

"Jamie, beautiful Jamie, you've given me back my life, made me strong again. No matter what happens now, I'll be okay. But do you think we could have a future? Is there hope for us?"

He waited breathlessly for her answer. But when it didn't come, he chanced a look at her.

She had passed out.

FOR THE SECOND TIME in only a few days, Jamie woke up in a hospital emergency room stuck with enough needles to turn her into a pincushion. This time it wasn't Robyn's face she saw when she opened her eyes, though. It was Daniel's.

"Jamie. Dear God."

Her arm throbbed, and she wished for a few seconds she could just sink back into that lovely, hazy nothingness. But Daniel was here; he wasn't a dream. That was his hand holding hers, warm and secure.

"I told you we should have waited in the car," she said.

He smiled through a pained expression. "I will listen to you from now on. I promise. How do you feel?"

"Ready for a dance marathon, can't you tell?" Then she thought to ask, "Am I okay?"

"Nothing a couple of gallons of blood and a whole lot of bed rest won't cure." It wasn't Daniel talking, but Dr. Novak. "I wasn't expecting to see you back here so fast."

"It's not like I was eager to return," Jamie shot back. "And no, I didn't try to cut my wrist and miss."

"You're never going to let me live that down, are you?" Dr. Novak checked the readings on various beeping machines. "Ah, your numbers look a whole lot better than when you came in here."

"Good. Can I go home?"

"Not yet, but it won't be long," Dr. Novak said. "Now, if you'll excuse me, I have rounds to make."

Once they were alone, Daniel took Jamie's hand. "I'm breaking you out of here just as soon as I can," he said. "You're coming home with me. I've appointed myself your twenty-four-hour nurse."

"Mmm, Jillian will love that."

"Jillian has already packed her things and moved out," Daniel admitted. "She said

I would be sorry, that without her my life would fall apart. She might be right," he said. "I haven't done a bang-up job running things so far. But I'm sure I'll get better at it. So you'll let me take care of you until you're stronger?"

"Anything to get me out of this place." But once she'd regained her strength, then what? She sighed. "Guess I'll have to get my résumé in order. Who will want to hire a prosecutor who mistakenly put a man on death row?"

"Are you kidding? When the true story comes out, you can write your own ticket. At the very least, Chubb will beg you to come back. But I was kind of hoping you'd come work for me."

"For you, personally?" She hoped he wasn't suggesting she should replace Jillian.

"For Project Justice. As an investigator. You're damn good at it. And we could use another attorney—I rely too much on Raleigh. Whatever the D.A.'s office is paying you, I'll double it."

His offer was tempting—for all of five seconds. She wanted a lot of things, but being Daniel's employee wasn't one of them.

"Daniel, it's not that I don't appreciate the

offer or your confidence in me, but I'm a prosecutor. I put bad guys away. It's what I love."

"But we're a team. You have to admit we work well together."

She nodded. "But Project Justice is your dream. And while I admire your passion, it's not mine."

"You're making this hard on me."

"Because I won't fall in line with your plans?"

"You don't remember what we talked about just before you passed out, do you?"

"Um, no. I remember you putting a pillow on my arm."

"Then I'll start over. I want you in my life. Any way I can get you. Offering you a job seemed the most expedient, but not the most effective, I guess."

Jamie's mouth opened, but nothing came out.

"I won't blame you if you walk away. I've been manipulative and high-handed, you've almost died because of me not once, not twice, but three times, and I cost you your job."

"You do show a lady a good time." Jamie's eyes were suddenly awash with tears.

"Oh, dear God, I've made you cry on top of everything else."

"Do you mean it, Daniel? I'm not just a...a diversion, or a novelty you'll get tired of after a while?"

"I wasn't going to bring this up, because I thought it was too much, too soon, but I am so sure that I will never grow tired of you that I want us to get married."

"Oh, boy..." Her tears spilled over. "Now I really am going to cry. I don't cry, Daniel. Nothing ever makes me cry."

He kissed her tears away.

"So are you crying because the answer is 'yes, I want to spend the rest of my life with you'? Or 'no, you're crazy as a bedbug and first chance I get, I'm filing a restraining order'?"

"Daniel. You *are* crazy as a bedbug." She kissed him with a lot more passion than she should have, given her health at the moment, and stopped only when she got light-headed from lack of oxygen. "But I do want to spend the rest of my life with you. I love you, Daniel."

"I love you, Jamie."

They would have kissed again, but the door opened and Abe Comstock entered, looking cocky. "Are you about done in here? I told you five minutes, and it's been fifteen."

"She just woke up," Daniel said with a shrug. Then to Jamie he explained, "I owe him an interview."

"Glad to see you're feeling better, Jamie," Abe said. "Don't get too comfortable. Your turn is next. I sure hope y'all's stories match, 'cause I'm ready for this stinkin' case to be over."

Daniel stood and squeezed her hand. "I'll see you later. Do what the doctor says."

"Yes, Nurse Daniel."

THE PODIUM HAD BEEN SET UP on the front steps of the Harris County courthouse, and Jamie's stomach was filled with butterflies.

It was January, the new year, more than a month since she'd almost died at Claude Morel's hands.

The actions she and Daniel had taken to free Christopher Gables had opened a pretty big can of worms. It had taken a lot of explaining, a lot of interviews. Evidence was checked and cross-checked, stories compared.

In the end, the Houston police and the Harris County district attorney's office had both grudgingly agreed they had made a mistake in sending Christopher Gables to prison. Claude Morel had been charged with two counts of first-degree murder, one count of attempted murder and two counts of felony assault.

Christopher Gables had been released from prison. Although Jamie hadn't talked to him, he had sent her a polite note, through his new attorney, thanking her for her role in his exoneration.

Project Justice had received another round of praise from the media and from various government officials, from the Houston mayor to the president of the United States, and donations for the important work Project Justice did rolled in. Daniel had started coming into work at the office three days a week.

It had taken Jillian exactly forty-eight hours to realize Daniel wasn't going to come crawling back, begging for her to resume her position as his assistant and/or his girlfriend, lover or wife. A penitent, subdued Jillian had asked Daniel for a second chance, doing whatever job he thought she would be good at. He'd offered her a couple of administrative positions at both Project Justice and Logan Oil. In the end she had surprised everyone by asking if she could be an intern at Project Justice, learning to investigate from the ground up.

Daniel had agreed to give it a try.

Jillian had also personally apologized to Jamie for her attitude. She admitted she was wrong about Jamie, and hoped they could someday be friends. Jamie, too happy with Daniel to bear a grudge, had told her all was forgiven.

Everyone in Daniel's circle, both his household staff and his employees, had seemed thrilled by the news of Daniel's engagement. The women, especially, had circled around Jamie, asking if she wanted help planning the wedding and in general trying to make her feel as welcome as possible. They all made it a point to say that her former—and possibly future—occupation didn't bother them.

Now here they all were, gathered around her and Daniel to show their support.

Daniel checked his watch. "It's about that time. Are you nervous?"

"Terrified."

"Me, too."

Daniel still didn't like crowds or closed-in spaces, and she couldn't get him inside a shopping mall. But he'd made remarkable progress since deciding to take back control of his life.

"What if they throw rotten tomatoes?" she asked.

"We'll duck."

At the appointed time, Daniel stepped up to the microphone. "Good morning, and thank you all for coming. I'm Daniel Logan, and this is former Assistant District Attorney Jamie McNair. We called you here to address a number of issues.

"A lot of rumors have been flying around since the arrest of Claude Morel. You've had to rely on often conflicting and confusing police reports as well as a lot of 'unnamed sources close to the story' who frankly didn't know what they were talking about.

"So here's the skinny. Ms. McNair and I cooperated in the investigation that led to

Morel's arrest and the overturn of Christopher Gables's conviction. Jamie was dismissed from the district attorney's staff as a result of philosophical differences over this case.

"Yes, Jamie and I both sustained minor injuries when we... When I made the unwise decision to confront a man who was cornered and desperate. But as you can plainly see, neither of us is in a coma on life support, neither of us has brain damage and Jamie still has both of her arms."

The crowd laughed a bit. Daniel was making reference to a couple of tabloid stories showing badly doctored photos of Jamie with only one arm, and Daniel in a hospital bed, hooked up to machines.

"How did you figure out Claude was the murderer?" one of the reporters shouted out.

"We can't comment on that—it's an ongoing investigation. In fact, we've told you pretty much all we can on that subject. So let's move on. Jamie has something she'd like to say."

Jamie stepped up to the podium.

"Good morning. The events of the last few weeks have brought home to me a few truths about crime and punishment—namely, things may not always be what they appear, and sometimes there are no right answers. As an assistant district attorney I wielded a lot of power. I had the ability to save lives by putting murderers behind bars and to ruin lives if I put the wrong person in prison.

"No one is immune to mistakes. Not cops, not judges and certainly not district attorneys. As you know, Harris County District Attorney Winston Chubb has announced he will leave office in May, before his term is up. There will be a special election held to fill the vacancy. This morning, I am announcing my candidacy. If elected, what I will bring to the office is an open mind. A commitment to looking for the right answers, even when they're not easy. A willingness to admit mistakes when they're made, and correct them.

"I'll have more specifics about my platform in the coming days and weeks. But right now, I'd like to change the subject one more time. Daniel?"

Daniel took the microphone again. "Rumors have been swirling for weeks now about the supposed relationship between myself and Jamie McNair. I want to be very clear about this. The rumors are absolutely...true. We are, in fact, engaged to be married."

Jamie was ready to step down. They had agreed that they wouldn't give out any details about their approaching nuptials.

But Daniel kept talking.

"I'm sure some of you think it's odd, that we're on different sides of the fence and how could that work? We'll keep each other on our toes, that's for sure. But I just want you to know, Jamie is the most wonderful thing to come into my life. She is passionate about her work, but she is filled with compassion, as well. I believe those qualities will serve her well—as district attorney, and as my wife.

"To you naysayers, I will add that I love this woman more than life itself. Love can overcome an awful lot. I'm living proof."

He hugged her and she hugged him back, heedless of how mushy they looked.

"Damn it, Daniel," she whispered in his ear, "you're making my mascara run in front of the TV cameras."

"You'll thank me later," he whispered

back. "Listen to that applause. I just got you elected."

Maybe she'd win the election, maybe she wouldn't. It didn't matter. With Daniel at her side, she was already a winner.

* * * * *